EMERGING IDENTITIES

Selected Problems and Interpretations in Canadian History

Paul W. Bennett
Upper Canada College

Cornelius J. Jaenen
University of Ottawa

with

Jacques Monet, s.j.
Regis College, University of Toronto

George A. Rawlyk
Queen's University

Richard A. Jones
Université Laval Québec

Prentice-Hall Canada Inc., Scarborough, Ontario.

Canadian Cataloguing in Publication Data

Bennett, Paul W., date
  Emerging identities

Includes bibliographies and index.
ISBN 0-13-274200-4

1. Canada - Historiography.   2. Canada - History.
I. Jaenen, Cornelius J., date   II. Title.

FC149.B45   1986   971′.0072   C85-099420-9
F1024.B45   1986

Prentice-Hall Inc., Englewood Cliffs, *New Jersey*
Prentice-Hall International, Inc., *London*
Prentice-Hall of Australia, Pty., Ltd., *Sydney*
Prentice-Hall of India Pvt., Ltd., *New Delhi*
Prentice-Hall of Japan, Inc., *Tokyo*
Prentice-Hall of Southeast Asia (Pte.) Ltd., *Singapore*
Editora Prentice-Hall do Brasil Ltda., *Rio de Janeiro*
Prentice-Hall Hispanoamericana, S.A., *Mexico*

ISBN 0-13-274200-4

Project Editor: Judith Dawson
Production Editor: Magda Kryt
Designer: Steven Boyle
Production: Irene Maunder
Composition: Attic Typesetting

Printed and bound in Canada by Imprimerie Gagné

1   2   3   4   5   6   7   IG   92   91   90   89   88   87   86

Table of Contents

Preface and Acknowledgements

This book has been a long time in the making. The grand idea of assembling a new collection of problems in Canadian history was first proposed six years ago. Many members of the Canadian historical community felt that the time had arrived for a new problems book; a few were foolhardy enough to actually join in the enterprise.

Emerging Identities is a uniquely cooperative venture. Over the six-year life of the project, P.W. Bennett served as the coordinating editor, spearheading the enterprise and transforming the various problem studies into a more integrated, cohesive collection. Cornelius Jaenen prepared six important chapters, specifically 1 through 4, 8, and 11. The initial preparation of Chapters 5, 7, and 9 was undertaken by Dr. Jacques Monet. Professor George Rawlyk developed two chapters focusing on aspects of Maritime history (6 and 10). Eight chapters in post-Confederation Canadian history were prepared by P.W. Bennett—namely, 12 to 18, and 20, and Professor Richard Jones contributed Chapter 19, utilizing his intimate knowledge and expertise to explore the dilemma of modern Quebec in crisis.

This book benefited greatly from the work of two resourceful research assistants. Kirk M. Baert, a talented undergraduate student at Queen's University, spent the summer of 1982 combing library stacks and archives—and helped assemble much of the original research materials found in the post-Confederation problems. Dr. Monet's research assistant, Paul Litt, did a fine job assembling documents and reshaping parts of the chapters dealing with the Quebec Act, political unrest in the 1830s and the union of the Canadas. Many of the original translations of work published in the French language were undertaken by professors Jaenen and Jones.

Assembling a collection of twenty problems in Canadian history is no easy task. We make no claim to cover all the important issues in such a changing and diverse field. In preparing *Emerging Identities*, the principal editors have drawn on the talents and expertise of a team of recognized scholars specializing in pre- and post-Confederation periods, regional and national approaches, and political, economic and social history fields. As editors of this collection, we benefited greatly from a careful analysis of the pioneering work in this genre: K.A. MacKirdy, J.S. Moir and Y.F. Zoltvany's *Changing Perspectives in Canadian History* (1971), and we acknowledge our debt to these scholars for blazing the trail which we have chosen to follow. While no collection of this size can hope to capture the whole spectrum of specialized interests among historians today, we hope that *Emerging Identities* will serve to introduce students to some of the critical sources, contentious issues and ongoing controversies which enliven the study of Canada's past.

No book of problems in Canadian history could be published without the generous cooperation of many. In particular, we would like to thank those Canadian historians, writers and artists who have agreed to allow their original work to be included in our sourcebook. It is their ideas and viewpoints which provide the book with much of its vigour and vitality. Over the course of the project, some twenty historians and prominent educators from across Canada reviewed parts of the manuscript and offered many valuable comments. Some of their ideas will undoubtedly be recognized in this final published collection. At Prentice-Hall Canada, Rob Greenaway took a personal interest in the project and offered valuable encouragement in those early years when it seemed that the book would never see the light of day. MaryLynne Meschino, Judy Dawson, and Magda Kryt steered the book through the protracted editing/publishing process with tact, skill and professionalism.

A few closing words. From the day in the spring of 1980 when this book was first proposed, until its eventual publication, Dianne Bennett has shared in the odyssey, suffering through the periodic setbacks, and typing the manuscript through innumerable drafts. Only she can fully appreciate the mixed feelings of relief and exhilaration with which we greet its publication.

Emerging Identities is the end result of a massive, adventuresome enterprise. To those who view all problems books as "scissors-and-paste" history, we think you will be surprised by this volume. If the book helps enrich and enliven the discussion of Canadian history in introductory survey courses, then we have succeeded in our purpose.

Paul W. Bennett
Upper Canada College

Cornelius J. Jaenen
University of Ottawa

Introduction for the Student

Emerging Identities invites you to explore a Canadian history that is lively, contentious and crowded with competing interpretations. Each chapter-length "problem study" provides you with a brief introduction identifying the critical questions, a set of documentary materials, a selection of key interpretations, and a bibliographic guide to further reading. The collection of twenty problems is designed primarily for use as a sourcebook for seminars, tutorials and essay-writing in introductory Canadian history survey courses. The problems are presented in such a way as to promote the discussion of major historical controversies and to whet your appetite for further historical inquiry and research.

This sourcebook presents students of Canadian history with two different types of raw materials—*contemporary sources* and *conflicting interpretations*. The distinction between contemporary sources and interpretations is an important one. A contemporary source consists of some direct record left behind from the period or *by* the people who are the subject of the historians' study. They are often purely primary sources—actual records by participants which have survived from the past. Contemporary sources may consist of records that are written (a personal memoir, a public speech, census data, or a newspaper report), or oral (a folk tale, a song or poem), or visual (a painting, a line drawing or a political cartoon). Whatever their form, they are the raw materials without which history is impossible.

The usefulness of contemporary sources rests on their reliability, and their reliability can vary greatly. An eyewitness account, for example, will not often tell how closely its author was personally involved with the events he or she describes, how much of the episode under discussion he/she was really a witness to, whether he/she got the information from hearsay, or whether he/she was influenced by personal biases. In analysing and assessing such sources, the wise student must approach the task with a critical eye and seek verification in other reliable accounts and records. As an historian, then, you learn to pass judgements of many kinds on the contemporary sources provided in each problem study.

The conflicting interpretations supplied in each problem/chapter are excerpts from selected secondary sources. A "secondary source", which can offer an impartial report, an informed opinion or a set of opinions (an interpretation), is an indirect record, something written *about* the people or period under study, rather than by them. While contemporary sources usually date from the time of the events being studied, a secondary source interpretation usually dates from a later time.

Analysing and assessing conflicting interpretations in *Emerging Identities* will introduce you to the world of Canadian historiography, or the debates among historians over interpretations of our past experience. For, like the history of any country, the story of Canada's past has been written within the framework of certain intellectual concepts and has reflected differing schools of historical thought. By delving into the conflicting interpretations, you become more aware of how the writing of Canadian history has been shaped by sharply different schools of thinking in Canada's English-speaking and French-speaking communities. Studying Canadian historiography can also produce new, revealing insights into questions of "national character", the importation of ideas, regional, ethnic and class perspectives, and the prevailing climate of opinion in various time periods.

In the 1970s and early 1980s the study of Canadian history has been undergoing its own "quiet revolution". Historians young and old have brought new perspectives and approaches to Canada's past, revealing areas previously overlooked and offering new interpretations of long-established themes. Our knowledge of Canada's regional, social and economic history has been broadened and deepened. While political history and biography remain a staple of historical writing, there is a growing recognition that "past politics" constitutes only one aspect of the complex texture of Canada's past. Much of the recent wave of Canadian historical scholarship has come to explore what historians Ramsay Cook and J.M.S. Careless once described as the "limited identities of region, culture and class" that lie at the root of the Canadian experience.* Indeed, the outpouring of recent writings has thrust these "emerging identities" into the mainstream of Canadian historical interpretation. Thus, the term "emerging identities" seemed an apt title for our new collection.

P.W.B., C.J.J.   September 1985

Publisher's Note:

1. Inconsistencies in spelling or punctuation appearing in the documentary sources are those of the original.
2. Square brackets have been used to indicate editorial clarifications or additions.
3. The sources of all visuals are listed at the back of the book.

---

* See J.M.S. Careless, "'Limited Identities' in Canada", *Canadian Historical Review*, Vol. L (March, 1969), pp. 1–10. The concept of "limited identities" was actually coined by Ramsay Cook in "Canadian Centennial Celebrations", *International Journal*, Vol. XXII (Autumn, 1967), p. 663. See also Careless, "Limited Identities—Ten Years Later", *Manitoba History*, Vol. 1, No. 1 (1980), pp. 3–9.

1

THE MEETING
OF TWO WORLDS

Who Benefited From Indian-French Contact?

Indian-French relations in the sixteenth and seventeenth centuries are part of a larger story of the meeting of two worlds. While we often think of Canadian history as beginning with Jacques Cartier's voyages of exploration or with the short-lived Norse settlements on the Atlantic coast, in fact, the first inhabitants came to Canada not hundreds but thousands of years ago, and not from Europe, but from Siberia and eastern Asia. These first settlers, who were the ancestors of our Native peoples, eventually migrated, it is thought, from Alaska across the continent from the Pacific to the Atlantic coast, and southward into Mexico and South America. By the time of the arrival of the European sailors and adventurers in the late 1400s, the indigenous peoples had adjusted to many different environments over many thousands of years and had developed many diverse and often complex cultures. In eastern Canada, the meeting place for the Indian and French worlds, there were two language stocks, Algonkian and Iroquoian, and many autonomous bands and nations, each with its own beliefs, customs and habitat. The nomadic Algonkian bands, such as the Montagnais (Quebec), the Beothuk (Newfoundland), the Micmac (Nova Scotia), and the Malecite (New Brunswick), engaged in hunting, fishing, fowling, food-gathering, and some agriculture. The sedentary Iroquoian nations, notably the Huron, whom the French befriended, and the Five Nations Confederacy, whom the French alienated, were basically agricultural peoples.

The initial contact of the Indians and the French in the sixteenth and early seventeenth centuries presented its share of challenges and benefits for both peoples. The French who came to North America brought with them deeply ingrained concepts of order, culture and "civility" that had been shaped in the Old World. Indian society, to the early French colonizers, was part of a new world, a new-found collection of "uncivilized" people, or natural people inhabiting a natural world. To the French, the fundamental challenge was to turn the Indians into "civilized" people—people refined in manners, improved in arts and learning, and worshipful of God. Evangelization or conversion to Christianity was thought to be essential to the accomplishment of this task. Indian-French contact was, however, a two-way process. The French who came as civilizers were often regarded by the Native peoples as intruders. Over time, many Indian ways, beliefs and social values had their influence on the European colonizers. And the question of who benefited more from contact—the Indians or the French—is the central issue in this problem study.

The nature and circumstances of early contact provide clues to the consequences of European colonization. The Indians and Inuit[1] of Eastern Canada first began sustained interaction with traders and colonizers from France in the seventeenth century. There had been earlier contact with the Vikings, beginning in the late tenth century, and with Western European fishermen since at least the fifteenth century. These early encounters, which appear to have been violent on occasion, probably led to the introduction of virulent diseases to which the Native population of the time had little immunity, and which seriously reduced the population levels. Permanent European settlements followed only later; not until 1604 in Acadia, 1608 in Canada, and 1639 in the upper country, did the Native peoples have to contend with a European presence. It constituted nothing less than an invasion, heralding permanent occupation and eventual domination.

Were the long-range consequences of colonization immediately apparent? New France began as a fishing ground and a commercial counter for the fur trade. It became a colony of European settlement, (almost exclusively on lands not inhabited at the time by Indians), and by the early 1700s it was seen in France as being of great strategic and military value. This evolution in the perception of, and the value attached to the colony affected France's relationship with the original peoples. First contacts had been largely with nomadic Algonkian hunting cultures, such as the Micmac and Montagnais, but later ones involved the agricultural Iroquoian confederacies of the Huron and the Five Nations Iroquois. New France eventually extended from Newfoundland and Acadia along the St. Lawrence Valley and Great Lakes Basin, into the hinterland as far away as the Mississippi Valley and the western prairies. With the passing of time, the fur trade and Catholic missions, which had occasioned the initial contact in many cases, became involved in a system of military alliances with various nations, friendship pacts and associations. The French found themselves in competition with the Anglo-American colonies and the Hudson's Bay Company (founded in 1670) for the trade in furs and sometimes also for the alliance and allegiance of nations of the interior.

---

1. Inuit—(Inuk in the singular)—is the term which has come to replace Eskimo and which is preferred by these inhabitants of our northern region. Eskimo was probably of Algonkian origin and referred to "eaters of raw flesh"; Inuit means "the people".

From the beginning, officials in France and in the colonies pondered the origin and culture of the Indians and planned to "civilize" them through policies of evangelization and assimilation ("francisation"). Samuel de Champlain, the founder of Quebec (1608), set out with the help of Catholic missionaries to create a kingdom of one people, based on the vision of a French-Indian-Catholic empire. Champlain's plan eventually gave way to the concept of a biracial colony peopled by Europeans and "civilized" Indians, which in turn was replaced by the less ambitious and idealistic notion of a Royal province containing French subjects and a few segregated communities of converted Indians. Each phase in the French plan of conversion and assimilation met with some acceptance but also resistance from Indians who sought to retain their ancestral ways and often found European ideas and life-styles peculiar or incomprehensible.

The evolving Indian-French relationship before 1760 was not without its contradictions. Although French sovereignty was proclaimed over the entire continent, missionaries, soldiers and settlers were directed to respect Indian self-government and land rights, particularly in the interior, or "upper country". The relationship was not mutually beneficial in all its aspects. Epidemics carried off an alarming proportion of the indigenous population in the early stages of contact. Depopulation was accompanied by a depletion of game, notably of beaver and moose. Exploitation of the first staple products—cod and furs—also led to the introduction of alcohol, the devastating effects of which were felt by Indians and all segments of French society. On the other side, the French were drawn into the existing pattern of warfare, which resulted in a long series of seventeenth-century wars with the Iroquois Five Nations, and later armed clashes with other nations in the Upper Great Lakes country, in the lower Mississippi River region, and on the western prairies.

Popular historical interpretations suggest that the aboriginal peoples, with their traditional customs and values, yielded before the advance of a techno-logically more sophisticated European civilization. Yet this popular view may rest on some misconceptions. For in fact many French travellers, mission-aries and traders left behind records which suggest that they had come to view the original inhabitants of Acadia and Canada as well-adjusted, self-reliant peoples possessing many positive qualities. Some of the French apparently learned to appreciate the diversity of Indian cultures, distinguishing between the customs of Micmac, Montagnais and Iroquois. Other French observers remarked on the degree of freedom, tolerance, equality and harmony which characterized Indian relations. For their part, the Indian peoples seem to have been remarkably discriminating in their adoption of French ways and beliefs. Newly introduced technology such as the musket and the wheel were not always seen by them as superior to traditional ways of hunting and transport like the bow and arrow and the birch bark canoe. French tools, implements, modes of transport, language, behaviour, social customs and religious beliefs were all examined—and some were adopted selectively. Many aspects of French culture were rejected outright as the Indians continued to value their own religion, manners and morals. Often they adopted the viewpoint so clearly stated by a Micmac who confronted a French Jesuit missionary: "That is the native way of doing it. You may have your way and we will keep ours. All value their own wares."

The meeting of the Indian and the European worlds produced a relationship which was more complex than has been popularly recognized. Who benefited more from the interaction of the French and the Indians as friends and as foes? To what extent were the aboriginal peoples exploited or robbed of their ancestral hunting territories and productive fields by the French? Is it possible that the French and Indian societies became so intertwined in often mutually satisfying relationships that neither wished to extricate itself? Or were the two societies bound together simply because neither partner could dominate or control the situation?

SELECTED CONTEMPORARY SOURCES

THE TWO WORLDS MEET—EARLY IMPRESSIONS OF EACH OTHER

The early impressions that the Indian and European peoples had of each other provided a glimpse of the possible challenges and benefits which lay ahead. The Spanish explorers of the late fifteenth century provided the French with their first perceptions of the New World and its peoples. However, the French were not long in condemning what they believed to be excessive Spanish cruelty in dealing with the Indians, and in proclaiming their own determination to establish a fruitful and peaceful relationship. Precise knowledge about the world discovered by the French expedition of 1524 (headed by Giovanni da Verrazzano) and the 1534–41 voyages of Jacques Cartier was scant. Early French impressions reflected a Europocentric (Europe-centered) view of the world and were usually closely related to European aspirations— political, economic and religious—in the New World. Likewise, the Indians viewed and measured the European intruders by the standard of their own ways and values.

An Early French View—Montaigne's Impressions of the New World and Its Inhabitants

Some of the first French impressions of America and its peoples were those recorded by Michel de Montaigne, a French essayist (1533–1592) known for his humane and broad-minded outlook. In attempting to describe America and its peoples to those with no first-hand experience of either, Montaigne remarked that "our world has just discovered another world". The concern he expressed for the Native peoples, whom he considered to be "in the infancy of mankind", was a theme that would recur. It suggested that they possessed an original and natural goodness which Europeans had lost and which the New World might also lose in contact with the Old World.

I am much afraid that we shall have very greatly hastened the decline and ruin of this new world by our contagion, and that we will have sold it our opinions and our arts very dear. It was an infant world; yet we have not whipped it and subjected it to our discipline by the advantage of our natural valor and strength, nor won it over by our justice and goodness, nor subjugated it by our magnanimity. Most of the responses of these people and most of our dealings with them show that they were not at all behind us in natural brightness of mind and pertinence.

> Donald H. Frame, ed., *The Complete Works of Montaigne. Essays, Travel Journal, Letters* (Stanford: Stanford University Press, 1957), Vol. III, p. 693.

Those people are wild, just as we call wild the fruits that Nature has produced by herself and in her normal course; whereas really it is those that we have changed artificially and led astray from the common order, that we should rather call wild.

> Donald H. Frame, ed., *Montaigne's Essays and Selected Writings* (New York: St. Martin's Press, 1963), p. 89.

A Europocentric Impression of North American Indians—The Fête at Rouen, 1550

Indians, even if from Canada, were long depicted in France of the sixteenth century dressed like indigenous South Americans. When King Henry II of France paid a visit to Rouen in 1550, a Brazilian village was built and some fifty Indians from New France were required to sing, dance and fight. A French woodcut captures the bizarre spectacle of this "Brazilian" fête at Rouen:

A meeting of two worlds—the fête at Rouen. 1550.

Two French Missionary Assessments of Indians, 1615 and 1627

Much of the work of evangelization and assimilation in New France was undertaken by two Catholic religious orders, the Récollets and the Jesuits, and by the secular priests of Saint-Sulpice at Montreal. The first concerted missionary activity was that of the Récollets, a Franciscan order, among the sedentary agricultural Huron who lived near the southern shores of Georgian Bay. When the Récollets found the burdens of missionary work beyond their meagre resources, the Jesuit order came to their assistance. In 1625, a small group of Jesuit missionaries arrived at Quebec. Soon the Jesuits were virtually the sole missionaries to the Indians in Canada. In terms of finance, intellect, power and prestige, they were the religious order best equipped to understand the challenge of massive conversion. Although among Europeans they probably had the best understanding of Indian spiritual beliefs and values, their goal was to uproot these in order to implant the Catholic religion.

Two early French missionary assessments of the Indians reflect views couched in seventeenth-century Catholic religious zeal. Both Denis Jamet, a Récollet friar, and Father Charles Lalemant, a Jesuit missionary, offered a revealing look at the diverse nations, and some insights into their difficulties in evangelizing the Indians.

A Récollet View, 1615

As for the stature of these people, they are all well-proportioned and sturdy, the Huron above all others are the strongest and have Flemish traits. The Nipissings are more slender in build but are courageous and quick. All wear their hair long, men as well as women, go bareheaded, dress in skins of beavers, martens and other animals, all are limited to their judgment and have little sense of values if it is not in their immediate profit. All live without worshipping any deity. The Montagnais, Algonkins and Nipissings invoke the devil through men they call *pilotois* and on several occasions I have heard them sing together in rhythm around their sick. An interpreter told me they were prayers to the devil....

...As for what touches us the most, which is the conversion of these barbarians, according to human reasoning it is a difficult matter; this is because the Montagnais and Algonkins are nomads and live scattered in diverse places only so long as they find fish and game there. Given the little we see of them and the impossibility of living among them, we will never learn the language and none now knows it. As for the Hurons, they are settled peoples living in large villages near a great lake the other end of which they have never seen.... All religious who go there can expect no comfort. Their food is usually Indian corn cooked in water; for their feasts they have bread baked in hot ashes. They have the advantage that the lake lacks no fish if they want to take the trouble to fish, but they are lazy and content themselves with one dish when they could have two. That is a bit annoying for us Frenchmen. But what matters most is that to win their friendship it would be necessary to live with them helter skelter in their cabins, which is a strange dissatisfaction, as you can imagine, Monseigneur....

Bibliothèque Nationale, Paris, 500 de Colbert, Vol. 483, Father Denis Jamet to Cardinal de Joyeuse, 1615, ff. 581–582v. trans. Cornelius J. Jaenen.

A Jesuit Missionary's View, 1627

...They attach great faith to their dreams. Some of them will tell you two days before the arrival of ships the hour of their arrival and will tell you nothing more except that they have seen it in their sleep. These people are reputed among them to be able to speak to the Devil. Their conversion will give us no little difficulty. Their licentious and lazy lives, their rude minds which can scarcely grasp things, the paucity of words which they have to explain our mysteries because they have never had any form of divine worship, will tax our wits. Yet we do not lose courage, thank God, because we trust in this truth that God will not take so much account of the fruit we produce as of the good disposition and the labour we undertake; furthermore, the greater the obstacles to their conversion, and the more distrust we have in ourselves, the more trust we will have in God....

> Lettre du Père Charles Lalemant, supérieur de la Mission du Canada de la Compagnie de Jesus (Paris: Jean Boucher, 1627), pp. 6–7, 13. trans. C.J.J.

Early Indian Views of the French, 1632

Since little recorded evidence exists of Indian views of the Europeans and their intrusions into Native societies, we must rely on reports of their impressions left by French missionaries and officials. The Récollet friar Gabriel Sagard offered these Europocentric observations based on his missionary work during 1623–24 in the Huron country.

> They call the French Agnonha in their language; that is, iron people. The Canadians [i.e., the Indians around Quebec City] and Montagnais surname us Mistigoche, which in their language means wooden canoe or boat; they call us so, because our ships and boats are made of wood and not bark as theirs are.
>
> Since they reckoned that the greatest captains in France were endowed with the greatest mind, and possessing so great a mind they alone could make the most complicated things, such as axes, knives, kettles, etc., they concluded therefore that the King...made the largest kettles, and regarding us in the capacity of captains they used sometimes to offer us kettles to mend.
>
> At Quicunonascaron there was the great captain and chief of the...Bears, whom they called *Garihoua andionxra*.... This *Garihoua andionxra* had no small opinion of himself, when he desired to be spoken of as brother and cousin of the [French] King and on an equality with him, like the two forefingers on the hands which he showed us touching one another, making a ridiculous and absurd comparison thereby.
>
> They have such a horror of a beard that sometimes when they try to insult us they call us...Bearded, You have a beard; moreover they think it makes people more ugly and weakens their intelligence. They speak very composedly.... This restraint of theirs leads them to call Frenchmen women, because they are too hasty and excited in their movements and speak all together and interrupt one another.

> Gabriel Sagard, *The Long Journey to the Country of the Hurons*. Edited by G.M. Wrong trans. H.H. Langton. (Toronto: Champlain Society, 1939), pp. 79, 183, 149, 137 and 140.

FRENCH POLICIES OF ASSIMILATION—BENEFITS FOR WHOM?

Converting the Indians to Christianity was part of a larger French strategy of assimilation, or making the Indians over into French-speaking "civilized" peoples. From the early days of Samuel de Champlain (1608–1635) the French invited Indians to convert to Christianity, and to become "francised"

through intermarriage with the French and the adoption of a settled agricultural way of life. Some French officials and missionaries were optimistic that
the Indians would soon see the advantages of the French way of life, but others
were more cautious, if not frankly pessimistic, observing that Native beliefs,
traditions and ways were well-established over centuries of living in the North
American environment. Nevertheless, French officials attempted, with
mixed success, means of assimilation ranging from integrated education and
intermarriage to evangelization and segregated settlement.

Creating "One People"—Two Views of the Assimilation Policy, 1618 and 1675

A plan to form "one people" with the Indians was first proposed by
Champlain and later reaffirmed by the French monarchy. Central to this plan
was the idea of assimilation into French colonial life by means of raising and
educating Indian children in a French environment. In the following documents, Samuel de Champlain explains in a 1618 memoir his dream of creating
"one people" and King Louis XIV (1638–1715) expresses his official support
for such a plan and its potential benefits.

Champlain's Plan of Colonization, 1618

... considering the advantage and profit to be derived therefrom, as well for the glory
of God as for the honour of His Majesty and for the good of his subjects, the Chamber
of Commerce has passed a resolution to represent to His Majesty and to the said Lords
of his Council on the measures which he should take for such a holy and glorious
enterprise....

... the said Sieur de Champlain declares and proposes, subject to the good pleasure
of His Majesty, should he see fit to undertake and pursue the said enterprise, to build at
Québec, the site of the Sieur Champlain's settlement situated on the river St. Lawrence,
at a narrow part of the said river, some nine hundred or a thousand yards in width, a
town almost as large as St. Denis, which shall be called, if it please God and the King,
Ludovica, in the centre of which will be built a fair temple, dedicated to the Redeemer,
and called the Church of the Redeemer, as a memorial and commemoration of the good
that it shall please God to do to these poor people, who have no knowledge of His holy
name, to incline the will of the King to bring them to the knowledge of the holy
Christian faith and to the bosom of our holy mother Church....

H.P. Biggar, ed., *The Works of Samuel de Champlain*, Vol. II. trans. John Squair
(Toronto: Champlain Society, 1922–36), pp. 326,337.

Louis XIV's Instructions on Assimilation, 1675

I am well satisfied with all you have done to attract the children of the natives in order to
have the girls fed and raised by the Ursulines, and the little boys by you.

The priests of the Seminary of Saint-Sulpice have made me the promise that they
will continue to raise some, and you could do nothing which would be more useful for
my service, for the benefit of the colony and that would be more pleasing to me than to
enjoin the religious communities and even individuals who are somewhat comfortable

to attract some and to raise them at home, because there is nothing which can contribute more to the welfare of religion and the growth of the colony than to diminish the number of those who live as savages in order to reduce them to a civil life and to render them capable of assuming all the offices of an honest life, each in the station in which God has placed him at birth.

Collection de Manuscrits (Quebec: Coté & Cie, 1883), Vol. I, Louis XIV to Governor Frontenac, 22 April 1675, pp. 235–6. trans. C.J.J..

Education and Conversion—Marie de l'Incarnation's Report on the Progress with Indian Girls, 1668

Indian children were originally sent to France to be educated, but this practice failed to produce the desired results. In 1639, a few Ursuline sisters and some Sisters Hospitallers arrived at Quebec to take up, among other duties in a missionary territory, the education and Christian upbringing of a select number of Indian girls. Thirty years later, the Ursuline Superior confided her feelings about the success of their work of conversion and assimilation in a private letter to her son.

Monseigneur our Prelate maintains in his residence a certain number of young Native boys, and as many French boys, so that being raised and nourished together the former may take on the ways of the latter and become francised. The Reverend Jesuit Fathers do likewise. The Gentlemen of the Seminary of St. Sulpice of Montreal are going to imitate them.

As for the girls, we have some Natives also with our French boarders for the same purpose. I do not know how it will all end because, to speak quite frankly with you, it appears very difficult to me. Since the many years we have been established in this country we have been able to civilize only seven or eight who became francised; the others, who were quite numerous, all went back to their relatives, although they were good Christians. The native way of life is so seductive, because of its freedom, so that it is a miracle to be able to captivate them with French ways.... Judge thereby if it is easy to change them, given the habits they pick up from childhood and which are as it were natural for them....

Claude Martin, *Lettres de la Vénérable Mère Marie de l'Incarnation* (Paris: 1681), Marie de l'Incarnation to her son, 17 October 1668, pp. 632–633. trans. C.J.J.

Segregated Settlement—A Report on Lorette Reserve, 1675

With the plan to form one French-Indian-Catholic people foundering, French authorities came to realize that conversion and assimilation might better be directed at whole communities. Beginning in 1637, a number of attempts were made to found settlements which might become ideal Christian communities. These settlements, called *réserves*, were modelled on similar Jesuit communities in Spanish America; it was intended that the Indians would not only become Christian but would also take up farming and adopt a French lifestyle. The original plan to attract nomadic hunting bands such as the Montagnais and the Algonkin to the reserves met with little success, and the French gradually replaced them with Huron and Iroquois, groups with more affinity to agricultural ways.

Some thirty-five years after the founding of the first reserve, a Jesuit priest, Father Claude Dablon, offered this hopeful report on the reserve at Lorette.

This Mission...now consists of about 300 souls, both Hurons and Iroquois. This number is small, in truth, compared with that of the other Missions; but they are all chosen persons, who openly profess Christianity and the most sublime virtues that are practiced therein.

This Christian settlement has the advantage, over the other Christian communities of natives of the country, of being a Church fully formed; and we no longer count therein the number of the baptized, except by that of the children who come into the world. Should it nevertheless happen that some Iroquois abandon their country to take refuge in this village, as in a sure port of safety, we baptize them after carefully instructing them; and this year we have administered baptism to twenty-two adults of this class. With respect to this, I must not omit to mention the zeal manifested for their countrymen by our Iroquois, of both sexes, who have dwelt in this mission many years; for I may say that the foundation of the instruction received by our newly-arrived neophytes is given them by the older residents, who very frequently go to seek them in their cabins, to instruct them in the mysteries of our holy Faith.

R.G. Thwaites, ed., *The Jesuit Relations and Allied Documents* (New York: Pageant Book Company, 1959, LX, pp. 27–29.

DIFFERING VIEWS OF THE RESERVES

Seven major reserves were eventually formed in New France and many Indians came to live on them for a variety of reasons: to escape from persecution in their home villages, to flee from enemies, and to take advantage of the material benefits offered there. Some reserves were set up as military buffer zones along the Anglo-American frontier, for the French respected the Indians' military abilities. Two reserves were created south of Trois-Rivières for the Abenaki people, on whose lands New England settlers had encroached. Opinions differed on the effectiveness of the reserves and the benefits of such settlements for both peoples. Although the reserves were often praised for their value in "civilizing" Indians and providing military buffers, critics pointed to them as an economic burden on the colony and as centres of illicit trade with the English. Periodic reports told of terrible hardships, like those experienced in 1742 at the Lorette Reserve, where the inhabitants endured hunger, poor soils and a worm infestation of their wheat crop. The following set of observations illustrates some of the costs and benefits of the reserve system.

Louis XIV's View of the Abenaki Reserves, 1705

His Majesty is persuaded that it is to a good end that he has influenced the Abenakis to come and settle among the French. This does not prevent him, however, from finding some inconvenience with the plan because a part of these Natives having remained in their former habitations, it is feared that the English may oppress them, that they may occupy the region of Pentagouet, and that as a consequence we should lose that buffer; also that those who have come to the colony should be a heavy burden to us.... Nevertheless, since the thing is done, we can only let it stand and you will let me know hereafter the consequences which this change will have produced.

Nouvelle-France. Documents historiques (Quebec: Coté, 1893), Vol. I, King to Governor Vaudreuil, 17 June 1705, pp. 47–48. trans. C.J.J.

Mutual Benefits of the Caughnawaga[2] Reserve—Louis Franquet's Report, 1752

The missionaries are the seigneurs of the place and its surroundings; they speak the native language.

The natives of this village are a mixture of five Iroquois nations. They allege that they have separated themselves from their people to embrace the Catholic religion, to which they are attached as far as it is in their own self-interest....

The natives of this village are rich. They are dressed in good cloth with gold and silver trimmings which they acquire most often from New England, where they are sold goods at better prices than at our place, with a view to attracting their confidence and friendship. There are among them several French half-breeds, and many English children taken prisoner during the last campaign, which they have adopted. These children are raised with native ways and inclinations; they are distinguished only by the colour of their skin which is paler. This liberty and license in which they are reared results in them not thinking of returning home when they grow up....

These natives have taken to building their houses in the French fashion, in rectangular shape, and even in masonry. To this end, they have drawn French workmen of all kinds. The missionaries urge them to undertake this sort of construction under the pretext that it is better; but I would be quite inclined to believe that being the seigneurs of the place, self-interest leads them into such views so that when the natives will be inconvenienced by the supervision, or when they are persuaded to it, they will suggest to them to go and settle elsewhere in order to enjoy their former freedom, and then as seigneurs all these dwellings will remain for their profit.

Voyage et Mémoires sur le Canada par Franquet (Montreal: Editions Elysée, 1974), pp. 37–39. trans. C.J.J.

PROBLEMS OF CONTACT

Indian-French relations were complicated by problems which arose both between—and within—the Indian and French colonial communities. Particularly disturbing to French authorities was the number of young men known as *coureurs de bois* who ran off to the hinterland, adopted Indian ways, and engaged in the collection of furs without official permission. Occasional friction cropped up with French fur traders and garrisons of soldiers who were dishonest in their dealings. The sale of intoxicants, mainly brandy, to the Indians produced its share of disorders and social disintegration and resulted in both Church censure and state intervention which, however, did little to

---

2. The spelling preferred by the *Confédération des Indiens du Québec* today is Kahnewake.

control "brandy trafficking". Another source of potential conflict was epidemic diseases, which began along the Atlantic coast and spread inland among the Native peoples. Neither the French nor the Indians fully understood the causes of the illnesses and some estimates of the death toll among Native populations who had little immunity to European disease ran as high as fifty or sixty per cent.

The *Coureurs de Bois*—A Governor's Opinion of the Problem, 1685

The effects of the *coureurs de bois*[3] and their activities on the "francisation" of Indians concerned many French officials. These young Frenchmen seemed to pose three problems for the Europeans. Firstly, they appeared to have been "Americanized", adopting the traditional Indian way of life instead of helping to "francise" the Indians. Secondly, their activities were linked, often unfairly, with the slow rate of growth and agricultural development in the colony. Thirdly, they represented dangerous rebellion against the authority of the church, the state and the family. One governor of New France, the Marquis de Denonville (1685–1689), summarized many of the popular complaints in a 1685 letter to the Minister of Marine and Colonies in Versailles, who had administrative authority over New France.

> It seems to me that this is the place, Monseigneur, that we have to take into account the disorders which occur not only in the woods but also in our settlements. These disorders have come to the Youth of this country only through the laziness of the children, and the great liberty which the light control of fathers and mothers and Governors have exercised over youth in allowing them to go into the woods on pretext of hunting or trading. This has reached the extremity, Monseigneur, that as soon as the children can shoulder a rifle the fathers can no longer restrain them and do not dare to make them angry. You may judge what evils may ensue from such a manner of living.... They have to pass their lives in the woods, where there are neither priests to trouble them, nor fathers nor Governors to constrain them. There are, Monseigneur, among those men some who distinguish themselves above others in these disorders and against whom I have promised to employ the authority which the King has entrusted to me to punish them severely.
>
> Monsieur de la Barre suppressed a certain gang called the Knights, but he did not take away its manners or disorderly conduct. A way of dressing up like savages, stark naked, not only on carnival days but on all days of feasting and debauchery, has been treated as a clever action and a joke. These manners tend only to maintain the young people in the spirit of living like savages and to communicate with them and to be eternally profligate like them. I could not express sufficiently to you, Monseigneur, the attraction that this savage life of doing nothing, of being constrained by nothing, of following every whim, and being beyond correction, has for the young men.
>
> P.A.C. MG 1, Series C11A, Vol. VII, Denonville to Minister, 13 November 1685, pp. 45–56. trans. C.J.J.

---

3. "Running the woods" was a feature of fur trade contact common to all Europeans in North America although never as pronounced as in the French experience. The Dutch had their *boschlopers*, the English their *wood rovers*, and the Russians on the Pacific coast their *promyshiliniki*.

The Effects of Brandy—A Variety of Views

Selling brandy to the Indians was raised as a serious moral and religious question, but economic considerations kept the trade alive. Although the question of the brandy trade was discussed at a consultative assembly called in 1678 (often erroneously referred to as the "Brandy Parliament"), the traffic persisted because it was considered to be a necessary evil in the competition with the English for furs and trading partners. Periodic prohibition campaigns spearheaded by Bishops Laval (1659–1688) and Dosquet (1733–1739) alleged that alcohol undermined missionary work, debased the French colonists and wreaked havoc among Indian families and nations. With only limited measures of prohibition undertaken by the state, the sale of intoxicants, and problems associated with it, continued almost unabated. Did the Indians regard the introduction of intoxicants as desirable? There are many documents which suggest an inordinate craving for liquor on their part—and which describe the disorders, disease and social disintegration promoted by their use. There is also the testimony of a Micmac who confronted the officer Claude-Sébastien de Villieu in 1701, and the vow of total abstinence of the Huron of Lorette ought to be considered. The results of alcohol use as reported among the Micmac give some indication of who suffered and who profited.

Remonstrance of a Micmac Elder, 1701

First when I learned that you were building a cabin near my village, I began to tremble with fear and I was apprehensive that the French who had previously given me prayer, should become the cause of my ceasing to pray; for I see my brothers who are, for example, in the direction of the St. John River, no longer pray so to speak because of the liquor. Similarly their relatives who are at Kennebec, since they trade with the English, have become stupid and no longer pray, because every day they are drunk... that is why I tell you that I do not want you to stay here.

H.R. Casgrain, *Les Sulpiciens et les Prêtres des Missions Etrangères en Acadie* (Quebec: Pruneau & Kirouac, 1897), citing a letter of abbé Antoine Gaulin, 24 October 1701, p. 239. trans. C.J.J.

Resolution of the Huron of Lorette, 1710

...they are wise Natives, obedient and who drink neither brandy nor wine, nor beer. It appears very surprising that Natives for whom one of the greatest passions is to drink, and to get drunk, have reduced themselves to never tasting strong drink although they have every day the occasion to do so, being always with us and among us in this city (Quebec) where they come to sell all the produce they have.

P.A.C., MG 1, Series C11A, Vol. 122, Letter 89, 1710, p. 245. trans. C.J.J.

Report on Micmac Depopulation, circa. 1720

This nation was previously very numerous and waged war on all others even to the Eskimo of the Brador Coast. There are still several descendants among them who came from the prisoners they took. But since the Europeans have frequented them, although they had never had any other drink except natural water, they gave themselves so much to Wine, and especially to Brandy, that the greater part died of it, which has reduced them to a very small number in comparison to what they were before.

> P.A.C., MG 3, Series K, Carton 1232, No. 4, Relation of the mission of abbé Antoine Gaulin (circa. 1720), p. 110. trans. C.J.J.

The Effect of Epidemic Diseases—Comments on the Human Costs

Epidemics caused much fear and despair, as well as severe depopulation, among the Indians. Neither were French settlers spared, because the virulent infections were transported by royal vessels and often spread throughout French settlements. While the reasons for the epidemics and Native depopulation were not clearly understood by either the French or the Indians, each had their own explanations. Le Maire's memorandum, although it deals specifically with Louisiana, describes a situation prevalent wherever there was contact. Father Marest's report indicates the degree of fear and despair that gripped Native communities. Given that Indians were the prime victims of epidemic disease, did the French gain anything by the unrelenting march of microbes?

Le Maire's Observations of Depopulation, 1717

Louisiana was previously more populated than it is today, which we know not only from reports from the natives but also by the great number of places which we recognize to have been heretofore cultivated and which we see now in the wild state. We are also convinced by the daily Experience we have of their decline in numbers. It is difficult to determine if it is diseases or wars which have contributed most to their destruction. If we are to believe the natives, they began to diminish markedly only after the arrival of Europeans in their Country. It is not because of the reason they advance, that is that the Spirit which presides over the preservation of the whites is stronger than theirs, but because, as I have stated above, they have been exposed since the arrival of Europeans to all the sicknesses of the latter, which added to those to which they were already subject, have taken a terrible toll of them.

> P.A.C., MG 7, I, A-2, Fonds français ms. 12 105, Le Maire's memorandum on Louisiana, 1717, pp. 41–42. trans. C.J.J.

Father Marest's Report of Illinois Despair, 1712

At that time a contagious disease desolated their village, and each day carried off many of the Indians: the medicine men themselves were not spared, and died like the rest. . . . The chief of the medicine men then imagined that their Manitou, being less powerful than the Manitou of the French, was obliged to yield to him. In this persuasion he many times made a circuit around the fort, crying out with all his strength, 'We are dead; softly, Manitou of the French, strike softly, do not kill us all'. Then, addressing himself to the Missionary, 'Cease, good Manitou, let us live; you have life and death in your possession; leave death, give us life'. The Missionary calmed him, and promised to take even more care of the sick than he had hitherto done; but notwithstanding all the care he could bestow, more than half in the village died.

W.I. Kip, ed., *The Early Jesuit Missions in North America* (New York: Wiley & Putnam, 1846), Fr. Gabriel Marest to Fr. Joseph Germain, 9 November 1712, p. 203.

THE BENEFITS OF CONTACT

Certain aspects of French contact with the aboriginal peoples were characterized more by collaboration and mutual benefits than by controversy and conflict. The French gained greatly from Native curative practices such as dieting, sweat baths, and the use of medicinal plants which provided alternatives to the favoured European remedies of bleedings, purges and emetics. For their part, the Indians benefited from French policies which recognized their ancestral land rights and reserved the "upper country" (inland beyond the confluence of the Ottawa river) as Indian hunting territories free from extensive French settlement. But many other aspects of Indian-French contact produced mutual benefits, such as cultural exchanges of technology, trade items and ceremonial practices. Both sides also gained from French-Indian military collaboration in which they seemed to develop the sense of kinship that comes from fighting common foes. Given these many examples of cross-cultural exchange, weighing the benefits derived by each side becomes difficult.

Iroquois Medicine—Jacques Cartier Benefits from A Cure for Scurvy, 1535–36

One of the most remarkable practices of immediate benefit to the French was the adoption and use of Indian medicine as a cure for scurvy. The first record of this practice was during Jacques Cartier's expedition of 1535–36, when Cartier and his men spent their first difficult winter near Stadacona on the shores of the St. Lawrence River. Cartier's journals record that, after twenty-five men had died of scurvy, the company survived when the Captain (Cartier) learned of a cure from Dom Agaya, an Iroquois. This resort to an Iroquois cure was a lesson which the French do not seem to have forgotten because apparently many years later, in 1757, officers of the regular French troops sent a detachment to gather spruce boughs for medicinal use.

...Dom Agaya whom he [Cartier] had seen ten or twelve days previous to this, extremely ill with the very disease his own men were suffering from; for one of his legs about the knee had swollen to the size of a two-year old baby, and the sinews had become contracted. His teeth had gone bad and decayed and the gums had rotted and become tainted...the Captain inquired of him what had cured him of his sickness. Dom Agaya replied that he had been healed by the juice of the leaves of a tree and the dregs of these, and that this was the only way to cure sickness...two squaws with our Captain...brought back nine or ten branches. They showed us how to grind the bark and the leaves and to boil the whole in water. Of this one should drink every two days, and place the dregs on the legs where they were swollen and affected. . . . The Captain at once ordered a drink to be prepared for the sick men . . . As soon as they had drunk it, they felt better. . . after drinking it two or three times, they recovered health and strength and were cured of all the diseases they had ever had . . . in less than eight days a whole tree as large and as tall as any I ever saw was used up, and produced such a result, that had all the doctors of Louvain and Montpellier been there, with all the drugs of Alexandria, they could not have done so much in a year as did this tree in eight days . . . .

H.P. Biggar, ed., *The Voyages of Jacques Cartier* (Ottawa: King's Printer, 1924), pp. 212–215.

Respect for Ancestral Land Rights and the Indian Nations—The Royal Policy on Indian Rights, 1665

The French colonizers were well known for laying official claim to North America through raising crosses bearing the King's arms and burying inscribed lead plates to mark the extent of their occupation. But they never dispossessed the Indians of any of their lands, never signed treaties involving land surrenders, and never used the reserves to spoliate Native culture. There is little doubt that the French shared with other Europeans the concept of the right of colonization—yet they asserted their claim only against other European contenders.

The official policy and royal intentions, from which the Crown never deviated, were clearly enunciated in the royal instructions to Governor Courcelles (1665–1672). Whether this policy represented a recognition of aboriginal title and rights is a fascinating question.

The King has two principal objectives with regard to the native Indians.

The first is to procure their conversion to the Christian and Catholic faith as soon as possible, and to achieve that, besides the instructions that will be given them by the missionaries whom His Majesty supports for this purpose under the direction of Msgr. de Petraea, his intention is that the officers, soldiers and all his other subjects treat the Indians with gentleness, justice and equity, without ever causing them any hurt or violence; that the lands which they inhabit never be usurped under pretext that they are better or more suited to the French.

The second objective of His Majesty is, in time, to make these Indians his subjects, working gainfully for the increase of commerce which will become established little by little in Canada, once it has been well brought under cultivation; but his intention is that all this be carried out in goodwill and that these Indians take it up out of their own interest. His Majesty knows that the males among these peoples do not want to devote themselves to the cultivation of the soil . . . but His Majesty also knows that the Indian females are very hard-working especially in the growing of maize which is their staple food.

Collection de Manuscrits contenant lettres, mémoires, et autres documents historiques relatifs à la Nouvelle-France (Quebec: Coté & Cie, 1883), Vol. I, Instructions to Governor Courcelles, 1665, p. 175. trans. C.J.J.

Cultural Exchanges—Some Examples of Mutual Benefits

Both the Indians and the French derived benefits from cultural interaction during the French régime. Early French colonists quickly adopted such Indian articles as birch bark canoes, snowshoes and moccasins, and Native practices like tobacco-smoking and soaking plant seeds to force germination. Reports from New France such as the *Jesuit Relations* indicated that the Indians readily accepted trade items obtained from French traders, including metal axes, blankets and iron cooking pots. One popular account by the French trader Nicholas Denys in 1672 reported that the Huron culture had been changed by the adoption of kettles, knives and muskets, articles that the Huron found "more convenient" than their traditional wares.

Few original illustrations of cultural practices in the French régime have survived. These pictorial representations afford us a glimpse of the impact of cultural exchange. What were the benefits—and possible undesirable effects—of this cultural exchange?

Canadian going to war on snowshoes, 1722

"Pie Island on Lake Superior"

Ceremonial Practices—Reports on Funeral Observances and Gift-Giving, 1723 and 1749

Many Native ceremonial practices, and the vocabulary attached to them, were adopted by the French. The French loved ritual and ceremony as much as did the Indians; they paid careful attention to etiquette and to protocol. From earliest contact the French gave presents to the Indians upon formalizing alliances, opening trade fairs and arming military expeditions. Gift-giving was widely practiced in all Native societies. It was not spontaneous and voluntary; it was required as tribute, as a token of hospitality, as a peace-keeping pledge, or as an offering to compensate the victims of crime. The

French fell into line with the obligatory nature of giving presents in their relations with the various nations. They found it essential to win and retain the favour of certain trading captains, warriors, guides and hosts. Two prime examples of the sharing of cultural practices were provided by Sister Duplessis de Ste-Hélène's brief description of an Indian-Catholic funeral observance, and a 1749 statement of the Royal policy of gift-giving.

Funeral Observances for a Chieftain, 1723

...When some great chieftain of our friendly tribes dies in the upper country, the Governor-General sends a representative on behalf of the French to that nation to lament the deceased and to 'cover his body'. These are performed with great ceremonial. The whole village gathers together, the representatives address the elders, he eulogizes the lamented one, then he unveils his presents, which are placed ceremoniously on the grave of the deceased. It usually consists of items the natives value—some red or blue blankets, some guns, some pointed knives, some strands of tobacco—those are the gifts offered. All these have their meaning and in offering each item an explanation is made why it is offered. For example, one will be to wipe away the tears, another to wash away the shed blood, another to revive courage, another to allay the spirits or to unite the hearts, and likewise for the others. And this whole assembly utters great sighs at each stage of the address as a sign of approval. All these presents go to the closest relatives of the deceased....

P.A.C., MG 3, Series T, Carton 77, Sr. Duplessis de Ste-Hélène to Mme Hecquet, 17 October 1723, pp. 32–33. trans. C.J.J.

Instructions Respecting Presents, 1749

The greater part of the nations have the custom of sending, in the spring of each year, some delegates to Montreal to receive the presents of ammunition and merchandise destined to them and whose distribution is presided over by the Governor, the Lieutenant-General, who in the month of May betakes himself to this town to see to this distribution and to the settlement of matters which concern these nations.

P.A.C., MG 18, G-1, La Jonquière Papers, King to La Jonquière, 30 April 1749, p. 11. trans. C.J.J.

CONFLICTING INTERPRETATIONS

The Heroism of the Civilizers—A Traditional Interpretation

American historian Francis Parkman (1823–93) captured in his writing both the heroism of the early French missionaries and the supposed French genius for getting along with the indigenous peoples. This romanticized view of early relations has become a dominant interpretation for this period of our history.

A life sequestered from social intercourse and remote from every prize which ambition holds worth the pursuit, or a lonely death under forms perhaps the most appalling,—

these were the missionaries' alternatives. Their maligners may taunt them, if they will, with credulity, superstition, or a blind enthusiasm; but slander itself cannot accuse them of hypocrisy or ambition. Doubtless, in their propagandism they were acting in concurrence with a mundane policy; but, for the present at least, this policy was rational and humane. They were promoting the ends of commerce and national expansion. The foundations of French dominion were to be laid deep in the heart and conscience of the savage. His stubborn neck was to be subdued to the 'yoke of the Faith.' The power of the priest established, that of the temporal ruler was secure. These sanguinary hordes, weaned from intestinal strife, were to unite in a common allegiance to God and the King. Mingled with French traders and French settlers, softened by French manners, guided by French priests, ruled by French officers, their now divided bands would become the constituents of a vast wilderness empire, which in time might span the continent. Spanish civilization crushed the Indian; English civilization scorned and neglected him; French civilization embraced and cherished him. Policy and commerce, then, built their hopes on the priests. These commissioned interpreters of the Divine Will, accredited with letters patent from Heaven and affiliated to God's anointed on earth, would have pushed to its most unqualified application the Scripture metaphor of the shepherd and the sheep. They would have tamed the wild man of the woods to a condition of obedience, unquestioning, passive, and absolute,—repugnant to manhood, and adverse to the invigorating and expansive spirit of modern civilization. Yet, full of error and full of danger as was their system, they embraced its serene and smiling falsehoods with the sincerity of martyrs and the self-devotion of saints.

Francis Parkman, *The Jesuits in North America in the Seventeenth Century* (Toronto: George N. Morang, 1899) pp. 130–132.

The Humanity of the Colonizers—Another Traditional Interpretation

Lucien Campeau, a Jesuit historian, has stressed the humanity of the French in their dealings with the Indians. Never doubting the obligation of the missionaries to undermine their traditional beliefs in order to implant Christianity, or of laymen to impose French ways, Campeau emphasizes the benefits of European civilization for Indians.

The French placed humanitarian considerations among the principles governing their relations with these peoples. The North American aborigines were not generally hostile at the outset. They were curious, hospitable, naturally good. The French had no difficulty approaching them and winning their confidence. And soon, French goods, axes, kettles, arrowheads, became a necessity for their clients. The merchants rejoiced over the peaceful access. But they did not go so far as to compromise their profits in making common cause with the indigenous peoples. It took a politician like Champlain to understand that a French alliance with the Montagnais implied obligations. The founder of Quebec quickly learned that the Indians were capricious, impulsive, undisciplined, vindictive, often sullen and dangerous. Attentive and respectful towards them, avoiding all expressions of repugnance or mockery, frank and faithful in his dealings with them, Champlain got their esteem and respect.

Lucien Campeau, *Etablissement à Québec (1616–1634)* (Quebec: Presses de l'Université Laval, 1979), pp. 97–98. trans. C.J.J.

Cultures in Conflict—An Early Critique of French Policy

Alfred Bailey was one of the first historians to seriously question both the achievements of the French intruders and the beneficial results of Western European contact. He emphasized the cultural conflict that had followed the arrival of fishermen, traders, missionaries, settlers and soldiers, as well as the moral disintegration of Indian societies as a result of sustained contact.

> Issuing as a secondary set of characteristics from the Canadian fur trade, closely interlocked with the economic disruption which followed the displacement of native materials by European [ones], intimately related to the disintegrating factors consequent to the spread of drunkenness and disease, and interacting with the elements of political modification which were outlined in the preceding chapter, was the social disorder that existed in eastern Algonkian life which was especially conspicuous in the customs and manners appertaining to love and war. These apparently superficial changes in customs and manners testify to an internal psychological turmoil which resulted from divergent sets of social values within the colony which dissolved the social solidarity of groups, and which dislocated the reproductive functions of formerly stabilized communities, all of which were fraught with serious consequences for the survival capacity of the native people....
>
> In the clash of cultures, even when one group is far superior to the other in most ways, both generally undergo considerable modification, and it is seldom, if ever, entirely beneficial. With the rise of that figure in New France which was known as the coureur de bois, life in the colony underwent a marked change.... Corruption at the trading posts, particularly those of the pays d'en haut, was the rule rather than the exception. And from cheating the Indian it was a short step to cheating his fellow Frenchman and the Government. The corruption and the weakening of the colony in its last days may be traceable to the lowering of standards which resulted from the French woodsmen having shaken off the shackles of their own society, and from social and commercial intercourse with a people of vastly different culture....
>
> Alfred Goldsworthy Bailey, *The Conflict of European and Eastern Algonkian Cultures, 1504–1700* (Saint John: New Brunswick Museum, 1937), pp. 96, 123.

The Colonial Model—An Assessment of the Colonizing Experience

In 1972, E. Palmer Patterson II undertook to write a comprehensive history of Canada's aboriginal peoples. He adopted the colonial model, assuming that the colonizing experiences of aboriginal peoples in different parts of the world would serve to illuminate the Canadian situation. His synthesis set up a "Red-White" opposition which has remained a popular characteristic of much writing about the Indians. However, in the case of French contact, as contrasted with Anglo-American, British and later Canadian contact, Patterson saw many areas of co-operation and mutual understanding.

> The French treatment of Indians, and their racial and cultural attitudes toward them, have frequently been written about. Their relations with the Micmacs, Malecites, and Abenakis, form an early illustration of French behaviour. It is usually pointed out that the French did not look down on the Indians or other non-whites as being racially

inferior, an attitude which is the reverse of that often characteristic of the English. The Jesuit evangelists stayed among their flocks as spiritual leaders and political advisors. The religious attachment made it possible for political ends to be served through their personal influence. The government of New France worked through the priests where possible, including using them to prosecute war against the English.

... The French settlers were few in number and the main thrust of the economy was the fur trade. This meant that the Indian was not threatened in his lands as he was in adjacent New England... The Indians, then, for their own advantage became engaged in wars of international scope. The Indians also profited from gifts from their French allies....

That the Indians regarded themselves as superior is attested to by reports of the Jesuits. The obvious desire for liaison which the French exhibited reinforced this conclusion of the Indians. Economic interdependence developed quickly as the Indians took up European tools, weapons, clothes, and food. Each became indispensible to the other. Other consequences followed the Indian contact with Europeans. The heightened rivalry among groups for the furs and resultant conflicts led to population decline. But disease also accelerated this frequent accompaniment to the European presence....

The European religious forms into which the Indians entered were interpreted by them as being political as well as spiritual. Baptism they took as a solemnization of their alliance with the French.... Conversion also meant the acquisition of French arms; that is, the French provided only Christianized Indians with guns and ammunition. Adherence to Christianity cut across tribal lines and introduced a new tie between peoples. Indians grouped together into intertribal alliances as the rivalry between French and English grew. As we have seen, the advantages of the French over the English were readily apparent to those eastern Algonkian-speaking Indians who witnessed or received reports of the land occupation of the English.

E. Palmer Patterson II, *The Canadian Indian: A History since 1500* (Don Mills: Collier-Macmillan, 1972), pp. 59–62.

The Reserves—A Response to a Crisis

Bruce Trigger, an anthropologist at McGill University who is best known for his history of the Huron people, has suggested that the creation of the first reserve at Sillery should be seen not so much as philanthropic planning for the assimilation of the Indian nomadic peoples, as a move to counter an immediate challenge or crisis.

Unlike the Montagnais at Tadoussac or the Algonkin bands farther west, these peoples did not live in an area from which as middlemen they were able to barter European goods among Indians living in the interior. Hence, in their desire to emulate the lifestyle of their neighbours, they overhunted their own land and then, as the beaver disappeared, became a sullen and unwelcome burden on the French trading company. To cope with this situation, the Society of Jesus founded a mission at Sillery in 1638, where these Montagnais were encouraged to settle and live a Christian life. To enable them to do this, the society provided them with houses, food and clothing purchased with funds the Jesuits had collected for such mission work.

Bruce Trigger in Shepard Krech III, ed. *Indians, Animals, and the Fur Trade* (Athens: University of Georgia Press, 1981), p. 28.

The Invasion of Canada—The March of Microbes

Howard Simpson has argued that the introduction of epidemic diseases had such a great impact, not only in terms of actual depopulation but especially in undermining the traditional cultures and beliefs, that Europeans actually "conquered" America by waging what was unknowing biological warfare.

> The conclusion is inescapable that the English, the French, and the Spanish were materially aided in establishing a beachhead in the New World by the infections they unwittingly introduced to a virgin area. Actually this was probably the determining factor that spelled for them the difference between success and failure. The natives, at full strength, doubtless would have flung the invaders back into the sea. As it was they melted away before a force they could neither combat nor comprehend. Their incantations could not thwart it, nor their wampum influence it.
>
> Howard N. Simpson, *Invisible Armies. The Impact of Disease on American History* (Indianapolis: Bobbs-Merrill Company, 1980), p. 8.

Russian Missions on the Pacific Coast—A Comparative View

The Russians began their fur trading and missionary activities along the Pacific coast of North America during the French régime in Atlantic America. Orthodox missionary activities among the Indians of the Pacific coastal region are particularly interesting when compared with the activities of Catholic missionaries among the Micmacs and Abenakis of the Atlantic coastal region. Sergei Kan, anthropologist and ethnohistorian of the Russian Orthodox missions in North America, argues that the Russians, especially compared to the Protestants in Alaska, were singularly successful—so much so that today, for example, some Tlingit identify Orthodoxy as a trait which distinguishes them from most Europeans and other Indian nations.

> In their work among the Tlingit, Donskoi and other priests were following the basic principles of Orthodox missionary theory and practice developed much earlier and introduced in Southeast Alaska by Fr. Ivan Veniaminov. Compared to most Protestant missionaries, the Orthodox showed greater tolerance of native culture, especially those aspects that did not radically contradict Orthodox dogma and ritual practices. The early Orthodox theologians and the more enlightened Russian missionaries in Siberia and Alaska did not necessarily equate Christianization with Westernization or even Russification.
>
> First and foremost, the Orthodox Church emphasized that the word of God had to be preached in the native language and similar to Catholicism, invested considerable time and effort in translating major prayers, liturgy, and the New Testament into various native languages.... [An] Orthodox seminary trained Tlingit deacons, song-leaders, interpreters, and other lay workers who were bi– and even trilingual and carried out missionary work among their own people, helping to maintain Orthodox parishes in those villages that for years lacked a resident priest.
>
> This emphasis on utilizing native languages in missionization was combined with considerable interest in indigenous customs and beliefs, exemplified in several ethno-

graphic studies of the Tlingit. . . .

Sergei Kan, "Russian Orthodox Missionaries and the Tlingit Indians of Alaska, 1880–1900", Unpublished paper presented at Second Laurier Conference on North American Ethnohistory and Ethnology, May 1983, pp. 13–15. With permission.

An Ethnohistorical Approach—The North American Overview

The study of indigenous peoples and their contacts with Europeans was long the preserve of anthropologists, ethnologists and sociologists. A number of historians, among them James Axtell of the College of William and Mary, have argued that the study of the Native peoples would be greatly enhanced if the critical methods of using documents and records and the expertise concentrated on the history of Western colonial cultures were brought to bear in the analysis of Native cultures. Axtell's survey of North American contacts has led him to conclude that the greatest cultural gap between European intruders and Indian hosts was intellectual and social, not technological. Furthermore, the Indians were not as receptive to European innovations, nor as underdeveloped, as often thought.

The invasion of North America by European men, machines, and microbes was primarily an aggressive attempt to subdue the newfound land and its inhabitants, and to turn them to European profit. Because it was not totally unlike that of Europe, the land itself could be brought to terms by the increasingly effective methods of western technology and capitalist economy. The American natives, however, posed a more serious problem. While they shared certain characteristics with the rest of mankind known to Europe, their cultures were so strange, so numerous, and so diverse that the invaders found it impossible to predict their behavior. If the Europeans hoped to harness, or at least neutralize, the numerically superior natives, they could ill afford to tolerate behavior that was as unpredictable as it was potentially dangerous. . . .

From its inception, the invasion of North America was launched on waves of pious intent. Nearly all the colonial charters granted by the French and English monarchs in the sixteenth and seventeenth centuries assign the wish to extend the Christian Church and to save savage souls as a principal, if not the principal, motive for colonization. . . .

The Indians were incredibly tenacious of their culture and life-style, but their traditionalism was neither blind nor passive. As the history of the missions clearly shows, the native peoples of the Northeast were remarkably resourceful in adjusting to new conditions, especially in using elements of European religious culture for their own purposes. According to the social and political circumstances in which they found themselves after contact, they accepted the missionaries' offerings in just the amounts necessary to maintain their own cultural identity. They may have made individual or short-term miscalculations of self-interest, white strength, and policy direction—no group is capable of a perfect functionalism—but in general they took what they needed for resistance and accepted only as much as would ensure survival. Because of their creative adaptability and the defects of the mission programs, many Indian people were never fully 'washed white in the blood of the lamb'. Although their outer lives could be partially 'reduced to civility', their inner resources were equal to the invasion within. As long as native people continued to think of themselves as 'original people', the religious frontiers of North America remained open.

James Axtell, *The European and the Indian, Essays in the Ethnohistory of Colonial North America* (New York: Oxford University Press, 1981), pp. 41, 43, 86.

An Ethnohistorical Approach—The Case of New France

Cornelius J. Jaenen of the University of Ottawa has called for the work of a vast number of disciplines—ranging from law, medicine, philosophy, and religious studies to the social sciences—to be applied in historical analysis and interpretation. This "new history" approach emphasizes the dynamism and adaptability of both Indian and French cultures in contact, attempts to understand the interaction in changing contexts, and leads to conclusions which often challenge the traditional and accepted views. Jaenen's emphasis is not so much on winners and losers, victors and victims, as it is on the constant evolution of all social groups in contact with each other.

Acculturation is a two-way process. The French were affected by contact too. When any culture is transplanted it changes and varies, but such adaptations are more marked when the society comes into contact and into conflict with other cultures. There follows an exchange and interaction of cultures which can, theoretically, enrich or impoverish both. Cultural *métissage* results, out of which a new culture can emerge. In a limited way, this is what began to occur in New France in the seventeenth century. The Indian societies were undermined and disoriented in several respects, as has been shown, without at the same time being afforded an opportunity to reorganize and consolidate themselves into Euro-Indian cultures. The French, on the other hand, did begin to develop a distinctive Canadian culture from a French Renaissance base, which was somewhat changed in both form and spirit by the North American environment and experience, and which was greatly enriched by and made the beneficiary of the centuries-old Indian experience in North America.

In the French experience, as in the Amerindian, paradoxes were to be found. The highest aboriginal civilizations were those which assimilated most readily to European society, but were also those best equipped to retain their ancestral beliefs and social structures and so resist losing their identity. In French society, the paradox was that in the seminal development of a distinctive Canadian-French culture, owing much to transplantation and to contact with Amerindians, the efforts to mould the colony in the image of metropolitan France increased with the passing of time. A result of the important contacts with the indigenous tribes of New France—contacts which absorbed much evangelical zeal, which sustained the economy, and which threatened or assured military and political survival—was a growing Canadian ethnocentrism. The colonists turned to their culture, particularly their religion, as a source of identity. There they found a sense of stability and security. As New France became more like Old France it follows that the cultural gap between French and Amerindian widened rather than closed.

Cornelius J. Jaenen, *Friend and Foe: Aspects of French-Amerindian Cultural Contact in the Sixteenth and Seventeenth Centuries* (Toronto: McClelland & Stewart, 1976), pp. 196–197.

A Guide to Further Reading

1. Overviews

Bailey, Alfred G., *The Conflict of European and Eastern Algonkian Cultures, 1504-1700*. Saint John: New Brunswick Museum, 1937.

Heidenreich, Conrad, *Huronia: A History and Geography of the Huron Indians, 1600-1650*. Toronto: McClelland and Stewart, 1971.

Jaenen, Cornelius J., *Friend and Foe*. Toronto: McClelland and Stewart, 1976.

_____, *The French Relationship with the Native Peoples of New France*. Ottawa: Department of Indian Affairs, 1984.

Jenness, Diamond, *The Indians of Canada*. Ottawa: Queen's Printer, 1967.

Kennedy, J.H., *Jesuit and Savage in New France*. New Haven: Yale University Press, 1950.

McGee, H.F., *The Native Peoples of Atlantic Canada*. Toronto: McClelland and Stewart, 1974.

Muise, D.A., ed., *Approaches to Native History in Canada*. Ottawa: National Museums, 1977.

Patterson, E. Palmer, *The Canadian Indian: A History Since 1500*. Don Mills: Collier-Macmillan, 1972.

Surtees, Robert, *The Original People*. Toronto: Holt, Rinehart and Winston, 1971.

Trigger, Bruce G., *The Children of Aataentsic: A History of the Huron People to 1660*. Montreal: McGill-Queen's University Press, 1976.

_____, *The Indians and the Heroic Age of New France*. Canadian Historical Association Booklet, No. 30. Ottawa: CHA, 1977.

_____, *Natives and Newcomers*. Montreal: McGill-Queen's University Press, 1985.

Upton, L.F.S., *Micmacs and Colonists: Indian-White Relations in the Maritimes, 1713-1867*. Vancouver: University of British Columbia Press, 1979.

2. Specialized Studies

French and Indian Images and Perceptions

Boucher, Philip, "French Images of America and the Evolution of Colonial Theories, 1650-1700", *Proceedings of the Sixth Annual Meeting of the Western Society for French History*. Santa Barbara: ABC-Clio, 1979, pp. 220-228.

Dickason, Olive P. *The Myth of the Savage*. Edmonton: University of Alberta Press, 1984.

Healy, George R., "The French Jesuit and the Idea of the Noble Savage", *William and Mary Quarterly*, Vol. XV (1958), pp. 143-167.

Jaenen, Cornelius J., "Amerindian Views of French Culture in the Seventeenth Century", *Canadian Historical Review*, Vol. LV (1974), pp. 261-291.

_____, "Conceptual Frameworks for French Views of America and Amerindians", *French Colonial Studies*, Vol. 2 (1978), pp. 1-22.

Smith, Donald B., *Le Sauvage: The Native People in Quebec Historical Writing on the Heroic Period (1534-1663) of New France*. Ottawa: National Museum of Man, 1974.

Policies of Assimilation

Dickason, Olive P., *Louisbourg and the Indians: A Study in Imperial Race Relations, 1713-1760*. Ottawa: Parks Canada, 1976.

Jaenen, Cornelius J., "The Indian Problem in the 17th Century" in J.M. Bumsted, ed., *Documentary Problems in Canadian History, Vol. 1— Pre-Confederation*. Georgetown:

Irwin Dorsey, 1969, pp. 1-24.

Pendergast, James F. and Bruce G. Trigger, *Cartier's Hochelaga and the Dawson Site*. Montreal: McGill-Queen's University Press, 1972.

Stanley, G.F.G., "The First Indian'Reserves' in Canada", *Revue d'histoire de l'Amérique française*, Vol. IV (1950), pp. 178-210.

_____, "The Policy of Francization as Applied to the Indians during the Ancien Régime:", *Revue d'histoire de l'Amérique française*, Vol. III (1949), pp. 333-348.

Warfare and Military Relations

Goldstein, R.A., *French-Iroquois Diplomatic and Military Relations 1609-1701*. The Hague: Mouton, 1969.

Hunt, George T., *The Wars of the Iroquois: A Study in Inter-Tribal Relations*. Madison: University of Wisconsin Press, 1940.

Trigger, Bruce G., "The French Presence in Huronia: The Structures of Franco-Huron Relations in the First Half of the Seventeenth Century", *Canadian Historical Review*, Vol. XLIX (1968), pp. 107-141.

Trade Relations

Innis, Harold A., *The Fur Trade in Canada: An Introduction to Canadian Economic History*. New Haven: Yale University Press, 1930.

Jacobs, Wilbur, *Wilderness Politics and Indian Gifts*. Lincoln: University of Nebraska Press, 1966.

Judd, Carol and Arthur J. Ray, eds., *Old Trails and New Directions*. Toronto: University of Toronto Press, 1979.

Martin, Calvin, *Keepers of the Game—Indian-Animal Relationships and the Fur Trade*. Berkeley: University of California Press, 1978.

Quimby, George I., *Indian Culture and European Trade Goods*. Madison: University of Wisconsin Press, 1966.

Ray, Arthur J., *Indians in the Fur Trade*. Toronto: University of Toronto Press, 1974.

Comparative American Studies

Axtell, James, *The European and the Indian: Essays in the Ethnohistory of Colonial North America*. New York: Oxford University Press, 1981.

Berkhofer, Robert F., Jr., *Salvation and the Savage*. Lexington: University of Kentucky Press, 1965.

Bowden, Henry Warner, *American Indians and Christian Missions*. Chicago: University of Chicago Press, 1981.

Jennings, Francis, *The Invasion of America*. Chapel Hill: University of North Carolina Press, 1975.

_____, *The Ambiguous Iroquois Empire*. New York: W.W. Norton, 1984.

Krech, Shepard, ed., *Indians, Animals, and the Fur Trade*. Athens: University of Georgia Press, 1981.

Salisbury, Neal, *Manitou and Providence*. New York: Oxford University Press, 1982.

Sheehan, Bernard, *Savagism and Civility*. Cambridge: Cambridge University Press, 1980.

Simpson, Howard N., *Invisible Armies: The Impact of Disease on American History*. Indianapolis: Bobbs-Merrill Company, 1980.

Vaughan, Alden T., *New England Frontier: Puritans and Indians, 1620-1675*. Boston: Little, Brown, 1965.

2

VISIONS OF NEW FRANCE

What Was the Colony's Role in the Empire?

"For the welfare, advantage, and the glory of the French name." These glowing words attributed to Samuel de Champlain are the ones which spring to mind when the question of what brought the French to Canada is raised. Many French colonizers who followed Champlain undoubtedly shared this vision of New France as a New World colony promising "riches in gold and glory", but most soon realized that this was not to be the colony's fate. Instead, New France yielded only the disappointing "treasures" of cod and furs, grew slowly compared to the neighbouring New England colonies, and eventually suffered conquest in 1760 by a foreign power.

Even though New France never fulfilled Champlain's grand expectations, it did come to occupy a significant place in the French empire. From the beginning, French and colonial officials joined in a continuing debate over New France's relationship to the mother country and its proper role in the seventeenth- and early-eighteenth-century French imperial system. Some officials in both France and the colony saw New France as a static, transplanted French society, with little value except as a base for the fur trade; others viewed the colony as a North American hinterland with potential for commercial expansion. Thus, throughout the French régime, disputes frequently arose about the colony's role—mostly in response to commercial, religious and military imperatives and to the changing needs and policies of old France.

In exploring New France's role in the Empire, we will focus on some of the contending visions of the period among Royal officials, colonial administrators, French traders and military leaders. Among the varied visions of New France to be considered are that of a new land of gold and riches, a New-

World Utopia[1], an expansionary commercial empire, a compact Laurentian colony, a mercantile supply base, and a strategic military outpost. Determining which role was of paramount importance to France—and to the colony itself—is the central task left for our readers.

Any serious study of New France's role in the Empire must begin with a review of the colony's history in relation to French imperial policy. The first French people to arrive are believed to have been fishermen plying the Newfoundland banks around 1504, although the presence of both cod and furs from there on the Rouen (France) market before that date attests to a much earlier contact. Both Jacques Cartier (1534–36), explorer of the St. Lawrence waterway, and Samuel de Champlain, the founder of the first permanent French settlement (1608), were searching for a route to the Western Sea and were motivated, at least initially, by visions of the gold and riches of the Orient. The merchant associations and commercial companies, which later were granted royal charters for the exploitation of the New World, all hoped, albeit in vain, for returns comparable to the riches in gold, silver and precious stones reaped by traders in the Spanish colonies. When New France became a Royal province of France in 1663, King Louis XIV assumed responsibility for the administration, defence and settlement of the North American colony and the state began to actively promote the search of lucrative mines and the elusive route to the Western Sea. For a century both objectives were pursued with little success, although the French did push their outposts down to the mouth of the Mississippi river, up the headwaters of the Missouri, and west to the foothills of the Rockies. Nevertheless, New France did not yield the wealth that New Spain had yielded.

Throughout its colonial development New France functioned as part of a French mercantile trading system. Mercantilism as a general concept envisaged colonies as existing primarily for the economic benefit of the mother country. In such a scheme, profitable colonies produced raw materials which were sent to the mother country for manufacturing or processing, then some of the finished products were sold in the colonies, the transportation both ways being assured by French vessels with French crews. Colonies were cast in the role of suppliers of raw materials (or staples) and markets for surplus goods. Canadian initiative was stifled, to the extent that local industries which might compete with those of the mother country were prohibited. Nevertheless, the colony did benefit to the degree that it had an assured market for its staple products and the investment, insurance and transportation risks (which were enormous at the time) were all assumed by French merchants.

The objective of the French government seemed to be to amass as much gold and silver bullion as possible because it was believed this would enable France to achieve world economic supremacy. It was also believed that the state should encourage the growth of population (numbers being equated with

---

1. Utopia was an imaginary island having a perfect social and political system, described by Sir Thomas More in a romance of that title, published in 1516 and widely known throughout Europe.

power) and should actively intervene in business affairs. The economy of the empire, in other words, was to serve the political and military objectives of the Crown and its administration. Disputes arose, however, when the Governor or Intendant, two appointed colonial officials, began advocating policies to expand the colony and make it more economically stable and self-sufficient.

By the beginning of the eighteenth century, the colonial situation was changing and New France seemed to be valued increasingly for its strategic military importance. New France had become more than a commercial outpost whose lifeblood was the fur trade. The growing rivalry of the Anglo-American colonies and the sometimes faltering support of the Indian nations (especially when a glut of furs on the French market occurred and there was talk of cutting down this trade upon which the Indians had come to depend to some extent) called for some reconsideration of the colony's role. The Treaty of Utrecht (1713), which marked the end of the War of Spanish Succession, dealt France a severe blow. It saw the loss of Acadia to Britain, the surrender of the captured Hudson's Bay Company posts and Newfoundland outports, and the recognition of British sovereignty over the Iroquois. Yet, in the face of these territorial losses and the colony's declining economic importance, French authorities reacted by adopting a more aggressive military strategy in North America, building the mighty fortress at Louisbourg and strengthening the Great Lakes-Mississippi chain of forts. At the very time that leading French social critics and philosophers were advocating the abandonment of all colonies, the Royal administration seemed to see a new military role for New France.

Over the course of New France's development from the first discoveries to the Conquest, a number of critical questions arise. What visions of New France motivated the French in their discovery, exploitation and colonization of America? How did French colonial policies—and the rivalry with Britain—affect the development of New France and ultimately decide its fate? And, during New France's 150 years of existence, what was its predominant role in the French empire?

SELECTED CONTEMPORARY SOURCES

EARLY VISIONS OF GOLD, GLORY AND GOD

The success of the Spanish in discovering the fabulous riches of Central and South America seems to have greatly influenced the earliest French hopes and objectives in Canada. At the time of French discovery the gold and riches of Spanish America were well known in France and it awakened a hope of the advent of another "Golden Age"[2]. Allied to these imperialistic dreams of

---

2. The idea of a "Golden Age" was based on a view that human history passed through "ages" or cycles of mankind in which empires rise and fall. The golden age, a period of fulfillment, contentment and simplicity, was considered the greatest of these ages.

commercial exploitation were visions conjured up by evangelical French Catholicism. For from the outset of New France, French kings also viewed their mission as one of bringing northern America under the dominion of a Christian God and of converting the Indians to the Catholic faith. Such visions of a new Golden Age and Christian dominion over the New World were strongly reflected in ideas of the colony's role, especially during the so-called early "heroic age" of New France from 1608 to 1663.

Jacques Cartier's Tale of A Kingdom of Fabled Riches, 1535

During his explorations of 1535–36 Jacques Cartier visited the island of Montreal and, from the summit of one of the mountains there, he saw in the distance the upper St. Lawrence River and the wide expanse of the Ottawa River. This magnificent view—and tales of promise and abundance related by the Iroquois chief Donnacona—awakened the desire to find the route to the land of fabled riches, whether in America or in Asia. Cartier's journal and the report of Lagarto, a Portuguese informer in the service of the King of France, set out this vision of fabulous wealth.

And they showed us furthermore that along the mountains to the north, there is a large river, which comes from the west like the said river [St. Lawrence]. We thought this river [Ottawa] must be the one that flows past the kingdom and province of Saguenay; and without our asking any questions or making any sign, they seized the chain of the Captain's whistle, which was made of silver, and a dagger-handle of yellow copper-gilt like gold, that hung at the side of one of the sailors, and gave us to understand that these came from up that river Ottawa, where lived *Agojuda*....

The Captain, on being informed of the large number of Indians at Stadacona, though unaware of their purpose, yet determined to outwit them, and to seize their Chief, Taignoagny, Dom Agaya and the headmen. And moreover he had quite made up his mind to take Chief Donnacona to France, that he might relate and tell to the king all he had seen in the west of the wonders of the world; for he had assured us that he had been to the land of the Saguenay where there are immense quantities of gold, rubies and other rich things, and that the men there are white as in France and go clothed in woolens.

H.P. Biggar, ed., *The Voyages of Jacques Cartier* (Ottawa: Acland, 1924), pp. 200–202, 220–221.

... and beyond the falls the King of France says the Indian King told him there is a large city called Sagana, where there are many mines of gold and silver in great abundance, and men who dress and wear shoes like we do; and that there is abundance of clove, nutmeg and pepper. And thus I believe he will again decide to send there a third time seeing his great desire; and thus he told me that he wished to build a fort well up the river, on the north side, and that commencing it in the summer, in the following year the brigantines may go there to pass the falls, for in that land the summer is short, and winter long and exceedingly cold.... And that there are certain animals whose hides as leather are worth ten cruzados each, and for this sum they are sold in France, and that ten thousand of these skins being brought they are worth 100,000 cruzados. Greatly praising the rich novelty of the land and telling these and other tales; and that there are men who fly, having wings on their arms like bats, although they fly but little, from the ground to a tree, and from tree to tree to the ground. And the said Jacques brought to the King a sample of gold, ten stones shaped like small goose quills, and he says it is fine gold and comes from the said city of Sagana.

H.P. Biggar, ed., *A Collection of Documents relating to Jacques Cartier and the Sieur de Roberval* (Ottawa: Public Archives of Canada, 1930), pp. 76–79.

Building a Community of God—A Récollet's View, 1615

The early dreams of a kingdom of great riches, taken up by the founding governor of New France Samuel de Champlain and his successors, held little attraction for French missionaries motivated by religious faith and evangelical zeal. From the time of their first arrival in 1615, missionaries attempted a Christianizing and civilizing mission in the colony and among the Indian peoples. Some early French missionaries were visionaries who sought to build a New Jerusalem on the banks of the St. Lawrence. Other Christian idealists even welcomed the French policy of sending undesirables, criminals and religious non-conformists to the colony because the New World might provide a form of redemption for the disadvantaged.

The most assured means, Monseigneur, is to settle French. The King can possess more in this country, at little expense, than he could elsewhere with great expenditure and shedding of blood. For thank God there is no enemy to fight here; the Natives wish it for their security. The Hurons promise to leave their country, although it is cleared and productive in maize, and to come to live next to the French, insofar as the hunting of moose, deer and other animals is very good. I advise parents to no longer constrain their children to become monks, in order to avoid dividing their estates, but to give them what it costs to become such and send them to this country where there are attractive lands. The nobility which takes up these lands in excess would do well to restrain themselves a bit and each undertake a settlement of fifteen people. This is also a matter for the King, which if he does not wish to depend on his own resources, there is in France every year such a large number of guilty persons, charged only with one or two misdemeanours and who indeed were honest persons. If they were relegated to these parts, I believe it would be exercising mercy and justice—mercy in granting them their lives, and justice in banishing them from their country. And if in a few years a second France were created, I promise only lovely lands and good rivers, good hunting and better fishing to whoever can make it his occupation.

If colonists were here we would stay among them in little houses apart; the Natives, even the nomads, would become domiciled little by little seeing the fruits of labour. Those who are in the upper country would come down and the French would push forward as much as they choose towards the south, and thus we would instruct them all, each according to his capacities....

Bibliothèque Nationale, Paris, 500 de Colbert, Vol. 483, Father Denis Jamet to Cardinal de Joyeuse, 15 July 1615, f. 582. trans. C.J.J.

Faded Dreams of Riches—Patoulet's Memorandum, 1672

By the middle of the seventeenth century it was clear that Canada did not possess abundant gold, silver, diamonds and precious stones. In 1665 the first

Intendant, Jean Talon, arrived at Quebec. On his way from France he had stopped at Gaspé to investigate the lead deposits he had heard about. The following year he discovered a seam of coal at Quebec, but it could not be mined. Instead, in 1670, coal mining operations were started at Cape Breton which, in fact, continue to the present day. Twenty barrels of iron ore from Trois-Rivières were sent to France for evaluation. Copper samples brought back from the north shore of Lake Superior by Jesuit missionaries led to a prolonged search for their source. But were iron, lead and copper the metals that France hoped to find in the colony? A bureaucrat cautioned the Minister of Marine, who was responsible for colonial affairs, about the prospects for New France.

> There appear to be many mines of iron, copper and lead in Canada. But Patoulet believes that the King ought not to undertake expenditures for their discovery. It must be the work of time. But as the iron mines are already known through the efforts of Mons. Talon, and that moreover Monseigneur is willing that the inhabitants should profit thereby, Patoulet believes that whoever will represent His Majesty in Canada could organize an association of merchants which could undertake its development.
>
> P.A.C., MG 1, Series C11A, Vol. III, Memorandum of Sieur Patoulet, 25 January 1672, p. 384. trans. C.J.J.

VISIONS OF A NEW-WORLD UTOPIA

In spite of the often discouraging prospects, some French idealists advanced greater dreams for the colony's role in the Empire. French policies which treated Canada as a virtual "dumping ground" for undesirables were looked upon as providing an opportunity to create a kind of New-World Utopia, or ideally perfect place.

Marc Lescarbot's Utopian Vision of New France, 1609

Under the pen of Marc Lescarbot, a learned lawyer and poet who wrote the first history of New France (1609), the vision of a penal colony was transformed into a Utopian dream. If Lescarbot's vision were pursued, New France would come to signify a truly new and better version of Old France, where new hope and a new life would be attainable not just for the condemned and fallen but also for the oppressed, the persecuted, and the disadvantaged.

> You must make an alliance, dear Mother, in imitation of the course of the sun. For as he daily carries his light hence to New France, so let your civilisation, your justice, your piety, in a word your light, be also carried thither by your children. . . . Even if they do not find there the treasures of Atabalippa and his like, which have whetted the appetite of the Spaniards and drawn them to the West Indies, yet shall they not be in want, for this province will be worthy to be called your daughter, the colony of men of courage, the Academy of Arts, and the retreat of those of your children who are not contented with their lot; many of whom, for lack of occupation, go to foreign lands, where they have already taught the crafts which of old were your special portion. But if, instead of

so doing, they take the road to New France, they will no longer wantonly turn aside from the obedience of their natural prince, but will carry on great enterprises upon the waters....

...The inducements are great enough to attract men of valour and of worth, who are spurred on by a goodly and honourable ambition to be the first in the race for immortality by this action, which is one of the greatest men can set before themselves.... [T]hose of your children who would fain leave this salt sea to go to drink of the fresh waters of Port Royal in New France, will soon find there, by God's aid, a retreat so agreeable, that they will greatly desire to go thither to people the province and to fill it with offspring.

W.L. Grant, ed., *The History of New France by Marc Lescarbot* (Toronto: Champlain Society, 1907), I, pp. 13–15, 17–18.

Robert Challes' Vision of a "Rich and Flourishing Kingdom", 1715

Another visitor to Acadia and Canada, this time in the latter part of the seventeenth century, was Robert Challes, described as a "King's scribe", who invested heavily in the sedentary fisheries at Ft. St. Louis (Guysborough, N.S.) and who prepared lengthy memoranda on colonial conditions and prospects for Seignelay, the Minister of Marine, in 1684. Challes was appalled when he learned that France in the Treaty of 1713 had ceded much of Acadia, as well as areas important to the cod fisheries and the fur trade, to Britain, believing that the colonization policies of Cardinal Richelieu and J.-B. Colbert had been betrayed.

God grant that I be a poor prophet; but I foresee that Quebec and Canada will soon be anglicized. That is part of what the plenipotentiaries of France should have foreseen, before signing the sad treaty of Utrecht which will certainly be the cause one day of numerous bloody wars, and in which this cession would not have been included if M. Colbert and M. Seignelay, his son, had been alive....M. Colbert knew that money spent wisely, for such a matter, was seed sown in the ground which would bring forth a hundredfold, both for the profit of the ploughman and that of the master of the field where the grain was sown.... He followed the principle of Cardinal Richelieu, sending reinforcements and help to the colonies which he had established and establishing some where as yet there were none....

I heard him say that it would have been better had France not kept galley fleets because instead of placing so many condemned to forced labour there they could have been sent, in chains, to Acadia, which being perceived as another world would have inspired more terror than the galleys; also because those who were sent there always have the hope of returning, instead of relegating them to a country which the common people regard as a lost land, the certitude of never returning to their motherland would have made those who wanted to imitate them in their crimes tremble with fear. Those unfortunates, obliged to clear the land, would have undergone a veritable corporal punishment for their mistakes. Besides, their labour would have been very profitable to the colonies and to France: to the colonies, through the cultivation of the land; to France because without loosening the purse strings it would have founded a kingdom as rich and flourishing as itself.

A. Augustin-Thierry, *Un colonial au temps de Colbert: Mémoires de Robert Challes, Ecrivain du Roi* (Paris: Plon, 1931), pp. 24, 26, 77–78. trans. C.J.J.

VISIONS OF A DYNAMIC COMMERCIAL EMPIRE

Dreams for New France like that of Robert Challes were also capable of inspiring ambitious colonial administrators with ideas of commercial expansion for the colony. As Minister of Marine and Colonies from 1669 to 1683, Jean-Baptiste Colbert pursued a policy of mercantilism, seeking to develop a trading system based on an economically powerful and self-sufficient France. His appointee as first Intendant in New France, the ambitious Jean Talon, (1665–68 and 1670–72) followed a similar policy by attempting to make Canada a self-sufficient and prosperous extension of the French kingdom. His boast, at one point, that he was clothed from head to toe in Canadian-made goods did not sit well with the Ministry of Marine, for it clearly meant that Canadian cottage industries were competing with those of France.

Jean Talon's Vision of A "Great and Powerful State", 1665 and 1671

In his correspondence with Colbert, Jean Talon described New France as a colony with great potential for commercial hinterland expansion.

... in order to give you a rough sketch, I have the honour to tell you that Canada is a very vast extent ... the limits so far distant are they from us, and that on the south nothing prevents us from carrying the name and arms of His Majesty as far as Florida, New Sweden, New Holland and New England, and by way of the first of these countries one can pass through to Mexico.

That all this country, watered variously by the St. Lawrence river and by beautiful rivers which flow into its bed from both sides, has communication by means of these same rivers with several native nations rich in furs....

That the climate, which by reason of its great cold causes apprehension about living in the country, is for all that so salubrious that one is rarely ill and that one lives long here.... The fertility for cereals is apparent to us by the abundant harvests which the cleared and cultivated lands yield each year....

But if His Majesty has regarded this country as a good project in which one can form a great Kingdom and found a monarchy, or at least a very considerable State, I cannot persuade myself that His Majesty will succeed in his design by leaving in other hands than his own the seigneury, the property, the lands, the nomination to cures, and I add even the trade which is the soul of the Plantation claimed.

P.A.C., MG 1, Series C11A, Vol. 2, Talon to Colbert, 4 October 1665, pp. 200–201, 206–207. trans. C.J.J.

... I am not a man of the Court and I do not say, out of a singular passion to flatter the King and without just foundation, that this portion of the French monarchy will become something great. What I discover about it at close range prejudices me in this direction, and these fragments of foreign nations bordering on the sea, so well settled, already tremble with fear at the sight of what His Majesty has done in seven years in the lands here. The measures we have taken to confine them to very narrow limits by means of the acts of possession which I ordered performed do not allow them to expand and at the same time do not give occasion to treat them as usurpers and wage war on them.

Pierre Margry, ed., *Découvertes et établissements des Français dans l'ouest et dans le sud de l'Amérique septentrionale, 1614–1754*, 6 vols. (Paris: D. Jouast, 1876–1886), I, Talon to Louis XIV, 2 November 1671, pp. 99–100. trans. C.J.J.

Building Up the Colony—An Account from the *Jesuit Relations*, 1666–67

From the time of his appointment as Intendant in 1665, Talon had attempted to act on the Royal Government's plans to strengthen the colony. To rectify an imbalance in the number of males and females in the colony and to help increase the colony's population by natural growth, the government of France—at Talon's urging—sent several shiploads of young women known popularly as *les filles du roi* to New France as prospective brides for settlers and soldiers. Through the offer of free land, Talon also induced many disbanded soldiers from the Carignan-Salières regiment to settle along the Richelieu River, bolstering the colony's defences. By the time Talon left New France in 1672, the colony's population had jumped from 3 200 to more than 7 000 souls.

An account in the *Jesuit Relation of 1666–67*, glowing with praise for Talon's activities, seemed to indicate that the Intendant worked hard trying to realize his vision of an economically self-sufficient colony.

... the first thoughts of Monsieur Tallon [sic], Intendant for the King in this country, were to exert himself with tireless activity to seek out the means for rendering this country prosperous. He does this both by making trial of all that it can produce, and by establishing commerce and forming business relations—which we can open not only with France, but also with the Antilles, Madeira, and other countries, in Europe as well as in America.

He was so successful in this that fisheries of all kinds are in operation, the rivers being very rich in fish....

The commerce which Monsieur Tallon proposes to carry on with the Islands of the Antilles will be one of this country's chief resources; and already, to ascertain its profitableness, he is this year shipping to those Islands fresh and direct codfish, salted salmon, eels, peas, both green and white, fish-oil, staves, and boards,—all produced in the country.

These cares, which cause him to investigate, with such assiduous devotion, all possible sources of profit in the St. Lawrence and other rivers of this country, do not prevent him from giving a share of his attention to the gain that may be derived from land so rich in every kind of product as is that of Canada.

Therefore, he is directing a careful search for Mines, which appear to be numerous and rich; he is causing the felling of all kinds of timber, which is found everywhere in Canada, and makes it easy for the French, and others who come here to live, to provide themselves with shelter upon their first arrival; he has started the manufacture of Staves, for export to France and to the Antilles, and of Masts, samples of which he is sending this year to La Rochelle for use in the Navy; and he is also giving his attention to wood suitable for ship-building, trial of which has been made in this country by the building of a bark which is found very serviceable, and of a large vessel which is all ready to be launched.

Besides the ordinary grains that have been hitherto harvested, he has started the culture of hemp....

We have this year seen eleven vessels, laden with all sorts of wares, anchored in the roadstead of Québec. We have seen land taken up by many workmen, and also girls, who people our colony and add to the number of our fields. Flocks of sheep meet our eyes, and many horses, which thrive finely in this country and render it great service. And the accomplishment of all this at his Majesty's expense obliges us to acknowledge all the results of his Royal kindness, by vows and prayers. . . . To him alone is due the whole glory of having put this country in such a condition that, if the course of events in the future correspond to that of the past two years, we shall fail to recognize Canada, and shall see our forests, which have already greatly receded, changing into Towns and Provinces which may some day be not unlike those of France.

> R.G. Thwaites, ed., *The Jesuit Relations and Allied Documents*, (New York: Pageant Book Company, 1959), L, pp 240–47.

VISIONS OF A COMPACT LAURENTIAN COLONY

Talon's entreaties to make Canada a "great and powerful" state met with resistance from the Minister of Marine, Colbert, and from the King, Louis XIV. His vision of a vast hinterland empire stretching into the continent of North America ran counter to Royal policy, which aimed at developing colonies primarily for the profit and glory of the mother country. Both Colbert and the King saw New France's proper role as that of a compact Laurentian colony, one which might be more easily defended and did not threaten to "depopulate" France.

Jean-Baptiste Colbert's Case Against Over-Expansion, 1666

Colbert, in a terse reply to Talon, cautioned the Intendant against over-extension which might lead to unwarranted commitments of men, money and materials on the part of France.

> The King cannot agree with all the arguments you make on the means of making Canada a great and mighty State, finding therein diverse obstacles which could be overcome only after a long lapse of time because even if he had no other matters and he could employ both his attention and his power thereto, it would not be prudent to depopulate his Realm as would be necessary to have Canada populated. Besides this consideration which will appear essential to you there is another matter which is that if His Majesty caused a larger number of men to go over than what the Country presently cleared could feed, it is certain that if they did not all perish at the outset at least they would suffer great extremities which by reducing them to continuous listlessness would weaken them little by little. . . . You will understand sufficiently from this discourse that the true means of strengthening this Colony is to have Justice reign there, to establish a good civil administration, to take good care of the inhabitants, to procure for them peace, repose, and abundance, and to inure them of all sorts of enemies, because all these things which are the Basis and foundation of all settlements being well observed the Country will become populated by slow degrees and with the passage of a reasonable period of time could become quite considerable. . . .
>
> You must always have in your mind the plan which I outline in a few words, which is in line with what is contained in greater detail in your Instructions, and to the conversations I had here with you. And never depart therefrom because it is notoriously impossible that all those ideas about forming great and mighty states can succeed if one does not have unprofitable People to send over to the places one wishes to settle.
>
> *Rapport de l'Archiviste de la Province de Quebéc, 1922–1923*, Colbert to Talon, 5 January 1666, p. 41. trans. C.J.J.

The Policy of Concentrated Settlement Reaffirmed, 1696

By 1696, a number of economic problems plagued the colony. These were seized upon in Versailles to emphasize the need to restrict activities by and large to the St. Lawrence Valley settlements in Canada and to avoid unnecessary expansion into the vast interior of North America. To begin with, there was a glut of furs, Canada's staple product, on the French market. The growing number of unlicensed traders or *coureurs de bois* who were going each year into the upper country in search of furs and adventure resulted in an unprecedented accumulation of furs and intensification of Iroquois hostility. This in turn was upsetting the interior nations and bands who were France's allies and trading partners. It was also charged that the drain of young men to the upper country was having an adverse effect on farming and settlement.

> . . . the estrangement of the Outawas and others proceeds from the fact that the French, by ranging the interior of the country, have usurped the trade these nations carried on with the Upper Tribes, and that some of the latter are, on the same account, waging war against the Allies, or obliged to rally themselves to the Iroquois; and that, finally, the ranging of the woods, more unrestricted last year than it ever was before—notwithstanding his Majesty's orders and the reduction of licenses to the number of 25—is the source of all the disorders of the Colony, and has given rise to establishments which by dividing, weaken its strength in such distant regions, and upset the views his Majesty has entertained and which alone ought to prevail—to concentrate it and employ the settlers in the cultivation of the soil, in the fisheries and other pursuits he has always recommended and which they can derive from the nature of the country and their own application and industry. . . .

> * * * * *

> They must, pursuant to his Majesty's invariable orders, observe as their main rule in all departments of the government of that Colony, to concentrate it, and to make it derive its support from the employment of the settlers within its confines and from their trade with the kingdom and with the Indians who will necessarily bring peltries into the Colony in order to procure there those goods of the Kingdom which they require. Such was their wont before the Canadians were permitted to go into the depths of the forest, where they contract every debauched and vicious habit which renders them useless and a burden to civil society; leaving out of consideration the extortions they are guilty of towards the Indians in the excessive prices of the merchandise they carry thither, and the irregularity on account of the bad beaver they accept indifferently from them, because they are sure of being equally paid for it. . . .

> E.B. O'Callaghan, ed., *Documents relative to the Colonial History of the State of New York* (Albany: Weed, Parsons & Co., 1855), Louis XIV to Frontenac and Champigny, 26 May 1696, IX, p. 638.

VISIONS OF A MERCANTILE COLONY

Closely allied to the notion of a compact Laurentian colony were visions of New France's role as that of purely a colony in the French mercantilist system. Such a position was clearly articulated by royal authorities in the early years of the eighteenth century, specifically in response to cases of expansion by missionaries, fur traders and explorers into the interior and to the establishment of French posts at Fort Frontenac (1673) and Detroit (1700). A set of general principles or guidelines, later called mercantilism, consigned New France and other colonies to a role as producers of raw materials, and markets for the manufactures of the mother country.

Pontchartrain's Vision of a Mercantile Colony, 1704

General guidelines for the colonies were developed along lines similar to those in the British imperial system and based on the mercantilist model. The Minister of Marine, Jérôme de Pontchartrain, outlined succinctly for Governor Vaudreuil and Intendant Beauharnois in 1704 how Canada should fit into that model.

His Majesty has been very pleased to learn that the growing of hemp has met with the success that we had hoped for. But he must explain that he never intended to allow cloth to be manufactured in Canada so that the settlers might do without that of France. Thus, no weavers will be sent to the colony. The settlers must forward their hemp to France to be sold either to the state for the servicing of the royal navy, or else to private parties to dispense them from buying this product from foreigners. Generally, they must observe that whatever can compete with the factories of France must never be produced in the colonies. Colonies must act as suppliers of raw materials to enable the factories of the kingdom to do without imports from foreign states. They must consider this as one of the principal purposes of colonies which are established solely for the benefit of the mother countries and never to permit them to do without those countries.

P.A.C., MG 1, Series B, Vol. 25, Memorandum of 14 June 1704, ff. 117–118. trans. C.J.J.

The Mercantilist Role Reaffirmed—A Royal Memorandum, 1705

Although triangular trade among Canada and Acadia, the French West Indies, and metropolitan France had been encouraged in the 1670s, it was felt by 1705 that such an arrangement did not coincide well with mercantilist policy. New France should be more directly tied economically, as it was politically and militarily, to the mother country—and not to other French colonies. In spite of these general guidelines, of course, illicit trade was still being carried on with Albany and the New England ports, providing the colony with other markets and enabling the French colonists to acquire some goods at cheaper prices.

... since colonies must be conceived only in relation to the Kingdom, they must be scrupulously prevented from supplying each other with the merchandise which they are used to drawing from France. It would not be proper, for example, for Canada to supply wheat to the islands [West Indies] in return for refined sugar because this would be prejudicial to the interests of the cities of La Rochelle, Bordeaux, Nantes and the others which send vessels to the colonies and which bear all the charges of the state.

It is equally important to prohibit every type of exchange between the inhabitants of Canada and the English, since the latter would only supply them with the goods they would otherwise obtain from France....

P.A.C., MG 1, Series B, Vol. 27, King to Raudot, 17 June 1705, f. 56. trans. C.J.J.

VISIONS OF A STRATEGIC MILITARY OUTPOST

French military victories in King William's War (1688–1697) seemed to awaken Royal authorities to the strategic value of colonies like New France. Much of the French success in North America was attributed to Pierre Le Moyne d'Iberville (1661–1706), the great Canadian military leader famous for his raids against Hudson's Bay Company posts, which severely disrupted English trade in the Bay. Aided by d'Iberville's naval attacks in the Bay and along the Atlantic coast of America, France successfully defended her empire in the war. Motivated by strategic considerations, d'Iberville pressed successfully for the establishment in 1701 of a permanent southern tidewater colony at the mouth of the Mississippi River—one designed to check English expansion and to strengthen France's North American defences. Following the loss of peninsular Acadia and Placentia (French Newfoundland) in the Treaty of Utrecht (1713), Governor Vaudreuil called for a more aggressive military policy to thwart British ambitions in America and the colony seemed to assume a greater strategic importance in the French empire.

King Louis XIV's Medal, 1690

A medal produced in 1690 celebrated French victories in the New World. The head on the medal was that of Louis XIV; the commemorative scene on its back showed the emblem of France (the fleur-de-lis) triumphant, with Neptune, representing England, dethroned. The medal also seemed to recognize New France's strategic role in the empire:

Louis XIV's medal, 1690

La Galissonnière's View of Canada's Strategic Role, 1750

The great imperial war between France and England, which began in 1744 and continued, after a brief respite, until the collapse of the French empire in 1763, caused Canadians and French alike to consider the strategic importance of Canada. Some French officials like the Comte de La Galissonnière, the interim Governor of New France, saw strategic value in the colony's ability to hobble the vastly superior British forces and to distract the English from French attacks in other theatres of war. In La Galissonnière's strategic plan, Canada's military importance warranted a greatly strengthened system of fortifications throughout the Ohio and Mississippi valleys as far south as Louisiana.

In this memoir, I shall consider Canada strictly as an unproductive frontier.... I will ask if a land, although sterile and a cause of great expenditure, can be abandoned if by its strategic position it provides its inhabitants with a great advantage over its neighbours.

This is precisely the case of Canada. We cannot deny that this colony has always been a burden to France and that it will probably continue to be so for a very long time to come. But it is also the most powerful obstacle we can use to check English ambitions. The only proof of this I need give are the many attempts the English have made against this colony over more than a century. However, I will also add that Canada alone can enable us to wage war on the English possessions in continental America, which are as dear to them as they are valuable in fact. Since their strength grows daily, they will soon swallow up our island colonies as well as those we have on the mainland unless we find a way of limiting their progress.

... if we do not interrupt the rapid progress of the English colonies on the continent, or, what is the same thing, if we do not build up a counterweight that is capable of containing them within their present limits and of forcing them to remain on the defensive, they will soon acquire such great facility for making formidable preparations for war in continental America....

...We should not deceive ourselves into thinking that we can have a navy that can compare to theirs for many years. Our only recourse is to attack them in their overseas possessions. To attempt this with troops launched directly from Europe would cost us dearly, and the chances of success would be slight. But by fortifying ourselves in America we can maintain the advantages we presently enjoy and even increase them by means of expenditures that are small compared to those European armaments would cost.

P.A.C., MG 1, Series C11A, Vol. 96, Memorandum on the Colonies in North America, 1750, pp. 182–4, 202–5, 211–12.

A Final Assessment of the Colony's Strategic Role—The Case for Retaining Canada, 1759

Although New France was conquered and occupied by the British in 1760, the eventual fate of the colony was decided by the peace negotiators, not the admirals or generals. And the success of the military could be undone by the diplomats. The debate continued in France, therefore, over the value of the colony in the Empire. A memorandum on the fate of Canada, prepared in 1759, suggested that Canada should be retained for its strategic position.

The territory owned by France in North America is vaster than the whole European continent. Its wealth is not yet known to us. The choicest areas remain to be settled. The glory of the King seems to require that we preserve such a vast country. In spite of the enormous sums of money we spend there, it is always sad to see the enemy grow greater at our expense. Besides, those expenses could be reduced considerably and are not so conspicuous in peacetime. It would even be easy for someone who is knowledgeable in finance to prove that the amounts of money France derives from the Canadian trade and from its exports to that colony are greater than those the King spends there. The reasons why it is important for a state to have colonies are related to this point.

It is wrong to object that it depopulates the realm. More men die during one year of European war than would be necessary to settle New France.... Once New France is populated, there will be no country easier to preserve. Our regular navy would guard Acadia and Louisbourg. But we can be certain that if France loses Canada, she will need more maritime forces than ever before, because the English will become absolute masters of the sea.

It is true that in the future these vast regions might break up into kingdoms and republics. The same will be true of New England. But how many centuries will this take? To look into a future so remote and so uncertain is to attempt to foresee too much.

And let us suppose that Canada will never be very useful to France and that it might even cost a little money. Must we regard it as of no consequence to prevent a rival nation from expanding, from establishing a despotic empire on the high seas, and from seizing all the trade?

P.A.C., MG 1, Series C11A, Vol. 104, Memorandum of 1759, pp. 600–605.

CONFLICTING INTERPRETATIONS

The varying visions of New France, expressed by both French authorities and Canadians during the French regime, have been strongly reflected in historical interpretations of the colony's role in the Empire. Out of the debates over the contending visions, two general interpretations seem to have emerged. The long-accepted, traditional interpretation suggests that New France was a static, transplanted French feudal colony, dominated by the oppressive weight of Royal absolutism and restrained in its economic growth by French mercantilism. The alternative view, arising from Jean Talon's dream, sees the colony as a dynamic, expansive North American state which had the potential for commercial development. While the traditional hypothesis of a transplanted French feudal colony suffering economic retardation once held sway, it is now being challenged on a number of fronts by historians.

The Classic Interpretation—Francis Parkman's Hypothesis

Much of English-language writing about New France and its place in the French imperial system has been influenced by the classic hypothesis first advanced by the American historian Francis Parkman. Following his strong bias against things French and Catholic, he argued that New France was a backward, authoritarian French feudal colony destined to experience failure and suffer defeat because of serious flaws in its founding philosophy, institutions and policies. According to Parkman, royal despotism, bureaucratic confusion, mercantilist restrictions and Catholic religious oppression all conspired to ensure that the dreams of a New-World Utopia or visions of a French mercantilist empire could never be realized.

It is easy to see the nature of the education, past and present, which wrought on the Canadians and made them what they were. An ignorant population, sprung from a brave and active race, but trained to subjection and dependence through centuries of feudal and monarchical despotism, was planted in the wilderness by the hand of authority, and told to grow and flourish. Artificial stimulants were applied, but freedom was withheld. Perpetual intervention of government,—regulations, restrictions, encouragements sometimes more mischievous than restrictions, a constant uncertainty what the authorities would do next, the fate of each man resting less with himself than with another, volition enfeebled, self-reliance paralyzed,—the condition, in short, of a child held always under the rule of a father, in the main well-meant and kind, sometimes generous, sometimes neglectful, often capricious, and rarely very wise,—such were the influences under which Canada grew up. If she had prospered, it would have been sheer miracle. A man, to be a man, must feel that he holds his fate, in some good measure, in his own hands....

In the building up of colonies, England succeeded and France failed. The cause lies chiefly in the vast advantage drawn by England from the historical training of her people in habits of reflection, forecast, industry, and self-reliance,—a training which enabled them to adopt and maintain an invigorating system of self-rule, totally inapplicable to their rivals....

While New England prospered and Canada did not prosper, the French system had at least one great advantage. It favored military efficiency. The Canadian population sprang in great part from soldiers, and was to the last systematically reinforced by disbanded soldiers. Its chief occupation was a continual training for forest war; it had little or nothing to lose, and little to do but fight and range the woods. This was not all. The Canadian government was essentially military. At its head was a soldier nobleman, often an old and able commander; and those beneath him caught his spirit and emulated his example. In spite of its political nothingness, in spite of poverty and hardship, and in spite even of trade, the upper stratum of Canadian society was animated by the pride and fire of that gallant *noblesse* which held war as its only worthy calling, and prized honor more than life. As for the *habitant*, the forest, lake, and river were his true school; and here, at least, he was an apt scholar. A skilful woodsman, a bold and adroit canoe-man, a willing fighter in time of need, often serving without pay, and receiving from government only his provisions and his canoe, he was more than ready at any time for any hardy enterprise; and in the forest warfare of skirmish and surprise there were few to match him. An absolute government used him at will, and experienced leaders guided his rugged valor to the best account.

Francis Parkman, *The Old Régime in Canada* (Toronto: George N. Morang, 1899) II, pp. 197–202.

The Colony's "Dream of Empire"—Mason Wade's Interpretation

Parkman's classic hypothesis has been directly challenged by many historians who have seen potential for colonial growth and expansion in New France. Drawing upon early visions of a land of "gold, glory and God" and on Jean Talon's dream for a mighty North American state, they have contended that such visions of the colony were both realistic and realizable had France given sufficient support in finance, colonization and trade. Some of these inter-preters suggest that New France was constrained by French bureaucratic controls and mercantilist polices and further imply that, if Canadians had been in control of the colony's affairs, the visions of Champlain or Talon would have been fulfilled.

One historian who summarized this popular interpretation is Mason Wade, a New England native, in his two-volume study of French Canada, *The French Canadians, 1760–1967* (1968).

Talon's vision was neither narrow nor dependent upon instructions from France. His mind was fascinated by the possibilities of the New World, and he dreamed great dreams, which sometimes alarmed the more cautious Colbert. . . .

The existence of English and Dutch settlements along the coast to the south was no bar to Talon's dreams of empire. He wrote home that 'nothing can prevent us from carrying the names and arms of His Majesty as far as Florida, New Sweden, New Holland, and New England.' To realize this dream, Lake Ontario was to be fortified, while the Iroquois were warned by the governor in 1671 to refrain from trading north of the lake. First Jolliet and Père Marquette, then La Salle, traced out the Mississippi waterway, which enabled the French to cut off the English advance and to monopolize the trade of the heart of the continent. The French empire in America soon stretched in a great crescent from the mouth of the St. Lawrence to that of the Mississippi, hemming in the other European settlements on the Atlantic seaboard.

But Talon had not heeded Colbert's significant warning of 1666: It would be better to restrict yourselves to an extent of territory which the colony itself will be able to maintain than to embrace so much land that eventually a part may have to be abandoned, with some consequent discredit to His Majesty's Crown. Talon was called back to France for good in 1672—he had once been briefly recalled because of his quarrels with Bishop Laval—and his successors lacked his genius. Then, in the same year, Louis XIV became involved in the long series of European wars which meant the waning of royal interest and support for the colony across the ocean, whose pleas for more colonists were rejected by Colbert on the ground that France would be depopu-lated. Despite the efforts of Talon, there were only 7,000 Europeans in Quebec and 500 in Acadia by 1675; there were not then, and never were to be, enough men to implement the French claim to the vast expanses labelled New France on the maps of North America. . . . When the final episode of the Seven Years' War opened in 1756, 1,500,000 Anglo-Americans were opposed to 70,000 French Canadians. The simple facts of population, plus the major factor of Britain's new sea power, settled the fate of New France.

Mason Wade, *The French Canadians, 1760–1967* (Toronto: MacMillan, 1968), I, pp. 19–20.

Visions of a New World Utopia—Marcel Trudel's View of the Ville-Marie Project

The Utopian visions of New France's role in the Empire have also been subjected to considerable historical study. One leading authority on the early "heroic age" of New France, Marcel Trudel of the University of Ottawa, has argued that such Utopian dreams soon evaporated when French colonists faced the harsh realities and stiff challenges of an alien land. His observations on a Christian Utopian experiment such as the founding of Ville-Marie by the *Société de Notre-Dame de Montréal pour la Conversion des Sauvages* in 1642 indicate how unstable were such visionary schemes. And yet, there must have been a measure of success because Montreal (formerly Ville-Marie) by the eighteenth century had surpassed Quebec to become the commercial centre of the colony.

The initial outburst of enthusiasm was not to last for long, although in 1644 there was much rejoicing over the first harvest of French wheat (an experiment recommended by the Sieur d'Ailleboust) and over the arrival of a detachment of soldiers. Already, undesirable elements were mingling with the devout first-comers. For a number of years, moreover, the colony ceased to develop: recruitment was at a standstill and the rate of natural increase was negligible....

Seemingly there were two factors behind this state of affairs: the instability of the backers of this new enterprise, and the incursions of the Iroquois.

The attacks of the Iroquois (almost always the Mohawks) were at first only isolated forays carried out by small, elusive groups; nothing compared to what they would be a few years later.... Each year there were peace talks and exchanges of wampum belts between the Mohawks and the Algonquins, but on both sides there were always deaths to be avenged. Since the new colony was situated above the mouth of the Richelieu River, the Mohawk invasion route, it was threatened with total isolation....

There was also the fact that the settlement, launched in the heat of missionary fervour, was not yet soundly based. This devout community was inspired by absolute confidence in God, and certain of its members' acts of devotion had brought forth truly astounding results, which served to excite their faith still further. But these pious people did not, generally speaking, have a very realistic view of things, and would launch blindly upon hazardous undertakings despite the advice of those with more experience. Furthermore, their benefactors tended to be temperamental.... The benefactors in France showed the same kind of instability in their support, giving more or less liberally as their zeal at the moment dictated, or, like La Dauversière, engaging in shaky financial operations, or else vanishing from the scene without replacement.

Marcel Trudel, *The Beginnings of New France, 1524–1663* (Toronto: McClelland and Stewart, 1973), pp. 189–191.

Settling in a "New World" Colony—The Case of the "Filles du Roi"

Central to the Utopian vision of New France was the hope that the colony would serve as a better world for the downtrodden, disadvantaged or oppressed of the Old World. While few historians today accept the validity of such Utopian visions, some have claimed that forced emigrants, and "undesirables" from France were, for the most part, "improved" by their New World experiences. It is true, at least, in the case of the "King's daughters" who arrived in New France in the 1660s and 1670s.

Coming for the most part from the lower classes in France, the morally healthiest of the realm, and also in a smaller proportion from the lesser nobility and middle class, these brave and honest girls courageously left their land of birth, the most prosperous and best organized of Europe at the time, to become exiled in a far-off colony, there to lead in difficult circumstances and through many perils an existence marked by daily sacrifices, while collaborating in the task of developing their land of adoption. That there were among them a few women whose conduct was later reprehensible is a fact which cannot be denied since documents prove it; but the number of these immigrants of little virtue is so minimal that it does not assail the generally good reputation of these New Canadians.

Silvio Dumas, *Les filles du Roi en Nouvelle-France* (Quebec: Société historique de Québec, 1972), p. 356. trans. C.J.J.

Compact Laurentian Colony or Hinterland Empire?—Abbé Groulx's Assessment

In considering the debate between the partisans of an optimistic continental expansionist policy and the metropolitan advocates of a restricted compact colony on the banks of the St. Lawrence, historians have expressed some definite opinions. Canon (abbé) Lionel Groulx (1878–1967), French Canadian nationalist writer, drew attention to the colonies' motives for hinterland expansion.

Who was right in this debate between the advocates of the Laurentian Valley colony and those of the Empire, the court or the colonial administrators? To answer this question we must examine the motives of French expansionism. Toward the Atlantic, at Ile Royale, in the Gulf, on the north shore, these motives were largely economic, namely the fisheries and the industries of oils and skins in which the colonials were encouraged to engage in order to complement the economy of the mother country. In the west and northwest, furs remained as important as ever. There were years like 1735, when la Vérendrye's furs saved the trade, threatened by a long period of troubles in the area of the Great Lakes. To those commercial preoccupations were joined as in the past the thirst for adventure and the curiosity of the explorer obsessed by the American enigma. The Laurentian Valley could not conceal from those of her sons who felt no inclination for agriculture the marvels of the Upper Country where impatient youths could freely roam. Yet it must be recognized that [after the treaty of Utrecht] the expansionist urge no longer came from the colony's inner self, from the irrepressible vital impulses of the missionary and the explorer. It came from an external pressure which is called Anglo-American expansionism. Let us look at each of the French advances in turn. In every case—Ile Royale, Crown Point, Niagara, Detroit, the Ohio, the West, the Prairies—a threatening shadow had appeared. To contain the English, bar his way, preserve the trade of the Upper Country, safeguard the alliance with the Indians, maintain communications between Canada and Louisiana, those were the imperatives that determined everything. . . .

Who then was right, the colonial or the French authorities? No doubt, it would have been preferable to settle a limited area, to build a compact colony instead of one so widely dispersed. But it remains to be known if the empire did not constitute a vital annex, an indispensable rampart for the inner colony and if the two did not somehow have to be reconciled. Suppose, after 1696, that the French had abided by Louis XIV's policy of withdrawal from the West; suppose, after the building of the fort at Oswego, that they had allowed the English and the Iroquois to hatch their intrigues in the Upper

Country; who would dare deny that such a policy would not have hastened the colony's fall by twenty years?

L. Groulx, *Histoire du Canada français depuis la découverte* (Montreal, 1962), I, pp. 209–210. trans. Yves Zoltvany in Kenneth A. MacKirdy et al., *Changing Perspectives in Canadian History* (Toronto: Dent, 1967), pp. 43–44.

New France's Role as a Strategic Military Outpost—W.J. Eccles' View

University of Toronto historian William Eccles saw New France as a kind of military outpost in the French imperial system, particularly in the last 70 years of the colony's existence. Whereas Groulx stressed the aggressiveness of the British, Eccles argued that it was in fact the aggressiveness of Louis XIV which aroused the British to press for the eventual conquest of Acadia in 1710 and of Canada in 1760. According to Eccles, Louis XIV's decision in 1701 to found a colony at the mouth of the Mississippi River started the overextension of the colony and precipitated the chain of events leading to economic, political and military disaster.

It was not expected that this new colony, when established, would be of great benefit to France in the foreseeable future. It was to serve mainly as a base, an anchor, for a series of posts to be built on the rivers flowing westward into the Mississippi from the Great Lakes to the Gulf of Mexico. Just as Governor Nicholson had foreseen six years earlier, these posts were to be used to weld all the Indian tribes between the Alleghanies and the Mississippi into an alliance with the French to bar the English from the west. If this were not done, it was feared that the English would soon begin to press south and west until they came into conflict with the Spanish in Mexico; in order to secure his grandson's hold on the throne of Spain, Louis XIV had to demonstrate to the Spanish people that France was able and willing to protect their colonial possessions from a common enemy. The French now found themselves committed to occupying the entire western section of North America from Hudson Bay to the Gulf of Mexico and to holding the English colonials on the eastern side of the Alleghanies—this at a time when the population of the English colonies was doubling every twenty-five years.

Essentially, it was a dog-in-the-manger policy. In 1696 Denis Riverin, one of the leading *bourgeois* in the colony and a staunch believer in Colbert's policy, had advocated what amounted to the abandonment of the Illinois country to the English, on the grounds that this whole area produced only poor-grade furs which were a glut on the market....

The consequences of Louis XIV's decision were certainly to be of great moment, not only for France and New France, but for England and her empire as well. Nothing is inevitable in history but what is made so by the decisions and acts of men. It may well be that had Louis not made this decision and had the French not attempted to hold western North America south of the Great Lakes, there would have been no conflict in the Ohio Valley, some fifty years later, between the French and the English colonials as the latter pressed on beyond the Alleghanies. Perhaps then the English would not have thrown their full weight against Canada in the Seven Years War and it would have remained under the French flag....

W.J. Eccles, *Frontenac, The Courtier Governor* (Toronto: McClelland and Stewart, 1959) pp. 335, 337.

The Colony's Role in the French Mercantilist System—The Case of the Shipyards

One scholar who has attempted to assess Canada's role in the French mercantilist system is Jacques Mathieu, a French Canadian economic historian. In his study of the royal shipyards (which enjoyed a fleeting success in the colony), he raised significant questions concerning the attitudes and quality of Canadian workers—and the industrial capabilities of New France itself. His observations bear comparison with Parkman's assessment of the colony and its people.

> ... royal naval construction at Quebec was a metropolitan industry in terms of its capital and its finality, in its methods, in the organization of the work force, in short, by its very nature. At the most important level, decisions were taken in France; they were conceived and valid for the metropolis, not for the colony. Thus Maurepas imposed on the Intendant a type of construction which did not suit the forest resources of New France. There was no greater success in adapting French methods to Canadian conditions. The skilled workers who came from France did not incite the Canadian worker to come out of his self-imposed seclusion. Was this attributable to the relationship between inferiors and superiors, to the influence of the Indians, or to the mode of life proper to the colony? At any rate, the Canadian preferred a quiet life on the land to the long hours of work in the shipyards, the cock's crow to the sound of the bell. He quickly lost his initial enthusiasm and concerned himself but little with acquiring greater competence.
>
> To the artificial character of this structure are tied nearly all the problems faced by this industry. The vision was too grand for the industrial capabilities of New France in the mid-eighteenth century. . . .
>
> Jacques Mathieu, *La Construction navale royale à Québec, 1739–1759* (Quebec: Société historique de Québec, 1971), p. 83. trans. C.J.J.

The Colony and the Empire—A Recent Synthesis

Among the recent works of synthesis which attempt to delineate the main features and explain the dynamic forces at work in a specific period, is University of Ottawa historian Susan Trofimenkoff's examination of the origins and roots of Quebec society. In her consideration of the visions of New France and the manner in which it fitted into the grand imperial schemes of Old France, she singles out economic and military factors as dictating expansion into the hinterland. This not only brought the small colony into open conflict with numerous stronger Anglo-American colonies but also enabled the French colony to survive and flourish. But the question of French priorities continued to be raised. How high was Canada, whatever its role or value, on the list of France's concerns?

> Just as the original trade had required a permanent, albeit small, presence in the St. Lawrence Valley, so now the expanding trade and the continuing peace with the Indians after 1701 required a French presence in the interior. Only if the French brought trade goods, and good ones, close enough, would the Indians refrain from establishing direct

trade links themselves with the English colonies. Only if the French military was somewhere in the vicinity would the Indians be sufficiently impressed or persuaded to stay on the French side in any skirmish with the English. And only if the French claimed, by physical presence, the right to the territory beyond the St. Lawrence and beyond the English colonies along the Atlantic coast, could France maintain its prestige in Europe. Hence the extraordinary expansion of New France from a colony clustered along a major river to a far-flung web of empire, north, west, and south across a continent.... As in the early seventeenth century, the lines of exploration became lines of mission, of trade, and then of defence. By the late 1730s the French had posts at all strategic locations in what would later be the Canadian and American mid-west.

The soldiers and the trade marched hand in hand. Defence of the empire offered the extra rewards of the fur trade. Sometimes even the high administrators were in on the profits. Governor Frontenac in the late seventeenth century may well have allowed the attraction of fur to decide the location of military posts financed by the French government. And once installed in defensive positions around the Great Lakes, a French garrison was bound to pass its time bartering with the Indians. Meanwhile, *voyageurs* in the employ of the troops packed as many trade goods as military materials into their canoes. Soon too many people were making too much money for the French government ever to be able to extricate itself with any delicacy from what soon became an overextended position.

But then France may not have wanted to withdraw. Although the French government recognized that, except for the fisheries, New France had become an economic liability in the eighteenth century, it remained keen to checkmate its European rivals, notably England. For that purpose, New France represented an enormous political and military asset. It could contain the English settlers along the Atlantic seaboard as well as the traders of the Hudson's Bay Company fringed around the northern sea; it could secure Louisiana's hinterland; and, in case of a major European conflict, it could keep many a British soldier entangled in the North American backwoods instead of on the battlefields of Europe. Such a conflict would also occupy the British fleet, bound to defend that country's prize colonies. And always there seemed to be an occasion for European conflict.

Susan Mann Trofimenkoff, *The Dream of Nation. A Social and Intellectual History of Quebec* (Toronto: Macmillan, 1982), pp. 10–11.

A Guide to Further Reading

1. Overviews

Eccles, W.J., *Canada Under Louis XIV, 1663–1701*. Toronto: McClelland and Stewart, 1964.

_____, *France in America*. New York: Harper & Row, 1972.

Lanctôt, Gustave, *A History of Canada*. Toronto: Clarke Irwin, 1964-8. 3 vols.

Nish, Cameron and Pat Harvey, eds. *The Social Structures of New France*. Toronto: Copp Clark, 1968.

Parkman, Francis, *The Old Régime in Canada*. Toronto: Musson, 1874.

Trofimenkoff, Susan Mann, *The Dream of Nation: A Social and Intellectual History of Quebec*. Toronto: Macmillan, 1982.

Trudel, Marcel, *The Beginnings of New France, 1524–1663*. Toronto: McClelland and Stewart, 1973.

_____, *Introduction to New France*. Toronto: Holt, Rinehart & Winston, 1968.

Zoltvany, Yves F., ed., *The French Tradition in North America*. Toronto: Fitzhenry & Whiteside, 1969.

2. Specialized Studies

Strategic and Military Issues

Bishop, Morris, *Champlain: The Life of Fortitude*. Toronto: McClelland & Stewart, 1962.

Eccles, William J., *Frontenac: The Courtier Governor*. Toronto: McClelland & Stewart, 1959.

Frégault, Guy, *Iberville le conquérant*. Montreal: Pascal, 1944.

Lamontagne, Roland, *La Galissonnière et le Canada*. Montreal: Les Presses de l'Université de Montréal, 1962.

Peckham, Harold H., *The Colonial Wars, 1689-1762*. Chicago: University of Chicago Press, 1964.

Steele, Ian K., *Guerillas and Grenadiers: The Struggles for Canada, 1689-1760*. Toronto: Ryerson, 1969.

Zoltvany, Yves, *Philippe de Rigaud de Vaudreuil, Governor of New France, 1703-1735*. Toronto: University of Toronto Press, 1974.

The Frontier Thesis

Burt, A.L., "The Frontier in the History of New France", Canadian Historical Association Annual *Report*, 1940.

Eccles, W.J., *The Canadian Frontier 1534-1760*. New York: Holt, Rinehart & Winston, 1960.

Trudel, Marcel, *Les débuts du régime seigneurial au Canada*. Montreal: Fides, 1974.

Mercantilism and Trade Relations

Blitz, Rudolph. "Mercantilist Policies and the Pattern of World Trade, 1550-1750", *Journal of Economic History*. (1967): pp. 39-55.

Cole, C.W. *Colbert and a Century of French Mercantilism*. New York: Octagon, 1939.

Galloway, Patricia. *La Salle and his Legacy*. Jackson: University Press of Mississippi, 1982.

Mathieu, Jacques, *Le Commerce entre la Nouvelle-France et les Antilles au XVIIIᵉ siècle*. Montreal: Fides, 1981.

Murat, Inez., *Colbert*. Charlottesville: University Press of Virginia, 1984.

Schaeper, Thomas J., *The French Council of Commerce, 1700-1715: An Administrative Study of French Mercantilism after Colbert*. Columbia: Ohio State University Press, 1983.

Society in the French Régime

Crowley, Terence, "'Thunder Gusts': Popular Disturbances in Early French Canada", Canadian Historical Association, *Historical Papers*, 1979, pp. 11-31.

Dumas, Silvio, *Les Filles du Roi en Nouvelle-France*. Quebec: Société historique de Québec, 1972.

Dechêne, Louise, *Habitants et marchands de Montréal au XVIIe siècle*. Paris: Plon, 1974.

Diamond, Sigmund, "An Experiment in 'Feudalism': French Canada in the Seventeenth Century", *William and Mary Quarterly*, Vol. 18 (1961), pp. 3-34.

Frégault, Guy, *La civilisation de la Nouvelle-France, 1713-1744*. Montréal: Fides, 1969.

_____, *Canadian Society in the French Régime*. Canadian Historical Association Booklet

No. 6. Ottawa: CHA, 1966.

Hamelin, Jean, *Economie et Société en Nouvelle-France*. Quebec: Presses de l'Université Laval, 1970.

Harris, R. Cole, *The Seigneurial System in Early Canada*. Madison: University of Wisconsin Press, 1966.

Lemieux, Denise, *Les Petits Innocents: L'Enfance en Nouvelle-France*. Québec: IQRC, 1985.

Munro, W.B., *The Seigneurial System in Canada: A Study in French Colonial Policy.* New York: Columbia University Press, 1907.

Nish, Cameron, ed., *The French Regime*. Scarborough: Prentice-Hall, 1965.

Séguin, Robert-Lionel, *La vie libertine en Nouvelle-France au dix-septième siècle*. Montreal: Leméac, 1972. 2 vols.

Trudel, Marcel, *L'Esclavage au Canada français: histoire et conditions de l'esclavage*. Quebec: Presses de l'Université Laval, 1960.

3

THE CHURCH
IN NEW FRANCE

How Extensive Was Its Influence?

The role of the Church is one aspect of the society of New France which has generated much historical discussion. The Church has been seen as an intolerant institution which not only excluded Protestants, Jews and non-practicing Catholics from the colony, but also imposed a severe moral code on the colonists and intervened in all aspects of daily life. It has also been portrayed as the driving force in French colonization, the rallying point for heroic efforts to build a New Jerusalem in an untamed northern wilderness. Both views assume that the Church's influence was extensive in the life of New France and in the colony's development. Yet historians are now asking if the Church's authority was really as great as these interpretations suggest. And exploring that central question involves a close assessment of the Church's actual role in such areas as enforcing religious uniformity, governing the colony, converting the Indians, regulating people's behaviour, and influencing daily life.

During the French régime the Roman Catholic Church was the national church of France and her colonies, presided over by the King. It was guided by the concept of Gallicanism which maintained that the Church was subject to the will and pleasure of the monarch who ruled by Divine Right. The French or Gallican Church jealously guarded its traditional rights and privileges against what was seen as the overweening power and influence of the Papacy in Rome. Yet church-state controversy did arise in New France over such contentious issues as parish organization, the treatment of minorities, the brandy trade, public morality and social decay in the colony. These issues also raised a larger, more fundamental question regarding the role and authority of the Church. Was the French Catholic Church powerful enough to be the dominant influence on life and society in New France?

The Church in New France was staunchly Catholic in its beliefs and practices. It had been transplanted into the colony along with the first wave of settlers and missionaries. Although French Protestants, or Huguenots, had been active in colonial ventures from 1540 to 1627, very few settled permanently in Canada. After 1627, when Cardinal Richelieu restricted immigration to practicing Catholics, life in Canada would be difficult for religious dissenters. Yet, in spite of the restrictions, a few continued to find their way to Acadia and Canada as fishermen, sailors, traders, soldiers, indentured servants, artisans, brides or *filles du roi* and merchants. In the closing years of the French régime, when the government of Louis XV became more tolerant of religious minorities, Protestant and Jewish interest in the colony increased.

Although New France was almost uniformly Catholic, the Church faced some serious challenges to its religious and social monopoly. First of all, the Native peoples, who were regarded variously by the French as having either no religion or else being addicted to Satanic rites, had to be converted, and there was some resistance to missionary work, in particular from the *shamans*.

Secondly, there was a challenge from within the Catholic community itself. Colonists often violated the teachings and practices of the Church by "running the woods", charging exorbitant prices during periods of shortages, or setting a poor moral example for Indians. Finally, the Church and its clerics faced a challenge from without. For, although New France was predominantly French and Catholic, most of the rest of the continent was occupied by English colonies and populated by Protestants.

On the whole, the Church in New France remained quite orthodox in doctrine and practice, rejecting both the rigorous puritanism of some reformers (Jansenists[1]) and the ecstatic or charismatic behaviour of some of its pioneer founders and patrons. The Utopian experiment of the Jesuits at Ste-Marie-among-the-Hurons fell before an Iroquois invasion, and that of the visionaries who founded Ville-Marie in 1642 gave way in time to the materialistic and military town of Montreal, a very secular place by any standard. Indeed, the history of the colonial Church can be divided into two periods: an initial "heroic age" of the zealots and martyrs during which the majority of the religious institutions were founded; and a later and more "normal" period of development during which the Church fell gradually into line with dominant patterns of Catholic practice in provincial France. The clergy in the colony, with some notable exceptions in Louisbourg and New Orleans, led exemplary lives. However, the reader will have to judge whether the colonists were as faithful in their religious practice as were their missionaries, curates and nuns.

The care of souls was the Church's normal spiritual and moral mandate, but education and social welfare—the care of the sick, handicapped, orphans, aged or unfortunates—fell within its broader range of responsibilities. The

1. Jansenism was a Catholic doctrine of the mid-seventeenth century based on the theories of Jansenius, Bishop of Ypres, and embodying a dissenting view of grace, predestination and other religious matters.

Church benefited from royal protection and financial support, in return for which it was expected to perform its duties and fulfil its responsibilities in the community. This gave it a prominent role which at one time or another touched each and every member of society. The extent to which the Church was able in this capacity to exercise any appreciable degree of control over civil society is another matter. It seems clear, however, that it found itself normally excluded from political affairs, except during the early colonization period, as well as from economic activities which were largely directed by—and from—metropolitan France.

Nevertheless, the Church taught that religion and morality were the foundation and core for all civic life and that the institutional Church—its hierarchy, religious orders, parish organization, seminaries, educational and charitable foundations—should be the dominant force in society. Catholicism ideally should permeate all aspects of social, political and economic thought and activity. It is not surprising that a college was established in New France before Harvard University was founded, that by 1639 there were hospitals and schools in the chief towns, and that by 1663 the secular clergy had a seminary in Quebec and one in Montreal. The presence of such institutions, however, cannot be assumed to indicate that the influence of the Church was oppressive or that the colonists were forced into abject docility and unquestioning subservience. The catechism, after all, taught a system of reasoning which could be applied to secular matters as well. The local government of the temporal affairs of each parish by elected trustees gave valuable experience in democratic expression and management. The Church also offered some opportunity for poor *habitants'* sons and daughters who showed promise to receive more advanced education which would fit them for a place in the ministry of the Church but also in a secular society. Furthermore, the Church was slowly becoming "Canadianized" with the admission of Canadians into its missionary, teaching and nursing orders, so that by the end of the régime it bore less resemblance to a "transplanted" French religious institution.

Although the Catholic Church had an important role to play in New France, the extent of its influence and control is still debated. Did the Church dominate colonial society or was it merely a reflection of the prevailing religious temper of the times? Was the government of New France controlled in any way by the clergy? Or was the reverse true? Did the Church in New France serve as largely an instrument of the administration? And if the Church's authority was less than all-encompassing, what were the actual limits of its power and influence?

SELECTED CONTEMPORARY SOURCES

THE EXTENT OF RELIGIOUS UNIFORMITY

Throughout the French régime, a concerted attempt was made to preserve "religious uniformity", or ensure that colonists conformed with accepted Catholic religious doctrine and practices. France in the sixteenth century had suffered from religious civil wars between Catholics and Huguenots and Royal authorities sought to prevent this dissension from spilling over into the colony. Efforts to rid the colony of religious non-conformists and their ideas provided a test of Church influence and authority.

Louis XIV's Policy of Uniformity, 1665

One of the clearest statements of the Royal policy of uniformity was found in King Louis XIV's April 1665 edict on the question. It was the Sun King's desire to reunite all sects and factions in the national Church of which he was the "eldest son":

> The design we have of seeing all our subjects reunited in the same belief in matters of faith and of religion, oblige us to watch incessantly to prevent the progress of all new ideas which might trouble the repose of consciences, and the peace of the Church and the State, there being no precaution that we have not taken to have all contentions cease and to arrest the course of errors that could alter the purity of the faith which we have received from our ancestors. In this design we have supported with our authority the decisions made by the Popes, and accepted by the Church, for the destruction of the new sect which has arisen by reason of the doctrine of Jansenius. . . .
>
> F. Isambert et al., *Recueil général des anciennes lois françaises* (Paris: 1822–33), XVII, p. 49. trans. C.J.J.

Bishop Laval's View of Protestants, 1670

From the beginning in New France, the Church feared that the influence of commercial interests, and notably of the Protestant Huguenots, would interfere with its religious mission of converting the Native peoples and with its attempt to foster its version of social justice and order among the colonists. In spite of official regulations under the Company of One Hundred Associates' rule (1627–1663), which barred non-Catholics from settling, Huguenots continued to maintain commercial relations with the colony and a few even took up permanent residence in Canada. It turned out that such presumably select groups of immigrants as the pious lay founders of Ville-Marie (Montreal) and the *filles du roi* harboured Protestant subjects!

In response to the problem, the first bishop, François de Montmorency Laval (1659–1688), called for a stricter enforcement of religious uniformity concerning Protestants.

> The Bishop of Quebec makes representation that the merchants of France send out Protestant agents, and that for a long time the clergy has made known the disadvantages thereof with respect to religion and with respect to the State.
>
> In what concerns Religion, the Bishop of Quebec affirms that they make numerous seductive speeches, that they lend out books, and that sometimes they even assemble together among themselves; and finally, he knows that a number of persons speak honorably of them and cannot be convinced that they are in error.
>
> Upon examining the matter from the perspective of the State it seems to be no less important. Everybody knows that Protestants in general are not as attached to His Majesty as are Catholics.

Quebec is not very far from Boston and other English towns; to multiply the number of Protestants in Canada would be to give occasion eventually for revolutions....

A prohibition to French merchants to send out Protestant clerks would suffice to remedy the abuse.

Collection de Manuscrits relatifs à la Nouvelle-France (Quebec: Coté, 1883), I, pp. 204–205. trans. C.J.J.

Lahontan's Criticism of Church Censorship, 1703

In the colony, as in France, there was censorship of reading material and of theatrical works. It has to be remembered that libraries were few, a printing press non-existent, and plays usually staged under the direction of the religious. In 1694, Governor Frontenac raised a furor at Quebec when he arranged to have an unsavoury officer of his household staff play the role of the seducer, dressed as a priest, in Molière's *Tartuffe*, a comedy which had aroused controversy at Versailles itself. Bishop Saint-Vallier succeeded in having the play banned and won his case on appeal to Versailles. In 1703, the Baron de Lahontan, a military officer, charged the Sulpician clergy in Montreal with prohibiting "the reading of Romances and Plays" and with burning all books which were not devotional in character.

When I think of this Tyranny, I cannot but be enrag'd at the impertinent Zeal of the Curate of this City. This inhumane Fellow came one day to my Lodging, and finding the Romance of the Adventures of Petronius upon my table, he fell upon it with an unimaginable fury, and tore out almost all the leaves. This book I valued more than my life, because 'twas not castrated: and indeed I was so provok'd when I saw it all in wrack, that if my Landlord had not held me, I had gone immediately to that turbulent Pastor's House, and would have pluck'd out the Hairs of his Beard with as little mercy as he did the Leaves of my book. These animals cannot content themselves with the study of Men's Actions, but they must likewise dive into their Thoughts....

R.G. Thwaites, ed., *New Voyages to North America by the Baron de Lahontan* (Chicago: A.C. McClurg & Co., 1905), I, pp. 89–90.

THE EXTENT OF THEOCRATIC RULE

The Church of the French régime was a national Church following the long-established principle of Gallicanism—that the Church was subordinate to the state, or civil authority. This Gallican principle was opposed in the seventeenth and eighteenth centuries by Catholic partisans who held the Romanist or *ultramontane* view that the authority of the Papacy transcended that of the state. Although Gallicanism remained the dominant philosophy until the period of British rule after the Conquest of 1760, the bishops did not hesitate to increase Church influence and power whenever possible.

Under Msgr. Laval in the 1660s and 1670s some alleged that colonial affairs bore some signs of theocratic rule, or government by the priesthood in the name of God. Episcopal influence was extended over the clergy, a system of parishes was established, and the Bishop actively resisted any policies or practices which might adversely affect the moral or spiritual life of the colony.

Whether Church influence under Laval constituted a form of theocracy remains a matter for debate. The presence of strong-minded civil officials— Governor Frontenac (1672–82) and Intendant Talon (1665–72), however, might suggest that such theocratic impulses were restrained.

The Reaffirmation of Royal Absolutism, 1614

At a meeting of the Estates-General of France in 1614 the paramountcy of Royal over ecclesiastical authority was reaffirmed. The commoners, or Third Estate, passed a resolution designed to block any attempt to assert the power of the Church in Rome over the state.

> In order to arrest the course of the pernicious doctrine which has been introduced during the past few years against kings and sovereign powers instituted by God by seditious minds which tend only to trouble them and subvert them: The King shall be supplicated to have decreed in assembly of the Estates, as fundamental law of the Realm, inviolable and binding on all, that, as he is the recognized Sovereign of his State, holding his Crown from God alone, there is no power whatsoever on earth, whether spiritual or temporal, which has any authority over his Kingdom to deprive the sacred persons of our Kings nor to dispense or absolve their subjects of the fealty and obedience which they owe them for whatever cause or pretext whatsoever.
>
> Bibliothèque Nationale Paris, Fonds Dupuy, No. 950, Resolution of the Chamber of the Third Estate, 1614, pp. 5–7. trans. C.J.J.

The Role of Bishop Laval—A Theocratic Influence

Any theocratic impulse that existed in New France came from the Bishop and the higher clergy. The first bishop, Laval, arrived in 1659, but not until 1674

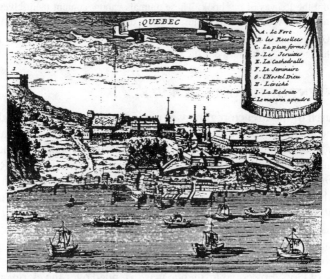

A view of Quebec, 1722

was a diocese created. From his arrival until 1688, Laval contended with governors and intendants for influence over the colonial administration of New France. His founding of the Seminary of Quebec, which was supposed to supply all the parishes with priests, his fight to prohibit the sale of intoxicants to the Indians, and his role in advising the Crown on the establishment of Royal government all seemed to reflect an *ultramontane* view of Church-state relations. Even the dominating presence of the Seminary and other religious institutions in the town of Quebec suggested a widespread church influence over the colony.

Clerical Influence on the Councils—Two Official Reports, 1647 and 1664

The appointment of members of the high clergy as voting members of the colonial councils in New France seemed to suggest the Church exerted considerable influence over the colony's administration. A report on the appointment of an administrative council under Company rule in 1647 appeared to recognize the extensive influence of the Jesuits in the early period. Opposition to this clerical influence mounted, however, after the establishment of Royal Government in 1663, when Bishop Laval was asked by the King to nominate the first Governor and the slate of colonial Councillors. Laval's prominent role in the government and clerical agitation for controls on immigration into the colony led to a confrontation with the Governor de Mézy (1663–65), who accused the Bishop and the Jesuits of conspiring to impose a theocracy in New France.

> I put at the head of a general council for the service of the King and the welfare of the country the Reverend Father Ragnaust, who has the honour to be known to your Highness, and who with three others deliberates every day public affairs. Because of his merit I thought I could do nothing better. If the occasion presents itself I beg Your Highness to authorize this conduct and to be altogether convinced that the Jesuits have worked more than any others in this country.
>
> Camille de Rochemonteix, *Les Jésuites et la Nouvelle-France au XVIIe siècle* (Paris: Letouzy et Ané, 1895–96), II, p. 527. trans C.J.J.

> The good understanding that was between them did not last long as the Jesuits accused Mézy of avarice and violence. He said that they wanted to take in hand the authority which the King had conferred upon him, in such a way that, there being only their placemen in the Sovereign Council, all decisions would be made according to their own wishes.
>
> P.A.C. MG 1, Series C11A, Vol. II, Instructions to Tracy, 15 November 1664, p. 123. trans. C.J.J.

Gallicanism Extended to the Colony—Instructions to Colonial Administrators, 1665

The Church was not without powerful friends and allies. It found support in France, even at the Court itself, "beyond the mountains" in Rome, and in the colony too. Gallicanism jealously protected the independence of the national Church and the sovereignty of His Most Christian Majesty, but it also emphasized the fact that the state was religious and that the New World would be brought under Christian dominion by the Christian Prince. It is not surprising therefore that seventeenth-century Governors and Intendants (for example, Talon) were reminded of the necessity of implementing the Gallican principles in New France.

It is absolutely necessary to hold in just balance the temporal authority, which resides in the person of the King and in those who represent him, and the spiritual authority, which resides there in the person of the said Bishop and the Jesuits, in such a manner nevertheless that the latter always be inferior to the former. The first thing which Sieur Talon will have to observe carefully, and about which it would be good for him to have firm convictions before leaving here (France), is to know perfectly well the state in which these two powers are at present in the colony, and the relationship in which they normally ought to stand.

P.A.C., MG 1, Series C11A, Vol. I, Instructions to Talon, 25 March 1665, pp. 50–51. trans. C.J.J.

The State Over the Church—The Oath of Fidelity of the Clergy, 1672

As a public acknowledgement of the proper role of the clergy within the state, Frontenac had the clergy take an oath of fidelity prescribed for them, in 1672, at a ceremony sometimes erroneously referred to as the "Colonial Estates-General". It was more a ceremonial occasion than an incipient form of parliamentary practice.

You swear and promise before God to labour with all your strength for the maintenance of the Catholic, Apostolic and Roman Religion, to promote it as much as you can through your example and care, by the purity of your doctrine and the proclamation of the Gospel, and to be faithful to the King as required under the authority of the charge with which he has honoured you in these provinces. You promise, in addition, that if a matter comes to your knowledge which is contrary to His Majesty's service you will advise us thereof, and in case it were not remedied by us, you will inform his Majesty thereof.

Collection de Manuscrits relatifs à la Nouvelle-France. (Quebec: Coté, 1883), I, p. 226. trans. C.J.J.

THE EXTENT OF EVANGELIZATION

The first challenge of the New World for the Church was the religious conversion of the non-Christian indigenous population.

The Récollet missionaries, soon followed by the more aggressive and financially and politically secure Jesuits, set to work with optimism and a self-sacrificing zeal born of the seventeenth-century Catholic revival in France. Yet these evangelizers often met stiff opposition from *shamans*. Whenever this resistance was overcome by skilled missionaries, the Indians adopted either the tolerant stance that each culture had the religion that best suited it, or a syncretic Catholicism which combined elements of both and enabled the traditional Indian belief systems to survive under a Catholic cloak. There were also zealous converts, yet some missionaries, and nearly all of their critics, doubted the depth and sincerity of these conversions.

A Christian Utopian View of Missions, 1648

Early French missionaries often expressed a Christian Utopian view of their evangelical purposes in Indian country. To one such Jesuit father, success seemed certain for such a "God-ordained" mission in that part of the world reserved to France.

> It seems as if innocence, banished from the greater part of the Empires and Kingdoms of the Universe, has withdrawn itself to the great forest where these people dwell. Their nature has something or other of the goodness of the Earthly Paradise before sin had entered it. Their practices have none of the luxury, nor the ambition, nor the avarice, nor the pleasures which corrupt our cities. Since Baptism has made them disciples of the Holy Spirit, that Teacher is very much at home with them; he teaches them away from the noise of courts and Louvres. He has made them more wise without books than are all the Aristotles with their weighty volumes.
>
> *Relation de ce qui s'est passe de plus remarquable es Missions des Peres de la Compagnie de Iesus, en la Novvelle France, es annees 1647. & 1648* (Paris: Gabriel Cramoisy, M DC XLIX), p. 112. trans. C.J.J.

The Resistance of the Shaman—Father Le Jeune's Account, 1634

Jesuits often learned that being received hospitably by Indian nations did not necessarily lead to mass conversions.

In some cases, they encountered hostile opposition, especially from the *shaman*, whom they usually referred to as a *jongleur*, or "trickster". Father Le Jeune gives a typical account of such an encounter. Just as annoying to the missionaries was the tolerant indifference of many hearers and the Indian conviction that although Catholicism was reasonable for Frenchmen, Indians were meant to live by their traditional beliefs.

> Neither hunger, nor thirst, nor the poverty and filth of their smoked foods, nor sickness, all these seemed of little account compared to the smoke of their lodges and the malice of the sorcerer, with whom I was always on bad terms for the following reasons.... First, Because having invited me to spend the winter with him, he had been let down.... Secondly, because I could not satisfy his greed; I had nothing which he asked me for.... In the third place, seeing that he played at being a prophet, amusing these people by means of a thousand stupid acts which to my mind he invented every day, I lost no chance to convince him of his foolishness and childishness, bringing to light the impertinence of his superstitions.... Sixthly, as he saw that the natives of other lodges had some respect for me, and knowing moreover that I was a great opponent of his impostures and that if I intruded into the beliefs of his adherents I would ruin him completely, he did everything possible to destroy me and make me look ridiculous in the estimation of his people.
>
> Paul Le Jeune, *Relation de ce qui s'est passe en la Novvelle-France en l'annee 1634* (Paris: Sebastien Cramoisy, M DC XXXV), p. 202. trans. C.J.J.

Success in Religious Conversion—A Tribute to Kateri Tekakwitha, 1715

Conversion efforts undertaken by Jesuit missionaries among the Iroquoian peoples and by the Ursuline Sisters with Indian girls did not always meet with success. Some "Black Robes" like Fathers Jean de Brebeuf and Charles Lalemant won the respect and support of the Huron, only to be put to death by the Huron's enemies, the Iroquois. Yet there were also some notable successes, such as the case of Kateri Tekakwitha, an Iroquois woman known to the French as "The Lily of the Mohawks". Tekakwitha showed a steadfastness in her faith that gradually earned her a following of devotees among colonists and converts and, eventually, canonization, the only time an Indian has been thus honoured. An early tribute to Tekakwitha was offered by Father Cholenec.

> The marvels which God is working every day through the intercession of a young Iroquois female who has lived and died among us in the odour of sanctity, have induced me to inform you of the particulars of her life.... All the French who are in the colonies, as well as the Indians, hold her in singular veneration. They come from a great distance to pray at her tomb, and many, by her intercession, have been immediately cured of their maladies, and have received from Heaven other extraordinary favors....
>
> Her father was an Iroquois and a heathen; her mother, who was a Christian, was an Algonquin, and had been baptized at the village of Trois-Rivières, where she was brought up among the French. During the time that we were at war with the Iroquois, she was taken prisoner by these Indians, and remained a captive in their country. We have since learned, that thus in the very bosom of heathenism, she preserved her faith even to her death....
>
> God did not delay to honor the memory of this virtuous girl by an infinite number of miraculous cures, which took place after her death, and which still continue to take place daily through her intercession. This is a fact well-known, not only to the Indians, but also to the French at Quebec and Montreal, who often make pilgrimages to her tomb to fulfil their vows, or to return thanks for favors which she has obtained for them in Heaven....
>
> William I. Kip, *The Early Jesuit Missions in North America* (New York: Wiley & Putnam, 1846), pp. 81, 114.

A Discouraging Report on Micmac Conversion, 1691

New Englanders were convinced that the missionaries wielded great influence over their converts, but missionaries like the Récollet Chrestien Le Clercq were less certain of the understanding and steadfastness of their charges. The fact that the Micmac remained Catholic after the British conquest of Acadia in 1710 may tell us something about their conversion.

> It is true that several of our Gaspesians hope at present to be instructed, ask for Baptism, and even seem externally quite good Christians after having been baptized, zealous in the ordinary morning and evening prayers, modest in Churches, and given to confessing their sins in order to approach the holy Communion worthily. But one may say that the number of those who abide by the rule of Christianity and who do not fall

back into the irregularities of a brutal and savage life is very small, either because of the natural insensibility of these people to matters of salvation or because of drunkenness, their delusions, their superstitions and other great defects to which they are addicted.

It is true that the slight progress I had made in four years of labour with all the application I could muster to convert these Peoples, in addition to the deep displeasure of not finding the response I hoped for on the part of our Gaspesians, the majority of whom were Christians only in appearance, the indefatigable labour of so many illustrious and zealous missionaries who preceded me notwithstanding caused me to hesitate to abandon the work but I had no cause to hope for a happier success in future. Meanwhile, not to rush matters in such a consequential affair, I asked the Holy Spirit for the light I needed in order to know the will of God and to give myself wholly to it. . . .

Chrestien Le Clercq, *Nouvelle Relation de la Gaspésie qui contient les Moeurs & la Religion des Sauvages* (Paris: Amable Auroy, 1691), pp. 276–79. trans. C.J.J.

THE EXTENT OF SOCIAL CONTROL

Along with providing spiritual comfort, converting the Indians and offering moral and ethical guidance, the Church was expected to promote public order, social stability and proper respect for established authority. Discharging this responsibility through pastoral letters and *mandements* meant that the Church and its bishops frequently appeared to be despotic in approach and puritanical in tone. Certainly the Catholic clergy complied, for the most part, with Church principles of piety, decency and social discipline. Some bishops and priests, however, deplored the "vices" of the Canadians. Their main complaints concerned the incidence of drunkenness, gambling, and quarrelling, and the poor behaviour of parishioners at worship services. Independence of spirit and disregard for the church's discipline by certain members of the upper classes were particularly upsetting. Some outstanding heroes of the colonial wars were even tried and convicted of such crimes as kidnapping, rape and seduction. Also frowned upon by the clergy were the activities of some Catholic merchants who engaged in profiteering during times of food shortages and famine. In view of these clerical worries, questions are being raised about how successful the Church was in imposing its standard of discipline and public order on the people of New France.

Tales of Disorderly Conduct—Madame Bégon's Letters, 1749

Many of the clergy were particularly concerned about the aping of Court life at Versailles which characterized Quebec in the closing years of the French régime. The casino, the lavish balls, the pompous display of wealth, and the open disregard for the moral code of the Church by some of the high-ranking officials stood in sharp contrast to the disciplined, dedicated and devout lives of their early seventeenth-century predecessors. In this period of so-called "social decay", the letters of Elizabeth Bégon to her son-in-law revealed much about upper-class manners and morals. The following excerpts recount some experiences related to the visit of the Intendant François Bigot to Montreal in February 1749, during the pre-Lenten Carnival season.

10th. Good day, dear son. I think that the whole town is sleeping except me, because they came away from the ball at six-thirty this morning....

11th. The whole court was very quiet today, although the two civil leaders dined at M. de Beaucor's, which surprised me as it did the rest of the town because we had been told that Mme. de Beaucor was dying, but you know what that woman is like, like many others she does with her body what she likes....

12th. It is fortunate, dear son, for all those who give themselves to the dance that they have two days to rest, or else I think they would die: they came away from the ball this morning at 6 o'clock. I don't doubt at all that some of them will not be taking Easter communion and especially those who will be going to the comedy which is to be staged during the three last days before the beginning of Lent.... De Muy told me after dinner that he did not want his wife and daughter to be there and that it was not decent to spend the nights dancing and the days sleeping while the Blessed Sacrament was exposed on the altar. I don't think that he will have his way very easily...

16th. A great feast, dear son, at the General's. This is the season when the talk is about nothing else but feasting and dancing....

... I think all the ladies and young women of the town will like it very much for this ball is tonight and Tuesday again. They begin at 8 o'clock and it ends only at dawn. I don't doubt that some lady will die of it all....

17th. I saw on rising, dear son, a party of ladies and gentlemen from the ball pass by. They hauled them away until 7 o'clock. I don't doubt that our priests are in despair. The General laughs heartily at it all....

18th. Here at last, my dear son, is the last day on which they'll do all they can to kill themselves. I am tired of hearing pass day and night the sleighs which prevent me from sleeping and I wish we were into Lent.

There is a great dinner at the General's and a ball this evening given by the Intendant, as usual at M. Varin's. They are to leave only when it is time to go and receive the ashes (Ash Wednesday). The Intendant asked Father Bonnecamps to have mass said at seven o'clock for him and his guests before they go to bed. But the father is not of the same mind. He is resolved to go to tell him that he would say mass for him at eleven o'clock, or eleven-thirty if he preferred; but to give him the ashes and say mass for him when he left the ball would in no wise be proper. I don't know if he will satisfy him with this arrangement....

19th. So many people with a hangover, dear son, this morning. No more balls, no more masquerades. The truth is that they pushed pleasure as far as possible since at seven-thirty they were still dancing....

("La Correspondance de Madame Bégon," *Rapport de l'Archiviste de la Province de Québec pour 1934–35* (Quebec: Rédempti Paradis, 1935), 36–39, 42.

An Ordinance Against Lower-Class Indiscipline, 1691

Independence and resistance were not confined to the upper levels of colonial society. The Church periodically reminded the common people to ensure that infant baptisms were properly conducted by the curate, to have marriages performed according to Church practice, to refrain from work on holy days, to cease frequenting taverns during the hours of worship services, and to pay their tithes and other levies for the support of the Church.

Bishop Saint-Vallier (1688–1727) was one clerical leader who addressed the problem of indiscipline among the lower orders of the colony. He touched on a number of issues in a general ordinance which he felt obliged to issue in 1691.

2. As we have been informed that some persons present themselves at the Sacrament of Matrimony without intentions of piety, modesty and the other required conditions, We enjoin all persons intending to marry to prepare for it through instructions in the matters which are necessary in order to receive this sacrament, and especially to approach it with piety and devotion, setting aside all the levity and other irreverent acts which sometimes are committed in church, as experience has shown....

5. We have been deeply grieved during the visits We made in the rural parishes to learn of the abuse which has slipped in among many to leave during the homily and announcements of the parish mass on Feast Days and Sundays without valid reason to go and gossip in houses during the sermon; this habit which has been introduced in diverse places in this diocese is an evident sign of lack of devotion and of irreligion.... We instruct the curates to refuse them even absolution if they do not wish to amend their ways upon sufficient warning; exhorting the priests to take into account the weak piety of their parishioners and not to have the Homily and announcements last more than one-half hour, especially during the severe cold....

7. And because we have been informed that in diverse meeting places dances and other entertainments were held on Feast Days and Sundays, and sometimes even during the hours of Divine Service, which is prohibited by the Ordinances of the King and by the Laws of the Secular Power, We exhort and adjure, in the love of Our Lord and the honour of Religion, all the Faithful of our Diocese to abstain in future from these kinds of things....

8. We have also learned with much sorrow that a great number of persons, especially the young men and boys, take the liberty to utter in all their gatherings unseemly discourses with double meanings, which causes in their behaviour a corruption which cannot be sufficiently deplored....

9. Having noticed that notwithstanding the precision with which we made known to the people the obligation they are under to pay the Tithes, many persons nevertheless dispense with doing so....

13. We cannot conclude this present Ordinance in a better fashion that by remarking to fathers and mothers the obligation they have not to permit children of the opposite sex to sleep together, or with them, when they reached an age of knowing naughtiness: for although this may derive from poverty it is nevertheless true that if parents were moved by a true love for the salvation of their children they would often find expedients to prevent such disorders. That is why we enjoin all Curates to be occupied therewith and to other confessors to question frequently their penitents on this matter in order to learn from them if they are performing their duties.

H. Têtu & C.O. Gagnon, *Mandements, lettres pastorales et circulaires des Evêques de Québec* (Quebec: Coté, 1888), I, pp. 275–81. trans. C.J.J.

Neglect of Church Obligations—A Pastoral Letter to Detroit Parishioners, 1720

If the Church had difficulty enforcing its legitimate authority, it appealed to the state for support. Such was the case with parishioners' neglect of Church obligations. In return for receiving the Church's services, the colonists—especially those who lived in organized parishes—were obliged to provide material support in the form of tithes, levied officially at 1/13th but reduced to 1/26th of cereal crops, and to supply money and labour for the construction or repair of the local church, the presbytery, the school and the cemetery. Collecting tithes from the *habitants* proved difficult enough for church-wardens, but inducing parishioners to provide extra money and labour could also present problems. In a few cases, like that of the Detroit parishioners in 1720, appeals were made to the Intendant who instructed the local Captain of the Militia to intervene in order to enforce the customary obligations.

> The extreme distance I am from you, my dearly beloved children, coupled with the very great difficulty wherein I find myself to send you priests to administer the sacraments to you, move me to have you take notice, by means of this Pastoral Letter, of the indispensable obligation you have to live a pure and Christian life, free from all the sins which can separate you from the grace of God and his love.... It is right that we exhort you to maintain the material Temple, which we learn is in lamentable state of disrepair, as well as the cemetery which you have allowed to remain open and exposed to all kinds of indignities because of the cattle which enter it, and which by this fact alone deserves to come under interdict. But above all we strongly urge and advise you to show a true obedience to your pastor, when it is so greatly in your interest to keep and accommodate him for we see here none in the regular or secular clergy who might succeed him....
>
> H. Têtu & C.O. Gagnon, *Mandements, lettres pastorales et circulaires* I, pp. 275–281. trans. C.J.J.

The Problem of *Métissage*, or "Country Marriages"—A Report on Clerical Control in Louisiana, 1721

It seems reasonable to suppose that the farther removed a parish or mission was from the centres of authority and control the greater the possibility of deviance and disorder. Distant Louisiana came under the jurisdiction of the Bishop of Quebec and presented Saint-Vallier and his successors with several problems. For example, the Church wavered on its views regarding racial intermarriage, or *métissage* as the union between French and Indians was called. At first it had promoted such unions as a means of uniting the two peoples, then it frowned on it because it seemed that the majority of the children of such unions were raised in the Native fashion. Eventually, the missionaries argued that sacramental marriages, and even the recognition of and blessing of "country marriages" contracted in the hinterland without benefit of clergy, were preferable to unsanctioned cohabitation.

> The news which reaches us from all quarters, from France as well as from the upper

country, about the little religion and purity with which the French newly arrived from Old France, of all social conditions, live in the vast country which they have come to inhabit along that great river, causing us to fear that they might bring down the cursings of God against those who do not want to live Christianlike and in keeping with their state, instead of the blessings promised in many places in the Holy Books to the people of goodwill who seek to serve God acceptably, resolve us to oppose with all our might the public vices and disorders which would be liable to bring these misfortunes upon us.

That is why in order to apply thereto the most efficacious remedies, We order those who under our authority direct souls to declare to them our intention is that we regard as public disgraces those who despising divine and human laws are led to commit impious scandals in word, or through their actions, by public concubinage of persons who in spite of all the prohibitions that are proclaimed are still determined to see each other and even live together. We do not wish that sort of persons to be received in church or at the sacraments until they have submitted to public penance....

H. Têtu & C.O. Gagnon, *Mandements, lettres pastorales et circulaires* I, pp. 502–3. trans. C.J.J.

Disregard for Social Teachings—A *Mandement* on Profiteering, 1742

The activities of colonial merchants who engaged in profiteering seemed—in the minds of the clergy—to show a complete disregard for the Church's social teachings. Those merchants of the Catholic faith who profited by raising prices during times of shortages were violating Church doctrines on "just price" in the marketplace. Thus, when the Superior Council at Quebec attempted to impose price controls to protect colonists, especially town dwellers, Bishop Pontbriand (1741–1760) issued an ecclesiastical order or *mandement* warning the faithful to obey the civil decree.

The Superior Council of this colony, Our dearly beloved Children, being duly informed of the odious cupidity of some of our rural inhabitants who profit from the shortages in which our cities find themselves by selling at an exhorbitant price wheat and flour, found itself obligated to issue a regulation on that matter.... We believe, Our dearly beloved Children, that we must warn you that those who would contravene the Council's regulation would render themselves guilty before God and man, that it is not permitted to go beyond the limits prescribed by a legitimate authority....

The towns, Our dearly beloved Children, are like the core or heart of this colony; would you become unjust members who would refuse the heart under attack the blood it requires? It is in the towns that you will find what is lacking in your countryside; it is in the towns that many of your children receive a Christian education; would you be so ungrateful as to violate the laws of perfect gratitude which heaven will reward a hundredfold? It is in the towns that the hospitals are open to receive you in your infirmities; grant to these houses which will ever be the august monuments of the piety of your parents, the help which they await with impatience; it is in the towns that justice settles your quarrels and renders to each what is rightfully his; it is there that resides in a special way royal authority and where His Majesty maintains a large number of troops for the defence of this Colony, the maintenance of public tranquility and your repose; finally it is in the towns that the poor of the countryside take refuge and come to burden the citizens.....

H. Têtu & C.O. Gagnon, *Mandements, lettres pastorales et circulaires* II, pp. 22–24. trans. C.J.J.

THE EXTENT OF INFLUENCE ON POPULAR BELIEFS AND PRACTICES

To what degree was the Church able to implant pious ideals and practices among the colonists, and to what degree was it able to uproot or suppress popular beliefs which were not fully in line with its teachings? The colonists were reported to stop to pray at the numerous wayside shrines, to recite the rosary in their homes, to say grace before and after meals, and to attach great importance and value to pilgrimages, relics, novenas and public prayers. But they also believed in diabolical possession, witchcraft, faith healers, soothsayers and a variety of folk superstitions. The Church felt an obligation to control and channel such popular beliefs.

Comments on St. Jean-Baptiste Day Observances, 1650

The official teachings of the Church and popular belief and practice could differ. The traditional celebration of the Feast of St. John the Baptist, or its eve on 23rd June, for example, had been introduced from Brittany. In Brittany the observances included allegedly Druidic practices, such as burning sweet grasses in a community bonfire. The Jesuits were not favourable to its celebration in New France, yet the custom survived and eventually it became the "national day" for the *Québecois*, the descendants of these colonists.

> The 23rd the St. John's bonfire, from which I excused myself foreseeing that they would have me to light it as usual, and not judging it proper to allow this custom to persist which had not been observed in the days of M. Montmagny, it was the Governor who lit the fire, Father La Place being present in surplice and stole, with St. Martin, to sing the *Te Deum*.
>
> Abbés Laverdière and Casgrain, *Le Journal des Jésuites* (Quebec: Léger Brousseau, 1870), pp. 41–42. trans. C.J.J.

Divine Displeasure and the Caterpillar Plague of 1743

The teachings of the Church and popular beliefs were sometimes quite compatible. The colonists placed great stock in magical formulas, in healing waters, in natural phenomena such as storms and earthquakes as omens of Divine displeasure, in the observance of taboos, and in the effects of spells. Such beliefs do not appear to have been distinguished from Catholic teaching regarding prayers and pilgrimages, religious processions and the power of the Blessed Sacrament. The Blessed Sacrament was carried in procession to stop plagues of grasshoppers and caterpillars, to put out fires, and to protect against storms and earth tremors. When a caterpillar plague threatened to wipe out the crops which were crucial to survival in 1743, for example, the Bishop ordered public prayers said. He took the occasion to support the popular view that such disasters were probably manifestations of Divine displeasure at the colonists' inadequate religious fervour.

> We exposed to you, our dearly beloved Brethren, in our *mandement* of 21 April of this year, the common dangers threatening us; we urged you to unite your prayers to those we enjoined in order to turn aside divine retribution so deservedly aroused . . . many use these more favourable days to offend God which gave to the sins committed a quality of the darkest ingratitude capable of calling down on us the most terrible punishments. Already the curse has appeared in one of the districts of our government: the prairies are almost eaten down completely by insects; in certain places even the cereal crops have suffered. You apprehend and perhaps with reason the same plague; we do not pretend to condemn this fear if you let it work out your salvation. . . .
>
> H. Têtu & C.O. Gagnon, *Mandements, lettres pastorales et circulaires* II, pp. 31–33. trans. C.J.J.

Stamping Out Sorcery: The Case of the Desecrated Crucifix, 1744

In an age when many people were superstitious it was not surprising there were alleged outbreaks of witchcraft and that there was both judicial pursuit and exorcism. An ordinance of 1682 had put an end to witchcraft trials in France, yet popular belief in the evil eye, the casting of spells and diabolical possession persisted. Among several celebrated cases in New France was that of a soldier named Havard, arrested for divination using a religious book and crucifix. When someone started the rumour that he had plunged a knife into the crucifix and that blood had spurted from it there was public outrage. The soldier was tried by the civil courts, but the Bishop who was making a pastoral visit to Montreal at the time decided to call for an act of public penance (giving way to popular sentiment) and to place the "desecrated crucifix" for safe-keeping as a holy relic with Hospital Nuns at Quebec.

> You took part, last year, our dearly beloved daughters, in the profound grief we felt on the occasion of the scandal which took place in Montreal. . . .
>
> Destined as you are by your vocation to succour in the persons of the poor the suffering members of Jesus Christ, a holy calling to which you consecrate yourselves with fervour, we believe that you will betake yourselves with greater zeal to make atonement for the insult which was offered to the very person of Jesus Christ, in his image. It was exposed to the flames: may your hearts aflame with his heavenly love redeem it from this abuse. They wanted to use it for gross superstition: use it as a buckler to defend yourselves against the attacks of the seducing spirit. Perhaps even heaven, favourable to our vows, will work wonders on behalf of those who adore in spirit and in truth Jesus Christ represented on that cross.
>
> We learned that at the time of the desecration, penetrated with grief you made honorable amends and a general communion. Persuaded that your dispositions have not altered, we confide to you, as to faithful spouses, this adorable cross and we order you to place it in your church and to choose a day of the week for its adoration and to join thereto a general communion.
>
> H. Têtu & C.O. Gagnon, *Mandements, lettres pastorales et circulaires* I, pp. 33–34. trans. C.J.J.

CONFLICTING INTERPRETATIONS

The Catholic Church and the Theocratic State—Francis Parkman's Interpretation

The interpretation that stands out and has influenced generations of readers was that of Francis Parkman, who saw the Catholic Church in New France as exercising an overweening and oppressive influence, and its clergy as intervening in all details of public and private affairs. In his view, Canada was no less than a theocracy with the clerical power dominant. Nevertheless, he did admit that in the face of adversity it was the Church that could provide some stability and continuity.

Against absolute authority there was a counter influence, rudely and wildly antagonistic. Canada was at the very portal of the great interior wilderness. The St. Lawrence and the Lakes were the highway to that domain of savage freedom; and thither the disfranchised, half-starved seignior, and the discouraged *habitant* who could find no market for his produce naturally enough betook themselves. Their lesson of savagery was well learned, and for many a year a boundless license and a stiff-handed authority battled for the control of Canada. Nor, to the last, were Church and State fairly masters of the field....

... Freedom is for those who are fit for it; the rest will lose it, or turn it to corruption. Church and State were right in exercising authority over a people which had not learned the first rudiments of self-government. Their fault was not that they exercised authority, but that they exercised too much of it, and, instead of weaning the child to go alone, kept him in perpetual leading-strings, making him, if possible, more and more dependent, and less and less fit for freedom....

One great fact stands out conspicuous in Canadian history—the Church of Rome. More even than the royal power, she shaped the character and the destinies of the colony. She was its nurse and almost its mother; and, wayward and headstrong as it was, it never broke the ties of faith that held it to her. It was these ties which, in the absence of political franchises, formed under the old regime the only vital coherence in the population. The royal government was transient; the Church was permanent. The English conquest shattered the whole apparatus of civil administration at a blow, but it left her untouched. Governors, intendants, councils, and commandants, all were gone; the principal seigniors fled the colony; and a people who had never learned to control themselves or help themselves were suddenly left to their own devices. Confusion, if not anarchy, would have followed but for the parish priests, who, in a character of double paternity, half spiritual and half temporal, became more than ever the guardians of order throughout Canada.

Francis Parkman, *The Old Régime in Canada* (Toronto: George N. Morang, 1899), Vol. I, pp. 198–199, 203.

The Church as an Agency of Social Control—Mason Wade on Parkman and the Church

Parkman's interpretation of the dominant role played by the Church has passed into twentieth-century Canadian history through the writings of both the French Canadian nationalist historians and the anglophone historians.

Mason Wade in his survey history of the French-Canadian people accepted the premise that the Church had been the most important institution of the *Ancien Régime*, although he did point to a number of challenges to its authority and to problems which it had difficulty solving.

> Parkman has justly stressed the fundamental importance of the Catholic Church in New France.... There can be little question that Bishop Laval had more influence in New France than Louis XIV during a long lifetime which appropriately paralleled Louis' reign. The development of the Church in New France may be said to be his work.
>
>   Laval came to the colony in 1659, having been named by Rome Vicar Apostolic of New France at the instigation of the Jesuits, who had maintained virtual ecclesiastical control of the colony since their arrival a quarter of a century before... at the moment of transition from mission to established church, the Church of New France was given an ultramontane rather than a gallican tendency. Under the regime of Laval, who had an inflexible will and an instinct for domination, ultramontanism was built into the very fabric of the Church in Quebec, which assumed a position very different from that which it held in gallican France....
>
>   Bishop Laval was an ultramontane centralizer, not a gallican or a believer in a national clergy. He was a churchman before he was a Canadian or a Frenchman; and under his guidance the Church in Quebec developed a tradition which it has preserved until today. Portraits of the Pope are found in French-Canadian homes more often than those of the Queen or of the prime ministers of Canada or Quebec, and the papal flag is displayed more frequently than at Rome.
>
>   In all, Laval guided the destinies of the Church in New France for thirty-four years, ruling in a more authoritarian and absolute fashion than any representative of the all-powerful Sun King. He left more of a mark upon the colony than any governor except the great Frontenac, with whom he had quarrelled violently, as might have been expected when two autocrats were thrown together in a small settlement.... The tradition of Bishop Laval has been a major force in the history of French Canada: his desire to subordinate state to Church, his authoritarianism, his Jansenism, his ultramontanism, have cropped up again and again in his spiritual heirs who have benefited from the prestige and ascendancy which the first Bishop of Quebec won by his domineering will, his zeal, and his ceaseless effort.
>
>   Mason Wade, *The French Canadians, 1760–1967* (Toronto: Macmillan, 1967), I, pp. 37, 39–40.

Theocracy in the "Heroic Age": Salone on Colonization

In his study of colonization in New France, the French historian Emile Salone distinguished between the early "heroic age" when the missions and the efforts of the Company of New France and a few noble seigneurs dominated colonial development and the later period under Royal Government when the role of the state became more directly felt.

> With the progress of the colony, with the growth of its population, New France escaped more and more from theocracy. Certainly the propaganda of the *philosophes* did not cross the Atlantic. The Canadians remain docile children of the Catholic Church. But the Jesuits lost a large part of their influence, if not over society in general at least in government, and the bishops of Québec, most of the time, [lacked] the wisdom to restrict themselves to their ecclesiastical functions. That is true especially after the

death of M. de Saint-Vallier. . . . At Québec as at Versailles the government has the sense of its power and makes no scruple about imposing its will.

Emile Salone, *La Colonisation de la Nouvelle-France* (Paris: E. Guilmoto, 1906), pp. 408–9. trans. C.J.J.

The Financial Status of the Church—A Revisionist View

One popular impression of the colonial Church is that it had been bequeathed enormous fortunes, that it owned vast and fertile agricultural lands, that its clergy, as a privileged order, had many opportunities to profit from investments, and that the common people were obliged to support it. Visually its massive stone monasteries and tall-spired churches dominated the landscape. Although there are elements of truth in these perceptions, historians have qualified all of these views. Guy Frégault in his analysis of Canadian society has given us a summary of the Church's financial status.

The first observation is that the Church has important revenues. Are they excessive? Are they sufficient? They seem to correspond quite well to the needs of society. The hospital services seem to conform to the standards of the time, as do the educational institutions. On this head, the only expression of dissatisfaction which we have found among the Canadians of the XVIIIth century is that of the Montrealers who, in 1727, request the establishment of a Jesuit college in their city. . . .

The second conclusion relates precisely to the contribution of the State to the works of the clergy. This contribution consists of three elements. The first is made up of the annual subsidies. . . . The second element is made up of the seigneuries which the king grants to the religious houses. . . . Finally come the tithes: no doubt, it is the State which supplies these when by reason of their insufficient revenues it pays the clergy a 'supplement'. . . . Besides these three sources of income, there exists only one which appears noteworthy: it is the totality of the endowments established from private fortunes in which are included certain benefices distributed by the Crown.

The considerable share which the latter assumes in financing the religious institutions raises an inevitable question: that of the relations between Church and State. An examination, even cursory, of this question will suggest another conclusion. It is certain that by reason of the extent of its role, the State is inclined to make intrusions into the affairs of the clergy. . . . It must be conceded that the very solicitations of the members of the clergy often oblige the civil government to intervene in questions which ought, it would seem, devolve upon the religious authorities. It may perhaps not be rash to conclude that, in general, the State, sure of its power, does not seem too inclined to abuse it, while the clergy manifests no dark susceptibilities towards the State. The statesmen are Catholics, the churchmen are the King's servants.

Guy Frégault, *Le XVIIIe Siècle Canadien. Etudes* (Montreal: Editions HMH, 1970), pp. 146–148. trans. C.J.J.

The Tyranny of Religious Uniformity—F.-X. Garneau's View

The French-Canadian nationalist historian François-Xavier Garneau argued long ago that the Church exerted far-reaching clerical influence in imposing its doctrine of religious uniformity. The decision to exclude Protestant

Huguenots from New France, according to Garneau back in 1845, was an example of excessive clerical influence which damaged the economic development of the colony. Subsequent editions toned down this criticism. The argument ignores the evidence that the Huguenots were not too interested in taking up permanent residence in large numbers in Canada before 1627, and that even after the Revocation of the Edict of Nantes in 1685 it was persecution, and not the attractions of emigration, that drove them abroad to Protestant lands.

> Thus Richelieu made a big mistake when he consented to having the Protestants excluded from New France; if it were necessary to expel one of the two religions, it would have been better in the interests of the colony to have this exclusion fall on the Catholics who emigrated little: it dealt a fatal blow to Canada by formally closing off admission there to the Huguenots by the act establishing the company of one hundred associates.
>
> ... The French colonial system would have had a very different outcome if they had lifted the barriers set up to keep away these sectarians from the country and if the doors had been left open to them....
>
> Richelieu by excluding the Huguenots from Canada undoubtedly committed an act of flagrant tyranny; but did not their conduct authorize him, or at least give him the plausible pretext to so act? It added weight to the assertion of Catholics who never ceased to repeat that there was no security in permitting them to establish themselves in the neighbourhood of English Protestant colonies....
>
> F.-X. Garneau, *Histoire du Canada depuis sa découverte jusqu'à nos jours* (Quebec: N. Aubin, 1845), pp. 156–7, 176. trans. C.J.J.

Abbé Groulx's Vision of the Church as the Creator of An Ideal Society

Like Garneau, abbé Lionel Groulx saw the Church's role as a dominant one in New France, but unlike his predecessor he contended that clerical influences played a creative role in shaping an ideal, purified Christian society. Groulx perceived no hint of theocratic oppression and looked upon the exclusion of "Huguenots and jailbirds" as part of the plan to create an "apostolic people". In his vision of New France the clergy provided important moral and spiritual leadership, while the parish was the centre of daily life and activity. An ideal Christian society, a sort of New Nation in embryo, was founded, he argued, on positive concepts of race, religion, language and social stability.

> To defend the race, there are two bastions, among others, that our bishops fashioned with their hands: the family and the parish. The French-Canadian family is one of the glories of our people, 'one of the greatest marvels of the Catholic Church in the past two centuries,' wrote one historian. The family deserves this great praise for the admirable manner in which it discharged its natural ends. But who created the French-Canadian family? Who gave it its laws, its soul, and those qualities of strength and purity where it found the courage to undertake and the power to accomplish its duty? Here again, let us have the fairness to recognize that the Church played the leading and the most active role....
>
> ... The feudal régime had established only judicial ties between the inhabitants of a

seigneury. The real public society, the one which raised an authority over the family groupings and brought them together so that they might progress in a manner both fuller and more perfect, was the parish, which was a purely ecclesiastical institution....

In the period of New France the parish meant that the man of God, the guardian of faith and morality, acted as a social leader; it meant that human relationships were regulated by Christian charity and justice....

[Our bishops] wished their activities to extend still farther and to reach as far as the state itself, or what was then our government organism. Councillors of the Sovereign Council and the only permanent ones, so to speak, our bishops held the first role in the *parlement* of New France. This suggests what orientation they would give to the colonial legislation, the origin of part of our present system of laws. We also know with what energy they defended the prerogatives of the spiritual power against the governors and the Gallican members of the council. To the best of their ability, they caused [the principle of] the proper subordination of powers to be recognized and to become a part of our public customs. And what does this mean if not to lay down the foundations of the social and political order? Those who appreciate the role of truth in the life of a people, the close relations that exist between the rights of man and the rights of God, will hail these men of the Church as real statesmen.

(Abbé Lionel Groulx, "Ce que nous devons au catholicisme," *Action française* (novembre 1923), 262–264)

The Church's Providential Mission Questioned—A Comparative Look at Louisiana and Canada

Recent studies of the Church in various parts of New France have taken a very different view. One such study, Charles O'Neill's analysis of Church-state relations in French colonial Louisiana, has called into question abbé Groulx's interpretation that the Church exercised massive influence throughout all of New France.

To the latter-day mentality it might seem unbecoming for the State to have been so clerical-minded and for the Church to have been so political-minded. The reader of history is shocked to see the State 'used as a tool' by the Church, and the Church 'used' by the State; yet the more he reads, the more he feels that his very phrasing of these relations is anachronistic. Seeing that things were this way, he seeks to penetrate them as they were, although it is not easy to understand the mentality of bygone epochs. In the mind of the period under study churchmen found it quite natural to depend upon the *roi très chrétien* in patterns unthinkable today. Yet there was a separation—a separateness that involved an intricate code or system of respect, distance-keeping, and consciousness of respective limitations. While in detail Church property might have been limited, and while precise rules for the clergy's respect for civil authorities in the sanctuary might have been imposed, a humiliation of the Church or its representatives was not formally to be thought of. Conversely, civil action in sacramental affairs, including marriage, and civil trial of those vested with canonical privilege might be contested, but a repudiation of the French King as protector of the French Church was an idea that hardly any mind of that day entertained....

One would err, however, in regarding the French monarch's Gallicanism as a monster in regard to the Church. It was inimical to an extent, but it must be remembered that the Church had neither the machinery nor the funds to carry on the missionary enterprise. It was the King's ships and the King's supplies that in reality kept the missions and the missionaries alive....

One can observe in the histories of Canada that the authors are often implicitly or explicitly arguing over the role of the bishop and clergy in the colonization and development of New France. Whatever may be the case for the northern colony, one can conclude that in Louisiana the clergy never obtained the influence that prelate and priest had (or were reputed to have) in Canada. On few points was there contention between the Louisiana civil government as such and the clergy as such. However, if an individual representative of the temporal authority contended with a cleric, the latter habitually lost....

In matters purely spiritual, the Louisiana colony never attained the religious fervor of the Canadian; indeed, while there was a formal structure which paid deference to Catholicism, the society and its political organization were wanting in depth and inspiration. One might say in retrospect that religion for the Louisiana of Louis XIV and Louis XV was a pervading, tempering influence but not a dynamic, decisive force.

Charles Edwards O'Neill, *Church and State in French Colonial Louisiana. Policy and Politics in 1732* (New Haven: Yale University Press, 1966), pp. 284–7.

A New Perspective: Practice vs. Precept

Cornelius J. Jaenen, author of *The Role of the Church in New France* (1976), has carried the process of reinterpretation one step farther. His assessment of the Church's influence in Canada is consistent with O'Neill's evaluation of the situation in Louisiana. By paying greater attention to popular beliefs and practices, by questioning the effectiveness of policy statements and clerical orders in changing behaviour, a new social dimension has been added.

At least a majority of the colonials, like the common people of the mother country, seem to have practiced their religion more out of social convention and habit than out of any overzealous conviction or superstitious fear. Most performed their Easter duties and took part at midnight mass at Christmas, although fewer attended mass faithfully every Sunday. Even those who did attend regularly did not always show the respect and attention that one might expect of them. In every decade there were priests who complained to the bishop and to the secular authorities about the laxity of religious practice. Nevertheless, the Canadians seem to have been a generally religious people. Their chief fault was that they performed their religious obligations in much the same way as they performed their social obligations, and in this they followed rather well the example of their Kings. Anyone who refused to conform to the conventional life-style was quickly marked.... It would be erroneous to suppose that religion was the chief motivational force behind all aspects of everyday living.... While it is true that, during the early missionary period when religious foundations of the colony were laid, a mystical and even fanatical Catholicism made itself felt, it did not dominate thought and action after 1663....

The colonists were far from docile, subservient, downtrodden, inarticulate, priest-ridden peasants. Contemporary documentation shows them to be remarkably independent, aggressive, self-assertive, freedom-loving and outspoken individuals. Saint-Vallier and Pontbriand both deplored their lack of respect for constituted authority, their brashness, their materialism and independence of mind....

At the end of the French period, the clergy were becoming concerned about the growing urbanization of the colony... even more disturbing was the strengthening of a

worldly outlook and the development of a courtier society, particularly at Quebec—
aping some aspects of court life in France—and also reproducing the worst features of
military garrison life, at Montreal, Louisbourg and Detroit. The clergy, from Pontbriand to the lowliest deacon, inveighed with good reason against the drunkenness,
sexual laxity, gambling, and the general worldliness and pleasure-madness of a
growing segment of colonial society. It was not surprising that some of the clergy
speculated that the British Conquest was some kind of Divine retribution, a sort of
'Babylonian captivity' to cleanse Israel of her filthy whoredoms.

Cornelius J. Jaenen, *The Role of the Church in New France* (Toronto: McGraw-Hill
Ryerson, 1976), pp. 150–1, 155–7.

A Guide to Further Reading

1. Overviews

Eastman, Mack, *Church and State in Early Canada*. Edinburgh: Edinburgh University
Press, 1915.
Frégault, Guy, *Canadian Society in the French Régime*. Canadian Historical Association
Booklet No. 3. Ottawa: C.H.A., 1968.
_____, *Le XVIIIe Siècle Canadien. Etudes*. Montreal: Editions HMH, 1970.
Groulx, Lionel, *Histoire du Canada français depuis la découverte*. 2 vols. Montreal:
Fides, 1962.
Jaenen, Cornelius J., *The Role of the Church in New France*. Toronto: McGraw-Hill Ryer-
son, 1976.
_____, "Church-State Relations in Canada, 1604–1685", Canadian Historical Associa-
tion *Report*, 1967.
Moir, John S., *Church and State in Canada, 1627–1867*. Toronto: McClelland and
Stewart, 1968.
Parkman, Francis, *The Old Régime in Canada*. Toronto: George N. Morang, 1899.
Plante, Hermann, *L'Eglise catholique au Canada de 1604 à 1866*. Trois-Rivières: Editions
du Bien Public, 1970.
Salone, Emile, *La Colonisation de la Nouvelle-France*. Paris: E. Guilmoto, 1906.
Voisine, Nive et al., *Histoire de l'Eglise catholique au Québec, 1608–1970*. Montreal:
Fides, 1971.
Walsh, H.H., *The Church in the French Era*. Toronto: Ryerson Press, 1967.
Zoltvany, Yves F., ed., *The Government of New France: Royal, Clerical or Class Rule?*.
Scarborough: Prentice-Hall, 1971.

2. Specialized Studies

Memoirs and Collected Documents

Collection de Manuscrits relatifs à la Nouvelle-France. Vol. 1. Quebec: Coté, 1883.
Martin, Dom Claude, *Vie de la Vénérable Mère Marie de l'Incarnation*. Paris, 1677.
Têtu, H. and C.O. Gagnon, eds., *Mandements, lettres pastorales et circulaires des
Evêques de Québec, 1659–1887*. 6 vols. Quebec: Coté, 1887–90.
Thwaites, R.G., ed., *The Jesuit Relations and Allied Documents*. 72 vols. New York:
Pageant, 1959.

Regional Studies of the Church

O'Neill, Charles, *Church and State in French Colonial Louisiana: Policy and Politics to 1732*. New Haven: Yale University Press, 1966.

Palm, Mary B., *The Jesuit Missions of the Illinois Country, 1673-1763*. Cleveland, 1933.

Johnston, A.J.B., *Religion in Life at Louisbourg*. Montreal: McGill-Queen's University Press, 1984.

The Bishops and the Institutional Church

Baillargeon, Noel, *Le Séminaire de Québec*. 2 vols. Quebec: Les Presses de l'Université Laval, 1972 and 1977.

Campeau, Lucien, *L'Evêché de Québec (1674): aux origines du premier diocèse érigé en Amérique française*. Quebec: Société historique de Québec, 1974.

Gosselin, Auguste, *L'Eglise du Canada depuis Mgr. de Laval jusqu'à la Conquête*. 3 vols. Quebec: Laflamme & Proulx, 1914-17.

Hurtubise, Pierre, "Jansenism, Gallicanism, Ultramontanism: The Case of François de Laval", in J.M. Bumsted, ed., *Canadian History Before Confederation*. Second Edition. Georgetown: Irwin-Dorsey, 1979, pp. 61-76.

Lacelle, Claudette, *Monseigneur Henry-Marie Dubreuil de Pontbriand: ses mandements et circulaires*. MA Thesis, University of Ottawa, 1971.

Religious Minorities

Bédard, Marc-André, *Les Protestants en Nouvelle-France*. Quebec: Les Presses de l'Université Laval, 1978.

Jaenen, Cornelius J., "The Persistence of the Protestant Presence in New France, 1541-1760", *Proceedings of the Second Meeting of the Western Society for French History*. Austin: Best Printing, 1975.

Vaugeois, Denis, *Les Juifs et la Nouvelle-France*. Trois-Rivières: Le Boréal Express, 1968.

Religious and Social Life

Falardeau, Jean-Charles, "The Seventeenth-Century Parish in French Canada", in Marcel Rioux and Yves Martin, eds., *French Canadian Society*. Toronto: McClelland and Stewart, 1964.

Moogk, Peter N., "'Thieving Buggers' and 'Stupid Sluts': Insults and Popular Culture in New France", *William and Mary Quarterly* (1979).

4

THE CONQUEST OF 1760

Were Its Consequences Traumatic?

It is sometimes asserted, on the basis of Canada's participation in the Boer War, two World Wars and the Korean conflict, that we have never endured the traumatic consequences of foreign invasion, military occupation and alien rule. This is not true, of course, for the inhabitants of Canada, Acadia, Newfoundland and Ile-Royale prior to 1812, who were very well acquainted with the sufferings and privations consequent to invasion and conquest. Canada, or Quebec, as the British came to call it, experienced not only the immediate consequences of military defeat but also the long-term consequences of cession to a foreign power.

While perceptions of the British Conquest of 1760 as a military invasion of Canada may have become blurred, the meaning of the Conquest remains one of the most controversial issues in all of Canadian history. For French—and English—Canadians, the Conquest stands out as a critical event which still evokes strong feelings and raises profound questions about the nature of Canada, and particularly, about the historic relationship between the country's two founding European peoples. Few events in Canada's past have attracted as much historical interest or generated as much dispute. The Conquest of 1760 has been alternately described as an "act of liberation" from French despotic rule, or as a "traumatic event", permanently and tragically deforming the "national development" of French Canada. A host of other interpretations fall somewhere between these two extreme positions. Outside the realm of scholarly study, ideas about the meaning of the Conquest still inform contemporary Canadian political thinking and behaviour.

The story of the Conquest of Canada in 1760 is a familiar one. The fall of New France was only part of a larger Anglo-French imperial struggle known as the Seven Years' War (1756–1763). The conflict in North America found its origins in both the eighteenth-century contest for imperial supremacy between England and France and a related competition between Canadian and Anglo-American colonists over control and use of the continent's interior. In the struggle, Acadians were expelled by the British from their homeland in 1755, the great French fortress Louisbourg fell in 1758, and Quebec capitulated after a British siege in 1759. Inland, determined French resistance staved off the final surrender for another year. Eventually, in September 1760, after six years of warfare, the Marquis de Vaudreuil, Governor of New France, surrendered the colony to the British, and some 65 000 French Canadians passed under British rule.

The Seven Years' War in North America was accompanied by the bloodshed, barbarism, and human suffering that accompanies all wars. Yet there has been a tendency in Canadian history to gloss over the military aspects of the Conquest, to present the struggle for Canada as a clean, disciplined economic and strategic struggle for control by two highly civilized powers. This popular representation is often enhanced by a laudatory reference to the two European commanders, General James Wolfe and the Marquis de Montcalm, both of which are depicted as heroes and both of which sacrificed their lives in the noble struggle. There is almost a romantic hope that from the Plains of Abraham, where the blood of two nations mingled, two founding peoples would blend their genius to build a greater New World community.

For the *Canadiens*[1], many of whose families had been in Canada for over a century, the British Conquest constituted a crisis threatening their ethnic survival, and elicited a variety of responses. Restoring a stable economy, safeguarding the Catholic religion, securing the customary civil and political rights, and salvaging financial investments were all matters of serious concern. Under British rule, new political institutions were established by usage and statute between 1763 and 1790 which conformed, for the most part, with the authoritarian French régime. Government was still by governor and council acting under the supervision of a minister in far-off Europe. Although the criminal law was English, French Canadian traditions in the area of civil law (concerning things such as marriage, commercial transactions and landholding) were continued, permitting *Canadiens* to maintain most of their traditional social structure. The Catholic faith was upheld by the appointment in 1766 of a new French Catholic bishop, Jean-Olivier Briand, even though the Church's operations were closely supervised by the new Protestant rulers. Education provided by the religious lost the support it had received from the French monarchy and was further hindered by the confiscation of the property of the Jesuit Order. Opinions differed, however, on whether such changes under British rule provided a measure of continuity or added to the trauma of conquest.

---

1. The term "Canadiens" or French Canadians applies to French-speaking/francophone Canadians in the post-Conquest period. Prior to the Conquest, French-speakers residing in Canada were termed "Canadians."

Almost since the fall of New France, the Conquest has been much more than just an historical issue. Canadian politicians, public figures and intellectuals, notably in Quebec, have often raised the issue of the Conquest in public debate. From the *Patriotes* of the 1830s to the Quebec *Péquiste* movement of today, the "tragic" event has been an important force in shaping and informing Quebec separatist thought. The Canadian public has been drawn into this political exercise too: some maintain that the issue of bilingualism and dualism was settled once and for ever on the Plains of Abraham, and others view the Conquest and its implications as "a sin against nationality". For some Canadians, it seems that the events of 1759–60 still have an upsetting effect today.

Were the consequences of the Conquest really traumatic? Or were the events of 1759–60 merely one incident in the historical evolution of French Canada? If the Conquest was a "catastrophe" for French Canadians, which groups in society were traumatized the most severely—and with what results? These are just some of the contentious questions addressed in this problem study by both French Canadian and English Canadian historians. Their interpretations are, as might be expected, often both widely divergent and the subject of acrimonious debate.

SELECTED CONTEMPORARY SOURCES

THE MILITARY EXPERIENCE OF CONQUEST

War had real meaning in New France in the 1750s. The *habitants* of the St. Lawrence Valley had crops and cattle requisitioned for the French armies and often had soldiers billeted in their homes during the Seven Years' War. Fathers and sons were often called away on militia duty, compulsory since 1669 for all able-bodied males between the ages of 16 and 60. And what of the added burdens that the women and children had to assume?— because war, after all, touched all members of society. When the British fleet appeared before Quebec in 1759 the inhabitants learned the meaning of naval bombardment. Even before the final battles had been decided the spectres of famine and epidemic appeared. The uncertainties, hopes and fears associated with war seemed real enough to both the military and Canadians at the time of the Conquest.

Initial Fears—General James Wolfe's Manifesto, 1759

For the colony of New France, the British advances of 1758 in the Seven Years' War seemed to spell doom. The fall of Louisbourg and the surrender of Fort Ticonderoga left many inhabitants of the French colony terror-stricken. Both the Lake Champlain overland route and the St. Lawrence naval approach to Canada lay open to the invading forces led by British generals, Amherst and Wolfe. Many *Canadiens* feared that the English conquerors would give vent to racial and religious prejudices and seek reprisals for alleged atrocities committed by France's Indian allies.

In this atmosphere of fear and anticipation, General James Wolfe adopted a strategy of psychological intimidation. His official manifesto, issued on June 28, 1759, sought to weaken *Canadien* resolve by threatening the populace with vengeful acts.

> The formidable sea and land armament, which the people of Canada now behold in the heart of their country, is intended by the king, my master, to check the insolence of France, to revenge the insults offered to the British colonies, and totally to deprive the French of their most valuable settlement in North America. For these purposes is the formidable army under my command intended. The King of Great Britain wages no war with the industrious peasant, the sacred orders of religion, or the defenceless women and children: to these, in their distressful circumstances, his royal clemency offers protection. The people may remain unmolested on their lands, inhabit their houses and enjoy their religion in security; for these inestimable blessings, I expect the Canadians will take no part in the great contest between the two crowns. But, if by a vain obstinacy and misguided valour, they presume to appear in arms, they must expect the most fatal consequences; their habitations destroyed, their sacred temples exposed to an exasperated soldiery, their harvest utterly ruined and the only passage for relief stopped up by a most formidable fleet. In this unhappy situation, and closely attacked by another great army, what can the wretched natives expect from opposition? The unparalleled barbarities exerted by the French against our settlements in America might justify the bitterest revenge in the army under my command. *But Britons breathe higher sentiments of humanity, and listen to the merciful dictates of the Christian religion . . . .* In this great dilemma, let the wisdom of the people of Canada shew itself; Britain stretches out a powerful yet merciful hand, faithful to her engagements, and ready to secure her in her most valuable rights and possessions: France, unable to support Canada, deserts her cause at this important crisis, and, during the whole war, has assisted her with troops who have been maintained only by making the natives feel all the weight of grievous and lawless oppression . . . .
>
> J.A. WOLFE.
>
> Brian Connell, ed., *The Siege of Quebec and the Campaigns in North America, 1757-1760 by Captain John Knox* (Mississauga: Pendragon House, 1980), pp. 135-6.

The Immediate Consequences—Views of the Siege of Quebec, 1759

Wolfe and the British were as good as their word. Crops were burned and homes destroyed before the British fleet attacked Quebec. In the ensuing battle on the Plains of Abraham, September 13, 1759, both Wolfe and the French commander, the Marquis de Montcalm, were killed in the discharge of their duties. While the encounter lasted only about fifteen minutes, it was not until five days later that the French capitulated and British troops were permitted to enter the devastated city. Sentries were quickly posted to prevent looting by the starving inhabitants as the French army withdrew. The British navy sailed back to Europe, leaving a garrison to brave a harsh winter, scurvy and guerrilla attacks by Canadian militia and Indian allies. In the siege, the

A British view of the Siege of Quebec, Sept. 13, 1759

heaviest toll had been borne by the civilian population. British bombardment destroyed more than three quarters of the buildings in the capital.

Popular interpretations and British soldiers' accounts of "The Taking of Quebec" tended to dramatize the event and to convey a different impression of its immediate military consequences.

A British Soldier's Account

... We then faced to the right, and marched towards the town by files, till we came to the Plains of Abraham; an even piece of ground which Mr. Wolfe had made choice of while we stood forming upon the hill....

About ten o'clock the enemy began to advance briskly in three columns, with loud shouts and recovered arms, two of them inclining to the left of our army, and the third towards our right, firing obliquely at the two extremities of our line, from the distance of one hundred and thirty, until they came within forty yards; which our troops withstood with the greatest intrepidity and firmness, still reserving their fire and paying the strictest obedience to their officers: this uncommon steadiness, together with the havoc which the grape-shot from our field-pieces made among them, threw them into some disorder, and was most critically maintained by a well-timed, regular and heavy discharge of our small arms, such as they could no longer oppose....

Hereupon they gave way, and fled with precipitation, so that, by the time the cloud of smoke was vanished, our men were again loaded and, profiting by the advantage we had over them, pursued them almost to the gates of the town and the bridge over the little river, redoubling our fire with great eagerness, making many officers and men prisoners. The weather cleared up, with a comfortably warm sun-shine....

Brian Connell, ed., *The Siege of Quebec*, pp. 195–198.

A Taste of Military Defeat—The British at Ste-Foy, 1760

The French and Canadians were not the only ones to suffer military losses in the "War of Conquest." In April 1760 the Marquis de Lévis led a French army down from Montreal for an attack on the British at Quebec, and Brigadier James Murray engaged the French force at Ste-Foy. Although the armies were evenly matched, the British lost this last battle and had to withdraw behind the walls of Quebec as Montcalm had done the previous year. Captain Smith's journal offered a glimpse of this British defeat in the afterglow of victory.

In the course of the action we were insensibly drawn from our advantageous situation into low swampy ground, where our troops fought almost knee-deep in dissolving wreaths of snow and water, whence it was utterly impracticable to draw off our artillery under those unhappy circumstances, after this infeebled army had performed prodigies of valour exceeding all description; having the whole force of the country to contend with, and our communication with the town in danger of being intercepted, we were obliged to give up the contest.

The troops being ordered to fall back, a command they were hitherto unacquainted with, as if sensible of the critical posture of our affairs, they drew a natural conclusion; and, growing impatient, some of them cried out, *Damn it, what is falling back but retreating?* The inference was immediately communicated to the whole, and accordingly put in execution. This discomfit was however so regularly conducted that the enemy did not pursue with that spirit which the vast importance of their victory required....

Brian Connell, ed., *The Siege of Quebec*, pp. 246–8.

POLITICAL EFFECTS OF THE CONQUEST

The arrival of a British naval force in 1760 decided the fate of Canada, and the capitulation of Montreal in September ended over 150 years of French rule in Canada, bringing certain political consequences. The colony was placed under the British military rule of General James Murray until a definitive treaty of peace was signed in 1763 and it was clear that Canada would not be returned to Louis XV of France. When Canada was ceded to Britain in the Treaty of Paris (1763), General Murray was appointed civilian Governor. In his instructions from Britain, he was urged to pursue a policy of conciliation towards the French Canadian "new subjects" and also towards the Indian nations of the interior of the continent, where a large reserve was being established. However, the Governor was to tolerate no extension of the privileges granted the Catholic Church. Although the British may have decided to keep Canada mainly to remove the threat of French aggression against their American colonies, it soon became clear that having acquired Canada, they hoped to make it British politically and socially—and to anglicize the *Canadiens* or "new subjects". Not until the Quebec Act of 1774 did the drive of this official policy of assimilation subside.

Dealing with the "New Subjects"—The Articles of Capitulation, 1760

The terms of surrender were set out in the Articles of Capitulation of Montreal, September 8, 1760. The articles consist of the conditions requested by Governor Vaudreuil, followed (in quotation marks) by the official comments of the British commander, General Jeffrey Amherst.

Article IST

Twenty-four hours after the signing of the present capitulation, the British General shall cause the troops of his Britannic Majesty to take possession of the Gates of the town of Montreal; and the British Garrison shall not enter the place till after the French troops shall have evacuated it.—'The whole Garrison of Montreal must lay down their arms, and shall not serve during the present war. Immediately after the signing of the present capitulation, the King's troops shall take possession of the gates, and shall post the Guards necessary to preserve good order in the town.'

Article IVTH

The Militia after evacuating the above towns, forts and posts, shall return to their habitations, without being molested on any pretence whatever, on account of their having carried guns.—'Granted.'

Article XXVII

The free exercise of the Catholic, Apostolic, and Roman Religion, shall subsist entire, in such manner that all the states and the people of the Towns and countries, places and distant posts, shall continue to assemble in the churches, and to frequent the sacraments as heretofore, without being molested in any manner, directly or indirectly. These people shall be obliged, by the English Government, to pay their Priests the tithes, and all the taxes they were used to pay under the Government of his most Christian Majesty.—'Granted, as to the free exercise of their religion, the obligation of paying the tithes to the Priests will depend on the King's pleasure.'

Article XXXIV

All the communities, and all the priests, shall preserve their moveables, the property and revenues of the Seignories and other estates, which they possess in the colony, of what nature soever they be; and the same estates shall be preserved in their privileges, rights, honours, and exemptions.—'Granted.'

Article XXXVI

If by the treaty of Peace, Canada remains to his Britannic Majesty, all the French, Canadians, Acadians, Merchants and other persons who chuse to retire to France, shall have leave to do so from the British General, who shall procure them a passage: and nevertheless, if, from this time to that decision, any French or Canadian Merchants or other persons, shall desire to go to France; they shall likewise have leave from the British General. Both the one and the other shall take with them their families, servants, and baggage.—'Granted.'

Article XXXVII

The Lords of Manors, the Military and Civil officers, the Canadians as well in the Towns as in the country, the French settled, or trading, in the whole extent of the colony of Canada, and all other persons whatsoever, shall preserve the entire peaceable property and possession of the goods, noble and ignoble, moveable and immoveable, merchandizes, furs and other effects, even their ships; they shall not be touched, nor the least damage done to them, on any pretence whatever. They shall have liberty to keep, let or sell them, as well to the French as to the British; to take away the produce of them in Bills of exchange, furs, specie or other returns, whenever they shall judge proper to go to France, paying their freight, as in the XXVIth Article. They shall also have the furs which are in the posts above, and which belong to them, and may be on the way to Montreal; and, for this purpose, they shall have leave to send, this year, or the next, canoes fitted out, to fetch such of the said furs as shall have remained in those posts.— 'Granted as in [a preceding article].'

Article XLII

The French and Canadians shall continue to be governed according to the custom of Paris, and the Laws and usages established for this country, and they shall not be subject to any other imposts than those which were established under the French Dominions.— 'Answered by the preceding articles, and particularly by the last.'

Adam Shortt & Arthur Doughty, eds., *Documents Relating to the Constitutional History of Canada, 1759–1791* (Ottawa: Taché, 1918), pp. 25–32.

The Policy of Conciliation—Instructions to Governor Murray, 1763

It is often contended that the lenient policy practised by the British after 1760 almost erased the military trauma of the Conquest and, indeed, won the loyalty of the *Canadiens*. Documents such as the British Secretary of State's instructions to Governor Murray in 1763 give some credence to this interpretation.

... I have no new Orders to transmit to you at present; But His Majesty thinks it very material, that you should be apprized, that He has received Intelligence, which give[s] some reason to suspect, that the French may be disposed to avail Themselves of the Liberty of the Catholick Religion granted to the Inhabitants of Canada, in order to keep up their Connection with France, and, by means of the Priests, to preserve such an Influence over the Canadians, as may induce them to join, whenever Opportunity should offer, in any attempts to recover that Country....

... the *Laws of Great Britain* prohibit absolutely all Popish Hierarchy in any of the Dominions belonging to the Crown of Great Britain, and can only admit of a Toleration of the Exercise of that Religion; This matter was clearly understood in the Negotiation of the Definitive Treaty; The French Ministers proposed to insert the Words, *comme ci-devant,* in order that the Romish Religion should continue to be exercised in the same manner as under their Government; and they did not give up the Point, 'till they were plainly told that it would be deceiving them to admit those Words, for The King had not the Power to tolerate that Religion in any other Manner, than *as far as the Laws of Great Britain permit:* These Laws must be your guide in any Disputes that may arise on this Subject; But, at the same Time, that I point out to you the necessity of adhering to Them, and of attending with the utmost Vigilance to the Behaviour of the Priests, The King relies on your acting with all proper Caution & Prudence in regard to a matter of so delicate a Nature as this of Religion; And that you will, as far as you can, consistently with your Duty in the Execution of the Laws, & with the Safety of the Country, avoid every Thing that can give the least unnecessary Alarm, or Disgust, to His Majesty's new Subjects.

Shortt & Doughty, *Documents*, pp. 168–9.

Conciliation of the Church—Bishop Briand's Appointment, 1766

The Conquest of 1760 did produce a state of trauma among Church leaders and French Catholics in Quebec. At the time of the capitulation, the death of Bishop Pontbriand had left the Church leaderless. The cathedral chapter at Quebec "elected" the Sulpician abbot Montgolfier to succeed to the episcopal chair but neither the British authorities at Quebec nor Rome would recognize him. The Royal Proclamation of 1763, like the terms of the peace treaty, tolerated the Catholics only so far as the laws of Great Britain allowed.

By the mid-1770s, however, it became clear to British authorities that the hoped-for "anglicization" of the French Canadians would not happen quickly. For political reasons Governor Murray gave up the idea of pushing Quebec into the Protestant fold and made arrangements for the appointment of a Catholic bishop who would be favourable to the British authorities. Officially, the Governor's candidate was "Superintendent of the Romish Religion" but he was regarded by almost everyone as Bishop.

> It was really affecting to see them congratulate each other wherever they met . . . and to see them afterwards run in crowds to the Parish Church to see this bishop, whom they look upon as the Support of their Religion, and as a Pledge of the King's Paternal goodness to them. In fact, at the same time that they publicly bless the Lord for having given them a Bishop, they loudly proclaim their Gratitude to His Majesty for having attended to their Requests: It is likely that this Favour confer'd on the Canadians by the King, will effectually attach them to the British Government.
>
> *Quebec Gazette*, July 3, 1766

THE SOCIAL EFFECTS OF THE CONQUEST

Following the Conquest, some 65 000 *Canadiens* became "new subjects" under a British régime from which they had much to fear and little to hope. Each of the four main classes of *Canadien* society—the seigneurs, the clergy, the bourgeois merchants and the habitants—was affected differently by the Conquest and responded in a different way to the uncertainties of British rule. Was the aftermath of the Conquest a "catastrophe" for any—or all—elements of *Canadien* society, or was it a relatively painless period of social adjustment?

The State of *Canadien* Society—A British Report, 1762

An instructive, though strongly biased, report on the condition of *Canadien* society after the Conquest was provided by General Murray. In his report, which was sent to the Colonial Office in June 1762, Murray made observations on the probable effects of the Conquest on many segments of the *Canadien* population.

General Murray's Report on Quebec, 5 June 1762

Observations

1st The Canadians are very ignorant and extremely tenacious of their Religion, nothing can contribute so much to make them staunch subjects to his Majesty as the new Government giving them every reason to imagine no alteration is to be attempted in that point.

5th... The Jesuites are neither loved nor esteemed in general, and this order may be easily removed whenever the Government shall think proper without giving offence...:

8th As to the communities of Women they are much esteemed and respected by the People, the narrowness of their circumstances will probably prevent their being filled up so easily as in former times; when the Canadians become a little more reconciled to British customs and Government, it may not be amiss under colour of serving those communities in their distressed situation, to restrict the admission of any under a certain sum; this regulation with another fixing a certain age, under which no vows to be taken, would probably soon reform the worst abuses of such institutions.

9th... There are some few French Protestants in this Country who no doubt will be willing to remain, it would be a great comfort to these, if a Church was granted for their use, and some French Clergyman of sound sense and good Character, with a tolerable salary, was invited to settle among them, such an establishment may be attended with the further good consequences of enticing many of their Brethren in France, to come and enjoy that religious liberty, after which they so ardently sigh, amidst a people sprung from the same origin, speaking the same language, and following the same Customs. It may likewise be conducive towards bringing about a Reformation, by slow degrees and must at least prove to the Canadians there is nothing in our Holy Religion repugnant to Virtue or Morality.

Character of the people

The Canadians may be ranked under four different classes

    1st The Gentry or what they call Nobility
    2d The Clergy
    3d The Merchants or trading part
    4th The Peasantry or what is here stilled, Habitant.

1st The Gentry. These are descended from the Military and Civil officers, who have settled in the Country at different times and were usually provided for in the Colony Troops.... They are in general poor except such as have had commands in distant posts where they usually made a fortune in three or four Years. The Croix de St-Louis quite completed their happiness. They are extremely vain and have an utter contempt for the trading part of the Colony, tho' they made no scruple to engage in it, pretty deeply too, whenever a convenient opportunity served; They were great Tyrants to their Vassals who seldom met with redress, let their grievances be ever so just.

This class will not relish the British Government from which they can neither expect the same employments or the same douceurs, they enjoyed under the French.

2d The Clergy. Most of the dignified among them are French, the rest Canadians, and are in general of the lower class of People, the former no doubt will have great difficulty to reconcile themselves to us, but must drop off by degrees. Few of the latter are very clever, however the Ecclesiastical state was once composed entirely of natives, they would soon become easy and satisfied, their influence over the people was and is still very great, but tho' we have been so short a time in the Country, a difference is to be perceived, they do not submit so tamely to the Yoke, and under sanction of the capitulation they every day take an opportunity to dispute the tythes with their Curés....

3d The Traders of this Colony under the French were either dealers in gross or retailers, the former were mostly French and the latter in general natives of this Country all of whom are deeply concerned in the letters of Exchange many are already gone to solicit payment and few of those who have any fund of any consequence in France will remain here.

4th... The 4th Order is that of the Peasantry, these are a strong healthy race, plain in their dress, virtuous in their morals and temperate in their living: They are in general extremely ignorant, for the former government would never suffer a printing press in the Country, few can read or write, and all receive implicitly for truth the many arrant falsehoods and atrocious lies, industriously handed among them by those who were in power....

...the daily instances of lenity, the impartial justice which has been administer'd, so far beyond what they had formerly experienced, have so alter'd their opinion with regard to us, I may safely venture to affirm for this most useful Order of the state, that far from having the least design to emigrate from their present habitations into any other of the French Colonies, their greatest dread is lest they should meet with the fate of the Accadians and be torn from their native Country.

Convinced that this is not to be their case and that the free exercise of their religion will be continued to them once Canada is irrecoverably ceded by a Peace the people will soon become faithful and good subjects to His Majesty, and the Country they inhabit within a short time prove a rich and most useful Colony to Great Britain.

Shortt & Doughty, *Documents*, pp. 71–78.

The Restoration of Rights—A Petition of the "New Subjects", 1765

In the early years of British rule a concerted attempt was made to anglicize the *Canadiens* or "new subjects". The Royal Proclamation of 1763 was intended to abolish the French laws, including the customary civil code governing property rights and inheritance. In 1764, Governor Murray set up a system of justice and police along British lines. The principal inhabitants petitioned because they did not wish to see their traditional civil law administered by those who had little knowledge of its content and procedures—or else altogether replaced. This expression of discontent was not without effect, because in 1766 *Canadien* jurors could sit and lawyers could plead in any court. The following year, an ordinance confirmed to the "new subjects" their former land laws.

... It has seemed to us indeed from the manner in which Justice has been administered among us up to the present time, that it was His Majesty's Intention that the Customs of our Fathers should be adhered to, so that what was done before the Conquest of Canada should be adhered to in the future in so far as it was not opposed to the Laws of England, and to the public good.

Our Governor, at the Head of his Council, has issued an ordinance for the Establishment of Courts, by which we were rejoiced to see, that to assist us in the settlement of family and other matters, a Lower Court of Justice was to be established where all cases between Frenchman and Frenchman could be decided.…

In proportion to the greatness of our Joy on seeing these wise regulations, was the distress with which we discovered that fifteen English Jurors as opposed to seven Jurors from the new Subjects had induced the latter to subscribe to Remonstrances in a language which they did not understand against these same Regulations.

With deep bitterness in our hearts we have seen, that after all the proofs of Your Majesty's Paternal Affection for your new Subjects, these same fifteen Jurors, with the assistance of the Lawyers have proscribed us as unfit, from differences of Religion, for any office in our country; even Surgeons and Apothecaries (whose professions are free in all countries) being among the number.…

We entreat Your Majesty with the deepest and most respectful submission to confirm the system of Justice which has been established for the French, by the deliberations of the Governor and Council, as also the Jurors and all others of different professions, to maintain the Notaries and advocates in the exercise of their functions, to permit us to transact our Family Affairs in our own tongue, to follow our customs, in so far as they are not opposed to the general Wellbeing of the Colony, and to grant that a Law may be published in our Language, together with the Orders of Your Majesty, whose most faithful Subjects, we do, with the most unalterable Respect, hereby declare Ourselves.

Shortt & Doughty, *Documents* , pp. 227–9.

Effects on the Indians—Provisions in the Royal Proclamation, 1763

The Indians, who had allied themselves with the French in the war of conquest, might well have expected harsh treatment under British rule. In the Articles of Capitulation, however, French authorities sought and secured an article (Article XL) preventing their Indian allies from being displaced from either their hunting and fishing lands or the French reserves. Under British rule, further efforts were made to conciliate the former French allies and to reassure them concerning their rights to "hunting territories" and ancestral lands. In order to prevent a flood of white settlers from intruding upon Indian lands and so threatening to set off a war in the Western frontier, the British Crown by proclamation in 1763 defined boundaries which effectively limited Anglo-American westward expansion and created a huge Indian "reserve" in the interior.

And whereas it is just and reasonable, and essential to Our Interest and the Security of Our Colonies, that the several Nations or Tribes of Indians, with whom We are connected, and who live under our Protection, should not be molested or disturbed in the Possession of such Parts of Our Dominions and Territories as, not having been ceded to, or purchased by Us, are reserved to them, or any of them, as their Hunting Grounds.…

And We do further declare it to be Our Royal Will and Pleasure, for the present as aforesaid, to reserve under Our Sovereignty, Protection, and Dominion, for the Use of the said Indians, all the Lands and Territories not included within the Limits of Our said

Three New Governments....

...We do, with the Advice of Our Privy Council, strictly enjoin and require, that no private Person do presume to make any Purchase from the said Indians of any Lands reserved to the said Indians...if any of the said Indians should be inclined to dispose of the said Lands, the same shall be purchased only for Us, in Our Name, at some publick Meeting or Assembly of the said Indians....

A Proclamation by the King. 1763. October 7 (London: Mark Baskett, 1763), pp. 4–6.

THE ECONOMIC CONSEQUENCES OF CONQUEST

The Conquest of New France was certainly accompanied by economic dislocation, trade difficulties and some shortages of commodities. Of all classes in *Canadien* society, the élite, made up of military officers, merchants and seigneurs, seems to have been most adversely affected, dependent as it was on the French system of military posts, trade and landholding. Most members of this *Canadien* élite found themselves in a colony which, although still predominantly French-speaking and Catholic, was now controlled by anglophone Protestants in the critical areas of trade and government. It has been argued that many of this *Canadien* élite, members of the nobility and bourgeoisie, seeing a loss of their economic and social status, chose to emigrate from the colony at the time of the Conquest. This emigration, along with the subordination of those who remained, left French Canadian society leaderless and in a state of "social decapitation". Whether the economic difficulties which followed the Conquest were the result of the emigration of the *Canadien* élite and the assumption of a dominant role by the British immigrants, or merely a reflection of inherent long-term weaknesses in the colony's economy, remains a central point at issue.

Two Views of the Economic Problems, 1763 and 1765

In the early years of British rule the colony's economic and financial woes were a main preoccupation of the *Canadien* élite. Some members of the bourgeois class complained of the effect of the Conquest on trade and business opportunities for *Canadiens*; others seemed willing to work constructively with the new British régime. The differing views were well expressed in a 1763 Canadian petition to the British government and a subsequent memorial to the Colonial Office two years later.

The scourges of war and famine, long before the surrender of Canada, afflicted its unfortunate inhabitants: expenditures of funds multiplied beyond reason had, long before its downfall, spread about an extraordinary quantity of paper: companies, as avaricious as they were powerful, were formed. All the trade was captured, and the merchants of Canada were helpless onlookers at business which should have been theirs. Would to Heaven that the ministry of France had been earlier informed as to these injustices! It would have imposed a check on abuses so antagonistic to the welfare of a colony!

These same merchants had made purchases of goods in France in the years 1757 and 1758. The fear of these goods running risks on the sea in time of war led them to take the resolution to await more favourable circumstances. They adopted the expedient of leaving their goods in warehouses until peace was restored. This peace, so dear to them and so much desired, aroused the hope of commencing their labours anew; but vain hope, Canada passed under the dominion of Your Majesty....

Still the future casts dread over the people of Canada. What will become of them if the payment for their money is long deferred? What will become of their families? The rural labourer will find in the fertility of the soil, at least, a reward for his labours; he will live, but, more unfortunate than he, the inhabitants of the towns will have no resources; they will do everything in their feebleness to assist one another, because they suffer in common.

Petition for British Intervention to Secure Payment of the Canada Papers, February, 1763 in Adam Shortt, ed., *Documents Relating to Canadian Currency, Exchange & Finance during the French Period* (Ottawa: King's Printer, 1925), Vol. II, p. 969.

We must give careful consideration at this point to the true export capability of the colony at the present time.... The cash broadcast by the military is no more; whatever the new subjects held in France is used up; their plate is being melted down; their paper has gone up in smoke; All these objects are in London—What resources, then, does the impoverished colony still command?... the only two resources now available, 700,000 livres supplied by the military and products to the value of 1,500,000 livres....

[This colony] is still in its infancy, and this may be the consequence of the bad policies of the French before its surrender, who would never allow freedom here and yet who feared nothing more than the depopulation of their own Kingdom...Great Britain, her interest now drawn to this colony and her own private reasons for taking steps to keep it, can expect nothing but certain gain if it is developed under her protection.... No one must be surprised that after 170 years or thereabouts of existence the country is incapable of supporting itself, but it will be able to do so when, under the freedom already allowed, a large population in the southern part will supply enough grain, hemp, and salted foodstuffs to overcome and more than overcome its present state of powerlessness.

P.A.C., Colonial Office, Series 42, Vol. 25 (Microfilm). Memorial of Some of the Principal New Subjects Concerning the Present State and Abilities of the Province, 1 May 1765.

The Emigration of the *Canadien* Elite—Francis Maseres' Account, 1774

One of the first observers to provide evidence that the *Canadien* élite had emigrated after the Conquest was Francis Maseres, an English lawyer of French Huguenot ancestry who served as attorney general of Quebec from 1766 to 1769. His report on colonial conditions was submitted in response to a petition from a group of notables asking for the right of *Canadiens* to hold public office. Maseres asserted that members of the Canadian bourgeoisie who saw their social mobility and channels of promotion blocked had emigrated to France and left the colony leaderless in the business community. The nobility, now deprived of military and administrative careers, was of little consequence.

...I am persuaded it would have been found impossible to...[elevate French Canadians to positions of 'trust and profit'] by reason of the want of a sufficient number of Canadians or Frenchmen in the province properly qualified for this purpose, most of those persons of ability who filled those offices in the time of the French government having either gone to Old France soon after the peace, or being dead in the course of the fourteen years that have elapsed since the conquest of the province. For, as to the Canadians themselves, as contradistinguished from the natives of Old France, it is in vain to seek for such persons amongst them, because their educations are not such as to qualify them for these employments; insomuch that in the time of the French government the most important civil offices in the province, such as those of the principal judges of the courts of justice, and the *procureur-général du roy*, as well as those of the governour and intendant, were filled by natives of Old France....

We have seen that the nobles of Canada are but few in number, in comparison of the whole body of the Canadians. We have likewise seen that they have no necessary connection with the seigniories, or other landed property, and some of little property of any kind. Yet some persons are apt to imagine (from their being called, as I suppose, by the same name as the nobility of England, who are, for the most part, owners of great landed estates,) that they are a very powerful and formidable body of men, and have a great lead and influence over the rest of the people. Now this is far from being the case. For they were never used, in the time of the French government to court the people, or try to gain an interest among them, having had no advantages to expect from them; but they paid all their devotions to the governour and intendant, and other officers of the crown, by whose interest they hoped to obtain preferment. And those of them who had seigniories, and were rich enough to live in the towns of Quebec and Montreal, did not use to reside on their seigniories, except perhaps for one month in a year, or less, to inspect the conditions of them, and collect their rents and other dues; but spent the rest of the year at Quebec and Montreal. And they will continue to do the same under the British government....

F. Maseres, *An Account of the Proceedings of the British and Other Protestant Inhabitants of the Province of Quebec in North America in Order to Obtain a House of Assembly in that Province* (London: 1774), pp. 143–69.

The Beginnings of British Dominance in Trade—Alexander Henry's Reminiscence

Even in the fur trade of the interior, the *Canadiens* found themselves displaced by British entrepreneurs after the American Revolution. *Canadiens* still found employment as voyageurs, guides and interpreters, of course. But there is little doubt that by 1790, French Canadian traders had been superseded by the Scots in the western fur trade. Alexander Henry's reminiscences give us some clue to the way in which the "old subjects" came eventually to dominate the fur trade.

The surrender of Montreal, and, with it, the surrender of all Canada, followed that of Fort de Levi, at only the short interval of three days; and, proposing to avail myself of the new market, which was thus thrown open to British adventure, I hastened to Albany, where my commercial connections were....

[Arriving in Quebec at Les Cèdres] I now learned, that Mr. Leduc, in the earlier part of his life, had been engaged in the fur-trade, with the Indians of Michilimackinac and

Lake Superior. He informed me of his acquaintance with the Indian languages, and his knowledge of furs....

I, who had previously thought of visiting Michilimackinac, with a view to the Indian trade, gave the strictest attention to all that fell, on this subject, from my host....

There being, at this time, no goods in Montreal, adapted to the Indian trade, my next business was to proceed to Albany, to make my purchases there. This I did in the beginning of the month of May, by the way of Lake Champlain; and, on the 15th of June, arrived again in Montreal, bringing with me my outfits. As I was altogether a stranger to the commerce in which I was engaging, I confided in the recommendations given me, of one Etienne Campion, as my assistant; a part which he uniformly fulfilled with honesty and fidelity.

A. Henry, *Travels and Adventures in Canada and the Indian Territories Between the Years 1760 and 1776* (Toronto: 1901), pp. 3 and 10–11.

CONFLICTING INTERPRETATIONS

THE MILITARY AND DIPLOMATIC CONSEQUENCES

The Conquest was first and foremost a military and diplomatic event. A number of historians have continued to present it essentially in those terms, although not all have approached the military and diplomatic questions from the same standpoint. Some have approached the topic in terms of leaders and negotiations, others from the standpoint of colonial objectives and policies, and still others from the angle of military strategy and tactics. But whatever the perspective taken, none deny that the cession of Canada to the British Crown in 1763 had special consequences for the strongly entrenched military tradition and establishment of New France.

A Popular Interpretation

The military and diplomatic consequences of the Conquest were clearly examined in a popular history of the period by Gordon Donaldson. Canada's fate, he argued, was decided more by diplomats than by generals. There was also the suggestion that Britain's decision to restore French institutions in Quebec contributed to her loss of the American colonies in the Revolutionary War.

... the fate of Canada was now being decided in the ornate chambers of the diplomats and in the counting-houses of Paris and London. The London merchants, unimpressed by the patriotic outbursts in the streets and alehouses, reckoned that possession of Canada meant, at most, a slight extension of the fur trade—and beaver hats were no longer the last word in elegance. The new King wanted to make peace with France, and this meant giving up some of his newly-won territory. A pamphlet, circulated in London, carried the argument that the French sugar island of Guadaloupe, also won by Britain, was far more valuable than Canada....

The French were thinking along the same lines. Guadaloupe had been more profitable and given less trouble. In a century and a half, Canada had cost the King millions of livres and returned no profit except to men like Bigot and Cadet, whose trial was still dragging on, with shocking revelations every few months. For a time it seemed that both Wolfe and Montcalm had died for nothing; neither side really wanted the land they had fought for....

George Washington, who had fired the first shots against the French at Fort Duquesne, led the Continental Armies to victory in the revolution that Murray and others had predicted. It followed a series of outstanding blunders by George III and his ministers—particularly Charles Townshend, whose mean little taxes infuriated the New Englanders—but it would almost certainly have happened anyway as the consequence of Wolfe's victory. The revolution might well have swept Canada, but for the cold, gray presence of Wolfe's quartermaster-general, Guy Carleton.

When he succeeded Murray as Governor at Quebec, he saw at once that the colony could never become a replica of the British possessions to the south. It was a feudal kingdom that had lost its king, but had no intention of changing its ways. English ideas of freedom and self-government had never penetrated there; the Canadians expected to be ruled by their seigneurs and their priests; if they wanted freedom they took to the woods. Carleton promoted the Quebec Act of 1774 which, in effect, restored the old French system while adding some English seigneurs to run it. French civil law was restored, although English law applied in criminal cases. The seigneurial land laws were confirmed, the Church was allowed to collect tithes, and the Ohio frontier lands were returned to Canada. New France was re-established in all but name. British parliamentarian Edmund Burke called this 'squinting at tyranny', but when the libertarian explosion blew the redcoats out of New England, most Canadians clung to their familiar tyranny and refused to join the revolution.

Gordon Donaldson, *Battle for a Continent. Quebec, 1759* (Toronto: Doubleday, 1973), pp. 237–240.

The Experience of Abandonment and Collaboration—G.F.G. Stanley's Interpretation

The military occupation of Canada was accompanied by another kind of conquest—*psychological conquest*. In his account of the last years of New France, George F.G. Stanley emphasized the pervasive psychological effects of military defeat on the French Canadians and their sense of "nationality".

The terms of the peace of 1763 were no great surprise to the Canadians, and yet they came as a stunning blow. They meant but one thing—conquest. And what did conquest imply? Who, in New France, really knew? War had meant empty stomachs, the flames of burning buildings, the blood upon the earth, the smell of death. What did conquest mean? The heavy drum-beat of the army of occupation, the hateful sight of enemy uniforms, the harsh sound of an unfamiliar tongue, the unwelcome triumph of a heretical religion. War had been the violent expression of something past; conquest opened the terrifying void of something yet to come....

In spite of the general willingness of the French Canadian élite to collaborate with the victors, the conquest profoundly affected the life of the Canadian community. Individually the Canadians survived as French Canadians—they did not have to forfeit their language, their religion, their laws, or their seigneurial system of land tenure—but as a community, as an emerging national entity, they were smothered. French Canada was not uprooted by the Treaty of Paris in 1763, but its growth was drastically curtailed. During the Ancien Régime—over the century and a half that had elapsed since Champlain built his Habitation below Cape Diamond—it had been developing its sense of identity, its consciousness of being Canadian. By the middle of the eighteenth century this community had become a small national group, possessing religious and ethnic homogeneity and with political, juridical and social institutions of its own, including an emergent bourgeoisie....

Thus, Canada during the last two generations of the Ancien Régime was on the way to becoming a sophisticated national community, not French, but French Canadian: a fiercely independent society, as almost every contemporary observer noted, despising domestic service and resentful of the assumption of superiority both by the ecclesiastical and by the military leaders of Old France.... Even if the country did not possess the outward strength of a national entity, by the mid-eighteenth century it did possess the inward mystique of nationalism.

As soon as Canada became a British possession this development came to an abrupt halt, not so much because the leaders of the Canadian community abandoned the country and emigrated... as because the cession of Canada to Great Britain slammed the door upon further opportunities for appointments of influence in the government, of rank in the army, of significance in the world of commerce.... Nearly two hundred years were to elapse before a second native-born French Canadian would sit in the chair of the Marquis de Vaudreuil.

George F.G. Stanley, *New France: The Last Phase, 1744–1760* (Toronto: McClelland & Stewart, 1968), pp. 268–273.

The Change in Warfare—A Military Historian's Analysis

Ian K. Steele's *Guerillas and Grenadiers: The Struggle for Canada 1687–1760* (1969) called greater attention to the military aspects of the Conquest and offered a fresh look at its consequences for warfare and military tactics. The conquest of New France, according to Steele, not only represented a British military triumph, but marked the supremacy of European military tactics over the North American strategy of "guerilla raids" in the wilderness. For military and defence strategists, it was nothing short of revolutionary.

In reflecting on the struggle for Canada it is possible to distinguish two related, but distinct, contests—the fight over the kind of weapons and rules, and the duel itself. This essay has argued that, while it did not precede the duel in time or importance, the struggle over weapons and rules was significant. North American pride in the ways of the New World has often led to the assumption that, in warfare as in everything else, the new men of the New World were better than the history-laden men of the Old.

It is very unlikely that Vaudreuil's policy [of guerilla raids] could have saved Canada or even have postponed its fall. He could not see, or would not see, that the Anglo-American offensive was aimed at capturing Quebec City, a European citadel in the physical and psychological sense. Nor did he fully appreciate that this war was different from its predecessors, in that winning time was no solution. The British were committed to victory in North America. Given the odds, there was very little chance ng could save Canada. By 1758 the Europeans, French and British alike, had ...pleted the imposition of their kind of fighting upon the struggle in North America. By doing so they increased the odds, which were already overwhelmingly in favour of those who were soon to win.

The fall of Canada may have had important cultural consequences, but it did not have cultural causes. Canada did not fall because of absolutism, paternalism, Catholicism or the seigneurial regime. Canada was not defeated primarily because of cheaper British trade goods, limited grain supply, a narrowly based economy, or the numerical preponderance of the American colonies. The British Army and the Royal Navy besieged Canada with an overwhelming military force. France could not send a force to lift the siege and, after a stout defence, Canada fell to fortune's favourite—the biggest army. Is this not sufficient reason for the fall of Canada?

Ian K. Steele, *Guerillas and Grenadiers. The Struggle for Canada, 1689–1760* (Toronto: Ryerson Press, 1969), pp. 131–134.

THE CULTURAL CONSEQUENCES OF CONQUEST

Many differing—and widely divergent—interpretations have been advanced to explain the cultural consequences of the Conquest for French Canadians. Both French Canadian and anglophone historians have applied themselves to studying the impact of the Conquest on race and religion, language and culture, often with dramatically different results. Some historians, following the lead of French Canadian nationalist writers, have contended that the Conquest marked the beginning of *la survivance*, or French Canada's long struggle for cultural survival under the rule of a foreign power. Other interpreters, influenced by Francis Parkman's interpretation, have argued that the fall of New France was an "act of liberation", freeing French Canadians from the oppressive weight of French colonial rule. The continued existence of a French Canadian cultural community has been attributed variously to the Catholic Church in the role of spiritual guardian, to the degree of liberty and freedom extended to the conquered by the British, or to the leniency and pragmatic good sense of British authorities. And the intensity of the continuing debate in both the French and English languages, shows no sign of subsiding.

The Struggle for National Survival—An Early French Canadian Nationalist Interpretation

One of French Canada's first historians, F.-X. Garneau, writing in the 1840s at the time of the hotly debated union of Lower and Upper Canada, depicted the conquest and its consequences as a series of tests and trials which French Canadians had to overcome in order to survive as a distinct people. The theme of national survival can be said to have been introduced with this patriotic portrayal of his people's history.

After three years passed in a state of alternate hope and fear, the Canadians had perforce to renounce their latest illusion. Their destiny was bound irrevocably to that of the

British people by the treaty of 1763. Consequent upon this event, a second emigration took place: numbers of commercialists, lawyers, ex-functionaries, with most of the leading men still remaining in the colony, left for France, after selling or abandoning estates.... None now lingered in the towns, but here and there a few subaltern place-men, some artisans, scarcely one merchant. The members of the different religious confraternities, with the rural populations, of course remained····

* * * * *

...The Canadians, meanwhile, felt all the chagrin arising from subjection to alien sway. The evils they had previously endured seemed light to them, compared to the suffering and humiliations which were in preparation, they feared, for them and their posterity. First of all, the British wished to repudiate whatever was Canadian, and to deprive the *habitants* even of the natural advantages Canada offered to them by its extent. The colony was dismembered....

From parcelling out territory, the British passed to relegislating. Their king, by his sole authority, without parliamentary sanction, abolished those laws of olden France, so precise, so clear, so wisely framed, to substitute for them the jurisprudence of England—a chaos of prescriptive and statutory acts and decisions, invested with complicated and barbaric forms... and the above substitution was effected, merely in order to ensure protection and the benefits of the laws of their mother country to those of the dominant race who should emigrate to Canada.

F.-X. Garneau, *History of Canada, from the Time of Its Discovery till the Union Year (1840–1)*, trans. Andrew Bell (Montreal: 1860), Vol. II, pp. 84–6.

An "Act of Liberation" from French Absolutism—The Parkman Thesis

Francis Parkman (1823–1893) saw the Conquest as a liberation of Canada from the oppressive weight of French despotism and bureaucratic authoritarianism. Unfortunately, he argued, the British had not broken the yoke of Catholic control and intolerance. His views, strongly tinged with Anglo-Saxon racism and Protestant pride, reflected those of the dominant American class into which he was born and for whom, essentially, he wrote, as well as fitting with the scientific view of the period.

This English conquest was the grand crisis of Canadian history. It was the beginning of a new life. With England came Protestantism, and the Canadian Church grew purer and better in the presence of an adverse faith. Material growth; an increased mental activity; an education, real though fenced and guarded; a warm and genuine patriotism,—all date from the peace of 1763. England imposed by the sword on reluctant Canada the boon of national and ordered liberty. Through centuries of striving she had advanced from stage to stage of progress, deliberate and calm,—never breaking with her past, but making each fresh gain the base of a new success,—enlarging popular liberties while bating nothing of that height and force of individual development which is the brain and heart of civilization; and now, through a hard-earned victory, she taught the conquered colony to share the blessings she had won. A happier calamity never befell a people than the conquest of Canada by the British arms.

Francis Parkman, *The Old Régime in Canada* (Toronto: George N. Morang, 1899), Vol. II, pp. 204–5.

With the Peace of Paris ended the checkered story of New France; a story which would have been a history if faults of constitution and the bigotry and folly of rulers had not dwarfed it to an episode.... Civil liberty was given them by the British sword; but the conqueror left their religious system untouched, and through it they have imposed upon themselves a weight of ecclesiastical tutelage that finds few equals in the most Catholic countries of Europe. Such guardianship is not without certain advantages. When faithfully exercised it aids to uphold some of the tamer virtues, if that can be called a virtue which needs the constant presence of a sentinel to keep it from escaping: but it is fatal to mental robustness and moral courage; and if French Canada would fulfil its aspirations it must cease to be one of the most priest-ridden communities of the modern world.

Francis Parkman, *Montcalm and Wolfe* (Toronto: George N. Morang, 1899), Vol. III, p. 259.

French Canada's "Providential Mission"—A Neo-Nationalist Clerical Interpretation

Canon Lionel Groulx, in the years between the World Wars, after French Canadians had weathered a series of school crises across Canada and a bitter debate over conscription, took a dramatically opposite stand to Parkman. He proclaimed a French Canadian homogeneity and racial superiority which had its roots in the French régime and which had survived the British conquest thanks in large measure to the role played by the Catholic church. French Canada, according to Groulx, had a Providential (God-ordained) mission to fulfil in North America.

In short, on the morrow of the Conquest, in that year 1766, there is a question full of anguish that the historian must ask himself. What will become, in the new environment tainted with creeping Protestantism, of the young, idealistic, and chivalrous race, sprung of such a pure history, the synthesis of the thoughts and labours of the ancestors, the offspring of those gallant knights with the flashing swords who had performed so many marvelous exploits? What will become of the race of New France so amorously moulded in the divine hands of the Church?

If the threats are great, thank God the protections are still greater and more powerful. In those arduous times the young nationality would be guided by a great bishop, a bishop in the best episcopal tradition... behind this leader was a clear-sighted and hardworking clergy whose devotion and attachment to the Holy See was without equal, as the abbé de La Corne once dared to inform the pope himself. Such noble qualities would enable the clergy to safeguard more effectively the integrity, the faith, and the customs of their people.

There also existed between the two races now facing one another—the one of Saxon background, the other of Latin descent—a mental opposition, an incompatibility of feelings, a lack of affinities that would reduce the dangers of contact. A juxtaposition of races took place but not a penetration. And ours being a historic race, one of those whose oneness is the result of the blending of several racial strains through environmental and institutional forces, ours kept this strength of never having mixed but homogeneous elements in its crucible. Perhaps the purest race on the whole continent, it would also have the quality of being the most impenetrable.

Finally, this is the time and the place to recall the memorable words of Mother Marie de l'Incarnation: 'Canada is a country specially guarded by Providence.' Mightier than all human protections was that of Divine Providence, the august guardian of our history, who has never abandoned the world, nor even a continent, to the disastrous uniformity of a single race or a single civilization.

L. Groulx, *Lendemains de conquête* (Montreal: 1920), pp. 234–5, trans. Yves Zoltvany.

The Church After The Conquest—A Period of Rising Clerical Power

Marcel Trudel, a historian at the University of Ottawa, agreed with Groulx with regard to the dominant role of the Church in post-Conquest society. But he saw its origins and consequences in a very different light—not as testimony to the foundations laid in the French régime, but rather a reflection of its increasingly *ultramontane* character under British rule. Whereas Groulx saw the Church as having exercised only a beneficial influence on society, Trudel suggested that it was, on occasion, capable of exerting a negative and baneful one.

These...years of English servitude profoundly marked the Canadian Church of Quebec. They first of all Canadianized it in its episcopacy and hierarchy. Because the State opposed the Church being directed by Europeans, Canadians got access to the episcopate by 1770, something that had not happened during the French régime. The Jesuits, all French of France in 1760, were completely eliminated. The Seminary of Quebec, composed also in 1760 of French of France would gladly recruit among Canadians; as for the Seminary of Montreal, similarly made up, it would end up by accepting Canadian Sulpicians in spite of itself and the interminable gnashing of teeth. Canadianization was not necessarily advantageous; the Church renewed its resources in a closed environment without being able to benefit from the ideas of the world beyond itself. It would take the ecclesiastical immigration of the 1840s to refresh its looks.

Moreover, it was the English régime that brought the Canadian Church to play a role in society which is not strictly a spiritual role. It is true that under the French régime the Church had been asked to take on hospital care and education, its registers had served the civil power, but it was unthinkable during the French régime that the Church should intervene in the political and economic domains. But, under the English administration it openly became the vehicle for government orders; it took the census of human and material resources, it held the people to their allegiance to the Crown.... A spiritual power, the Church became a political power which would soon unleash the crisis of undue influence. Finally, the traditional Gallicanism of this Canadian Church was transformed into a ferocious Romanism. Gallican since the days of Mgr. de Saint-Vallier, the Canadian Church found itself cut off from the sources of Gallicanism....

Marcel Trudel, "La Servitude de l'Eglise catholique du Canada français sous le Régime Anglais", Canadian Historical Association *Report, 1963*, Vol. 43, pp. 63–64. trans. C.J.J.

A Triumph of Imperial Conciliation—A Consensus Interpretation

Mason Wade gave a different interpretation of the same events. While he did not deny that conquest brought significant changes in Canadian society, he emphasized the generous policy of the British conquerors, the spirit of survival of the Canadians, and the general success of the Imperial policy of conciliation.

It is still possible today to start bitter controversy in Quebec by pointing out that the first British rulers of Canada did not try to crush the French Canadians under the yoke of military government, but on the contrary actually befriended them against the pretensions of the swarm of campfollowers and commercial adventurers who descended upon the newly conquered land like a cloud of locusts. Such, however, is the picture which emerges from sober study of the contemporary documents. In this age of ruthless oppression of conquered peoples the peaceful transition of Quebec from French to British rule is remarkable and noteworthy. The English conquest might well have meant the end of French Canada as a cultural unit in North America, and of the French Canadians as an ethnic group; instead the survival of both was assured by legislation adopted a decade after the peace treaty had been signed.... But their survival was not dependent, however, upon either British magnanimity or the force of circumstances; for French Canada possessed an indomitable will to live, witnessed in the first decade after the conquest by the attainment of the highest birthrate ever recorded for any white people. The whole history of Quebec since 1760 reveals how completely the French Canadians concentrated their resources and devoted them to the struggle for survival.

Mason Wade, *The French Canadians 1760–1945* (Toronto: Macmillan, 1955) pp. 47–8.

THE ECONOMIC CONSEQUENCES OF CONQUEST

The greatest debate which the cession has generated revolves about the economic consequences of 1760–63. This debate among historians and economists is in fact largely an attempt to arrive at some explanation for the economic retardation of Lower Canada in the nineteenth century, or the anglophone domination of the Quebec economy in the twentieth century.

Maurice Séguin's Thesis—A Social "Decapitation" of *Canadien* Society

In 1947, Maurice Séguin of the University of Montreal presented a doctoral thesis dealing with the role of agriculture in French Canada. Subsequently a great debate developed over his contention that the Conquest had brought about a social decapitation, the economic consequences of which were still determining factors in Quebec life. His attacks on the viability of a French Canadian agrarian society were politically volatile in a Quebec where youth was becoming preoccupied with decolonization.

In practical terms, the *Canadiens* were isolated from the higher reaches of trade because of a change of empire in the age when mercantilism was in force. The obligation to concentrate trade within the foreign world of the British empire, the difficulty for the *Canadiens* of developing relations with the unknown businessmen of the new metropolis or the other colonies, as opposed to the ease with which Britons could arrange exports and imports among themselves, plus the British monopoly on ocean transport were so many causes that combined to annihilate the external trade the *Canadiens* had carried on before 1760, and even to force them out of a large portion of the internal trade, chiefly in activities closely linked to the external trade.

Similarly, the *Canadiens* were excluded from the primary exploitation of the great natural resources other than agriculture. The exploitation of furs or timber by owners or employers was dominated by the trading group and thus fell primarily to the British. These important sources of wealth, particularly the forest, one of the bases of the Quebec economy, eluded the *Canadiens*.

Since they were excluded from the lucrative primary products as masters of exploitation and trade, the *Canadiens* could build up capital only in small farm savings. Deprived of the capital built up in the country itself, the *Canadiens* also could not, by reason of the occupation, seek European capital able to serve their nationality. Only the British could easily import into their conquest the capital all young colonies need. This strengthened their position.

Finally, because trade and capital sources in the wake of the Conquest were virtually monopolized by the occupying power, the *Canadiens* were unable to industrialize their country for their own benefit, and in the proportion their numbers would have required, when the time came....

This process of segregation resulted logically in the conquerors' grasp on Quebec economic life. Only the British were in a position to direct the development the country called for in the name of economic progress, while the *Canadiens*, who had become like the blacks of the African colonies of exploitation, were pushed out to the fringes of economic life in their own native land. Relegated to a single sector, unable to remain there indefinitely, facing the foreigner already firmly lodged in every other part of the economy, the *Canadiens*, servants of this foreigner, were reduced to leaving agriculture.

To the British went the leadership and ownership of most large businesses; the *Canadiens* would supply the manpower. The die was cast long before the age of industrial expansion.

M. Séguin, "La Conquête et la vie économique des Canadiens", *Action nationale* (1947), Vol. 28.

The Conquest Hypothesis Clarified—Michel Brunet's Formulation

The clearest expositions of Séguin's decapitation thesis came from his colleague at the University of Montreal, Michel Brunet. Brunet contended that New France had been a "normal society" possessing a secular leadership class composed of administrators, soldiers, and businessmen. This naturally ambitious élite, he believed, would have played a more and more important role in the economic development of the colony. But the cession cut off all opportunity of fair competition for these *bourgeois*. The colony was exploited thereafter by anglophone entrepreneurs.

...The present-day historian of French Canada sees what the *Canadien* leaders at the end of the eighteenth century did not see... He realizes that the *Canadiens*, barred from *haut commerce*, were unable to acquire the habits of big business. Kept in a minority and in subordinate positions in the public administration, they were deprived of a truly political class with strong traditions. The Canadian nation, thirty years after the Conquest, no longer possessed the framework necessary for the normal development of an Atlantic community. This was one of the results of the Conquest: a sociological phenomenon in no way due to the malignant designs of men. This colonial populace had lost its nourishing metropolis prematurely. Reduced to its own resources, it was destined to an anaemic collective survival. It would no longer benefit from the enlightened and dynamic direction of an economically independent bourgeoisie...

Michel Brunet, *La Présence Anglaise et les Canadiens* (Montréal: Beauchemin, 1958), p. 111.

A Critique of the French Canadian Nationalist Interpretations

The thesis of traumatic Conquest was soon challenged by professors at Laval University who were already greatly influenced by the socio-economic, quantitative approach of the *Annales*[2] school of history in France. Fernand Ouellet, for example, cast doubt on the origins of French Canadian national feeling and national consciousness going back as far as the French régime.

In the very wake of Conquest, so far as most of the nationalist historians are concerned, the struggle for survival began, never to cease; for others, meanwhile, the same conquest ushered in an age of great decline and emasculating compromises.... For Brunet and Séguin, this social mutilation was the thing that reduced French Canada to slavery; severing all contacts with the old motherland, the tragedy of the Conquest traumatized the still delicate Canadian nationality.... And so in spite of appreciable differences between Canon Groulx's reassuring position and Michel Brunet's pessimism, they do share a common starting point: the existence before 1760 of a French-Canadian nationality. The whole of their interpretation of Canada's history logically flows from this initial observation.... The positing of a nationality in New France depends on an extremely thin and, in my opinion, highly unsatisfactory case, one which I think is more the product of the historian's mind than of strong evidence.

Fernand Ouellet, as quoted in Dale Miquelon, ed., *Society and Conquest* (Toronto: Copp Clark, 1977), pp. 171–3.

Ouellet also challenged the view that the cession was responsible for the economic weakness of French Canada. His quantitative studies indicated that the *Canadiens* after the cession got access to the important new markets of the British Empire for their wheat and that they continued to dominate in the fur trade until the American Revolution, when the Scots displaced them.

The Conquest did not engender any essential change in the life of the inhabitants of the Laurentian valley. It even, by eliminating the profiteers of the old system, clarified many situations and benefitted a number of merchants.... Immediately after 1760, the citizen of New France is not a being whose psychological buoyancy has been shattered and whose single destination is bondage. Fruitful perspectives open before him, multiple choices are evident in the challenges that bring themselves to his attention. His fate thus is related to the quality of his responses.

Under these conditions, it would be difficult to explain why the Conquest should

---

2. The *Annales* school of historians pioneered the application of systematic, quantitative analysis to the study of French and European society. Its work is characterized by a global, socio-economic approach, detailed documentation, and techniques of analysis based on statistics and social science theories.

have unleashed the famous struggle for survival, or the deterioration of French Canadian society. Between 1760 and 1791 there existed conflicts, but these had no national character. They were, properly speaking, social, and placed the governors, administrators and *seigneurs* of all origins in opposition to the commercial classes. At this period the fundamental cleavage was not yet ethnic but social....

> Fernand Ouellet, as quoted in Cameron Nish, *The French Canadians, 1759–1766; Conquered? Half-Conquered? Liberated?* (Toronto: Copp Clark, 1966), p. 128.

The Decapitation Hypothesis Denied

Another challenge to the decapitation thesis came from Jean Hamelin, also at Laval University, who doubted the very existence before the Conquest of a significant Canadian bourgeoisie for the British to decapitate. On this point he was in complete agreement with Fernand Ouellet who believed that both before and after the Conquest a spirit of capitalism and a true bourgeois mentality were absent. If a decapitation took place at all, it was of the military and administrative caste, the Canadian nobility.

> Much is said about the French Canadian bourgeoisie in the period before 1760. Its origins are traced back to the formation of the Company of Habitants in 1645; the Conquest marked its decline. A part of this bourgeoisie then emigrated to France, and the other part, cut off from its economic bases (the fisheries and trading posts) by the revision of the boundaries of New France, died of asphyxiation. Thus the annihilation of the French Canadian bourgeoisie in 1760 becomes the major historical factor which dominates and determines the economic development of French Canada down to Confederation.
>
> The thesis is attractive, but does it correspond to the real facts? It is a legitimate question to ask because the hypothesis has been put forward without any exhaustive research to support it. Hence the case is not closed; it remains open to discussion...
>
> There is nothing in our findings which authorizes us to speak of a French Canadian bourgeoisie before 1760, and even less of an upper middle class, in the strict meaning of the term. The explanation of this economic and social weakness is no doubt complex. It would be a distortion of reality to try to reduce it to a few simple factors....
>
> Jean Hamelin, *Economie et Société en Nouvelle-France.* (Quebec: Les Presses de l'Université Laval, 1970), pp. 127, 131–2. trans. C.J.J.

Cook's Thesis of *Canadien* Optimism

Professor Ramsay Cook of Toronto's York University provided the debate on the Conquest with a new twist. Cook argued that the *Canadiens* remained preoccupied with cultural survival, and were not aware, at first, of the implications for their economy. Instead of producing trauma, British rule after the Conquest may have helped nourish their cherished hopes of survival.

> This *Canadien* nation, unfortunately, inhabited a land that no longer belonged to it. The Conquest had fostered new colonization in the fifteenth English colony of America. At the beginning the influx of English immigrants was not very great. A few hundred came from 1760 to 1775. Such a tiny minority, however, possessed an influence that

was much greater than that of the *Canadiens*, whose only strength was their number. England naturally entrusted the administration of its new colonies to its own subjects. When *Canadiens* gained the right to hold public office, they had to be content with subordinate posts. In less than fifteen years the whole of foreign trade and a considerable proportion of domestic trade had passed into the hands of English merchants. Because of their connection with the London market they had quickly supplanted the *Canadien* merchants, who were cut off from the support of a metropolis. Control of the political and economic life of the vanquished colony belonged to a group that the *Canadiens* now called 'Londoners' or 'the English'.

The conquered were not unduly alarmed by the situation. Since they could not foresee the ultimate consequences of the Conquest, they remained optimistic. Their illusions were nourished by the marks of sympathy they received from the first two English governors, and by generous concessions from the Imperial government. The colony was relatively prosperous. After a few years there remained no trace of the ruin caused by the war. The *Canadiens* knew that they constituted an immense majority of the population, and everything seemed to indicate that this would always be the case. Carleton himself was convinced of it. The *Canadiens* did not doubt that sooner or later they would regain political and economic control of the country that they still considered as their own, a country belonging to them by right. They secretly thought that the 'Londoners' would not always be on top. A day would come when they would once again be masters of their own destiny. They cherished this fond hope and believed it to be both legitimate and realistic because they refused to see, or had not yet seen, that a new Canada—an English Canada this time—was in the process of rising on the ruins of the old French Canada.

Ramsay Cook, ed., *French Canadian Nationalism: An Anthology* (Toronto: Macmillan, 1969), p. 285.

The Meaning of the Conquest Today—A Recent Perspective

Was the Conquest really a traumatic experience? And if so, for whom? A number of answers have been proposed to this central problem. Yet the prevailing interpretations seem to reflect contemporary perspectives on Quebec society as much as historical analysis of the past. For Maurice Séguin and the so-called Montreal school, the cession of 1760 was intimately connected with post-Conquest economic problems and the evolution of a form of French Canadian nationalism leading to separatism for Quebec. Such contentions have been completely rejected by the rival "Laval school" of historians. If the Séguin/Brunet hypothesis is correct then it could be argued that to gain full "national" identity and avert assimilation, Quebec should secede from Canada. But if the Ouellet/Hamelin thesis proved more conclusive, then the best interests of French Canadians would lie in rejecting separatism.

One historian who has attempted to approach the Conquest from a fresh perspective is Susan Mann Trofimenkoff, member of an emerging group of scholars known as the "Ottawa school" of French Canadian history. Her analysis confirms the observation that although historians write about the past, it is often present-day concerns which influence their research.

By the early twentieth century, as French Canadians reeled under successive blows of English Canadian intolerance, industrialization, and imperial wars, the Conquest emerged as a challenge to French Canada's survival instincts. Misreading the society of New France as agricultural and clerical, the historian Lionel Groulx saw the persistence of such traits in the Quebec of the 1910s as a sure sign that struggle and survival were the valued, perhaps even providential, legacy of a nonetheless tragic Conquest. The more secular historians of the mid-twentieth century saw fewer clerics and fewer farmers in New France; rather Frégault, Brunet, and Séguin spotted a normal society in infancy, arrested in its growth by the Conquest. This view of Conquest-as-thalidomide, hotly contested by Hamelin and Ouellet, raised the question of the nature of society in New France, one of the more fruitful although by no means yet resolved historical enquiries engendered by the Conquest debate. Most historians in Quebec today have turned resolutely away from the debate: the older among them concentrating on the early adaptability, or lack thereof, of French Canadians to economic and social changes of the early nineteenth century; the younger asking similar questions about the late nineteenth and early twentieth centuries.

Behind the varying interpretations of the Conquest are two very different approaches to the place of French Canada in North America. Each recognizes the minority position of French Canadians, but one makes of it a problem, the other a challenge. For some French Canadians, being a minority has entailed subordinate economic, political, and social status. They have been able to point to foreign observers such as Lord Durham in the nineteenth century who said it would be so or to federal enquiries such as the Royal Commission on Bilingualism and Biculturalism in the twentieth century that recorded the fact. And they have sought the cause in the Conquest, and the cure, albeit with some reluctance, in independence. For other French Canadians, however, being a minority has entailed a complex challenge, rather than an obstacle. For some, meeting this challenge has meant arguing and displaying a certain superiority to English Canadians. For others it has meant denying the ethnic dimension altogether and claiming that the interests of class and politics are paramount. This approach thus emphasizes either healthy competition or interested co-operation between French and English Canadians and implies, for its adherents, adaptation and coping rather than blaming and whining. To its opponents it spells compensation or, worse still, collaboration. The two approaches have fuelled the debates of historians, intellectuals, and politicians throughout the history of French Canada. René Lévesque and Pierre Trudeau are merely the latest manifestations of the two points of view. Without the Conquest neither would have existed.

Susan Mann Trofimenkoff, *The Dream of Nation. A Social and Intellectual History of Quebec* (Toronto: Macmillan, 1982), pp. 19–20.

A Guide to Further Reading

1. Overviews

Brunet, Michel, *Les Canadiens après la Conquête, 1759–1775*. Montreal: Fides, 1969.

Burt, A.L., *The Old Province of Quebec, 1760–1791*, 2 vols. Toronto: McClelland and Stewart, 1968.

Creighton, Donald G., *The Commercial Empire of the St. Lawrence*. Toronto: Macmillan, 1958.

Eccles, W.J., *France in America*. New York: Harper & Row, 1972.

Miquelon, Dale, ed., *Society and Conquest: The Debate on the Bourgeoisie and Social Change in French Canada, 1700–1850*. Toronto: Copp Clark, 1977.

Neatby, Hilda, *Quebec: The Revolutionary Age, 1760–1791*. Toronto: McClelland and Stewart, 1966.

Nish, Cameron, ed., *The French Canadians, 1759–1766: Conquered? Half-Conquered? Liberated?*. Toronto: Copp Clark, 1966.

Parkman, Francis, *The Old Regime in Canada*, Vol. II. Toronto: George N. Morang, 1899.

Stanley, G.F.G., *New France, the Last Phase, 1744–1760*. Toronto: McClelland and Stewart, 1969.

Wade, Mason, *The French Canadians: Vol. 1, 1760–1911*. Toronto: Macmillan, 1968. Revised Edition.

Zoltvany, Yves F., ed., *The French Tradition in North America*. Toronto: Fitzhenry and Whiteside, 1969.

2. Specialized Studies

Historiography of the Conquest

Blain, Jean, "Economie et société en Nouvelle France: le cheminement historiographique dans la première moitié du XXe siècle", *Revue d'histoire de l'Amérique française*, Vol. 26 (juin, 1972), pp. 3–31.

_____, "Economie et Société en Nouvelle France: l'historiographie des années 1950–1960—Guy Frégault et l'école de Montréal", *Revue d'histoire de l'Amérique française*, Vol. 28 (septembre, 1974), pp. 163–86.

Brunet, Michel, "The British Conquest: Canadian Social Scientists and the Fate of the Canadiens", *Canadian Historical Review*, Vol. XL (June, 1959).

Cook, Ramsay, *Canada and the French-Canadian Question*. Toronto: Macmillan, 1966.

_____, *The Maple Leaf Forever: Essays on Nationalism and Politics in Canada*. Toronto: Macmillan, 1977. New Edition.

Eccles, W.J., "The History of New France according to Francis Parkman", *William and Mary Quarterly*, Vol. 18 (April, 1961).

Jaenen, Cornelius J., "Military History and the Conquest", in D.A. Muise, ed., *A Reader's Guide to Canadian History*, Vol. 1: Beginnings to Confederation. Toronto: University of Toronto Press, 1982, pp. 40–42.

Ouellet, Fernand, "M. Michel Brunet et le problème de la Conquête", *Bulletin des Recherches historiques*, Vol. 62 (avril-mai-juin, 1965), pp. 92–101.

_____, "Compte rendu: la Nouvelle-France et la bourgeoisie", *Journal of Canadian Studies*, Vol. 4 (August, 1969), pp. 57–60.

Military Aspects of the Conquest

Eccles, W.J., "The French Forces in North America during the Seven Years' War", in *Dictionary of Canadian Biography*, Vol. III. Toronto: University of Toronto Press, 1974. Introductory essay.

Frégault, Guy, *Canada: The War of the Conquest*. Toronto: Oxford University Press, 1969.

Kennett, Lee, *The French Armies in the Seven Years' War*. Durham: Duke University Press, 1967.

Parkman, Francis, *Montcalm and Wolfe*. Toronto: George N. Morang, 1899.

Stacey, C.P., *Quebec 1759: The Siege and the Battle*. Toronto: Macmillan, 1959.

Steele, Ian K., *Guerillas and Grenadiers: The Struggle for Canada, 1689–1760*. Toronto: Ryerson Press, 1969.

Wrong, George M., *The Fall of Canada: A Chapter in the History of the Seven Years' War.* Oxford: Oxford University Press, 1914.

The Conquest and French Canadian Nationalism

Chapais, Thomas, *Cours d'histoire du Canada*, Tome 1, 1760–1791. Montreal: Bernard Valiquette, 1919.

Cook, Ramsay, ed., *French Canadian Nationalism: An Anthology.* Toronto: Macmillan, 1970.

Gagnon, Serge, *Le Québec et ses historiens de 1840 à 1920: La Nouvelle-France de Garneau à Groulx.* Quebec: Les Presses de l'Université Laval, 1978.

Garneau, F.X., *History of Canada, from the Time of Its Discovery till the Union Year*, Vol. II. Montreal: Aubin, Fréchette and Lovell, 1860.

Groulx, Lionel, *Lendemain de conquête.* Montréal: Bibliothèque Action française, 1920.

Trofimenkoff, Susan Mann, *The Dream of Nation: A Social and Intellectual History of Quebec.* Toronto: Macmillan, 1982.

The Debate on the Bourgeoisie and Social Change

Brunet, Michel, *French Canada and the Early Decades of British Rule 1760–1791*, Canadian Historical Association Booklet No. 13. Ottawa: CHA, 1963.

Hamelin, Jean, *Economie et société en Nouvelle-France.* Québec: Les Presses de l'Université Laval, 1960.

Igartua, José, "A Change in Climate: The Conquest and the Marchands of Montreal", Canadian Historical Association *Historical Papers 1974*, pp. 115–134.

————, "The Merchants of Montreal at the Conquest: Socio-Economic Profile", *Histoire sociale/Social History*, Vol. VIII (November, 1975), pp. 175–93.

Miquelon, Dale, *Dugard of Rouen: French Trade to Canada and the West Indies, 1729–1770.* Montreal: McGill-Queen's University Press, 1978.

Nish, Cameron, "The Nature, Composition and Functions of the Canadian Bourgeoisie, 1729–1748", Canadian Historical Association *Report*, 1966, pp. 14–28.

Ouellet, Fernand, "French-Canadian Nationalism: From Its Origins to the Insurrection of 1837", in Miquelon, ed., *Society and Conquest*, pp. 171–186. Translated from the *Canadian Historical Review*, Vol. XLV (December, 1964).

Séguin, Maurice, *L'Idée de l'indépendance au Québec: genèse et historique.* Trois-Rivières: Les Editions Boréal Express, 1968.

5

THE QUEBEC ACT

Magnanimous Statesmanship or Selfish Expediency?

Victory over the forces defending New France in 1760 was celebrated by both Britain and its American colonies, who together had feared and coveted the French Empire in North America for decades. They had gained a new colony that offered seemingly unlimited opportunities for commercial and territorial expansion. After the celebration, however, there came a sobering recognition of the problems of possessing a colony developed by another empire. The military conquest did not change the fact that the Canadians were French and Catholic—still different, still to be feared by their neighbours along the Atlantic seaboard. Yet the mother country could no longer share its colonies' outright antagonism. Britain now had a responsibility for the Canadians; they had become the King's "new subjects".

Exactly how to govern the colony was an unprecedented and complex problem for the British. For the first time in modern history an imperial European power found itself in possession of a major colony as culturally sophisticated as itself, yet different in many fundamental ways. These approximately seventy thousand Canadians were firmly settled in a unique social pattern that was rich with its own traditions, language, religion, laws, and government. Of these cultural differences, the last three in particular posed problems for the establishment of British government. The British had to decide how a Roman Catholic colony should be governed by a British king, the "Defender of the Faith" of the Church of England. They also had to determine whether British law could or should be applied to a population that knew only the legal system it had had for a century and a half under the French régime. Finally, they wondered whether they should incorporate traditional British representative institutions into a colony that was accustomed to an authoritarian form of government under a Governor appointed by the king.

A decade and a half after the Conquest the British addressed the problem with the Quebec Act. Faced with the choice between attempting to assimilate the French Canadians or trying to integrate the two cultures into a workable governmental system, they settled on the latter course—adopting a policy which confirmed the rights of French Canadians to preserve their language, religion, and customary civil laws, and establishing a colonial government— though without an Assembly. It was a crucial decision for Canada's future development. The Act acknowledged the coexistence of the two founding European peoples in Canada. Ever since, it has been cited as the first official recognition of Canadian cultural duality.

What motivated the British authorities to adopt such a policy is a matter which still sparks controversy among historians. And out of the many-sided debate over the Quebec Act, two diametrically opposed positions have emerged. One long-standing view is that the Act was a prime example of British leniency, justice and humanity—a triumph of magnanimous states-manship. The other side contends that the Quebec Act was more the product of selfish expediency, born of a realistic assessment of the French Canadian presence in Quebec and the need to secure the loyalty of *Canadiens* in the event of a revolt in the American colonies. Most historians agree that the real answer lies somewhere between these two poles.

Deciding on the proper policy for dealing with the new colony of Quebec did not come easily for the British. In the early years of British rule the policy was formed gradually, perhaps unconsciously, through the interaction of members of the British government, the governors of the colony, and the French Canadians. The surrender of New France in September, 1760, was followed by two and a half years of military rule, tempered only by the terms of the Articles of Capitulation. When the Seven Years' War ended with the Treaty of Paris on February 10, 1763, Canada was formally ceded to Great Britain. The next October, a Royal Proclamation was issued to introduce civil administration into the colony, now called the Province of Quebec. It would serve as the constitution of the colony until a specific policy for the province was set out in the Quebec Act in 1774.

These constitutional developments occurred at a time when other events further complicated the issue. Soon after the Conquest, a small but highly vocal and influential minority of British merchants, mostly from New En-gland, established themselves in Quebec to take advantage of the commercial opportunities that the new colony offered. These "old subjects" expected their customary privileges under British rule, including the right to an Assembly. But under British law, Catholics were denied the right to hold public office and if an assembly were granted, such a government would likely be dominated by the British minority. At the same time, the "old subjects" in the Thirteen Colonies were becoming restless under British rule. While the Quebec Act was being formulated, American colonists began to organize armed resistance (against British trade and tax laws known as the "Intolerable Acts"), assembled a "Continental Congress" in Philadelphia, and formed a united opposition to British policies. Three weeks before the proclamation of the Quebec Act, the first shots of the American Revolution were fired at Lexington and Concord. It was amid these turbulent events that the Act had its genesis.

The Quebec Act, officially proclaimed in May 1775, reaffirmed the rights of Britain's "new subjects", established a new colonial government without an elected assembly, and greatly extended the colony's boundaries southwestward to include the Ohio Valley so coveted by expansionists in the Thirteen Colonies. Clearly the British sought to win the loyalty of French Canadians rather than to command their obedience. But why had they chosen such a policy? What were its immediate and its long-term effects? It is around these two questions that most historical debate about the Quebec Act has revolved.

Debate over the short-term effects of the Act has focused on its relation to the American Revolution. The Quebec Act did anger American colonists by denying them lands for settlement in the Ohio Valley and by sanctioning authoritarian government and Catholicism in North America. Historians have thus argued that the Quebec Act was partly responsible for inciting the American Revolution. They have also debated the effectiveness of the Act in keeping the French Canadians from joining the Thirteen Colonies in revolt against the British.

But a more fundamental issue in Canadian history has been the long-term effect of the Quebec Act in protecting French Canadian rights and ensuring the development of Canadian duality. And while discussing this issue, historians have inevitably raised the related problem of whether the effects of the Quebec Act were what the British government had intended.

What makes the nature of the Quebec Act such a fascinating problem is that it involves ascertaining motives. Historians have asked whether the Quebec Act was an example of an enlightened and humane imperial policy, or whether it was little more than an act of political manipulation, a desperate attempt by the British to strengthen their position in Quebec as relations with the Thirteen Colonies deteriorated. Analyzing the motives behind the Quebec Act thus raises the larger question of whether or not Canadian cultural duality was originally based on good faith between the two European founding peoples, the French and the English. In this problem study, the crucial questions are left for the reader to decide: Was the Quebec Act the only possible policy for the British, or was it a humane course freely and deliberately chosen? If there had been no American Revolution, would the French Canadians have been granted the legal means to preserve their way of life? Was the Quebec Act an example of magnanimous statesmanship, or of selfish expediency?

SELECTED CONTEMPORARY SOURCES

The sources available for study of the Quebec Act consist for the most part of the constitutional documents preceding the Quebec Act, the dispatches that passed between the Governors-General and the Colonial Office, petitions to the British government from the inhabitants of Quebec, and the reports of

British officials advising their government about the Quebec situation. These materials provide some insight into the issues at stake and the opinions of certain parties.

They are inadequate, however, for providing a definite answer about the motivations behind the Quebec Act. Among the important documents that are missing are the private papers of Governor Guy Carleton, who played a large part in composing the Quebec Act. Nor are there extant any other important confidential papers that deal with the formulation of the Quebec Act. A further problem is that few records exist conveying the views of French Canadians on the Act. As a result, conclusions can be drawn based only on speculation about the circumstances in which the Act was passed and on what is known of the sympathies of its authors from limited sources.

THE CONSTITUTIONAL GENESIS OF THE ACT

The Quebec Act is usually credited with alleviating political uncertainties posed by the Conquest of 1760. But as such, did it represent a major British departure from policy? Or did it merely confirm established practice in Quebec? It is necessary to examine the constitutional documents which preceded the Quebec Act to find an answer to this question. In doing so, it may be possible to shed some light on the motives behind the Act. Assuming, for example, that the Quebec Act was indeed little more than an authorization of policies developed by British administrators in Quebec since the Conquest, would this support the "magnanimous" or the "expedient" interpretation of the motives behind the Act?

The Articles of Capitulation, Montreal, 1760

The rough outlines of the British responsibilities to the conquered Canadians were set out in the Articles of Capitulation. The first of these was signed after the Battle of the Plains of Abraham on September 13, 1759, and the second, parts of which appear below, was signed a year later at Montreal. Together they provide for the protection of the *Canadiens'* property and their legal system, as well as for the practice of the Roman Catholic religion.

Article XXVII

The free exercise of the Catholic, Apostolic, and Roman Religion, shall subsist entire, in such manner that all the states and the people of the Towns and countries, places and distant posts, shall continue to assemble in the churches, and to frequent the sacraments as heretofore, without being molested in any manner, directly or indirectly. These people shall be obliged, by the English Government, to pay their Priests the tithes, and all the taxes they were used to pay under the Government of his most Christian Majesty.—'Granted, as to the free exercise of their religion, the obligation of paying the tithes to the Priests will depend on the King's pleasure.'

Article XXX

If by the treaty of peace, Canada should remain in the power of his Britannic Majesty, his most Christian Majesty shall continue to name the Bishop of the colony, who shall always be of the Roman communion, and under whose authority the people shall exercise the Roman Religion.—'Refused.'

Article XXXVII

The Lords of the Manors, the Military and Civil officers, the Canadians as well in the Towns as in the country, the French settled, or trading, in the whole extent of the colony of Canada, and all other persons whatsoever, shall preserve the entire peaceable property and possession of the goods... [lands], merchandizes, furs and... even their ships...—'Granted as in [a previous article].'

Article XLI

The French, Canadians, and Acadians of what state and condition asever, who shall remain in the colony, shall not be forced to take arms against his most Christian Majesty, or his Allies, directly or indirectly, on any occasion whatsoever; the British Government shall only require of them an exact neutrality.—'They become Subjects of the King.'

Article XLII

The French and Canadians shall continue to be governed according to the custom of Paris, and the Laws and usages established for this country and they shall not be subject to any other imposts than those which were established under the French Dominions.—'Answered by the preceding articles, and particularly by the last'....

Adam Shortt and Arthur Doughty, eds. *Documents Relating to the Constitutional History of Canada 1759–1791* (Ottawa: Taché, 1918), pp. 25, 30–34.

The Treaty of Paris, 1763

In the Treaty of Paris, which ended the Seven Years' War, the property rights of the French Canadians who had stayed on their land after the Conquest were not even mentioned, and the religious rights granted in the Articles of Capitulation were cited only briefly. Included for the first time was a qualification about the status of Catholics under British law which introduced a vague (but ominous) limitation to the freedom of worship previously granted to the Canadians.

IV. His Most Christian Majesty [the King of France] renounces all pretensions which he has heretofore formed or might have formed to ...the said countries, lands, islands, places, coasts, and their inhabitants, so that the Most Christian King cedes and makes over the whole to the said King, and to the Crown of Great Britain.... His Britannick Majesty, on his side, agrees to grant the liberty of the Catholick religion to the inhabitants of Canada: he will, in consequence, give the most precise and most effectual orders, that his new Roman Catholick subjects may profess the worship of their religion according to the rites of the Romish church, as far as the laws of Great Britain permit. His Britannick Majesty farther agrees, that the French inhabitants, or others who had been subjects of the Most Christian King in Canada, may retire with all safety and freedom wherever they shall think proper, and may sell their estates, provided it be to the subjects of his Britannick Majesty, and bring away their effects as well as their persons, without being restrained in their emigration....

Shortt and Doughty, *Documents*, pp. 113–117.

The Royal Proclamation of 1763

Military rule ended with the Proclamation of 1763, which applied to Quebec as well as to other new British possessions in which civil government was about to be established. It also set a new boundary that limited the territory of Quebec to little more than the area occupied by seigneurial lands, effectively cutting off the St. Lawrence Valley from its historic hinterland in the Ohio Valley.

> ...We have thought fit to publish and declare, by this Our Proclamation, that We have...given express Power and Direction to our Governors of our Said Colonies respectively, that so soon as the state and circumstances of the said Colonies will admit thereof, [The Governors] shall, with the Advice and Consent of the Members of our Council, summon and call General Assemblies within the said Governments respectively, in such Manner and Form as is used and directed in those Colonies and Provinces in America....
>
> ...and in the mean time and until such Assemblies can be called as aforesaid, all Persons Inhabiting in or resorting to our Said Colonies may confide in our Royal Protection for the Enjoyment of the Benefit of the Laws of our Realm of England; for which Purpose We have given Power under our Great Seal to the Governors of our said Colonies respectively to erect and constitute, with the Advice of our said Councils respectively, Courts of Judicature and public Justice within our Said Colonies for hearing and determining all Causes, as well Criminal as Civil, according to Law and Equity, and as near as may be agreeable to the Laws of England....
>
> We have also thought fit, with the advice of our Privy Council as aforesaid, to give unto the Governors and Councils of our said Three new Colonies, upon the Continent full Power and Authority to settle and agree with the Inhabitants of our said new Colonies or with any other Persons who shall resort thereto, for such Lands, Tenements and Hereditaments, as are now or hereafter shall be in our Power to dispose of; and them to grant to any such Person or Persons upon such Terms, and under such moderate Quit-Rents, Services and Acknowledgments, as have been appointed and settled in our other Colonies....
>
> Shortt and Doughty, *Documents*, pp. 163–8.

Instructions to Governor James Murray, 1763

The official instructions issued to Governor James Murray in December 1763 followed the established pattern of instructions to a colonial governor, but permitted a temporary modification of the provisions of the Proclamation of 1763. The oaths of allegiance that Murray was instructed to administer, not only to office-holders but to all subjects, finally elaborated on what limitations "the Laws of Great Britain" could place upon Catholic freedom of worship. Rigidly applied, the instructions would have eliminated any such freedom. But there was a loophole: even though it was planned that the colony would become English and Protestant, the French Canadians temporarily retained the rights they had been granted previously and the schedule for introducing the changes was left to the governor's discretion. Although it seemed inevitable that British courts of law would be introduced, the instructions asked that more information be gathered before settling the question of the property rights of the "new subjects". Here again, some latitude was given to Murray in applying the laws.

... You are in the next place to nominate and establish a Council for Our said Province, to assist You in the Administration of Government....

11. And whereas it is directed, by Our Commission to You under Our great Seal, that so soon as the Situation and Circumstances of Our said Province will admit thereof, You shall, with the Advice of Our Council, summon and call a General Assembly of the Freeholders in Our said Province.... But, as it may be impracticable for the present to form such an Establishment, You are in the mean time to make such Rules and Regulations, by the Advice of Our said Council, as shall appear to be necessary for the Peace, Order and good Government of Our said Province....

16. ... You are authorized and impowered, with the Advice and Consent of Our Council, to constitute and appoint Courts of Judicature and Justice... apply your Attention to these great and important Objects....

28. And whereas We have stipulated, by the late Definitive Treaty of Peace concluded at Paris the 10th Day of February 1763, to grant the Liberty of the Catholick Religion to the Inhabitants of Canada... Our new Roman Catholick Subjects in that Province may profess the Worship of their Religion, according to the Rites of the Romish Church, as far as the Laws of Great Britain permit....

29. You are, as soon as possible, to summon the Inhabitants to meet together, at such Time or Times, Place or Places, as you shall find most convenient, in order to take the Oath of Allegiance... and in case any of the said French Inhabitants shall refuse to take the said Oath, and make and subscribe the Declaration of Abjuration, as aforesaid, You are to cause them forthwith to depart out of Our said Government.

32. You are not to admit of any Ecclesiastical Jurisdiction of the See of Rome, or any other foreign Ecclesiastical Jurisdiction whatsoever in the Province under your Government.

33. And to the End that the Church of England may be established both in Principles and Practice, and that the said Inhabitants may by Degrees be induced to embrace the Protestant Religion, and their Children be brought up in the Principles of it; We do hereby declare it to be Our Intention... [that] all possible Encouragement shall be given to the erecting [of] Protestant Schools... and you are to consider and report to Us, by Our Commissioners for Trade and Plantations, by what other Means the Protestant Religion may be promoted, established and encouraged in Our Province under your Government....

42. And it is Our further Will and Pleasure, that all and every [one of] the French Inhabitants in Our said Province, who are now possessed of Lands within the said Province... do, within such limited Time as you in your Discretion shall think fit, register the several Grants, or other Deeds or Titles, by which they hold or claim such Lands....

44. And whereas it is necessary, in order to the advantageous and effectual Settlement of Our said Province, that the true State of it should be fully known; You are therefore, as soon as conveniently may be, to cause an accurate Survey to be made of the said Province....

Shortt and Doughty, *Documents*, pp. 189–93.

Governor Guy Carleton's Proposals, 1767–68

While Governor Murray believed that anglicization was desirable, he developed a sympathetic attitude toward the French-speaking Roman Catholics in the colony and practiced leniency in his application of the laws affecting their customary practices. Murray was recalled, however, after a series of disputes with the "English party" of merchants who were angered at his refusal to grant an elected assembly. His successor, Guy Carleton, grew to share Murray's sympathy for the "new subjects" and seemed to continue his policies. As a career soldier and a pragmatic governor, Carleton anticipated the military need for French Canadian loyalty in the event of further trouble in the Thirteen Colonies, and practically assessed the likelihood that a British minority could assimilate the preponderant French Canadian majority in Quebec. In his correspondence with the Colonial Secretary, Lord Shelburne, during 1767 and 1768, Carleton offered advice and recommendations concerning British policy.

December 24, 1767.

> To conceive the true State of the People of this Province... 'tis necessary to recollect, they are not a Migration of Britons, who brought with them the Laws of England, but a Populous and long established Colony, reduced by the King's Arms, to submit to His Dominion, on *certain Conditions*: That their Laws and Customs were widely Different from those of England, but founded on natural Justice and Equity....
>
> The most advisable Method, in my Opinion, for removing the present, as well as for preventing future Evils, is to repeat that Ordinance [of 17th Sept. 1764]... and for the present leave the Canadian Laws almost entire; such Alterations might be afterwards made in them....

November 25, 1767.

> Having arrayed the Strength of His Majesty's old and new Subjects, and shown the great Superiority of the Latter, it may not be amiss to observe, that there is not the least Probability, this present Superiority should ever diminish. On the Contrary 'tis more than probable it will increase and strengthen daily: The Europeans, who migrate never will prefer the long unhospitable Winters of Canada, to the more chearful Climates, and more fruitful Soil of his Majesty's Southern Provinces; The few old Subjects at present in this Province, have been mostly left here by Accident, and are either disbanded Officers, Soldiers, or Followers of the Army, who, not knowing how to dispose of themselves elsewhere, settled where they were left at the Reduction; or else they are Adventurers in Trade, or such as could not remain at Home, who set out to mend their Fortunes, at the opening of this new Channel for Commerce... some, from more advantagious Views elsewhere, others from Necessity, have already left this Province, and I greatly fear many more, for the same Reasons, will follow their Example in a few Years; But while this severe Climate, and the Poverty of the Country discourages all but the Natives, its Healthfulness is such, that these multiply daily, so that, barring Catastrophe shocking to think of, this Country must, to the end of Time, be peopled by the Canadian Race, who already have taken such firm Root, and got to so

great a Height, that any new Stock transplanted will be totally hid, and imperceptible amongst them, except in the Towns of Quebec and Montreal.

January 20, 1768.

...the better Sort of Canadians fear nothing more than popular Assemblies, which, they conceive, tend only to render the People refractory and insolent; Enquiring what they thought of them, they said, they understood some of our Colonies had fallen under the King's Displeasure, owing to the Misconduct of their Assemblies, and that they should think themselves unhappy, if a like Misfortune befell them....

Shortt and Doughty, *Documents*, pp. 288–290, 284 and 294.

THREE POINTS OF VIEW—PETITIONS FROM QUEBEC

The Royal Proclamation angered both the French Canadians and the British in Quebec for different reasons. The British merchants who had settled in the ports of Quebec and Montreal wanted an Assembly to be convoked immediately, and they resented both their exclusion from the Ohio Valley and other trading territories as well as other trade regulations. The Proclamation also disappointed French Canadian seigneurial and clerical leaders, who did not find in it the expected recognition of their laws and religion. They particularly disliked the fact that the dispositions of the Test Act barred them, as Catholics, from careers in administration and deprived them of public rights in their own country. If an Assembly were granted, they would be governed, in effect, by the British merchant minority.

From 1763 onward, several groups in Quebec joined in agitating for a new constitutional settlement. These groups included the English-speaking merchants and traders, French Canadian notables and a dissenting faction of *Canadiens*. Their petitions to the King provide some basis for evaluating how well the Quebec Act later satisfied the desires of the citizens of Quebec. But the third petition printed here illustrates that the French Canadians, at least, were not unanimous in their opinions about the most suitable form of government. Although it is alone among surviving sources in the opinion it expresses, it illustrates the impossibility of making sweeping generalizations about what the French Canadians really wanted from the British.

Petition of the Quebec English Traders, circa 1764

Our Settlement in this Country with respect to the greatest part of us; takes its date from the Surrender of the Colony to your Majesty's Arms; Since that Time we have much contributed to the advantage of our Mother Country, by causing an additional Increase to her Manufactures, and by a considerable Importation of them, diligently applied ourselves to Investigate and promote the Commercial Interests of this Province and render it flourishing. To Military Government, however oppressive and severely felt, we submitted without murmur, hoping Time with a Civil Establishment would remedy this Evil.

With Peace we trusted to enjoy the Blessings of British Liberty, and happily reap the fruits of our Industry: but we should now despair of ever attaining those desirable ends, had we not Your Majesty's experienced Goodness to apply to....

The Governor instead of ... giving a favorable Reception to those of your Majesty's Subjects, who petition and apply to him on such important Occasions as require it, doth frequently treat them with a Rage and Rudeness of Language and Demeanour, as dishonorable to the Trust he holds of your Majesty as painful to those who suffer from it.

His further adding to this by most flagrant Partialities... to keep your Majesty's old and new Subjects divided from one another, by encouraging the latter to apply for Judgment of their National Language....

Your Petitioners therefore most humbly pray your Majesty... to appoint a Governor over us, acquainted with other maxims of Government than Military only... to order a House of Representatives to be chosen in this as in other your Majesty's Provinces; there being a number more than Sufficient of Loyal and well affected Protestants, exclusive of military Officers, to form a competent and respectable House of Assembly; and your Majesty's new Subjects, if your Majesty shall think fit, may be allowed to elect Protestants without burdening them with such Oaths as in their present mode of thinking they cannot conscientiously take....

Shortt and Doughty, *Documents*, pp. 232–4.

Petition of the *Canadien* Notables, 1770

From the Moment, Sire, of the union of this Province to the Dominion of your Crown, your most humble servants have taken the Liberty of frequently representing to you, of what importance to their interests it was to be judged and governed according to the Laws, Customs and regulations under which they were born, which serve as the Basis and Foundation of their possessions, and are the rule of their families, and how painful and at the same time how humiliating it has been to them to be excluded from the offices which they might fill in this Province, for the Service of Your Majesty, and the Comfort of Your Canadian People,—the only way to excite emulation.

Could the religion we profess, Sire, and in the profession of which it had pleased you to assure us that we shall never be disturbed, though differing from that of your other subjects, be a reason, (at least in Your Province of Quebec) for excluding so considerable a number of Your submissive and faithful Children from participation in the favours of the best of Kings, of the tenderest of fathers? No Sire, prejudice has never reached Your Throne you love equally and without distinction all your faithful subjects....

Restored to our customs and usages administered according to the forms with which we are familiar every individual will know the extent of his rights & the way to defend himself without being obliged to spend more than the value of his property to maintain himself in his possessions.

Thus rendered able to serve our King and our country in every situation we shall no longer groan under this state of humiliation, which, so to speak, makes life unbearable to us, and seems to have made of us a reprobate nation.

Shortt and Doughty, *Documents*, pp. 421–2.

Opinion of *"Canadiens Vrais Patriotes"*, 1773

... We are told that it is the intention to leave to this Province its local laws of property, therefore giving a reasonable interpretation to the Proclamation... That is fair... Is it possible to alter, or to repress or abolish the laws which govern these goods, since without these Laws we cannot enjoy them as they should be enjoyed and as we always have enjoyed them?... But he [the Minister] wishes... against the promises given to the Canadians by the Royal Proclamation that they would enjoy together with all British subjects the benefits and advantages of English laws, to take these from them, in granting to the Governor with the Council, without the help of the House of Assembly, full legislative power... full right (without consulting the people and their true interests) to change, alter, reform, or even abolish their ancient laws of property according to his caprice and his will, and to impose on them all such taxes that he judges proper. Such a prerogative cannot be granted to a Governor and Council without totally debasing the prudent and wise constitution of the British Government. His Most Excellent Majesty and his honourable Parliament... will without doubt refuse to accept any such plan which tends only towards the eradication of our personal rights, which His Most Excellent Majesty by his Proclamation has promised that we should enjoy as British subjects and assuring us that we should profit entirely from the benefit of English laws of which this part is one of the foremost advantages which is granted and promised by the said Proclamation. If it is not possible according to the British Constitution to establish in this Province a House of Assembly into which Canadians of the French Catholic Church should be allowed we cannot reasonably consent to the establishment of one from which they must be excluded... The Governor, with an adequate council may have... power to make laws only on police matters in keeping with former practices... provided this power should not... change... the basic laws regarding property in the smallest detail. Nor are we against granting the right to anyone to renounce for himself and his family the local laws of the province concerning marriage, dowry, and inheritance... to fulfil the promise of His Most Gracious Majesty that we should enjoy the benefit and the advantages of English law and satisfy in every way the old subjects who are established here already and to those who in the future may come here to settle. There is not the least difficulty in the laws of England being followed in this province in cases relating to the admiralty and commercial matters, because these do not concern real property rights.

The inhabitants of the province cannot reasonably oppose the establishment of a House of Assembly if it is to be composed (as it should be) of old and new subjects without distinction.... The irreproachable conduct that the latter have followed since the Conquest, their submission to the British Government, should be a sure guarantee to the mother country that they will not abuse any change in its ancient laws that may be made in their favour. His Most Excellent Majesty... has promised them that they will have all of its advantages and that as British subjects they will be allowed representation in the House of Assembly by Canadians of their own communion. The Mother Country cannot refuse this favour because, contrary to its own statutes, it is already allowed to them to be sworn as Jurors not only in civil but also in criminal cases.

The old subjects who are reasonable... are not against such a House of Assembly composed of old and new subjects... The inhabitants of this province know that if such a House is established it will be necessary to impose taxes in order to meet the expenses of government.

P.A.C., Baby Collection (Transcripts), *Political Papers*, Vol. XLVIII, 30938. "Address... to His Majesty, July 24, 1773." trans. J.M., s.j.

CONFLICTING LEGAL OPINIONS

By 1772 the British government, anxious about the situation in the Thirteen Colonies, began to consider the Quebec situation a serious priority. The Attorney General, Edward Thurlow, was asked to make recommendations, and the Advocate General, James Marriott, was also asked for his considered opinion. Their reports contain the best expressions to date of the differing legal positions that could be taken on the rights of new subjects. The fact that each came to a different conclusion belies a simple interpretation of the Quebec Act as the logical result of standard British legal practice. The two reports are valuable because they illustrate the concerns of the British government and delineate the constitutional issues in dispute.

The Case for Retaining French Law and Custom—Report of Attorney General Edward Thurlow, 1773

The Canadians seem to have been strictly entitled by the *jus gentium* to their property, as they possessed it upon the capitulation and treaty of peace, together, with all its qualities and incidents, by tenure or otherwise, and also to their personal liberty; for both which they were to expect your Majesty's gracious protection.

It seems a necessary consequence that all those laws by which that property was created, defined, and secured must be continued to them. . . .

When certain forms of civil justice have long been established, people have had frequent occasions to feel themselves and observe in others the actual coercion of the law in matters of debt and other engagements and dealings, and also in the recompense for all sorts of wrongs. The force of these examples goes still further and stamps an impression on the current opinion of men and puts an actual check on their dealings; and those who never heard of the examples or the laws which produced them, yet acquire a kind of traditional knowledge of the legal effects and consequences of their transactions, sufficient and withal absolutely necessary for the common affairs of private life. It is easy to imagine what infinite disturbance it would create to introduce new and unknown measures of justice. . . .

The same kind of observation applies with still greater force against a change of criminal law, in proportion as the examples are more striking, and the consequences more important. The general consternation which must follow upon the circumstance of being suddenly subjected to a new system of criminal law, cannot soon be appeased by the looseness or mildness of the code.

From these observations, I draw it as a consequence that new subjects, acquired by conquest, have a right to expect from the benignity and justice of their conqueror the continuance of all these old laws, and they seem to have no less reason to expect it from his wisdom. It must, I think, be the interest of the conqueror to leave his new subjects in the utmost degree of private tranquillity and personal security; and, in the fullest persuasion of their reality, without introducing needless occasion of complaint and displeasure, and disrespect for their own sovereign. He seems, also, to provide better for the public peace and order, by leaving them in the habit of obedience to their accustomed laws than by undertaking the harsher task of compelling a new obedience to laws unheard of before. And if the old system happens to be more perfect than anything which invention can hope to substitute on the sudden, the scale sinks quite down in its favor.

Shortt and Doughty, *Documents*, pp. 437–44.

The Case for Asserting British Sovereignty—Report of Advocate General James Marriott, 1774

It is very observable, that in the XLIId article of the capitulation for Montreal and Canada, the demand was, *that the Canadians shall be governed according to the custom of Paris, and the laws and usages established for that country.* This neither granted nor refused, but *reserved.* The answer is, *'they become your Majesty's subjects.'* The consequence is, their laws are liable to be changed....

Every new mode is considered as a hardship by the old inhabitants, and so might they equally complain of the conquest. Their minds naturally revert to their ancient usages, and *their wishes return to their ancient government.* It is no reproach to them; they must feel as men; and to men every political change which brings an uncertainty of rights, and of the mode of pursuing them, is of necessity painful.

...in the civil proceedings carried on in the new superior court of king's bench, the forms of all actions, the style of the proceedings, the method of trial, the rules of taking evidence, are such as are prescribed by the English law, and are universally known by the Canadians to be so....

...the English laws of bankruptcy are well received by many of the ancient Canadians, as being agreeable to the spirit of the French laws in cases of *déconfiture* or insolvency. It is agreed on all hands, in criminal proceedings, *that the Canadians do as well as English universally understand the criminal laws of England to be in full force; that no other are ever mentioned or thought of; and that the Canadians seem to be very well satisfied with them....*

As men move forward, the laws move with them, and every constitution of government upon earth, like the shores of the sea from the agitation of the element, is daily losing ground or gaining something from one side or the other.

Shortt and Doughty, *Documents*, pp. 445–58.

THE TERMS OF THE QUEBEC ACT

Finally, in 1774, after years of debate, the Quebec Act was passed by the British parliament. The difficulty of the issue had not been the only reason for the delay. A series of unstable British ministries had been concerned with little more than staying in power, and had proposed only the most pressing legislation. But now it seemed that the Quebec situation could wait no longer. Perhaps the ominous developments in the Thirteen Colonies prompted the British government to turn its attention to Quebec. Or was it merely a coincidence that the resolution of the Quebec problem came just before the outbreak of the American Revolution? In any case, the Quebec Act received royal assent from King George III on June 22, 1774, establishing an unprecedented policy in British colonial rule.

An Act for making more effectual Provision for the Government of the Province of *Quebec* in *North America.*

...the said Proclamation [of 1763], so far as the same relates to the said Province of *Quebec*, and the Commission under the authority whereof the Government of the said Province is at present administered...are hereby revoked, annulled, and made void, from and after the First Day of May, One thousand seven hundred and seventy-five.

And, for the more perfect Security and Ease of the Minds of the Inhabitants of the said Province, it is hereby declared, That His Majesty's Subjects, professing the Religion of the Church of *Rome* of and in the said Province of *Quebec*, may have, hold, and enjoy, the free Exercise of the Religion of the Church of *Rome*, subject to the King's Supremacy, declared and established by an Act, made in the First Year of the Reign of Queen *Elizabeth*, over all the Dominions and Countries which then did, or thereafter should belong, to the Imperial Crown of this Realm; and that the Clergy of the said Church may hold, receive, and enjoy, their accustomed Dues and Rights, with respect to such Persons only as shall profess the said Religion.

Provided nevertheless, That it shall be lawful for His Majesty, His Heirs or Successors, to make such Provision out of the rest of the said accustomed Dues and Rights, for the Encouragement of the Protestant Religion, and for the Maintenance and Support of a Protestant Clergy within the said Province, as he or they shall, from Time to Time, think necessary and expedient.

Provided always, and be it enacted, That no Person, professing the Religion of the Church of *Rome*, and residing in the said Province, shall be obliged to take the Oath required by the said Statute passed in the First Year of the Reign of Queen *Elizabeth*, or any other Oaths substituted by any other Act in the Place thereof; but that every such Person who, by the said Statute is required to take the Oath therein mentioned, shall be obliged, and is hereby required, to take and subscribe the . . . [Oath of allegiance to His Majesty King George].

And be it further enacted by the Authority aforesaid, That all His Majesty's *Canadian* Subjects, within the Province of *Quebec*, the religious Orders and Communities only excepted, may also hold and enjoy their Property and Possessions, together with all Customs and Usages relative thereto, and all other their Civil Rights, in as large, ample, and beneficial Manner, as if the said Proclamation, Commissions, Ordinances, and other Acts and Instruments, had not been made, and as may consist with their Allegiance to His Majesty, and Subjection to the Crown and Parliament of *Great Britain*; and that in all Matters of Controversy, relative to Property and Civil Rights, Resort shall be had to the Laws of *Canada*, as the Rule for the Decision of the same . . . .

And whereas the Certainty and Lenity of the Criminal Law of *England*, and the Benefits and Advantages resulting from the Use of it, have been sensibly felt by the Inhabitants, from an Experience of more than Nine Years, during which it has been uniformly administered; be it therefore further enacted by the Authority aforesaid, That the same shall continue to be administered, and shall be observed as Law in the Province of *Quebec*, as well in the Description and Quality of the Offence as in the Method of Prosecution and Trial; and the Punishments and Forfeitures thereby inflicted to the Exclusion of every other Rule of Criminal Law, or Mode of Proceeding thereon, which did or might prevail in the said Province before the Year of our Lord One thousand seven hundred and sixty-four. . . .

And whereas it may be necessary to ordain many Regulations for the future Welfare and good Government of the Province of *Quebec*, the Occasions of which cannot now be foreseen, nor, without much Delay and Inconvenience, be provided for, without intrusting that Authority, for a certain Time, and under proper Restrictions, to Persons resident there: And whereas it is at present inexpedient to call an Assembly; be it therefore enacted by the Authority aforesaid, That it shall and may be lawful for His Majesty, His Heirs and Successors, by Warrant under His or Their Signet or Sign Manual, and with the Advice of the Privy Council, to constitute and appoint a Council for the Affairs of the Province of *Quebec*, to consist of such Persons resident there, not exceeding Twenty-three, nor less than Seventeen, as His Majesty, His Heirs and Successors, shall be pleased to appoint; and, upon the Death, Removal, or Absence of any of the Members of the said Council, in like Manner to constitute and appoint such and so many other Person or Persons as shall be necessary to supply the Vacancy or Vacancies; which Council, so appointed and nominated, or the major Part thereof, shall have Power and Authority to make Ordinances for the Peace, Welfare, and good Government, of the said Province, with the Consent of His Majesty's Governor, or, in his Absence, of the Lieutenant-governor, or Commander in Chief for the Time being....

Excerpts from the Act, in Shortt and Doughty, *Documents*, pp. 570–76.

REACTIONS TO THE ACT

The following sources provide examples of some of the reactions that the Quebec Act provoked in the new colony and in the American colonies to the south. When considering these reactions to the Quebec Act it is important to distinguish between the intention of the Act and its effects. The impact of the Quebec Act does not necessarily reveal the original motivations for its policy, although the British government might have had a good idea of how its legislation would be received.

Appeal of the Continental Congress 1774

To the Thirteen Colonies the Quebec Act appeared to be a continuation of the "Intolerable Acts" that had been passed earlier in the same British Parliament. Recognition of the Roman Catholic church grated against their Protestant religious convictions. They interpreted the Quebec Act's sanctioning of authoritarian government as the first step of a British plan to deny civil liberties throughout the colonies. The extension of Quebec's boundaries to include the Ohio Valley would help the St. Lawrence fur trade, but the American colonists believed that it was really intended to restrain their westward expansion. In the opinion of the Continental Congress, the Quebec Act was designed to further oppress the American colonies just as they were struggling to shed the last chains of colonial rule.

...the dominion of Canada is to be so extended, modelled, and governed, as that by being disunited from us, detached from our interests, by civil as well as religious prejudices, that by their numbers daily swelling with Catholic emigrants from Europe, and by their devotion to Administration, so friendly to their religion, they might become formidable to us, and on occasion, be fit instruments in the hands of power, to reduce the ancient free Protestant Colonies to the same state of slavery with themselves.

This was evidently the object of the Act:—And in this view, being extremely dangerous to our liberty and quiet, we cannot forebear complaining of it, as hostile to British America.—Superadded to these considerations, we cannot help deploring the unhappy condition to which it has reduced the many English settlers, who, encouraged by the Royal Proclamation, promising the enjoyment of all their rights, have purchased estates in that country.—They are now the subjects of an arbitrary government, deprived of trial by jury, and when imprisoned cannot claim the benefit of the habeas corpus Act, that great bulwark and palladium of English liberty:—Nor can we suppress our astonishment, that a British Parliament should ever consent to establish in that country a religion that has deluged your island in blood, and dispersed impiety, bigotry, persecution, murder and rebellion through every part of the world.

Worthington Chauncey Ford, ed., *Journals of the Continental Congress*, Vol. I, pp. 87–8.

A Canadian Seigneur's View

Those who perceive the Quebec Act as a policy of selfish expediency by the British government contend that the British strategy was to win the French Canadians' loyalty in the imminent revolutionary war by forming an alliance with the seigneurial and clerical leaders of Quebec society. The following extract, however, shows that the wishes of at least one Canadian seigneur were not fully accommodated into the Act. Seigneur Chartier de Lotbinière travelled to London to give evidence during the Westminster debates on the Quebec Act, and later recorded his dissatisfaction with the concessions the Act granted to Canadians.

... shall the governor have the right to make statutes which might annul the fundamental laws of Canada?... Should his process not rather be restricted to only making police regulations, and that strictly in accordance with the fundamental laws of the country without ever being able to step outside the spirit of these laws...? What I can state as positively certain is that in the request [the Canadians] are making for their own laws, there is no question of excepting such of them as relate, to criminals; and they would not have failed to express their opinion if they had preferred the English law on this point... Besides the Canadian understands the criminal law which has been followed from the beginning in this country... He believes too that he can see a danger, under the English law, of his being looked upon as a criminal, on the bare oath of a man, without any offence or crime being proved... This is the most fearful danger that it is possible to imagine, and one to which the Canadian is certain never to be exposed under the French law....

With regard to the establishment of the legislative power in Canada, I have already had occasion to demonstrate to the honourable chamber how essential it was to entrust it only to the largest landed proprietors in this country; owners only of properties recognized all over the world as solid, any others being liable to ruin from a sudden fire, or a few bankruptcies. It is from them only we can hope for the attention and care necessary to foresee the evil, and to develop all the natural advantages which the country may possess, seeing that they are the most prominent and the most interested in the success of the matter: this cannot reasonably be expected from those who have no interest, or only a very slight one in the public good, and especially if their personal interests are opposed to public ones.

Shortt and Doughty, *Documents*, pp. 564–7.

Confusion or Alarm?—An Artist's Conception of Reaction to the Act, 1774

Among the many reactions to the Quebec Act was an artist's rendering of its reception in the streets of the colony. The drawing in question, published in 1774 and bearing the caption "This Sr. is the meaning of the Quebec Act", has been subject to several different interpretations. Which national group and social class is being depicted? Is the animated talk a sign of confusion or anger? Does the drawing suggest, as historians have argued, that by blending English and French law the Act confused many?

"This S^R. is the meaning of the Quebec Act"

A Call to Loyalty—*Mandement* of Bishop Jean-Olivier Briand, 1775

When the American Revolution did break out, Quebec was, in fact, invaded by the American rebels, and the loyalty of the French Canadians was put to the test. The Catholic church was one element of Canadian society that appeared to have been favourably influenced by the Quebec Act. Bishop Briand, the highest authority in the Quebec church hierarchy, spoke out in favour of the British rulers on May 22, 1775.

> A band of rebels who have revolted against their lawful Sovereign, who is also ours, has just invaded this Province, less in the hope of being able to hold it fast than in the design of drawing you off into their revolution, or at least to get you to promise not to

oppose their pernicious plan. The singular kindness and gentleness with which we have been governed by His Very Gracious Majesty King George III, since by the fate of arms we have become subject to his dominion; the recent favours which he has bestowed upon us in returning to us the use of our laws, the free exercise of our religion, and allowing us to participate in all the privileges and advantages of British subjects would be sufficient to excite your gratitude and zeal in upholding the interests of the Crown of Great Britain. But more pressing motives must speak to your hearts at the present time. Your oaths, your religion, impose upon you duties from which you cannot be dispensed to defend with all your might your native land and your King.

Close your ears therefore, dear Canadians, and do not listen to rebels who would make you unhappy.... Take up joyously whatever you may be commanded by a benevolent Governor who has no other interest but your welfare and happiness....

H. Têtu & C.O. Gagnon, *Mandements, lettres pastorales et circulaires des Evêques de Québec* (Quebec: Coté, 1888) Vol. II, pp. 264–5. trans. J.M., s.j.

The Limits of Canadian Gratitude—Chief Justice Hey's Comments, 1775

It is debatable, however, whether the seigneurs and clergy had much influence on the French Canadians' allegiance during the revolutionary war. In the opinion of one British official, the Quebec Act did little to win the loyalty of Canadians. On August 28, 1775, Chief Justice Hey wrote home to Lord Chancellor Apsley, expressing his disappointment with the attitude of the "new subjects".

...what will be Your Lordship's astonishment when I tell you that an act passed for the express purpose of gratifying the Canadians & which was supposed to comprehend all that they either wished or wanted is become the first object of their discontent & dislike. English officers to command them in time of war, & English Laws to govern them in time of Peace, is the general wish, the former they know to be impossible (at least at present) & by the latter if I understand them right, they mean no Laws & no Government whatsoever—in the mean time it may be truly said that Gen. Carleton had taken an ill measure of the influence of the seigneurs & Clergy over the lower order of people whose Principle of conduct founded in fear & the sharpness of authority over them now no longer exercised, is unrestrained, & breaks out in every shape of contempt of detestation of those whom they used to behold with terror & who gave them I believe too many occasions to express it. And they on their parts have been and are too much elated with the advantages they supposed they should derive from the restoration of their old Priviledges & customs, & indulged themselves in a way of thinking & talking that gave very just offence, as well to their own People as to the English merchants....

Shortt and Doughty, *Documents*, pp. 670–1.

CONFLICTING INTERPRETATIONS

From the different interpretations of the Quebec Act that follow it is evident that the historical evidence available can be used to support a variety of opinions about the motivations behind the Act and its implications for the subsequent history of Canada. Many historians judge the Quebec Act to be a constitutional document that was fundamental to the development of the present character of Canada. Because of this direct linking with the present, the Quebec Act has engendered much controversy. But it is important to recognize that present-day concerns can prejudice an objective evaluation of the Quebec Act. Opinions about the French-English duality of modern Canada can be unwittingly reflected in what ostensibly are historical studies of the Quebec Act in its eighteenth-century context. For example, a conclusion that "selfish expediency" was the motivation behind the Quebec Act could provide moral support for a French Canadian separatist view of modern Canada, while a judgement that the British government displayed "magnanimous statesmanship" in its policy could strengthen the position of an advocate of a bilingual and bicultural Canada. Given the intrusion of modern bias and the paucity of relevant source material, the Quebec Act presents a complex challenge to Canadian historiography.

An Act of British Expediency—An Early French Canadian Nationalist View

François-Xavier Garneau, who wrote in the 1840s, was the first historian to examine the policies which led to the Quebec Act. He did not have access to all the sources that we have today, so his conclusions about the motives of the British government are based chiefly on deductive reasoning. Garneau exhibited French Canadian liberal nationalist sentiments that were typical of his compatriots, and he assumed that French Canadians of the previous century had shared his beliefs. He established an interpretation that has been echoed many times since.

> The Petitions of the Canadians were received, as they were bound to be in the context of the situation in England, and served as the basis of the Act of 1774, which itself was part of a much larger plan regarding all the British colonies on the continent. The increasing power of these colonies was causing more and more alarm in Britain, and their attitude since the treaty of 1763 . . . provides an explanation of the true motives of Britain's policy towards Canada.
>
> In 1764 the spirit of the government was quite hostile to the Canadians; by 1774 things had changed; its prejudices were now turned against the Americans and their colonial assemblies. Interest triumphed over ignorance and passion. The permanent abolition of their language and ancient laws would inevitably have the effect of uniting Canadians with the discontented of the other provinces; this was well understood, and consequently the regulation of the Canadian question was delayed from year to year until the authorities were obliged to act against Massachusetts and the provinces in the South. Thus the re-establishment of French laws for long depended on the result of the attempt to tax the colonies. The unconquerable opposition of the Americans helped to persuade the ministry to listen to the petitions of the Canadians. Yielding to Canadian wishes served a double purpose; it attached the clergy and nobility to the imperial cause, and it persuaded the people to recognize Britain's right to tax them; in the opinion of Canadians this recognition was a small price to pay for the preservation of their nationality, and for the granting to them of political privileges from which the other British subjects wished to exclude them.
>
> François-Xavier Garneau, *Histoire du Canada depuis sa découverte jusqu'à nos jours* (Quebec: 1852), pp. 406, 414–5. trans. J.M.,s.j.

Unnecessary in its Provisions/Disastrous in its Results: An American Perspective

A study dealing specifically with the Quebec Act appeared in 1886. Entitled *The Province of Quebec and the Early American Revolution*, it was the product of the research of a professor at the University of Wisconsin, Victor Coffin. He distinguished the Quebec Act from the Intolerable Acts, arguing that it had been intended only for the better government of Quebec and not to punish (indirectly) the Thirteen Colonies. But this did not prevent him from condemning the Quebec Act as a disastrous piece of legislation.

> ... the Quebec Act is really one of the most unwise and disastrous measures in English Colonial history. It will be shown below that it was founded on the misconceptions and false information of the Provincial officials; that though it secured the loyal support of those classes in Canada,—the clergy and the noblesse,—whose influence had been represented as all important, at the critical juncture this proved a matter of small moment.... Without the Act the old ruling classes, there is every reason to believe, would have taken precisely the same attitude, and the people would not have been exposed to those influences which ranged them on the side of the invader. Apart from Canadian affairs, the disastrous effect of the measure on public feeling in the older provinces must be strongly considered in any estimate as to its expediency....
>
> ... the main desire of the authors of the measure was to further the security and prosperity of the Province and fulfill treaty obligations toward the French Canadians, and will show that there is practically no evidence of more insidious aims with regard to colonial affairs in general. But it will also appear that the step was accompanied by manifestations of an arbitrary policy, and that it was taken at a moment when its authors were exhibiting in other ways real evidences of hostility to the free spirit of American self-government....
>
> ... What else could have been done, we are asked,—usually with extravagant laudation of the humanity and generosity of the British government in thus pursuing the only path open to it. It has been one of my objects to try and show that something else, something very different, *could* have been done; that the policy that was adopted with such far-reaching and disastrous consequences was precisely also the one that was the most dangerous with regard to the conditions of the moment....
>
> ... it should be manifest from the above examination that the alternative course was simply to set the new English Province firmly and definitively upon an *English* instead of a *French* path of development.... The way was clearly pointed out by other advisers as well qualified to speak as those whose advice was taken in 1774....
>
> It therefore does not seem an extreme view to regard the great difficulties that have beset English rule in Canada, as well as the grave problems that still confront the Dominion, as a natural and logical development from the policy of the Quebec Act.
>
> Victor Coffin, *The Province of Quebec and the Early American Revolution* Bulletin of the University of Wisconsin, (Madison: 1896), pp. v-vi, 431–43.

Strengthening the Imperial Tie—A Canadian Imperialist View

W.P.M. Kennedy, a historian at the University of Toronto, presented his interpretation of the Quebec Act in 1922 in his book, *The Constitution of Canada*. Kennedy's argument contradicted Coffin's and followed the same lines as Garneau's. He placed more emphasis than Coffin had on the role of Governor Carleton in the formulation of the Quebec Act, accepting many of

Carleton's recommendations to the British government as the ultimate rationale for the Act.

We know that the reports were practically pigeon-holed for years and were only considered in relation to practical politics late in 1773. We know that when the Act assumed its final form, almost every legal and expert opinion was rejected, and Carleton's ideas were almost completely incorporated. It is necessary to trace the causes behind these facts....

As early as 1767 he [Guy Carleton] had begun to relate Canada to the world, and to see the strategical position which the province would hold should the southern colonies prove recalcitrant.... While Carleton had his mind fixed on what appeared to him the only vital issue as far as Quebec was concerned, he was informed that the Cabinet was seeking light on a new parliamentary constitution for the province, especially in connection with the blending of laws to satisfy all the inhabitants.... To a mind full of a military situation the Cabinet brought a political problem, and in all the dispatches that follow, that problem is seen through the eyes of a soldier, who anticipated a war in which he and the province over which he presided would play perhaps a decisive part....

... [under the scheme] Canada was to be a military base, held quiet by an endowed church, a vast hinterland, a satisfied *noblesse*, a recognized priesthood, French civil law, and a disciplined and obedient population....

The provisions granted in the Act to the Roman Catholic Church are remarkable, when the legal disabilities in England are recalled. It was a blessing for Canada that the Quebec Act settled the status of the Roman Catholic church and removed it for generations out of that *damnosa haereditas*—religious politics. Had its position been left in the air without a statute behind it, the coming of the United Empire Loyalists might have added another war of religion to the tragedies of history. As it was, the transition to a new constitution was infinitely less complicated....

It is also claimed that the presence of a solid French Canadian group in modern Canada with all its attendant political difficulties can be traced to the folly of the Act. Many political thinkers, quite apart from racial and religious prejudices, believe that a less complete recognition of French-Canadianism in 1774 would have been acceptable to the French Canadians and would have eliminated such problems as are evident today in relation to race, creed and education....

...Quebec has brought essential and vital and characteristic gifts to the life of Canada, and they can be traced to the influence of the Roman Catholic church satisfied in 1774.... One thing is certain, the Quebec Act strengthened the imperial tie, and we may too lightly exaggerate the defects and too lightly appreciate the virtues.

W.P.M. Kennedy, *The Constitution of Canada* (Oxford: Oxford University Press, 1922), pp. 58–9, 64, and 68–70.

An Act of Statesmanship and Practical Politics

Sir Reginald Coupland's study of the Quebec Act, published in 1925, arrived at very different conclusions. Unlike Kennedy, he thought there had been no expedient motives behind the Quebec Act. Instead, he contended that the British had had very little choice but to implement a policy such as that of the Quebec Act because of their obligations under the Treaty of Paris and the

Articles of Capitulation. Although his interpretation agreed with Coffin's up to this point, he parted from his American predecessor by concluding that the Quebec Act had been a factor in keeping French Canada British during the American Revolution. He then expanded upon the implications of the Quebec Act. As an enthusiastic historian of the British Empire, he found in the thinking that led to the Quebec Act a remarkable preview of the policy of toleration and acceptance of diversity which led later to the foundation of the new Commonwealth.

... Did the Quebec Act, like some ghastly injury of childhood, stunt and spoil the future life of Canada?

If the facts of that distant time have been truly stated in this essay, the first answer to such doubts and questions is evident. It is probable, in the highest degree, that, if the policy of the Quebec Act had not been adopted, Canada would have been lost to the British Empire in 1775, and no distinct Canadian nation could ever have come into being.

And the second answer is also clear. The contrary policy—the suppression of French-Canadian nationality—was in its essentials precluded by the terms of the Capitulations and the Treaty of Paris. Apart, moreover, from the antecedent treaty-rights and apart from the subsequent dangers of the American invasion, it is difficult to believe that the policy of suppression was really practicable. The French-Canadians might have been deprived of their law, their Church of its legalized tithes, and their language of all official recognition. But would such measures, would even harsher measures, have succeeded in destroying French-Canadian nationality? .... For nationality is at root a spiritual thing and difficult to kill. Nor was it in New France in 1774 a young and tender growth: the French-Canadians had been rooted there for a century and a half. Nor, again, were they, like the French of Louisiana when it was annexed to the United States, a small minority in a great English-speaking state: the position was precisely the reverse. Under these circumstances, the French-Canadians might have been compelled to obey the English law; but, once the spirit of national revolt had been aroused, no power could have compelled them to speak the English tongue. Nor could penal laws have forced the French-Canadians any more than they could force the Irish, to abjure their faith; and so long as their Church survived, the mainspring of their nationality would have remained unbroken. Forcible fusion; in fact, must have proved if it had ever been adopted, a futile policy....

... only the blackest pessimists can refuse to believe that, in due course of time, Canada will grow into a unity as real and lasting as the unity of Britain. When that day comes, the last doubt as to the statesmanship of the authors of the Quebec Act will have faded away. No one will claim, then or now, that Carleton and North and the rest were gifted with superhuman foresight or inspired by the ideals of a later age. They were only concerned to meet the needs of their own day... but their achievement was greater and more lasting than they knew. For they had acted in accordance with political principles of permanent force and universal application—that, in the long run, the unity of the whole is still the stronger for the diversity of its parts, and that on fidelity to the old, deep loyalties of local or provincial or national life, and only indeed on that sure foundation, can be built, if men are wise and patient, a broader and more general communion of human fellowship and service.

Reginald Coupland, *The Quebec Act* (Oxford: Clarendon Press, 1925), pp. 194–6.

A Charter of French Canadian Rights—Thomas Chapais' View

In his history of Quebec written during the same period, Sir Thomas Chapais, a French Canadian historian at Laval University, also concluded that the Quebec Act set a constitutional precedent, but chose to emphasize its effect in preserving the French Canadian way of life in Quebec. Borrowing a phrase from another Canadian historian, Sir George Bourinot, he described the Quebec Act as a charter of the special characteristics which constitute the foundation of the French Canadian nationality. In Chapais' estimation, the beneficial effects of the Act fulfilled its generous intentions.

[The Quebec Act] marked a critical point, a step forward along the new path in which the mysterious decrees of Providence were directing our destiny. To a régime of uncertainty and of arbitrary rule, there succeeded a régime of familiar law and order. We emerged from a vague condition to assume definite status. We were freed from a precarious toleration and were put in possession of a legal guarantee. For the last ten years we had been struggling against a group, small in numbers but arrogant, who claimed to dominate us by right of conquest. Arbitrating between this group, English in race and Protestant in faith, and us, French in race and Catholic in faith, the English Parliament, whatever may have been its motives and its plan, decided in our favour and proclaimed our rights. For the first time since 1760, it determined by legislation our government and our institutions.... The Quebec Act was perhaps more important for what it implied than for what it decreed. For us it suppressed the Oath of Supremacy; and this necessarily meant that Catholicism was fully recognized and on an equality with official Protestantism. It granted to parish priests the legal right to collect the tithe; and that willy-nilly meant that the Catholic Church was recognized in Canada by the British state. It re-established incontestably our ancient French civil law, because it was better adapted to our outlook, to our principles, our customs and our traditions; this inevitably involved the acknowledged survival of these traditions, customs, manners, and this outlook, essential elements of our French nationality....

A currently accepted opinion is that it had as almost its only determining cause the imminence of the American Revolution and the necessity of satisfying us at all costs in order to ensure our loyalty in an imminent conflict. Does the study which we have just completed together in the course of these last lectures allow us to accept this theory? For my part I do not find it supported by the direct observation of the events. The warning signs of the American crisis may have had some usefulness to our cause, but only as a secondary consideration. Let us not forget that it was only at a later date that England came to believe in the reality of the American danger. The fundamental principles of the Quebec Act were approved by British jurists and ministers long before that danger became apparent.... when we look at the mass of reports, of communications, of confidential notes relating to Canadian affairs and to which we now have access, nothing indicates that that argument had a preponderant influence in the solution adopted, except, perhaps, for the refusal to initiate a legislative assembly.

No, the Quebec Act was due principally to our demands, to the doctrines and principles of natural law and of right professed by the great English jurists.... Finally it was due to the persistent action of one man who, among British officials, could do more than any other to vindicate honour. That man was Carleton. For eight years he pleaded in favour of French law and the ending of religious discrimination. He saw his views adopted and his advice followed. Our victory was his victory.

Thomas Chapais, *Cours d'Histoire du Canada* (Quebec: J.-P. Garneau, 1919), Vol. I, pp. 167–172. trans. Hilda Neatby.

An Economic Historian's Revisionist View

More recent work on the Quebec Act has approached the subject from different perspectives. In his economic history of Quebec from 1760 to 1850, Fernand Ouellet of the University of Ottawa interpreted the motivations of the British in terms of the economic development of the colony after the Conquest. He wrote of the Quebec Act as a reversal of policy after the Proclamation of 1763, a realistic acceptance by the British that Quebec was not going to develop rapidly with a large English immigration, as they had first predicted.

> The Royal Proclamation, it was too often forgotten at the time and since, had not been conceived with the purpose of setting up the rule of a minority over a majority; nor with the view of bringing about, at any price, the subjugation of the French Canadians. The originations of this constitution had believed that thanks to the superior techniques of British business and to a massive immigration from New England, it would be possible in a few years to build in the St. Lawrence Valley a mercantile state peopled by an Anglo-Saxon majority, which would justify the measures taken in 1763. These utopian visions were contradicted by the facts. That is why a radical and rapid reversal of English policy took place....
>
> As the English authorities, through the intervention of Murray and Carleton, came to realize the bankruptcy of their hopes, they abandoned little by little the objectives pursued until then, in order to adopt a new conception of Quebec's future. It was from this angle and because of the steadily increasing tensions between Britain and New England that the personal influence of the governors could be freely exercised. From then on, we witness the disintegration of the Royal Proclamation. Slight economic progress, the scarcity of immigrants, the strong natural increase of the French, and difficulties with New England, such were the fundamental sources of essential sections of the Quebec Act....
>
> If such an interpretation reduces the famous themes of the 'struggle for survival' and the 'miracle of survival and persecution' to insignificance, at the same time it illustrates the realism of British policy. This policy did not lead a crusade; it was, while reserving fleeting notions of assimilation, above all sensitive to the realities of the situation. By supporting themselves with these facts, Murray and Carleton were able to get their point of view accepted, and thus to work to perpetuate Quebec's traditional society in opposition to the 'mercantile spirit'. Throughout this period, the bourgeoisie did not enjoy governmental favour; it was in opposition. In the eyes of the leaders in London, it was not yet of a size or economic importance to deserve preferred treatment, indeed, any equality whatsoever. This helps explain the social tensions of the time.
>
> The weight of the sentiments and opinions of the British régime's first governors on the Colonial Office has been grossly exaggerated. If we believe our historiography, the French Canadians, at odds with the vexatious policy of 1763, found in Murray and Carleton almost providential heralds. Because it fails to take into account the *conjoncture* of this period, this interpretation belongs to the realm of poetic fantasy. Can we believe that the program of 1763 would have been so quickly abandoned if economic growth had been rapid, if there had been a massive immigration into the province, and if there had been no American threat? Between 1763 and 1768, the overall development of Quebec took such a form that the original policy would have seemed incomprehensible even to those who had fashioned it....
>
> ... in Canada and England the government leaders of that time were clearly aware of the real trends of Quebec's evolution. The presence of Murray and Carleton in the colony, however, helped the British leaders to gain insight into the Canadian problem.

Without them, the realization would have come later. But with them and without the basic *conjoncture*, the program of 1763 would have prevailed.

Fernand Ouellet, *Economic and Social History of Quebec, 1760–1850* (Toronto: Macmillan, 1980) pp. 95–7

A Continuation of—Not A Radical Departure From—British Practice

Dr. Hilda Neatby of the University of Saskatchewan studied the Quebec Act more closely than any other historian in recent years. In her conclusions she disagreed with Ouellet concerning the importance of the Royal Proclamation. She saw it instead as a measure passed for a group of colonies which did not particularly apply to Quebec and was never seriously acted upon. Nor did she perceive the Quebec Act as a radical new policy for Quebec. In the concluding chapter of *The Quebec Act: Protest and Policy*, published in 1972, she argued that the Quebec Act simply recognized unofficial British policies that had developed over the years since the Conquest. If it had not been for the provisions expanding the borders of the province, she claimed, the Quebec Act would never have become very controversial.

Britain, after 1763, was faced with two problems inextricably entangled with one another, but in their nature distinct. One was the disposition of the Ohio country (where the local war had started in 1754) and the development of just and peaceful relations with the Indian peoples living there. The other was the determination of a mode of government consistent with the general law and practice of the British Empire, for a former French colony. The second problem was undoubtedly difficult, but the main lines of the settlement had already been sketched in the Articles of Capitulation and in the Peace Treaty. All that was needed was to apply the principles agreed on consistently with the general law of the British Empire....

It can be said...that the continuation of much of Canadian civil law was never seriously threatened. Although the Proclamation of 1763 appeared to contemplate a change, any such intention was repudiated by British ministers, and condemned by Britain's law officers. The evidence indicates that no legislation by the British Parliament was needed, and that none would have been passed, but for the apparent blunder of the Proclamation in promising to confide legislative power to a hypothetical assembly which in the circumstances could hardly be summoned....

In fact the Quebec Act recognized a situation already universally accepted....

It may therefore be said that the essential concessions of law and religious freedom could be and were claimed under the capitulations. Apart from a constitutional technicality, the continuation of Canadian law could have been assured without any Parliamentary statute; and the Act, while enforcing, perhaps unnecessarily, the tithe, and providing in the instructions a salary for the 'Superintendent,' provided in the same instructions orders which can only be called harassing and degrading to the Church. If the Quebec Act was a charter for Canadians, like some other charters it may be said only to have confirmed, and with some restrictions, what had already been conceded in practice.

One important exception must be noted to this statement. The granting of civil equality to Canadians by instituting a new oath of office which Roman Catholics were at liberty to take removed a degrading distinction. Even this, however, important as it was, was an application and an extension of the principle enunciated by the law officers in 1765 when they stated that Roman Catholics in colonies abroad ceded to the King were not subject to the disabilities imposed on Roman Catholics in the United Kingdom. Presumably, therefore, without a statute the Governor might have been authorized to admit Canadians to office on condition of their taking a modified oath.

The main function of the Quebec Act so far as the Canadian community was concerned was to provide for a legislative body other than the promised assembly. Had an assembly been given it could not have been one from which Roman Catholics were excluded, as they must have been, had the usual colonial pattern been followed. The authorities, as was shown by the plan of 1769, were willing to experiment, but by 1773 they had decided that the risks from ignorance, inexperience, and 'turbulence' were too great.... Some years later they did get an assembly—and there is good reason for thinking that for all the talk of the seigneurial party about the Quebec Act, most politically-minded Canadians dated their 'charter' from 1791 rather than from 1774.

So much for those parts of the Quebec Act that applied specifically to the internal affairs of the conquered French colony. Had the Act, or the British authorities without an Act, done no more than this, there would have been little controversy....

What made the Act a centre of the most violent and continued controversy was the geographical, economic and historic connection of the St. Lawrence community with the Ohio country which inspired the boundary clause; and the coincidence in time of the evolution of a policy for the newly-conquered colony with the upsurge of revolutionary activity in the older colonies on the Atlantic coast.

Hilda Neatby, *The Quebec Act: Protest and Policy* (Scarborough: Prentice-Hall, 1972), pp. 137–8, 140–1.

A Guide to Further Reading

1. Overviews

Burt, A.L., *The Old Province of Quebec*. Minneapolis: University of Minnesota Press, 1933.
Creighton, D.G., *The Empire of the St. Lawrence*. Toronto: Macmillan, 1956.
Lanctôt, Gustave, *Canada and the American Revolution 1774–1783*. Toronto: Clarke Irwin, 1967.
Neatby, Hilda, *The Quebec Act: Protest and Policy*. Scarborough: Prentice Hall, 1972.
_____, *Quebec: The Revolutionary Age, 1760–1791*. Toronto: McClelland and Stewart, 1966.
Trofimenkoff, Susan M., *The Dream of Nation: A Social and Intellectual History of Quebec*. Montreal: Macmillan, 1982.

2. Specialized Studies

Brunet, Michel, *Les Canadiens après la Conquête*. Montreal: Fides, 1969.
_____, *French Canada and the Early Decades of British Rule, 1760–1791*. Canadian Historical Association Booklet No. 13. Ottawa: CHA, 1968.
Burt, A.L. *Guy Carleton, Lord Dorchester, 1724–1808*. Canadian Historical Association Booklet No. 5, Ottawa: CHA, 1960.
Chapais, Thomas, *Cours d'Histoire du Canada*, Vol. I. Quebec: J.-P. Garneau, 1919.
Coffin, Victor, *The Province of Quebec and the Early American Revolution*. Madison: Bulletin of the University of Wisconsin, 1896.
Coupland, Reginald, *The Quebec Act: A Study in Statesmanship*. Oxford: Clarendon Press, 1925.

Editions Fides, 1966.

Rawlyk, George A., *Revolution Rejected 1775–1776*. Scarborough: Prentice-Hall, 1968.

Reynolds, Paul R., *Guy Carleton: A Biography*. Toronto: Gage, 1980.

6

REVOLUTION REJECTED

Why did Nova Scotia Fail to Join the American Revolution?

During the American War of Independence, from 1776 to 1783, most people in the scattered British-American colonies which are now a part of Canada chose not to become American republican revolutionaries. In the case of Quebec, the timely passage of the Quebec Act (1774) and a basic fear of change helped to secure the loyalty of most *Canadiens*, who rejected an appeal from the Continental Congress to become the "fourteenth colony". In Ile-St-Jean (later Prince Edward Island), inhabited by a tiny, isolated population of some 1 000 recent British immigrants and Acadians, the Revolution had little appeal. In Newfoundland, the bulk of the small Anglo-Irish population engaged in fishing remained strongly oriented toward Britain, the centre of their Atlantic trade. Yet, in Nova Scotia the decision whether or not to join the Revolution proved more difficult. Of Nova Scotia's 17 000 to 20 000 settlers in 1775, some three fifths were New Englanders, who might be expected to have strong economic and family ties with the New England colonies. Much more than Quebec and the other British-American colonies, Nova Scotia resembled a northern outpost of New England. Thus, Nova Scotia's refusal to join in the revolutionary struggle seemed most puzzling.

Nova Scotia's response to the American Revolution has long intrigued historians, especially American scholars, who have seen the colony as merely a northern extension of New England. Traditionally, Nova Scotia's "neutrality" in the revolutionary period has been explained by the strong British naval and commercial presence at Halifax, by the colony's geographic position jutting out into the British-controlled Atlantic ocean, and by the flexibility of British colonial rule during the period of crisis. More recently, however, historical studies have begun to challenge this standard interpretation by calling attention to the role of religious influences on most Nova Scotians to accept neutrality. Some scholars now contend that many Nova Scotia "Yankees", who had emigrated from New England before 1765, never experienced the later American revolutionary fervour, and, further, that a so-called "Great Awakening" sparked by the "New Light" evangelism of Henry Alline acted to channel much of the colony's social protest into a "revolutionary" religious revival.

By the outbreak of the American Revolution Nova Scotia was not merely a New England Yankee colony. For the influx of Yankee fishermen and farmers to the colony—which in the 1770s consisted of all of present-day New Brunswick and Nova Scotia—had virtually come to an end, and an outflow back to New England had begun. Immigration from Great Britain, however, continued and even expanded. As a result, a little more than 750 Yorkshire settlers, some destitute Scots and some Irish Roman Catholics had entered the colony before the outbreak of the Revolution and substantially strengthened the non-Yankee element of the population. Of an estimated total population of twenty thousand, only approximately 60 percent was of New England origin. Nova Scotia, therefore, was not a homogeneous New England colony. Indeed, the name was little more than a political expression for a number of widely scattered and isolated communities stretching from what is now the Maine-New Brunswick border to the northernmost extremity of Cape Breton Island, to Yarmouth at the southeast corner of the province.

During the Revolutionary decade, there were at least two distinct Nova Scotias, Halifax and the outer settlements. Halifax was the chief seaport, the colony's seat of government, and the site of a large British naval and military base. Although Halifax's naval establishment engendered a healthy respect for British authority, and its military and governmental personnel provided much of the specie that circulated in the colony, the actual influence of the capital may not have extended much beyond the surrounding Bedford Basin region. Not surprisingly, it was in Halifax that pro-British and anti-revolutionary sentiment found its strongest expression.

The outer settlements were populated largely by Nova Scotia Yankee settlers, except for pockets of British and German Protestant immigrants in the regions of Chignecto-Minas Bay, Pictou, and Lunenburg. The Yankee inhabitants of the coastal strip of the southern half of peninsular Nova Scotia and of the valley of the St. John River had strong cultural and economic ties with their former homeland. They also were sullenly suspicious of the small clique of Halifax merchants who controlled the legislative and executive functions of government and who attempted to impose central control over the isolated townships. Consequently, when the revolutionary crisis engulfed North America, the Halifax authorities, not without reason, expected their so-called "bitter bad subjects" to flock to the American side.

Only in the two western frontier settlements of Maugerville, near present-day Fredericton, and Cumberland, near Sackville, New Brunswick, was there any noteworthy indigenous revolutionary activity. And the so-called "contagion of disaffection" afflicted merely a minority of the population of these two regions and only for a period of a few months in 1776. Pressed between the millstones of contending forces, most of the Chignecto and St. John River Yankees, like those New Englanders in other areas of Nova Scotia, did not at that moment want to commit themselves to one side or to the other. They would patiently wait, aloof from the conflict, until they were either "liberated" by the Americans or absolutely certain that the British would retain effective control of Nova Scotia.

Most other Nova Scotians shared the basic vacillation of the so-called "Yankee response". In a very real sense the essence of Nova Scotia's response to the Revolution was acute confusion. The activities of American privateers and British press-gangs merely added to the existing chaos. Almost every Nova Scotian settlement, with the exception of Halifax, was ravaged by American privateersmen. This was indeed a strange way to make American converts of Nova Scotians. Meanwhile, large numbers of Nova Scotians were either impressed or threatened by British impressment. This, in turn, was a strange way to persuade Nova Scotians to remain loyal to the British crown.

Nova Scotia's behaviour and experience during the revolutionary period was further complicated by the occurrence of an intense religious revival amid the chaos and confusion of war. This "Great Awakening", as it came to be called, was led by a charismatic young Nova Scotian farmer and tanner,

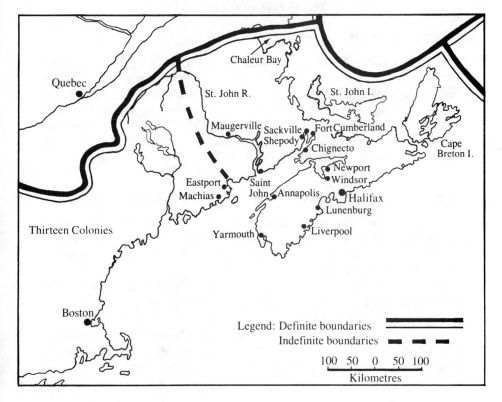

Nova Scotia and the American Revolutionary War, 1775–76

Henry Alline. It has been argued that this social movement, growing out of feelings of insecurity and acute disorientation, diverted potential revolutionary ardour into a struggle for religious reorganization, and even generated among Nova Scotians a sense of themselves as a unique people with their own identity and destiny before the arrival of the United Empire Loyalists in the post-revolutionary years.

A few essential questions arise concerning Nova Scotia's position of neutrality during the American Revolution. Why did so many Nova Scotians refuse to endorse the American bid for "life, liberty and the pursuit of happiness" and join in the revolutionary cause? Did the British naval presence and their relative isolation from the Thirteen Colonies serve as a deterrent? Were they asserting an attachment to British ideals of "peace, order and good government"? Or were they conditioned to "neutrality" by confusion, and a complete breakdown in their system of loyalties? Did Nova Scotia Yankees (who had mostly arrived in the colony before 1765) "miss" a crucial decade of revolutionary ferment in the thirteen American colonies? And can the religious revival inspired by Henry Alline explain the enigmatic response of most Nova Scotians to the Revolution?

SELECTED CONTEMPORARY SOURCES

THREE VIEWS OF THE REVOLUTION

The American War of Independence evoked a variety of responses from the pre-Loyalist Nova Scotia population, divided as the people were between Halifax and the outer settlements, and from one isolated community to another. Out of the range of colonial opinion, however, three main viewpoints can be discerned in the "Critical Years", 1775–76. Each view drew its support from a different locality and urged Nova Scotians to pursue a different course of action in the revolutionary period.

The Call to Join "The Cause"—Responses of Western Nova Scotians, 1776

Pro-revolutionary sentiment emanated largely from a small but vociferous minority residing in the Chignecto and Maugerville areas, parts of the western section of the colony. Those "hearty in the cause" regarded themselves as Americans and were especially critical of British authorities in Halifax. Some supporters of the American Revolution demanded to be liberated by General George Washington, the colonial commander who would later become first President of the United States. Two separate documents—a written appeal to Washington from an anonymous Chignecto region inhabitant in February 1776, and a set of resolutions from the Maugerville inhabitants dated May 1776—both express strong support for the revolutionary movement.

Anonymous Letter to General George Washington, February 8, 1776

The great contest between *Britain* and *America* has hitherto been only treated with speculation amongst us. A spirit of sympathy, I presume, for our brethren on the Continent, reigns in the breasts of the generality of the inhabitants. With gladness and cheerfulness would we be active in the glorious struggle, had our situation and circumstances been any way such that there was the least glimpse of success; but our remoteness from the other Colonies, and our form of Government, joined with the indigent circumstances of the inhabitants, render it in a manner impossible, without succour from some other quarter.... the rulers in Government [have laid]...certain restraints on the people....

A bill was passed for raising a regiment by ballot; and another for raising a tax to support them. The preamble to the latter was such, that, in my view, it carried the greatest implication of a declaration of war against the Colonies. This flagrant proof of the intention of these miscreants roused a spirit among the people, and publick declarations were made which before were not heard. Some were immediately for applying to your Excellency. Business was entirely stagnated. Nothing to be heard but war—this Country in particular. The inhabitants being called to appear by the Commanding Officer of Militia, they complied with the order; and, when met, they all, to a man, charged the officers, on their peril, to draw a person. The inhabitants then agreed that an Address, Remonstrance, and Petition, be sent to the Governour, praying his suspending the execution of said acts, and to dissolve the House of Assembly, and call a new one to meet immediately. The Governour gave no other answer than ordering the officers of Militia and tax-gatherers to desist, for the present, the putting the acts into execution....

...The straggling manner in which people have settled this new country makes it very difficult, and, in a manner, almost impossible for them to act either offensively or defensively. The people, in general, have great families, which will occasion a lamentable scene should *British* Troops arrive here before any succour comes from your Excellency. We would greatly rejoice could we be able to join with the other Colonies; but we must have other assistance before we can act publickly. I would observe to your Excellency, concerning the *Acadians*, I have dwelt among them near six-and-twenty years. I am well acquainted with their manners and ways. I have taken great pains in conversing with them concerning their commotions. They are, to a man, wholly inclined to the cause of *America*. I have often pitied them in their situation, and the manner of proceedings against them from time to time....

Peter Force, *American Archives*, Fourth Series (Washington: 1844), Vol. 5, pp. 936–938.

Resolutions of the Maugerville Inhabitants, May, 1776

1stly Resolved. That we can see no shadow of Justice in that Extensive Claim of the British Parliment (viz) the Right to Enacting Laws binding on the Colonies in all Cases whatsoever. This System if once Established (we Conceive) hath a Direct tendency to Sap the foundation, not only of Liberty that Dearest of names, but of property that best of subjects.

2ndly Resolved. That as tyrany ought to be Resisted in its first appearance we are Convinced that the united Provinces are just in their proceedings in this Regard.

3rdly Resolved. That it is our Minds and Desire to submit ourselves to the government of the Massachusetts Bay and that we are Ready with our Lives and fortunes to Share with them the Event of the present Struggle for Liberty, however God in his Providence may order it.

4ly Resolved. That a Committee be Chosen to Consist of twelve Men who shall Immediately make application to the Massachusetts Congress or general assembly for Relief....

5ly Resolved: That we and Each of us will most strictly adhere to all such measures as our S[ai]d Committee or the Major Part of them shall from time to time prescribe for our Conduct and that we will support and Defend them in this Matter at the Expence of our Lives and fortunes if Called thereto.

6ly Resolved. That we will Immediately put ourselves in the best posture of Defence in our power, that to this End we will prevent all unnecessary use of gun Powder or other ammunition in our Custody.

7ly Resolved. That if any of us shall hereafter, Know of any person or persons that shall by any ways or means Endeavour to prevent or Counteract this our Design, we will Immediately give notice thereof to the Committee that proper Measures may be taken for our Safety.

8ly Resolved.... we will share in and submit to the Event of this undertaking however it may terminate, to the true performance of all which we bind and obligate ourselves firmly each to other on penalty of being Esteemed Enemies and traitors to our Country and Submitting ourselves to popular Resentment.

F. Kidder, *Military Operations in Eastern Maine and Nova Scotia During the Revolution* (Albany: J. Munsell, 1867), pp. 64–65.

A Call to British Loyalty—The Voice of the Pro-British Element, 1776

A second body of opinion in the colony was that of the pro-British element. Although Nova Scotia was virtually New England's northeastern frontier and populated largely by former Yankees, British, German and French-born citizens formed a significant minority of the population. For some of these Nova Scotians, the American sympathizers seemed utterly rash and irresponsible, needlessly "disturbing the peace". A sharply worded letter to the editor of a Halifax newspaper, dated September 10, 1776, clearly expressed their views.

...The Demagogues, which raised this disturbance, are a motley crew of hungry lawyers, men of broken fortunes, young persons eager to push themselves in the world, others, gentlemen of opulence, vain & blustering—Amongst this medley there are several of good party, and great reading, but withal little versed in the complicated interests, and springs, which move the great political world, because untutored in the Courts of Europe, where alone that science is to be acquired—These could not miss perceiving the growing importance, as they call it, of America, and what she might one day arrive to: so far indeed they judged with propriety, if they would only give time, and leave her to herself; but the greatness of the object dazzled the eyes of their understanding; and they began to think Empire, without considering the infant state of their country, how much it is [in] want of every requisite for war, what a mighty nation they have to contend with, & that the united interest of every other nation in Europe likewise forbids their being anything more than dependent colonies—However, as if envying their prosperity, they hastened to bring on the great and glorious day, which would hail them masters of a quarter of the globe; and set up claims which, they thought, would either place them in that elevated station or in one more suitable to their present condition viz. to make the Mother Country drudge and slave to support, and protect them, for yet a while longer, without contributing a farthing more towards that expence that they should think proper. . . .

The menaces of the Americans to run to arms, their violent proceedings in the first stage of the insurrection, their levying troops, which every where belongs to the executive branch, so notoriously. . . their collecting warlike weapons . . . were all such strong acts of rebellion as no government could put up with, it destroyed the merits of their cause, were it otherwise good . . . .

Had they acted in a moderate, dutiful, and justifiable manner, like subjects averse to break with their Sovereign, like men, who even in their own cause wished only for material justice, and not actuated by any indirect views but by the force of the principles, they protested; there is no doubt but whatever appeared to them harsh and dangerous, in the claims of Great Britain, would have been departed from, and matters settled on the basis of indulgence to the Colonies, and justice to the Mother country. But his Majesty's Paternal voice was bar'd access to his beloved subject; He could not treat with them, but thro' the false, and villainous medium of the proud demonogues, who paid no regard to truth, to loyalty, to peace or justice . . . .

Nova Scotia Gazette and the Weekly Chronicle, September 10, 1776. Modern spelling has been used to clarify the meaning of the letter.

An Appeal for Peace and Safety—The Position of the "Neutral New Englanders", 1775

A completely different viewpoint was that expressed by Nova Scotia's New Englanders who favoured steering a course of neutrality. This "neutral Yankee" view found its strongest support in what is now western Nova Scotia, as well as in the Yarmouth region and among settlers who had family, friends or relatives still living in the Thirteen Colonies. For the most part, they were not willing to fight against their relations in New England nor were they eager to participate actively in the revolutionary cause against their beloved monarch, George III. They wanted to be certain in which direction the bandwagon was rolling before they jumped on it. Until that time they were content to remain neutral even though their basic sympathies probably lay with the rebels. Such instinctive loyalties, however, were tempered by the practical considerations that came from living in the shadow of a British naval base and on a maritime peninsula removed from the main theatre of war.

Torn by contending loyalties, most New Englanders in Nova Scotia seemed to want simply to be left alone. Their point of view can best be seen in two oft-quoted petitions from the Yarmouth area and the Amherst-Sackville region:

We do all of us profess to be true Friends & Loyal Subjects to George our King. We were almost all of us born in New England, we have Fathers, Brothers & Sisters in that Country, divided betwixt natural affection to our nearest relations, and good Faith and Friendship to our King and Country, we want to know, if we may be permitted at this time to live in a peaceable State, as we look on that to be the only situation in which we with our Wives and Children, can be in any tolerable degree safe....

P.A.C., Nova Scotia Series A, Vol. 94, Memorial of the Inhabitants of Yarmouth, December 8, 1775, p. 300.

The dispute arising between Great Britain and her Colonies has no way reached this quarter nor can we find any grounds of complaint wherein any act[s] of violence have been committed...nor are we any ways apprehensive of any danger...except this Militia Bill is enforced. Those of us who belong to New England, being invited into the Province by Governor Lawrence's Proclamation it must be the greatest piece of cruelty and imposition for them to be subjected to march into different parts in Arms against their friends and relations. Still should any person or persons presume to molest us in our present situation, we are always ready to defend ourselves and property.

Public Archives of Nova Scotia, Vol. 364, The Inhabitants of Cumberland to Governor Legge, December 23, 1775.

THE INFLUENCE OF STRATEGIC AND PRACTICAL CONSIDERATIONS

A variety of strategic and practical considerations weighed heavily in determining the responses of both Nova Scotians and the American revolutionary leaders to proposals for involving the colony in the Revolution. From the outset of the War of Independence, the colony's rather insular position and its formidable British naval establishment served as a practical deterrent to actions of either "liberation" from British rule or overt military support for the revolutionary cause. Although the Government at Halifax did attempt to raise a militia and levy a tax for its support, British authorities did not make an issue of the matter, and showed some flexibility in acceding to the demands of the Halifax merchant class for the recall of an unpopular colonial governor, Francis Legge. For some Nova Scotians, notably the Halifax merchants, neutrality had its economic benefits in the form of increased trade with the British forces, supplemented by some illicit commerce with the rebel colonies. Whatever the factors, most Nova Scotians stayed neutral during the Revolution. Aside from a series of raids on British provision ships and forts on the Bay of Fundy, and some privateering by sea, only a small band of inhabitants came out openly on the side of the Revolution in a short-lived 1776 uprising at Fort Cumberland on the Isthmus of Chignecto.

The British Naval Deterrent—General George Washington's View, 1775

General Washington's official response to a daring plan for an American invasion of Nova Scotia in August 1775 provided a prime example of the daunting effect exerted by the Halifax garrison and British sea power. In ruling out the risky venture, Washington set out the strategic military considerations.

It might, perhaps, be easy, with the Force proposed to make an Incurrence into the

Province and overawe those of the Inhabitants who are Inimical to our cause; and, for a short time prevent the Supplying The Enemy with Provisions; but the same Force must Continue to produce any lasting Effects. As to the furnishing Vessels of Force, you, Gentn, will anticipate me in pointing out our Weakness and the Enemy's Strength at Sea. There would be great Danger that, with the best preparation we could make, they would fall an easy prey either to the Men of War on that Station, or someone who would be detach'd from Boston... our Situation as to Ammunition absolutely forbids our sending a single ounce out of the Camp at present.

General George Washington to Committee of the Massachusetts Legislature, August 11, 1775, cited in J.B. Brebner, *The Neutral Yankees of Nova Scotia* (Toronto: McClelland and Stewart, 1969), p. 281.

Dependence on British Protection—Two Observations on the Impact of Privateering

Many Nova Scotians seemed strangely ambivalent in their attitudes to the Americans. Some settlers actively helped American privateers and prisoners escape from British authorities, while at the same time fearing and resenting the disturbances caused by plundering raids and threats of invasion. Faced with the prospect of American aggression, however, most settlers had no option but to turn to the British authorities for protection.

Two prominent Nova Scotians, the Reverend Jonathan Scott, a Congregational Church minister in the Yarmouth area, and Simeon Perkins, a native of Connecticut and leading merchant at Liverpool, Nova Scotia, offered these observations on the impact of American privateering on their respective communities.

Wednesday, November ye 29, 1775. ... some of the Company went on Board two Vessels that had just come into the Harbour, and in about an Hour there came a number of armed Men from the Vessels, headed by Nathan Brown, and entered into Esq. Durkee's House, and took from thence, Capt. Jeremiah Allen, Capt. Hebard, Lieut. Brown, and Nehemiah Porter Clark, and carried them all on board the Vessels; without any Resistance, there being no Power sufficient to relieve these who were Apprehended: this happened about 3 o Clock P.M. In the Evening following, a number of men from the same Vessels, came to Jebogue and took my brother David Scott, (a Lieutenant in the Infantry Company, who did not meet with the Officers at Esq. Durkee's, because he had been Sick, and was not recovered so as to be able to go so far) and took him and carried him on board the same Night.

Upon enquiry into this sudden and alarming Affair, it was made to appear, that the two Vessels were from New-England, Armed Schooners, mounting eight carriage Guns each, and a number of Swivels, and full Man'd; and came out with a design to oppose all that they took to be their Enemies: and having been in to Barrington, and there got intelligence (from some of our own people who were there) that there was this new Establishment, and that this was the Day in which they were to be Imbodied, they made all possible Speed, and got here at the nick of Time when the Officers were met, and took them without any previous Notice.

The unfortunate Sufferers were not suffered to come ashore to see their Families, tho' the Vessels tarried Friday towards night: but what appeared most Unnatural and

Barbarous was, that most people seemed Glad at the Calamity of the Sufferers; and looked upon it a good Providence, because thereby the Infantry Company was like to be broken up...

Henry E. Scott, Jr., ed. *The Journal of the Reverend Jonathan Scott* (New England Historic Genealogical Society: 1980), pp. 70–72.

Liverpool, Thursday, June 4th,—Cloudy, and some rain, and foggy. A small Privateer comes into the Harbour, early in the morning, and halls along side the wreck of the French Ship. We hear a report that a Malagash schooner was retaken by some Dutchmen yesterday, at Port matoon, and also hear the Blonde has three privateers stroped in at the Ragged Islands, and the Aburthnot two stroped in at Port Roseway. I hear some of the Privateers men, that belonged to the retaken Schooner, are in Town. We double the Guard on acct. of the Privateers being in the Harbour, and the said Men on shore.

Fryday, June 5th,—Rains, and foggy. The Privateer still remains at ye wreck, and I understand towards night, that Seth Freeman and John Kinney are entered on board her. She has thrown out her ballast, and is loading with iron. I understand it is the same Privateer that carried Ebenezer Herrington to New England.

Satterday, June 6th,—Still continues rainy and foggy. The Privateer remains in the Harbour, at ye wreck. Capt. Cole sails. H. Collins goes with him. I hear they carry some guns and other things out of ye wreck.

Sunday, June 7th,—Wind continues easterly, and clears a little. The Privateer goes out this forenoon, about ten or eleven o'clock, having layed by the wreck (and got loaded with iron,) this three days and nights, none of the King's Cruisers appearing to disturb her. Thus our coast is guarded after all the Promises we have had from Government. Our people are much Discouraged, and seem to be looking out to leave the place. Two young men are entered on board the Privateer, or gone in her, viz: Seth Freeman and John Kinney. Rob. Doliver, and Joseph Virge gone with Cole.

Harold A. Innis, ed. *The Diary of Simeon Perkins, 1766–1780* (Toronto: Champlain Society, 1948), pp. 202–23.

The Commercial Advantages of Neutrality—A Governor's View of the Loyalties of Nova Scotians, 1776

Material incentive and the prospect of war profits secured the vocal support and loyalty of some Nova Scotians, and particularly of those in the Halifax merchant class. The colony's principal role from 1774 to 1776 was to supply the British with all kinds of provisions from beef, barley and flour to flaxseed. And not surprisingly, most Halifax merchants (and some in the more distant areas) responded to the demand for provisions with zest. Dependent upon the British navy for protection and respectful of it as well, many merchants, the so-called "substantial people", resolved to remain in Halifax, to supply the British troops, and to reap the handsome profits. Although evidence of the merchants' motives remains sketchy, Lieutenant-Governor Mariot Arbuthnot, who succeeded Legge in 1776, did see loyalty among the "wealthy people" and restiveness among the New Englanders.

...the truth is My Lord the wealthy people in general are loyal, the sectaries [the Yankees] are not so, nor ever will until their clergy are under some control...the New England people...are bitter bad subjects....

Public Archives of Nova Scotia (P.A.N.S.), Vol. 45, Lieutenant-Governor Arbuthnot to Lord George Germain, December 31, 1776.

THE INFLUENCE OF NOVA SCOTIA'S "GREAT AWAKENING"

While the American War of Independence was being fought in the colonies to the south, Nova Scotia was experiencing its own "Great Awakening". At the centre of this religious revival was Henry Alline, a Nova Scotia farmer turned "New Light" preacher. After undergoing an emotional conversion in March 1775 at the age of twenty-seven, Alline turned to preaching and seemed to ignite a great religious revival that swept the colony during and after the American revolutionary war. To the extent that the Revolution fostered popular anxieties, it has been argued that Alline's personal vision of evangelical Christianity appealed to confused, disoriented Nova Scotians seeking some peace of mind amid the uncertainties of war. How much influence this religious revival had on the behaviour of Nova Scotians in the revolutionary decade is a critical point at issue.

The Dawn of the "Great Awakening"—Henry Alline's Account of His Religious Conversion, 1775

Henry Alline's own description of his religious conversion gave some indication of the depth of feeling generated by the evangelical movement among its adherents. His was not the first conversion to "New Light" Christianity, and it was an experience destined to be repeated by hundreds of other Nova Scotians during the Revolution.

These discoveries continued until I went into the house and sat down, which was but a short time, though I saw more than I could express or had seen for some time.... Being almost in an agony, I turned very suddenly round in my chair and seeing part of an old bible laying in one of the chairs, I caught hold of it in great haste; and opening it without any premeditation, cast my eyes on the 38th Psalm, which was the first time I ever saw the word of God: it took hold of me with such power, that it seemed to go through my whole soul, and read therein every thought of my heart, and raised my whole soul with groans and earnest cries to God, so that it seemed as if God was praying in, with, and for me. This so affected me, that I could not refrain from tears, and was obliged to close the book.... At the same time I could not bear the thoughts of falling short, but hungered, thirsted and longed after God and his love. O help me, help me, cried I, thou Redeemer of souls, and save me or I am gone for ever, and the last word I ever mentioned in my distress (for the change was instantaneous) was, O Lord Jesus Christ, thou canst this night, if thou pleasest, with one drop of thy blood atone for my sins, and appease the wrath of an angry God.... At that instant of time when I gave up all to him, to do with me, as he pleased, and was willing that God should reign in me and rule over me at his pleasure: redeeming love broke into my soul with repeated scriptures with such power, that my whole soul seemed to be melted down with love; the burden of guilt and condemnation was gone, darkness was expelled, my heart humbled and filled with gratitude, and my will turned of choice after the infinite God, whom I saw I had rebelled against, and been deserting from all my days. Attracted by the love and beauty I saw in his divine perfections, my whole soul was inexpressibly ravished with the blessed Redeemer, not with what I expected to enjoy after death or in heaven, but with what I now enjoyed in my soul: for my whole soul seemed filled with the divine being. My whole soul, that was a few minutes ago groaning under mountains of death, wading through storms of sorrow, racked with distressing fears, and crying to an unknown God for help, was now filled with immortal love, soaring on the wings of faith, freed from the chains of death and darkness, and crying out my Lord and my God; thou art my rock and my fortress, my shield and my high tower, [Ps. 18:2] my life, my joy, my present and my everlasting portion.

Henry Alline, *Life and Journal of the Rev. Mr. Henry Alline* (Boston: 1806), pp. 33–35.

Awakening the Christians—Alline's Recollections on the Revival, 1776–78

Beginning in April 1776, Alline launched a public preaching campaign which over the next two years took him to almost every settlement in the Minas Basin, farther afield to the Annapolis Valley, and to the town of Annapolis itself. In April 1779, after being ordained by his followers as an itinerant preacher, he journeyed to all areas of pre-Loyalist Nova Scotia. Such an astute observer as Simeon Perkins could only compare the effect of Alline's charismatic preaching to the "Great Awakening" that had stirred the New England colonies in the late 1730s and early 1740s. A few selected excerpts from Alline's own journal give an indication of the religious fervour that he aroused in the first two years of his preaching.

April (1776)

It being reported at this time that Henry Alline was turned New-Light preacher, many would come from other towns, even whole boat-loads. Some came to hear what the babler had to say; some came with gladness of heart that God had raised up one to speak in his name; and some come to make a scoff, but it did not seem to trouble me much; for I trust God was with me and supported and enabled me to face a frowning world....

In July 1776, I was invited by one Joseph Bailey to preach at his house at Newport. I accordingly went over, and found a great number of people attending: God gave me great boldness and freedom of speech in declaring the wonders of redeeming love: and although many came to watch for my halting, yet they seemed to be struck with awe, and some of the christians after meeting gave me the hand of fellowship....

November 3d, [1776]. As I was invited to Horton, I preached there two sermons on the Sabbath-day, which seemed to have much effect, and gained the attention of the people. I was desired to preach again in the evening, which I did, and the Lord was there. It was a strange thing to see a young man, who had often been there a frolicking now preaching the everlasting gospel. The people seemed to have hearing ears, and it left a solemn sense on some youths. I remained there till Tuesday evening and preached again; when there was such a throng of hearers, that the house could not contain them; and some of them were that evening convicted with power....

February (1777)

...I went to Newport, and being in haste, preached there but two sermons, and then returned to Falmouth, where I remained until the 15th of February. The christians seemed revived, and some sinners under a load of sin inquiring after salvation. I then rode to Horton, and preached there, and found the Lord kind to me beyond all expression. O that I could continually live to his praise. I then went to Cornwallis, and got there in the evening; but as they had heard of my coming, there was a great throng of people that attended, and there began now to be a considerable work in the town....
I went from Cornwallis again to Falmouth and Newport, and preached every day, for there seemed to be a thirst for the word....

August the 14th [1777]. I set out with a young man, who came for me to go again to Annapolis. I rode through all the county of Annapolis, preached night and day, and visiting the people, found the work of God increasing; some souls born to Christ rejoicing in the Redeemer's love, and others having no rest night nor day; but groaning under a sense of their condition.... I preached so often and rode so much, that sometimes I would seem almost worn out; and yet in a few hours would be so refreshed, that I could labour again for twelve hours in discoursing, praying, preaching and exhorting, and feel strong on my lungs....

September (1778)

After I had seen, preached to, and conversed with all the societies in the country, I returned to Cornwallis.... Nothing was scarcely talked of now among numbers where I preached but religion. Wherever they met, their language was the language of Zion, and telling what they had enjoyed. I then rode to Horton where I saw the work of God among his children. The day following I rode with 9 or 10 to Falmouth to meet the christians there, and to commune with them; and thus the Lord increased the numbers and boldness of his children. The christians at Falmouth seemed at first to be but weak, and few in number, but were now increased in gifts, graces and numbers. O the happy days that we enjoyed, while anti-christ was raging all around us, and said that we were all under a delusion....

Henry Alline, *Life and Journal*, pp. 47–49, 51, 58, 60, 66.

Revival and Reaction—An Appeal from the Residents of Cornwallis, 1778

Not all people in pre-Loyalist Nova Scotia joined in the Alline revival. The charismatic preacher won most of his converts from the Congregational Church, representing the great majority of former New Englanders. While Alline was well received by the Methodists (mostly Yorkshire settlers), he made little headway in converting Presbyterians of Scotch-Irish stock. The fiercest resistance of all, however, came from defenders of the old Congregational doctrines and institutional practices.

Alline's principal antagonist was Reverend Jonathan Scott, pastor of the Congregational Church of Jebogue near present-day Yarmouth. The surviving church records reveal that Scott was extremely alarmed over Alline's theological views, his emotionalism and his itinerant religious practices. Yet even Scott found himself caught up in the religious revival. The residents of

Cornwallis on the Bay of Fundy, concerned that Alline's evangelism was undermining and dividing their Church, invited Scott to become their minister. Scott accepted their offer, and soon found himself in demand, with invitations to visit other areas and to shore up other crumbling Congregational bastions. The original letter of invitation, dated June 16, 1778, gives some insight into the mood and concerns of the time.

> We, the dissenting Church and Congregation in Cornwallis, have been without any fixed Pastor over us for several Years; during which Time we have however, been more or less every Year occasionally favoured with Preaching. Several Visits we have had from the Rev. Mr. Smith of Londonderry, Mr. Cock of Truro, Mr. Morse of Annapolis, and Mr. Murdock of Horton, the last of which hath preached with us several Times, (every other Sabbath) for six months. Thus our christian Brethren, and their Reverend Pastors have been exceeding kind and indulgent to us in our desolate and broken Circumstances. We are greatly desirous of having the Gospel resettled among us; but whether ever we shall be indulged with that invaluable Blessing, God only knows. But as our blessed lord hath purchased Gifts for Men, even for the rebellious, we have been Encouraged to hope in his Mercy, (although the Times are so dark, and the Danger and Confusions on every quarter around us, so great, that, the Application we have made for Relief from Abroad, hath hitherto been denied) and we hereby supplicate your Compassion and Assistance.
>
> P.A.N.S., The Records of the Church of Jebogue in Yarmouth, Elkanah Morton, Cornwallis, to The Reverend Mr. Scott, June 16, 1778.

CONFLICTING INTERPRETATIONS

Opening the Debate—A Key Interpretation of Nova Scotia's Response

In 1931 Professor Viola Barnes launched a decade of stimulating historical debate concerning the problem of Nova Scotia's response to the American Revolution. In an early article in the *New England Quarterly*, she contended that the Halifax merchants and Governor Francis Legge were responsible for keeping Nova Scotia loyal to the Crown. Barnes emphasized the influence of potential commercial advantages in determining the response of Halifax and its merchants. In analyzing Nova Scotia's reaction to the 1774 Continental Congress boycott against Britain, Ireland and the British West Indies, she set out the essential points of her thesis:

> The merchants of Nova Scotia saw in the impending boycott of West India trade a golden opportunity to escape from the economic bondage to New England under which the Province had suffered since the French and Indian War. A report in 1764 shows that of Nova Scotia's total exports, valued at £64,790, fish and furs worth £17,000 were disposed of through New England. The rich farm lands around the Bay of Fundy produced quantities of grain, which was marketed chiefly through Boston, because it was easier to sell to New England vessels than to ship to Halifax....
>
> Suddenly the whole horizon of her economics opened up. If the twelve rebellious colonies chose to cut themselves off from trade with Nova Scotia and the West Indies,

perhaps Nova Scotia could control her own fisheries monopolistically and appropriate the West India trade. But first she must rid herself of the impost act....

[A new act passed in November 1774] seems immediately to have stimulated trade. Several vessels [were] fitted out and left for the West Indies stocked with the products of Nova Scotia. More ships were needed, but luck was on the side of Nova Scotia again, for refugee loyalists were beginning to arrive with their vessels and other equipment....

The loyalist party, which comprised a majority of the House, the greater part of the Council, and many of the chief officers, triumphed at last over the spreading radicalism on the one hand and the Governor's authority on the other. These men were not interested in wrangling over the theory of empire. They accepted the dependent status of colonies and admitted the right of Parliament to tax them, believing they should share imperial expenses. Having found the mother country sympathetic to their appeals for redress of local grievances, even to the point of removing a governor who was out of harmony with the Province, they had no constitutional cause for joining the rebellion. Furthermore, the Association and the Restraining Acts, followed by the Prohibitory Act of 1775, suddenly opened up new trade opportunities which independence of the rebel colonies promised to make permanent. The merchants of Nova Scotia in the government and out of it, warmly supported the loyalist cause because the imperial trend was to their advantage, and they minded less the restrictions of the mother country than they did the rivalry of the New England colonies. In short, Nova Scotia remained loyal because the merchant class in control believed the Province profited more than it lost by the connection with the mother country, and because the Governor, with their help, was able to prevent the radicals from stirring the people to revolt. Legge's type of governor in the rebel colonies might at an early stage of the Revolution have been able to beat out the flames of disaffection, but too often the governors avoided a vigorous policy lest they be driven from their posts. True to his military training, Legge showed a dogged determination to do his duty, irrespective of the consequences. The results speak for the relative effectiveness of tact and vigor in the execution of office. He saved his Province; himself he could not save.

Viola F. Barnes, "Francis Legge, Governor of Loyalist Nova Scotia 1773–1776", *The New England Quarterly* (July, 1931), pp. 424–427, 446.

The Barnes Thesis Questioned—An Explanation of the Absence of National Feeling

A Canadian historian, Professor W.B. Kerr, questioned the validity of Viola Barnes' thesis in two separate articles published early in 1932 in the *Canadian Historical Review* and the *Dalhousie Review*. Kerr also offered his own explanation for events in Nova Scotia, stressing the "almost total want of sympathy among artisans, fishermen, and farmers for the American cause". Although Kerr challenged the "Halifax merchant" hypothesis, his own interpretation has been criticized for underestimating the sympathy among some Nova Scotians for revolutionary principles; for failing to explain how "national feeling" was measured; and for mistaking the neutrality of most Nova Scotians for "tepid loyalty".

...Reluctance of merchants to join the agitations was no feature peculiar to Nova Scotia. It was marked in New Hampshire and Georgia as well; and when the crisis came it was evident even in the more revolutionary colonies. This merchant, says Mr. Schlesinger,[1] speaking of the New Englanders of 1774–5, could not see 'any commercial advantage which might accrue from pursuing the will o' the wisp of the radicals. The uncertain prospect which the radical plans held forth was not comparable with the tangible benefits which came from membership in the British Empire under existing conditions....' The position of the merchants was at the bottom much the same from Halifax to Savannah. But in thirteen colonies the radicals overbore both merchants and economic interests; in one they did not. The decisive factor was not the attitude of the merchants but that of the urban populace and farmers. Hence in Nova Scotia also the decisive factor was the apparently loyal attitude of populace and farmers.

In the second place it is doubtful that even the merchants of Nova Scotia were influenced by economic motives to the extent assumed by Miss Barnes. She believes that they resented their 'economic bondage' to New England, such bondage consisting in the near-monopoly of Nova Scotian carrying trade by New Englanders. But the Nova Scotians were New Englanders themselves, with nothing to prevent them from doing that carrying trade if they so desired. If they allowed their New England brothers and cousins to do it for them, they must have been satisfied with the situation. The writer has failed to find in the Nova Scotia documents any trace of hostility to New Englanders over the carrying trade or any other economic matter. As for desire to capture West Indian trade from the New Englanders, we may recall that Nova Scotia merchants had shown themselves singularly indifferent to similar opportunities in 1768–1770. Further, such capture would have been of no more than very temporary benefit, of less benefit than the loss caused by the continental boycott, unless the thirteen colonies were to become actually independent. One has serious doubts that anyone in Nova Scotia in 1774 really believed that the thirteen colonies would achieve complete independence.... But if not, another factor beside the purely economic must have been at work in New England proper and not in Nova Scotia, the factor of common sympathy, the feeling of nationality. The absence of national feeling, then, was the decisive factor in the Nova Scotia situation rather than the presence of doubtful economic opportunities.

From every point of view it appears that Nova Scotia's New Englanders remained cold and impervious to the feeling of nationality which was impelling the thirteen colonies to try the difficult ways of revolution in those critical years....

W.B. Kerr, "The Merchants of Nova Scotia and the American Revolution", *Canadian Historical Review* (April, 1932), pp. 33–36.

The Factors of Deterrence—D.C. Harvey's Assessment

For D.C. Harvey, the superiority of the British Navy as well as British Colonial policy were largely responsible for keeping Nova Scotia in British hands in 1775 and 1776. Harvey, the former Archivist of Nova Scotia, argued that the shrewd Nova Scotians were "inclined to submit to the will of the stronger". And since British naval power was infinitely superior to that of the rebels in 1775 and 1776 there was only one possible choice for the Nova Scotians to make. However, had the French come to the assistance of the

1. The reference is to Arthur M. Schlesinger, *The Colonial Merchants and the American Revolution, 1763–1776* (New York: 1918).

American revolutionaries in 1775 rather than in 1778, the general reaction in Nova Scotia might have been radically different.

Harvey also argued that the relative absence of revolutionary activity in Nova Scotia might be explained by the degree of control exerted by the Halifax government over the democratic tendencies and local autonomy of Nova Scotia's "New Englander" communities. The argument, however, assumed that Halifax authorities possessed the means of communication and authority to force their will upon the various isolated settlements.

> In principle, the Act (An Act for the Choice of Town Officers and regulating of Township, 1765) was more conservative than either the Act of 1759 or that of 1761. They had left the choice of the officers mentioned exclusively to the Grand Jury; but by the Act of 1765 the Grand Jury could only nominate two or more persons for each office; and then, out of these, the Court of Quarter Sessions (appointed by the Halifax authorities) was to *choose* and *appoint*....
>
> This Act was a complete repudiation of the New England form of Township government; and it no doubt had some influence upon the attitude of the rural townships towards the American Revolution. Certainly, some of the settlers left the Province because of their dissatisfaction with what they regarded as broken pledges. But it prevented the formation of some 20 little republics in Western Nova Scotia, and it enabled the central government both to establish communication with the Townships and to retain a check upon their activities.
>
> D.C. Harvey, "The Struggle for the New England Form of Township Government in Nova Scotia", Canadian Historical Association *Report* (1933), p.22.

The Neutrality of the Nova Scotia Yankees—J.B. Brebner's Synthesis

No historian has written as perceptively and as authoritatively about seventeenth- and eighteenth-century Nova Scotia as has J.B. Brebner. Brebner's *Neutral Yankees of Nova Scotia*, published in 1937, took full advantage of the various studies on Nova Scotia and the Revolution published earlier in the decade. It is still widely regarded as the "classic account".

> ...the explanations for Nova Scotian behavior; active and passive, must be sought in the persistent peculiarities of the Province itself, of its peoples, and of the positions in which both were placed by the actions of Great Britain and of some of her American Colonies....
>
> There was not even a sense of solidarity in Nova Scotia. Settlements were scattered at intervals along the edges of a long, narrow peninsula whose rough surface defied the road makers. The unpredictable sea was the road between settlements.... There simply could not be an integral Nova Scotia.
>
> Perhaps, then, the principal clue to Nova Scotian behavior in this, as in many other problematical situations, lies in her insulation from the rest of North America. The northeastward trend of the coast, the Appalachian uplands of Maine and New Brunswick, the deep invasion of the Bay of Fundy, push her outward toward Newfoundland and Europe from the main body of North America. Nova Scotia has always had to contemplate the possibility that she may be in North America but not of it, and this mold of circumstances has pressed with varying weight on some generations of Nova Scotians to modify their traditional loyalties and inclinations....
>
> All in all, both external and domestic circumstances operated to dilute very

considerably in Nova Scotia the clash of opinion which prevailed elsewhere. It is now generally believed that in most of the thirteen rebellious American Colonies the majority of the population was passive, but that the radicals formed the larger of the two active minorities and thereby involved their communities. As events proved, the majority in Nova Scotia was also passive, and neither minority was able to rouse its members beyond individual acts or minor joint enterprises for or against Government. . . .

With the probable exception of Halifax, the available evidence demonstrates the quite natural refusal of most Nova Scotians to risk becoming involved in fratricidal strife with the rebellious Colonies. Inevitably this attitude was interpreted by the official loyalists as being synonymous with treason to Great Britain and with the desire actively to assist the rebels. The resident officials of a colony who had vigorously represented it to be ultra-loyal were loath to allow this embarrassing belief to reach London, but such persons as Legge, Gibbons, and various naval or military officers felt no such compunctions. Yet it is permissible to doubt the many assertions that Nova Scotians' sympathy with the revolutionaries was so great that only their own weaknesses prevented them from joining the America[n] Revolution. In all parts of the Province, outside of Halifax, there were a few men who did participate in the Revolution by emigrating or by conspiring at home to aid the rebels and overthrow British authority. They appear to have been distinctly more numerous and more active than the similarly scattered minority who had the courage actively to assist Great Britain. But both groups were negligible as compared with the mass of Nova Scotians, whose former affiliations and present environment put them in the paradoxical position of being positive only in a negative action. They refused to fight their blood brothers, even, as we shall see, to the point of failing in their professed willingness to defend their homes against them. They felt incapable, even when they were willing, to take overt action to destroy British control. They were desperately concerned by the interruption in their economic intercourse with New England. The Nova Scotian settlers were weak and exposed, and knowing this, like the Acadians whom they had supplanted, asked that the belligerents treat them as neutrals. . . .

J.B. Brebner, *The Neutral Yankees of Nova Scotia* (New York: Columbia University Press, 1937), pp. 291–293, 298–300, 313–314.

Neutrality and Religion—An Early Attempt to Make the Connection

In his analysis of Nova Scotia during the Revolution, J.B. Brebner, like his predecessors, did not take into account the impact of the "Great Awakening" upon the colony. Aware of the significance of religion in eighteenth-century life and society, Professor M.W. Armstrong felt compelled to ask—Was there any direct relationship between the revival and neutrality?

Hitherto, little attention has been paid to the fact that in Nova Scotia the years of the Revolution coincided exactly with a revival of religion which swept through every New England settlement in the province with the most far-reaching and profound social and spiritual results. Such a widespread and vital movement was bound to exert an influence upon Nova Scotians' attitude towards the Revolution. The extent of that influence and the interaction of neutrality and religion have yet to be estimated, but there can be little doubt that the two were at least mutually dependent, and that the 'Great Awakening' in Nova Scotia was an expression of democratic ideals and spiritual independence which shows that these sons of New England were neither so mercenary nor so lethargic as they may at first appear. . . .

Cut off from New England (in 1775 and 1776) with little chance of refilling their pulpits or recuperating their losses in membership and wealth, the outlook of Nova Scotian Congregationalism must have seemed particularly dark....

It was to people in this discouraging situation, faced with the loss of their religion in addition to being 'divided betwixt natural Affection to our nearest Relations, and good Faith and Friendship to our King and Country' that the revival of religion offered at once an escape and a vindication....

Such emphasis on 'spiritual' interests and such wide spread preoccupation with other worldly affairs was bound to have an influence upon Nova Scotians' attitude towards the Revolution. The colonial question necessarily appeared less important as men's minds placed more and more value upon 'heavenly' things. After all, in the light of eternity what comparison was there between the claims of King George and the claims of King Jesus?

To assume, that while their brothers in the Thirteen Colonies were engaged in a life and death struggle for the high ideals of 'Life, Liberty and the pursuit of Happiness,' Nova Scotians were unmoved by any higher considerations than safety and profits is unfair. Indeed, the Great Awakening itself may be considered to have been a retreat from the grim realities of the world to the safety and pleasantly exciting warmth of the revival meeting, and to profits and rewards of another character. Although this psychological law of compensation undoubtedly played a part in the eagerness with which [Henry] Alline's doctrines were accepted by his countrymen, it is not the whole explanation of their conduct. Besides the possibilities for release offered by the revival to emotionally starved and mentally perplexed people, there was also a large element of self-assertion and revolt in the movement.

The emotional extravagances of the enthusiasts and the lengths to which they carried their peculiar beliefs in 'Christian Liberty' were the subject of constant criticism by their opponents, yet even these may be interpreted as the exaggerated assertions of personal independence.... The same individualism which found expressions in other molds in the Thirteen Colonies, activated the religious extraverts to the northern outpost.

Negatively, an escape from fear and divided loyalties; positively, an assertion of democratic ideals and a determination to maintain them, the Great Awakening in Nova Scotia gave self-respect and satisfaction to people whose economic and political position was both humiliating and distressing....

In comparison with the physical and economic factors which held the province within the British Empire, 'the Great Reformation under Mr. Henry Alline,' may seem insignificant and remote, yet psychologically it played a part. Not only Mr. Alline, but lesser exhorters in every township pointed out the blessings of peace and turned men's minds away from the political issues of the day. In a state of divided loyalties and impotence the Neutral Yankees found an indirect method of asserting their independence. Political neutrality was superseded by religious enthusiasm.

M.W. Armstrong, "Neutrality and Religion in Revolutionary Nova Scotia", *The New England Quarterly* (March, 1946), pp. 51, 53, 54, 57–58, 60–61, 62.

The Frontier Thesis Applied to Nova Scotia

Frederick Jackson Turner's frontier thesis, first propounded in a paper to the American Historical Association in 1893, has had a considerable impact upon North American historiography. But it was not until 1959 that the Turner thesis was applied in a sophisticated manner to the case of Nova Scotia during the early years of the Revolution. S.D. Clark, who undertook this task, was a sociologist rather than a historian, and he viewed Nova Scotia's reaction as one of many genuine movements of political protest which grew out of radical democratic impulses born in settlements in the frontier areas.

To the people of Nova Scotia the question at issue in the revolution was largely that of their relationship with New England. The plea of the inhabitants of Yarmouth that they be allowed to remain neutral in the war represented truly their position. They had no positive desire to break free from Britain. What they were concerned about was that they should not be cut off from New England....

Closely related to the connection with New England as a force determining the position of Nova Scotia in the revolution was the intense localism of the village communities. British authority, as represented by the government in Halifax, constituted a direct threat to the right of these communities to govern their own affairs. To them, as a result, independence in 1775 meant not so much the freedom of the colonies from interference by the motherland as freedom of the local community from interference by colonial governments. Like all frontier people, the Nova Scotians were separatists. Compelled to act on their own, and dependent largely on their own resources, they had no strong interest in the affairs of the state. In this attitude of mind, the American revolutionary movement of independence had strong roots in Nova Scotia....

Maintenance of close proprietory control over the early settlement of New Englanders in Nova Scotia had emphasized the character of the village structure as a 'closed social system,' but unrest in New England, evident in the Great Awakening in religion and in local movements of political protest, made its effects felt in the new frontier communities of Nova Scotia. The people who moved to the frontier were the people least socially accommodated within their home communities, and efforts to impose upon them the kind of controls from which they were seeking an escape met with vigorous resistance....

Impoverished and without leadership of its own, the great mass of the population could offer no effective resistance to the system of control being imposed upon it. Random individual protests against authority, evident in occasional refusals to conform to the rigid Puritan code of morals, the development of an attitude of shiftlessness and general irresponsibility, and, in the more isolated areas, the growth of a spirit of lawlessness, reflected an underlying social philosophy of nonconformity which weakened the sense of solidarity of the village community but provided no positive force of social reorganization. Development of such a force of social reorganization came with the rise of the Newlight movement of religious revival....

Yet there developed out of Newlight religious teaching no clearly formulated social or political philosophy. Rather, an ignorance of social or political questions tended to be characteristic of the Newlight religious following. It was, however, in this very cultivation of an attitude of ignorance or indifference to social and political questions that the influence of Newlightism gained much of its political significance....

The Newlight religious community, in a sense, seceded from the larger political community and developed complete within itself a social world of its own. Here within the religious revival was to be found the fullest expression of that spirit of local independence which permeated the whole American revolutionary movement. In its intense separatism, Newlightism constituted a more serious challenge to established political authority than did any of the more purely political manifestations of social protest. Only smuggling, perhaps, in the Nova Scotia out-settlements gained as great importance as a force of resistance to the state. . . .

The widespread growth of political sympathy for the American revolutionary cause, together with the rise of the Newlight religious revival, offered an indication of the extent of the social unrest of the outlying population in Nova Scotia in the years immediately preceding the outbreak of the war between Britain and the English colonies. Growing resentment against the rule of the narrow governing party in Halifax strengthened the sense of solidarity of the village communities and gave to the town meeting a new importance as a vehicle for the expression of local discontent. On the other hand, the weakening social position of local village and church leaders reflected the strength of democratic influences growing out of the conditions of frontier settlement and emphasized the importance of the Newlight religious revival as a force of social reorganization. Though the Cumberland rebels were defeated by the forces of the Crown, and [the rebel leaders] were driven from the province, the spirit of revolt which found expression in religious revival could not so easily be crushed. The revolutionary movement in Nova Scotia was rooted in the strong separatist attitude of mind of the outlying fishing and farming population and that attitude of mind survived the military and political developments of the revolution though the province remained, by the fortunes of war, a part of the British Empire.

S.D. Clark, *Movements of Political Protest in Canada 1640-1840* (Toronto: University of Toronto Press, 1959), pp. 6, 69-74.

The "Missing Decade" Thesis

In 1972, reacting against the prevailing Brebner hypothesis, Professor Gordon Stewart, together with Professor George Rawlyk, introduced into the historiographical debate what has been called the "Missing Decade" thesis. In essence, Stewart and Rawlyk suggested that the Nova Scotia Yankees rejected the Revolution because they did not understand its motivating ideas.

As Britain persisted in the years after 1763 in her attempts to tax the Thirteen Colonies and to bring her American possessions under tighter control, the New England colonists organized political resistance and carefully defined the legally limited dependence they believed the colonies were subject to. As John Adams explained many years later, it was in those ten years of political debate that many Americans, fearing what the Patriots believed was a British 'conspiracy' to destroy American 'liberty', began to discard their loyalty to Britain. 'The real American Revolution' occurred in the decade preceding the military events of 1775-76 and, observed Adams, consisted in the 'radical change in the principles, opinions, sentiments and affections of the people.'

Those thousands of Yankees who had emigrated to Nova Scotia in the early 1760s did not, however, undergo this radical change. . . . During this decade of transformation in New England and most of the Thirteen Colonies, the Yankees in Nova Scotia remained remarkably untouched by these contemporary currents of opinion that were radically changing America's view of the relationship with Britain.

Nova Scotia's response to this decade of radical change was an exception to the general pattern of political transformation that affected New Englanders in the 1760s and 1770s. . . . The failure of colonial revolutionary ideas to take root in Nova Scotia was not simply the result of remoteness, sparseness of settlement and the lack of homogeneity in the population, although these were important background factors. What primarily decided that the Nova Scotia Yankees would not conform to the general

American pattern was that the form of government and the nature of society precluded the development of what some historians have described as the necessary 'general enlightenment' of key sections of the population. Some of the rhetoric of protest may have appeared to be the same but in Nova Scotia it always tended to be hedged with limitations and weakened by self-doubt. The Nova Scotia Yankees were, throughout these years, an isolated group of colonists whose traditional values and assumptions failed to transcend their traditionality and become the foundation for novel revolutionary opinions....

For the Nova Scotia Yankees this period was the missing decade. It was during these years that the other American colonies left Nova Scotia behind while they created for themselves a new sense of identity and constructed a new version of their position and purpose in the world. The Yankees in the outsettlements of Nova Scotia could still join in opposing the Stamp Act in small groups but there was no general movement of protest and no sense of solidarity among the settlements. Above all, there was no sense of participation in the 'Union' of 1765 that John Adams believed so significant....
Insofar as the Nova Scotia Yankees protested British policy in the 1760s they did so at a much less intense level than the other colonists, and the protests were never generalized into a popular, colony-wide movement. Such ideas of protest remained submerged and limited in their application; they were not brought into the public consciousness and pressed into service as the basis for a coherent attack on British designs for enslaving the colonies. In Nova Scotia such ideas remained in a stunted form, uncertain of their legitimacy, incapable of raising men's passions and sustaining a revolutionary ideology.

Gordon Stewart and George Rawlyk, *A People Highly Favoured of God* (Toronto: Macmillan, 1972), pp. 3–4, 43–44.

The Critical Role of a Charismatic Religious Leader, Henry Alline

The "Missing Decade" thesis is only one part of the argument put forward by Stewart and Rawlyk in *A People Highly Favoured of God* to explain Nova Scotia's reaction to the American Revolution. The other part, which stresses Henry Alline's crucial role, is briefly explored in an article written by Rawlyk in 1976—the year of the Bicentennial of the American Revolution. Rawlyk has developed this theme at much greater length in his *New Light Letters and Songs* (1983) and his *Ravished by the Spirit: Religious Revivals, Baptists and Henry Alline* (1984).

Henry Alline was one Nova Scotian who was able to perceive a special purpose for his fellow colonists in the midst of the confused Revolutionary situation. He was the charismatic leader of the intense religious revival which swept the colony during the war period. This revival was not merely a 'retreat from the grim realities of the world to the safety and pleasantly exciting warmth of the revival meeting', and 'to profits and rewards of another character.' Nor was it basically a revolt of the outsettlements against Halifax or an irrational outburst against all forms of traditionalism and authority. The Great Awakening of Nova Scotia may be viewed as an attempt by many Yankee inhabitants to appropriate a new sense of identity and a renewed sense of purpose. Religious enthusiasm in this context, a social movement of profound consequence in the Nova Scotian situation, was symptomatic of a kind of collective identity crisis as well as a searching for an acceptable and meaningful ideology. Resolution of the crisis came not only when the individuals were absorbed into what they felt was a dynamic fellowship of true believers but also when they accepted Alline's analysis of contemporary events and his conviction that their colony was the centre of a crucial cosmic struggle....

In his sermons preached as he crisscrossed the colony, Alline developed the theme that the Nova Scotia 'Yankees', in particular, had a special predestined role to play in God's plan for the world. It must have required a special effort for Alline to convince Nova Scotians of their special world role. But Alline, striking deep into the Puritan New England tradition that viewed self-sacrifice and frugality as virtues, contended that the relative backwardness and isolation of the colony had removed the inhabitants from the prevailing corrupting influences of New England and Britain. As a result, Nova Scotia was in an ideal position to lead the world back to God....

The implication of the conjunction of events, of civil war in New England and an outpouring of the Holy Spirit in Nova Scotia was obvious to Alline and the thousands who flocked to hear him. God was passing New England's historical mantle of Christian leadership to Nova Scotia.... In the world view of those New Englanders fighting for the Revolutionary cause, Old England was corrupt and the Americans were engaged in a righteous and noble cause. There was therefore some meaning for hostilities. But to Alline the totally 'inhuman War' had no such meaning. Rather, along with all the other signs of the times, it could only indicate one thing, that the entire Christian world, apart from Nova Scotia, was abandoning the way of God.

G.A. Rawlyk, "Nova Scotia and the American Revolution", *New Edinburgh Review*, No. 35/36 (1976), pp. 107–108. Footnotes omitted.

Nova Scotia's Enigmatic Response—A Few Unanswered Questions

There are some obvious flaws in the "Missing Decade" thesis. It assigns great significance to the decade of 1765–1775, which, it has been argued, transformed Anglo-Americans into patriots and revolutionaries. Did all the Nova Scotia Yankees, in fact, miss this crucial decade of ideological transformation? Indeed, was there actually such a decade in the Thirteen Colonies? And were the Nova Scotian communities really as isolated from unfolding events in New England as Stewart and Rawlyk suggest? And even if Alline had a "sense of Mission", how can one be certain that Nova Scotians responded favourably to him because of this? Can one, in other words, generalize from Alline's experience and make it all of Nova Scotia's? These are some of the questions which must be raised as one considers critically the strengths and weaknesses of the Stewart-Rawlyk approach. It is noteworthy that Stephen Marini, in his *Radical Sects of Revolutionary New England* (Harvard University Press, 1982), has argued that Alline's Great Awakening profoundly affected events and personalities in northern New England during the American Revolution and, moreover, considerably encouraged neutrality in the region. Thus, Nova Scotia's enigmatic response to the Revolution, shaped by the colony's special relationship with New England, in turn may actually have influenced the way in which many New Englanders reacted to the American War of Independence.

A Guide To Further Reading

1. Overviews

Armstrong, M.W., "Neutrality and Religion in Revolutionary Nova Scotia", *The New England Quarterly*, Vol. IX (March, 1946), pp. 50–62.

Barnes, Viola F., "Francis Legge, Governor of Loyalist Nova Scotia 1773–1776", *The New England Quarterly* (July, 1931), pp. 424–446.

Beck, J.M., *The Government of Nova Scotia*. Toronto: University of Toronto Press, 1957.

Brebner, J.B., *The Neutral Yankees of Nova Scotia: A Marginal Colony during the Revolutionary Years*. Toronto: McClelland and Stewart, 1969.

Clark, S.D., *Movements of Political Protest in Canada 1640–1840*. Toronto: University of Toronto Press, 1959.

Harvey, D.C., "Machias and the Invasion of Nova Scotia", Canadian Historical Association *Report* (1932), pp. 22–24.

_____, "The Struggle for the New England Form of Township Government in Nova Scotia", Canadian Historical Association *Report* (1933), pp. 18–22.

Kerr, W.B., "The Merchants of Nova Scotia and the American Revolution", *Canadian Historical Review* (March, 1932), pp. 20–36.

_____, "Nova Scotia in the Critical Years, 1775–76", *Dalhousie Review* (April, 1932), pp. 97–107.

Macnutt, W.S., *The Atlantic Provinces: The Emergence of Colonial Society*. Toronto: McClelland and Stewart, 1965.

Rawlyk, G.A., "Nova Scotia and the American Revolution". *New Edinburgh Review*, No. 35/36, 1976, pp. 104–111.

_____, "Nova Scotia and the American Revolution Reconsidered", *Dalhousie Review*, Vol. XLIII (Autumn, 1963), pp. 379–394.

_____, ed., *Revolution Rejected, 1775–1776*. Scarborough: Prentice-Hall, 1968.

Stewart, Gordon T. and George A. Rawlyk, *A People Highly Favoured of God: The Nova Scotia Yankees and the American Revolution*. Hamden, Conn.: Archon Books, 1972.

2. Specialized Studies

The American Revolution

Ahlin, J.H., *Maine Rubicon: Downcast Settlers during the Revolution*. Calais: Calais Advertiser Press, 1966.

Bailyn, Bernard, *The Ideological Origins of the American Revolution*. Cambridge: Harvard University Press, 1967.

Heimert, A., *Religion and the American Mind from the Great Awakening to the Revolution*. Cambridge: Harvard University Press, 1966.

Kerr, W.B., "The Stamp Act Crisis in Nova Scotia", *New England Quarterly*, Vol. VI (September, 1933), p. 558.

Kidder, F., *Military Operations in Eastern Maine and Nova Scotia during the American Revolution*. Albany, N.Y.: J. Munsell, 1867.

Marini, Stephen A., *Radical Sects of Revolutionary New England*. Cambridge, Mass.: Harvard University Press, 1982.

Rawlyk, G.A., *Nova Scotia's Massachusetts: A Study of Massachusetts–Nova Scotia Relations, 1630–1784*. Montreal/Kingston: McGill-Queen's University Press, 1973.

Journals, Diaries and Memoirs

Beverley, James and Barry Moody, eds., *The Journal of Henry Alline*. Hantsport, Nova Scotia: Lancelot Press, 1982.

Fergusson, C.B., ed., "The Life of Jonathan Scott", *P.A.N.S. Bulletin*, No. 15. Halifax: 1960.

Harvey, D.C., ed., *The Diary of Simeon Perkins, 1780-1789*. Toronto: Champlain Society, 1958.

Innis, H.A., ed., *The Diary of Simeon Perkins*. Toronto: Champlain Society, 1948.

Scott, Henry E. Jr., ed., *The Journal of the Reverend Jonathan Scott*. New England Historic Genealogical Society, 1980.

Stewart, Gordon T., ed., *Documents Relating to the Great Awakening in Nova Scotia*. Toronto: Champlain Society, 1982.

The Great Awakening in Nova Scotia

Armstrong, M.W., *The Great Awakening in Nova Scotia 1776-1809*. Hartford, Conn.: American Society for Church History, 1948.

Bumsted, J.M., "Church and State in Maritime Canada, 1749-1807", Canadian Historical Association *Historical Papers* (1968), pp. 41-58.

_____, *Henry Alline, 1748-1784*. Toronto: University of Toronto Press, 1971.

Clark, S.D., *Church and Sect in Canada*. Toronto: University of Toronto Press, 1948.

Rawlyk, G.A., "Henry Alline and the Canadian Baptist Tradition", *Theological Bulletin*, McMaster Divinity College (1977), pp. 2-17.

_____. *Ravished By The Spirit: Religious Revivals, Baptists and Henry Alline*. Montreal/Kingston: McGill-Queen's University Press, 1984.

Stewart, Gordon T., "Charisma and Integration: an Eighteenth Century North American Case", *Comparative Studies in Society and History*, Vol. 16 (1974), pp. 138-149.

_____, "Socio-economic Factors in the Great Awakening", *Acadiensis*, Vol. III (1973), pp. 18-34.

7

POLITICAL UNREST IN THE CANADAS IN THE 1830s

What Lay at the Root of the Struggle?

The rebellions of 1837–38 in Upper and Lower Canada have long been seen as a major watershed in the history of Canada. Some sixty years after the American Revolution, rebels in both Canadas rose against British colonial government in insurrections which seem too similar to be merely coincidental. By the 1830s demands for reform were emanating from all the British North American colonies, but only in the two Canadas did rebellion erupt. What caused this apparent disruption in the orderly political development of Britain's two largest North American colonies? What lay at the root of the struggles in Upper and Lower Canada? And were these disturbances separate—or, in fact, closely related?

Like most historical events, the rebellions of 1837–38 in the two Canadas can be interpreted in a variety of ways. Of course, they had their similarities as well as their differences. But since they occurred at about the same time in neighbouring colonies, historians invariably ask the same questions about both of them.

By the 1830s a political crisis had arisen in both provinces over the constitution of colonial government. The lack of any connecting link between the elected assemblies and the appointed governors and councils enraged assembly members who desired an effective voice in government. Were the rebellions attempts to introduce new forms of government to break the constitutional deadlock? If so, did the rebels want British parliamentary government, or a republican constitution that would create a democracy like that of the United States?

At the same time, both Canadas were suffering from financial troubles which lent socio-economic and class dimensions to the rebellions. Was the real cause of the rebellions a deep-seated and ongoing struggle between agriculture and commerce? Were the economic goals of the merchants in Montreal and Toronto in conflict with the interests of the farming population in the hinterland?

Then again, both rebellions showed some signs of being popular revolutions. Were the *patriotes* of Lower Canada engaged in a struggle to achieve "national" independence for *Canadiens*, and were the rebels of Upper Canada determined to overthrow British colonial rule and establish an independent frontier democracy? Serious consideration of these questions leads us back to the circumstances surrounding the insurrections themselves.

The rebellions came after years of constitutional conflict in Lower and Upper Canada. The Constitutional Act of 1791 had granted assemblies to each province, but had made no provision for the Legislative and Executive Councils to be responsible to the wishes of the Assembly. It seemed as though the people had been given a forum for political expression while being denied the means for political action. Frustration resulted. Between 1822 and 1836, the Legislative Council of Lower Canada refused 234 bills passed by the Assembly, while in Upper Canada over 300 bills were dismissed. Both Assemblies reacted by attempting to gain more control over government revenues to force the Governor and his Councils to accept their demands.

In Lower Canada, the "Château Clique", an oligarchy composed primarily of the British merchants and their sympathizers, occupied the appointed positions on the Executive and Legislative Councils and controlled government policy and patronage. The elected Assembly, on the other hand, was dominated by a majority of French Canadians who over time grew embittered about their lack of political power. In 1831 the British government ceded control of most provincial revenues to the Assembly, but by this time the protracted conflict within Lower Canada had made the French Canadian reformers truculent and intransigent.

The struggle in Lower Canada reached its breaking point in the mid-to late 1830s. Some of the more radical reformers, spearheaded by the *parti patriote* leader Louis Joseph Papineau, issued reports on government misdeeds and began to advocate far-reaching changes such as an elected Legislative Council. When Lord John Russell, the British Colonial Secretary, responded to the radical reformers' demands in August, 1837 with his "Ten Resolutions", rejecting any greater measures of self-government, demonstrations of protest broke out and the Assembly (controlled by French Canadian reformers) refused to provide the council with its required revenues. In a cycle of retaliation, the Governor prorogued the Assembly and the *patriotes'* protests intensified in the capital as well as in towns across the province. In early November, 1837, there was a bloody clash in the streets of Montreal between supporters of the *patriotes* and the "British party". It was the beginning of the unsuccessful 1837 rebellion in Lower Canada. Rebel forces banded together in the country, but in a series of sharp encounters were defeated by troops raised by the British authorities. A second insurrection by the *patriotes* in November of 1838 was likewise crushed by the government forces.

Upper Canada had a constitutional battle of its own taking place during the 1830s. There, another clique, the "Family Compact", controlled the governing councils. Unlike the Château Clique, the Family Compact did not represent a "racial" minority, but the Upper Canadian reformers nevertheless saw it as a self-appointed aristocracy dedicated to advancing its own economic, social and religious interests at the expense of the general welfare of the province. Settlers complained that the development of the province was deterred by poor roads and by the Compact's grants of large tracts of land to absentee owners, who would hold the property undeveloped until it could be sold for a large profit. In a province of many religious denominations, it was also bitterly resented that the Family Compact was attempting to entrench the rights of the Church of England. Leaders of the Methodists, the fastest-growing Protestant church, led the protest against the Anglican Church's pretensions to all the revenue from the Clergy Reserves and its monopoly over higher education.

As in Lower Canada, the rule of the colonial oligarchy was challenged by a reform party in the Assembly. By the 1830s the reformers, like their counterparts in the lower province, had split into two groups, the moderates favouring parliamentary changes and the radicals, led by William Lyon Mackenzie, advocating broader democratic institutions. The political conflict reached the critical point when a newly appointed Lieutenant-Governor, Sir Francis Bond Head, ignored moderate reformers in his appointed Legislative Council and successfully orchestrated (through questionable tactics) the election of a Tory majority in the 1836 Assembly elections. This setback further radicalized Mackenzie's group, which pledged its support to the Lower Canadian *patriotes* and then, in early December 1837, launched a poorly organized march down Yonge Street in a futile attempt to overthrow the government of Upper Canada. Shortly afterwards, another radical member of the Assembly, Dr. Charles Duncombe, led a similar uprising in southwestern Upper Canada. Like the Yonge Street rebellion, Duncombe's revolt was crushed by "loyalist" forces.

Few events in pre-Confederation Canadian history have generated as much controversy as the rebellions of 1837–38, and their aftermath[1]. What lay at the root of the disturbances? Did the rebellions arise primarily out of the political problems of constitutional deadlock and financial control? Could they have been symptoms of an economic struggle between the contending forces of agriculture and commerce? Or were these revolts actually incipient revolu-

---

1. Canadian social historians have placed the rebellions in an illuminating context by emphasizing that violence was more common in the politics and society of the 1830s than it is today. The rebellions of 1837 and 1838 occurred during an era that was marked by labour struggles on the canals of Upper and Lower Canada, as well as by social disorder stirred up by a band of Irish desperadoes, the Shiners, in the Ottawa Valley. While space does not permit a full study of these disturbances here, they should be kept in mind when studying the political, economic and social conditions in which the rebellions erupted.

tions motivated by French Canadian nationalism in Lower Canada and democratic-republican ideas in Upper Canada? Finally—were the insurrections simply simultaneous but unrelated outbreaks?

SELECTED CONTEMPORARY SOURCES

ELEMENTS OF A POLITICAL-CONSTITUTIONAL STRUGGLE

Louis Joseph Papineau's Call for Democratic Institutions, 1834

Leaders of the Reform movements in both Upper and Lower Canada often claimed that democratic institutions were superior to the existing British colonial political system. Radical Reform leaders like Louis Joseph Papineau became republicans and promoted solutions such as elective institutions. To them the "system of privilege"—which included the banks, the land companies, the Established Church and the appointed councils—had to be eliminated in all its forms.

The following extract, from a speech given by Louis Joseph Papineau in February of 1834, sets out some of his arguments against the existing form of government. As a leader of the French Canadians in the Assembly, Papineau naturally desired more political power, but it is interesting to examine the other ways in which he justified his demand for an elected Legislative Council.

In the colonies the people need democratic institutions because they are less costly and less burdensome than more expensive institutions. A new country needs robust men accustomed to hard work, to privations, and to the techniques needed to exploit the forests. It is in the customs, the nature and the common interests of colony and mother country that government institutions should be economical, for everything that is taken from the enjoyment of luxury is an endowment for new families that will marry earlier, will clear new land, will create a new productive capital to buy the useful manufactured products of cloth and iron rather than silks and liquors. . . .

Give institutions where there is no cause for flattery, and national distinctions will cease. In the present situation the Government is reaping the fruits that it has sown. There is need, they say, of a council to defend one part of the population that can't be a majority in the Assembly. A party is needed in the House to support the Council. . . . The complaints of this country against the evils of the Council's composition are too unanimous to make it necessary to say more on this subject. The Constitutional Act has given the Council a disastrous preponderance that allows it to paralyze all the work of the House of Assembly. It had been desired to give the latter body influence, since the Province of Quebec had been divided so that the original population in Lower Canada could protect its own institutions. But the Constitutional Act provided an easy way to destroy that hope: that was by installing Upper Canada in the Legislative Council of Lower Canada. And so it was done.

La Minerve, February 27, 1834, in Fernand Ouellet, *Papineau: Textes choisis et présentés* (Quebec: Les Presses de l'Université Laval, 1958), p. 54.

Reverend Egerton Ryerson's Attack on the "Blighting System", 1831

In Upper Canada, reformers demanded what they called "responsible government" as a way of correcting a different system of privilege. Although much of their criticism was directed at Compact rule, it was often linked with attacks on the special privileges of the province's established Church. Under the Constitutional Act of 1791, about one seventh of all Crown lands had been set aside for the support of the Protestant clergy and the Family Compact had given these "Clergy Reserves", as they became known, to the Church of England. By the late 1820s and early 1830s, however, the majority of Upper Canadians belonged to other Protestant denominations and many deeply resented the system of privilege which endowed the Anglican Church with great wealth, disrupted the uniform development of farming communities, and often reduced the supply and affordability of arable land.

The Methodists were the largest Protestant sect in the province, and one of their ministers, Egerton Ryerson, led a campaign against religious privilege that added considerable impetus to the Reform movement. As editor of the *Christian Guardian*, Ryerson urged that the Clergy Reserves should be sold and the proceeds put towards public education.

> No means are too low for the high church party in this Province to descend to, in order to preserve their blighting system . . . the burden of their arguments was, that if you take away the Reserves, the Clergy of our venerable Church will starve. Learned, able, legitimate Ministers of the Apostolic Church, and yet will starve, languish, and die, if they are placed in the same relation to their flocks with those Ministers who are prosperous and successful, whom they affect to despise as unapostolic intruders, as poor ignoramuses!! What consistency! But, say they, 'the people of Upper Canada are too ignorant to value talent and acquirements, therefore, a learned Clergy cannot be supported without some government provision for that purpose.' . . . The advocates of equal religious freedom and liberal institutions wish to have these lands converted from their present unjust and worse than useless application, to the very purpose of educating the people generally. . . .
>
> We know the policy of the high Church party now. They see that the one seventh of the Province, as reserve lands, cannot be retained . . . and therefore they try to delay any decisive proceedings on the application of the proceeds of these lands for the general good of the country, until they can dispose of them and vest the proceeds of the sale of them in a permanent fund for the advancement of their Clergy. But can an administration or a government, with one spark of wisdom or justice in its councils, tolerate this? A moment's glance upon the past, present and probable future progress of public opinion on this subject, must show the impossibility as well as impolicy of erecting and perpetuating any dominant Church Establishment in this country, and more especially when it is known that the funds which support that Establishment should have been, upon just and constitutional principles, applied to the general benefit of the Province . . . .
>
> [The] aggressions of the high Church on the characters, principles, conduct and rights of other denominations of Christians have created a feeling of abhorrence, on the part of the people generally, against the system that gave rise to them . . . .
>
> Rev. E. Ryerson, "The High Church Party 'Blighting System'", *Christian Guardian*, March 26, 1831.

The Demands of the Lower Canadian Reformers—The Ninety-Two Resolutions, 1834

By 1834, the conflict in the governments of both Canadas had become increasingly bitter. The Assembly of Lower Canada passed the "Ninety-Two Resolutions", a confused summary of every grievance—real or imagined—of the *patriotes* against the oligarchy. John Neilson, a Scottish Lower Canadian reformer who broke with the radical reformers on this issue, described the *Resolutions* thus: "...eleven stood true, six contained both truth and falsehood; sixteen stood wholly false; seventeen stood doubtful; twelve were ridiculous; seven were repetitions; fourteen consisted only of abuse; four were false and seditious; five were good or indifferent."

In spite of this harsh judgement, the main resolutions are worth examining:

9. Resolved, That the most serious defect in the Constitutional Act...the most active principle of evil and discontent in the province...is that injudicious enactment...which invests the Crown with that exorbitant power (incompatible with any government duly balanced, and founded on law and justice, and not on force and coercion) of selecting and composing without any rule or limitation, or any predetermined qualification, an entire branch of the legislature, supposed from the nature of its attributions to be independent, but inevitably the servile tool of the authority which creates, composes and decomposes it, and can on any day modify it to suit the interests or the passions of the moment....

14. Resolved, That this House is nowise disposed to admit the excellence of the present Constitution of Canada, although His Majesty's Secretary of State for the Colonies has unreasonably and erroneously asserted, that it has conferred on the two Canadas the institutions of Great Britain; nor to reject the principle of extending the system of frequent elections much further than it is at present....

52. Resolved, That since a circumstance, which did not depend upon the choice of the majority of the people, their French origin and their use of the French language, has been made by the colonial authorities a pretext for abuse, for exclusion, for political inferiority, for a separation of rights and interests; this House now appeals to the justice of His Majesty's Government and of Parliament, and to the honour of the people of England; that the majority of the inhabitants of this country are in nowise disposed to repudiate any one of the advantages they derive from their origin and from their descent from the French nation, which...has never been behind the British nation, and is now the worthy rival of the latter in the advancement of the cause of liberty and of the science of Government; from which this country derives the greater portion of its civil and ecclesiastical law, and of its scholastic and charitable institutions, and of the religion, language, habits, manners and customs of the great majority of its inhabitants....

64. Resolved, That the claims which have for many years been set up by the Executive Government to that control over and power of appropriating a great portion of the revenues levied in this province, which belong of right to this House, are contrary to the rights and to the constitution of the country....

75. Resolved, That the number of the inhabitants of the country being about 600,000 those of French origin are about 525,000, and those of British or other origin 75,000; and that the establishment of the civil government of Lower Canada for the year 1832...contained the names of 157 officers and others receiving salaries, who are apparently of British or foreign origin, and the names of 47 who are apparently natives

of the country, of French origin: that this statement does not exhibit the whole disproportion which exists in the distribution of the public money and power, the latter class being for the most part appointed to the inferior and less lucrative offices... that the accumulation of many of the best paid and most influential, and at the same time incompatible offices in the same person, which is forbidden by the laws and by sound policy, exists especially for the benefit of the former class; and that two-thirds of the persons included in the last commission of the peace issued in the province are apparently of British or foreign origin, and one-third only of French origin....

84.   Resolved, That besides the grievances and abuses before mentioned, there exist in this province a great number of others....

1stly. The vicious composition and the irresponsibility of the Executive Council...

2dly. The exorbitant fees illegally exacted in certain of the public offices,

3dly. The practice of illegally calling upon the judges, to give their opinions secretly on questions which may be afterwards publicly and contradictorily argued before them....

4thly. The cumulation of public places and offices in the same persons, and the efforts made by a number of families connected with the administration, to perpetuate this state of things for their own advantage, and for the sake of domineering for ever, with interested views and in the spirit of party, over the people and their representatives....

5thly. The intermeddling of members of the Legislative Councils in the election of the representatives of the people, for the purpose of influencing and controlling them by force, and the selection frequently made of returning officers for the purpose of securing the same partial and corrupt ends....

6thly. The interference of the armed military force at such elections, through which three peaceable citizens, whose exertions were necessary to the support of their families, and who were strangers to the agitation of the election, were shot dead in the streets....

7thly. The various faulty and partial systems which have been followed ever since the passing of the Constitutional Act, with regard to the management of the waste lands in this province, and have rendered it impossible for the great majority of the people of the country to settle on the said lands....

W.P.M. Kennedy, *Statutes, Treaties and Documents of the Canadian Constitution, 1713-1929* (Toronto: Oxford, 1930), pp. 272-90.

William Lyon Mackenzie's List of Grievances, 1833

In 1833, William Lyon Mackenzie listed the grievances of the Upper Canadian reformers in a book that was sub-titled "The Constitutional Reformer's Text Book". Mackenzie later chaired the Upper Canadian Assembly's Select Committee on Grievances, and the "Seventh Report on Grievances" that it produced in 1835 expanded on earlier criticisms of the government. Radical opposition to the Family Compact coalesced around Mackenzie during these years as he used his newspaper, the *Colonial Advocate*, to attack the entrenched interests of the ruling party.

1. The people are taxed without their consent. 2. The money so raised is appropriated without their leave. 3. They are unequally represented in the Assembly, and the laws they pray for are always negatived and refused by a Legislative Council of persons

chosen by the Governors for life, and chiefly dependent on the colonial revenues for the means of existence. 4. They are afflicted with Military Officers as their Civil Chief Magistrates, persons more accustomed to command slaves than preside over freedom. 5. Their Judges and every Officer of the Government are entirely dependent on the Military Power for their incomes and continuance in office. 6. Magistrates and other officers are not usually selected from among the most respected of the population, but the contrary. 7. The Executive Council are unchangeable, and irresponsible to public opinion. 8. A host of priests, bishops, and such like are made Government Pensioners, out of the people's money, and these the priests of the minority; while the majority have to pay both for their own and the others.... 9. The University Charter is bigoted and sectarian. 10. The control of the Funds for Education is in bad hands. 11. Improper persons are forced into the Assembly, and undue influence is used to place them there. 12. Sheriffs pick Juries at their pleasure; and, being themselves dependent persons, they labour under strong suspicion of picking Juries from the worst of motives and for the worst of purposes. 13. No court for trying Impeachments of Public Delinquents in office, no means of bringing them to punishment. 14. Bodies of armed men kept in the country, independent of the civil power, to awe and coerce the native population. 15. Banking Monopolies, flooding the country with paper of a doubtful character, no security being afforded for its redemption, and the Banks being used as political party engines to destroy the liberties of the country. 16. The Post-Office Tax on Letters and Newspapers £4000 of which are pocketed by the secret manager, and the rest shipped to London without the consent of the Province. 17. Wanton and partial Prosecutions and Sentences for alleged Political Libel. 18. Violent Expulsions of Members of the Assembly on frivolous and illegal pretexts, countenanced by the Authorities. 19. An enormous Public Debt, the money borrowed being chiefly squandered in accordance with the system. 20. Delay, uncertainty, doubt and suspicion, in all matters relating to the Law Courts, and enormous expense. 21. 700,000 Acres of the Lands of the Country sold for a song, to make fortunes to a few speculators and increase the ill-applied patronage of the Justice of the Peace. 22. Trade and Commerce subjected to innumerable restrictions, regulations, and prohibitions, ever changing, and in which the country is never consulted. 23. The Petitions of the People for Relief disregarded in England by Mr. Stanley, and the guilty promoted as an example to others.

> W.L. Mackenzie quoted in Patrick Swift, *A New Almanack for the Canadian True Blues: with which is incorporated the Constitutional Reformer's Text Book; for... 1834* (York: Colonial Advocate Press, 1833), p. 21.

ELEMENTS OF AN ECONOMIC STRUGGLE

Agriculture vs. Commerce—A French Canadian's Analysis, 1829

In the Canadas the interests and ambitions of merchants often clashed with those of farmers. Many rural settlers in Upper Canada wanted the colonial government to spend money to improve roads and other services that they knew were necessary for their prosperity. Government support for canal-building appeared to them to be nothing more than a handout of public money to a few rich capitalists. In Lower Canada, where the British merchants had control of the government, the *parti patriote* saw commercial development as a direct threat to French Canada's agrarian society, which they believed to be the bastion of their cultural heritage. Tension between the two groups escalated as the *patriotes* did everything they could, with their limited powers in the Assembly, to block the British merchants' plans. One French Canadian, who favoured more *Canadien* participation in the world of commerce, offered this assessment of the economic condition of his people.

> Let us talk about commerce. Perhaps it is in this field that Canadiens have the greatest impediment to overcome. They have not done as well as they could in this area. First, very few Canadiens know commerce as a subject of study and learning. . . . The Canadiens who used to be involved in trade have slowly withdrawn. They did not form any significant establishments. Even now there is hardly what could properly be called an association, a Canadien trading association. Yet without this it is practically impossible to conduct extensive trade. It cannot be said that they have always been and are still now completely without capital. It is said that they have often had reason for complaint about the lack of precision of those they have dealt with here and in England, in attempting to get merchandise from them when they wanted to try overseas trade. It is possible to suspect that these complaints were well-founded. But why trust others to do something you can do yourself? When, especially in trade, have we ever found that we could rely on the care, attention, and the vigilance of an agent as we could rely on ourselves? In any case, trade in this country requires particularly local knowledge. Only Canadiens can make a good choice of merchandise that will suit the inhabitants of the province. Are there many Canadiens who cross the ocean on their own to supervise the purchase or choice of goods to be imported? If they did this they would save the commissions, discounts, by which the intermediary agents between them and the European manufacturer or producer profit. . . .
>
> *La Minerve*, July 13, 1829.

The Lot of An Upper Canadian Squatter—A Plea for Help, 1833

In Upper Canada, many rural settlers were beset by financial worries and the threat of losing their land. The practice of squatting on lots without legal title was widespread in areas like Peel County in the late 1820s and early 1830s. One such settler, David Long of Albion Township, was threatened with eviction in June of 1833 and offered this plea for help. (The appeal was futile. His land was put up for auction and he was dispossessed.)

> [It cost] $23 five journeys to York and back making 180 miles . . . with loss of my toenails and three weeks idleness [sic] it is a pity if I lost it I being prepared to go on direct, having some utensils a yoke oxen 3 cows and what is better four sons . . . who are all desirous of being their own servants . . . I hope you will pardon me, theres [sic] now [sic] man a greater object for land than I am at present . . . I beseech you for God-almightys [sic] sake to assist me . . . .
>
> Ontario Archives, CLP, Township Papers, Albion Township, Concession IV, Lots 34, 35 (1833), cited in David Gagan, *Hopeful Travellers: Families, Land and Social Change in Mid-Victorian Peel County, Canada West* (Toronto: Ontario Historical Studies Series, 1980).

The Economic Imperatives of the Mercantile Interests—Two Views

While both provinces faced agricultural difficulties, merchants in the cities and towns sought to increase trade by improving transportation through the waterways of the Canadas. Many Upper Canadian entrepreneurs and members of the Lower Canadian English mercantile community sought government revenues to help finance the construction of canals. Such government aid to commercial interests was, not surprisingly, strongly opposed by both Upper Canadian rural farmers and elements of French Canadian agrarian society. Two separate letters, written by Adam Thom, a Scottish-born defender of Lower Canadian mercantile interests, and by William Merritt, a leading Upper Canadian promoter of canal-building, express some of the frustrations and aspirations of the merchant class in the 1830s.

Adam Thom's "Anti-Gallic" Viewpoint, 1835

Will the French faction, my lord [Governor, Lord Gosford], devote the public revenue to the improvement of the commercial facilities of the province? Will the demagogues deepen Lake St. Peter? Will they improve and extend the wharves of Montreal? Will they complete the magnificent line of communication so nobly undertaken by their tributary victim of Upper Canada? Will they make one effort to render Montreal, what nature destined her to be, the rival of New York? No, my lord; they will not do anything, that at all tends to inundate the sacred soil of a French province with British, or Irish, or American foreigners.... They will appropriate [the funds]...to local objects, which ought to be accomplished by local assessments, and thus buy the support or at least the neutrality of individuals, who are too shortsighted to see the fatal consequences of French supremacy....

Adam Thom, *Anti-Gallic Letters; Addressed to His Excellency, the Earl of Gosford, Governor-in-Chief of the Canadas* (Montreal: 1836), p. 42.

William Merritt's Appeal for Increased Trade, 1839

From our defective system (based on separate Legislatures), we have lost the trade of the entire Country bordering on Lake Champlain at the North, and from thence as far West as Lake Superior—lying within the boundaries of the United States—It now behooves us to regain what we have lost by the negligence, ignorance, supineness and powerless situation of two divided Legislatures—as well as by the want of attention to our best interests on the part of the Home Government—and to open [the Line of our Water] communication on such a scale as will ensure the *transit* in all time to come...

The St. Lawrence and Mississippi Rivers are the two natural outlets in a North and South direction, from the interior of this continent.... Nature has placed their trade and commerce within our reach—and future ages will applaud the wisdom of the Legislature who commenced the St. Lawrence Canal on a sufficient scale to insure its full and complete usefulness....

William Hamilton Merritt to Sir George Arthur, St. Catharines, February 6, 1839, in H.A. Innis and A.R.M. Lower, eds., *Select Documents in Canadian Economic History, 1783–1885* (Toronto: University of Toronto Press, 1933), pp. 183–4.

The Condition of Agriculture—A Report on Lower Canada, 1837

The unsatisfactory state of agriculture was a major source of discontent among reformers in agrarian areas of the two provinces. In August of 1836, the *Quebec Gazette*, for example, published a report on agricultural conditions in Lower Canada. Its publisher, John Neilson, was a loyal British subject who very much admired the French Canadian way of life. If his report of the agricultural conditions was accurate, it would seem that many French Canadians joined the protests of 1837 with empty stomachs.

> During the sixteen years that we have furnished Agricultural Reports for the Quebec *Gazette*, we never sat down to the task with such unfavourable forebodings as at present.
> The drought noticed in our report for June has continued during two months; till the 29th July, nothing but some light showers occurred to allay its destructive effects on every kind of vegetation. The heat was excessive in the first week of the month; the thermometer having been, on several days, at 98° in the shade. It was succeeded by parching, clear, easterly winds, and then, alternately, cool, clear, and warm days, till the close of the month. All the rains that fell never penetrated more than an inch into the ground, which remained underneath like a dry cake. . . .
> Hay-making commenced about the middle of the month, or rather, on more than one-half of the meadows the mowers cut down a dried stubble, or withered grass, not worthy of the name of hay. It is only on low, rich lands that there is anything like a crop.
> Turnip-seed sown at the usual time did not come up for want of moisture . . .
> The late sown potatoes did not come up or only here and there a stalk. The early sown ones, although presenting a tolerable appearance above ground, have no tubers. . . .
> The oats and peas are stunted, and will be unproductive excepting on low lands. Barley is also short and of doubtful appearance.
> Wheat is the best crop, and will probably be an average on all low lands. . . .
> In fact, never in the memory of the oldest inhabitants have the prospects of the harvest been so unfavourable in this vicinity. It behoves the poorer classes to exert all their industry and practise the greatest economy and foresight, to provide the necessaries of life for the ensuing winter. It behoves the wealthier classes to remember that they are the 'stewards of the poor', to waste nothing, and be prepared for the calls that will be made on them. . . .
> *The Quebec Gazette*, August 1, 1836.

ELEMENTS OF A "NATIONAL-DEMOCRATIC REVOLUTION"

Strains of Republican Influence—William Lyon Mackenzie's Revolutionary Writings, 1837

Democratic freedom and republican ideas of national independence were sometimes cited by rebels and *patriotes* as their ultimate goals. Although early expressions of revolutionary ideas were rare, by 1836 and 1837 rebel leaders, perhaps out of accumulated frustration, began to exhort their supporters to revolt with stirring slogans of liberty, democracy and nationality. It is questionable whether such ideals truly motivated the rebels, or whether they were merely rhetorical fuel which, added to the smouldering sources of discontent, provided a noble rationale for rebellion.

Elements of American republican ideas could be seen in William Lyon Mackenzie's writings of 1836–37. Much of this radical outpouring was found in *The Constitution*, a newspaper founded by Mackenzie shortly after his crushing personal defeat in the election of 1837. A casual reading might suggest that he had become strongly attracted to American revolutionary thought and Jacksonian democracy. Yet Mackenzie himself in 1836 disclaimed any strong attachment to American republican institutions and his regular "epistles" also contained ideas rooted in British Whiggism[2] and conservative reaction. Two examples from Mackenzie's revolutionary writings seem to provide contradictory evidence.

BRAVE CANADIANS! God has put into the bold and honest hearts of our brethren in Lower Canada to revolt—not against "lawful" but against "unlawful authority". The law says we shall not be taxed without our consent by the voices of the men of our choice, but a wicked and tyrannical government has trampled upon that law—robbed the exchequer—divided the plunder—and declared that, regardless of justice they will continue to roll their splendid carriages, and riot in their palaces, at our expense—that we are poor spiritless ignorant peasants, who were born to toil for our betters. But the peasants are beginning to open their eyes . . . —too long have they been hoodwinked by Baal's priests—by hired and tampered with preachers, wolves in sheep's clothing, who take the wages of sin, and do the work of iniquity. . . .

CANADIANS! Do you love freedom? I know you do. Do you hate oppression? Who dare deny it? Do you wish perpetual peace, and a government founded upon the eternal heaven-born principle of the Lord Jesus Christ—a government bound to enforce the law to do to each other as you would be done by? . . .

Up then, brave Canadians! Get ready your rifles, and make short work of it; a connection with England would involve us in all her wars, undertaken for her own advantage, never for ours; with governors from England, we will have bribery at elections, corruption, villainy and perpetual discord in every township, but Independence would give us the means of enjoying many blessings. . . . Woe be to those who oppose us, for 'In God is our trust.'

Margaret Fairley, *The Selected Writings of William Lyon Mackenzie* (Toronto: Oxford University Press, 1960), pp. 222–5.

. . . We, the people of the State of Upper Canada, acknowledging with gratitude the grace and beneficence of God, in permitting us to make choice of our form of government, and in order to establish justice, ensure domestic tranquility, provide for the common defence, promote the general welfare, and secure the blessings of civil and religious liberty to ourselves and our posterity, do establish this Constitution.

10. The military shall be kept under strict subordination to civil power. No soldier shall, in time of peace, be quartered in any house without the consent of the owner, nor in time of war but in a manner to prescribed by law . . . .

22. The Legislative authority of this State shall be vested in a General Assembly, which shall consist of a Senate and House of Assembly, both to be elected by the people . . . .

40. Any bill may originate in either House of the Legislature; and all bills passed by one House may be amended or rejected by the other. . . .

56. There shall never be created within this State any incorporated trading companies, or incorporated companies with banking powers. Labour is the only means of creating wealth . . . .

---

2. British Whiggism refers to a political philosophy popular in the eighteenth and nineteenth centuries associated with a strong belief in "the rights of all Englishmen" and opposition to Tory ideas of aristocratic rule.

58. The Executive power shall be vested in a Governor. He shall hold his office for three years. No person shall be eligible to that office who shall not have attained the age of thirty years....

78. All powers not delegated by this Constitution remain with the people....

81. This Constitution, and the laws of this state, which shall be made in pursuance thereof, and all treaties, made, or which shall be made under the authority of this State, shall be the supreme law of the land, and the judges shall be bound thereby.

The Constitution, November 15, 1837.

A Revolt of the French Canadians—The "British Party" View, 1837

In Lower Canada the insurrections of 1837–38 seemed to bear the signs of a conflict rooted in the differences between the French Canadians and the British. While the rebel forces consisted mainly of *Canadiens* who called themselves *patriotes* and later *Frères Chasseurs*, the strongest defenders of the Château Clique were the commercial interests that dominated the appointed councils and were known as the "British party". When rebellion broke out in the fall of 1837, the British party's Constitutional Association quickly concluded that the conflict was a nationalist struggle caused by the misguided ambitions of French Canadians.

When sedition and rebellion have boldly proclaimed themselves, in the most populous and prosperous portions of this once contented and apparently loyal Province, and when anarchy and confusion have set the laws at defiance, and outraged the harmony and quiet of social life, the question naturally arises, to what circumstances of oppression, or to what unredressed grievances such a calamitous state of things is to be ascribed....

The possession of the right of almost universal suffrage, and of a numerical popular majority of the provincial constituency, gave the complete command of the Representative branch of the Legislature to the French Canadians, who soon exhibited a perfect knowledge of their advantage....

The French Canadian population were...not only nationally inclined to mark their active opposition to their fellow-subjects of British and Irish origin, but they have been taught to consider them as strangers and trespassers upon their soil...they have in fine been taught to believe themselves oppressed by their fellow-subjects of British and Irish origin...desperate men made an open livelihood by influencing the population of French origin to acts of violence.... In all cases, the object was attained, active discontent was introduced into the passive population, and noon day meetings gradually ripened into sedition and rebellion.

It is this exclusive French Canadian spirit alone which has given rise to all the discontent existing in this Province, it is this which has in fact made the question one of national origin and not of political party, in it is to be discovered the source of all the disturbances which have brought sedition and rebellion in their train, and in it alone is to be found a full and complete answer to the enquiry, to what causes the present unhappy condition of this Province is to be ascribed.

Address of the Constitutional Association of the City of Montreal to the Inhabitants of the Sister Colonies, December 13, 1837, in W.P.M. Kennedy, *Statutes, Treaties and Documents of the Canadian Constitution, 1713–1729* (Toronto: Oxford, 1930), pp. 347–50.

Motivations of the *Patriotes*—Images of A National "People's Revolution"

It was not only the British party that viewed the risings of 1837 and 1838 in Lower Canada as a struggle between the French and English. The armed clashes of November and December 1837 between Sir John Colborne's militia forces and the *patriotes* have been depicted visually in ways that conjure up images of a French Canadian "national resistance". The two illustrations which follow, for example, have served as powerful nationalist reminders of the rebellions. A famous lithograph of the Battle of St. Eustache (December 14, 1837), originally published in 1840, captured the spectacle of a small band of *patriotes* led by Dr. Jean-Olivier Chénier scattering before the advancing militia. Another well-known representation, a portrait of an armed *patriote* of '37, was later used as a symbol of Quebec separatism and could be found emblazoned on F.L.Q. communiqués during the October Crisis of 1970.

An Impressionistic View of the Battle of St. Eustache, 1837

Battle of St. Eustache, 14 December 1837

A *Patriote's* Call for Independence—Chevalier DeLorimier's Political Testament, 1838

Judging from statements issued after the insurrections, some *patriotes* believed that they were engaged in a popular uprising aimed at overthrowing their British conquerors and establishing an independent French Canadian state. One of the twelve who were hanged for treason, the Montreal notary, Chevalier DeLorimier, offered this final testament to the cause: .

> I die without remorse; all that I desired was the good of my country, in insurrection and in independence...For 17 to 18 years I have taken an active part in almost every popular movement, always with conviction and sincerity. My efforts have been for the independence of my compatriots; thus far we have been unfortunate...

But the wounds of my country will heal—the peace-loving Canadian will see liberty and happiness born anew on the St. Lawrence....

I have only a few hours to live, and I have sought to divide them between my duty to religion and that due to my compatriots: for them I die on the gallows the infamous death of a murderer, for them I leave behind my young children and my wife, alone, for them I die with the cry on my lips: *Vive la Liberté, Vive l'Indépendance!*

Chevalier DeLorimier, "Political Testament". Reprinted in Stanley B. Ryerson, *Unequal Union: Confederation and the Roots of Crisis in the Canadas, 1815–1873* (Toronto: Progress Brooks, 1968), p. 81.

CONFLICTING INTERPRETATIONS

The nature of the struggle which erupted in the rebellions of 1837–38 is a subject which has generated extensive historical debate. Since the early works of Charles Lindsey (1862) and J.C. Dent (1885), traditional Whig interpretations of the rebellions have portrayed the disturbances as part of a political struggle between the forces of "popular reform" and the established, oligarchical colonial order. Following this view, Liberal nationalist scholars of the early twentieth century tended to treat the uprisings as an important catalyst in the country's political progress—a rare violent outburst in the otherwise peaceful and paper-strewn path toward responsible government. Yet in recent decades interpreters have argued variously that the rebellions were at root part of an economic struggle, an abortive national-democratic revolution, or two concurrent, but only loosely related, political outbreaks.

VIEWS OF THE POLITICAL-CONSTITUTIONAL STRUGGLE

"Democracy" vs. "Privilege"—A Traditional Whig View of Political Unrest

Much of the traditional interpretation of the rebellion in Upper Canada was set down in J.C. Dent's *The Story of the Upper Canadian Rebellion* (1885). Adopting a view sympathetic to the Reform cause, Dent interpreted the rebellion as a classic struggle between "democracy" and "privilege". In the 1920s this line of interpretation was further pursued and developed by Aileen Dunham in *Political Unrest in Upper Canada*, an account of the political steps leading to rebellion. Like previous commentators, Dunham contended that the problems of Lower Canada were more severe than those of the upper province. Dunham's analysis of the causes of discontent in Upper Canada focused on the ongoing struggle between the Family Compact and the Assembly.

During most of the period...upper classes the world over were dominated by the conservative reaction after the American and French Revolutions, and it was natural for government to be composed wholly of tories. If the people tended more and more to push men of liberal political ideas to the foreground, it is not surprising that the old tories looked askance at these upstarts . . . . The Upper Canadian officials wrapped their robes of office tightly about them, and had to submit, willy nilly, to the popular nickname, the family compact. In Lower Canada, under similar conditions, the situation was even worse, for there a racial division was added to the political and social one . . . Certain general evils resulted, however, from this type of government . . . . The machinery of government was too heavy for the sparse population. This defect is common in pioneer lands and is remedied naturally by time. The constitution, by depriving the assembly of any real responsibility or power, tended to draw into public activities men who were grievance-mongers and agitators rather than men who were statesmen and administrators. The complete separation of powers between the nominated and elected branches of the government invited friction. The constitution, with all its defects, was difficult to modify. The impossibility of legislative reform in the face of the Canadian executive threw the hope of advance entirely on acts of the imperial parliament, and statesmen in England were not sufficiently in touch with provincial affairs to devote much attention or interest to the subject. The high degree of centralization needed in 1791 had served its purpose before 1840, and should have given way to greater popular control. As, however, the constitution remained rigid, political unrest ensued. In such a state of affairs a certain degree of unrest was the natural accompaniment of growth. Had the people not agitated for reform, they would not have been worthy of the small amount of power already accorded them.

Aileen Dunham, *Political Unrest in Upper Canada 1815–1836* (Toronto: McClelland and Stewart, 1963), pp. 45–46.

Mackenzie's Rebellion—An Early Revisionist View

Not every historian saw the Upper Canadian rebellion as a struggle of "the people" against the privileged order. William Dawson LeSueur, an early critical biographer of Mackenzie[3] contended that the causes for discontent in Upper Canada were not as extensive as those in Lower Canada, and that Mackenzie's uprising was by no means inevitable or even necessary. The Yonge Street rebellion, according to LeSueur, delayed more than it advanced the reformers' cause by inviting repressive action and disrupting the previous slow but steady progress toward constitutional reform.

. . . while in [Lower Canada] the rebellion was the almost inevitable outcome of a prolonged and hopeless quarrel between an overwhelming majority of the legislature and the executive, involving a continued withholding of the supplies, in Upper Canada the executive was on the best possible terms with a large majority of the legislature and the so-called rebellion was solely due to the turbulence and mad spirit of adventure of one man, and the fatuous ignoring by another of the plain beginnings of mischief. The conjunction of William Lyon Mackenzie and Francis Bond Head made the Upper Canada rebellion such as it was. Without Mackenzie there would have been no rebellion; but neither could Mackenzie have made it under such a governor say as Sir John Colborne, or any man of ordinary prudence, firmness and good sense . . . .

3. LeSueur's critical biography, written in the 1920s, so enraged the Mackenzie family that court action blocked its publication (i.e., by denying permission for use of family documents) until recently.

As to his influence on the political development of Canada very different views have been expressed; but the best opinion of today, unless the writer of this volume is wholly in error, is that it was retardatory rather than otherwise.... Rebellion, if unsuccessful, is always followed by reaction—sometimes even if successful—and it is not difficult to trace in the policy of the three governors who preceded Lord Elgin, and even in the early policy of Lord Elgin himself, a less favourable disposition towards responsible government than the Colonial Office had begun to manifest in the days of Sir Francis Head. The problem of Upper Canada, as it presented itself to the home authorities, was complicated, it should always be remembered, by the companion problem of Lower Canada.... Lower Canada had taken the bit in its teeth in a way that Upper Canada had not. There the government was face to face with a permanently hostile majority of the legislative Assembly. In Upper Canada the government had from time to time the support of the Assembly, and was strongly supported in that body for over a year before the rebellion broke out.... Mackenzie—we have his own word for it—had pledged himself to support a rising in Lower Canada by a similar movement in Upper Canada; and thus it was that the latter province was most needlessly dragged out of a course of steady and peaceful, if not very rapid, constitutional development....

William Dawson LeSueur, *William Lyon Mackenzie: A Reinterpretation*, Carleton Library No. 111 (Toronto: Macmillan, 1979), pp. 353–4, 388–9.

Constitutional Reform or Racial Nationalism?—A Traditional View of the Revolt in Lower Canada

Helen Taft Manning, an American scholar specializing in British imperial history, was one historian who saw the political unrest in Lower Canada as a struggle of constitutional principles, rather than one of races. In her major study, *The Revolt of French Canada* (1962), Manning argued that the *patriotes* were concerned more with political issues than with questions of language and race in the pre-rebellion years. Her analysis of the election of 1834, for example, rejected the common assumption that French Canadians were fighting for an elected Legislative Council as a means to achieve *Canadien* supremacy in government. Referring to a contemporary pamphlet in English, entitled "What is the Result of the Elections?", Manning wrote:

[the] author sets out to prove that the election turned entirely on the political issues involved, and that questions of race and language were scarcely raised except by members of the English party...

The election, according to this writer, turned entirely on the question of how members voted on the Ninety-two Resolutions, which he regards as the embodiment of the 'elective principle', the new slogan of Mackenzie in Upper Canada as well as of Papineau in the lower province. Twenty-seven persons had voted against the Resolutions or were known to be against them. Of this number seventeen had withdrawn from the contest, seven Canadians and ten English-speaking members. In the election twelve of the seventeen were replaced by members 'favourable to the elective principle'....
The only part of the province where no striking changes occurred was the county of the Gaspé where two members opposed to the elective principle were returned. Of the ten members of the moderate party who offered themselves for re-election six were defeated. In all only four men who had voted against the Resolutions were re-elected and they were able to add to their number only three or four of the new arrivals.

On the whole, if the writer of this pamphlet is accurate in his classifications, his point that national prejudice played little part in the selection of members is established. There were, in fact, two more Englishmen in the new assembly than in the former one, the same number of Irish, Swiss and Germans, two less Americans and two more Canadians. Of members not born on Canadian soil there were twenty-five, and they were, in several cases, returned by constituencies whose voters were mostly Canadian. The Irish leader, [Dr. E.B.] O'Callaghan, had defeated a Canadian in the county of Yamaska where the voters were for the most part, habitants. 'The reply of the Canadian electors [says the pamphleteer] was characteristic of their extraordinary steadiness to principle: "Better, said they, a good Irishman than a bad Canadian."

H. T. Manning, *The Revolt of French Canada 1800–1835* (Toronto: Macmillan, 1962), pp. 362–4.

VIEWS OF AN ECONOMIC STRUGGLE

A Laurentian Interpretation of the Rebellions

The late Donald G. Creighton offered a view of the rebellions within the context of the history of the St. Lawrence commercial waterway system. In his classic work, *The Empire of the St. Lawrence* (1956), he argued that the rebellions found their roots in an economic contest between agrarian interests and British colonial governments which favoured the commercial class.

... the quarrel between settlement and commerce, which had begun with the beginning of the Canadian fur trade, was inevitably aggravated under the régime of the new staples. There were those who looked upon the Canadas simply as a great imperial trading system: there were those who regarded the St. Lawrence as the centre of a new homeland, of future North American communities....

... it was only natural that the trades of the St. Lawrence should form the main economic basis for the controlling political and social group. While the merchants were anxious enough to use the strength and seek the favours of government, the professional men were often ready to accept directorships in commercial companies and to promote commercial projects; and the 'Family Compact' in both Upper and Lower Canada was less a company of blood-relations than it was a fraternal union of merchants, professional men and bureaucrats. The group was relatively small; and the names of a few dozen persons turn up again and again, with almost equal regularity in the affairs of business and of government, until the extent of their monopoly control suggests the practical identification of the political and commercial state....

In one important respect, the rebellions were the final expression of that hatred of the rural communities for the commercialism of the St. Lawrence; and the defence of constituted political authority was an exciting incident in the ceaseless effort to protect the interests of the Canadian commercial state. The rebellions came, and had to come, from the countryside; but the existing order found its most violent supporters among the magistrates, the civil servants and the merchants. The towns were the citadels of the governing class; they were, in particular, the strongholds of the powerful and determined commercial group; and it was appropriately enough in Montreal, the focus of the whole northern trading system, that toryism found its most provocative and violent expression. Even in the tiny villages of the countryside, as Mackenzie found to his cost, the local shopkeepers were energetic in opposing the radicals....

Thus the governing class, a small and fairly compact body, inspired by a common purpose and speaking a common language with great conviction and authority, stood ready for its final battle with the agricultural interest of the two provinces. In sharp contrast with the opposition, it was, as it had always been, the party devoted to the realization of the commercial empire of the St. Lawrence; and this connection with big business, with the economic development of the country by private capital and public expenditure, was the strength as well as the weakness of the group....

Donald Creighton, *The Empire of the St. Lawrence* (Toronto: Macmillan, 1956), pp. 260–4, 269, 286, 316.

The Harvest of Economic Crisis—Fernand Ouellet's Interpretation.

The "agricultural crisis" in Lower Canada during the mid-1830s has been cited as an important factor contributing to the outbreak of the 1837 rebellion in that province. This thesis, first proposed by W.H. Parker, a Canadian historical geographer, holds that the real source of discontent in the rural districts was a decline in wheat production that left the usually comfortable *habitant* in dire financial straits. Since Parker's article, a historical debate has raged over the nature and severity of the crisis affecting Lower Canada's agricultural economy in the decades before the rebellions. While all historians agree that the Lower Canadian economy was transformed by changing world markets, they are divided regarding the effects of such changes on Lower Canadian agriculture in the pre-rebellion years. Professor Fernand Ouellet, the French Canadian historian, has adopted the Parker thesis and defended it against the critics.

In the following passage, Ouellet contends that the crisis was severe enough to ravage the agricultural sector and to spark a wave of French Canadian discontent born of economic despair.

To understand fully the nature and real repercussions of the rebellions of 1837–1838, it is not sufficient simply to cite the reactions to [Lord John] Russell's Resolutions, any more than it is to emphasize the preceding political conflicts. It is just as important to take into consideration the economic, social, demographic, and psychological aspects of this revolutionary attempt, since it is impossible to believe that the rural population with its low level of education and its traditions could have been aware of the constitutional principles involved in the debate. They were not trying to promote a democratic society by their action. The reaction of the habitant sprang from sources more intimately connected with his everyday existence and his mental outlook....

The economic trends taking form at the turn of the century were thrown into sharper relief after 1815. As the decline of the fur trade gathered momentum, the agricultural situation of Lower Canada was becoming more critical. The lower prices which had prevailed for so long accentuated the problems facing the inhabitants of Lower Canada. This economic crisis was not, however, universal. The development of the lumbering industry and the expansion of agriculture in Upper Canada, in spite of violent fluctuations, did a great deal to alleviate the existing problems. Nevertheless, the economic situation remained, on the whole, unfavourable.

The decline in wheat production, in spite of occasional increases, continued without interruption after the War of 1812. Surpluses for export became progressively smaller, until after 1832 the deficits became chronic. At this stage the consumer in Lower Canada was obliged to import a large part of the grain necessary for subsistence either from Upper Canada or from the United States. The decline could not be attributed to a lesser demand from foreign markets, for as time went on these demands increased. Nor was its main cause the epidemic of wheat rust, since this did not occur in full force until 1835. It was owing, rather, to the continuance of outmoded techniques which inevitably caused an exhaustion of the land; however, it has a much greater significance for it was an expression of the deep agricultural crisis existent in Lower Canada during these times.

This decisive turn of events resulted in the restriction of agricultural production until it was aimed at mere subsistence. The habitant, in order to feed himself, was obliged to increase the number of his cattle and swine and resort to replacement crops, such as the potato, that had no foreign outlets. Furthermore, the impoverished farmer found it more difficult to obtain textiles and wools imported from Great Britain, and therefore was forced to devote more attention to the raising of sheep and the production of linen. In concentrating his efforts in this direction the habitant, instead of participating in the internal markets, was rather obeying a defence mechanism which led him to assert his agricultural independence. This reaction explains why Lower Canada remained a heavy importer of dairy products and butchered meats during this period. Technical progress did not keep pace with the increase in the quantities produced. Thus, after 1832, when the crisis forced the agricultural producer to substitute commodities, he was inevitably forced to watch a reduction in animal husbandry.

The extent of the crisis became more apparent as 1837 approached; it plunged the peasantry into debt, imperilled patrimonies and engendered rancour and discontent. Instead of looking for a remedy to his problems through technical improvements, the French-Canadian farmer was led to look outward for the responsibility for his misfortunes. The political élite, although occasionally rather patronizing toward the agricultural groups, did help the farmers to find scapegoats in the capitalist, the immigrant, the local government, and, before long, in the British Government as well—in a word, the *English*.

> Fernand Ouellet, "The Insurrections" in P.G. Cornell et al., *Canada: Unity in Diversity* (Toronto: Holt, Rinehart, Winston, 1967), pp. 216–17.

Land Granting and Social Class—A Critical Analysis of the Upper Canadian System

The extent of contemporary complaints about the government's methods of granting land has prompted historians to study the effects of Upper Canada's land policy on the settlement patterns, development, and social structure of rural areas of the province. In an article entitled "Land Policy, Population Growth and Social Structure in the Home District," 1793–1851, historian Leo A. Johnson examined the way in which an inequitable system of land grants contributed to the settlers' discontent in the years leading up to the rebellion in Upper Canada.

> Of all the problems which faced the government of Upper Canada in its early years, perhaps none was so important nor proved so vexatious as the disposition and settlement of the crown lands. Impoverished in all else, Upper Canada possessed an abundance of good land which, in the early years at least, seemed to be inexhaustible.

In the absence of money, land was viewed as capital, to be accumulated .nd spent as needed. When Loyalists demanded repayment for losses, land was awarded; when militia and military begged rewards for valour and service, land was given; when Lieutenant-Governor John Graves Simcoe and his successors dreamed of creating an aristocracy, land was seen as its basis, and when the Colonial Office decided to create a class of labourers and servants in Upper Canada, land policy was seen as the means.

Yet if land was to be viewed as capital, it carried with it two serious defects: its value was only potential, and it was not readily convertable into other kinds of assets. Its very abundance reduced its desirability and made it hard to dispose of at a price. Thus it was in the interest of the immigrants to demand free land and to oppose speculation and monopoly, but once in possession of his land, it was equally to his benefit to oppose cheap land policies and to reject interference with his control of his most important asset....

...Farmers, merchants, colonial officials, and the Upper Canadian government all found themselves at odds with each other and with the land-capitalists over the land question. The results of these tensions and ensuing conflicts would do much to embitter Upper Canadian politics, and to shape the society which would ultimately emerge....

* * * * *

...In the long run, Government land policy in Upper Canada was concerned with much more than mere distribution of lands. In effect, it became the medium through which policy makers attempted to shape not only the manner in which land was acquired and held, but also the very nature of society itself. In Home District the effects of these policies were deeply felt. Since few could escape, or hope to escape, the drastic consequences of such policy decisions, they remained the centre of political controversy and conflict all through the period.

Leo A. Johnson, "Land Policy, Population Growth and Social Structure in the Home District, 1793-1851", *Ontario History*, Vol. LXIII, 1, (March 1971).

VIEWS OF A "NATIONAL-DEMOCRATIC" REVOLUTION

The Revolt in Lower Canada—A National-Democratic Revolution

Few major events in nineteenth-century Canadian history fit into a Marxian frame of analysis as neatly as the rebellions of 1837 in the Canadas. Much of the Marxist-nationalist interpretation finds its origins in the general interpretive works of Stanley B. Ryerson.

In his best known book, *Unequal Union: Confederation and the Roots of Crises in the Canadas, 1815-1873* (1968), Ryerson combined his Marxist perspective with a neo-nationalist interpretation. According to this scholar, the revolt of the *patriotes* was a French Canadian "national-democratic revolution" against their British colonial masters which ended in defeat and brutal repression.

...Inseparable from one parliamentary contest was the wide-ranging struggle over the innumerable economic and political grievances that landlordism and colonial-compact rule engendered. Gradually as the struggle sharpened, the fundamental political issue of *Canadian independence* was thrust to the fore. It was to be proclaimed in 'declarations of independence' in both the Canadas....

In Lower Canada, the struggle involved not only colonial self-government, as in the other provinces, but the right of national self-determination for the French-Canadian nation. From the Conquest onward, this was to become the burning issue in the valley of the St. Lawrence.

The leader of this powerful national-democratic movement in French Canada was Louis-Joseph Papineau....

...Growing up in the years that followed the French Revolution, he was profoundly influenced by that historic upheaval, and to the end of his life bore the imprint of its revolutionary-democratic thought, interwoven with the national-democratic spirit of French Canada's fight for survival. In his last public speech before his death, Papineau summed up in these words his life-long creed as a democrat: 'The good teachings of modern times, I have found condensed, explained, and given over to the love of peoples...in a few lines of the Declaration of Independence of 1776 and of the Declaration of the Rights of Man and the Citizen of 1789.'

The struggle in Lower Canada started with the resistance of the French Canadians to national oppression. It soon embraced the issues of legislative control of the revenue, freedom of press and assembly, and colonial self-government. It thus paralleled the struggles in Upper Canada and those (in a less acute form) in the Atlantic provinces. Soon, as the contest sharpened, there came the first beginnings of joint effort and mutual support on the part of the national-democratic, patriotic forces in all three areas....

But inseparable from the question of representative government was the issue of French-Canadian national rights. To the growth of the sentiment of nationality, of the existence of a 'nation canadienne,' Colonial Secretary Huskisson counterposed England's 'duty and interest': having 'carried our language, our free institutions, and our system of laws, to the most remote corners of the globe,' it was now imperative to 'imbue (the colony) with English feeling, and benefit it with English laws and institutions'....

[In an attempt to stifle French-Canadian rights] newspapers were prosecuted, judges removed from office, French-Canadian militia battalions dissolved. Petitions addressed to London protesting against the repression gathered the signatures of no less than eighty-seven thousand persons....

Stanley Ryerson, *Unequal Union: Confederation and the Roots of Crisis in the Canadas, 1815–1873* (Toronto: Progress Books, 1968), pp. 44–7.

The Roots of the Western Upper Canada Rising—A Recent Differing Interpretation

Few historians have seen any evidence of a "people's revolution" in Upper Canada. Indeed, most scholars have tended to accept the view taken by Gerald M. Craig in 1963 in his survey of Upper Canada that the rebellion was mainly a "comic episode" springing more from local conditions than from the infusion of British or American democratic ideas. Colin Read's recent study of the Duncombe rising in the London area, however, does shed some new light on the nature of the disturbances.

Read has raised some questions about whether the rebels were representatives of the "common people". The followers of Duncombe, according to Read, were mostly mature, prosperous men of property, but largely American by birth or origin, which may have made them more receptive to radical republican ideas.

> ...the Duncombe rebels may be divided roughly into three occupations: an agrarian 'proprietorial' group of farmers and farmer's sons; a more or less skilled 'middle class' of craftsmen, millers, professionals, and so on; and a 'lower class' of labourers and hired farm hands. Contemporary evidence suggests that the insurgents were not economically disadvantaged but were rather a reasonably mature, well-established body of men....
>
> Most known to have mustered under Duncombe were relatively mature, well-settled, prosperous members of an agrarian community. This seems to have been true, documentary evidence suggests, of the Duncombe insurgents generally. In the regional society of the west neither clear economic nor social conditions distinguished loyalists from rebels. There is no basis for arguing that the rebels comprised a clearly disadvantaged sector of society and hence were driven to arms by economic despair or the prospect of plunder....
>
> The majority of rebels were either American-born or the offspring of American parents and may well have retained or adopted the deep American dislike of Britain and have been more willing to rebel, hoping to sever the provincial ties to Great Britain....
>
> ...Whether or not most rebels understood that the revolt was to establish an independent government or just to reform the one they had, their American birth or parentage probably conditioned their response to the rebel call....
>
> ...the Duncombe rising would never have occurred had the rebels known the true state of affairs at Toronto. Those who answered the call to arms believing Mackenzie's revolt successful were certainly misled. Doubtless some men had their own reasons for turning out, a particular grievance against the government, for example, the loss by executive decree of a disputed lot to another claimant or the confiscation of property for non-payment of taxes. Others were driven by the desire for material gain, while others simply did not appreciate the significance of their actions. None the less most rebels turned out for similar reasons and purposes. Most were not members of the Church of England and so had not been exposed to its teachings about the necessity of loyalty to the Crown and the sanctity of the colonial tie. Most were North American in lineage as their local communities were in character. They were thus inclined to welcome change in a government which could be construed as British and colonial.
>
> Colin Read, *The Rising in Western Upper Canada* (Toronto: University of Toronto Press, 1980), pp. 180, 211.

A RECENT SYNTHESIS OF THE STRUGGLE

Two Separate But Interrelated Explosions—Michael Cross' Thesis

Only recently have scholars turned their attention to a thorough examination of the underlying struggle in each of the two provinces. One historian who has offered a comprehensive synthesis of recent research is Michael S. Cross of Dalhousie University. In an "Afterword" to *The Wait Letters*, a collection of correspondence of Benjamin Wait, an Upper Canadian rebel, Professor Cross interpreted the rebellions as two separate, but strangely interrelated, disturbances.

...The troubles of 1837–1838 in British North America grew out of local conditions and local problems; the rebellion movements developed with their own logic.

The rebellions in the two Canadas were quite separate but interrelated explosions. On the political level, it was hard for many contemporaries to share the rosy view of colonial development that hindsight has given historians. In Lower Canada, politics had become polarized between a popular assembly, dominated by French speaking members, and the appointive branches of government, which were overwhelmingly English.... The fact that this political division corresponded to ethnic divisions between English and French made the conflict more bitter, but did not cause it. For similar conflicts arose in Upper Canada, where the assembly as well as the executive was English speaking. There the Reformers had gained control of the assembly between 1828 and 1830 and between 1834 and 1836. On each occasion they found their attempts to reform provincial institutions blocked from above, the business of the province brought to a halt by an intransigent executive which checked and vetoed the legislation brought forth by the Reform assemblies....

This mood of disillusionment, this sense of betrayal, was heightened by the coercion of Lower Canada. Radicals in the upper province had the last vestiges of their faith in Britain shattered; if fundamental rights could be stripped from French Canadians, they could be stripped as well from English Canadians. A powerful feeling of political desperation had seized radicals in both colonies.

Economic distress added to this feeling. Lower Canada had been troubled through-out the 1830's by agricultural depression, the attacks of insects on crops and crop failures. Upper Canada was plunged into depression in 1836 by the stoppage of all public works in the province as the result of cutting off of government funds in the dispute between Bond Head and the assembly. To these domestic problems was added the impact of a general international depression in 1837. Benjamin Wait was far from alone in having to flee Upper Canada to escape from his debts.

Economic causes went deeper than the immediate depression. The rebellions in the Canadas, as with all revolutions, were rooted in the economic relationships of their societies.... By the nineteenth century big business was not an arena ambitious *Canadiens* could even consider attempting to enter. That situation helped add bite to political controversies. Young French Canadians of ambition, business closed to them, entered the liberal professions, law, medicine. And politics. Politics became a surrogate for business, a way of climbing in society, the power and patronage of politics replacing the status and economic rewards of business success. To find the higher reaches of politics closed off by the English as well was frustrating and enraging.

To the degree that this is an accurate picture of the French Canadian political elite, their agitation was selfish, their movement towards rebellion *was* a "conspiracy" to improve their own positions, not a liberal attempt to improve the lot of the people. Some of the so-called 'popular' leaders had little interest in or regard for the people. Louis-Joseph Papineau, the dominant figure in the opposition movement, was a seigneur, a man who owned a great estate on the Ottawa river and whose primary concern was not to help his peasants progress but, rather, to extract the highest possible income from them. Haughty, filled with aristocratic pretensions, Papineau used the rhetoric of democracy but shared few of its basic assumptions....

That the rebellion was not simply a race war is shown by the heavy involvement of Lower Canadian Irish. At the level of leadership there were men such as Dr. Edmund Bailey O'Callaghan, one of the major organizers and theoreticians of the movement. And among the shock troops were Irish workers from Montreal, men with a traditional hatred of England, men frustrated by the discrimination and exploitation they faced in their working lives. They, as with the French Canadian masses, had their own reasons for rebellion, reasons quite distinct from those of the middle class elites who led the revolution.

There were similar political frustrations for middle class men in Upper Canada, their ambitions thwarted by the local elite at Toronto, the Family Compact. But the frustrations did not have the added edge of ethnic tensions and the economic system was far more open to them than it was to their French Canadian counterparts. They might be driven to more extreme political positions by the intransigence of the Compact, but they would not be driven to the extreme of rebellion. . . .

If their backgrounds differed, so did their ideas about what would emerge from rebellion. The middle class leaders foresaw a liberal, laissez-faire society—much like the United States—in which their ambitions would have free rein. Mackenzie, and some of his rural supporters, expected an agrarian utopia of small farms and educated, honest yeomen. Most, perhaps, had no clear vision of the future. Indeed, most probably had no desire to engage in a full-scale revolution. Many rebels later reflected that their goals were much more limited. In Lower Canada it was fighting between the Tory Doric Club and *patriote* organizations which escalated into the rebellion in November 1837. . . .

Was [the Upper Canadian rebellion] a comic and foolish episode, irrelevant to the real political progress of the Canadas? That is certainly the usual view. . . .

Such an interpretation rests on a whole set of dubious assumptions. One is that the rebellion movement had no wide popular support. Given the rapid defeat of the internal rising, thanks to its poor execution, it is an assumption which cannot be tested, for only the foolhardy would have rallied to a losing cause. One could argue with equal plausibility that a body of support existed which could not be mobilized because of the fiasco on Yonge Street in December 1837; certainly government observers of the time feared that such support for rebellion existed and might emerge to the surface under certain circumstances. . . .

The interpretation assumes, as well, that the rebels were 'simple people,' people incapable of making political judgements. However, . . . they in fact tended to be men of substance, established agrarians. . . . Whether or not those involved thought they were engaged in full-scale revolution, they were aware they had undertaken armed resistance to the government. And they knew why they were resisting, they knew they were trying to change an oppressive and unjust society.

. . . The real victors of 1837–1838 were the men who were uninvolved, the men who supported neither side. The suppression of the rebellions destroyed the radicals, the political factions of Papineau and Mackenzie. The revulsion which followed destroyed the executive elites, the Chateau Clique and the Family Compact. In the 1840's, new forces filled this created vacuum. New business-minded men came to the forefront, modern men, men devoted to the interests of a new capitalist order. . . .

The fall of the radicals and their aristocratic opponents left Canada to the mercies of the 'corporations, monopolies, banks of issue', to the men of 'mercinary character'. That was the ultimate tragedy of the failure of the rebellions of 1837.

Michael S. Cross, ed., "Afterword" in *The Wait Letters* (Erin, Ontario: 1976), pp. 145 ff.,159.

A Guide to Further Reading

1. Overviews

Craig, Gerald M., *Upper Canada: The Formative Years, 1784–1841*. Toronto: McClelland and Stewart, 1963.

Creighton, Donald, *The Empire of the St. Lawrence*. Toronto: Macmillan, 1956.

Cross, Michael, "Afterword" in Benjamin Wait, *The Wait Letters*. Erin, Ontario: Porcupine's Quill Inc., 1976.

Lucas, C.P. ed., *Lord Durham's Report on the Affairs of British North America*, 2 Vols. London: Oxford, 1912.

McCallum, John, *Unequal Beginnings: Agriculture and Economic Development in Quebec and Ontario until 1870*. Toronto: University of Toronto Press, 1980.

Ouellet, Fernand, *Lower Canada 1792–1841*, trans. Patricia Claxton. Toronto: McClelland and Stewart, 1980.

Ryerson, Stanley B., *Unequal Union: Confederation and the Roots of Conflict in the Canadas*. Toronto: Progress Books, 1968.

2. Specialized Studies

The Rising in Lower Canada

Bergeron, Léandre, *The History of Quebec: A Patriot's Handbook*, trans. Baila Markus. Toronto: NC Press, 1971.

Harris, R. Cole, "Of Poverty and Helplessness in Petite-Nation", *Canadian Historical Review*, Vol LII (1971), pp. 23–50.

Le Goff, T.J.A., "The Agricultural Crisis in Lower Canada, 1802–1812: A Review of a Controversy", *Canadian Historical Review*, Vol. LV (March, 1974), pp. 1–31; and "A Reply", *CHR*, LVI (June, 1975), pp. 162–168.

Manning, Helen Taft, *The Revolt of French Canada 1800–1835*. Toronto: MacMillan, 1962.

Ouellet, Fernand, *Louis Joseph Papineau: A Divided Soul*, Canadian Historical Association Booklet no. 11, Ottawa: CHA, 1964.

Paquet, G. and J.-P. Wallot, "Crise agricole et tensions socio-ethniques dans le Bas Canada, 1802–1812", *Revue d'histoire de l'Amérique française*, Vol. XXVI (septembre, 1972), pp. 185–237.

———, "The Agricultural Crisis in Lower Canada, 1802–12: A Response to T.J.A. LeGoff", *Canadian Historical Review*, Vol. LVI (June, 1975), pp. 133–161.

Schull, Joseph, *Rebellion: The Rising in French Canada*. Toronto: Macmillan, 1971.

Séguin, M., *La Nation Canadienne et l'Agriculture 1760–1850*. Trois-Rivières: Express Boréal, 1970.

Discontent in Upper Canada

Cross, Michael, ed., *The Frontier Thesis and the Canadas*. Toronto: Copp Clark, 1970.

Dent, J.C., *The Story of the Upper Canadian Rebellions*, 2 Vols. Toronto: C.B. Robinson, 1885.

Dunham, Aileen, *Political Unrest in Upper Canada 1815–1836*. Toronto: McClelland and Stewart, 1963.

Earl, David W. L., ed., *The Family Compact: Aristocracy or Oligarchy?*. Toronto: Copp Clark, 1967.

Head, Sir Francis Bond, *A Narrative*. Toronto: McClelland and Stewart, 1969.

Johnson, Leo A., "Land Policy, Population Growth and Social Structure in the Home District, 1793–1851", *Ontario History*, Vol. (1971).

Kilbourne, William, *The Firebrand*. Toronto: Clarke, Irwin, 1964.

Lindsey, Charles, *The Life and Times of William Lyon Mackenzie*. Toronto: Morang and Co., 1912.

Rasporich, Anthony W., ed., *William Lyon Mackenzie*. Toronto: Holt, Rinehart and Winston, 1972.

Rea, J.E., "William Lyon Mackenzie—Jacksonian?", *Mid-America*, Vol. L (1968), pp. 223.

Read, Colin F., *The Rising in Western Upper Canada, 1837–8*. Toronto: University of Toronto Press, 1982.

Wilson, Alan, *The Clergy Reserves of Upper Canada: A Canadian Mortmain*. Toronto: University of Toronto Press, 1968.

Document Collections

Craig, Gerald M., ed., *Discontent in Upper Canada*. Toronto: Copp Clark, 1972.

Robeson, Virginia R., et al., eds., *Lower Canada in the 1830s* and *Upper Canada in the 1830s*. Toronto: OISE Press, 1977.

8

THE SOCIAL REFORM IMPULSE IN MID-NINETEENTH-CENTURY BRITISH NORTH AMERICA

Altruism or Social Control?

The mid-nineteenth century was a period of crucial social, economic and political ferment in the British North American colonies. A massive influx of immigrants, mainly from the United States and Britain, had brought a measure of prosperity but also drastic social inequalities. Wave after wave of immigration had begun to transform the colonies from frontier communities into more urban, pre-industrial societies in which public concerns began to develop about crime, health care, schools and social welfare. As the immigrants of the late 1820s and early 1830s swelled the ports of the maritime colonies and filled in the empty lands in the two Canadas, the primitive, spirit-breaking struggle of the pioneer increasingly faded into memory. This growth of settlement meant an end to the physical isolation of frontier communities and an increasing concentration of population in new commercial centres, towns and villages. Much of the impetus for reform seemed to come from an emerging middle class that confronted the problems of rapid social change with the particular outlooks shaped by this more urban and commercial society.

Changing social conditions in mid-nineteenth-century cities and towns seemed to arouse the Victorian social conscience as well as popular anxieties. From the early 1840s onwards, a rising faith in social progress and "improvement" among the colonies' middle classes found expression in public debates over social welfare, poverty relief, crime, temperance, public education and the role of minorities. Such a social reform impulse has traditionally been interpreted as a genuine benevolent desire to care for others in society. It is thanks to the humanitarian efforts of mainly middle-class citizens, it has been said, that fundamental social institutions such as schools, workhouses, prisons, asylums and hospitals sprang up in the colonies.

Recent studies in mid-nineteenth-century social history, however, have suggested a different interpretation of social reform and its motivations and purposes. It has been argued that public-spirited individuals and groups, drawn mainly from the middle classes, actually were seeking to restore order and a sense of stability in tackling society's ills. A determination to assert Victorian values of propriety, order and social improvement, rather than an altruistic desire to help others, is said to have been the driving force motivating most social reformers of the time.

Large-scale immigration to the British-American colonies after 1815 had much to do with awakening the social reform spirit. The colonies, boasted many promoters of British immigration, were a "good poor man's country". And they did indeed prove to be so. Between the early 1820s and 1860 British North America saw the arrival of a succession of immigrant groups ranging from rural Americans, Scottish crofters and poverty-stricken Irish farmers to refugee blacks from the U.S. slave states. In the ports and towns of the Atlantic colonies, heavy overseas immigration and severe economic recession after 1815 forced social ills and the need for state assistance to the forefront of public affairs. In the province of Canada the population swelled and, although most inhabitants still lived in rural areas, there was a marked increase in the number of urban dwellers. Public demand for schooling, apprenticeship, and correctional services rose dramatically, since by 1841 over half the population in the Canadas was under 16 years of age. Unlike the Atlantic colonies, the province of Canada until 1849 lacked both a tradition of state-sponsored welfare and effective institutions of local self-government.

By the 1840s the British-American colonies were ripe for social reform. Cities like Halifax, Montreal, Toronto (York) and Saint John periodically bulged with new immigrants, many of whom were able-bodied paupers or unfortunates, sometimes called "the friendless, homeless and vagrant". Some state poverty relief was offered in cities and towns of the Atlantic region, but voluntary and religious societies and the churches shouldered the responsibility, for the most part, in the Canadas. Along with the rise in the urban population came poverty and attendant increases in crime, particularly in juvenile delinquency. Nor was all well in the field of medical care. Health services in the Atlantic colonies and the Canadas were minimal. No institutions existed for the care and education of the deaf or blind, though in Canada East the religious orders sometimes took them in as charity cases. The insane were cared for in private institutions in the French section of the province, but politicians could not agree on public support of these institutions. Cholera epidemics which ravaged the colonies in the 1830s, and typhoid in later decades, forced governments to set up quarantine facilities and to establish initially temporary, then permanent, local boards of health. Although alcohol was regarded as one of the principal causes of crime, insanity and indigence, few facilities for inebriates, as found in the United States and Europe, were opened. Instead, the campaign against alcohol abuse was left to the churches, popular evangelists and temperance societies. Penal institutions were used to house not only hardened criminals, but also the able-bodied unemployed on the popular Victorian assumption that poverty in most cases was the result of vagrancy and unwillingness to work or save.

A variety of possible motivations have been identified to explain Victorian efforts toward social reform. Some reformers undoubtedly sought to help others not only at the insistence of church leaders, but also out of a sense of Christian duty, for in a society steeped in Christian values, the laws of God and humanity would likely have provided a spur to action. For other reform-minded citizens, involvement in the creation of social institutions may have grown out of a personal or collective search for enhanced status and self-esteem. Signs of such motivation can be seen, for example, in the local pride and public boasting associated with the building of the first lunatic asylums in the Atlantic colonies. The reforming impulse, on the other hand, may well have arisen among middle-class Victorian reformers seeking less to provide humanitarian assistance *per se*, than to expand the role of the state in an increasingly unstable society by attempting to mediate between groups and to control their behaviour. To such reformers, institutions like schools, hospitals and prisons, as well as workhouses and temperance halls, might have been designed to minimize disorder and provide a needed measure of social control.

Canada in the mid-nineteenth century experienced, to be sure, the awakening of a Victorian social conscience. Yet economic and social inequality was a predominant characteristic of life with which middle-class reformers often failed to grapple. What motivated the public-spirited reformers of the 1840s and early 1850s in their efforts to expand the role of the state and private agencies in colonial society? Were the social institutions that were created, like schools, workhouses, hospitals and prisons, designed to help the needy or to correct social offences? And most importantly, were those reformers who promoted social welfare, health care services, public schools and prison reform, particularly in the 1840s, more concerned with protecting traditional values and the established order with which they felt comfortable, than with truly humanitarian change? In other words, were they promoting only those changes which would assure stability, social tranquility and established order, i.e., their own interests—or were they genuinely prepared to promote some fundamental changes which would benefit the disadvantaged? Which motives predominated among these reformers will be left to the reader to decide in the course of this problem study.

SELECTED CONTEMPORARY SOURCES

THE PRECONDITIONS—ORIGINS OF A SOCIAL REFORM IMPULSE

The Experience of the "Hopeful Travellers"—The Immigrant's Welcome in British North America, c. 1820

The rapid social changes of the years from 1820 to the early 1840s touched virtually every area of colonial life. Although such changes were creating more urban, pre-industrial communities, most British North Americans remained farmers in the 1840s. Most newcomers became pioneers, engaged in the arduous task of taming an unfamiliar environment which was a far cry from the cultivated landscape of the mother country. Transportation was a serious problem: the land had to be cleared of trees, swamps had to be drained and roads built, and cash was in short supply even for essentials. Farmers in Canada East were plagued with bad harvests and mounting debts and could not accommodate their numerous children. Immigrants were therefore seen as unwelcome competitors for the few jobs available in the towns. Already out-migration to the New England states had begun. Canada West, unlike the St. Lawrence Valley, still had some good farmland available. However, many of the immigrants who arrived, especially those fleeing the Irish famines of the early 1830s and 1846–47, were destitute. A large number became "hopeful travellers", or squatters who shifted about from one farm to another.

After a difficult voyage, many poor British immigrants found that life, particularly in the "wilderness" or countryside of British North America, was anything but easy, and very different from what the glowing promises made to prospective emigrants had led them to expect.

The immigrant's welcome to British North America, ca. 1820.

The Experience of the "Poorhouse"—A Register of Inmates at the Halifax Poorhouse, 1833–37

Heavy immigration also brought a dramatic increase in the indigent population of the cities and towns. For along with comfortable and affluent colonists, immigrant ships frequently carried the poor and disadvantaged, ranging from poverty-stricken Irish settlers and runaway black slaves to orphan children and the permanently disabled. In the case of the Atlantic colonies the most significant group in sheer numbers was the Irish who, on arrival, crowded into the poorhouses of Halifax, St. John's and Saint John. A register of inmates at the Halifax poorhouse showed the extent and composition of the urban poor in the mid-1830s.

Table 8–1 Residence Indicated for Inmates, 1833–37

	Halifax*N.S.		England	Scotland	Ireland	NFLD.	N.B.	US	OTHER
1833	300	99	94	27	299	17	17	12	32
1834	339	79	80	27	330	27	20	22	41
1835	298	64	77	27	248	10	10	10	47
1836	280	98	71	23	243	9	12	8	62
1837	350	74	53	25	270	10	20	8	45

* With no orphanage or laying-in hospital in Halifax, more than half the town inmates were children.

Journals of the Legislative Assembly, Nova Scotia, 1834–38, as reported in Judith Fingard, "The Relief of the Unemployed Poor in Saint John, Halifax, and St. John's, 1815–1860," *Acadiensis* Vol. 5, No. 1 (1975), p. 32.

The Problem of Alcoholism—A Temperance Hymn, 1844

One of the main sources of social instability in the 1840s and early 1850s was thought to be the problem of alcoholism. Many colonists, new immigrants, and Indians were evidently addicted to the "demon rum". Among groups of temperance crusaders and other social reformers, intemperance was often linked with conditions of poverty, crime, domestic violence and even disease, which made life miserable for a great many. A popular hymn sung by temperance choirs and mechanics' bands[1] in the Canadas in the 1840s provides a glimpse of the problem and an earnest temperance message.

A baby was sleeping; its mother was weeping,
For her husband, a drunkard had left her forlorn;
And the tempest was swelling round their woe-stricken dwelling;
And she cried, oh! my Edward, from folly return.
The hours while she numbered, her baby still slumbered,
Unconscious its father was breaking those vows
He made to its mother that he would protect her,
And watch o'er their offspring when wild winter blows.
But while he is straying, God's law disobeying,
And plunging still deeper and deeper in woe,
His wife is yet praying, that he would bethink him,
And turn from those wild drinks that sink him so low.
Ye husbands and fathers, a voice is now sounding—

---

1. Mechanics' bands were fraternal associations of craft workers, intended for self-help and also educational advancement. They were the predecessors of the Mechanics' Institutes.

The 'water of life' in the tee-total stream
Is speaking to thousands, with blessing abounding;
Then rise! see the truth in its silvery beam.

Canadian Temperance Advocate, 16 August 1844, p. 91.

Social Conditions in An Atlantic Colony—Sir Richard Bonnycastle's Description of Newfoundland, 1842

Conditions varied from one part of British North America to another, but the class structure exhibited certain common features in all of the colonies. Reports on the structure of colonial society often suggested that colonization had resulted in a "levelling" of classes so that there were fewer differences between the upper, ruling class and the "commoners" than in Britain. Sir Richard Bonnycastle, who served as commanding officer of the Royal Engineers in the early 1840s in Newfoundland, has left us a useful description of that colony's social classes.

The upper class, which at home would almost without exception be the middle class, consists of the clergy, judges, councillors, and officers of the state, with the oldest and most wealthy of the merchants holding office.

The middle class—that class so well named in England as the 'shield of society'—consists here of the newer merchants, the conductors of the business of the extensive firms at home, and a growing, most important, and rapidly-increasing number of the sons and daughters of those respectable men who have chosen Newfoundland as the country of their children....

The third class I have no name for, as neither that of labourer nor that of peasantry is applicable.

The third class in Newfoundland are small farmers, small shop-keepers, and fishermen, or fishermen exclusively....

In the towns, of course, there is a still lower class, which is engaged, as elsewhere, in domestic or in menial offices, or employed in hewing wood and drawing water, or as carters, farm servants, etc.

But still, with all these advantages, there are miserable and destitute citizens enough in St. John's, and plenty of poverty in the out-harbours, for which two causes may be assigned.

The fisherman, formerly, during seven months of winter weather, had no resources but idleness or drink. If he was industrious, it is true, he might employ himself, when he resided near the towns, in cutting and hauling fuel with his dogs, from the woods, which have hitherto been looked upon as common property; but since the opening of the coal-mines in Nova Scotia and Cape Breton even this source of profit has been diminished at the capital.... The consequence has been, until the successful introduction of temperance pledges and societies, that those unfortunates, from the accidental causes of a failure in the fishery, from constitutional idleness, sickness, or inability, either took to drinking, or suffered indescribable miseries.

The other cause has been the want of roads and the extensively scattered nature of the coast population. There, if the fishery was unproductive, or the winter very rainy, the solitary settler had no means of answering the cries and wants of his family, however industrious.

...they live on fish dried or salted, and potatoes, if they have been provident enough to raise them, with occasionally the milk of a goat; numbers of these animals being kept, and suffered, like the dogs, to forage for themselves.

These are the very poor, and I am sorry to say, they are somewhat numerous; but even in the capital, they are not clamorous nor obstinate beggars, and to the credit of the higher and middle classes be it said, every exertion is made to ameliorate their condition.

Sir Richard Henry Bonnycastle, *Newfoundland in 1842* (London: Henry Colburn, 1842), Vol. 2, pp. 120–123, 125–126.

THE IMPULSE FOR SOCIAL WELFARE AND PUBLIC HEALTH REFORM

From the 1820s onwards, the incessant flow of immigrants to the British American colonies imposed a heavy strain on their fragile economies and limited social service facilities. Shiploads of immigrants often arrived destitute or weakened by disease. The British-American colonies tried to meet the problem of what Janet Noel has aptly called "the growing numbers of redundant hands, diseased bodies and homeless families" by erecting orphanages, hospitals and "houses of industry". Self-help was another resort of the populace in need of more direct and immediate results than could be hoped for over the long-term from provincial legislation and an improved educational system. Thus, certain enterprising colonists set about organizing mechanics' institutes, agricultural societies, model farms and penny savings banks.

Aiding the Destitute—An Act Concerning Debtors, 1843

Many colonists and new immigrants fell quickly and hopelessly into debt. The problem reached such severity by the early 1840s that colonial officials and public-spirited citizens began to consider seriously the possible remedies. In the united province of Canada, the government came to the relief of the destitute in December 1843 by abolishing imprisonment in execution of debt.

Whereas Imprisonment for Debt where fraud is not imputable to the Debtor, is not only demoralizing in its tendency, but is as detrimental to the true interests of the Creditor as it is inconsistent with that forbearance and humane regard to the misfortunes of others which should always characterize the Legislation of every Christian country; and whereas it is desirable to soften the rigor of the Laws, in that part of this Province called Upper Canada, affecting the relation between Debtor and Creditor, as far as a due regard to the interests of commerce will permit. Be it therefore enacted . . . that from and after the passing of this Act, no person shall be arrested or held to bail, upon any cause of action arising in any foreign country where the defendant would not have been liable to have been arrested or held to bail, had such defendant continued within the jurisdiction of the Courts of such foreign country, or in any civil suit where the cause of action shall not amount to ten pounds of lawful money of this Province, and where the cause of action shall amount to ten pounds and upwards, it shall not be lawful for the Plaintiff to proceed to arrest the body of the defendant or defendants, unless an affidavit be first made by such plaintiff, his servant, or agent, of such cause of action, and the amount justly and truly due to the said Plaintiff from the said defendant, and also that such Plaintiff, his servant or agent, hath good reason to believe, and doth verily believe that the defendant is immediately about to leave the Province of Canada with intent and design to defraud the Plaintiff of the said debt, and that no person shall be taken or charged in execution in any such action for any sum whatever, whether the party shall originally have been held to bail, or been merely served with common process....

Statutes of Canada, 1843, An Act to Abolish Imprisonment in execution of Debt, 7 Victoriae, Cap. 31, 9 December 1843, pp. 239–240.

Dealing with Disease—An Act to Provide for the Care of Immigrants, 1848

Disease was a horrible fact of life in the 1840s. A fear of typhus and cholera epidemics swept the British North American colonies with each new influx of settlers. After the serious cholera epidemics of 1832 and 1834 in Quebec, Montreal and parts of Upper Canada, the government began to adopt quarantine procedures and rudimentary provisions for medical care.

Following the arrival of thousands of poor and disease-weakened "paupers" in 1847, an Act was passed in the Province of Canada requiring the shipping companies to assume the costs of caring for indigent immigrants.

Whereas the amount of the rate or duty now levied under the provisions of the [current] Provincial Act... hath been found to be inadequate for the purposes contemplated by the said Act; and whereas it is necessary to increase the said amount, and to make such further provisions generally in reference to Emigration as will tend to prevent the introduction into the Province of a pauper class of Emigrants, labouring under disease and incapable of supporting themselves; and it is expedient to amend the said Act accordingly.... That Instead of the rate or duty of five shillings currency, payable for each Passenger by any ship arriving in the Port of Quebec, or in the Port of Montreal, from any Port in the United Kingdom or in any other part of Europe, directed to be levied under the provisions of the said Act, there shall be raised, levied, collected and paid the rate or duty of ten shillings currency for every Passenger, irrespective of age, who shall have been embarked in such ship.

II.   And whereas it is expedient to hold out inducements to Masters of Ships carrying passengers, to maintain proper cleanliness, ventilation, and regularity on board, during the voyage: Be it therefore enacted, That the rate or duty payable for Passengers embarked on board of any such ship as aforesaid, shall be increased in proportion to the time during which such ship shall be detained in Quarantine....

III.   And whereas it is necessary to prevent, if possible, the arrival of Passengers at so late a period of the year as to render it almost impossible that they should be able, during the winter season, to provide for their own subsistence: Be it therefore enacted, That the said rate or duty of ten shillings, shall be doubled for every Passenger in any ship arriving in either of the said Ports of Quebec or Montreal, between the tenth day of September and the first day of October in any year, and shall be trebled for every Passenger in any ship so arriving on or after the first day of October in any year.

V.   And be it enacted, That in addition to the particulars heretofore required in the list of passengers to be delivered on each voyage, by the Master of any ship carrying passengers and arriving in either of the Ports of Quebec or Montreal, to the Collector or Chief Officer of Her Majesty's Customs at such Port, the Master shall report in writing to the said Collector or Chief Officer, the name and age of every passenger embarked on board of such ship on such voyage, and shall designate all such passengers as shall be lunatic, idiotic, deaf and dumb, blind or infirm, stating also whether they are accompanied by relatives likely to be able to support them; and shall also designate all such passengers as shall be children not members of any Emigrant family on board, or widows having families, or women without their husbands having families with the names and ages of their children....

> *Statutes of Canada*, 1848, An Act to make better provision with respect to Emigrants, and for defraying the expenses of supporting Indigent Emigrants, 11 Victoriae, Cap. 1, 23 March 1848, pp. 5–6.

Criticism of the Temperance Campaigns—A British Officer's Observations, 1842

The temperance campaigns undertaken in the Canadas and the Atlantic colonies did not meet with universal approval. Sir Richard Bonnycastle, in his books of impressions of the colonies, made some stinging criticisms of the temperance movement and its activities in both parts of British North America. The motives of the temperance campaigners, according to Bonny-castle, were highly questionable.

> Dancing to a fiddle is a favourite winter amusement of the fishermen; and, until lately,—when soberness and reflection are coming over the people, like the shadow of a summer cloud, cooling and invigorating,—the number of grog and spirit shops in St. John's were, with the quantity of money squandered in midnight revelry, incredible. The very servants stole out of their beds to enjoy these hurtful amusements, and such was the taste for them that they materially interfered with their duties.
>
> Spruce beer and tea have superseded rum and whiskey, and if it were not that wholesome malt liquors are included, there appears nothing to disapprove in the great exertions which the Roman-catholic clergy, who tread in the footsteps of Father Mathew, have made, and are still making, to rescue the ignorant and idle from the baneful and deadly consequences of strong drinks.
>
> Nevertheless, I cannot alter an opinion expressed in a former work on Canada, that these temperance movements are worse than useless when fostered by designing politicians, by people who have an object in view, and who, under the cloak of evangelism, merely want to render their otherwise obscure names conspicuous, or to serve some professional or private purpose. The spouter upon religious topics at public meetings and the spouter upon temperance are often much alike. Let the clergy do the work: the ministers of the gospel of peace are assuredly the fittest instruments in this moral reform, and it is disgusting to see it paraded, as it was in Canada before 1837, by political and fanatical theorists, whose minds are so narrowed from early education or prejudice, that they cannot permit a fellow Christian to remain in possession of quiet opinions, but, with Bible in one hand and the sword or the rod in the other, would force him to take heaven by storm, in their own peculiar and dogmatic enterprise. 'Every man to his trade' is an old and safe aphorism, and more harm has been done towards

ensuring a return to the healthy regimen of our great patriarchal ancestors by these meddlers, than all the alcohol which all the grain of the earth ever yielded. Excess on the one part has met the extreme on the other, and both have joined hands.

Sir Richard Henry Bonnycastle, *Newfoundland in 1842* (London: Henry Colburn, 1842), Vol. 2, pp. 142–143.

THE IMPULSE FOR "CORRECTION"—APPROACHES TO POVERTY, CRIME AND MORAL IMPROVEMENT

Public attitudes and values prevalent in Victorian Canada often dictated that the able-bodied poor as well as the mentally ill and the criminal were in need of "correction". In confronting poverty, mental disabilities and crime, politicians, social agencies and the churches held to a firm belief in self-help, that only the "deserving poor" be given a chance to support themselves in workhouses and other institutions. Houses of industry, insane asylums and prisons were all considered not only houses of refuge, but also places of correction.

Helping the "Deserving Poor"—A Plea for a Montreal Workhouse, 1843

While voluntary relief associations and poorhouses dated back to the 1820s and 1830s in the Atlantic colonies, few attempts were made to establish "houses of industry" in the Canadas until the early 1840s, and such institutions were designed primarily for the "deserving poor" in need of correction. Inmates were to be "diligently employed in labour" and to be punished for failure to work or to observe house rules. The case of the Montreal workhouse established in 1843 illustrated how the public viewed social assistance and why demands were often voiced to keep out the immigrant poor. A letter from a public-spirited citizen to the *Montreal Transcript* provided some insight into the motives of reformers.

Sir,—The attempt now being made to establish a House of Industry is very commendable. It is most astonishing that a permanent institution for the accommodation of the poor has not been in operation long ago, as nearly £2000 was left by Mr. Marteller, and other friends, for that purpose, more than twenty years ago. It is most devoutly hoped that those to whom those funds were entrusted, will exert themselves to see that they may be applied according to the design of the donors.

Can it be possible, that a city like Montreal, shall continue to allow the poor to wander from door to door seeking bread and clothing, when the labour of those destitute persons, if wisely directed, could feed and clothe them. It has been found in a neighbouring government, that the labour of the poor can furnish the necessary support; why not in Canada?

The house now occupied as the House of Industry must soon be given up for the use of emigrants, and unless an effort be made to provide other accommodations, the poor will be going about our streets begging, or stealing, as they formerly have done.

The vase importance of this object will excite the attention of all friends to the destitute. No time is to be lost. That ministers and magistrates may employ their influence in providing a house and farm for the poor of Montreal, is the prayer of

T. Osgood.

Montreal Transcript, 2 March 1843

Caring for the Mentally Ill—A New Use for the Jail, 1841

Care for the chronically ill in the colonies was a different matter from dealing with poverty and crime. Reform-minded citizens with a Christian outlook expressed great concern that while funds were being lavished on facilities for transportation and commerce, the provision of social services was sadly neglected. No institutions for the care of the chronically ill, for example, existed until the opening of the first lunatic asylum in Saint John, New Brunswick in 1836. And even after that date some of the earlier asylums offered merely custodial care rather than assistance, consistent with Victorian notions of self-improvement.

Temporary measures were often taken to provide care for the mentally ill. In the case of Canada West, special facilities were only provided after years of petitions from families and jail wardens unable to cope with the supervision of the insane. Finally, a petition from the justices of the Ottawa district in 1839 did move the legislature to authorize the erection of an asylum. Since nothing happened for about ten years, as an interim measure in 1841 a prison in Toronto was designated as an asylum.

That for a number of years past, the peace of the said District has been repeatedly disturbed and the moral feelings of its inhabitants shocked, by the appearances among them of maniacs, and insane persons, for the most part strangers to the country, or to the district.

That although the magistrates have, in every case, promptly interfered, both to protect the public, and to secure the unfortunate beings in question, yet their measures have been unavoidably attended with great public expense and inconvenience, owing to the necessity of confining and maintaining the deranged persons in the Common Gaol of the District.

A Petition of Justices of Ottawa District to Lieutenant-Governor, 16 February 1839, cited in Richard B. Splane, *Social Welfare in Ontario, 1791–1893* (Toronto: University of Toronto Press, 1965), p. 203.

Attitudes to Crime and Punishment—A Humanitarian View of Prison Reform, 1849

Custodial care was considered by most people to be the sole function of prisons in the British American colonies. Even so, some public-spirited reformers did express concern over cases of brutal and excessive punishment and a few considered the possibilities of rehabilitating criminals in penal institutions. The report of an 1848–49 Royal Commission, formed to investigate charges of inhuman punishment, tensions between guards and inmates, and waste and misappropriation of funds at the Kingston penitentiary offered a grave indictment of conditions. It also provided an indication of some of the more progressive attitudes toward crime and punishment emerging in Canada West.

> The time has been when the Prison was regarded as a mere place of punishment, when fear was deemed the only passion by which prisoners could be swayed, and the law of terror the only rule of discipline; when a discharged Convict, no matter what his crime, was shunned as the leper, and driven by the cold unpitying cruelty of his fellow-beings to despair, too often sought revenge by plunging into the lowest abyss of guilt. But the labours of the great and good men who have devoted their lives to the cause of the outcast of society, have not been fruitless; public attention has been gradually awakened to the errors of the prevailing systems of prison discipline, and great ameliorations have been effected. The dungeon gave way to the well regulated apartment—healthful labour has replaced vicious idleness—and now the general aim is to find in what manner the security of the public, the prevention of crime and the reformation of the criminal can be best obtained without the appearance of revenge. And when it is considered that a large proportion of the inmates of prison are the victims of circumstances; that many are condemned for the first act of crime, and many more for the act of a moment of passion or intemperance; and that the great majority of prisoners have been born and reared in ignorance of everything but vice—how strong is the claim on a Christian people to see well that their prisons shall not become the moral tomb of those who enter them, but rather schools where the ignorant are enlightened and the repentant strengthened—in which expiation for crime is not lost sight of, but the permanent reform of the Convict is the chief aim.

> Canada, *Journals*, 1849, Appendix B.B.B.B.B.

THE IMPULSE FOR PUBLIC EDUCATION REFORM

The public school system of Canada West (Ontario), created in the 1840s, serves as a fascinating case study in the motivations behind educational reform in the period. This centralized system, designed by the Reverend Egerton Ryerson and based on schooling in Prussia and Massachusetts, was important not just for its lasting impact on education in Ontario but also for its influence on developing systems of other colonies. Public schooling, following Ryerson's philosophy, was to become centrally regulated general education aimed at preventing pauperism and criminality among the poorest classes. But what was the prime motive of Ryerson and the public school promoters—to achieve administrative efficiency, to aid the poor and disadvantaged, or to extend social control in the interests of the dominant classes?

The Concept of Universal Public Education—Egerton Ryerson's View, 1846

Reverend Egerton Ryerson's blueprint for educational reform was found in his *Report on a System of Public Elementary Instruction*, published in 1846. As the Superintendent of Schools in Canada West, Ryerson recommended the creation of a highly centralized system, in the hands of a small network of bureaucrats, which would turn out patriotic and morally sound citizens.

By Education, I mean not the mere acquisition of certain arts, or of certain branches of knowledge, but that instruction and discipline which qualify and dispose the subjects of it for their appropriate duties and employments of life, as Christians, as persons of business and also as members of the civil community in which they live.

The basis of an Educational structure adapted to this end should be as broad as the population of the country; and its loftiest elevation should equal the highest demands of the learned professions, adapting its gradition of schools to the wants of the several classes of the community, and to their respective employments or profession, the one rising above the other—the one conducting the other; yet each complete in itself for the degree of education it imparts; a character of uniformity as to fundamental principles pervading the whole; the whole based upon the principles of Christianity, and uniting the combined influence and support of the Government and the people.

The branches of knowledge which it is essential that all should understand, should be provided for all, and taught to all; should be brought within the reach of the most needy, and forced upon the attention of the most careless. The knowledge required for the scientific pursuit of mechanics, agriculture and commerce, must needs be provided to an extent corresponding with the demand, and the exigencies of the country; while to a more limited extent are needed facilities for acquiring the higher education of the learned professions. . . .

First, such a system of general education amongst the people is the most effectual preventative of pauperism, and its natural companions, misery and crime.

To a young and growing country, and the retreat of so many poor from other countries, this consideration is of the greatest importance. The gangrene of pauperism in either cities or states is almost incurable. . . .

Now, the Statistical Reports of pauperism and crime in different countries, furnish indubitable proof that ignorance is the fruitful source of idleness, intemperance and improvidence, and these the fosterparent of pauperism and crime. The history of every country in Europe may be appealed to in proof and illustration of the fact,—apart from the operation of extraneous local and temporary circumstances,—that pauperism and crime prevail in proportion to the absence of education amongst the labouring classes. . . .

1. The first feature then of our Provincial system of Public Instruction, should be *universality*; and that in respect to the poorest classes of society. It is the poor indeed that need the assistance of the Government, and they are proper subjects of their special solicitude and care; the rich can take care of themselves. The elementary education of the whole people must therefore be an essential element in the Legislative and Administrative policy of an enlightened and beneficent Government.

2. Nor is it less important to the efficiency of such a system, that it should be *practical*, than that it should be universal. The mere acquisition or even the general diffusion of knowledge without the requisite qualities to apply that knowledge in the best manner, does not merit the name of education.

The state of society, then, no less than the wants of our country, require that every youth of the land should be trained to industry and practice,—whether that training be extensive, or limited.

Now, education thus practical, includes Religion and Morality; secondly, the development to a certain extent of all our faculties; thirdly, an acquaintance with several branches of elementary knowledge. . . .

J. George Hodgins, ed., *Documentary History of Education in Upper Canada* (Toronto: Warwick & Rutler, 1897), IV, Egerton Ryerson's Report on a system of public elementary instruction, 1846, pp. 142–163.

An Alternative to the Common Schools—The Toronto Industrial School, 1945

Yet the common public school system was not deemed suitable for the education of all young people. Privately owned and financed Industrial Schools, emphasizing a more job-oriented curriculum, while not ignoring the religious, moral and patriotic qualities or rudimentary intellectual skills, were organized. These philanthropic institutes resembled a combination of the reformatory and trade school. The opening of one such institution, the Toronto Industrial School, was heralded by an advertisement which gave some indications of its purposes.

'It is better to prevent than to punish crime—it is more humane,—it is more Economical.'

The following is the Prospectus of an Industrial School, which will be commenced as soon as possible, in the vicinity of the City of Toronto, for the benefit of Orphans and other poor and Neglected Children. It will be under the superintendence of Mr. Wilson, whose experience enables him to undertake the task with confidence, and he will perform it gratuitously with pleasure.

The pupils will be treated with the greatest paternal kindness, and receive a good Mental, Moral, Religious and Physical Education; each will be taught a Trade, and all will be occasionally employed in Agriculture and Gardening. One-half of each day, (except Sunday,) will be spent in suitable labour, and the other half in the School Room. The exercises shall be varied with agreeable and instructive recreation. The Sabbath will be employed in religious duties, such as are unexceptionable, and Sacred Music.

The pupils may be visited by their friends at all times, provided it does not interfere with the arrangements of the School.

To carry into successful operation such a useful and laudable Institution, it is necessary to raise a small sum to purchase provisions, and pay rent for the first year; also to purchase Furniture, Tools, Stock, etcetera, to begin with; and, for this purpose, several benevolent Gentlemen of the City have subscribed liberally. . . .

William H. Boulton, Esquire, Mayor of Toronto; the Honourables Robert Baldwin and Henry Sherwood; H. J. Boulton, Esquire; and Doctors O'Brien, Hamilton and Sewell.

Toronto, 22nd of December, 1845.

J. George Hodgins, ed., *Documentary History of Education in Upper Canada*, Vol. V, 22 December 1845, p. 271.

Benevolence or Social Order—The Manual Labour Schools for Native Peoples, 1846

Special educational provisions, in the form of Manual Labour Schools, were also to be provided for Native peoples in Canada West. A general council of Native representatives was summoned to meet at Orillia in July 1846, under the direction of Captain Thomas G. Anderson, the Superintendent of Indian Affairs. These representatives were not consulted on educational matters or policy, but were informed that the missionaries who would manage the Manual Labour Schools "will perhaps explain". Anderson's opening address on the occasion gave some indication of the reformers' motivations.

BRETHREN ... As great changes are taking place in your condition, and your Great Mother, the Queen, having directed the Indian Department to make arrangements for your future benefit and guidance, I have obtained permission of Lord Cathcart, the Governor General, to assemble the Chiefs and Principal Men, under my superintendence, in General Council, to deliberate on the following subjects. . . .

Firstly—That the Indian Tribes shall use every means in their power to abandon their present detached little Villages, and unite, as far as practicable, in forming large Settlements—where,

Secondly—Manual Labour Schools will be established for the education of your children; and the Land, to which you may now, with the consent of the Government, remove, the Government will secure, by written documents to you and your posterity forever.

Thirdly—That you shall devote one-fourth of your annuities, which many of you promised me last fall that you would do, for a period of from twenty to twenty-five years, to assist in the support of your children of both sexes, while remaining at the Schools. It is to be hoped, by that time, that some of your youth will be sufficiently enlightened to carry on a system of instruction among yourselves, and that this proportion of your funds will, therefore, no longer be required after that period.

Fourthly—That you give up your hunting practices . . . (etcetera).

Fifthly—That the present practice of paying for putting up your Houses shall cease, and that each man shall put up his own Buildings . . . (etcetera).

It has, therefore, been determined that your children shall be sent to the Schools, where they will forget their Indian habits, and be instructed in all the necessary arts of civilized life, and become one with your White brethren. In these Schools, they will be well taken care of, be comfortably dressed, kept clean, and get plenty to eat. The adults will not be forced to leave their present locations. They may remove, or remain, as they please; but their children must go to the Schools . . . .

The Management of the Manual Labour Schools will be entrusted to your Missionaries, under the direction of your Great Father, the Governor General, who takes a deep interest in your prosperity. . . . And the Missionaries will perhaps explain to you in what manner they intend to conduct these Schools . . . .

J. George Hodgins, ed., *Documentary History of Education in Upper Canada*, Vol. IV, Address of Captain Anderson, July 1846, p. 296.

THE IMPULSE FOR AIDING MINORITIES

Social reformers in the 1840s also turned their attention to the condition and treatment of racial, religious and ethnic minorities. Concerns were raised about encroachments on Native ancestral lands and reserves, not only by colonists, settling in various parts of the Canadas, but also by lumbering and mining companies in the hinterland areas. For many reformers, a policy of "civilizing" (i.e., Christianizing and Europeanizing) the Native peoples had supplanted the older idea of conciliating them. Religious strife between Protestants and Catholics was a common occurrence—and attempts to redress grievances on occasion further worsened relations. Evidence of prejudice directed against racial minorities, notably black children, also prompted reforms which, however, may have served the interests of the majority population rather than those of the afflicted minority.

The Attempt to "Civilize" the Native Peoples—Lord Elgin's Report on Violations of Native Land Rights, 1849

From 1830 onward Reform politicians, Wesleyan missionaries, and British humanitarians actively pursued a programme of "civilizing" the Native peoples. The Bagot Commission Report of 1842 recommended improved Indian Department organization, registration of Native title deeds, eviction of interlopers and squatters on Native lands, the creation of a corps of Rangers for each reserve, and the establishment of industrial boarding schools for children in addition to the maintenance of a common school on each reserve. Still, Lord Elgin had to report in 1849 that Native peoples' rights were being violated by mining companies in the Lake Superior region of the Canadas. Could the agitators, or the "unprincipled white men" who supported the Indians in their legitimate claims have been reformers?

> I regret to State that I have found it necessary to dispatch a Detachment of Soldiers from this place to the Eastern shore of Lake Superior in order to protect the Miners settled in that District from an attack with which they are threatened by certain Indians and others professing to act on their behalf....
>
> 2.   ...It appears that in the year 1845 permission was given by the Provincial Government to certain individuals to explore the Northern and Eastern shore of Lake Superior for minerals, and that in the following year grants for mining purposes alone were made to these persons of portions of the Territory in question on specified conditions. Soon after my arrival in the Province complaints were addressed to me by certain Indian Tribes who alleged that the miners were trespassing on their property... With the Concurrence of the Council I sent Mr. Anderson a very efficient officer of the Indian Department in the summer of 1848, to examine into these Indian Claims, and I enclose for your Lordship's perusal a Copy of his report which was favorable to the Indians; and of the correspondence which ensued upon it with the Crown Lands Office....
>
> 3.   I cannot but think that it is much to be regretted that steps were not taken to investigate thoroughly and extinguish all Indian claims before licences of exploration or grants of land were conceded by the Government in this Territory. This omission is the pretext for the present disturbances and renders the Indians much more difficult to treat with.
>
> At the same time it must be admitted that their claims are of a questionable character, and as they are a docile people and cognizant of the steps which the Government is now taking to ascertain and satisfy them, there can be little doubt that they are seduced into violent courses by the evil counsels of unprincipled white men....
>
> Arthur G. Doughty, ed., *The Elgin-Grey Papers, 1846–1862* (Ottawa: King's Printer, 1937), Vol. 4, pp. 1485–1486.

The Motives of the Clergy and Fraternal Societies—James Johnston's Report on Religious Strife, 1851

Although the civil rights of Catholics had been assured and religious minorities, like the Quakers and Mennonites in Upper Canada, had won some concessions, strong religious feeling often spilled over into noisy demonstrations and street riots. Richard Bonnycastle was caught in the middle of a religious riot in Harbour Grace, Newfoundland and James Johnston had a similar narrow escape in Woodstock, New Brunswick. Religion and politics made a particularly explosive mixture, and both Protestant and Catholic clergy, as well as fraternal and patriotic organizations such as the Loyal Orange Lodge, engaged in politicking.

At Woodstock, in the evening, we were gratified with an interesting musical entertainment. It seems that the Orangemen are numerous in some parts of New Brunswick, and that Woodstock has its full share of them. Some twelve months or more ago, a riot took place between them and the Romanists, (Mickeys, as they are here called,) attended by the destruction of a considerable amount of property, which the county of course was called upon to pay. But the county applied to the provincial House of Assembly, to have the sum in whole or in part paid out of the provincial treasury; and in reference to this matter, my fellow-traveller, Mr. Brown, as a member of the assembly, had given a vote which was unsatisfactory to the Woodstock Orangemen. Hearing of his arrival, therefore, instead of lynching him, as they might have done a little farther West, they serenaded us all at the hotel until near midnight with a charivari of all the most discordant noises, vocal and instrumental, which the tongs, kettles, saucepans, and throats of Woodstock could produce. There were also tar-barrels and bonfires on the occasion, and finally a burning in effigy. Fortunately the budding Orangemen did not personally know the man they thus delighted to honour; so that Mr. Brown himself flitted about the blazing barrels, and enjoyed the burning fun as much as any of them.

James F. W. Johnston, *Notes on North America. Agricultural, Economical, and Social* (Edinburgh: William Blackwood and Sons, 1851), Vol. 1, pp. 55–56.

Separate Schools for Black Children—A Hamilton Police Commission Report, 1843

Blacks were another minority who felt the burden of reforming zeal. In both Nova Scotia and Upper Canada black separate schools not only existed by law but the courts upheld the view that all black children should attend such schools once they were established. Before this position became firmly entrenched, some black parents in Hamilton petitioned the Governor-General in October 1843, to confirm their right of access to public schools. A written report prepared by the Hamilton board of police commissioners in 1843, and submitted to Lord Elgin, revealed much about why the separate schools were established in that locality.

I am favoured with your Letter, respecting the Petition of the coloured inhabitants of this Town upon the subject of their exclusion from the benefits of the established Common Schools....

First, There appears to be about twenty coloured children in Hamilton, within the ages of five and sixteen years.

Secondly, I regret to say that there is a strong prejudice existing amongst the lower orders of the whites against the coloured people. The several Teachers, as well as others acquainted with the extent of this prejudice, fear that if coloured children are admitted into the Schools, the parents of the greater part of the white children will take them away.

Thirdly, The coloured population belong chiefly to the Methodist and Baptist persuasions.

Fourthly. The Board of Police are unanimous in their opinion, that whatever may be the state of feeling with respect to the admission of the coloured children into the same School with the white, it would not be advisable to yield to it, but that the law ought to be enforced without distinction of colour. They think that if a firm stand be taken at first, the prejudice will soon give way.

J. George Hodgins, ed., *Documentary History of Education in Upper Canada* (Toronto: 1897), Vol. 4, Board of Police Commissioners of Hamilton to Robert Murray, 9 November 1843, p. 313.

CONFLICTING INTERPRETATIONS

Mid-nineteenth-century British North American society is one subject which has received much attention from Canada's most recent generation of social historians. Traditionally, the social developments of the 1840s and 1850s were treated as humanitarian efforts closely associated with Canada's emerging political and social institutions. Such standard studies had tended to emphasize institutional changes, generally implying that they were undertaken for altruistic purposes. Over the past fifteen years, however, historians young and old have brought new approaches and new perspectives to bear on the society of early Victorian Canada. Studies of the social reform impulse in the 1840s have broadened our knowledge of reform attitudes and activities and raised some serious questions about the apparently benevolent motivations of reformers.

Much of the historical controversy has centred on the attitudes and activities of public-minded reformers in the united province of Canada. This is merely a reflection of the orientation of research into social reform in the 1840s and early 1850s, which has, for the most part, focussed on developments in Canada West and Canada East. Yet, in spite of the limitations of current research, early indications are that there were comparable initiatives in social reform in the maritime British-American colonies. Indeed, a few recent studies of poverty relief, cholera epidemics, temperance and schooling in Atlantic region ports and cities have turned up evidence of attitudes and actions similar to those in the Canadas.

THE IMPULSE FOR SOCIAL WELFARE AND PUBLIC HEALTH REFORM

The Origins of Social Welfare—A Traditional Institutional Analysis

Early studies of social welfare in the British-American colonies tended to treat such developments as institutional responses to genuine welfare needs. Though the tradition of self-help and volunteerism remained strong, it was recognized that new demands were being placed on governments to provide for the needy and unfortunate. Richard B. Splane's study of social welfare in

Canada West, attempted to assess the response of the state to the call for reform. Taking a purely institutional approach, Splane had much to say about the organization of public and private bodies but little about the people they were supposed to help.

> Throughout the period, the development of social welfare depended, as always, on the willingness of governments, voluntary bodies, and individuals to express their interest and concern in meeting social welfare needs through the provision of the funds required to support the necessary programmes and services. In the primitive economy of the early decades in Upper Canada, the paucity of social welfare services was a reflection of the poverty in the province—poverty at least in terms of the lack of capital which could be spared from the vital tasks of developing the basic economy. The limitation of taxable resources, combined with the scale of priorities of the early communities, was such that even the gaols, often the sole social welfare resource, were financed with difficulty. The plight of the gaols and of other welfare programmes bore early testimony to the flaws in provincial-municipal relationships and the resulting problem of determining what social welfare functions should be delegated by the province to the municipality and how such functions, if delegated, should be financed. As a result, from the 1830's to the end of the Union period, although municipal expenditures on social welfare expanded sporadically and unevenly, voluntary giving in the development of hospitals, houses of refuge, and orphanages increased, probably in rough proportion to the growth of private wealth, and there was a manifold expansion of provincial expenditures on correctional institutions, mental hospitals, and other charities. By 1867, the social welfare costs borne by the province were close to a quarter of provincial expenditures.
>
> Richard B. Splane, *Social Welfare in Ontario, 1791–1893* (Toronto: University of Toronto Press, 1965), pp. 59–60.

The Reform Impulse of Temperance Evangelism—A Revisionist View

Several recent studies in social history have probed into the motivating influences behind largely middle class reform in early Victorian Canada. Departing from the traditional institutional approach, Janet Noel has looked at the motivations and socio-economic underpinnings of the temperance movement in the Canadas. In a doctoral thesis at the University of Ottawa (1978) she argued that the movement succeeded in attracting wide public attention because it moved beyond the purely religious sphere to campaign for social and political reforms as well.

> This thesis interprets the temperance agitation of 1840–1854 as the translation of radical religion into social and political conduct. Beginning as a spiritual revival which mobilised people to reform their own lives, it soon evolved into an emotional and self-confident campaign for social and political reform. At a time when political radicalism was effectively checked, temperance channelled popular discontent into a less direct attack on a reactionary colonial elite and an irresponsible government. As such, it served as a positive or 'progressive' force which united a broad segment of the population in an active struggle for reform.

By the late 1840's, then, temperance was moving back to the political stance of pre-Rebellion days, as an attack on the social and political establishment. This time, though, there was a difference: the movement had numerous and militant supporters in nearly every community in Canada, including many merchants, doctors, lawyers and magistrates. Invoking the names of both religion and progress, temperance had emerged as the first reform campaign that was at once popular *and* respectable.

Preached as a social gospel, the temperance movement acquired prestige and a political clout it had not previously possessed. Where revivalists had stressed drinking as personal sin, secular reformers presented it as a social disaster—the leading source of the appalling misery of the 1840's. Many were convinced. The public demand for temperance reforms grew so strong that Parliament finally, in 1849, appointed a committee to enquire into the effects of intemperance. Relying heavily on the testimony of gaolkeepers, doctors, and directors of asylums, the committee confirmed all the worst charges against drink. Its Report opened with the statement that intemperance did indeed lie at the root of one-half of the crimes annually committed, two-thirds of the cases of insanity, and three-fourths of the pauperism.

Few people today would agree with the public and Parliamentary assertions that drink was the main cause of the poverty and crime of the 1840's. In retrospect, it seems obvious that the deeper source was a grossly unfair distribution of wealth both in Canada and in Ireland, from which so many of the paupers came.... But while the attack on alcohol dealt with a genuine problem and cannot be dismissed as nativist paranoia or middle class conspiracy, it created a new problem at the same time that it tackled an old one. Evolving from religious revival to social reform, temperance retained the rigid dogmatism of fundamentalist religion. The narrow focus on drink as the source of all evil deflected attention from other environmental sources of human misery. Temperance reformers, in fact, drew public attention to a whole range of social problems, such as violence against women, neglect of children, and the acute shortage of urban housing; but temperance convictions tended to preclude a more diversified attack on these problems.

The linking of drink with the social crises of the 1840's did have one clear effect. It mobilized a large segment of the population, composed of the working and the middle classes, women, farmers and church leaders to demand social reform. By associating drink with the most pressing colonial problems, it removed the temperance campaign from the spiritual realm. The issue would be resolved not in the hidden recesses of the soul or beyond the grave; the showdown between 'wets' and 'drys' would be an historical battle fought in the legislative chambers, town councils and village streets. Temperance had emerged as a major drive for social reform. Within a few years, hundreds of thousands would turn to it as a form of worldly salvation....

Janet Noel, *Temperance Evangelism. Drink, Religion and Reform in the Province of Canada, 1840–1854* (Unpublished Ph.D. thesis, University of Ottawa, 1978), pp. 5–6, 105–107, 165–166.

Controlling Cholera—A New Look at Public Health Reform

Geoffrey Bilson, a social historian at the University of Saskatchewan, has called attention to the important impact of disease on nineteenth-century Canadian society. His recent studies of cholera seem to indicate that responses to the threat—and occurrence—of the disease in the 1830s and 1840s were conditioned largely by self-interest and limited by prevailing *laissez-faire* attitudes toward state action.

While people learned to live with cholera, they were not indifferent to it and each epidemic brought demands that government act....

Cholera led to a temporary rediscovery of the poor with every epidemic. The first epidemics occurred in cities and towns where poor and rich lived close together. When it became clear that the disease would not confine its attacks to the poor, the wealthier citizens often felt obliged to do something to change the conditions of the poor, if only in self-defence. In later years, patterns of urban settlement changed and the wealthier citizens withdrew to parts of town more distant from the poor. The young doctor starting his practice and the clergyman were among the few middle-class people with any regular experience of the conditions in which the poor lived. When cholera struck, it forcibly drew the attention of the richer citizens to those conditions. Their response was ambivalent, a compound of self-interest and charity. In each epidemic some people argued for the need to improve the services of the towns and raise the living standards of the poor. These were goals beyond the scope of local governments of the time. The epidemics, therefore, stimulated considerable charitable efforts in support of hospitals, aid for the destitute, food for the hungry, and shelter for widows and orphans....

The operations of charitable institutions were shaped by middle-class attitudes to the poor. The operators had to reassure their prospective supporters that they would not be the dupes of the 'undeserving poor'. The understanding of cholera suggested that it could be the product of immoderate behaviour and intemperance. When it fell heavily on the poor it could confirm prejudices and encourage moralizing. If the Irish or the French suffered, it was perhaps because they were debauched. The poor might be responsible for the conditions in which they lived by preferring drink and sloth to good food and hard work with the scrubbing brush. The moralizing became less certain as the rich began to die, and it faded in the later epidemics—but it never completely disappeared; the rediscovery of the poor did not necessarily bring fresh attitudes.

It did, however, become clear in the course of the epidemics that the poor could not be acted on without reaction. The poor were individuals, capable of helping one another, and holding strong opinions about what governments could do to them. The operation of public health laws was restricted by the public attitude and the poor could act violently against laws which they felt to be unfeeling or intrusive. Even those who could not articulate their objections could express themselves by resisting the health wardens and forcing them to seek police protection, by ignoring regulations, reoccupying condemned buildings, and opposing efforts to remove their friends and relatives to hospitals....

The most forceful expression of popular opposition to public health measures was directed against the hospitals. Hated by the poor, who alone were sent to them, and feared by those who lived nearby, the hospitals were fought with petition, crowbar, and torch. In some towns, too, the houses of victims of the disease were burned by mobs. The mob did not turn out only in opposition however, but could sometimes be found supporting health regulations. Vessels which ignored regulations were attacked or threatened, boats were turned back if they came from infected ports, and men erected road-blocks and tried to close their villages to outsiders.... Canada's regulations were made by temporary bodies and enforced, slowly and ineffectively, through the courts. That helped to save Canada from worse violence than did occur....

Geoffrey Bilson, *A Darkened House: Cholera in Nineteenth-Century Canada* (Toronto: University of Toronto Press, 1980), pp. 169, 175–177.

THE IMPULSE FOR CORRECTION—STUDIES OF POVERTY, CRIME AND MORAL IMPROVEMENT

Controlling Juvenile Delinquency—Susan Houston's Interpretation

The intimate connections between poverty, crime and social attitudes have served as a major focus for much social history being written about mid-nineteenth-century Canada. Professor Susan E. Houston of York University, in two articles and a later collection of documents, emphasized that the founders of Canada West's public schools shared mid-Victorian attitudes toward "correction" markedly similar to those of promoters of temperance and penal reform.

THE VICTORIAN SOCIAL CONSCIENCE was troubled on many accounts, and perhaps no more so than by the plight of delinquent youngsters. Few causes cut so deeply into the delicate weave of moralism and economy out of which much nineteenth-century social policy was fashioned....

Crime was not, in itself, a novel preoccupation of Canadian reformers.... The provincial penitentiary, started in 1833 after the plan of the New York State Prison at Auburn, was witness to the enthusiasm of this earlier generation for penal reform. Reformers at midcentury were quite as susceptible to the consolation provided by prison structures and police, but they perceived their problem as less tangible and therefore more alarming. Chronically inadequate jail provision and an increase in felonies were now only part of the story, the tip of an iceberg. What was glimpsed were the consequences of a way of life, of a commitment to certain values and goals exemplified by the city, railroads, mechanics, Progress, Democracy, and Steam....

...The Romanticism that tinged the mid-Victorian Canadian's acceptance of the dark side of city life also contributed a cynicism and world-weariness to his analysis of existing social ills. Crime was the hub of the problem. Crime represented 'an evil under which all cities, however prosperous they may be (those of this continent especially) suffer from.' Moreover, the problem was quite specific; Toronto in the 1850s seemed in danger from 'crime which appears to have come in like a flood into our usually quiet and well-ordered community.' The 'crimes' that swelled the gaol statistics—vagrancy, disorderly conduct, and intoxication—were precisely those to which juveniles were most susceptible, while being 'some of the elements that demoralize society, that supply the place as the ranks of detected criminals are thinned, and that must be reformed, if any important progress is made by man in the course of virtue and civilization.' A touchstone to Victorian morality was provided by the equation of conduct and character. An emphasis on character provided the thread that linked shades and waves of reform opinion through much of the nineteenth century. It also lent essential plausibility to the strategy of reformation that provided the chief rhetorical justification for experiments in social engineering. All of this was buttressed by the religious emphasis of the Victorian years that functioned in Canadian society as a particularly pervasive social norm. Thus the campaign against ignorance (and the mandate of the school system) encompassed more than reading; illiteracy was deplored, but more as the visible sign of that other ignorance that was the root of personal and social deviance. In this ideological context, the necessity to provide for neglected children could appear a crusade 'to civilize the street-arab and convert the vagrant from the alarming vice of idleness to habits of honesty and industry.'

The obvious existing institution that might transform the street-arab was the common school. Few school supporters needed the urging of the Chief Superintendent to link the promotion of education with 'administration of justice, organized systems for the repression or prevention of crime, and other important subjects.' The existence and promised redemption of ignorant, ill-mannered street children proved to be a stock argument of free school promoters. It effectively dramatised the ingredients of character formation and social mobility that contributed much to the appeal of the common school idea....

> Susan E. Houston, "Victorian Origins of Juvenile Delinquency: A Canadian Experience", reprinted in Michael B. Katz and Paul H. Mattingly, eds., *Education and Social Change: Themes From Ontario's Past* (New York: New York University Press, 1975), pp. 83, 86–7 and 88–9. Footnotes deleted.

Urban Poverty, Crime and Poor Relief—A Comparative Look at the Atlantic Colonies

Recent studies of life in the Atlantic colonies have also drawn strong connections between Victorian attitudes toward poverty and crime, and other reform initiatives of the 1840s and 1850s. Professor Judith Fingard's work on poverty relief in the Atlantic cities of Saint John, Halifax and St. John's serves as a case in point.

> ...goaded by tender consciences and insistent churches, some colonists regarded benevolence as a christian duty. Within a society that prided itself on its christian ethos, the laws of God and humanity dictated that the poor could not be permitted to starve; the sick and aged poor must be cared for. But starvation did occur, and the numerous sick and aged poor in the towns necessitated the erection of institutions to minister to their afflictions. In the absence of this kind of large-scale capital expenditure which city councils or provincial legislatures were reluctant to undertake, privately organized dispensaries and societies for the relief of the indigent sick played a vital role in treating accidents and common illnesses. For the chronically ill, however, circumstances were different. Halifax, for example, possessed no specialized institution for dealing with any category of sick poor until the opening of the lunatic asylum in 1859. The failure 'to ameliorate the condition of suffering humanity' offended christians who witnessed ample investment in facilities for transportation and commerce; the neglect of social amelioration seemed to be at odds with mid-Victorian notions of progress.
>
> In these circumstances townspeople responded sympathetically to acute destitution because they considered the existing forms of poor relief outdated and unprogressive. The purely custodial care of destitute lunatics in the temporary asylum established in St. John's in 1846, for example, was said to be inconsistent with the age of improvement. Citizens were particularly outspoken when their local pride was offended. To lag behind other towns in the provision of specialized facilities for the poor seemed unpatriotic as well as undesirable. The example of Saint John, where a lunatic asylum was opened in 1836 and firmly established in a permanent edifice in 1848, was constantly paraded by social critics before the lethargic citizenry of Halifax and St. John's. This call for imitation grew out of search for self-esteem, since colonial towns aspired to social responsibility and an acknowledgement of their benevolence and modernity....
>
> * * * * *
>
> Citizens' attitudes towards poor relief were also influenced by the need to distinguish between the honest, deserving, labouring poor and those who were undeserving,

profligate, or even criminal. For the public remained anxious that the poor should not endanger the social order of the towns and that relief should preserve a properly balanced relationship between the 'haves' and the 'have-nots.' This determination to ensure that the 'haves' maintained the upper hand goes far to explain the universal abhorrence of mendicancy; begging transferred the initiative to the poor when it ought to remain with their economic betters. Mendicancy was a form of free enterprise, an activity not to be encouraged in the poor who were certain to misuse it. A successful beggar might see in crime his road to further advancement.... Such unbecoming and potentially subversive behaviour in the poor might be avoided if the rich took it upon themselves to seek out poor families in their dwellings and investigate their degree of penury and deservedness....

Despite the need for precautionary measures to safeguard the interests of the town and the welfare of the honest poor, it was often that same apprehension for the good order of society that stimulated citizens to urge generous public relief in times of severest want.... The spectre of hungry mobs of workers conjured up in the mind of the authorities frightening thoughts of uncontrollable outrage and seething insubordination. Poverty was regarded as an 'evil' which could not be allowed to reach 'that stage where it is not stopped by stone walls, or locks, bolts, or bars.'

Judith Fingard, "The Relief of the Unemployed Poor in Saint John, Halifax and St. John's, 1815-1860", *Acadiensis* Vol. 5, No. 1 (1975), pp. 34 and 38. Footnotes omitted.

THE IMPULSE FOR PUBLIC EDUCATION REFORM—THE CASE OF CANADA WEST

Reverend Egerton Ryerson and the Public Education System—A Traditional Interpretation

Early interpretations of the public school movement in Canada West tended to reflect the attitudes and perspectives of the chroniclers, mostly trained educators. Schools and school systems were generally taken for granted, as requiring little or no explanation of their origins, or purposes. Much of the writing about public education, tended to focus on its chief heroes—or villains. In the case of Canada West, this approach led early analysts to concentrate largely on the dominant personality and achievements of Reverend Egerton Ryerson, superintendent of the provincial system from 1844 to 1876.

On March 27, 1846, Ryerson forwarded to the Hon. Dominick Daly, Secretary of the Province of Canada, his completed *Report on a System of Public Elementary Instruction for Upper Canada*...The experience of some twenty countries visited and the views of numerous authorities on education were arrayed in support of the theories presented. The best in Europe and in the United States was sought for Canada, and adapted to Canadian conditions....

He at once challenged opposition by laying down two principles: that a universal and compulsory system of primary and industrial education is justified by considerations of economy as well as of humanity; and that religion and morality, though not sectarianism, must have a central place in any system of education. Here for the first time we learn that he regarded Separate Schools as unnecessary....

* * * * *

The School Act of 1846 was merely a beginning. Ryerson had to wait until 1850 for a partial realization of his hopes, and until 1871 for their consummation. The Province was not yet ready for free schools, nor was it possible by law at once to purge the schools of unenlightened superintendents, feeble teachers and antiquated textbooks....

...In the local management of school affairs a general interest was stimulated and maintained, and at the same time an opportunity afforded electors and elected to apply the principles of democracy in the control of matters of vital and immediate concern. To many a Canadian the office of school trustee became the first step in public life. Cohesion and consistency, however, were essential, and this was provided by the Chief Superintendent assisted by an advisory Board of Education....

C.B. Sissons, ed., *Egerton Ryerson: His Life and Letters* (Toronto: Ryerson Press, 1947), Vol. 2, pp. 94–5 and 103–4.

Public Schools As Agents of Social Control—A Revisionist Interpretation

Recently the traditional view of Ryerson and the "school promoters" in Upper Canada has come in for some heavy attack. Historians such as Alison Prentice and Susan Houston have sought to dispel the so-called "mythology" of Ryersonian reformism. In her major study, *The School Promoters* (1977), Prentice explored the underlying motivations of public school reform in the 1840s.

...School promoters had several aims in mind. The promotion of an intelligent and respectable class was one aspect of their programme; another the general elevation and improvement of the labouring poor. They were concerned about those Upper Canadians whose occupational status was threatened by industrial change, change which nevertheless they strongly supported. The only hope for these displaced people seemed to be an education designed to prepare them for the new order....

* * * * *

Certainly, the very complexity of educational change during this period precludes any interpretation that would brand Ryerson and his supporters as a monolithic group of enthusiasts determined to press at all costs and at all times a single conception of education upon the people of Upper Canada. Partly because of the length of his career, and the extent of his public and private writings, the thought of Egerton Ryerson does not form a consistent whole. He started out attacking one establishment, and ended up defending, if not virtually creating, another one....

Yet the contradictions are in many ways the keys to the man as they are to an understanding of the era. The school promoters were essentially divided men, individuals who were at once fascinated and repelled by their rapidly changing environment. Their dominant feeling about the world around them seems, in the end, to have been one of profound distrust. They claimed to believe in progress; indeed they promoted it. They hailed educational change as a great reformation in society. Yet one cannot ignore their even greater pessimism. The world, as they saw it, verged on chaos; the question uppermost in their minds often seems to have been how to tame rampant nature and the devil in man, and their real quest a quest for control. There was accordingly the desire, on the part of those who saw themselves as the reasonable, civilized and respectable elements of society, to exert control over the unreasonable, savage and disreputable at all social levels, but especially among the poor. This control, they hoped, would be exercised through the schools....

The response of school reformers in Upper Canada to the social dislocations of their times was, in sum, to promote an essentially inegalitarian view of society and an equally inegalitarian approach to schooling. Control of the uncivilized poor, on the one hand, and the promotion of middle class respectability and achievement on the other, were clearly their fundamental aims. Their approach to educational reform, moreover, was governed by a view of the middle class state as genuinely representative of society in its competitive quest for advancement. The schools could not help but reflect these social and political biases.

Alison Prentice, *The School Promoters: Education and Social Class in Mid-Nineteenth Century Upper Canada* (Toronto: McClelland and Stewart, 1977), pp. 170-1 and 182-4.

A Critique of the New Revisionism

Revisionist interpretations of the school promoters in Upper Canada have not gone unchallenged. Professor Bruce Curtis, a sociologist at McMaster University, has adopted a fresh approach to the question and suggests that the educational revisionists have made far too much of poverty and crime and have been hobbled by their view of education simply as a system of social control.

The educational reforms advocated by Ryerson sought to overcome class antagonism in civil society by creating harmony and personal contact between members of different social classes at school. 'Common' schooling in the late 1840s meant the schooling of different social classes in common. Common schooling meant placing 'the poor man on a level with the rich man'.

It meant providing a common intellectual property to members of all social classes and to a certain extent as well it was an attempt to compensate the urban proletariat for its real propertylessness with an intellectual property. This property was to be distributed by the state, and through the appropriation of it, members of all social classes would occupy a common position in relation to the state.

Common schooling and common Christianity as a theory and practice, then, sought to create social harmony by creating political subjects predisposed to act in keeping with principles of respect for existing relations of authority. This phenomenon in Upper Canada may be understood as an attempt on the part of religious dissent to create forms of civil and religious universality. Its class character is thoroughly petty-bourgeois. It did not attempt to alter existing relations to the means of production in Upper Canadian society. On the contrary, by modifying some of the consequences of existing relations among social classes, school reform sought to preserve these relations. Educational reform sought to create a new form of governance. . . .

Educational reformers in Canada and elsewhere in the initial period of reform frequently thought of and described themselves as creating 'systems of public instruction'. They were somewhat mistaken. In Upper Canada during the period covered here there was no public to instruct. The political life of the colony was lived in disparate ethnic and religious groups, antagonistic social classes and isolated rural communities. There was no population sharing a common set of rights, duties and obligations in a national state. The very form of the state itself was in dispute. There were no 'general' nor 'common' interests which a state could appear to represent.

In fact, the process of educational reform can better be understood as one of the processes involved in the *construction* of a public. Educational reform sought to create a new political universality. . . .

Educational reformers in effect sought to create a new domain, a new terrain out of the political conflicts which shook Upper Canadian society. This would be a sphere of social harmony and political universality in which the state would rule. Educational reform was directly involved in the construction of the formal elements of universality which constitute the public.

Bruce Curtis, *Preconditions of the Canadian State: Educational Reform and the construction of a Public in Upper Canada, 1837–1846* (Toronto: Structural Analysis Programme, University of Toronto, 1981), Working Paper Series No. 24, pp. 29, 31, 33–34. Rev. ed. in: *Studies in Political Economy*, No. 10 (winter, 1983).

ALTRUISM OR SOCIAL CONTROL—THE BROADER DEBATE

Social Developments and the Growth of Canadian Institutions—A Standard Interpretation

A clear expression of the traditional view of "social developments" in the 1840s and early 1850s can be found in J.M.S. Careless' synthesis of the 1841–51 period, *The Union of the Canadas* (1967). Although the book deals solely with the Canadas, it suggests that Canada's basic social institutions took shape in this period. In addition, the social policies adopted in the united province of Canada, in Careless' view, were, by implication, administrative responses of the state to legitimate social needs.

The sixteen years' experience of the Canadian union had . . . produced . . . patterns of lasting significance: in education, in public administration, and in social policy. In these respects, the later Canadian confederation and provinces of Ontario and Quebec owed a sizable debt to the old province of Canada. Most notably, the union period virtually set the outlines of the school systems of Ontario and Quebec, almost as two alternative modes, with profound consequence both for the course of their cultural development and for educational issues that subsequently emerged in the federal Canadian union after 1867. . . .

[In Upper Canada] the system of public education that concerned the large majority was under non-sectarian state authority at the centre and lay control in the localities. It was really the reverse of the Lower Canadian pattern, where the pre-eminent influence was the church, though the state was a necessary agent. . . .

* * * * *

Administrative development under the union of the Canadas of course comprehended education. It also entered the realm of social policy, and both of these would fall generally to provincial authority in the federal structure after 1867. Social policy, as it first emerged in the union, particularly concerned penal institutions. Apart from the state maintaining a provincial asylum in Toronto and a marine hospital and quarantine hospital at Quebec, social welfare functions such as poor relief, correctional training and care of the sick and aged were essentially left to the municipalities and voluntary interdenominational bodies in Upper Canada and to the Roman Catholic Church in Lower Canada; though with some aid from varied public grants. Prisons, however, were seen as a provincial responsibility; and on that inauspicious foundation, state action in the social sphere began to grow. . . .

At Confederation, since social welfare responsibilities went to the provinces, they followed separate courses of development thereafter under the jurisdictions of Quebec and Ontario. Yet unquestionably, the emergence of an experienced group of officials within this field during the 1850's was of major consequence for the future growth of provincial social services and welfare legislation. It eased the transition from pioneer self-reliance and family care to the colder world of urban industrialism, and reduced the application of stern doctrines of laissez-faire—always, however, more recited in theory than applied in practice. Indeed, the evolution of prison inspectors in the Canadian union as effective instruments of state social policy is analogous to the evolution of factory inspectors in contemporary Britain. That the one sprang out of colonial prison brutality and the other from British industrial prisons may be regarded as a tribute to the realistic humanity of those Canadian and British Victorians who put first things first.

J.M.S. Careless, *The Union of the Canadas: The Growth of Canadian Institutions*, 1841–1857 (Toronto: McClelland and Stewart, 1967), pp. 213–14, 215, 216–7, 220 and 221–2.

Social Change in Pre-Industrial Canada—A Reinterpretation

Two practitioners of the new social history, Michael S. Cross and Gregory S. Kealey, have recently offered a different perspective on the social changes and reforms of the mid-nineteenth century. In their introduction to a series of readings on pre-industrial Canada, Cross and Kealey contend that the conditions of economic and social instability (after the ending of British preferential trade) prompted the British North American reformers to seek a larger role for the state in many areas of social life.

... In the 1840's, England embraced free trade, the removal of barriers to commerce, the philosophy of free enterprise. Now the predominant industrial power in the world, able to compete successfully in markets everywhere, Britain no longer needed artificial protection. Nor, incidentally, did she need either the markets or the produce of the colonies. So the mainstays of Canadian development, the timber duties and the Corn Laws—which had provided a protected market for colonial wheat—disappeared between 1842 and 1846.

These British actions produced a panic in Canada. The situation was worsened by a general depression in the western world and by the Irish famine migration. The failure of the potato crop in Ireland caused widespread starvation and disease. Tens of thousands fled the disaster; in 1847 alone, some 100,000 set out for the North American colonies. Many died along the way, but the survivors arrived in the colonies bringing with them their diseases and their poverty. An economy already disrupted by depression and free trade reeled under the impact of the Irish hordes. The colonial mind, conditioned by the experience of the imperial system of the past, could conceive of few solutions to the compound crisis of the 1840's....

* * * * *

England turned on the taps after the Napoleonic Wars and poured her surplus population on British North America. Her requirements shaped the character of the migration and ultimately of Canadian society. British North America received large numbers of the poor and unskilled and an undue proportion of gentle folk—retired military officers on half-pay, younger sons of the upper middle class, and the like. Compared to the United States, Canada received relatively few of the most productive workers, artisans, and capitalists. After the early 1830's, the immigration was dominated by Irish, fleeing their dying country and encouraged to leave by landlords and the British government. The contours of Canadian society were shaped by this selective immigration.

It was in many ways an unstable society.... The rapidity of the peopling of Canada almost guaranteed that instability as disparate elements, different nationalities, different religions, and different classes were thrown together in a new environment. Friction and disorder were inevitable, especially when one of the elements, the Irish, had long traditions of disrespect for authority and of violence. To these factors were added ethnic and religious discrimination, as well as the economic oppression that tormented groups such as the canal workers.

The state played an increasing role in mediating between groups and in controlling their behaviour. This was especially true in the 1840's. The Rebellions had shown the danger in unrest and the necessity to control it before it grew into insurrection. The friction in a mixed society suggested the need to establish common patterns of behaviour and common economic, social, and political goals. Institutions of social control emerged to meet this need. Some were frankly coercive, such as police forces and prisons, mechanisms to frighten people into appropriate behaviour. Others were more subtle. The school became the most important institution of social control, a place where good citizenship, personal hygiene, the idea of progress, and respect for authority all would be inculcated in the young. Many in 1849 believed that if the schools were successful the disorder of a pioneer society would be a thing of the past....

Michael S. Cross and Gregory S. Kealey, Introduction to *Pre-Industrial Canada, 1760–1849: Readings in Canadian Social History*, Vol. 2 (Toronto: McClelland and Stewart, 1982), pp. 10–11 and 13–14.

A Guide to Further Reading

1. Overview

Careless, J.M.S., *The Union of the Canadas: The Growth of Canadian Institutions, 1841–1857*. Toronto: McClelland and Stewart, 1967.

Clark, S.D., *The Social Development of Canada*. Toronto: University of Toronto Press, 1942.

Cross, Michael S. and Gregory S. Kealey, eds., *Pre-Industrial Canada: Readings in Canadian Social History*, Vol. 2, 1760–1849. Toronto: McClelland and Stewart, 1982.

Houston, Susan E., "Politics, Schools and Social Change in Upper Canada", *Canadian Historical Review*, Vol. LIII (September, 1972), pp. 249–270.

Katz, Michael B., *The People of Hamilton, Canada West: Family and Class in A Mid-Nineteenth Century City*. Cambridge, Mass.: Harvard University Press, 1976.

Lower, A.R.M., *Canadians in the Making*. Toronto: Longmans, 1958.

Moir, John S., *Church and State in Canada West, 1841–1867*. Toronto: University of Toronto Press, 1959.

Morton, W.L., ed., *The Shield of Achilles: Aspects of Canada in the Victorian Age*. Toronto: McClelland and Stewart, 1968.

Ouellet, Fernand, *Economic and Social History of Quebec, 1760–1850*. Toronto: Macmillan, 1980.

Parr, Joy, ed., *Childhood and Family in Canadian History*. Toronto: McClelland and Stewart, 1982.

Prentice, Alison L. and Susan E. Houston, eds., *Family, School and Society in Nineteenth-Century Canada*. Toronto: Oxford University Press, 1975.

Sutherland, Neil, *Children in English-Canadian Society: Framing the Twentieth-Century Consensus*. Toronto: University of Toronto Press, 1978.

2.   Specialized Studies

Population, Land and Settlement

Cowan, Helen I., *British Emigration to British North America*. Toronto: University of Toronto Press, 1961.

Craig, Gerald M., ed., *Early Travellers in the Canadas 1791-1867*. Toronto: Macmillan, 1955.

Duncan, Kenneth, "Irish Famine Immigration and the Social Structure of Canada West", in Michiel Horn and Ronald Sabourin, eds., *Studies in Canadian Social History*. Toronto: McClelland and Stewart, 1974, pp. 140-63.

Gagan, David, *Hopeful Travellers: Families, Land, and Social Change in Mid-Victorian Peel County, Canada West*. Toronto: Ontario Historical Studies Series, 1981.

Johnson, Leo A., *History of the County of Ontario, 1615-1875*. Whitby: Ontario County Council, 1973.

Parr, C.J., "The Welcome and the Wake: Attitudes in Canada West toward Irish Famine Migration", *Ontario History*, Vol. LXVI (June, 1974), pp. 101-114.

Social Welfare and Public Health

Bilson, Geoffrey, *A Darkened House: Cholera in Nineteenth Century Canada*. Toronto: University of Toronto Press, 1980.

Fingard, Judith, "The Relief of the Unemployed Poor in Saint John, Halifax and St. John's, 1815-1860", *Acadiensis*, Vol. 5 (1975), pp. 32-53.

Noel, Janet, "Temperance Evangelism: Drink, Religion and Reform in the Province of Canada, 1840-1854". Unpublished Ph.D. Thesis, University of Ottawa, 1978.

Splane, Richard B., *Social Welfare in Ontario, 1791-1893*. Toronto: University of Toronto Press, 1965.

Trudel, Marcel, *Chiniquy*. Trois-Rivières: Le Boréal Express, 1955.

Whalen, J.M., "Social Welfare in New Brunswick, 1784-1900", *Acadiensis*, Vol. 2, No. 1 (Autumn, 1972).

Crime and Punishment

Beattie, J.M., *Attitudes to Crime and Punishment in Upper Canada, 1830-1850*. Toronto: Centre for Criminology, 1977.

Bellomo, J. Jerald, "Upper Canadian Attitudes Toward Crime and Punishment, 1832-1851", *Ontario History* Vol. LXIV (March, 1972).

Cross, Michael S., "'The Laws are Like Cobwebs': Popular Resistance to Authority in Mid-Nineteenth Century British North America", in Peter B. Waite, Sandra Oxner, and Thomas Barnes, eds., *Law in a Colonial Society: The Nova Scotia Experience*. Toronto: Carswell, 1984, pp. 103-123.

Fingard, Judith, "Jailbirds in Mid-Victorian Halifax", in Peter B. Waite et al., eds., *Law in a Colonial Society*, pp. 81-102.

Houston, Susan E., "Victorian Origins of Juvenile Delinquency: A Canadian Experience", *History of Education Quarterly* (1972).

Public Education Reform

Hodgins, J. George, ed., *Documentary History of Education in Upper Canada*, Vols. IV and V. Toronto: Warwick and Rutler, 1897.

Katz, Michael B., and Paul H. Mattingly, eds., *Education and Social Change: Themes from Ontario's Past*. New York: New York University Press, 1975.

Lajeunesse, M., "L'évêque Bourget et l'instruction publique au Bas-Canada, 1840–46", *Revue d'histoire de l'Amérique française* (1970).

McDonald, Neil and Alf Chaiton, eds., *Egerton Ryerson and His Times*. Toronto: Macmillan, 1978.

Prentice, Alison, *The School Promoters: Education and Social Class in Mid-Nineteenth Century Upper Canada*. Toronto: McClelland and Stewart, 1977.

Wilson, J. Donald, "The Ryerson Years in Canada West", in J.D. Wilson, R.M. Stamp and L.-P. Audet, eds., *Canadian Education: A History*. Scarborough: Prentice-Hall, 1970, pp. 214–240.

9

THE UNION OF THE CANADAS, 1841–1864

An Emerging Bicultural Community or "Two Scorpions in a Bottle"?

The Union of the Canadas is usually remembered for the turbulence with which it began and the factious strife in which it ended. Both periods featured political struggles, sectional tensions, and constitutional dilemmas. In the wake of the rebellions of 1837–38 came Lord Durham's famous description of "two nations warring in the bosom of a single state". Two decades later, as Upper Canada and Lower Canada came to a political standoff that seemed impossible to resolve, the description could still have applied. In fact, modern French Canadian nationalist historians, echoing a metaphor of René Lévesque's, have described the Union as a political arrangement equivalent to "two scorpions in a bottle".

But was this really the case? Within months of the publication of Lord Durham's pessimistic assessment, French Canadian and English-speaking Canadian Reformers were working together in a political alliance that led to the political triumph of responsible government in 1849. The Union of 1841, which was proposed by Lord Durham as a way to anglicize French Canadians, may in fact have provided the two peoples with the opportunity to learn co-operation. Every student of Canadian history knows that the deadlock that killed the Union of the Canadas soon led to the phoenix-like birth of Confederation. Were these developments not indisputable evidence of a developing bicultural community? To the French Canadian nationalist contention that the two nations were like embattled scorpions, historians sympathetic to federalism have countered that the Union in fact laid the groundwork for a federal bicultural state.

Thus, the historical debate over the Union has moved, in a sense, from the scholarly to the public realm. It has become bound up in—and has been to some extent sustained by—the clash of ideologies in contemporary relations between Canada and Quebec. And only a close look at the historical background and evidence can really settle the question for serious students of history.

Between 1841 and 1864, the Canadas—that is, the former colonies of Upper and Lower Canada—operated within a single government. The rebellions of 1837 and 1838 had brought to a boil many of the simmering problems of the day. In the aftermath, John George Lambton, Lord Durham, had recommended that Lower Canada, the homeland of the French Canadians, be joined in a legislative union with its English-speaking neighbour, Upper Canada. The Act of Union, proposed by the British government in 1840 and officially proclaimed in February, 1841, incorporated many of Durham's proposals and linked the two provinces in a common legislative system.

The debate over the Union embroiled the two Canadas in a continuing political controversy. Despite Durham's recommendation for representation by population, each "section"—Canada East (Lower Canada) and Canada West (Upper Canada)—had been given an equal number of seats in the new assembly. Thus the two sections were equally balanced in political power. Far from being absorbed by an English-speaking majority, French-speaking Canada preserved its own special character, religion, and laws. Lord Durham's recommendation for assimilation succeeded only in arousing racial and nationalist feelings. While English Canadians in Canada West were divided into different religious and political groups, the majority of French Canadians reacted as one body to safeguard their cultural interests. Wielding considerable power, the *Canadien* representatives could—and regularly did—demand and gain an equal share in the long succession of governments formed between 1841 and 1864 in the province of Canada.

The politics of the decade that followed Lord Durham's Report were dominated by the struggle for responsible government. A Reform alliance, first forged in 1839–40 by Louis-Hippolyte LaFontaine and Francis Hincks and later headed by LaFontaine and Robert Baldwin, campaigned hard through the 1840s for the principle. While Baldwin favoured reform which extended parliamentary practice to the colony, LaFontaine saw responsible government as the means by which French Canadian rights and culture might be preserved. After years of constitutional struggle and periodic concessions, the British government finally relented. Formally approved by Lord Grey, the Colonial Secretary, and Lord Elgin, the Governor-General, in 1848, the principle was confirmed in practice in April 1849 when Elgin signed the Rebellion Losses Bill for Lower Canada into law. This development has long been viewed as the beginning of the end of colonial status for the Canadas; and has been more recently cited as the point of origin of bicultural, biracial party government in Canada.

In the standard accounts of the Union, the politics of the 1850s have been treated as a period of growing schisms between Canada East and Canada West; between Reformers and Tories. Largely because of continued British immigration, the population of Canada West surpassed that of Canada East. Leading Reform politicians, such as Oliver Mowat and George Brown among the Grits, complained that the government was under "French domination". Canada West, they argued, paid more taxes, but most public money was spent in Canada East, and the life of every ministry depended on the support of a sizable bloc of *Canadien* representatives in the assembly. The Reform alliance worked out by LaFontaine and Baldwin dissolved as the cry arose in the western section for "representation by population", a scheme that would give Canada West a working majority of seats in parliament. Prominent *Canadien* leaders, such as A.A. Dorion of the *Rouges*, fiercely resisted this demand, fearing that it would drown the French Canadian vote and lead to total assimilation.

Most historians have judged that by the late 1850s and early 1860s the Union had failed as a government. The legislative process seemed to be arrested in a state of "double majority" paralysis, and both Reformer and Tory alliances appeared to be in a shambles. This preoccupation with the sectional struggles of the 1850s, however, may have obscured the signs of a growing sense of bicultural community. It was during this period that a new and lasting political partnership emerged out of the political deadlock. The main *Canadien* faction, the *Parti bleu*, headed by George-Etienne Cartier, and the English-speaking "Liberal-Conservatives" led by John A. MacDonald, worked out a new partnership which resisted the demand for "rep by pop" and sought other constitutional solutions. This new entente, it has been argued, formed the uneasy but enduring foundation for the "Great Coalition" of 1864 which led to Confederation.

The politics of the Union raise a number of critical historical questions. What dilemma did the Union of the Canadas pose for the colonies of Upper and Lower Canada, for French- and English-speaking Canadians? Was the struggle for responsible government primarily a question of "party" or "race"? If the Union was designed to assimilate the French Canadians, why did it fail? Were the years preceding Confederation a period of continual acrimony and political deadlock between two incompatible nationalities? Or did the Union of the Canadas lay the initial foundation for a bicultural community of shared ideals and institutions?

SELECTED CONTEMPORARY SOURCES

THE ORIGINAL PLAN OF UNION

Lord Durham—known in British politics as "Radical Jack" for his part in the reform movement of the 1820s and 1830s in Britain—arrived in Quebec City at the end of June, 1838, as Governor-General and Special High Commissioner. He came to inquire into the causes of the rebellions of 1837 in the two Canadas and to make recommendations about their future government. On his return to Britain in November, 1838, he wrote his celebrated *Report*, which was published early in February, 1839. In this monumental document, he set down his famous analysis of French Canadian society and proposed the unification of the Canadas. It is generally agreed that Lord Durham saw the struggle as one of the two warring "races" and recommended legislative union as the most effective means of anglicizing, or assimilating, the French Canadians of Lower Canada.

Lord Durham's Constitution Solution, 1839

In these passages from his Report, Durham set out his plan for a union of the two Canadas and explained clearly its purposes. Although he had shown an earlier preference for a federation of all the British North American colonies, his investigations convinced him that the urgency of the problem in Lower Canada required an immediate legislative union to assimilate the French Canadians.

> ...A plan by which it is proposed to ensure the tranquil government of Lower Canada, must include in itself the means of putting an end to the agitation of national disputes in the legislature, by settling, at once and for ever, the national character of the Province. I entertain no doubts as to the national character which must be given to Lower Canada; it must be that of the British Empire; that of the majority of the population of British America; that of the great race which must, in the lapse of no long period of time, be predominant over the whole North American Continent. Without effecting the change so rapidly or so roughly as to shock the feelings and trample on the welfare of the existing generation, it must henceforth be the first and steady purpose of the British Government to establish an English population, with English laws and language, in this Province, and to trust its government to none but a decidedly English Legislature....
>
> There can hardly be conceived a nationality more destitute of all that can invigorate and elevate a people than that which is exhibited by the descendants of the French in Lower Canada, owing to their retaining their peculiar language and manners. They are a people with no history, and no literature....
>
> ...In any plan, which may be adopted for the future management of Lower Canada, the first object ought to be that of making it an English Province.... With this end in view, the ascendancy should never again be placed in any hands but those of an English population....
>
> ...I believe that tranquility can only be restored by subjecting the Province to the vigorous rule of an English majority; and that the only efficacious government would be that formed by a legislative union.
>
> If the population of Upper Canada is rightly estimated at 400,000, the English inhabitants of Lower Canada at 150,000, and the French at 450,000, the union of the two Provinces would not only give a clear English majority, but one which would be increased every year by the influence of English emigration; and I have little doubt that the French, when once placed, by the legitimate course of events and the working of natural causes, in a minority, would abandon their vain hopes of nationality....
>
> C.P. Lucas, ed., *Lord Durham's Report on the Affairs of British North America* (Oxford: Clarendon Press, 1912), Vol. 2, pp. 288, 294–6 and 306–9.

Lord Durham's Call for Responsible Government, 1839

Lord Durham's Report recommended more than the assimilation of the French Canadians and the union of the two Canadas. Agreeing with a suggestion by the Upper Canadian reformer Robert Baldwin, Durham recommended that "responsible government" be granted to the legislature of the united Canada. This was a constitutional principle just beginning to be recognized at Westminster, meaning, essentially, that the ministry, or "cabinet", which governed was responsible as a body to the majority of the elected House. In this passage from the Report, Durham outlined his conception of the "great principle".

It is not by weakening, but strengthening the influence of the people on its Government; by confining within much narrower bounds than those hitherto allotted to it and not by extending the interference of the imperial authorities in the details of colonial affairs that I believe that harmony is to be restored, where dissension has so long prevailed; and a regularity and vigour, hitherto unknown, introduced into the administration of these Provinces. It needs no change in the principles of government, no invention of a new constitutional theory, to supply the remedy which would, in my opinion, completely remove the existing political disorders. It needs but to follow out consistently the principles of the British constitution, and introduce into the Government of these great Colonies those wise provisions, by which alone the working of the representative system can in any country be rendered harmonious and efficient. . . .

I would not impair a single prerogative of the Crown; on the contrary, I believe that the interests of the people of these Colonies require the protection of prerogatives which have not hitherto been exercised. But the Crown must, on the other hand, submit to the necessary consequences of representative institutions; and if it has to carry on the Government in unison with a representative body, it must consent to carry it on by means of those in whom that representative body has confidence. . . .

I admit that the system which I propose would, in fact, place the internal government of the colony in the hands of the colonists themselves; and that we should thus leave to them the execution of the laws, of which we have long entrusted the making solely to them. Perfectly aware of the value of our colonial possessions, and strongly impressed with the necessity of maintaining our connexion with them, I know not in what respect it can be desirable that we should interfere with their internal legislation in matters which do not affect their relations with the mother country. The matters, which so concern us, are very few. The constitution of the form of government,—the regulation of foreign relations, and of trade with the mother country, the other British Colonies, and foreign nations,—and the disposal of the public lands, are the only points on which the mother country requires a control . . . .

C.P. Lucas, ed., *Lord Durham's Report*, Vol. 2, pp. 277-8 and 281-2.

THE STRUGGLE FOR RESPONSIBLE GOVERNMENT

In the decade following Durham's report a struggle developed in the Canadas over the introduction of responsible government. In spite of Durham's claim that French Canadians would be anglicized in a legislative union of the two provinces, a group of moderate Lower Canadian Reformers came to believe that responsible government might provide the means by which *Canadiens* could preserve their culture and institutions within the Union.

A political alliance based on political principles rather than race was the key. If they could join forces with English Canadians of similar Reform views, together they could form a majority in the Assembly. Under responsible government the French Canadians would thus be assured a share in governing the colony. Even before the Act of Union was proclaimed, the leaders of the moderate Reform parties in the two provinces pledged to cooperate in the attainment of responsible government.

Origins of Reform Party Collaboration—The Hincks-LaFontaine Correspondence, 1839.

One of the earliest signs of an emerging bicultural co-operation can be found in a correspondence between Upper Canadian Reformer Francis Hincks and Lower Canadian Reform leader Louis-Hippolyte LaFontaine. In an exchange of letters in the months preceding Union, they promised that their parties would work together in a united legislature.

This collaboration furthered the objectives of both parties. For Upper Canadian Reformers it increased the chances of obtaining responsible government and political power which would enable them to introduce long-sought-after reforms. As Reformers, LaFontaine's Lower Canadian followers stood to gain similar benefits. LaFontaine believed that the reform alliance also offered an unexpected and peaceful means for protecting French Canadian interests, though this was not one of the purposes of co-operation set out in Hincks' initial letter to LaFontaine:

Hincks' Appeal, April 12, 1839

Though I have not the honour of personal acquaintance with you, yet entertaining a high respect for your political and private character, I take the liberty of addressing you on the subject of Lord Durham's report, which you have doubtless attentively perused long ere this. I am most anxious to know how that document is received by you and your political friends, and your press is at present so completely gagged that it is not a true index of public opinion. With respect to the principles of government recommended by Lord D. I presume there cannot be a doubt, that they will be as satisfactory to you as to us. With regard to the Union I fear it will be unsatisfactory, but I am anxious to know. You may be afraid that in this promotion of liberal and economical government the Reformers of this province will cooperate with those of Lower Canada. On national questions it is not likely that they would. Lord Durham ascribes to you national objects; if he is right, union would ruin you, if he is wrong, I think you are really desirous of liberal institutions and economical government, the Union would in my opinion give you all you could desire, as an United Parliament would have an immense Reform Majority. I should be much gratified if you would inform me candidly and confidentially how you like the report, and what you think of present prospects. The British party below calculate as does Lord Durham on the French Canadian party being destroyed in the United Legislature. This as I have already said might be the case so far as national objects are concerned, but if we combine *as Canadians* to promote the good of all classes in Canada there cannot be a doubt that under the new constitution, worked as Lord Durham proposes, the only party which would suffer would be the bureaucrats.

P.A.C. Louis-Hippolyte LaFontaine Papers, Francis Hincks to L.-H. LaFontaine, April 12, 1839 (Vol. 7–2623), trans. J.M., s.j.

"Two Nations in A Single State"—Lord Durham's Analysis, 1839

Lower Canadians who opposed LaFontaine's strategy of collaboration frequently cited Lord Durham's observations on the nature of the problem in the Canadas. In his Report, Durham saw the struggle as one of "races" rather than of "political principles". Any possibility for bicultural cooperation was precluded by the fundamental incompatibility of the two peoples. If this analysis of the situation was accepted, it followed that Union could lead only to the victory of English Canadians over their French Canadian rivals.

> ... I expected to find a contest between a government and a people: I found two nations warring in the bosom of a single state: I found a struggle, not of principles but of races; and I perceived that it would be idle to attempt any amelioration of laws or institutions until we could first succeed in terminating the deadly animosity that now separates the inhabitants of Lower Canada into the hostile divisions of French and English....
>
> The national feud forces itself on the very senses, irresistibly and palpably, as the origin or the essence of every dispute which divides the community; we discover that dissensions, which appear to have another origin, are but forms of this constant and all-pervading quarrel; and that every contest is one of French and English in the outset, or becomes so ere it has run its course....
>
> ... It is scarcely possible to conceive descendants of any of the great European nations more unlike each other in character and temperament, more totally separated from each other by language, laws, and modes of life, or placed in circumstances more calculated to produce mutual misunderstanding, jealousy and hatred.
>
> C.P. Lucas, ed., *Lord Durham's Report*, Vol. 2, pp. 17, 19–20 and 27.

The "Great Measure" of 1842—Governor Charles Bagot's Report on Its Outcome

During the first session of the new Parliament of the Union, the Reformers began to act together. In fact, so much so that by the summer of 1842, the new Governor-General, Sir Charles Bagot, realized that Durham's recommendations against French Canadian participation in the government were impossible to carry out. He advised the Colonial Secretary, Lord Stanley, of his intention to include French Canadian representatives in his government. Then, shortly after Parliament opened in September, 1842, he invited LaFontaine to enter the Council. Bagot's initiative, popularly known as the "Great Measure", had more than symbolic importance. LaFontaine accepted office after a round of intensive negotiations that in effect consolidated the Reform alliance and secured for the government French Canadian support. Bagot's report to Lord Stanley in late September 1842 seemed to suggest that the measure produced a brief *rapprochement* between the two peoples.

> Various circumstances induced me to postpone the meeting of the Legislature to the latest period allowed by the law; I accordingly fixed it for the 8th of Sept. As the time approached, my Executive Council in a more formal manner urged upon me the expediency of admitting some French Canadians to my Govt. to which, on mature reflexion I could no longer offer sufficient reasonable objection. I felt satisfied that the

distrust and ill will which had been engendered among the French Canadians by their long exclusion from a share in the administration of public affairs, would be dispelled by such a measure; that they would receive it as a boon with gratitude, and would give in exchange for it their support in the Legislature and their assistance throughout the lower province in carrying out the main provisions of the Union. . . .

The House of Assembly has already expressed 'its unmingled satisfaction' at the course which I have taken. From the principle of it there was not *one dissentient voice*. I may confidently state that the same feeling exists in the other branch of the Legislature. . . . I have met the wishes of a large majority of the population of Upper Canada and of the British Inhabitants of Lower Canada. I have removed the main ground of discontent and distrust among the French Canadian population; I have satisfied them that the Union is capable of being administered for their happiness and advantage, and have consequently disarmed their opposition to it. I have excited among them the strongest feeling of gratitude to the Provincial Government, and if my policy be approved by H.M.'s Govt. I shall have removed their chief cause of hostility to British Institutions, and have added another security for their devotion to the British Crown. . . . The Union did not offer [the occasion for developing loyalty:] it was imposed upon them without their being consulted, (for they had no representation in the Special Council) and without regard to their remonstrance.

The present crisis, however, has offered the occasion; I have seized it; and I cannot use terms too strong in expressing to yr. Lp. my conviction that the result will, without the least sacrifice of British interests, or the least danger to British Institutions in the Province, tend to establish and confirm the principles and main intentions of the Union, and thus conduce to make United Canada one of the most happy, contented, loyal and prosperous portions of H.M.'s Dominions.

P.A.C., Sir Charles Bagot Papers, Charles Bagot to Lord Stanley, September 26, 1842.

The Double Triumph of Responsible Government—Lord Elgin's Explanation for Signing the Rebellion Losses Bill, 1849

For the Reform alliance, the campaign for responsible government was a slow, halting, ten-year struggle. From the beginning LaFontaine had to convince doubtful compatriots that French Canadian rights could be protected best by political co-operation with English-speaking Reformers. By the late 1840s LaFontaine's moderate Reformers faced a new challenge from within Lower Canada. A group of radical democrats known as the *Parti rouge* and radical Lower Canadian Reformers, spurred by the return of rebellion leader Louis Joseph Papineau to Quebec in 1845, had begun to condemn LaFontaine's strategy as the work of *Canadiens vendus*, or "sell-outs" to the English.

The signing into law of the Rebellion Losses Bill for Lower Canada represented an important test on two counts. First, the Bill—which compensated persons who had lost property during the 1837–38 uprisings, and was personally opposed by the Governor-General—served as a critical test of responsible government in practice. And secondly, it was a bill sponsored by LaFontaine and thus represented a severe test of the viability of French-English partnership and collaboration. In explaining his decision to grant "royal assent" in a March 1849 dispatch, Lord Elgin made it clear he had considered both the constitutional and bicultural aspects of the problem.

Mar. 1, 1849

A good deal of excitement and bad feeling has been stirred in the Province by the introduction of a measure by the Ministry for the payment of certain Rebellion losses in Lower Canada—I trust that it will soon subside and that no enduring mischief will ensue from it; but the opposition leaders who are very low in the World at present, have taken advantage of the circumstance to work upon the feelings of the old loyalists as opposed to Rebels, of British as opposed to French, and of Upper Canadians as opposed to Lower, and thus to provoke from various parts of the Province the expression of not very temperate or measured discontent.... The measure itself is not indeed altogether free from objection, and I very much regret that an addition should be made to our debt for such an object at this time. Nevertheless I must say I do not see how my present Govt could have taken any other course in this matter than that which they have followed. Their predecessors...had already gone more than half way in the same direction—though they had stopped short and now tell us that they never intended to go further—If this Ministry had failed to complete the work of alleged justice to Lower Canada which had been commenced by the former administration M. Papineau would most assuredly have availed himself of the plea to undermine their influence in this section of the Province....

Discussions of this class place in strong relief the passions and tendencies which render the endurance of the political system which we have established here and of the connexion with the Mother Country uncertain and precarious. They elicit a manifestation of antipathy between races, and of jealousy between the recently united Provinces, which is much to be regretted. This measure of indemnity to Lower Canada is however the last of the kind and if it be once settled satisfactorily, a formidable stumbling block will have been removed from our path....

A. Doughty, ed., *The Elgin-Grey Papers, 1846–1852* (Ottawa: 1937), Vol. 1, pp. 299–300.

Reaction to the Bill—Signs of Hostility between the Two Races

Giving royal assent to the Rebellion Losses Bill in April 1849 touched off a violent reaction among those in Lower Canada's English minority who had opposed the legislation. For members of the Tory party who had so recently lost control of the Executive council, and for many of Montreal's commercial class, already suffering the effects of an economic recession, the issue aroused deep passions. Enraged with the primitive and panic-striken fury of the recently dispossessed, Tory mobs took to the streets of Montreal, attacked the Governor-General's carriage, and set fire to the parliament buildings.

Graphic illustrations and news reports of the violent events left the impression that the signing of the Rebellion Losses Bill had re-opened old wounds between the two races. Interpreters, however, seemed divided on where to lay the blame for the tragedy. A famous lithograph of "The Destruction of the Parliament House" seemed to dramatize the wanton destruction wreaked by the Tory mobs. Yet a bitter *Punch* caricature and commentary alleged that the real responsibility rested with L.-H. LaFontaine, the French Canadian leader who sponsored the legislation which would compensate the rebels of 1837.

"The man wot fired the
Parliament House"

"Destruction of the Parliament House, Montreal,
April 25th, 1849."

THE SECTIONAL TROUBLES OF THE 1850S—A CLASH OF VIEWS

For the Union, the early 1850s were years of passage. Public concerns in the Canadas changed from those of recession to those of prosperity, from responsible government to railways, from Union to a larger scheme, Confederation. LaFontaine, the architect of the Reform policy of collaboration, gave way as French Canadian leader to another, George-Etienne Cartier; and John A. Macdonald succeeded William Draper at the head of the Upper Canadian Conservative party. A new and forceful voice, that of George Brown, editor of *The Globe*, arose to express the radical reform and sectarian interests of Canada West, while French Canadian republican and anti-clerical views came to the fore, espoused by the newly formed *Parti rouge* in Canada East. Material growth, rapid industrial development and the sense of accomplishment that went with them impelled British North Americans to look beyond their own provincial boundaries. But as the 1850s wore on, friction between the two sections of the province of Canada, between Catholics and Protestants, between French, Irish and English, between Tories and Reformers, seemed to be undermining the bases of French-English collaboration.

A Struggle of Races—George Brown's View of Sectional Rivalries, 1852

George Brown, a leader of the Upper Canadian Reform party, was one who showed a growing consciousness of the deep sectional rivalries. Still stinging from defeat in an 1851 by-election, he charged that French Canadian opposition to "Clear Grit" reform measures revealed a basic incompatibility between the two races.

On almost every issue the ministerialists were obliged to take up the defensive; they acknowledged that it would be well if such views could be carried out—but they voted as if they thought the contrary, and palliate their inconsistency on the unworthy plea of expediency. It would have been desirable, they admit, to have had a vote of the Assembly in favour of secularizing the [Clergy] Reserves—but the French Canadians were opposed to it, and it was dangerous to insist on it. It would have been well to apply the 550,000 acres at once to educational purposes—but the French Canadians thought it best to await the settlement of the whole Reserve question. It would have been well to prevent new incumbents being placed on the pension-list—but the French Canadians were in the way.... The sectarian clause of the Upper Canada School Bill is a great evil—but the Roman Catholics demand Separate Schools; the French Hierarchy of Lower Canada have taken up their cause—and what can we do?... Population is the only true basis for Parliamentary Representation; but it would swamp the French Canadians, and they will never consent to it....

And in what a contemptible attitude does all this place the Reformers of Upper Canada! Does it not confess them the abject vassals of the French Canadian priesthood? Mark the long list of important reforms from which we are debarred by the *fiat* of Popery. And mark, too, the humiliating draughts we have been compelled to swallow under compulsion of the same power. What has French Canadianism been denied? Nothing. It bars all it dislikes—it extorts all it demands—and it grows insolent over its victories. And is this a state of things to delight the Reformers of Upper Canada? All this humiliation, all this sacrifice of principle, all this iniquitous legislation under the sanction of Western liberalism—for the noble consideration that '*the party*' is in office! Shame, shame on such degradation!...

But the Tories would come in, if we acted honestly—and they might remain in for ten years! And what if they did? It is our duty to act uprightly and leave consequences in higher hands. Shall we do evil that good may come? And such a good!—a base vassalage to French Canadian Priestcraft.

The Globe, December 30, 1852.

Conciliation and Entente—John A. Macdonald's Response to Sectional Divisions, 1856

John A. Macdonald took a decidedly different view of the sectional troubles. In this note to an English-speaking Lower Canadian journalist who had been railing about "French domination", he argued that cooperation was a practical necessity and pointed out the political benefits of respecting French Canadian "nationality".

...But the truth is you British L. [Lower] Canadians never can forget that you were once supreme—that Jean Baptiste was your hewer of wood and drawer of water—You struggle like the Protestant Irish in Ireland—like the Norman Invaders in England not for equality, but ascendency—the difference between you and those interesting and amiable people being that you have not the honesty to admit it—You can't & [sic] won't admit the principle that the majority [in Lower Canada] must govern....

...No man in his senses can suppose that this country can for a century to come be governed by a totally unfrenchified govt.—if a Lower Canadian Britisher desires to conquer he must 'stoop to conquer'—He must make friends with the French—without sacrificing the status of his race or lineage he must respect their nationality—Treat them as a nation and they will act as a free people generally do—generously. Call them a faction, and they became factious—Supposing the numerical preponderance of British in Canada becomes much greater than it is. I think the French could give more trouble than they are said now to do—At present, they divide, as we do, they are split up into several sections—& are governed more [or] less by defined principles of action—As they become smaller & feebler, so they will be more united—from a sense of self preservation—they will act as one man & hold the balance of power. . . . So long as the French have 20 votes they will be a power, & must be conciliated—I doubt much however if the French will lose their numerical majority in L.C. in a hurry. . . .

    P.A.C. Brown Chamberlin Papers, John A. Macdonald to Brown Chamberlin, Editor, Montreal *Gazette*, January 21, 1856.

THE LEGACY OF THE UNION—BICULTURAL COLLABORATION OR INCOMPATIBILITY?

Out of the Union of the Canadas eventually grew a movement for the larger confederation of all British North American colonies. In spite of the efforts of Macdonald and the Lower Canadian *Parti bleu* leader, George-Etienne Cartier, to build a workable political partnership, by the late 1850s increasing sectional tensions seemed to make a new form of government necessary. When in August of 1858, Alexander T. Galt entered the Cartier-Macdonald ministry on the condition that it accept his scheme for Confederation, a federal union of British North America became government policy. Yet Macdonald and Cartier initially favoured different forms of "confederation" and the Lower Canadian *Parti rouge* came out in strong opposition to any larger scheme of union. In the debates leading to Confederation, the experience of Union government was regularly held up as either an experiment which made larger forms of French-English collaboration possible or a graphic example of the utter incompatibility of the two peoples under one government.

The Legacy of Partnership—G.-E. Cartier's Conception of Federal Union, 1865

Much of G.-E. Cartier's optimism about a federation of the British North American colonies seemed to be based on his experience in an uneasy, but enduring, partnership with Macdonald's "Liberal-Conservatives" during the Union period. While Macdonald's initial preference was for a legislative union, Cartier succeeded in convincing Macdonald and other Canadian leaders of the need for a federal form of union. In his landmark February 1865 address on the Confederation proposals, Cartier argued that a "federation" of the colonies would quite adequately protect French Canadian "nationality" and also assure that the rights of anglophones in Quebec would be respected.

Some parties—through the press and by other modes—pretended that it was impossible to carry out Federation, on account of the differences of races and religions. Those who took this view of the question were in error. It was just the reverse. It was precisely on account of the variety of races, local interests, &c., that the Federation system ought to be resorted to, and would be found to work well. (Hear, hear.) We were in the habit of seeing in some public journals, and hearing from some public men, that it was a great misfortune indeed there should be a difference of races in this colony.

...Now, he (Hon. Mr. Cartier) desired on this point to vindicate the rights, the merits, the usefulness, so to speak, of those belonging to the French Canadian race. (Hear, hear.) In order to bring these merits and this usefulness more prominently before his hearers, it would be only necessary to allude to the efforts made by them to sustain British power on this continent, and to point out their adherence to British supremacy in trying times....

These historical facts taught that there should be a mutual feeling of gratitude from the French Canadians towards the British, and from the British towards the French Canadians, for our present position, that Canada is still a British colony. (Hear, hear)....

Nations were now formed by the agglomeration of communities having kindred interests and sympathies. Such was our case at the present moment. Objection had been taken to the scheme now under consideration, because of the words 'new nationality.' Now, when we were united together, if union were attained, we would form a political nationality with which neither the national origin, nor the religion of any individual, would interfere. It was lamented by some that we had this diversity of races, and hopes were expressed that this distinctive feature would cease. The idea of unity of races was utopian—it was impossible. Distinctions of this kind would always exist.... But with regard to the objection based on this fact, to the effect that a great nation could not be formed because Lower Canada was in great part French and Catholic, and Upper Canada was British and Protestant, and the Lower Provinces were mixed, it was futile and worthless in the extreme. Look, for instance, at the United Kingdom, inhabited as it was by three great races. (Hear, hear.)... ...He [Cartier] viewed the diversity of races in British North America in this way: we were of different races, not for the purpose of warring against each other, but in order to compete and emulate for the general welfare. (Cheers.) We could not do away with the distinctions of race. We could not legislate for the disappearance of the French Canadians from American soil, but British and French Canadians alike could appreciate and understand their position relative to each other. They were placed like great families beside each other, and their contact produced a healthy spirit of emulation. It was a benefit rather than otherwise that we had a diversity of races.

Parliamentary Debates on the Subject of the Confederation of the British North American Provinces, February 7, 1865 (Quebec: Hunter Rose and Company, 1865), pp. 57, 59–60.

The Legacy of Incompatibility—A.-A. Dorion's Case Against Federal Union, 1865

Cartier's optimistic view of federal union and French Canadian "nationality" met stiff opposition from the *Rouges* of Lower Canada, led by Antoine-Aimé Dorion. As leader of the anti-confederates, Dorion intervened in the Confederation debates several times, and his greatest speech, delivered on February 16, 1865, summed up his critique of the federal proposals.

...whenever the question came up I set my face against it. I asserted that such a confederation could only bring trouble and embarrassment, that there was no social, no commercial connection between the provinces proposed to be united—nothing to justify their union at the present juncture. Of course I do not say that I shall be opposed to their Confederation for all time to come. . . .

But the Confederation I advocated was a real confederation, giving the largest powers to the local governments, and merely a delegated authority to the General Government—in that respect differing *in toto* from the one now proposed which gives all the powers to the Central Government, and reserves for the local governments the smallest amount of freedom of action. . . .

Honourable members from Lower Canada are made aware that the delegates all desired a legislative union, but it could not be accomplished at once. This Confederation is the first necessary step towards it. The British Government is ready to grant a Federal Union at once, and when that is accomplished the French element will be completely overwhelmed by the majority of British representatives. What then would prevent the Federal Government from passing a series of resolutions in a similar way to those we are called upon to pass, without submitting them to the people, calling upon the Imperial Government to set aside the Federal form of government and give a legislative union instead of it? (Hear, hear.) . . . .

Confederation Debates, February 16, 1865.

CONFLICTING INTERPRETATIONS

The history of the Union has been written largely as another distinct stage in Canada's political and constitutional evolution. Since the 1920s, historians of the "Whig" and "Political Nationhood" schools[1] have focused on the demise of the old British colonial system, and on the consequent growth of Canadian political institutions.

Much of the historiography of the Union period has been concerned with explaining and applauding the ultimate success of responsible government. LaFontaine's main arguments and evaluations of his own activity have been regularly appropriated by historians. Popular stereotypes of the "good" and the "bad" British governors, the equation of responsible government with French Canadian survival, and the advantages of cultural duality owe much to the partisan opinions of LaFontaine and George-Etienne Cartier.

Recent political studies of the Union period have focused more on the conflict of ideologies. Historians of the modern Quebec nationalist school

---

1. Two schools of English-Canadian historical writing popular from the turn of the century until the 1930s. Whig historians, like J.L. Morrison (author of *British Supremacy and Canadian Self-Government*, 1919), stressed Britain's role in extending the rights of Englishmen to the colonies and interpreted events according to their effect on colonial "progress" toward representative institutions. Historians of the Political Nationhood School, like Chester Martin and R.G. Trotter in the 1920s, focused their attention more on Canada's long struggle to move beyond colonial status and towards the ideal of autonomous Dominion or independent political nationhood. Unlike the Whig interpreters, the Liberal nationalists of the Political Nationhood School treated responsible government as the joint product of personalities and forces on both sides of the Atlantic.

have explored the tragic aftermath of the 1837 and 1838 uprisings, the racial clashes generated by the "two scorpions" warring within the Union "bottle", and the consequent revival of separatist feelings. Other scholars, often with strong federalist leanings, have found the origins of our bicultural federal state in the sectional pressures and cooperative experiments that marked the Union.

VIEWS OF THE STRUGGLE FOR RESPONSIBLE GOVERNMENT

A Triumph of Reform Cooperation—The Political Nationhood View

Traditional interpretations of the struggle for responsible government, harking back to the historical writings of the 1920s and 1930s, have seen the events of 1848–49 as the critical turning point on the long road to Canadian self-government. In the following excerpt, Chester Martin, a historian of the Political Nationhood School, offers an assessment of the Reform alliance's achievement in transforming Lord Durham's proposal for responsible government into practice.

> The solid phalanx of French-Canadian Reformers under LaFontaine were the shock troops that won the most cherished of all Durham's recommendations. The ink was scarcely dry on the *Report* when Francis Hincks, the real architect of the party which won responsible government in Canada in 1848, opened a secret and confidential correspondence with LaFontaine designed to command a working majority in the legislature. The friendship which followed between Baldwin and LaFontaine was the sheet-anchor of the Reform cause. It was they who forced the Bagot incident in 1842; and when the Reformers were beaten in Canada West in 1844 LaFontaine had to find a constituency for Baldwin himself in Rimouski. It was LaFontaine in the greatest speech of his life and in the French language who carried the caucus of the Reform party against Papineau's bitter invective. It was LaFontaine to whom Elgin turned to form the first responsible ministry in the old province of Canada.... The long story of co-operation between Baldwin and LaFontaine, between Hincks himself and Morin, between Cartier and Macdonald is surely an ironical commentary upon Durham's prophecy: 'never again will the present generation of French Canadians yield a loyal submission to a British Government.' I should be inclined to say that the greatest achievement of the French race upon this continent was not before the conquest in 1763 but after it; not before but after the War of 1812; not before but after Lord Durham's *Report*.

> Chester Martin, "Lord Durham's Report and Its Consequences", *Canadian Historical Review*, Vol. XX (June, 1939), pp. 185–6.

The Great Political Invention—A Liberal Nationalist Interpretation

Frank H. Underhill, the late University of Toronto historian, interpreted the 1840s as a crucial formative period in the evolution of the Canadian political party system. Drawing on the political analyses of Wilfrid Laurier and his Liberal nationalist sympathizers, Underhill pointed out that the struggle for responsible government had given birth to a unique Canadian invention—the biracial, bicultural governing party.

> ...the composite bi-racial, bi-cultural party, uniting both French and English voters... [has] been one of our great political inventions. It has been the only effective instrumentality that we have been able to devise for overcoming the deep cleavages between the two communal groups and for keeping them going along together in some kind of rough jolting co-operation.
>
> The experiment began with the Reform party of LaFontaine and Baldwin in the 1840s, which won Responsible Government....
>
> These successful bi-racial governing parties are marked by certain characteristics. Whatever their name, they are really coalitions of the moderate men in each of the French and English communities. Above all, their leaders are moderates. The extremists after 1854, the Grits and Rouges, never quite succeeded for a long time in forming a nation-wide party that was a going concern....
>
> This composite party, with membership from the two races, is always in a state of internal tension, and is frequently torn by dissension. Its unity is always somewhat doubtful, for French and English find it difficult to understand each other even when they can speak one another's language. What holds the party together in the end is the quality of its leaders, their determination to stick together personally through thick and thin, their loyalty to one another and fondness for one another—usually, also, their similarity in temperament as well as in political philosophy. The party, in effect, has had a joint leadership when it was most successful....
>
> To judge from the fact that this experiment has been going on with more or less success continuously since the 1840s, this kind of a bi-racial party would seem to be essential if political co-operation between French—and English-Canadians is to work in practice.
>
> Frank H. Underhill, *The Image of Confederation* (The Massey Lectures, 1963) (Toronto: Canadian Broadcasting Corporation, 1964), pp. 53–5.

A Triumph of "Divide-and-Rule" Colonialism—A Radical Quebec Nationalist View

Radical Quebec historians and writers have in recent years interpreted the attainment of responsible government in starkly different terms. Writing from the perspective of a Quebec separatist in the early 1970s, Léandre Bergeron saw LaFontaine's triumph as part of the British plan to co-opt and integrate "Canayen" leaders into colonial institutions. In this excerpt from his popular history, *A Patriote's Handbook* (1971), Bergeron further contends that responsible government was not "won" by Canadian reformers, but rather "granted" by the British for their own purposes.

> LaFontaine, the timid 'moderate,' the Patriote-turned-collaborator, sees his chance as sell-out leader of a vanquished people. He decides to run for office and issues a proclamation clearly indicating that he will lick English boots. He speaks of a Canada, homeland of French Canadians but, also the adopted country of the English. Our happiness is to depend on social equality and political freedom!
>
> He denounces the Union, all right, but agrees to play ball with the English. Instead of refusing to collaborate with the regime, as a self-respecting Patriote would do, he

urges the Canayens to participate, to vote, to accept the 'democratic game.' LaFontaine behaves just like the obedient *Negro-King* who knows that he will never rule in his own right but hopes against all hope for a few crumbs from the colonizer. . . .

England can easily grant responsible government to her Canadian colony now that there is no longer any Canayen threat. The Canayens have been definitively defeated; their leaders play the parliamentary game, speak English on command and integrate themselves into British institutions. A few concessions are even in order—to bind them all the more strongly to the colonial masters. The French language becomes official in 1849.

Everything has been well planned. Colonial principles well-applied can prevail over the Canayens. The foremost is *divide-and-rule*. Lord Elgin conceals nothing in his letters to Grey at the Colonial Office: 'I believe that the problem of how to govern Canada would be solved if the French would split into a Liberal and a Conservative Party and join the Upper Canadian parties bearing the corresponding names. . . . The national element would be merged in the political if the split to which I refer were accomplished.'

Léandre Bergeron, *The History of Quebec: A Patriote's Handbook*, trans. Baila Markus (Toronto: NC Press, 1971), pp. 109 and 111.

VIEWS OF THE NATION

The Union As a "Second Conquest"—A Quebec Nationalist View

Maurice Séguin, the intellectual father of the French Canadian nationalist school at the Université de Montréal, argued that the Union of the Canadas was a "disaster" for French Canada, because the Union's assimilationist intentions were largely realized. According to him, the Union was torn by the conflict of "two incompatible nationalities", and, in the end, the *Anglais* prevailed in what amounted to a "second conquest".

The two nations, through the instrumentality of their most advanced elements in Lower Canada, were reaching the point of exasperation. A general paralysis resulted. No more government, no more administration of justice, no more schools; capital fled, immigration languished, public works were suspended and Upper Canada was bankrupt. This was the result of the conflict of two incompatible nationalities. . . .

Finally (in 1840) the union of the English forces of the two Canadas over the French Canadians was effected . . . It was the veto by all British Montreal, and behind this veto, by all of British North America, of the separatism of Quebec.

The union, the only logical solution, was imposed by force of circumstances. It was ordained by the higher interests of English colonization. . . . Masters since 1760 of all levels of command, the British, by the union, consolidated their hold not only on the valley of the St. Lawrence, but on Quebec itself. The union of 1840 confirmed, first through political inferiority, and afterwards through economic inferiority, the minority status of a French colonization that had failed. Faced with the inevitable democratic, political, economic and social inferiority of the small French Canadian population, some British seriously asked themselves whether it would not be better, even in the interests of the French Canadians, to work towards the total assimilation of the minority to assure social peace in the valley of the St. Lawrence. But as the solution to the French Canadian problem, assimilation is as unrealizable as the solution of independence.

If in 1840 . . . English Canada out-classed [in economic control and industrialization] all the sectors of French Canada, it was still impossible for it to assimilate the latter. The relations between the two nationalities congealed. As early as 1841 the legislative union, which contained some concessions to the minority of a federal character, functioned spontaneously as a federation, and since that day, the French Canadians survived, annexed, provincialized, in a greater *British North American* Empire.

This solution which could not be rejected, LaFontaine and his successors accepted very easily. They even accepted it with a certain enthusiasm, for they found in it the application of the principle of federalism which contained no material inconveniences for them. The capitulation of Vaudreuil had led infallibly to the unconscious capitulation of LaFontaine, a necessary capitulation, even explicable, but one that remains nonetheless a capitulation. A population is forced to live, and must accept life, as a minority under a foreign majority, without being able to measure the gravity of the situation.

The political history of French Canada cannot be well understood unless one takes into account the inevitable disaster of these two times, forecast in 1760 by English colonization, and consolidated in 1840 by the union of the English forces. . . .

. . . A majority of the population, and having a majority in the legislative assembly, a majority in the executive council, and supported by metropolitan capital, English Canada had completely declassed French Canada without being able to assimilate it. French Canada was literally annexed, provincialized in politics and in economics, transformed into a French appendix attached to a British nation. And English Canada could not avoid this without compromising her own chances of development, without placing her own separatism *vis-à-vis* the United States in danger.

Maurice Séguin, "Genèse et historique de l'idée séparatiste au Canada français", from a series of three talks on the CBC radio program *Conférences*, March 18, March 25 and April 1, 1962. Reprinted from Elizabeth Nish, ed., *Racism or Responsible Government: The French Canadian Dilemma of the 1840s*, (Toronto: Copp Clark, 1967), pp. 178–180, trans. E. Nish.

The Union in the 1840s—The Germination of Canadian Nationalism

Not every French Canadian historian accepts the French Canadian nationalist view. Jacques Monet, s.j., a scholar versed in the political and constitutional issues of the Union period, has interpreted the 1840s as a time of rebirth for French Canada. In his major work, *The Last Cannon Shot* (1969), he contended that the Union failed in its assimilationist intentions and, instead, served as a catalyst for the germination of a new French Canadian nationalism.

Perhaps the *Canadiens'* greatest problem was learning to live with their neighbours. Geography, economics, and history linked them to British Upper Canada, and to that other world with joys and sorrows all its own, the English-speaking commercial class of Montreal and Quebec City. In solving this problem, the years after 1837 proved crucial. For Durham's proposal to make French Canada and English Canada one state forced the French Canadians for the first time to face the issue squarely. And the quality of their response during that decade has marked the evolution of Canadian history ever since. . . .

By 1850 it would be clear that French Canada had succeeded in reforming its systems and institutions to meet the challenges of another century; that both French and English Canadians could live together within the bosom of a single state—and from this bicultural point of view, the protocol of 1867 was only a readjustment, not a new departure; and, finally, that it was the flexibility of British political institutions that could best reconcile Canada's autonomy and the imperial connection. In particular, the new beginnings and new dimensions of the decade made clear how truly interdependent these three—*la survivance*, the success of the Canadian experiment, and the British Constitution—had become.

LaFontaine's party won the struggle for responsible government. And the magnitude of their victory gave a lasting strength to most of the themes they contributed to *Canadien* nationalism. There is the theme that *la survivance* can be achieved only by the united effort of all *Canadiens*; the theme of the struggle to win the right to speak French; and the multitudinous variations on the theme of the language as the guardian of the faith.... But, above all, it was with the theme of the last cannon shot that LaFontaine placed himself and his followers directly in the mainstream of nineteenth-century French-Canadian nationalist thought.

This fundamental idea that just as British dominion depended on French Canada so the national aspirations of French Canada could not be adequately fulfilled unless linked with the British connection, that just as a non-American, non-republican state could not exist in northern North America without a self-governing French Canada, so without British North America there could be no *Canadiens*, this theory of mutual dependence, begun years before Parent's and LaFontaine's era of power, has continued long since in the thunder of oratory and the sweep of history....

LaFontaine accepted the Union, and by winning responsible government, guaranteed for the *Canadiens* their right to be themselves. He then went on, by defeating annexation, to guarantee the British connection. Of such stuff then did French Canadians fashion their nationalism. They insisted on their right to be themselves. Convinced that this right was best redeemed in a British North America, they remained firmly loyal. An unemotional loyalty, true; one founded not on sentiment, or quick-lived stirring passion. Indeed, this is its strength, that it is securely rooted in self-interest. If allowed to remain himself the French Canadian will be the last to defend what Etienne Parent described in 1840 when he approved the uniting of the two Canadian peoples, 'une grande nationalité Canadienne assez forte pour se protéger elle-même et vivre de sa propre vie.'

Jacques Monet, s.j., *The Last Cannon Shot: A Study of French Canadian Nationalism, 1837–1850* (Toronto: University of Toronto Press, 1969), pp. 5–6, 397–399.

VIEWS OF THE UNION'S LEGACY

A Formative Period for Canadian Duality—J.M.S. Careless' Interpretation

Many historians of the pre-Confederation years have presented the Union period as a formative one in the growth of Canadian cultural duality. In his standard history of the Union of the Canadas from 1841 to 1857, J.M.S. Careless, a professor of history at the University of Toronto, offered this synthesis of the widely accepted interpretation:

The persistence of duality: that indeed had been the most profound experience of the union. Assimilation and an unqualified single majority were unreal, as [Governor Charles] Bagot had first been compelled to recognize. Equally unreal was an absolute double majority, pointing to paralysis and the politics of 'race'—whereby minority racialism invited majority racialism, and a return to coercion and violence. There were English Canadians who would hold to the delusive simplicity of the one, recast as representation by population; there were French Canadians who would not abandon the superficial logic of the other. But the general attitude in both communities, expressed in conduct more than doctrine, was to accept an empirical duality in Canadian life. Nevertheless, this was restricted also by the plain necessity of majority rule, for, under free institutions, the only known mode of decision was still by counting votes. There might be two nations in society and culture, as [Francis] Hincks had said, but they formed one politically self-governing state.

Here, indeed, was the obvious lesson that seemed to emerge from the life of the Canadian union: that dualism had to be combined far more effectively with majority rule, thus demanding equal representation of distinct communities in the one house and representation on the basis of numbers in the other. The character of Canadian federation might owe much to American example, much to the experience of living in the British colonial system. But it owed a great deal as well to the old union of the Canadas.

That union, which by 1857 was well on its course to ultimate disunion and sectional deadlock, was succeeding even as it failed. It had tied the two Canadas inextricably together; inextricably, at least, in all the circumstances of that day. It would have to be changed, not abandoned; built on, not destroyed; and the wider horizons that were opening invited conceptions of a greater state. In the apparent pattern of disunion, the threads were already being woven for a design far more vast and enduring than this first union of the Canadas.

J.M.S. Careless, *The Union of the Canadas: The Growth of Canadian Institutions, 1841–1857* (Toronto: McClelland and Stewart, 1967), pp. 222–3. Footnotes omitted.

A Necessary and Fruitful Bicultural Partnership—W.L. Morton's View

The late W.L. Morton was another English Canadian historian to assess the legacy of the Union. Like Careless, he stressed the importance of the Union in shaping an "organic" British-French community in the Canadas. Here Morton examines the Union of the Canadas within the broader context of political developments in the Victorian age:

Amid so many, the chief trait of the age remained that of the External Ties. There were two, simply because the people of Victorian Canada were British and French; because two languages, English and French, were in use, both privately and publicly; and because each community had different concepts of society and of a society's expression and behaviour—of its civilization.

There was thus in Canada neither a traditional common heritage, as in England and France, nor a fusing ideology, as in the United States. And this duality of cultures was, in the Victorian era, to be underlined and exaggerated by the duality of the External Ties. One was the tie of British Canada with the Empire, and the other, the tie of Canada with the Papacy.

Both communities, of course, were exposed to the same environment: both had to struggle with a severe climate and an often gruelling terrain. Both, in consequence, were Canadian, having much in common in their response to a common country. It was this possession and experience of a common environment, rather than the historical accident of the Conquest, that made political union necessary.... It was also this that made their fruitful partnership in the great staple trades—and in politics—both necessary and possible.

How intensive the partnership had become any close study of the Union of the Canadas reveals. The decade of the forties, with its elaboration of responsible government, provided the means to place French beside British Canadians in the public service. Place had been made for the rising French middle class. The new political conventions allowed both communities to carry those measures of reconciliation and reform, the Rebellion Losses Act, the creation of the school and local government systems, the abolition of seigneurial tenure and the clergy reserves—the institutions and principles of government each community desired. It was their organic development of a British-French community that made Confederation possible as a means of expansion for a society equipped with complete resources of self-government. Confederation made no fundamental change in Canadian life; it merely opened the way to the wider growth of communities that had already realized themselves.

W.L. Morton, "Victorian Canada", in W.L. Morton, ed., *The Shield of Achilles: Aspects of Canada in the Victorian Age* (Toronto: McClelland and Stewart, 1968), pp. 312–14.

A Union of "Warring Scorpions" and Divergent Peoples—The Quebec Government's Official View, 1980

Heavily influenced by the writings of the neo-nationalist school of the Université de Montréal and by the ideology of separatism, René Lévesque and his government did much to popularize the historic struggle of the *Québécois* to fashion their own "nation". This excerpt from the White Paper released for the referendum of May, 1980, tells the story of the "warring scorpions" trapped in the bind of Union, yet seeking separate destinies.

...[Lord] Durham, in his famous report, recommended that the government be entrusted to a single Legislature that was decidedly English. The ideal solution would have been to federate all the British Colonies, but there was not enough time. Aiming at essentials, London decided to join together in a single legislature the Assemblies of Upper and Lower Canada, and in 1840 passed the Act of Union. Even though the population of Lower Canada was larger than that of Upper Canada, the two provinces had the same number of representatives in the Assembly; moreover, Lower Canada had to assume an equal share of the substantially higher debt of Upper Canada.

Since all the representatives from Upper Canada were Anglophones—as were some from Lower Canada—Governor Sydenham could, at last, count on an English majority. Thinking it had made the Francophones powerless, England granted to the Parliament of the Union responsible government and the control over taxes and spending that Upper Canada, and in particular Lower Canada, had demanded in vain. Because they were a minority, however, Francophones would be unable to reap the benefits of those measures.

The Act of Union abolished the use of French in the Legislature. However, the

Francophone representatives quickly discovered that British parliamentary procedures allowed them to bring the debate to a standstill and that the interaction of the parties required mutual concessions: since they did not have real political equality, they sought at least parliamentary equality. Accordingly, they succeeded in having the use of the French language reestablished in the Assembly in 1849; they stopped several attempts at assimilation; they were able to defend and promote their interests and, in particular, to hamper Anglophone territorial and commercial expansion....

In 1864, when debates on the projected federation began, the situation of the two peoples had changed considerably since 1763. Thanks to a strong immigration policy, Anglophones had added the supremacy of numbers to the political, economic and military supremacy they already enjoyed...

Francophones were also in a better position than before: thanks to 'the revenge of the cradle' they had increased their population considerably and extended their hold on the territory; they had developed good, solid institutions—social, educational and cultural—since the 1837 rebellion. They had developed not only a new elite, but also an original way of life and a culture of their own as manifested by the work of their craftsmen, artists and thinkers. And though their determination and skills had won them major gains in the political arena, albeit limited and precarious, in the economic field, big business and industry were more difficult of access than ever and they had control only in agriculture.

At the constitutional conferences in 1864 and 1866, the Quebec delegates and those from other provinces were pursuing very different goals. Upper Canada in particular wanted a supraprovincial parliament, endowed with as many important powers as possible, to preside over the destiny of the new country; Quebec on the other hand wanted its own responsible government, with a large degree of autonomy, that would guarantee once and for all the existence and progress of the Quebec people—a government that would be their real government. Opposition between a centralized federation and a decentralized federation was felt from the start.

> *Quebec-Canada, a New Deal. The Quebec Government Proposal for A New Partnership between Equals: Sovereignty-Association* (Quebec: Editeur officiel du Québec, 1979), pp. 6–7.

A Guide to Further Reading

1. Overviews

Careless, J.M.S., *The Union of the Canadas: The Growth of Canadian Institutions, 1841–1857.* Toronto: McClelland and Stewart, 1967.

Cornell, Paul G., *The Alignment of Political Groups in Canada, 1841–67.* Toronto: University of Toronto Press, 1962.

Hodgetts, J.E., *Pioneer Public Service: An Administrative History of the United Canadas.* Toronto: University of Toronto Press, 1955.

Lucas, C.P., ed., *Durham's Report on the Affairs of British North America.* Oxford: Clarendon Press, 1912.

Martin, Chester, *Empire and Commonwealth.* Oxford: Clarendon Press, 1929.

Monet, Jacques, "The Foundations of French Canadian Nationality", *Culture*, Vol. XXVI (December, 1965), pp. 456–66.

Morton, W.L., *The Critical Years: The Union of British North America, 1857–1873.* Toronto: McClelland and Stewart, 1964.

_____, ed., *The Shield of Achilles: Aspects of Canada in the Victorian Age*. Toronto: McClelland and Stewart, 1968.

Ryerson, Stanley B., *Unequal Union: Confederation and the Roots of Conflict in the Canadas, 1815-1873*. Toronto: Progress Books, 1968.

Wade, Mason, *The French Canadians, 1760-1967*. Toronto: Macmillan, 1968

2. Specialized Studies

Responsible Government in the 1840s

Bernard, Jean-Paul, *Les Rouges, Libéralisme, Nationalisme, Anticléricalisme, au milieu du XIXᵉ, Siècle*. Montreal: Les Presses de l'Université du Québec, 1971.

Brebner, J.B., "Patronage and Parliamentary Government", *Canadian Historical Association Report*, 1938.

Careless, J.M.S., ed., *The Pre-Confederation Premiers: Ontario Government Leaders, 1840-1867*. Toronto: University of Toronto Press, 1980.

Chapais, T., *Cours d'histoire du Canada*, Vols. 5 and 6. Quebec: Librairie Garneau, 1934.

Falardeau, Jean Charles, *Etienne Parent, 1802-1874*. Montreal: Les Editions de la Presse, 1974.

Leacock, Stephen, *Baldwin, LaFontaine, Hincks: Responsible Government*. Toronto: Morang & Co., 1907.

Metcalf, George, "Draper Conservatism and Responsible Government in the Canadas, 1836-1847", *Canadian Historical Review*, Vol. XLII (December, 1961).

Monet, Jacques, S.J., *The Last Cannon Shot: A Study of French Canadian Nationalism 1837-1850*. Toronto: University of Toronto Press, 1968.

Morison, J.L., *British Supremacy and Canadian Self-Government, 1837-54.* Toronto: Gundy, 1919.

Nish, Elizabeth, ed., *Racism or Responsible Government: The French Canadian Dilemma of the 1840s*. Toronto: Copp Clark, 1967.

Séguin, Maurice, *L'idée d'Indépendance au Québec: Genèse et historique*. Trois-Rivières: Les Editions Boréal Express, 1968.

Confederation and the Canadas

Bonenfant, Jean Charles, *The French Canadians and the Birth of Confederation*, Canadian Historical Association Booklet No. 21. Ottawa: CHA, 1966.

Careless, J.M.S., *Brown of the Globe: The Voice of Upper Canada*. Toronto: Macmillan, 1959.

Cook, Ramsay, ed., *Confederation. Canadian Historical Readings Series*. Toronto: University of Toronto Press, 1967.

Creighton, Donald G., *John A. Macdonald: The Young Politican*. Toronto: Macmillan, 1952.

_____, *The Road to Confederation*. Toronto: Macmillan, 1964.

Desilets, Andrée, *Hector-Louis Langevin: Un père de la Confédération canadienne*. Quebec: Laval University Press, 1969.

Sweeney, Alastair, *George-Etienne Cartier: A Biography.* Toronto: McClelland and Stewart, 1976.

Young, Brian, *George-Etienne Cartier: Montreal Bourgeois*. Kingston and Montreal: McGill-Queen's University Press, 1981.

10

CONFEDERATION
AND THE MARITIMES

Why Did Maritimers Respond
With Such Ambivalence to
the Idea of Federal Union?

On the eve of Confederation, Nova Scotia, New Brunswick and Prince Edward Island—the three Maritime provinces[1]—had relatively little in common with the two Canadas. For the Upper and Lower Canadians, beset by the sectional strife and political deadlock of their Union, change was essential, and that knowledge drove them on to seek new political solutions. But for Maritimers a scheme of federation with the Canadian provinces seemed unlikely. The society and economic life of the Maritimes were, by the late 1850s, strongly oriented towards the Atlantic and, despite residual historic ties to New England, towards Britain, the mother country. Colonies situated up the St. Lawrence River, in the interior of North America, did not figure prominently in the outlook of most Maritimers. To them, perched on the Atlantic and shaped by different historical experiences, the ports of Britain, the British West Indies and the eastern United States seemed much closer than the remote provinces of Canada East and Canada West. Union with these provinces appeared, at the outset, to offer few solutions to the region's pressing political and economic problems. And in the face of such opposition, it took a steady application of pressure by the British Colonial Office, as well

---

1. Newfoundland responded in its own unique way to the Confederation proposals of the 1860s. The island of Newfoundland had experienced a pattern of historical development quite distinct from that of Nova Scotia, New Brunswick and Prince Edward Island and resisted joining Confederation until 1949. Since the province is not properly a Maritime province, its response to the Confederation movement of the 1860s will not be considered here.

as the concerted efforts of local Confederationists, Canadian politicians and railway promoters to win over all three of the Maritime colonies to the Confederation scheme between 1864 and 1873.

Many attempts have been made to explain the seeming ambivalence of the Maritimes and their people to Confederation, but two distinct lines of interpretation are popular among historians. Traditionally, the mixed response of the Maritimers has been attributed to local conservatism and their abiding preference for the "steady ways" of their own colonies. From this perspective, a federal union of the British North American colonies was seen as a dubious "Canadian scheme", promoted by Canadian politicians seeking to resolve their own problems of political deadlock. Although federation offered some possible material advantages, most Maritimers felt it held few answers to their particular political problems. Not only did federal union fail to address Maritime concerns, it also raised the prospect of some vast and unsettling constitutional changes. Resisting the scheme, according to the traditional view, was a practical political response springing from the conviction that Confederation would not in fact solve any of the difficulties particular to the Maritimes.

Recently an alternative interpretation has begun to emerge. The Maritimes by the late 1850s, as recent social and economic studies have suggested, were a collection of colonies caught in a paradoxical situation. The three colonies shared a common "Atlantic outlook" and were reaching social and political maturity as colonies of Britain. But it has been argued that at this juncture their maritime economies, based on the Atlantic trade in timber, shipbuilding and fish, were being challenged as a result of the development of steam and steel technology and the advent of a new railway-building age. In this period of economic transition and changing relationships, Confederation appeared to represent yet another threat, this time to their "painfully won collective identities". Thus, it is concluded that most Maritimers reacted to the scheme with feelings of ambivalence, and many sought security by resisting federation with a strong defence of traditional Maritime ways.

Only by looking back at the history of Confederation in the Maritimes can we really weigh these two interpretations. For, while one can generalize about the Maritime response, each colony reacted in subtly different ways. And a close examination of the response in each province is necessary to gauge the overall response of Maritimers to federal union in the 1860s.

Although the idea of British North American union had first been put forward around 1790, it was not until the late 1850s that conditions and circumstances allowed a movement to take shape and gain momentum. A.T. Galt, a leading Canada East politician and railway financier, revived the idea of a general union with an 1858 resolution in the Canadian assembly. When, in August of 1858, Galt entered the John A. Macdonald-G.-E. Cartier ministry, it was on the condition that the Liberal-Conservative party accept his scheme for a union of the British North American colonies. After this development, federation became government policy and such a scheme became a distinct possibility. The next year the Upper Canadian Clear Grits (the forerunners of the Liberals) followed suit, adopting British North American union as a political objective at their great Liberal Reform Convention in Toronto.

Galt's initiative provoked an almost immediate response in the Maritimes. A proposal for a smaller union of the "Lower Provinces" surfaced shortly after the Galt resolution and was at least in part a reaction against the larger scheme. In spite of strong encouragement for the Maritime Union idea from the lieutenant-governors of Nova Scotia and New Brunswick, however, it was not until September of 1864 that a conference of Maritime politicians was held to discuss the matter. And then, after Canadian representatives, with the assistance of Governor-General Lord Monck, obtained an invitation to attend the conference and present their case for a broader union, the whole idea of Maritime Union was quietly dropped from the political agenda of the colonies.

With the sudden death of Maritime Union, the Maritime delegates joined fully in the movement for a larger union. At the 1864 Charlottetown Conference, John A. Macdonald, George-Etienne Cartier and Charles Tupper of Nova Scotia emerged as the leading advocates of the Confederation scheme. And before the conference was over, the assembled Maritime and Canadian delegates had endorsed the idea of a broader British North American union.

The Charlottetown Conference of September 1864 put the colonies on the road to Confederation. A number of the significant features of the eventual federation were in principle decided upon at Charlottetown: a federal system was proposed, dividing powers between central and provincial governments; regional representation was to be accommodated in the Upper House; and the Lower (elected) House was to be based on "representation by population". The details were worked out at a second conference at Quebec, only one month later, and formally embodied in the Seventy-Two Resolutions. Then the Canadian and Maritime politicians returned to their home provinces to campaign for the acceptance of the proposals by their respective colonial assemblies.

The scheme for Confederation enjoyed general support in only one of the colonies, Canada West. Elsewhere, responses ranged from ambivalence to violent opposition. Nova Scotia seemed, at best, cool to the scheme and only Tupper's efforts kept the issue alive. In New Brunswick sentiments toward the project were decidedly mixed. In Canada East it ran into stiff opposition from the anti-Confederate *Parti rouge* under Antoine-Aimé Dorion, and the motion to adopt Confederation was only carried after an acrimonious, divisive debate. The two island colonies, Prince Edward Island and Newfoundland, which looked eastward, not westward, rejected the proposals outright, joining Confederation only later. With such apparent opposition, particularly in the Maritimes, it is still something of a wonder that Confederation was ever achieved.

In exploring the response of the Maritimes to Confederation, a number of key questions should be kept in mind. Why did Maritimers, with the exception of the leading Confederationists, so strongly oppose the federation idea? Was it a reflection of their traditional preference for the "steady ways"? Or was the opposition, and later, the ambivalence, the product of anxieties brought about by changes affecting the economic underpinnings of the Maritime colonies? And, in the absence of widespread popular support, how were the Maritime colonies actually brought into Confederation?

SELECTED CONTEMPORARY SOURCES

THE MARITIMES AND THE ORIGINS OF CONFEDERATION

The Idea of Maritime Union—A Lieutenant-Governor's View, 1858

The passage of A.T. Galt's Resolution in the Canadian Assembly in 1858 provoked an almost immediate response in the eastern British North American colonies. It awakened interest in the idea of union and generated an alternate proposal calling for a smaller legislative union of the Maritime colonies only. From the beginning, the proposal for Maritime Union was strongly promoted by British colonial officials rather than by Maritime politicians. Here, in one of the first dispatches on the question in October 1858, Lieutenant-Governor John Manners-Sutton of New Brunswick (1854–61) set out some serious objections to Galt's "larger union" proposal and then made a strong case for Maritime Union.

There are... no such objections (at least in my opinion) to a Legislative union between the Lower Provinces, viz., New Brunswick, Nova Scotia, and Prince Edward's [sic] Island. On the contrary, I believe that such a union would confer incalculable benefits on all the three Provinces, and that it would form an additional security for the continuance of harmony between Her Majesty's Government and the Provincial Government, and of the existing connection with the mother-country.

The close contiguity of the three Provinces, the identity of their interests, and the existing facilities of the inter-communication between them, which will be materially increased when the railway from Halifax joins the railway from St. John to Shediac Point to such a union, and the fusion of the three Governments and Legislatures into one would not be regarded by the people of any one of the provinces in the light in which they would regard the transference of power now vested in their own Governments and Legislatures to a Government and Legislature stationed at Quebec or Montreal....

* * * * *

But the institution of the inquiry proposed by the Canadian Government would, even if that inquiry should embrace the Legislative as well as Federal union of some, as well as of all, the British North American provinces, certainly place new and most formidable difficulties in the way of attaining this object; and if this inquiry be now instituted, it will, I think, be difficult to prevent a Federative union of all the British North American provinces, not because the people of New Brunswick, or (so far as I am aware) of Nova Scotia and Prince Edward's Island, are in favour of such a scheme, but because Canada will exercise an overpowering influence in the decision of the question.

Lieutenant-Governor John Manners-Sutton to Sir Edward Bulwer-Lytton, October 2, 1858, private and confidential. Public Records Office 30/6/69.

The Ambitions of Colonial Politicians—Two Conflicting Viewpoints, 1860 and 1864

The lure of larger political opportunities apparently influenced some of the more ambitious Maritime politicians who supported Confederation. In a speech in Halifax in 1860, Charles Tupper, the Conservative Premier of Nova Scotia, commented on the opportunities a small colony like Nova Scotia provided for ambitious men. On the other hand, critics of the Confederation scheme, like the editor of the *Halifax Citizen*, saw a somewhat different motivation.

> One of the greatest evils that can ever befall a country is that men of character, ability and position, should withdraw from her public concerns.... The highest offices we have to offer and the largest salaries we have to give afford no adequate temptation, no significant remuneration.... In the absence of larger questions of statesmanship... we see men of ability desecrating their talent by fomenting sectional or sectarian discord and placing one section or one religious class in deadly antagonism with another.
>
> Sir Charles Tupper, *Recollections of Sixty Years in Canada* (Toronto: Cassell, 1914), pp. 17 ff.

> [Those who support Confederation are] a few ambitious individuals, who feel our legislature too small for their for their capacity, and its rewards too trifling for their acceptance; who feel anxious to strut in embroidered court suits... before a Viceroy at Ottawa, and enjoy fat salaries far away from the provinces whose best interests are to be shamefully voted away in return for a fortnight's feasting and a few private promises.
>
> *Halifax Citizen*, November 24, 1864.

An Invitation to "Colonial Union"—John A. Macdonald's Halifax Appeal, 1864

The three Maritime Provinces were formally invited to join in a scheme of colonial union at the Charlottetown Conference, held in September 1864. Although the negotiations were conducted in secret, the Canadian delegates did publicly air their views at a banquet held on September 12th in a Halifax hotel. On this occasion, John A. Macdonald stated his reasons for urgently advocating the union of the provinces of British North America.

> The question of 'Colonial Union'... absorbs every idea as far as I am concerned. For twenty long years I have been dragging myself through the dreary waste of Colonial politics. I thought there was no end, nothing worthy of ambition; but now I see something which is well worthy of all I have suffered in the cause of my little country.... There may be obstructions, local difficulties may arise, disputes may occur, local jealousies may intervene, but it matters not, the wheel is now revolving and we are only the fly on the wheel... we cannot delay it—the union of the colonies of British America, under one sovereign, is a fixed fact....
>
> The dangers that have risen from this system we will avoid if we can agree upon forming a strong central government—a great central legislature—a constitution for a union which will have all the rights of sovereignty except those that are given to the local governments. Then we shall have taken a great step in advance of the American

Republic. If we can only obtain that object—a vigorous general government—we shall not be New Brunswickers, nor Nova Scotians, nor Canadians, but British Americans, under the sway of the British Sovereign.... In the conference we have had [the Charlottetown Conference] we have been united as one man—there was no difference of feeling, no sectional prejudices or selfishness exhibited by any one;—we all approached the subject feeling its importance; feeling that in our hands were the destinies of a nation....

In the case of a union, this railway must be a national work, and Canada will cheerfully contribute to the utmost extent in order to make that important link, without which no political connection can be complete. What will be the consequence to this city [Halifax], prosperous as it is, from that communication? Montreal is at this moment competing with New York for the trade of the great West. Build the road and Halifax will soon become one of the great emporiums of the world. All the great resources of the West will come over the immense railways of Canada to the bosom of your harbour. But there are even greater advantages for us all in view. We will become a great nation; and God forbid that it should be one separate from the United Kingdom of Great Britain and Ireland....

Edward Whelan, ed., *The Union of the British Provinces*. Originally published 1865 (Toronto: 1927), pp. 45, 47 and 48–50.

NOVA SCOTIA AND CONFEDERATION

The Confederation scheme ran into stubborn resistance from leading elements of Nova Scotian society and particularly from those conservative Nova Scotians whose way of life and values were grounded in the traditional Atlantic mercantile economy. Charles Tupper, elected premier of Nova Scotia in May 1864, seemed to threaten their favoured position. He had come to power at the head of a pro-Confederation party committed to, among other things, a "new industrial ideology".

The Nova Scotia Anti-Confederation League was slow to get organized. But the defeat of Samuel L. Tilley's pro-Confederation government in New Brunswick in March 1865 seemed to galvanize Nova Scotia's anti-Confederation forces into action. As spokesperson for the "Old Order" in Nova Scotia, Joseph Howe, who had guided the colony to responsible government in the late 1840s, now rallied his province's anti-Confederation forces in the mid-1860s.

The Anti-Confederation Case—Joseph Howe's Critique of the Scheme, 1866

Joseph Howe whipped up much anti-Confederation sentiment by playing upon popular distrust of the "Canadians". In presenting his criticism of the scheme during 1865 and 1866, he referred to the Province of Canada spitefully as "a nation with a helot race in its midst" and raised fears about the dire Canadian threat to Nova Scotian autonomy. His 1866 speech is a classic critique of the Confederation scheme.

Let us see what the Canadians desire to do. They are not, as we have shown, a very harmonious or homogeneous community. Two-fifths of the population are French and three-fifths English. They are therefore perplexed with an internal antagonism which... must ever be a source of weakness. They are shut in by frost from the outer world for five months of the year. They are at the mercy of a powerful neighbour whose population already outnumbers them by more than eight to one... on the opposite side of a naturally defenceless frontier. Surely such conditions as these ought to repress inordinate ambition or lust of territory on the part of the public men of Canada. The wisdom of Solomon and the energy and strategy of Frederick the Great would seem to be required to preserve and strengthen such a people, if formed, as it appears they desire to form themselves, into 'a new nationality'... but it is evident that a more unpromising nucleus of a new nation can hardly be found on the face of the earth, and that any organized communities, having a reasonable chance to do anything better, would be politically insane to give up their distinct formations and subject themselves to the domination of Canada.

... When franchises were conferred upon the people of the Maritime Provinces, and legislatures given to them, these could only be yielded up by voluntary consent, or be forfeited by misconduct. When self-government was conceded, it could never afterwards be withdrawn, unless upon ample proof, elicited by legal forms or deliberate parliamentary inquiry, that it has been grossly abused. Even the colonial legislators themselves, entrusted for a definite time with limited powers and sacred trusts, could not strip the people of their rights without their own consent, or transfer to others the power of legislation....

... Until the people of Nova Scotia, Prince Edward Island and Newfoundland Forfeit, by corruption or abuse, the privileges conferred, or voluntarily relinquish them, they cannot be reclaimed by the Crown or swept away by Parliament without a breach of faith; nor can they be transferred by the local legislatures....

Unfortunately these plain principles of legal construction and constitutional law have, in dealing with the Maritime Provinces, been strangely overlooked. When all the parties to the Quebec scheme of confederation found that they had made an egregious blunder, they should have abandoned the project and left the Province in peace; and above all, the Government of England should have withdrawn from a controversy into which, for no imperial objects, as has been clearly proved, they had been artfully drawn....

J.A. Chisholm, *The Speeches and Public Letters of Joseph Howe* (Halifax: 1909) Vol. II.

In Defence of Colonial Union—A Refutation of Howe's Claims, 1866

Not all Nova Scotians concurred with Howe's analysis of the Confederation scheme. Charles Tupper, who had headed the Nova Scotia delegation at the Confederation conferences, vigorously responded to Howe's arguments. In a published letter in 1866, he took deliberate aim at *Confederation Considered*, a Howe brochure outlining the case against union.

Mr. Howe has ventured to affirm throughout his *brochure*, [*Confederation Considered*] that this policy of a Union between Canada and the Maritime Provinces is an ambitious and unscrupulous attempt at 'spoliation' and 'appropriation' on the part of

Canada. What must be thought of his temerity in making such a statement, when viewed in the light of the fact, that when Mr. Howe was Leader of the Government of Nova Scotia, in 1861, he moved the resolution ... declaring 'that many advantages may arise' from such a Union, and wrote an official letter to the Government of Canada based upon that resolution, which had been unanimously carried in the Assembly of Nova Scotia, asking Canada to entertain his overtures for Union, and proceeded to Quebec, in 1862, a Delegate to press his suit?

Now, when the policy of Union, for which for many years he professed such devotion, is likely, in other hands, to be more successful, he denounces it as an attempted 'spoliation'.... For twenty years he has been advocating the construction of an Intercolonial Railway and the Union of the Provinces, as the best means of advancing their interest, promoting their prosperity, and the only means of securing, in any part of British America, the permanence of British institutions....

Mr. Howe not only treats the proposed Confederation as an attempt at 'spoliation' on the part of Canada, but says the ambition of her public men overleaps that of 'Bismarck or Louis Napoleon.' Does he not perceive that if it be true, as he asserts, that Canada is shut out from the sea during the winter months, and can never become a really great country, and that the equally balanced state of the Legislature between Upper and Lower Canada made a change in her Constitution indispensable, it was not strange that she should seek, in a Confederation, the means of obtaining access by railway to the ocean, and of removing that embarrassing provision of her present Constitution by which the two great sections of the country were equally represented in the Legislature irrespective of their growth or population? The reflection that Mr. Howe had himself endeavoured to induce Canada to unite with the Maritime Provinces, for the obvious reason that it would make the latter the 'ocean frontage' for a great country lying behind them, teeming with wealth and industry, ought for ever to prevent him from charging Canada with attempted 'spoliation'. That neither Canada nor the Maritime Provinces can ever attain any real greatness, except in such a combination as is now proposed, cannot but be seen by anybody in the least acquainted with the position they occupy relatively to each other....

When Mr. Howe wishes to prove that Canada, Nova Scotia, and New Brunswick, dependent upon each other for the advancement of all, and drawn together by a common interest and a common danger, had better remain isolated, he presents the United States as riven by internal discord and breaking up into a half-dozen different and antagonistic Governments....

[W]here, I would ask, can he expect to find another Nova Scotian who would be content with a position of isolation so utterly fatal to that progress and importance to which, with her great natural resources and position, as the Atlantic frontage of British America, she may now look confidently forward?

Charles Tupper, Letter to the Editor, 1866, concerning Joseph Howe's *Confederation Considered*, reprinted in G.A. Rawlyk, R.P. Bowles and B.W. Hodgins, eds., *Regionalism in Canada: Flexible Federalism or Fractured Nation?* (Scarborough: Prentice-Hall, 1979), pp.205–7.

In or Out?—A Nova Scotia Call for Repeal, 1867

Even after Confederation in 1867, anti-Confederation sentiment remained alive in Nova Scotia. The union scheme was a major issue in the Dominion's first general election—and Joseph Howe's anti-Confederates captured 18 of the province's 19 seats. In the Nova Scotia provincial election held in the autumn of 1867, Howe and his Liberal party swept 36 out of 38 seats in the assembly. Once elected, Howe sought to fulfil the mandate given to his party by bringing about the secession of the province. When the British government refused to grant repeal, Howe launched a campaign to secure "better terms" within Confederation for Nova Scotia. The repeal movement itself withered soon after Howe was "co-opted" into Macdonald's government in January 1869.

At the time of Confederation, much of the Nova Scotia opposition was focused on Charles Tupper and his government. Howe's anti-Confederates capitalized on the fact that Tupper had secured approval "in principle" from the Assembly, then arranged the terms of union without calling an election. Perhaps this editorial, published shortly after Tupper's disastrous defeat in September 1867, best captures the mood of the disaffected province.

> After weary months of waiting the people's turn came. They were required to render a verdict upon the actions of their rulers. Have they not brought in a verdict of 'GUILTY, without extenuating circumstances?' The people have spoken upon the question of Confederation, and what have they said? They have said with a unanimity never before known in the history of a free people that they are opposed to the measure of Confederation and to the manner in which it has been brought about. They have declared that they desire no political connection with Canada, that they wish to manage their own affairs, that they desire to remain loyal subjects of their gracious Queen. And they have declared that the legislature of the Province had no right nor power to take away the constitution of the country, without the sanction of the popular voice. . . . In a word we desire to have Responsible Government with all the blessings and privileges restored to us. Those privileges, while we did enjoy them, we never abused, and we cannot consent that they should be ruthlessly taken from us without just cause. We want to be restored to our former status as an independent Province of the British Empire.—- In order to accomplish this, the Act of Union, so far as Nova Scotia is concerned, must be repealed. This is all we ask, and we will be satisfied with nothing less.
>
> *New Glasgow Chronicle*, September 25, 1867.

NEW BRUNSWICK AND CONFEDERATION

As in the case of Nova Scotia, the debate over Confederation in New Brunswick reflected a deeper division within the colony's political and mercantile elite. The government of Samuel Tilley based its support for the Confederation scheme on the promise of an intercolonial railway and the prospect of material progress. Tilley and the pro-Confederates met strong resistance from a group of Saint John merchants who favoured a "Western Extension" railway from Saint John to Portland, Maine, where it would link with a variety of American railways. Among the more conservative elements of the province the Confederation scheme was viewed as an "Upper Canadian" proposal which might result in higher taxes and few benefits for New Brunswick. Indeed, many New Brunswickers saw little reason to sacrifice their prized political autonomy to the mistrusted Canadians.

The Anti-Confederation View—A New Brunswick Appeal to Colonial Loyalty, 1865

W.H. Needham, a leader of the New Brunswick anti-Confederates, saw little to be gained, and much to be lost, by joining Confederation. In this frequently quoted speech delivered in the New Brunswick legislature on April 3, 1866, he appealed to the people's sense of colonial loyalty.

> ... I know there are men whose souls soar away beyond us, who are satiated with all that little New Brunswick can give them, and they reach forward to the celebrated towers and palaces of the far-off Ottawa; for this they would let New Brunswick go to the winds and be lost for ever. Bring us near to the darling of our souls, the far away Ottawa, with its miles of cornice and its acres of plaster and let us revel there in vice-regal glory. But there are loyal sons of New Brunswick who will not be carried away by all this splendor, and when the time comes, it will be seen that this splendor has been like a dissolving view to their eyes, become 'the baseless fabric of a vision which leaves not a wreck behind.'...
>
> * * * * *
>
> When I forget my country so far as to sell it for Confederation, may my right hand forget its cunning, and if I do not prefer New Brunswick, as she is, to Canada with all her glory, then let my tongue cleave to the roof of my mouth. When the day comes when we shall have... Confederation deposited in the grave, those that will be there will not be there as mourners, but as glorifiers, and they will sing, with hearts elate with patriotic joy:
>
> Then safely moored, our perils o'er
We'll sing the songs of Jubilee,
For ever and for ever more,
New Brunswick, Land of Liberty.

New Brunswick, *Debates of the House of Assembly for 1866*, p. 89.

The Unionist Appeal of Defence and Loyalty—A Fenian Circular, 1865

Defence and loyalty were immediate considerations that weighed heavily in New Brunswick's ultimate decision to join Confederation. The main threat came from the American branch of the Fenian Brotherhood, a radical organization founded in 1858 for the purpose of liberating Ireland from British rule. By the mid-1860s a militant faction had decided that Ireland's liberation could be more quickly and easily won by attacking British North America. While a serious invasion was unlikely, Fenian groups—consisting often of demobilized Irish-born Civil War troops—did gather at various scattered points along the border to engage in boundary raids. The most serious Fenian attack came in June 1866 in Upper Canada, but the most influential threat, from the point of view of the Confederation movement, was posed by a Fenian convention held at Portland, Maine, in April 1865, shortly after the election of New Brunswick's short-lived anti-Confederate government.

Fenian circulars, like this one found posted in Saint John, New Brunswick, in 1865, were regularly used by Unionists in their campaigns.

CITIZENS OF NEW BRUNSWICK

Republican institutions have become necessary to the peace and prosperity of your Province. English policy, represented by the obnoxious project of Confederation, is making its last effort to bind you to the effete forms of Monarchism. Annexation to the United States is not necessarily the only means of escape. Independence for the present is the best one and will assure you the supreme and sole management of your affairs. Mercenary bayonets cannot—shall not—prevent your asserting your independence if you desire it. Signify your wishes and you will become the founders of a Free State, untrammeled by Royalty, unchecked by Misrule and certain to secure all the lost benefits of Reciprocity.

A Fenian Circular in Saint John, New Brunswick, 1865, cited in H.A. Davis, "The Fenian Raid on New Brunswick", *Canadian Historical Review* (December, 1955), p. 322.

An Early Expression of Disillusionment—The New Brunswick Reporter, 1868

New Brunswick eventually did join in the Confederation project. The anti-Confederate government of 1865, headed by A.J. Smith, quickly collapsed because of a combination of forces. An initial financial crisis, delays in proceeding with the promised Western Extension railway, the failure to work out a free trade agreement with the United States, and growing interference from Lieutenant-Governor Arthur Gordon and the pro-union British Colonial office had all conspired to put the Smith government on the defensive. Finally, in April 1866, it caved in under pressure from Gordon, and an election was called. In the ensuing campaign, Samuel Tilley and the Confederates were returned to power because of fears generated by the Fenian raids along the New Brunswick-Maine border.

As one of the four original provinces in the union of 1867, New Brunswick was the keystone in the Confederation arch. Yet much of the initial enthusiasm for Confederation seemed to dissipate during the first session of the Canadian Parliament. Even pro-Confederation supporters in New Brunswick grew disheartened with events unfolding in Ottawa. An editorial in the *New Brunswick Reporter*, a pro-Confederate weekly paper, seemed to express this growing sense of disillusionment.

With very little of the ostentation which marked the occasion of its opening, the first session of the first Parliament of the Dominion came to a close last Friday. Most of the members had left for their homes, when the principal matters had been determined, some before, thus rendering the closing scene tame enough. In looking back at this session as the test of Confederation, we wish it were in our power to say that it has been satisfactory, and that the future looks bright and encouraging. But we cannot. Whether too much was promised, or too much expected, certain it is the facts fall far short of the expectations, and the very best friends of Confederation shake their heads ominously. For this state of affairs the men, and not the measure, are responsible; the omissions and commissions of Parliament are not the sins of Confederation. The cause for which we struggled in this Province necess-tated [sic] no tax upon the necessari[e]s of life, no bill stamps, no newspaper postage, and although these may not be of vital importance in themselves, the very fact that our representatives stood up against their adoption and were powerless to prevent it, is in itself, sufficient to damp the ardor of Unionists in New Brunswick. We were told at the outset that Canada's necessity was our opportunity; but the worst of it is, Canada has too many necessities, while New Brunswick has the delightful opportunity of paying her proportions. This would be cheerfully done were the measures of the day in harmony with the interests of New Brunswick, and were our representation regarded instead of being ignored. We expected that Confederation would induce a line of national instead of sectional policy; that it would give a general impetus to trade, emigration and commerce; that men like Cartier would see something more noble in the Union of the British Provinces, than a mere opportunity to advance the interests of their respective localities. But we have been disappointed; not in the cause which, being right, is sure to succeed eventually, but rather in the petty, selfish policy of some of the men who have given caste to the first operation of Confederation.

New Brunswick Reporter, May 29, 1868.

PRINCE EDWARD ISLAND AND CONFEDERATION

While the Confederation issue provoked widespread debate in the two mainland Maritime provinces, Prince Edward Island was almost unanimous in its rejection of the union. The prospect of being a small province in a large country seemed to generate a sense of peril among Island politicians and within the community. At the Charlottetown Conference of 1864, some Island delegates had been attracted to the Confederation principle, but later at the Quebec Conference support for union dissolved when the delegates resisted several possible infringements on their colonial autonomy.

The Charlottetown Conference, September 1864

The Problem of Absentee Landlords—An Underlying Island Issue, 1866

Much of the fertile farmland of Prince Edward Island, which had been granted to a group of "proprietors" after the Seven Years' War, was still in the hands of absentee British landlords in the 1860s, and many Island farmers were tenants who paid rents to these. A commission appointed in 1860 to investigate the situation had recommended an imperial loan to assist farmers in the purchase of their lands, but the British government refused and no further progress had been made on the matter.

By 1864 and 1865, while Confederation was being debated, Island farmers had formed a "Tenant Union" and were beginning to organize protests. Supporters of Confederation, moved by strongly worded tenant resolutions, like those which follow, promised that, under the plan of union, monies would be made available to buy out the absentee landlords.

Resolved, That we, the tenantry of... individually and collectively, virtually and solemnly pledge our honour... to withhold... rent... to resist... coercion, ejection, seizure and sale for rent.

Resolved, That it is our duty to unite as tenants for mutual protection and sympathy in order to put an end to the leasehold system.

Resolved, That every member provide himself with a bugle to sound the note alarm on the approach of the rent-leeches.

Prince Edward Island *House of Assembly Journals*, 1866. (Charlottetown: 1866), Appendix G.

Union Rejected—A Resolution from Prince Edward Island, 1866

Promises to aid Islanders in buying out the landlords did little to alter the colony's resistance to federal union. Prince Edward Island's strong opposition to Confederation found firm expression in a formal resolution, introduced into the Island House of Assembly on May 7, 1866.

Resolved, As the deliberate opinion of this House, that any Union of the British North American Colonies which would embrace P.E. Island, upon the terms and principles set forth in the Resolutions of the Conference of Quebec, held on the 10th October 1864, would not only be to unjust to the inhabitants of this Colony but prove disastrous to their dearest and most cherished rights and interests as a free people enjoying the blessings of a priceless constitution guaranteed to them by the Imperial Government of Great Britain.

That considering the isolated, peculiar and exceptional position of Prince Edward Island, as contrasted with the other British North American Provinces and Colonies, this House deems it to be its duty... to reaffirm the decision so early and unequivocally declared by this House in the Resolutions passed by it, in its last session, upon the subject of a Union of the British North American Colonies....

Resolved further, that even if a Union of the Continental Provinces of British North America should have the effect of strengthening and binding more closely together these Provinces, or advancing their material and commercial interests, this House cannot admit that a Federal Union of the North American Colonies that would include Prince Edward Island, could ever be accomplished upon terms that would prove advantageous to the interests and well-being of this Island, cut off and separated as it is, and must ever remain, from the neighbouring Provinces by an immovable barrier of ice for many months in the year; and this House deems it to be its sacred and imperative duty to declare, as it now does, that any Federal Union of the North American Colonies that would include Prince Edward Island would be as hostile to the feelings and wishes, as it would be opposed to the best and most vital interests, of its people.

The Charlottetown Examiner, May 14, 1866 Vol. XVI, no. 27, p. 2.

In Defence of Island Rights and Liberties—Cornelius Howatt's Case for Rejection, 1866

Conscious of their unique Island identity and defensive about their autonomy, Islanders rejected the union scheme as they had rejected annexation threats in the past. Cornelius Howatt, an ardent anti-Confederate, seemed to capture the prevailing mood in this impassioned speech in support of the P.E.I. resolution, delivered on May 7, 1866 in the House of Assembly. Howatt was not merely speaking for himself. He was expressing the deeply-felt views of the Island majority—a majority which felt threatened by political forces beyond its control. It was not until 1873 that the Island, facing a hefty railway debt, economic uncertainties, and steady British pressure, reluctantly joined the Confederation.

... I believe the day has come when we must make a stand for the preservation of our independence; for when we see a pressure brought to bear upon the other Colonies, we may be sure that our turn is coming. If the other Colonies go into Confederation, no doubt a pressure will be brought to bear upon us also, and then does it not remain for us to make a united effort to resist any attempt to take away our constitution, our revenue, and, I might almost say, everything else belonging to us? I was opposed to Confederation last year, for I saw there was danger even in admitting the principle of it, and I am just as much, or more opposed to it now. Suppose, for argument['s] sake, we should even go into Confederation with terms with which we would be satisfied, would we be safe then? I should say no. Does not the British Government recognize the right to change the constitution? Now, if this is the case, though I do not profess to have any great knowledge in constitutional matters, I believe that, even if we should go into it with the most favourable terms, the Federal Government would have power to change the constitution, and therefore we would not be secure....

.... And, considering that we would be such a small portion of the Confederacy, our voice would not be heard in it. We would be the next thing to nothing. Indeed I would almost as soon be without any voice in it at all. We would be as small a minority as the hon. member on my right (Mr. Laird) and myself are in this House. Are we then going to surrender our rights and liberties? It is just a question of 'self or no self'. Talk about a local Legislature! It would be a mere farce. We would not even have the control of our local affairs, for every trifling or petty bill would have to be sent to Ottawa for the approval of the Federal Government. This House would be dwindled down to a level with the small municipal bodies throughout Canada, for the management of local affairs. Again, I say that, for the good of the country, I will waive any objections I have to the Resolutions of his Honor the Leader of the Government, and will give them my hearty support; believing, as I do, that we require a united effort to resist any invasion of our rights and liberties.

The Charlottetown Examiner, August 27, 1866, Vol. XVI, no. 42, p.1.

CONFLICTING INTERPRETATIONS

The Maritime response to Confederation has long interested historians despite the fact that so much Canadian history is written from a Central Canadian or a Western perspective which tends to ignore Maritime history. Various points of view have been put forward by a variety of historians. Usually those scholars from within the region have viewed the anti-Confederation movement in a sympathetic way while outsiders—especially central Canadians—have found it difficult to understand why Maritimers were so opposed to Canadian "progress". The debate concerning the advantages and disadvantages of Confederation is still active in the three Maritime Provinces—especially in Prince Edward Island. The historians, however, have replaced the politicians as the major participants.

Far too much of the history of the Maritimes in Confederation has been written from the viewpoint of colonial politicians, newspaper editors, and other so-called leaders of society. Many Maritime historians of the recent generation are turning to social and economic history, and just beginning to explore the experiences of ordinary people—the farmers and the fishermen, craftsmen and labourers, townsfolk and settlers—in the decades before and after Confederation. When this "new social history" is written, a dramatically different picture of the Maritimes and Confederation may, in fact, appear.

HISTORICAL OVERVIEWS

The Maritime Reaction to Confederation—A Standard Interpretation

Perhaps the first scholarly treatment of the Maritime reaction to Confederation was found in W.M. Whitelaw's volume, *The Maritimes and Canada Before Confederation*, originally published in 1934. Though not a Maritimer, Whitelaw had a great sympathy for the Maritime point of view and spent much time teaching and doing various types of research in the region.

Although the maritime provinces were accustomed to compare their external security and internal harmony with that of Canada, to the great disadvantage of the latter, they looked wistfully and with no slight jealousy at Canada's spectacular economic development. With some disregard of the complexity of the factors involved, they commonly regarded the Canadian development as the result of the union of 1841. While attacking with his most vitriolic pen the chronic political turmoil in Canada, Joseph Howe was accustomed to laud the economic advantage of the Canadian union as the foundation of the material prosperity of that province. The moral was easily drawn. Might not a complete legislative union of the maritime provinces also lead to enhanced credit in the world's money markets, to increased immigration, as well as to the development of industry and commerce? A union comparable to that of Canada would be not only economical but would create a country of which its people might well feel proud, a union on whose ampler stage local politicians could play a larger rôle. . . .

[T]he close connection between maritime union and British North American federation was no mere accidental coincidence of 1864. Throughout its whole history maritime union had grown in the most intimate and complex relationships with the larger movement. Sometimes regarded as an important or essential preliminary to the larger union, frequently as a necessary antidote to it, maritime union was seldom urged, or even thought of, except in some relation to Canadian expansion eastward....

In area and population alike the maritime provinces were small in comparison with either section of Canada. To the outside world they were liable to be thought of as virtually a part of Canada. More and more they were being swept into the Canadian vortex. Many noted with anticipation these signs of the emergence of a larger whole in which the provinces by the sea would play their small but important role. Others as definitely fought against the expansiveness of Canadian life. But whether the people of the maritime provinces looked westward with apprehension or with hope, they were becoming increasingly aware of Canadian centrality in British North America.

It was not primarily, however, on the advantages of location and resources that the maritimes had built their hopes. To them a country's greatness lay in the character of its people. It may have been inevitable—it was certainly unfortunate—that the maritimes should have based their estimate of themselves so largely on comparisons with their sister colonists, the Canadians. Invidious distinctions proved all too easy.

Not only was the rebellious character of the Canadians contrasted with the loyalty of maritime sentiment, this Canadian characteristic was commonly held to be the result of poorer stock.

When all due allowance is made for the truth in this comparison made by the people of the maritimes between themselves and Canadians—and it was largely true in fact—one cannot but feel, after much reading in the debates, editorials and correspondence of the period, that the comparison contained an unusual amount of bitterness. It is difficult to avoid the conclusion that much of it was mere pique at the extraordinary, almost spectacular, development of Canada both in wealth and population during this period. Coupled with this was the almost complete lack of contact between Canadians and the people of the maritimes. Much of the suspicion, to use no stronger word, of the latter toward Canadians was doubtless due to the fact that so few of them had ever seen one.

William Menzies Whitelaw, *The Maritimes and Canada Before Confederation* (Toronto: Oxford University Press, 1934), pp. 3–7, 24–26, 52–53, 158, 274.

The Role of External Pressures—An Often-Neglected Interpretation

Another general overview of the historical problem was presented in Donald F. Warner's *The Idea of Continental Union* (1960). Warner maintained that the initial resistance of many Maritimers to federal union was gradually overcome by a combination of American—and British—external pressures. Warner argued that fear of American military force, of annexation and of an economic depression following the end of reciprocity (1865), along with British imperial influences, eventually worked to win over many reluctant Maritimers.

Hostility in the Maritimes... doomed the drive for a speedy completion of confederation. Their people had initiated the movement for union and expected that leadership would be the reward of authorship. Instead, it was painfully apparent that Canada would assume the dominant position in the federation and the Maritimes would be a minority with particular interests which might be subverted by the majority. A psychological factor complicated the situation: particularism was a salient characteristic of political thinking in Nova Scotia, New Brunswick, and Prince Edward Island.

The people of these colonies lived in their own world, geographically separated from the St. Lawrence Valley and with little desire to be politically coupled to it; they lived by and from the sea and tended to look out upon it and not toward the heart of the continent. Moreover, confederation would strike them in the pocketbook. The Maritimes had been wedded to free trade, for they depended upon lumbering and fishing for their livelihood and had to import much of what they consumed. Canada, on the other hand, dreamed of industrialization and would surely girdle the new union with its tariff wall. . . .

The eight years from 1860 to 1867 constitute a significant era in Canadian history because the Dominion of Canada came into being then. The threat of annexation was an important immediate cause of this development. Though the colonial agitation to join the United States was weak, loyalists feared that the impending depression and American hostility would harry the colonies into joining the United States.

This fear of American aggression was groundless. The Civil War period illustrates the general American indifference to the acquisition of Canada and the peaceful intent of most of the annexationists in the United States. . . .

The history of the period also reiterates the connection between Canadian-American trade and the annexation question. The colonial movement for annexation produced reciprocity, and the death of reciprocity revived annexation. A large number of Canadians were becoming convinced that their real prosperity demanded permanent free trade with the United States, whatever the political basis.

As in 1849, the mother country reacted to the impact of annexationism. Some British might be indifferent to the fate of the colonies, but those who formulated foreign and colonial policy were determined to prevent their accession to the United States. The Republic was a brawny young giant, a dangerous rival whose strength must be circumscribed. Confederation would, so the authorities in London fondly hoped, prevent annexation and keep the power of the United States in leash. The union was consummated more to keep the colonies out of the Republic than to keep them in the Empire, for British statesmen believed that the new Dominion would soon become independent. Federation would better enable the provinces to stand on their own feet and would bolster their resistance to the pull from the south.

Donald F. Warner, *The Ideal of Continental Union* (Lexington: University of Kentucky Press, 1960), pp. 51–55, 57–58.

NEW BRUNSWICK AND CONFEDERATION

Anti-Confederation Sentiment in New Brunswick—The Bases of Resistance to Union

New Brunswick's response to Confederation has been approached from two different perspectives. Professor Alfred G. Bailey, a Maritime historian, in the early 1940s offered an overview of the source of New Brunswick opposition and also suggested the reasons for the collapse of the anti-Confederation movement. His interpretation tied together the complex of forces impinging upon the politics of New Brunswick in the critical years from 1864 to 1867.

It is evident that in the early stages of the union movement there was a misapprehension of its significance, together with some degree of apathy, rather than a reasoned opposition. There was an inclination to regard Confederation 'as intended to produce, by its agitation, some immediate effect on the condition of existing political parties rather than as designed to inaugurate a new constitutional system.' But apathy and a 'willing ignorance' of the whole matter gave way to an increasing hostility throughout the autumn of 1864 on the part of influential sections of the press.... Politicians, editors, farmers, manufacturers, and financiers, wrestled with the crucial problem of hard cash. What was Confederation to cost? Would it increase taxes? Would it stimulate business? Would it facilitate trade, ensure the safety of New Brunswick and the Empire generally? How were the signs of the times to be read and interpreted?

... In the railways to the North-West the Maritime Provinces could have no present or future interest, but they would bring upon present or future generations large burdens of taxation. It seemed clear... that New Brunswick, with its small representation in the proposed federal Assembly, could not hope to block a large expenditure on public works from which the unionists conceived she would derive no benefit.

If the development of the West were the price the Maritime Provinces would have to pay for securing the Intercolonial Railway, provided this railway were held out as a bait on the hook of Confederation, what constitutional guarantee was there that the railway would be built forthwith?...

... There is no doubt that the measure of uncertainty with regard to the railway contributed to the defeat of the unionists in March, 1865.

While the different sections fought over the railway route, speculation ran rife concerning the possible effects of Confederation upon the industrial structure of the province. The cleavage of opinion seems not to have followed either occupational or class lines. The manufacturing interests were divided, some strongly favouring union. Having viewed it 'in all its bearings', they felt satisfied that it would prove beneficial not only to domestic manufacturers, but to every other interest throughout the province.

Equally decisive was the action of the Catholic section of the population. Fear of the Protestant influence of Canada West and especially of Grand Trunk control of the Intercolonial railway were salient motives. Control of the project railway, if it were secured by the Grand Trunk, would give that company a guiding hand in land settlement adjacent to the railway line. The Bishop of Saint John had for years taken a great interest in the settlement of his co-religionists on the wilderness land of New Brunswick. But by far the strongest single element opposed to union with Canada was the business fraternity who had been endeavouring for a decade to integrate the commerce of the province more closely with that of the United States, and thus to make the most of New Brunswick's historic position as the north-eastern extension of the Atlantic geographic province. Separated as New Brunswick was from Canada by the Appalachian barrier, trade with that province was negligible in comparison with her expanding commercial relations with the United States....

Alfred G. Bailey, "The Basis and Persistence of Opposition to Confederation in New Brunswick", *Canadian Historical Review*, Vol. 23, no. 4 (December, 1942), pp. 374, 377–79, 382–383.

A Struggle of Ideologies—A New Look at New Brunswick's Response

David G. Bell, a New Brunswick historian trained at Queen's University, has focused on the response to the Confederation debate of residents in one New Brunswick locality—Charlotte County. The Unionists, he contended, held out the promise of material improvement possible within a large federation, while the "Antis" appealed to the province's satisfaction with the *status quo* and to an underlying fear of losing the advantages of responsible self-government and prosperity by becoming simply one part of Canada. Moreover, Bell has argued that the Unionists made very good use of the so-called "Loyalty Cry", branding all dissidents as "rebels".

The confederation issue did not provoke the same emotional commitment among its friends that it evoked in its foes. The Antis were convinced that they were defending their Country from machinating Canadians without, and *vendus* within. Their only goal was to 'stave off a union with Canada'. But even for its most vocal Charlotte County supporters, the Quebec Scheme was difficult to get excited about. The abstract ideal of a great British American union was certainly a grand vision, but it was much easier to become aroused over considerations of local pride. . . .

Charlotte County's Unionists were confronted by a formidable task. *Prima facie*, they had to explain the merits of radical constitutional innovation to an audience which had no reason to be dissatisfied with its existing system of government. . . .

The union alluded to was far more an abstract ideal of the kind the people of Charlotte had long heard in relation to railway promotion, than it was a practical proposal. Instead of elucidating the Seventy-Two Resolutions the Unionists conjured visions of the immense local benefits confederation would yield. As a minor accompanying theme they pointed to some negative aspects of the province's current situation. To do so when New Brunswickers were congratulating themselves that the twin blessings of responsible self government and prosperity had created the best of all plausible worlds, and at a time when the Antis were fanning the flames of provincial patriotism, risked offending voter sensibilities. Nevertheless, advocacy of such profound change was inextricably linked to a critique of the status quo. . . .

It would be natural to suppose that the principal thrust of the Unionists' 1866 campaign was an emphasis upon the defense issue against the background of the Fenian threat[2]. . . .

One might [reason] that the people of Charlotte, like New Brunswickers in general, had opted for the status quo in 1865 because they had no great reason to be dissatisfied with it. But fifteen months later this view of the world was no longer tenable. Reciprocity was dead and New Brunswick was in the midst of a recession. The local government was diametrically opposed to Imperial policy. And, most alarming of all, the province was threatened with invasion, and was manifestly unable to defend itself. Developments over which they had little control shocked New Brunswickers into the realization that provincial life could not go on as it had. Their collective self-confidence evaporated. They discovered that their provincial house was, after all, built upon the sand, and that their only recourse in a stormy world was to cleave to the rock of confederation. One can thus readily hypothesize how the Unionists' use of the defense argument might have been the critical element in their 1866 triumph. . . . But while this line of argument is a common one, it is not the dominant theme in confederate election rhetoric. Or, the Unionists may have made surprisingly little use of the defense argument simply because they realized that they had at their disposal an even more potent campaign weapon, related to but distinguishable from the defense issue: the Loyalty Cry.

2. See Peter B. Waite, *The Life and Times of Confederation, 1864–1867* (Toronto: 1962), p. 275.

The inevitable aftertaste produced by [much of the rhetoric used in Charlotte County] was the feeling that those who opposed the Unionist ticket were disloyal.

David G. Bell, *The Confederation Issue in Charlotte County, New Brunswick* (unpublished M.A. thesis, Queen's University, 1976), pp. 69, 72–76, 80–82, 152–153, 155, 160–162.

PRINCE EDWARD ISLAND AND CONFEDERATION

Prince Edward Island's Aloofness—F.W.P. Bolger's Interpretation

Much of the twentieth-century writing on Prince Edward Island's response to Confederation reflects the strong influence of the "Antis" at the time of the Confederation debate. One historian who has cut against the grain of interpretation, however, is Francis W.P. Bolger. In a 1964 book and most recently in *Canada's Smallest Province* (1973), a collection of essays published by the P.E.I. Centennial Commission, Bolger has set out an assessment of the Island's ambivalent reaction.

The aloofness of Prince Edward Island resulted, in the first place, from a deep-seated provincialism and insularity. Situated in the Gulf of St. Lawrence and practically isolated from the mainland for five months of the year, Prince Edward Island had very limited contact with the other British North American provinces.... Moreover, the people of the Island were deeply preoccupied with land and religious controversies. These unsolved problems assumed a place of such supreme importance that the broader forces encouraging Confederation in other parts of Canada were not strong enough to distract the Islanders from questions intimately affecting their material and spiritual lives....

On July 1, 1873, the people of Prince Edward Island accepted their destiny with mixed feelings of disappointment and satisfaction. They expressed disappointment because economic necessity alone had induced them to declare in favor of Confederation....

...For ten years, in spite of protestations from her mother, Great Britain, the Island had categorically rejected all proposals because she did not consider the terms of union sufficiently attractive to compensate her for her highly prized independence. And it was only when economic forces threatened to undermine her financial security that she consented to unite with Canada....

Political reasons were also responsible for Prince Edward Island's lack of interest in Confederation. The Islanders cherished the political independence they had enjoyed since 1769, and when they attained Responsible Government in 1851 they had even a profounder attachment to their independence. Furthermore, their failure to persuade the British Government to resolve their proprietary land tenure question left them with an innate suspicion of distant administrations. And, finally, the realization that they would have an insignificant voice in a centralized legislature, led them to fear that their local needs would be disregarded....

Economic reasons also accounted for Prince Edward Island's aloofness to Confederation. The Island in the 1850's and 1860's enjoyed a high degree of economic self-sufficiency. The finances of the province were satisfactory, since revenue usually exceeded expenditure, and the public debt was little more than the revenue for a single year. Shipbuilding was an important and lucrative business. The products of the Island's staple industries, agriculture and fishing, were readily sold in Europe, the West Indies, and especially in the United States where the Reciprocity Treaty of 1854 had opened up a steady market. Since Canada was essentially agricultural and also possessed extensive fisheries, it did not provide, and could not be expected to provide, a market for the staple commodities of the Island. Since the Island, because of the complete absence of minerals, could hardly hope to become a manufacturing province, the people concluded that Confederation would mean economic extinction. And to complete the dreary economic outlook, the people feared the effects of a Canadian tariff and an oppressive federal taxation from which they would derive little financial benefit. In fine, Islanders maintained that Confederation would decrease revenue and increase taxation, and as a result prove financially disastrous.

F.W.P. Bolger, ed., *Canada's Smallest Province: A History of P.E.I.* (Charlottetown: P.E.I. Heritage Foundation, 1973), pp. 135-7 and 230-1.

The Conflict of Economic Interests—A Neo-Marxist View of the Island's Response

Completely different treatment of the question is to be found in Errol Sharpe's *A People's History of P.E.I.* (1975), a neo-Marxist perspective. While Bolger proposed a variety of different factors influencing the Islanders response, Sharpe singles out "economic interests" as the basis for the conflict between pro- and anti-Confederate elements.

In the years leading up to Confederation, the Island's economy continued to depend upon agriculture and shipping. But the merchant bourgeoisie of Canada were ushering in the railway age of steel and steam. The merchants, who of course dominated the Canadian provincial legislature, were voting themselves huge sums of public money to finance their ventures and granting to the chartered railway companies, of which they were the principal shareholders, vast blocks of crown land....

When the [colony's] delegates [to the Charlottetown Conference] returned to the Island, they found outright opposition to the Confederation plan. The tenants saw no advantage in joining a union to remain under the tutelage of British landlords. Freehold farmers and workers who had fought against British imperialism, were reaping the benefits of expanded trade and wanted no part of a union with the Canadas.

The bourgeoisie was split. Small manufacturers like Coles had built up flourishing businesses in the colony. They saw only increased competition at best and outright bankruptcy at worst as the centralised economy proposed by the union wiped out their small enterprises. Political-military careerist John Hamilton Gray and journalist Edward Whelan saw that the larger union would be to their advantage. W.H. Pope spoke for a group of wholesale merchants who stood to gain with a greater volume of imported manufactured goods from central Canada under Confederation....

When the debate opened in the Island legislature the Conservative government was torn with dissension. The pro-Confederate group advocated union until it was clear no amount of persuasion was going to change the minds of the overwhelming majority of the legislators or the people. They then changed their tactics—speaking publicly against union or saying nothing, while secretly working to bring it about.

The tenant uprising of 1865 strengthened the arguments of the anti-Confederates. The Confederation scheme offered no solution to the biggest problem on the Island— the leasehold tenure system. When the vote finally came in the legislature the scheme for union was defeated by a resounding 23 to 5.

In 1871, the pro-Confederates pulled their ace out of their sleeve. They convinced the merchants that the Island needed a railway, and a bill to authorise the building of a railway from Tignish to Souris was passed in the legislature. It was proposed that the money to build the railway be raised by selling Island notes to London bankers. . . .

. . . In 1873, the Island was faced with an enormous debt for railway construction and the work was far from complete. Because the Island had accumulated no debt until railway building began there is little doubt that it could have absorbed the cost and eventually finished the railway. But the pro-Confederates insisted that the only way out was to join Confederation. They negotiated with the Canadian Cabinet and an agreement was reached. . . .

Errol Sharpe, *A People's History of Prince Edward Island* (Ottawa: Steel Rail Publishing, 1976), pp. 114–116, 118–119, 121–122.

The Island at Confederation—A Neo-Conservative Interpretation

In stark contrast to Sharpe's interpretation, David Weale and Harry Baglole have offered what might be called a neo-conservative view of mid-nineteenth-century Island reality. In *The Island and Confederation* (1973), Weale and Baglole have taken a somewhat iconoclastic approach and provided the following concise summary of the Islanders' "sentimental and intangible" fears of losing their identity, institutions and traditions by agreeing to the Canadian initiatives of 1864.

More than any other event in the history of the Island the Confederation controversy, and the resistance of Islanders 'as one man', demonstrated that the inhabitants were united by a strong underlying sense of themselves as fellow members of a single community. And although they were racial, religious and regional issues which divided Islanders—and over which they frequently quarrelled in a truly energetic fashion— there were other important factors which bound them together and provided the basis for a shared identity. . . .

. . . . Geography dictated separateness; the smallness and isolation of the Colony fostered inwardness and an attitude of protectiveness; the overwhelmingly rural nature of the society allowed for the existence of a set of common values and ideals; and the unique political development which was always inextricably bound up with the Land Question had created a tradition of self-assertion and self-reliance. Working together these various elements had helped to create by the 1860's a deep sentiment of attachment and belonging to the Island. And although the distinctive cultural traits of the different founding peoples had by no means been effaced, most of the residents had come to regard themselves, first and foremost, as Islanders. . . .

It was at this point, just when the community was becoming firmly established and rooted, that the Confederation issue intruded upon the scene. Suddenly there was a demand that the focus of Island loyalty and identification be expanded or diffused to take in the whole of a great sprawling country which, according to some, would one day extend across the entire continent. It was a step which required an enormous, and in many ways painful, psychological adjustment, and the first instinct of most Islanders was that it simply was not worth it. . . .

It would be a mistake to suggest that the Islanders' response to the various offers and overtures was determined solely by 'principle' and had nothing whatever to do with their pocketbooks. They were, of course, worried about terms, taxation, tariffs and the prospect of having to help pay for the railways and canals of the 'extravagant' Canadians. But that was by no means all that concerned them. They were also worried about their political institutions and traditions, and even about such sentimental and intangible matters as the identity and honour of the Island as an independent community, and the necessity of preserving the way of life which had evolved there.

These latter issues were mentioned at least as often as the economic aspects of Union—and generally with greater ardor. And while it is impossible to isolate the various ingredients of the Confederation debate so as to assess precisely their relative importance, it would appear that at its centre the anti-Confederation movement was not based on economic considerations, but rather on the Islanders' desire to maintain their established practice of looking after their own affairs in their own way....

David Weale and Harry Baglole, *The Island and Confederation: The End of an Era* (Summerside: Williams and Crue Ltd., 1973), pp. 105–107, 113, 130–131, 148.

NOVA SCOTIA AND CONFEDERATION

An Economic Interpretation of Nova Scotia's 1867 Anti-Confederate Reaction

Nova Scotia, perhaps because of the intensity of its pre-Confederation debate, has generated the widest and most specialized literature concerning its Confederation experience. D.A. Muise's 1968 essay on the 1867 federal election in Nova Scotia stands out as one which casts the anti-Confederation movement within the context of economic changes affecting the province. According to Professor Muise, a native of Nova Scotia now teaching at Carleton University in Ottawa, important "sectional" economic forces were at work in Nova Scotia in the 1860s and 1870s—forces which would eventually make Confederation virtually inevitable.

The fifteen years preceding Confederation had been a veritable golden age for the economy of Nova Scotia. The general loosening of world trade in the 1850's combined with the Reciprocity Treaty with the United States to provide the stimulus needed for a rapid expansion of the resource-based Nova Scotia economy. Fishing and lumbering expanded especially quickly, and the related ship-building industry and carrying trade underwent its period of most rapid expansion. By the early sixties, the age of 'Wood, Wind and Sail' had reached its apogee. Yet, even while this amplification of the traditional economy was underway, there was emerging, at least in terms of economic importance, a very substantial competing sector.

In compensation for its refusal to admit Nova Scotia built vessels to its coasting trade as part of the Reciprocity Treaty of 1854, the United States had agreed to the inclusion of coal on the free list established. Nova Scotia had the only large coal deposits in the whole Atlantic seaboard. The effect was little short of phenomenal.

In 1864 the Conservative government of Charles Tupper, having failed once again to initiate construction of the much desired Intercolonial, undertook a policy of provincial expansion....

Tupper's determination to meet the demand for increased railway construction brought forward the first signs of a new political dichotomy for the province. As the interests spawned by the growth of the coal mining industry began to challenge the old line interests for the attention of the government, a marked reaction began to set in....

... The leadership of the more traditional economy was politically astute and moved quickly to meet the challenge of their domination of public policy. The scheme of union offered by the Quebec Resolutions was immediately labelled antipathetic to the established interests of the province and the proposal was temporarily shelved. But ultimately the British North America Act was passed. The pressure for Confederation in Nova Scotia came primarily from those areas which were committed to the emerging economy. By the early sixties, the older wood, wind and sail economy had been joined by the more continental realities of coal, steam and steel. The iron rails and pit-blackened men of the Northern Counties had challenged the wooden ships and iron men of the old economy, and had won the first round. The election of 1867 was to be the first instance in which they were pitted in a struggle for the electorate.

D.A. Muise, "The Federal election of 1867 in Nova Scotia: An Economic Interpretation", *Collections of the Nova Scotia Historical Society*, Vol. 36, 1967, pp. 330, 332–335, 338.

Entry by Default—An Interpretation of Nova Scotian "Acquiescence"

Kenneth Pryke's recent synthesis, *Nova Scotia and Confederation* (1979), encapsulates and advances much that has been written on the Nova Scotian response. A central feature of Pryke's interpretation is his explanation of Nova Scotia's eventual acquiescence to colonial realities. For Pryke, the "balance of power" pushed Nova Scotians into Confederation—almost "by default".

During the long months of debate on the proposal for colonial union there was a marked tendency to examine the scheme from the very narrow view of provincial interests. Much time was spent in estimating how much taxes would be increased by union and which local interests would be damaged. A similar approach was adopted by some Canadian advocates of union.... Support for union thus did not always indicate a broadsighted vision nor did opposition to it necessarily indicate a reactionary sectionalism.

The immediate pressure for change was based on the sound conclusion that the existing legislative union of Canada West and Canada East was no longer operative and had to be altered to allow greater freedom for the differing ambitions of the constituent parts. The search for a new political formula became a blueprint for the future. Some, but by no means all Canadians, saw a way whereby a solution to the political impasse could assist in meeting their defence problems, as well as absorb the colonies to the east and territories to the west. Unlike the suggestion for maritime union, the scheme in the Canadas became identified with broad political and economic goals which embraced a vision of a new nation.

Once this plan was presented by the Canadians the Nova Scotians had little alternative but to acquiesce, particularly since the Colonial Office had concluded that it was a workable solution to colonial ills. The scheme did have an internal logic in its solution to the growing resentment by the Nova Scotians to the increasing control over Nova Scotian affairs by the Canadians. While Nova Scotia objected to Canadian influence, the balance of power had unalterably tipped to the advantage of the Canadians. The solution, ironical and bitter as it was, was for Nova Scotia to enter into a political union with the Canadas.

Colonial union was a realistic recognition of the existing balance but it nonetheless caused bitterness in Nova Scotia during the debate over union and a sullen reception to union after 1867. The necessity of accepting an unwelcome subordination, no matter how it might be presented by the advocates of union, contributed to the many cross-currents in Nova Scotia after 1867. Each faction, whether confederates, anti-confederates, Howe compromisers, or local compromisers, ultimately was forced to work within a framework being imposed on the province. . . . Nor after 1867 did any political leader manage to extricate himself from the morass. This factionalism not only precluded a clear and consistent Nova Scotian role in dominion politics but prevented the strong pursuit of repeal with anything like a consensus of opinion. By default, then, Nova Scotia entered into and remained in confederation.

Kenneth Pryke, *Nova Scotia and Confederation 1864–74* (Toronto: University of Toronto Press, 1979), pp. 6, 7, 15.

SYNTHESIZING INTERPRETATIONS

The Maritime Response of Ambivalence—A Widely Accepted Interpretation

Much of the prevailing view of the Maritimes' response to the 1864 proposals has its origins in the first of the post-World War II studies of Canadian Confederation, Peter B. Waite's *The Life and Times of Confederation, 1864–1867* (1962). This account, based on research into newspaper sources, seems to capture the ambivalent attitude of the Maritimers to Confederation.

. . . Though the fundamentally empirical character of Confederation was dictated largely by the temper of the men who shaped it and by the immediate circumstances that gave rise to it, the newspaper suggestions for Confederation, and comments upon it, reveal why it came to be what it was. . . .

What was sought by the Quebec Conference and later by the Colonial Office was a mean between the federation of the United States and the legislative union of Great Britain. . . .

The general view was that the new central government at Ottawa would be the old colonial legislatures rolled into one, with a few more powers added. To Canadians the government at Ottawa would be a familiar one, but it was a type that all the provinces had known before. . . . It was the local governments that were new. They were the uncertain quantity. Much of the confusion about the way the new federal system would work stemmed from the fact that the role of the local governments was extraordinarily obscure. . . . The existing colonial system seemed to have little or no application to the circumstances of the local governments. American state governments were not any help either. They were sovereign. Most British Americans did not consider that sovereignty was an attribute of the local governments. . . . The truth probably was, as Professor Brady has suggested[3], that a federation has never been easy to understand by people who have never lived under it.

Perhaps the most remarkable, and certainly the most pervasive characteristic of British Americans was their passionate desire for a place in the world. Galt's sensitivity to the patronizing in London and the colonists' resentment at the ignorance about them

---

3. The reference is to Alexander Brady, *Democracy in the Dominions* (Toronto: 1952).

in England are of a piece. 'Colonial' was not yet a word generally resented; some were even proud of being 'British colonists', but it was not enough....

British North Americans were purposive yet hesitant, surer of what they wanted than they were of themselves. They were still adolescent with high dreams and fancies; nationality was the most golden of them all. July 1, 1867 was the beginning of a long and difficult maturity....

But no one knew, not [G.-E.] Cartier, not even [John A.] Macdonald, what really was involved in the creation, administration, and maintenance of a transcontinental state. An empire of this size had been created before; it could be done—that was the great example the Americans provided. But it had been done by a rich and powerful nation of twenty millions. The contemplation of the same thing by a struggling group of still discordant provinces, with a population of four millions, was surprising; perhaps it was absurd. The railway that might have given such a union a semblance of reality did not yet exist. Union of the colonies was achieved in 1867; but it was hardly more than a beginning. The railways at Riviere du Loup and Truro that stared into the empty miles between marked a cause not yet won, a nationality not yet realized. These still lay in the difficult years ahead.

Peter B. Waite, *The Life and Times of Confederation 1864–1867* (Toronto: University of Toronto Press, 1962), pp. 325–329. Footnotes omitted.

A Guide to Further Reading

1. *Overviews*

Beck, J.M., *The History of Maritime Union: A Study in Frustration*. Fredericton: Maritime Union Study, 1969.

Bercuson, David Jay, ed., *Canada and the Burden of Unity*. Toronto: Macmillan, 1977.

Cook, Ramsay, ed., *Confederation*. Canadian Historical Readings Series No. 3. Toronto: University of Toronto Press, 1967.

Creighton, Donald, *Macdonald: Vol I—The Young Politician*. Toronto: Macmillan, 1952.

_____, *The Road to Confederation: The Emergence of Canada, 1863–1867*. Toronto: Macmillan, 1964.

Forbes, Ernest R., *Aspects of Maritime Regionalism, 1867–1927*. Canadian Historical Association Booklet No. 36. Ottawa: CHA, 1983.

_____, *The Maritime Rights Movement, 1919–1927: A Study in Canadian Regionalism*. Montreal: McGill-Queen's University Press, 1979.

Fraser, Joan, "Canada's First Forgotten Separatists", *Financial Times of Canada*. Vol. 65 (November 22, 1976), p. 25.

MacNutt, W.S., *The Atlantic Provinces: The Emergence of Colonial Societies, 1713–1857*. Toronto: McClelland and Stewart, 1965.

Morton, W.L., *The Critical Years: The Union of British North America, 1857–1873*. Toronto: McClelland and Stewart, 1964.

Rawlyk, G.A., *The Atlantic Provinces and the Problems of Confederation*. Halifax: Breakwater Press, 1979.

_____, "The Maritimes and the Canadian Community", in Mason Wade, ed., *Regionalism and the Canadian Community, 1867–1967*. Toronto: University of Toronto Press, 1969.

_____, R.P. Bowles and B.W. Hodgins, eds., *Regionalism in Canada: Flexible Federalism or Fractured Nation?* Scarborough: Prentice-Hall, 1979.

Waite, P.B., *The Charlottetown Conference*. Canadian Historical Association Booklet No. 15. Ottawa: CHA, 1970.

_____, *The Life and Times of Confederation, 1864-1867*. Toronto: University of Toronto Press, 1962.

Whitelaw, W.M., *The Maritimes and Canada Before Confederation*. Toronto: Oxford University Press, 1966. Originally published 1934.

2. Specialized/Regional Studies

New Brunswick

Baker, W.M., *Timothy Warren Anglin, 1822-96: Irish Catholic Canadian*. Toronto: University of Toronto Press, 1977.

Bailey, Alfred G., "The Basis and Persistence of Opposition to Confederation in New Brunswick", *Canadian Historical Review*. Vol. XXIII, No 4 (December, 1942), pp. 374-398.

_____, "Railways and the Confederation Issue in New Brunswick", in Bailey, *Culture and Nationality*. Toronto: McClelland and Stewart, 1972.

Bell, David G., "The Confederation Issue in Charlotte County, New Brunswick", Unpublished M.A. Thesis, Queen's University, 1976.

MacNutt, W.S., *New Brunswick: A History 1784-1867*. Toronto: Macmillan, 1963.

Thorburn, Hugh G., *Politics in New Brunswick*. Toronto: University of Toronto Press, 1961.

Wallace, Carl, "Albert Smith: Confederation and Reaction in New Brunswick 1852-1882", *Canadian Historical Review*, Vol. XLIV. (1963)

Nova Scotia

Beck, J.M., *The Government of Nova Scotia*. Toronto: University of Toronto Press, 1957.

_____, *Joseph Howe: Anti-Confederate*. Canadian Historical Association Booklet No. 17. Ottawa: CHA, 1968.

_____, ed., *Joseph Howe: Voice of Nova Scotia*. Toronto: McClelland and Stewart, 1964.

_____, *Joseph Howe*. 2 vols. Montreal: McGill-Queen's University Press, 1983.

Fergusson, C.B., *W.S. Fielding: The Mantle of Howe*. Windsor, N.S.: Lancelot Press, 1970.

Muise, D.A., "The Federal Election of 1867 in Nova Scotia: An Economic Interpretation", *Collections of the Nova Scotia Historical Society*. Vol. 36 (1967).

_____, "Parties and Constituencies: Federal Elections in Nova Scotia, 1867-1896", Canadian Historical Association, *Historical Papers*, (1971).

Pryke, Kenneth, *Nova Scotia and Confederation, 1867-1871*. Toronto: University of Toronto Press, 1979.

Rawlyk, G.A., ed., *Joseph Howe: Opportunist? Man of Vision? Frustrated Politician?* Toronto: Copp Clark, 1967.

Prince Edward Island

Bolger, F.W.P., ed., *Canada's Smallest Province: A History of P.E.I.* Charlottetown: P.E.I. Heritage Foundation, 1973.

_____, *Prince Edward Island and Confederation, 1863-1873*. Charlottetown: St. Dunstan's University Press, 1964.

MacKinnon, Frank, *The Government of Prince Edward Island*. Toronto: University of Toronto Press, 1953.

Sharpe, Errol, *A People's History of Prince Edward Island*. Toronto: Steel Rail Press, 1975.

Weale, David and Harry Baglole, *The Island and Confederation: The End of An Era.* Summerside: Williams & Crue, 1973.

Newfoundland

Fraser, A.M., "The Issue of Confederation, 1864–1870", in R.A. MacKay, ed., *Newfoundland: Economic, Diplomatic and Strategic Studies.* Toronto: Oxford University Press, 1946.

Hiller, J.K., "Confederation Defeated: The Newfoundland Election of 1869", in J.K. Hiller and P. Neary, eds., *Newfoundland in the Nineteenth and Twentieth Centuries.* Toronto: University of Toronto Press, 1980.

11

MÉTIS RESISTANCE AND REBELLION, 1869–1885

What Were the Roots of Conflict?

The Métis, like other peoples of Canada, are a distinct group with their own history and traditions, yet rarely have they played a dominant role in the chronicles of our national history since the days of the early fur trade. The Métis, sometimes referred to even with the present-day awareness of aboriginal rights and revisions of the Constitution as "Canada's forgotten peoples", are often seen only as the hapless victims of colonial exploitation, political manipulation, and racial and religious prejudice. In fact, the Métis, led by the charismatic Louis Riel in the Red River Resistance of 1869 and the 1885 North-West (or Saskatchewan) Rebellion, achieved both military and constitutional victories. It is largely thanks to their struggles that in 1870 Manitoba entered Confederation as a province rather than as a territory; the Métis also contributed to the eventual adoption of a federal policy to promote Western settlement. Clearly the Red River Resistance and the later North-West Rebellion are two events which cannot be fully understood except in the context of Métis history and aspirations, and represent only one aspect of the larger story of a people who survived and live on in Canadian society today.

From the moment the Hudson's Bay Company permitted European settlers at Red River the Métis population in the West had reason to be troubled about its future. Tension was generated between this community on the "frontier" and external power and authority, whether in London or in Ottawa. But what precisely were the roots of this conflict? Were the troubles at Red River and later in the North-West caused by similar Métis grievances? Or were the two disturbances different in their sources, nature and political objectives?

The Métis of Manitoba and the North-West were a mixed-blood population that had arisen out of early fur trade contacts between the French and the

Indians. By the end of the French régime in 1760, intermarriage between French men and Indian women had produced sizeable Métis communities around the Upper Great Lakes region. Soon other mixed-blood communities began developing in the Red River district and later in the Saskatchewan territory. Some Métis found employment either with the North-West Company or the Hudson's Bay Company, while others quite independently played an important role in provisioning. It was probably not before the early years of the nineteenth century, when the Earl of Selkirk established a European colony at Red River, that the Métis became conscious of themselves as a distinct people, as the "New Nation". Although the French element seems to have formed the nucleus of this "New Nation" at Red River, the English and Protestant element would make common cause with them by the late 1860s.

Métis settled in the Red River district found themselves caught in the middle of a mounting rivalry between the Hudson's Bay Company and the North-West Company for control over the western fur trade. The Nor'Westers, based in Montreal, strongly objected to Lord Selkirk's plans to settle indigent Scots at Red River. Such a colony, they believed, would disrupt the North-West Company's communications between Montreal and the North-West, ruin their western trade, and bring them under the control of the Hudson's Bay Company. To block Selkirk's plans, the Montreal traders first tried to frighten off prospective settlers, then enlisted the help of the Métis. In a skirmish near Seven Oaks in 1816, a band of Métis—acting to resist encroachments on their lands and in the interests of the Nor'Westers—met and killed a newly appointed governor, Robert Semple, and nineteen of his armed escorts, who had been sent to the Red River colony to enforce the Hudson's Bay Company's claims. The Métis had met an external threat head-on. Thereafter, they kept their "para-military force" or militia on the alert against possible external threats and Sioux attacks from the south.

The Métis at Red River slowly gained representation and a voice in the government of their district, known as Assiniboia. After 1836, the Métis were represented on the Council of Assiniboia which functioned as a legislature for the Red River settlement. The Council governed only with popular consent, as was evident in 1849 when an attempt to enforce the Hudson's Bay Company's unpopular trade monopoly was successfully challenged. The local court acquitted a notorious free trader, Guillaume Sayer, and many Métis publicly expressed their disaffection with the rule of the Company (which had been reorganized and amalgamated with the North-West Company in 1821). According to Métis leaders, it was more concerned with the careers of its agents than with the welfare of the Red River inhabitants.

The transfer of control over the Red River region from the Company to the Dominion government in 1869 was an unsettling event which galvanized the Métis people into action once more. The British government had the Hudson's Bay Company sell their territory to Canada for a mere £300 000, and this transfer of sovereignty was effected without consulting—or even officially informing—the people at Red River. At a public meeting at Fort Garry in July,

William Dease, a well-known Métis leader and member of the Council of Assiniboia, demanded that the £300 000 payment be made to the Métis proprietors of land and not to the Hudson's Bay Company. When William McDougall, governor-designate, arrived at Red River in October, 1869, in anticipation of the transfer scheduled to take place on December 1st, the Métis set up barricades at St. Norbert and easily convinced him to withdraw to American territory. Louis Riel, another local leader, halted a survey party sent from Canada which was running survey lines through the hay lands of his relatives and friends.

Louis Riel and John Bruce organized the National Métis Committee along the lines of their traditional famine relief committee. As the men returned from the autumn buffalo hunt and the voyageurs of the northern fur brigade came back to their homes in the valley, a force was assembled to occupy Fort Garry in the name of the Métis council. The Red River Resistance had begun. The local inhabitants were determined not to be sold and bought like "poor dumb driven cattle". They had rights and these must be protected. If they were to be a part of Canada, their interests had to be safeguarded. And Ottawa should negotiate, not impose, entry into Confederation.

The Red River Resistance of 1869–70 secured a temporary triumph for the Métis people. Under the leadership of Louis Riel, they proposed a "List of Rights" and in negotiations with the Dominion government won major concessions to end the conflict. Riel and the Métis succeeded in gaining some legal redress for their grievances in the Manitoba Act of 1870, which brought the postage-stamp-sized province into Confederation. Indeed, the inept transfer of sovereignty over the Red River colony had proved costly to the government. Both the armed resistance and the tough bargaining of the Métis should have served as important lessons to the Macdonald government.

Yet Macdonald and his politicians seem to have learned nothing and forgotten nothing. The old hatreds and tensions so evident in the 1870s resurfaced in the 1880s—this time over Métis rights in the North-West Territories. The Métis people once more saw their lands threatened by settlement and their freighting business threatened by the railway. Besides, the buffalo herds were fast disappearing. When they could get no unequivocal assurances of protection from Macdonald's government in Ottawa, the Métis in desperation called once more on Louis Riel, now a naturalized American citizen living in Montana, to come to their aid. The Riel who returned to his Métis "nation" in July 1884 was a changed man. He now claimed to be a Métis religious leader and called himself Louis "David", the Son of God. And this time the Métis forces were ably organized and commanded by Gabriel Dumont, the legendary leader of the buffalo hunt.

Edgar Dewdney, Commissioner of Indian Affairs in the North-West, mistakenly believed that Riel was organizing a Métis-Cree rebellion, though in fact the Cree at the time were agitating for their own Indian territory. The Métis rising provided the government with the opportunity, when troops were sent into the North-West to suppress the Métis, to destroy the Cree movement as well. After several brief skirmishes with the North West Mounted Police, the Métis were unable to stand up to the overwhelming advantage in men and equipment of the Canadian militia.

The apprehension of Louis Riel in May 1885 set the stage for a full-blown national crisis. Riel was taken to Regina and there tried and found guilty of treason—by an all-white, all-Protestant jury. With cries in Ontario for Riel's death, Macdonald's government chose to ignore a jury recommendation for mercy and allowed the Métis leader to be hanged. In the end, the people in the hinterland lost once more.

The Métis protest movements of 1869 and 1885, and particularly the role of Louis Riel in leading the cause, are encrusted with popular and historical mythology. Today, one hundred years after the crisis, the struggle of Louis Riel and the Métis for justice still generates a host of contentious questions. What lay at the root of the conflict leading to resistance and rebellion? Did the Red River and North-West disturbances spring from similar sets of causes? In leading the Métis, was Louis Riel a frontier rebel, a Western separatist, a religious prophet of the New World, or at bottom merely the victim of partisan politics and racial and religious prejudices? And why is Riel often regarded as a Canadian folk hero, while the Métis people and their cause are only now beginning to emerge from the mists of history?

SELECTED CONTEMPORARY SOURCES

THE ROOTS AND NATURE OF THE RED RIVER RESISTANCE—A VARIETY OF VIEWS

The Agitation of the Canadian Party—Alexander Begg's Observations, 1869

Many of the seeds of fear and apprehension among the Métis of the Red River were sown by an English-speaking faction in the colony composed of British and former Ontario settlers and calling itself the "Canadian Party". This small group, led by Dr. John Christian Schultz, agitated for union with Canada as a means of opening the North-West for settlers of their own kind. In his famous Red River Journal of 1869–70, Alexander Begg blamed Schultz and his Canadian Party for stirring up much of the trouble.

> ... This bold, ambitious and aggressive man [John Schultz] had become the focus of all the dislike and distrust of Canadians and things Canadian in Red River. Schultz was the outspoken advocate of Canadian annexation... he would himself be a beneficiary of the transfer.... The handsomest of men, tall, solid, and quick in movement, he was yet reserved, studious and low-voiced; able but not popular; winning men, if at all, by the force of intellect, not by the power of affection. His reputation among the leading men of Red River was that he was a selfish and unscrupulous adventurer; his friends thought him a champion of popular rights and a Canadian patriot....

> W. L. Morton, ed., *Alexander Begg's Red River Journal and Other Papers Relative to the Red River Resistance of 1869–1870* (Toronto: Champlain Society, 1956), pp. 22–23.

Encroachment on Métis Lands—Two Perspectives on the Threat, 1874

The activities of surveyors laying out the Dawson Road, a route linking Fort Garry to the Lake of the Woods, and the appointment in 1868 of Governor William McDougall, fostered much uneasiness among Métis about the future of their lands and the territory. Two Red River observers of widely different backgrounds, John McTavish of the Hudson's Bay Company and Thomas Bunn, a Red River farmer who served in Louis Riel's Provisional Government, agreed that the apprehensions caused by surveying and the transfer of sovereignty contributed greatly to the Métis resistance.

John McTavish's Testimony, 1874

... There was a feeling of uneasiness on the part of all as to what was proposed to be done with regard to the transfer of the country, the first symptoms of which discontent occurred in the autumn, when the facts of the proposed transfer became known. In the same summer there was a public meeting, called by Mr. William Dease, which was, however, but poorly attended. At that meeting Mr. Dease spoke against the Government of the Council of Assiniboia, but did not prove any very great cause of complaint or ill-feeling against said Government. There was no ill-feeling against Canada at that time. When the appointment of Governor McDougall was heard of, the feeling of uneasiness began to take a very marked form, and a determination to resist his entry into the country was expressed at meetings held amongst themselves.

Some surveys which were made at that time were also displeasing to the French half-breeds, through whose lands said surveys were made. These surveys were first made at Oak Point. These surveys, followed up by the appointment of Governor McDougall, caused great discontent. The discontent of the half-breeds arose from the fact of their lands being measured by the surveyors, without explanation being made as to the object; which lands were being cultivated by the French half-breeds. Very little was known as to the different steps of the rising until it actually broke out in the form of a congregation of people, determined to oppose the entry of the Governor, which meeting took place nine miles from Fort Garry. Witness was in constant communication with the inhabitants in a business way, and knew that dissatisfaction arose....

1st. From the surveys.

2ndly. From the appointment of a Lieutenant Governor.

3rdly. From the fact of the transfer being made without their being taken into account.

Report of the Select Committee on the Causes of Difficulties in the North-West Territory in 1869–70 (Ottawa: I.B. Taylor, 1874), John McTavish's testimony, 10 April, 1874, p. 1

Thomas Bunn's Testimony, 1874

The first symptoms of discontent of which I am aware were on the 21st Oct., 1869. That was the day that notice was sent to Governor McDougall not to enter the territory. I did not however know of this notice till a few days afterwards. There was before this a feeling of discontent in the territory, among the French Métis, and among a small portion of the English-speaking population, as well whites as Métis. This discontent was caused by the conduct of Mr. Snow, the Superintendent of the Dawson route, on account of the manner in which he was said to have disposed of the provisions which were sent in aid of the population which was then suffering from the ravages of the grasshoppers.

It was very generally believed or apprehended among the people generally, but to a greater extent among the French half-breeds, that the whole country would be appropriated or monopolized by new comers. I myself shared that apprehension. I mean by the new comers purchasing the lands from the Indians, and thereby extinguishing the Indian title.[1] . . . .

I understood that the French Métis claimed that the country belonged to the half-breeds under the same kind of title by which Indians claim, namely, by birth, residence and occupation.

They claim no transfer from the Indians. The English half-breeds do not make this kind of claim, though, as I have said, they probably would have taken some action if the surveyors had come into their neighborhood.

Report of the Select Committee, Thomas Bunn's testimony, 4 May 1874, pp. 114–115.

The Mismanagement of the Transfer—John A. Macdonald's Private Opinion, 1869

Prime Minister John A. Macdonald acknowledged privately that the preparations for the transfer of sovereignty of the North-West to Canada had been a fiasco.

You see we have commenced the extension of our sovereignty with a war of which I informed you by cable. It appears that the half-breeds have been soured by all kinds of stories as to the intention of Canada to deprive them of their lands and to govern them without any reference to the residents. These stories have been industriously propagated, and *entre nous*, I fear that the people that McDougall sent up there—Snow and Mair and Stoughton Dennis have not helped at all to smooth matters.

These French half-breeds have always been truly loyal to the Hudson's Bay Company, greatly dislike Schultz and that small section who published the *Nor'Wester* and are opposed to the Company. I am afraid that Snow and Dennis fraternized too much with that fellow, who is a clever sort of man but exceedingly *cantankerous* and ill-conditioned. To make matters worse, Governor McTavish is dying and unable to arrange matters with a firm hand. However, we must possess our souls in patience, and deal with these refractory people as best we may.

Joseph Pope, ed., *Correspondence of Sir John A. Macdonald* (Toronto: Oxford University Press, 1921), Macdonald to John Rose, 23 November 1869, p. 106.

The Threat to Métis "Nationhood" and Sovereignty—The Métis Declaration of A Provisional Government, 1869

The transfer of the Red River colony to Dominion control seemed to awaken a sense of national consciousness among Métis leaders like Louis Riel and William Dease. In response to the government's action, they argued for the protection of their rights as a condition of union with Confederation, not as

---

1. "Extinguishing the Indian title" means acquiring ownership of land held by the aboriginal peoples by right of birth and possession.

merely a promised aftereffect of annexation. In late November 1869, Riel and his associates declared their Métis council to be the colony's "provisional Government", since Hudson's Bay rule had lapsed. The Métis Declaration voiced their case that the intervention of a "foreign power" in the North-West had threatened Métis sovereignty and precipitated the resistance.

And, whereas, it is also generally admitted that a people is at liberty to establish any form of government it may consider suited to its wants, as soon as the power to which it was subject abandons it, or attempts to subjugate it, without its consent to a foreign power; and maintain, that no right can be transferred to such a foreign power. Now, therefore, first, we, the representatives of the people, in Council assembled in Upper Fort Garry, on the 24th day of November, 1869, after having invoked the God of Nations, relying on these fundamental moral principles, solemnly declare, in the name of our constituents, and in our own names, before God and man, that, from the day on which the Government we had always respected abandoned us, by transferring to a strange power the sacred authority confided to it, the people of Rupert's Land and the North-West became free and exempt from all allegiance to the said Government. Second. That we refuse to recognize the authority of Canada, which pretends to have a right to coerce us, and impose upon us a despotic form of government still more contrary to our rights and interests as British subjects, than was that Government to which we had subjected ourselves, through necessity, up to a recent date. Thirdly. That, by sending an expedition on the 1st of November, ult., charged to drive back Mr. William McDougall and his companions, coming in the name of Canada, to rule us with the rod of despotism, without previous notification to that effect, we have acted conformably to that sacred right which commands every citizen to offer energetic opposition to prevent this country from being enslaved. Fourth. That we continue, and shall continue, to oppose, with all our strength, the establishing of the Canadian authority in our country, under the announced form . . . furthermore we do declare and proclaim, in the name of the people of Rupert's Land and the North-West, that we have, on the said 24th day of November, 1869, above mentioned, established a Provisional Government, and hold it to be the only and lawful authority now in existence in Rupert's Land and the North-West which claims the obedience and respect of the people; that, meanwhile, we hold ourselves in readiness to enter in such negotiations with the Canadian Government as may be favourable for the good government and prosperity of this people. . . .

Issued at Fort Garry, this Eighth day of December, in the year of our Lord One thousand eight hundred and sixty-nine.

JOHN BRUCE, Pres.
LOUIS RIEL, Sec.

Canada Sessional Papers, 1870, Vol. 5, No. 12

The Demand for Self-Government—The Métis' Fourth "List of Rights", 1870

Riel and his Provisional Government grew more insistent in their demands for Métis self-government, particularly after the quelling of an armed coup against them by the Canadian party, and the public execution of the Ontario Orangeman, Thomas Scott, for his role in the plotted overthrow. By early 1870 the council had revised its List of Rights asking for provincial status for both Assiniboia and the North-West Territories, land grants for the Métis, and treaties with the Indians. Judge John Black, Alfred Scott and abbé Ritchot were chosen as delegates to negotiate in Ottawa. Archbishop Taché returned hurriedly from the First Vatican Council in Rome, at the urgent request of the Canadian government, and discussed the terms of union with the delegates before they left. A further revised List of Rights, the fourth, was carried to Ottawa as the basis of negotiations. This Fourth List of Rights read:

> 1. That the territory of the North-West enter into the Confederation of the Dominion of Canada as a province....
> 7. That the schools be separate, and that the public money for schools be distributed among the different religious denominations in proportion to their respective population according to the system of the Province of Quebec.
> 9. That in this province, with the exception of the Indians who are neither civilized, nor settled, every man having attained the age of twenty-one years, and every foreigner being a British subject, after having resided three years in this country, and being possessed of a house, be entitled to vote....
> 11. That the Local Legislature of this province have full control over all the lands of the North-West.
> 13. That treaties be concluded between Canada and the different Indian tribes of the North-West, at the request and with the co-operation of the Local Legislature.
> 14. That an uninterrupted steam communication from Lake Superior to Fort Garry be guaranteed within the space of Five years....
> 16. That both the English and French languages be common in the legislature, and in the courts; and that all public documents, as well as Acts of the Legislature, be published in both languages.
> 17. That the Lieutenant-Governor to be appointed for the Province of the North-West be familiar with both the English and French languages.
> 18. That the Judge of the Supreme Court speak the English and French languages....
>
> W.L. Morton, *Manitoba: The Birth of a Province* (Toronto: 1965)   (Altona: D.W. Friesen & Sons, 1965), The Fourth List of Rights, pp. 248–250.

The Responsibility of the Dominion Government—Louis Riel's View, 1874

Louis Riel himself published a defence of the Provisional Government's actions in forcing Ottawa to negotiate terms of union in 1870. He considered it a great moral victory for the Métis people that the Red River settlement was recognized as a province with guarantees of property rights, dual confessional schools,[2] and two official languages.

> This simple account of the principal events during our troubles from the autumn of 1868 up to the last part of February 1870, together with the testimony of Lord Granville, prove: (1) that the Canadian government provoked the troubles which broke out in the North West Territories over the transfer of these territories to its power, consequently the government should bear the sole responsibility for these troubles.

---

2. A system of parallel Protestant and Catholic public schools independent of each other and each having full control over its finances, administration, curriculum and teacher training.

(2) That it was the employees of Canada who, by destroying little by little the Hudson's Bay Company government in 1869, forced the inhabitants of these territories to provide themselves with a provisional government whose legality was thus not in doubt....

Louis Riel, *L'Amnistie* (Montreal: Le Nouveau Monde, 1874), p. 12.

THE ROOTS AND NATURE OF THE NORTH-WEST REBELLION, 1885—A VARIETY OF VIEWS

By the 1880s many groups of Métis had left Manitoba and moved westward to resettle in the Saskatchewan River valley. The Métis land reserve guaranteed in the Manitoba Act of 1870 had been depleted as a result of the encroachment of new settlers and the activities of land speculators, who often acquired "half-breed land scrip"[3] in return for cash payments to Métis seeking food and supplies or escape from debt. In addition, most Métis lived from the buffalo hunt, and thus had moved westward in search of the herds, beyond the line of advance of settlement.

Like the Métis resistance of 1869–70, the North-West Rebellion of 1885 was the product of accumulated grievances and the frustrations of the Métis people. But the conditions and concerns were often different among Métis in the Saskatchewan River valley. Louis Riel had returned from exile with a religious mission and a determination to found a "Métis nation". The further encroachment of settlers and surveyors into the North-West territory, the depletion of the buffalo herds, and the introduction and sale of alcohol all added to their fears and frustrations. Also, by the mid-1880s, the Métis had been joined in their grievances by some thirty thousand Plains Indians and scattered groups of settlers disgruntled by Dominion government policies in the North-West.

The Crisis Among the Cree—Lieutenant-Governor Archibald on the Stone Fort Treaty, 1872

By the late 1860s signs of desperation and resistance began to appear among the Indians of the Prairies. The buffalo were rapidly disappearing, so the Cree, faced with possible starvation, moved into traditional Blackfoot country in 1869. At the same time, epidemics carried off thousands and American whiskey traders moved into Canadian territory. Those who survived the scourges of pox, famine and whiskey soon found themselves involved in a fierce confrontation between the Cree and the Blackfoot.

Although the Cree-Blackfoot hostilities were eventually brought to a satisfactory resolution, the Canadian government remained aware of the social and economic crisis that had produced such an outburst. In addition to

---

3. In the early 1870s the Dominion Government set aside 1 400 000 acres (560 000 hectares) of land for the Métis people. The father of each Métis family was given a piece of paper called a *scrip*, which could be used to claim 160 acres of land or traded for money. This land scrip was also granted to Métis children.

some ten thousand Métis in the prairie West, there were at least 30 000 Indians (as defined in the British North America Act) whose interests fell under federal jurisdiction. In order to avoid concerted opposition by the Native peoples to plans for European settlement of the West, the question of aboriginal title had to be faced and some guarantees made with respect to the future welfare and subsistence of the first inhabitants. Three treaties were signed in 1871–72 to secure title to the lands of southern Manitoba and north-western Ontario.

> When we met this morning (July 29th), the Indians were invited to state their wishes as to the reserves, they were to say how much they thought would be sufficient, and whether they wished them all in one or in several places.
>
> In defining the limits of their reserves, so far as we could see, they wished to have about two-thirds of the Province. We heard them out, and then told them it was quite clear that they had entirely misunderstood the meaning and intention of reserves. We explained the object of these in something like the language of the memorandum enclosed, and told them that it was of no use for them to entertain any such ideas, which were entirely out of the question. We told them that whether they wished it or not, immigrants would come in and fill up the country; that every year from this one twice as many in number as their whole people there assembled would pour into the Province, and in a little while would spread all over it, and that now was the time for them to come to an arrangement that would secure homes and annuities for themselves and their children.
>
> Alexander Morris, *The Treaties of Canada with the Indians of Manitoba and The North-West Territories* (Toronto: Belfords, Clarke & Co., 1880), p. 34

The Violation of Métis Land Rights—A Law with Unintended Effects, 1873

Much of the Métis' disillusionment of the 1880s stemmed from the violation and loss of their land rights, in spite of these being guaranteed under the Manitoba Act. The Act had provided for a large Métis land grant and subsequent orders-in-council in 1871 permitted "every halfbreed resident. . . and every child" to share in the grant. Yet lengthy delays occurred because no census had been undertaken. No major amounts of land were distributed until 1876, several years after new settlers had begun taking up Métis lands.

One Manitoba law, the 1873 Half-Breed Land Act, illustrated how legislation designed to protect Métis land rights actually worked to their detriment. In this case, Manitoba merchants reacted to the Act by refusing to extend credit to Métis, believing erroneously that debts were unrecoverable under this legislation.

> 2. No promise or agreement, verbal or in writing, made by any half-breed, previous to the issue of the patent,[4] or to the allotment and receipt by him or her, as the case may be, of the same, or publication of the allotment, either for or without a money consideration, to convey to any person, after the patent should or shall issue or the allotment be made, the title of such child of half-breed in the portion of the said grant

---

4. Patent refers to the grant of land scrip issued to Métis in settlement of their claims.

which might fall to his or her share shall be binding on such child of half-breed, and no damages shall be recoverable against him or her either at law or in equity, by reason of his or her refusing to carry out such promise or agreement.

3. Any sale for a valuable consideration, and duly made and executed by deed, from and after the first day of July in the year one thousand eight hundred and seventy-seven by any child of half-breed, having legal right to a portion of land out of the one million four hundred thousand acres of land in the Province set apart for the children of half-breeds by the Parliament of Canada, of such portion, shall be legal and effectual for all purposes whatsoever, and shall transfer to the purchaser the rights and estate of the vendor thereto and therein.

Revised Statutes of Manitoba, 1892, I, p. 741.

Métis Impoverishment and Despair—Louis Riel's Observations, 1885

Long-standing tensions between the Métis and Dominion authorities seemed to be coming to a head with an agricultural depression which beset the North-West after 1883. Farmers (including some Métis) were affected by the loss of markets for their produce; and the Plains Indians were even harder hit because the Dominion government reduced their rations in order to cut costs. With buffalo and other game nearly gone from the prairies, the Métis and Indian peoples were facing the prospect of starvation. A personal letter written by Louis Riel in June 1885 provided some indication of the depth of their poverty and despair.

...the time was hard, especially in the Saskatchewan; there was nothing to do; there was no money; the crops had failed, as you could have learned it from the newspapers. Certain merchants in bad fix, half ruined or on the eve of being totally ruined, did not know what to do; by means of intrigues they worked to have as many Mounted Police as they could. Others, who were the pronounced enemies of the Half-Breeds rights, went as far as threatening a war of extermination upon us.

Glenbow-Alberta Institute Archives, Louis Riel to Romuald Fiset, June 16, 1885.

Unreasonable Métis Claims—John A. Macdonald's Assessment, 1885

Sir John A. Macdonald and his government in Ottawa seemed preoccupied with other matters, such as the financial difficulties of the Canadian Pacific Railway project and the possibility of an Indian rising in the North-West. In defending his government's handling of the Métis problem, the Prime Minister admitted that many of the Métis in Manitoba had lost their lands, but maintained that some of their claims were "unreasonable".

... The causes of the rising are what I have expressed. The half-breeds have had a great many claims, some of them, as I have stated, reasonable enough, but some of them are not reasonable. The House knows that at the time the arrangement was made for the settlement of land titles in Manitoba, on the creation of that Province, a large number of Indians settled on the Assiniboine and Red River who had got places, localities, little properties, in possession under the direct sanction, though perhaps not by any other title, of the Hudson Bay Company. Those claims were recognized and a certain quantity of land was appropriated for their satisfaction. Land scrip was issued to those Indians to the value of their holdings. The half-breeds scattered over the plains had no such rights from the Hudson Bay Company or any one, but as they heard that the half-breeds had received certain moneys, or money's worth, within the Red River settlement, they claimed that they all had the same rights. Among those half-breeds that are at Prince Albert and along both banks of the Saskatchewan, there are a number who received their land scrip for their land on the Red River, who have left Manitoba and are on the plains beyond the bounds of Manitoba. They made their claims and they pressed them, thinking they would not be recognized again. They pressed their claims again; they said they were half-breeds, and they tried to enforce a double claim on their behalf. A great many of these have been identified and have been refused. As a whole the half-breeds have been told that if they desire to be considered as Indians there are most liberal reserves that they could go to with the others; but that if they desired to be considered white men they would get 160 acres of land as homesteads. But they are not satisfied with that; they want to get land scrip of equal quantity—I think upwards of 200 acres— and then get as a matter of course their homesteads as well. Then there was some difficulty about the plots on which these half-breeds had been settled along the Saskatchewan. No man has been disturbed in his settlement, and he has been told that he would not be disturbed.

Canada, *House of Commons Debates*, 26 March 1885.

The Religious Mission—Louis Riel's Vision of A "Métis Nation", 1885

When Riel returned to the North-West from Montana in July 1884, he fashioned himself Louis "David" Riel, a religious leader with a prophetic mission to lead "God's chosen people" to freedom. In the nine-month period between his return and the rebellion, he formed an *Exovedate*,[5] or provisional government, and exhorted his followers with prophetic visions of the Métis as a "sacerdotal people" who would one day see the papacy transferred to St. Boniface (Manitoba) and enter a glorious future. His notebook contained passages which suggest religious motivations may have contributed to the 1885 Métis uprising.

O my *Métis* Nation. You have long offended me with your horse races, with your wagers on the subject of your horse races, by your obstinacy, by your hateful contentions over the wrongs of your horse races. This is why said the Eternal Christ, that yesterday, while sparing you I killed your horses. The Eternal remembers the sinful attachment you have for your horses: that is why he greatly diminished their number yesterday. Another time, when I ask you the use of the horses I have lent you, you will not refuse me. O my *Métis* people! I punish you lightly. That which I ask of you, is obedience. The spirit of God said to me while speaking of the *Métis* Nation: 'I will end up becoming angry at her for she is too negligent; she is not sufficiently vigilant, obedient.'

O my God! Do not punish the *Métis* Nation. Because of Jesus, Mary, Joseph have mercy on her. See how she is charitable, how she is gentle and easy to lead. Consider favourable, O my God, the great works the *Métis* Nation performs for your greater

---

5. Riel's council in 1884–85 bore the peculiar name *Exovedate*, from the Latin words *ex* "from" and *ovile* "flock".

glory, for the honour of the religion, for the salvation of souls, for the good of society. The Diary of Louis Riel, March—May 1885, as translated in *The Nor'Wester*, July 15, 1970, Manitoba Centennial Publication, p. 54.

Neglect of the Métis Claims—A *Grip* Commentary, 1885

Many close observers of the North-West Rebellion blamed the Macdonald government for negligence and inefficiency in handling Métis claims. Even sworn enemies of Riel like prominent Ontario lawyer George T. Denison conceded that the "obstinacy" of the Interior Department in pursuing its land surveying plan caused great unease among the Métis. Such criticisms of the Macdonald government's neglect of Métis complaints were reflected in *Grip* cartoonist J.W. Bengough's proposal for a bizarre medal to commemorate the Rebellion.

DESIGN FOR THE MEDAL

The Motive of Personal Gain—Reports on Riel's attempts to obtain a Personal Indemnity—1884–1885

Louis Riel's attempts in the winter of 1884–85 to secure for himself a personal indemnity from the Canadian government are still shrouded in controversy. According to participants in the pre-Rebellion negotiations, Riel began to speak about getting money in early December 1884, and by January 1885, attempts to have his personal claims satisfied took priority over any other work on behalf of the Métis. Riel had spoken of his personal claims before, in the early 1870s, but what was new about these efforts was his apparent willingness to separate his own interests from those of the Métis and possibly to create a false impression in order to obtain money. Was Riel motivated by greed or merely attempting to acquire money with which to wage the Métis struggle?

Father [Alexis] André has just arrived from St. Laurent, and he has spoken with this unfortunate man [Riel], who, after having defended impractical theories and the most heterodox opinions for a long time, finally gave in and admitted to Father André that he was in an impasse, and that he wanted to get out of it at any price. He asked him to get in touch with Mr. [D.H.] McDowall, that the latter might try to get from the government a certain sum of money to permit him to leave the country, while making the public believe he was going as a delegate to the Federal government.

Louis Schmidt, "Notes: Mouvement des Métis à St. Laurent Sask. T.N.-O. en 1884", AASB, T 29794. Entry for 12 December 1884.

His claims amount to the modest sum of $100,000.00, but he will take $35,000.00 as originally offered [by Father Proulx in 1873], and I believe myself that $3,000.00 to $5,000.00 would cart the whole Riel family across the boundary. Riel made it most distinctly understood the 'self' was his main object, and he was willing to make the claim of his followers totally subservient to his own interests.... Riel's last statement was that he would not believe in any promise that might be made to him but that if money were sent for him he would carry out his part. He said, 'My name is Riel and I want material,' which I suppose was a pun. He wished the money principally as a provision for his wife and family in case of his death.

P.A.C., D.H. Macdowall to Edgar Dewdney, December 24, 1884. MG 26A, 42959–60.

... if he got the money he would go the United States and start a paper and raise the other nationalities in the States. He said that before the grass is that high in this country you will see foreign armies in this country. He said I [Riel] will commence by destroying Manitoba, and then I will come and destroy the North-West and take possession of the North-West.

Desmond Morton, ed., *The Queen v. Louis Riel* (Toronto: University of Toronto Press, 1974), Charles Nolin's Testimony (1885), p. 195.

The Result of Government Failures—Wilfrid Laurier's Observations, 1886

Critics of the Macdonald government offered a startlingly different view of the roots of conflict. In the House of Commons, Wilfrid Laurier, a Quebec Liberal whose political star was beginning to rise, blamed the Macdonald government for the unfortunate events at both Red River and in North Saskatchewan.

Sir, what is hateful—I use the word which the hon. gentleman made use of—what is hateful is not rebellion, but is the despotism which induces that rebellion; what is hateful are not rebels, but the men who, having the enjoyment of power, do not discharge the duties of power; they are the men who, having the power to redress wrongs, refuse to listen to the petitions that are sent to them; they are the men who, when they are asked for a loaf, give a stone.... Where would be the half-breeds to-day if it had not been for this rebellion? Would they have obtained the rights they now enjoy? I say, Sir, that the Canadian Government stands convicted of having yielded their rights only to rebellion, and not to the just representation of the half-breeds and of having actually forced them into insurrection.... Though, Mr. Speaker, these men were in the wrong; though the rebellion had to be put down; though it was the duty of the Canadian government to assert its authority and vindicate the law, still, I ask any friend of liberty, if there is not a feeling rising in his heart, stronger than all reasoning to the contrary, that these men were excusable?.... I am a British subject, and I value the proud title as much as anyone in this House. But if it is expected of me that I shall allow fellow countrymen unfriended, undefended, unprotected and unrepresented in this House, to be trampled under foot by this Government, I say that is not what I understand by loyalty, and I would call that slavery.

Canada, House of Commons Debates, March 16, 1886.

CONFLICTING INTERPRETATIONS

The "French-English Conflict—A Traditional Interpretation

There are numerous ways of approaching the Métis resistance. Some people still refer erroneously to the events of 1869 as a "rebellion", although the legitimacy of the Provisional Government, with whose representatives Ottawa negotiated, is well established constitutionally. The oldest, and it could be said, the traditional, interpretation is that the confrontations at Red River and later in the North-West Territories were extensions of the struggles and tensions felt in Canada between English and French, Orange Ontario and Catholic Quebec, the partisans of a bicultural nation and those committed to making it a "British" country. Even the French-Canadian nationalist historian abbé Lionel Groulx tended to see the events of 1869–70 and 1885 in traditional terms. Here is how Groulx summarized the once pervasive interpretation:

... at the hour of crisis the conduct of the government at Ottawa was indeed strange. Strange also was the poorly disguised disdain of certain ministers for the 'miserable Métis' of the North-West. And most strange of all was the body of politicians and administrators, composed almost entirely of those who spoke English, sent to the Red River region where the majority were French. It is impossible to avoid the impression that at the heart of this conflict there was a confrontation in the West, brought about by the equivocations of Ottawa, of divergent interpretations of the Canadian reality, on one side the natives, wanting to see in the future of Manitoba and all the Territories a loyal extension of the Canadian duality of culture and religion; and on the other side those, determined to build there an annex to Ontario. Deplorable events. And if they are related to what was happening at the same time in New Brunswick, where the first conflict over the school question was breaking out, are they not to be regarded as the tragedy at the cradle of Confederation?

Lionel Groulx, *Histoire du Canada français depuis la découverte* (Montréal: Action Nationale, 1952), Vol. 5, pp. 117–118. trans. C.J.J.

A Clash of Societies—G.F.G. Stanley's Frontier Interpretation

The traditional interpretation was a reflection of an ethnocentric view of Canadian history. In 1936, Professor George Stanley brought in the Métis component, but he played down the implications of such a perspective by also interpreting the events in the context of Frederick Jackson Turner's famous frontier thesis of American historical development. (For Turner the frontier was an advancing line of settlement where the dynamism was provided by the non-Natives, and the Native peoples were largely an encumbrance). The Red River and Saskatchewan disturbances were, for Stanley, the last-ditch attempts of the Native peoples to preserve their ancestral lands and their traditional cultures.

In essence the troubles associated with the name of Louis Riel were the manifestation, not of the traditional rivalries of French Catholic Quebec and English Protestant Ontario, but of the traditional problems of cultural conflict, of the clash between primitive and civilized peoples....

Louis Riel was not a great man; he was not even what Carlyle would call a near great. Nevertheless he became, in death, one of the decisive figures of our history. By historical accident rather than by design he became the symbol of divisions as old as the Franco-British struggle for the control of northern North America. It is this historical accident which has obscured the fundamental character of the two risings which bear Riel's name; for the Riel 'rebellions' were not what the politicians argued and what the people believed, a continuation on the banks of the Red and the Saskatchewan of the traditional hostilities of old Canada. [They were, instead, the typical, even inevitable results of the advance of the frontier, the last organized attempts on the part of Canada's primitive peoples to withstand what, for want of a better word, may be termed progress, and to preserve their culture and their identity against the encroachments of civilization.] To present-day Canadians Riel appears, no longer as the wilful 'rebel' or 'murderer' of Thomas Scott, but as a sad, pathetic, unstable man, who led his followers in a suicidal crusade and whose brief glory rests upon a distortion of history. To the métis, the people whom he loved, he will always be, mad or sane, the voice of an inarticulate race and the prophet of a doomed cause.

George F.G. Stanley, *Louis Riel: Patriot or Rebel?* (Ottawa: Canadian Historical Association, 1954), CHA booklet No. 2, pp. 3,24.

The "New Nation" Idea—A Corollary to the Stanley Thesis

Professor Stanley also established in our historiography the idea that the Métis had come to see themselves as a distinctive race, as a "New Nation". According to Stanley, what Riel and his followers had attempted to establish was the independence of that national group, perhaps as a sub-group at first of the French-Canadians. He wrote in 1972 that Riel's downfall was also the collapse of the New Nation concept.

...it was a Pyrrhic victory. The New Nation did not long survive the events of 1869–1870. Persecuted and discriminated against, many of those *métis* who had taken the most active part in the events of 1869–1870, sold their rights in the land grant in

Manitoba and fled to the valley of the Saskatchewan, where, for a few years, they were able to reconstruct the traditional *métis* society. But only until the immigrants caught up with them. An attempt to repeat what he had achieved in Manitoba, led to an armed conflict and military defeat in Saskatchewan, and Louis Riel was brought to a trial in Regina presided over by the ghost of the dead Thomas Scott.

Riel's execution in 1885 marked the death of the New Nation. Some *métis* succeeded in coming to terms with the times and moved... into the white man's society. These, the *métis* elite, French and Scottish, fused physically and mentally with the whites. In doing so they gained stability and ambition, but lost their separate national identity. Others, particularly those who remained in Manitoba after 1870, made a modest adaptation, and are now to be found living south and east of their spiritual centre at St. Boniface. These, of all the *métis* peoples in Western Canada, are the ones who retain most tenaciously a sense of history and a reverence for the memory of their national hero, the father of Manitoba, Louis Riel. Hanging about in the periphery of the white and Indian societies, are those poor lost souls, the *métis* who are unable to find any strength in their past or see any hope in their future.

The New Nation has ceased to exist, but its achievement remains for all Canadians to recognize, the Province of Manitoba.

G.F.G. Stanley, *Manitoba 1870—A Métis Achievement* (Winnipeg: University of Winnipeg Press, 1972), pp. 26–27.

The War for a "Strange Empire"—A Sympathetic View

More recent work in Native Studies in Canada would tend to question the characterization of the Métis as a primitive people attempting to preserve their particular culture. American writer Joseph Kinsey Howard as early as 1952 saw the Riel risings as part of a larger continental pattern of resistance to the invasion of America by Europeans.

Philippe Régis de Trobriand, one of the most brilliant of the many intellectuals who were drawn to the far Western frontier, noted in his journal in 1867, 'The destiny of the white race in America is to destroy the red race.' Yet the native cause was not quite so hopeless as our histories have led us to believe. There were times when Manifest Destiny slid off the trail and bogged down. There were times when the defenders, given a little more skill, could have wrested a better bargain from white civilization....

American and Canadian military commanders knew that their task of subjugating or destroying the primitive peoples of the West would be hopeless, at least for many years, if the native races should unite. This idea came to Sitting Bull—too late; it came still later to the leaders of another but related people in Canada. Had there been time for them to act upon it there might have been independent, semiprimitive tribal societies in North America such as still exist on other continents as near neighbors to modern states.

The native defenders of the West in this period were for the most part Sioux, Cree and Blackfeet Indians and their 'cousins,' the Métis or 'half-breeds.' Their 'empire' was the great mid-continent buffalo range now designated the Northern Great Plains; as the Indians doggedly retreated from it, the Métis and whites moved in. But the Métis inherited all of the Indians' problems while the whites gained strength and cunning. The Métis therefore were the worst sufferers, and this book concerns itself chiefly with their nation because their tragedy climaxed and epitomized the whole struggle of red man, or brown, against white.

When the Métis sought to achieve nationhood in the strange empire of the West, white men called it treason, the greatest of crimes....

...And 'backward' peoples, then as now, could be used as puppets in the power politics of dynamic 'civilized' states....

Those with whom this book deals clung to the old loyalties, defied science and the machine—and perished. Of course they were an illiterate people, primitive and unstable, not even white. And their spokesman and symbol, who believed the old values to be good, became thereby a traitor.

He died on the gallows and his nation with him—his nation, and the dream of a strange empire in the West.

Joseph Kinsey Howard, *Strange Empire, a Narrative of the Northwest* (New York: William Morrow & Co., 1952), pp. 14–17.

In Defense of a Civilized Community—W.L. Morton's Interpretation

William L. Morton rejected the idea that the Métis constituted a primitive society in 1869 and also rejected the applicability of the frontier thesis in the case of the Red River Resistance. He submitted that concepts of cultural corporateness and ethnicity were more useful approaches in gaining an understanding and appreciation of the events of 1869–70 and 1885.

[The] Resistance of the *métis* was an event of major significance at the time, and its consequences were momentous for the future. Involved in its course and outcome were the relations of half-breed and Indian with the white immigrant in the North-West, and the relations between French and English, their language and institutions, in one-third of Canada, and this affected also their political relations in Old Canada. Involved also was the question as to whether the North-West was to be Canadian or American; and within that was the more important question whether, in the face of a United States stretching from Alaska to Florida, old Canada would be able to maintain its independence. Red River was the key to the North-West, the North-West to the future of the new Dominion; and in October, 1869, Louis Riel and his followers seized and held that key to win for themselves and the people of the North-West guaranteed rights as civilized men. Their error was not so much that they risked rebellion, as that they used this great lever to exact what in due course would have been generously given.

If they used means disproportionate to their ends, however, the ends were neither ignoble nor mistaken. The half-breeds claimed as their birthright the civil and political rights of British subjects. This they were entitled to do, for they were civilized men, their leaders educated, the main body of the people simple and honest folk, intelligent, if illiterate. That the majority of the *métis* of Red River were hunters and freighters did not make them nomads. The long contest between nomadism and settlement was being ended on the whole in favour of the latter. The colony was their settled abode, and in the farther North-West were new Red River Settlements in the making. To describe Red River as a frontier is to use a term of such general application and of so little local relevance as to possess slight scientific value. By 1869 Red River had had a government, courts, churches and schools for nearly fifty years. It had become a civilized society, largely of mixed white and Indian blood, it is true, but civilized by every test except that of self-government; and that test in no forced sense of the word it could also meet.... The *métis*, one half of its people, were unique also in that they thought of themselves as a 'new nation', a 'peculiar people', as Riel termed it. Neither French nor Indian, but intermediate, they claimed to unite the civilization of their fathers' with the rights of their mothers' people in a new nationality of the North-West. The 'new nation' was a unique ethnic and political reality, sprung from the continental fur-trade; and it was not unaware both of its uniqueness and of its dependence on the old way of life, and also of its need to adapt itself to the changes which had been foreseen for at least a decade before 1869.

It is in this sense of nationhood of the *métis* that an understanding of the Resistance of 1869 is to be found. They sought guaranteed rights as a community of civilized people. The Canadian government was entirely ready to grant the normal rights of British subjects to all civilized individuals in the North-West, without respect to race. But it had no idea that it was dealing with a corporate entity, a 'nation' by sentiment and by their own claim.

It is in this conflict between the half-articulated demand for *corporate* rights by the *métis*, and the intention of the Canadian authorities to grant *individual* rights in due course, that the true character of the Resistance is to be found....

W.L. Morton, ed., *Alexander Begg's Red River Journal*, pp. 1–3.

The Disintegration Thesis—An Alternative View of Red River Society

More recent research has looked for other contexts. Frits Pannekoek, for example, seeks to explain the background of the Red River Resistance in terms of the social and political disintegration of local society before 1869. While his thesis, on the surface, may appear appropriate for the English-speaking community, it does not appear to fit well what is known about the francophone Métis community at Red River. The fact that there was a Saskatchewan Rebellion suggests also that the Métis did not find in Canada a satisfactory point of reference.

The 1840s were becoming, then, years of crisis, of disorientation, and disintegration for Red River. Those who knew the relatively more generous and prolific years of the early 1830s, must have despaired at the increasing unpleasantness of their world. For Red River the scapegoats were obvious: the Company and the Church. Red River did not realize that it was in the clutches of an inexorable dilemma which had no solution and for which no scapegoat could be found.

The Company, because of its economic, political, and social dominance, was an obvious target for dissatisfaction. It was the only employer, the only route by which sons of the first and second generation could acquire the position of respect and wealth held by their fathers. The Company seemed to hold the keys to the door that had shut forever on the golden decade of the 1830s. There seemed no alternative to smashing the Company, for by 1840 the only other legitimate and popular source of prosperity, the land, was closed by overcrowding. But a wholesale destruction of the Company's monopoly would not have brought back the closeness and the security offered by the extended family and close neighborhoods in the 1830s—it would offer only anarchy. In fact during the 1850s and 1860s the settlement edged closer and closer to total social and political disintegration.

The church was equally responsible for exacerbating the crisis. Both the Catholic and Protestant churches had taught the value of subservience, of hierarchy, and of family; and the Protestants the value of an agricultural existence. Throughout the 1830s the teachings of the clergy had struck a responsive chord, reinforcing as they did patterns taught by the fur trade and the European traditions of Red River. The church had, in fact, in a few years won an astounding following. By 1840, however, the goals of farm and family set by the church were no longer possible. The failure to achieve these goals must have served again and again to underline the desperateness of the situation. As important were the social pretensions of the clergy, and more important their support of the Company, which meant, too, that they were unable to empathize with the dilemma of the mixed-bloods.

By 1845, then, the second generation of mixed-bloods of the settlement were in a state of confusion. The major points of reference for nineteenth century society, the farm, the state (the Hudson's Bay Company), and the church were in disrepute. Red River would have to seek new reference points, a new identity. In the end they found it not in Red River or the fur trade, but rather in Canada.

Frits Pannekoek, "A Probe into the Demographic Structure of Nineteenth Century Red River", in Lewis H. Thomas, ed., *Essays on Western History* (Edmonton: University of Alberta Press, 1976), pp. 88-89.

The Roman Catholic Conspiracy Hypothesis

One of the most popular theories concerning the Red River Resistance stresses the role of the Catholic clergy. In 1920 Chester Martin affirmed that it was the Roman Catholic clergy who roused the Métis to resistance in 1869 and briefed them on the terms of union they should demand. In the Saskatchewan troubles, of course, the demands were very similar to those made in 1870 but this time the Catholic clergy was staunchly opposed to Riel and his Métis followers. The thesis of "a conspiracy among the Roman Catholic clergy" had been articulated in 1874 by a certain James Lynch who had spent nine months in Red River during the troubled period. It was a thesis taken up again by Professor Donald Creighton in 1967 who denied the intention of the Canadian politicians to extend the bilingual dualism of the United Canadas to Manitoba in 1870.

It will not be necessary to trace in detail the course of the Riel Insurrection, but the political difficulties at Red River undoubtedly arose from the French and Roman Catholic section of the community; and French obstruction to the Union in 1869-70 has undoubtedly left its mark upon the subsequent political history, not only of Manitoba, but of the whole Dominion.

The policy of building up a smaller Quebec upon the banks of the Red River had been patiently and successfully pursued for more than fifty years. The French *Métis*, the chief charge of a devoted clergy, had not lost the characteristics which [Alexander] Ross [the historian] had attributed to the preceding generation. They were 'generous, warm-hearted and brave, and left to themselves, quiet and orderly.' Living still largely by the buffalo hunt, their credulous good-nature and their very improvidence left them responsive to clerical control. They were correspondingly dependent upon their clerical guardians for knowledge and counsel.

...The English-speaking population of Assiniboia long remained in ignorance of the influences which resulted in provincial status under the Manitoba Act.

These influences were undoubtedly French and Roman Catholic in origin, and their cogency is very easily understood. Special terms of union, safeguarding by statute the official use of the French language, separate schools, control of lands by the local legislature, etc., were much more enduring guarantees of French claims than the most explicit declaration of policy....

Chester Martin, "The First 'New Province' of the Dominion", as cited in H. Bowsfield, ed., *Louis Riel: Rebel of the Western Frontier or Victim of Politics and Prejudice?* (Toronto: Copp Clark, 1969), pp. 10–11.

The Métis Struggle—A Quest for a Working Duality

W.L. Morton, on the contrary, saw demands for biligualism and dual confessional schools arising naturally out of the earlier Métis struggle with the London-based Company and fitting well into the pattern already established in eastern Canada.

The Red River Resistance had many causes, but the root of one was the same as that of the rising of 1849, to force recognition of the rights of the half-breed to participation in the trade and government of Red River. Because of the relatively backward conditions of the *métis*, or French half-breeds, and because of the background of their leaders, the two Riels, it became a struggle to obtain recognition of the rights of the French to equality in the government of Red River and the Northwest. Thus the issue raised by the entrance of the Northwest in Confederation was, on what terms should it enter, and what particular terms should the French have. Out of this issue came the Province of Manitoba with both French and English as official languages and with a dual and confessional school system. The same rights were entrusted to the Territories in 1875.

Thus the Northwest entered Confederation on the basis of duality and equality. That duality and equality rested on the realities of population. Had the equality of numbers been continued, how different Canada would be today. But few French came to Manitoba and the Northwest; many English Canadians, many British, some Europeans did. The balance of numbers tilted against the French.

W.L. Morton, "Manitoba's Historic Role", *Transactions of the Historical and Scientific Society of Manitoba*, Series III, No. 19 (1964), pp. 18-19.

A Refutation of the American Conspiracy Thesis

There have been suggestions that, apart from a clerical plot to create a "second Quebec" in the West to counterbalance the influence of Ontario in Confederation, it was the Americans who fomented the Red River troubles so that they might have the opportunity of annexing the Canadian West. Professor Morton has dealt with this hypothesis:

The question of American influence on the Resistance is an obscure and subtle subject. Riel himself was not anti-American in feeling, and seems to have had some admiration of American institutions. This probably was the general attitude of the *métis*. Many of them made freighting trips to St. Paul, and most had American relatives and friends at

Pembina, St. Joseph's, and St. Paul. On the other hand they had reservations with respect to union with the United States. One cause of this was the failure of the Pembina Indian Treaty of 1851; another was the refusal of the American Government to recognize half-breeds as a group intermediate between Indian and white; and perhaps the American school system was a third. But there was no hostility, and American influence upon the course of the Resistance had no deep-seated aversion to American institutions to overcome. Riel's statement to Donald A. Smith that he was for annexation 'only if the people wished it' meant that he did not expect them to do so, but would not oppose them if they did.

American attempts to influence Riel and his councillors—the distorted news concocted in Pembina; the visits of [Enos] Stutsman, Joseph Rolette, Jr., and Joseph Lemay to Fort Garry; the open hope of the Americans in Winnipeg for annexation; and finally, the frankly annexationist tone of the *New Nation*—were all obvious enough. It seems clear, however, that these factors did not inspire the Resistance or to any degree affect its course. The rising of the *métis* was spontaneous and autonomous, and the Americans simply attempted to use it for their own ends.... What these American activities did in fact produce was a readiness on the part of the Canadian Government to conciliate and finally to negotiate with the people of Red River. Riel presumably anticipated this result. He knew also that, if negotiations with Canada failed, then the alternative of annexation to the United States lay ready to hand. Riel, in short, could not quarrel with the Americans until he was sure of terms with Canada.

W.L. Morton, ed., *Alexander Begg's Red River Journal*, pp. 85–86.

The North-West Rebellion—A "Repeat Performance"

Some historians have argued that, in the case of the North-West rebellion, history may have repeated itself. In his work on Riel, George Stanley argued that in Saskatchewan the Métis once again took up arms simply because Ottawa seemed to have learned nothing from the 1869–70 experience. Following in the footsteps of Stanley, Mason Wade, a New England historian specializing in French Canadian history, offered this assessment of the second Métis resistance.

The North-West Rebellion of 1885 was largely a sequel and repetition of the Red River troubles of 1869–70, though in the second instance the rising was against unquestioned authority. The French and Scottish *Métis*, who made up most of the population west of the new province of Manitoba, began to petition Governor [David] Laird of the North-West Territories and Ottawa as early as 1874, for their semi-nomadic culture was threatened by the westward advance of agricultural civilization and the decline of the buffalo. An 1877 ordinance restricting the buffalo-hunting upon which *Métis* life was based was followed by the rapid disappearance of the beast from the Saskatchewan country, thanks to the ruthless slaughter of the migratory herds by American hunters seeking buffalo robes. As the telegraph and the Canadian Pacific Railway advanced across the plains, bringing settlers in their wake, the buffalo retreated southward over the frontier and the *Métis* were left in sad straits, prey to land speculators who often robbed them of their homes. Their chief grievances—the government's failure to meet their claims for land scrip and to supply aid in making the transition from semi-nomad to agricultural and commercial life—went unheard in an Ottawa which was preoccupied with vast land-grant schemes devised to lessen the heavy financial burden of railroad construction.

Once more Eastern expansionists were little concerned with the rights of Western pioneers; once more trouble arose out of the government's decision to survey lands after the American square section system, without regard for the Quebec-type river-strip holdings of the *Métis*. One of the North-West missionaries, Father Végreville of Saint-Louis-de-Langevin, made urgent representations to Ottawa in 1884 about the need to consider existing land divisions. Captain [E.G.] Deville, the Chief Inspector of Surveys, worked out a compromise between the chosen plan of survey and the *Métis* wishes, but this solution of the difficulty was buried, thanks to red tape in the Ministry of the Interior and to the unwillingness of English-speaking land agents in the West to take extra trouble to meet the wishes of the French-speaking pioneers of the country. With the language difficulty increasing the misunderstanding resulting from the inability of the largely uneducated *Métis* to grasp the complexities of surveying and land regulations drawn up in Ottawa by lawyers unacquainted with the country, new unrest developed.

Its growth was fostered by Ottawa's interminable delay in answering *Métis* petitions.

Mason Wade, *The French Canadians, 1760–1945* (Toronto: Macmillan, 1955), pp. 405–406.

The "Prophet of the New World"—Thomas Flanagan's Thesis

Professor Thomas Flanagan, a political scientist at the University of Calgary who is involved in the ongoing Riel Research Project, drew some interesting conclusions in 1979 about Riel's messianic, prophetic and millenarian religious views. This interpretation brings together the different strands of his political Utopianism, sense of religious mission and resistance strategy.

Riel's ideas were developed from Christian themes. His new religion was an exaggerated version of the ultramontanism that he had learned from the French-Canadian clergy. He was probably also inspired by Catholic prophetic literature on the margin of orthodoxy.... And he may have derived some secondary inspiration from contemporary Protestant millenarians in the United States.... In any case, all his important ideas have Christian rather than pagan sources.

But Riel's situation resembled those of typical native resistance movements. He created a religion which promised deliverance to a small people whose identity was threatened by the expansion of Western civilization. He could speak the traditional idiom of Catholic millenarianism rather than a more exotic blend of paganism and Christianity because the métis were already firmly Catholic....

To the extent that Riel's religion was a personal matter, it arose from the frustrations of his own life. To the extent that it was social, it stemmed from the métis perception that their existence as a people was in danger. The métis were threatened in several ways at once. Their traditional economy was destroyed by the disappearnce of the buffalo, the decline of the fur trade, and the introduction of new forms of transport superior to their cart trains and boat brigades. Their language and religion were jeopardized by massive English and Protestant immigration. Their ownership of the land was threatened.... There would have been no new religion without Riel: but without the malaise of the métis there would have been no one to listen to the prophet.

Thomas Flanagan, Louis "David" Riel: "Prophet of the New World" (Toronto: University of Toronto Press, 1979), pp. 180, 182, 183.

The Mythology of Louis Riel—A Critical Perspective

Professor Desmond Morton, specialist in Canadian military history, has offered some insights into the controversy over Louis Riel's trial and punishment. Moving beyond the military aspects, Morton has argued that our generation tends to judge Riel differently from Riel's own generation. In his introduction to a 1974 editon of *The Queen v. Louis Riel*, he ventured some answers based on the "community morality" and "stock of wisdom" existing at Regina in 1885.

That he was essentially guilty as charged not even his lawyers attempted to deny. That he was the author and inspiration of an armed uprising against the government was amply demonstrated by witnesses and documents. His own intermittent attempts to blame Dumont or to claim half-heartedness in his cause were neither consistent nor convincing. Assuming the authority of the Canadian state to protect itself (and at least one British petitioner for Riel's life was prepared to deny it), Riel had committed treason.

That Riel was insane enough to satisfy modern legal and medical criteria hardly now seems in question. That he was shamming, as the Crown had inferred during the trial, seemed impossible, even to Jukes, by November. That he was insane by the standards of his own day remains open to doubt.

The real dilemma had rested with the six jurors for their decision, in effect, was final. According to the correspondent for the Toronto *Mail*, three of them later explained their plea for mercy on the grounds that while Riel was 'not absolutely insane in the ordinary accepted meaning of the word, he is a very decided crank.' To be a crank, however, as even Dr. Clark must had admitted, was not to enjoy the protection of the McNaughten rules.

Finally, could Riel claim justification? That was the plea he would have made for himself if his counsel had permitted, and it was the burden of both his long addresses to the court. However, his lawyers did not reject the approach from perversity—as partisans it would have suited their purposes admirably—but because it is not a defence against the charge of high treason. No grievance of injustice could entitle a subject to take arms against his sovereign. At best it was a plea in mitigation of sentence.

As such, it might seem persuasive. Certainly it is the Riel version of government policy in the North-West which occupies the history books. A generation which faces the genuine dilemmas as well as the rhetoric of aboriginal rights and native claims should have more sympathy for the difficulties which confronted Macdonald and his colleagues. However, the problems of politicians and officials were not the concern of Indians, Métis, or westerners generally. They could not afford patience and they would not wait for insights. The rebellion brought answers and if, as native people might now argue, they proved to be wrong and even disastrous, they seemed at the time to be a vindication of Riel's actions. The Liberal press may have been right: the recommendation of mercy did condemn the government. Later, Edward Blake would read the House of Commons a letter from one of the jurors: 'had the Government done their duty and redressed the grievances of the half-breeds of Saskatchewan . . . there would never have been a second Riel Rebellion, and consequently no prisoner to try and condemn.'

Desmond Morton, ed., *The Queen v. Louis Riel* (Toronto: University of Toronto Press, 1974), pp. xxix-xxx.

Riel, The Métis and Ottawa—A Reconsidered Interpretation

After a closer examination of Riel's writings in 1884 and 1885, Thomas Flanagan began to question his own earlier view of the Métis leader and his movement. Two key passages from Flanagan's recent study, *Riel and the Rebellion of 1885 Reconsidered* (1983), signalled both a dramatic change in his position and the beginning of a new phase in the reinterpretation of Riel's role in the Métis resistance.

As I sifted the evidence, this [the conventional] view became less and less convincing to me, until I concluded that the opposite was closer to the truth: that the *Métis* grievances were at least partly of their own making; that the government was on the verge of resolving them when the Rebellion broke out; that Riel's resort to arms could not be explained by the failure of constitutional agitation; and that he received a surprisingly fair trial. When I came to these conclusions, I knew I had to publish them, especially because of the gathering movement to grant Riel a posthumous pardon in 1985, something which now strikes me as quite wrong . . . .

* * * * *

No easy moral judgments can be made about the North-West Rebellion. For its part, the government of Canada certainly deserves some censure. With respect to the river-lot issue much hard feeling could have been avoided if the whole settlement of St. Laurent had been surveyed at the outset according to the wishes of the *Métis*, or if a resurvey had been carried out as was ultimately done. Also, the government was wrong in procrastinating so long over the half-breed land grant in the North-West. . . .

These are severe criticisms, but they must be kept in proper perspective. They were mistakes in judgment, not part of a calculated campaign to destroy the *Métis* or deprive them of their rights. Under political pressure, the government did implement a land grant and did adjust the river-lot claims. Government is never perfect; it is difficult to ask more of a system than that it be capable of correcting mistakes in a reasonable period of time. I believe the Canadian government's performance in these matters passed that test.

Judgments about Louis Riel are also necessarily complex. No one will deny that he was the greatest leader the *Métis* have produced and that he made the advancement of his people the overriding purpose of his life. But it is clear that he had little real concern for the issues of river lots and the land grant which had goaded the *Métis* of St. Laurent into seeking his help. For him, these were only stepping stones to his vast scheme of a new settlement of aboriginal claims. To that extent, he might be accused of using his followers as pawns in his own game. It is also beyond dispute that Riel was pursuing a private strategy of getting money from the government and that this sometimes took precedence over his efforts on behalf of the *Métis*.

As regards the aftermath of the Rebellion, the evidence shows that Riel's trial was as procedurally fair as was obtainable within the limitations of the Territorial courts. There was a rational argument for the cabinet to commute the death sentence to a lesser penalty; but this was a matter of discretion, not of right, and there were also strong arguments for letting the sentence be carried out. The only way in which the government acted improperly was in its manipulation of the medical commission[6]— admittedly a shameful episode.

Thomas Flanagan, *Riel and the Rebellion 1885 Reconsidered* (Saskatoon: Western Producer Prairie Books, 1983), pp. viii and 146–147.

A Guide to Further Reading

1. Overviews

Bowsfield, Hartwell, ed., *Louis Riel: Rebel of the Western Frontier or Victim of Politics and Prejudice?* Toronto: Copp Clark, 1969.
_____ , *Louis Riel: The Rebel and the Hero*. Toronto: Oxford University Press, 1971.
Davidson, W.M., *The Life and Times of Louis Riel*. Calgary: Albertan Printers, 1952.
Flanagan, Thomas, ed., *The Diaries of Louis Riel*. Edmonton: Hurtig, 1979.
_____ , *Louis 'David' Riel: Prophet of the New World*. Toronto: University of Toronto Press, 1979.
_____ , *Riel and the Rebellion 1885 Reconsidered*. Saskatoon: Western Producer Prairie Books, 1983.
Groulx, Lionel, *Histoire du Canada français depuis la découverte*, Vol. V. Montreal: Action Nationale, 1952.
Hill, Douglas, *The Opening of the Canadian West*. Don Mills: Longmans, 1967.
Howard, Joseph Kinsey, *Strange Empire: A Narrative of the Northwest*. Toronto: James Lorimer, 1974.
Lamb, R.E., *Thunder in the North: Conflict over the Riel Risings of 1870 ... 1885*. New York: Pageant Press, 1957.
Owram, Douglas, "The Myth of Louis Riel", *Canadian Historical Review*, Vol. LXIII (September, 1982), pp. 315–336.
Rumilly, Robert, Histoire de la Province de Québec, Vol. 5: Riel. Montreal: Editions Bernard Valiquette, 1942.
Ryerson, Stanley B., "Riel vs. Anglo-Canadian Imperialism", *Canadian Dimension*. Vol. VII (July, 1970).
Silver, Arthur, "French Quebec and the Métis Question, 1869–1885" in Carl Berger and Ramsay Cook, eds., *The West and the Nation*. Toronto: McClelland and Stewart, 1976.
Stanley, George F.G., *The Birth of Western Canada: A History of the Riel Rebellions*. London: Longmans Green, 1936.
_____ , *Louis Riel*. Toronto: Ryerson Press, 1963.
Trémaudan, Auguste Henri de, *Histoire de la Nation Métisse dans l'Ouest Canadien*. Montreal: Editions Albert Lévesque, 1935.
Wade, Mason, *The French Canadians 1760-1945*. Toronto: Macmillan, 1955.

2. Specialized Studies

Memoirs and Journals

Begg, Alexander, *The Creation of Manitoba: A History of the Red River Troubles*. Toronto:

---

6. A comment on the medical commission headed by Dr. Michael Lavell, Warden of the Kingston Penitentiary, and Dr. F.X. Valade of Ottawa, which was appointed by the Macdonald Government to investigate Riel's sanity before he was hanged.

A.H. Hovey, 1871.

Boulton, Charles A., *Reminiscences of the North West Rebellions*. Toronto: Grip Printing & Publishing, 1886.

Riel, Louis, *L'Amnistie*. Montreal: Le Nouveau Monde, 1874.

Métis Histories

Alberta Federation of Métis Settlement Associations, *The Métis People of Canada: A History*. Toronto: Gage, 1978.

Brown, Jennifer. *Strangers in Blood: Fur Trade Company Families in Indian Country*. Vancouver: University of British Columbia Press, 1980.

Foster, John. "The Metis. The People and the Term", *Prairie Forum*. Vol. 3 (1978), pp. 79–90.

Lusty, Terry, *Louis Riel: Humanitarian*. Edmonton: 1975.

Pelletier, Emile. *A Social History of the Manitoba Métis*. Winnipeg: Manitoba Métis Federation Press, 1977.

Peterson, Jacqueline. "Prelude to Red River: A Social Portrait of the Great Lakes Métis", *Ethnohistory*. Vol. 25 (1978), pp. 41–67.

Redbird, Duke, *We Are Métis*. Toronto: Ontario Métis and Non-Status Indian Association, 1980.

Sealey, D. Bruce, *Statutory Land Rights of the Manitoba Métis*. Winnipeg: Manitoba Métis Federation Press, 1975.

———, and Antoine S. Lussier, *The Métis: Canada's Forgotten People*. Winnipeg: Manitoba Métis Federation Press, 1965.

Trémaudan, Auguste-Henri de, *Hold High Your Heads—History of the Métis Nation in Western Canada*. Winnipeg: Pemmican Press, 1982.

Van Kirk, Sylvia. *"Many Tender Ties": Women in Fur Trade Society in Western Canada, 1670–1870*. Winnipeg: Watson & Dwyer, 1980.

The Manitoba Resistance

Morton, William L., ed., *Alexander Begg's Red River Journal and Other Papers Relative to the Red River Resistance of 1869–1870*. Toronto: The Champlain Society, 1960.

———, ed., *Manitoba: The Birth of A Province*. Altona: D.W. Friesen & Sons, 1965.

Pannekoek, Frits, "A Probe into the Demographic Structure of Nineteenth- Century Red River", in L.H. Thomas, ed., *Essays in Western History*. Edmonton: University of Alberta Press, 1976.

The North-West Rebellion

Anderson, Frank W., *The Riel Rebellion, 1885*. Calgary: Frontier Publishing, 1965.

Morton, Desmond, *The Last War Drum*. Toronto: Hakkert, 1972.

———, and Reginald A. Roy, eds., *Telegrams of the North-West Campaign, 1885*. Toronto: Champlain Society, 1972.

Spry, Irene M., "The Tragedy of the Loss of the Commons in Western Canada", in Ian A.L. Getty and Antoine S. Lussier, eds., *As Long as the Sun Shines and Water Flows*. Vancouver: University of British Columbia Press, 1983.

Woodcock, George, *Gabriel Dumont: The Métis Chief and His Lost World*. Edmonton: Hurtig, 1975.

The Trial and Execution of Riel

Beal, Bob and Rod Macleod, *Prairie Fire: The 1885 North-West Rebellion*. Edmonton: Hurtig, 1984.

Morton, Desmond, ed., *The Queen versus Louis Riel*. Toronto: University of Toronto Press, 1974.

Osler, E.B., *The Man Who Had to Hang—Louis Riel*. Toronto: Longmans Green, 1961.

12

NATIONALISM, CONTINENTALISM AND IMPERIALISM, 1878–1896

Where Did Canada's Destiny Lie?

The 1880s and early 1890s were times of trial for the young Dominion. Canada had expanded from four to seven provinces with the entry of Manitoba, British Columbia and Prince Edward Island. John A. Macdonald's national policies seemed to hold out the promise of industrial development, a transcontinental railway and eventual Western settlement. But there were signs of doubt and uncertainty. Canada seemed to be at a crossroads. Public debates of these years revolved around three distinct possibilities for Canada's future—nationalism, continentalism and imperialism. These options raised questions of critical importance—questions which challenged Canadians' faith in the national experiment of Confederation, in their own views of each other, and, among some groups, in the very structure and destiny of the nation.

During the three decades after 1867 the initial promise of Confederation still seemed largely unfulfilled. The National Policy,[1] formally adopted by Macdonald in the 1878 election, had established a system of tariff protection for Canada's infant industries, but the tariff policy generated little lasting prosperity and provided little relief from the continuing problem of large-scale emigration to the United States. Regional interests and discontent found expression in thriving "provincial rights" movements, most notably in Ontario, Nova Scotia and Quebec. Tensions between French- and English-speaking Canadians were aggravated by crises over the execution of Louis Riel, by the passage in 1888 of Quebec's Jesuit Estates Act, and by conflicts

---

1. Following the original convention, the "National Policy" refers to the protective tariff policy introduced by John A. Macdonald's government in 1879, while the term "national policy" applies to the three-pronged set of Canadian nation-building policies.

over the future of Manitoba separate schools. Underlying the political difficulties and crises of the period, and affecting most of them, was a world-wide economic depression which began in the early 1870s and, except for a few small spurts of prosperity, gripped the country until the latter half of the 1890s.

In view of these problems, three major political and economic alternatives presented themselves to Canadians. While each alternative assumed a variety of different forms, they were, in broadest terms: political and economic nationalism, continentalism, or closer ties with the United States, and British Canadian imperialism. Each prescription for the nation had its own leading proponents, its preferred policies, and its idealized vision of Canada's destiny. For many Canadians—and for most of Canada's leading thinkers and public figures—the fundamental "Canadian question" lay in determining which held out the brightest hope for Canada's future.

Late-nineteenth-century Canadian nationalism was most clearly symbolized and embodied in Sir John A. Macdonald's policies for national development. In governing the Dominion from 1878 to 1891, Macdonald developed a series of nation-building policies—the protective tariff, a transcontinental railway, and the settlement of the West—calculated to unify the nation economically and to transform it into a self-reliant kingdom within the Empire. Macdonald's policies of nationalism were inspired by many sources. Confederation had opened up the possibility of creating what its founders called a "new nationality" out of Canada's diverse regions, groups and communities. Some of Macdonald's ideas bore strong resemblance to those proposed by the "Canada First" movement, a political association formed in the early 1870s by a small group of Toronto's foremost public figures to promote Canadian national pride and work for greater political independence. As a skilful and experienced politician, he was, of course, keenly aware of the political and economic considerations. But whatever Macdonald's motivations, the program was essentially nationalist in appeal. Its public aims were to create a "Canada for Canadians", expressing a basic impulse for national survival on the North American continent and giving form and substance to the fragile political entity forged at the time of Confederation.

For a significant number of Canadians, continentalism in its various political and economic forms seemed to offer a viable arrangement for Canada's future. By the 1880s Canada faced such severe political and economic difficulties that many were predicting the nation's collapse. Out of the general feeling of despondency arose several contentious proposals for closer relations with the United States. Reciprocity in trade, commercial union, and even annexation were proposed by prominent Canadian intellectuals, politicians and businessmen as solutions to the dilemma of the 1880s. The idea of free trade with the United States gained popularity as an economic panacea which would provide Canadian producers with freer access to the huge American market and effectively reduce the cost of U.S. imported goods for Canadian consumers. A commercial union movement, led by Goldwin Smith, a professor and free trade advocate, and Erastus Wiman, a wealthy

Canadian-born Wall Street financier, surfaced in Canada to actively promote and lobby for the "C.U." idea. The opposition Liberal party, led first by Edward Blake, and after 1887 by Wilfrid Laurier, pronounced Macdonald's National Policy a failure and committed itself to a policy of freer trade with the United States. Popular support for lower tariffs and freer trade was so strong that the Liberal continued to advocate unrestricted reciprocity or "U.R." until shortly after the triumph of Macdonald and his National Policy in the 1891 federal election.

As a response to the challenge of continentalism, imperialism—and particularly schemes of closer imperial unity—also held strong appeal in the late 1880s and early 1890s. Supporters of imperial unity believed fervently that Canada could be strengthened as a nation by maintaining the connection with the Empire and by acquiring a greater influence within its councils. Like continentalism, Canadian imperialist sentiment arose out of the widespread mood of pessimism about Canada's destiny at that time. But the catalyst for its emergence was the Liberal party's adoption in 1887 of a policy of unrestricted reciprocity with the United States. To Canadian imperialists, this decision realized their worst fears, committing the Liberal party to a policy they identified, rightly or wrongly, with continentalism and Canada's eventual political extinction. At this point—in 1887 and 1888—the Imperial Federation League, an imperialist organization founded in England in 1884, began to set up branches in Canada which quickly became active centres of British imperial loyalty. As an alternative to reciprocity, leading spokesmen for imperial unity, like Colonel G.T. Denison, George R. Parkin, and George M. Grant, advocated an economic union of the Empire to be secured through preferential tariffs.

Supporters of imperial unity played a central role in the late-nineteenth-century clash of ideas about Canada's destiny. While the Canadian imperialist movement attracted much support in parts of English-speaking Canada, it met with hostility and indifference from many French Canadians. Prominent French Canadian leaders, most notably Quebec Premier Honoré Mercier, saw little appeal in British imperial federation, but it was not until the Boer War (1898–1902) that anti-imperialism emerged and grew in intensity as an organized force in French Canada. Nevertheless, Canadian imperialists claimed some successes. In the 1891 election, supporters of imperial unity campaigned fiercely against the threat of commercial union, contributing to the narrow victory of Macdonald's National Policy. Later, in 1897, the tariff introduced by the new Liberal government of Wilfrid Laurier set a preferential tariff on British manufactured goods, further testifying to the influence of imperialist ideas.

The late nineteenth century saw Canada in a state of turbulence and almost continuous crisis. Confederation seemed to have established a workable federal system, but the nationalism of Macdonald's national policies was now being called into question. Canada's relationship with Britain and the Empire had become a focus for public debates among English Canadian imperialists, advocates of Dominion autonomy, and French Canadian nationalists. The economic concerns of Canadians in a time of depression simply added fuel to the raging fires of controversy between nationalists and continentalists, between protectionists and free traders, and between imperialists and nationalists.

In exploring nationalism, imperialism and continentalism in the 1880s and early 1890s, this problem study focuses on the great debates of the time over Canada's future. What conception of nationalism was embodied in John A. Macdonald's national policies? Did Macdonald's nation-building program help to bridge—or to widen further—the deep fissures in the foundation of Canadian Confederation? What relationship should Canada seek with Britain and the Empire? Should Canada continue the national experiment of Confederation or seek continental union with the United States? Would closer imperial unity strengthen Canada by giving her greater influence over British imperial policy, or restrain the development of the Dominion's self-government? In short, where did the most fruitful prospect for Canada's destiny lie?

SELECTED CONTEMPORARY SOURCES

NATIONALISM—EXPRESSIONS OF FAITH IN CANADIAN CONFEDERATION

The Introduction of the National Policy—John A. Macdonald's Conception of Nationalism, 1878

The "National Policy" of John A. Macdonald, a policy of tariff protection, was to some, a reflection, to others, a symbol of late-nineteenth-century Canadian nationalism. The idea of establishing a "National Policy" tariff, like the idea of Confederation, was one which John A. Macdonald found in political debates during the Conservative party's time in opposition before 1878, and adopting it as his own, made popular. Macdonald seems to have recognized the appeal of tariff protection for Canadian nationalists, and his speech introducing the National Policy tariff illustrated the essential bases of a dominant form of late-nineteenth-century nationalism. Although Macdonald may have advocated a protective tariff for reasons other than nation-building, it was presented in 1878 as a "National Policy" intended to benefit manufacturers, labourers and farmers alike.

> I move: 'That... this House is of the opinion that the welfare of Canada requires the adoption of a National Policy, which, by a judicious readjustment of the Tariff, will benefit and foster the agricultural, the mining, the manufacturing and other interests of the Dominion; that such a policy will retain in Canada thousands of our fellow countrymen now obliged to expatriate themselves in search of the employment denied them at home, will restore prosperity to our struggling industries, now sadly depressed, will prevent Canada from being made a sacrifice market, will encourage and develop an active interprovincial trade, and moving (as it ought to do) in the direction of a

reciprocity of tariffs with our neighbours, so far as the varied interests of Canada may demand, will greatly tend to procure for this country, eventually, a reciprocity of trade.'... We have no manufacturers here. We have no work-people; our work-people have gone off to the United States. They are to be found employed in the Western States, in Pittsburg, [sic] and, in fact, in every place where manufactures are going on. These Canadian artisans are adding to the strength, to the power, and to the wealth of a foreign nation instead of adding to ours. Our work-people in this country, on the other hand, are suffering for want of employment.

Have not their cries risen to Heaven? Has not the Hon. Premier been surrounded and besieged, even in his own Department, and on his way to his daily duties, by suffering artisans who keep crying out: 'We are not beggars, we only want an opportunity of helping to support ourselves and our families'?

...if Canada had had a judicious system of taxation [a protective tariff] they would be toiling and doing well in their own country....

...As John Stuart Mill said in the celebrated passage so often quoted: the very fact that a nation commenced a particular industry first gives them a control over that industry. By getting the start in this way, capital is generated and a system of manufacture is formed which will prevent any rivals from successfully competing with them. So long as we have a Free-trade system, we can only have substantially one description of industry, and that is—agriculture. Agriculture must be, and will be, in our time, at all events, and for many ages, the backbone of the Dominion of Canada. It will be a chief, a paramount interest. That interest claims and requires in this country, as in the United States, a home market. But no nation has arisen which had only agriculture as its industry. There must be a mixture of industries to bring out the national mind and the national strength and to form a national character....

House of Commons *Debates*, March 7, 1878.

The Building of the CPR—Sir Charles Tupper's View, 1880

For many Canadians, the construction of a transcontinental railway in the 1880s seemed to epitomize Macdonald's approach to nation-building. The building of a railway to the Pacific was part of the 1874 "bargain" which brought British Columbia into Confederation. If the Northwest was to be settled, a Pacific railway seemed essential. In addition, a Canadian Pacific Railway held out the promise of binding the nation together with rails of steel.

Although most Canadians saw the ultimate need for a Pacific railway, many disagreed over the proper approach to national expansion. Critics of the scheme focused on the lucrative contract and the railway monopoly granted to the private syndicate (The Canadian Pacific Railway Company) by the Macdonald government. Opponents of the CPR project, like Liberal leader Edward Blake, objected to the terms of the contract which turned the project over completely to private interest and granted millions of acres of land, without taxation, to the company in the North-West.

In the debate on the CPR contract, Macdonald's Conservatives argued that building the CPR was a great national enterprise. Sir Charles Tupper, for example, appealed to national sentiment when he introduced the CPR bill in Parliament in April 1880.

...No person can look abroad over the Dominion without feeling that the Great North-West Territory is the district to which we must look for our strength and development. Just as the older of the United States look to their Great North-West, with its rapidly increasing population... not only may we look for strength by reason of an additional Customs Revenue from the increased population of that Territory, but we must look upon that western country as a field for the manufacturing industries of the older and more settled parts of Canada.... we must look forward not only to building up thriving centres of industries and enterprises all over this portion of the country, but to obtaining a market for these industries after they have been established; and I say where is there a greater market than that magnificent granary of the North-West, which, filled up with a thriving and prosperous population, will make its demands upon Ontario, Quebec, Nova Scotia and New Brunswick for those manufacturing products that we, for many years, will be so well able to supply? ... At this moment the eyes of a large portion of the civilized world are centred upon the Great North-West of Canada, and hundreds of thousands of people in every foreign country, as well as the British Empire, are studying the question as to whether they shall come with their capital and industry and build up Canada into a great, prosperous and progressive country.... let us, on the great national question of the Canadian Pacific Railway, unite as a band of brothers... to do all that men can do to strengthen the hands of those who are engaged in a great national enterprise, upon the success of which the rapid progress and prosperity of our common country depends.

House of Commons *Debates*, April 15, 1880, pp. 1424–25.

Nation-Building or "Centralization"?—A Provincial View of Canada's Destiny, 1882

John A. Macdonald's approach to nation-building rested on maintaining a strong central authority, and regularly ran afoul of the provinces in the late 1880s and early 1890s. While Macdonald had accepted the idea of a "federal union" in 1867 and yielded on occasion to provincial demands for better financial terms within Confederation, he generally sought to preserve the power of the national government and resisted, where possible, attempts to expand provincial powers. In the 1880s this conception of a centralized federal system was directly challenged by a rising "provincial rights" movement. Provincial leaders in the 1880s held a view of Canada's destiny different from that of Macdonald's government. In the case of Ontario, the Dominion government's repeated disallowance of Ontario Rivers and Streams Acts and interference in a Manitoba-Ontario boundary dispute led Premier Oliver Mowat to publicly reject the concept of a centralized federal system.

Why is it that our rights in that territory are so persistently withheld from us? I would like to know some reason, some real reason.... What is the meaning of the Dominion Government? Is it to make Ontario the smallest of the great Provinces?... Does not the Dominion owe the greater part of its prestige to Ontario? (applause) Is not Ontario the great taxpayer—the Province that puts more money into the Treasury than she takes out of it? (applause) Why the difficulty, the obstacle that stands in the way?... I cannot account for it except that there is a little hostility somewhere against this Province as a Province.... There is hostility somewhere, and those who ought to stand up for

Ontario are not doing so. . . . Well, it is for the people of Ontario to say whether they will yield or not. . . . If they have been asleep, I venture to say that they are aroused now—(applause)—and that they will be asleep no more, and that they will not rest until every mile of awarded territory is surrendered to us—(Renewed cheering)—and our constitutional freedom and our Provincial rights are both respected and secured for ever. (Loud and long-continued cheering)

> Report of Proceedings in the Ontario Legislature, January 26, 1882, from *The Globe*, January 27, 1882.

CONTINENTALISM—PROPOSALS FOR CLOSER UNION WITH THE UNITED STATES

As the severe economic problems facing Canada dragged on into the late 1880s, the debate on economic policy dominated much of public discussion. For the first time prominent Canadians began to question whether Confederation was worth preserving. Some Canadians like Goldwin Smith and Erastus Wiman proposed commercial union with the United States; others in the opposition Liberal party, like Sir Richard Cartwright, favoured what amounted to unrestricted reciprocity. This economic debate focused attention on Canada's present state and the viability of proposals for closer continental relations.

Goldwin Smith and the Challenge of Continentalism, 1891

The disappointments of the 1880s led many Canadians to seek salvation in the idea of commercial union. Goldwin Smith was an English-born liberal who had taught history at Oxford and Cornell universities and had settled in Toronto in 1871. As a prominent and influential Canadian journalist, he first espoused the nationalism of the Canada First movement; then, having witnessed the fading of national hopes in the 1880s, he concluded that the only solution to Canada's problems was continental union. Smith's book *Canada and the Canadian Question* (1891), offered a cogent critique of the Canadian experiment and a classic case for North American continentalism.

> Whoever wishes to know what Canada is, and to understand the Canadian question, should begin by turning from the political to the natural map. The political map displays a vast and unbroken area of territory, extending from the boundary of the United States up to the North Pole, and equalling or surpassing the United States in magnitude. The physical map displays four separate projections of the cultivable and habitable part of the Continent into arctic waste. The four vary greatly in size, and one of them is very large. They are, beginning from the east, the Maritime Provinces—Nova Scotia, New Brunswick, and Prince Edward Island; Old Canada, comprising the present Provinces of Quebec and Ontario; the newly-opened region of the North-West, comprising the Province of Manitoba and the districts of Alberta, Athabasca, Assiniboia, and Saskatchewan; and British Columbia. The habitable and cultivable parts of these blocks of territory are not contiguous, but are divided from each other by great barriers of nature, wide and irreclaimable wildernesses or manifold chains of mountains.
>
> . . . Between the divisions of the Dominion there is hardly any natural trade, and but little even of forced trade has been called into existence under a stringent system of

protection. . . . Between the two provinces of Old Canada, though there is no physical barrier, there is an ethnological barrier of the strongest kind, one being British, the other thoroughly French, while the antagonism of race is intensified by that of religion. Such is the real Canada. Whether the four blocks of territory constituting the Dominion can for ever be kept by political agencies united among themselves and separate from their Continent, of which geographically, economically, and with the exception of Quebec ethnologically, they are parts, is the Canadian question. . . .

. . . The two sections of the English-speaking race on the American continent . . . are in a state of economic, intellectual, and social fusion, daily becoming more complete. Saving the special connection of a limited circle with the Old Country, Ontario is an American State of the Northern type, cut off from its sisters by a customs line, under a separate government and flag. . . .

To force trade into activity between the Provinces and turn it away from the United States, giving the Canadian farmer a home market, and consolidating Canadian nationality at the same time, were the ostensible objects of the adoption in 1879 of a Protective tariff. The real object perhaps was at least as much to capture the manufacturer's vote and his contributions to the election fund of the party in power. . . .

In the want of a real bond among the members of Confederation, the anti-national attitude of Quebec, the absence of real Dominion parties, and the consequent difficulty of holding the Dominion together and finding a basis for the administration must be found the excuse, if any excuse can be found, for the system of political corruption which during the last twenty years has prevailed. . . .

Annexation is an ugly word; it seems to convey the idea of force or pressure applied to the smaller State, not of free, equal, and honourable union, like that between England and Scotland. Yet there is no reason why the union of the two sections of the English-speaking people on this Continent should not be as free, as equal, and as honourable as the union of England and Scotland. We should rather say their reunion than their union, for before their unhappy schism they were one people. Nothing but the historical accident of a civil war ending in secession, instead of amnesty, has made them two. . . .

That a union of Canada with the American Commonwealth, like that into which Scotland entered with England, would in itself be attended with great advantages cannot be questioned, whatever may be the considerations on the other side or the reasons for delay. It would give to the inhabitants of the whole Continent as complete a security for peace and immunity from war taxation as is likely to be attained by any community or group of communities on this side of the Millenium. Canadians almost with one voice say that it would greatly raise the value of property in Canada; in other words, that it would bring with it a great increase of prosperity. . . .

Goldwin Smith, *Canada and the Canadian Question* (Toronto: Hunter, Rose & Co., 1891), pp. 1–3, 207–224, 267–70, 279–80. Selected excerpts.

Questioning Commercial Union—Edward Blake's West Durham Letter, 1891

Seeing the strength of continentalist sentiment, and seeking a way to revive its political fortunes, the Liberal party embraced the idea of commercial union by adopting a trade policy of unrestricted reciprocity with the United States in 1887. Although the new Liberal leader, Wilfrid Laurier, personally favoured lower tariffs, the strong influence of Sir Richard Cartwright's free trade views were reflected in the party's official platform. From 1887 to 1891 unrestricted reciprocity formed the basis of Liberal trade policy.

Shortly before the 1891 federal election, however, the former Liberal leader, Edward Blake, openly questioned the party's flirtation with commercial union. Returning to the House in 1890 after an illness, and angered partly by his loss of influence in the party, Blake penned his famous West Durham letter attacking the Liberal policy of unrestricted reciprocity. While Laurier eventually persuaded Blake not to publish the letter until after the 1891 election, the episode reflected deep divisions within Liberal ranks over the right approach to Canada's economic future. By 1893 the policy of "U.R." had been dropped from the Liberal party platform.

(7) In our present political condition a moderate revenue tariff approximating to free trade with all the world and coupled with liberal provisions for reciprocal free trade with the States, would be, if practicable, our best arrangement. . . .

On the other side it seems to be the settled policy of the States to decline a limited reciprocity.

So that what would be best is not now attainable. . . .

* * * * *

(21) The tendency, in Canada, of unrestricted free trade with the States, high duties being maintained against the United Kingdom, would be towards political union; and the more successful the plan the stronger the tendency, both by reason of the community of interests, the intermingling of population, the more intimate business and social connections, and the trade and fiscal relations, amounting to dependency, which it would create with the States, and of the greater isolation and divergency from Britain which this would produce. . . .

* * * * *

(27) . . . whether we like or dislike, believe or disbelieve in political union, must we not agree that the subject is one of great moment, towards the practical settlement of which we should take no serious step without reflection, or in ignorance of what we are doing?

Assuming that absolute free trade with the States, best described as commercial union, may and ought to come only as an incident, or at any rate as a well-understood precursor of political union, for which, indeed, we should be able to make better terms before than after the surrender of our commercial independence.

Then so believing—believing that the decision of the trade question involves that of the constitutional issue, for which you are unprepared and with which you do not even conceive yourselves to be dealing—how can I properly recommend you not to decide on commercial union?

The Toronto *Globe*, March 6, 1891.

IMPERIALISM—PROPOSALS FOR CLOSER IMPERIAL UNITY

Imperialism arose in Canada—and revived in Britain—at a time when, in the world, the primacy of the British empire was being challenged by the rise of imperial Germany and a changing balance of power in Europe. Although the movement drew upon the traditional loyalties of Canadians to the "British connection", its ideas and beliefs were, to some extent, home grown in British North America. In late-nineteenth-century Canada imperial unity meant closer union of the British Empire through greater economic (and later, military) cooperation and through political changes which would give the Dominion influence over imperial policy. And for many imperialists, supporting imperial unity was one of the ways of expressing their "Canadian nationality".

The Imperial Federation Scheme—George R. Parkin's Case for Imperial Reorganization, 1888

By the late 1880s British imperialism was on the rise and, in Canada, a scheme of imperial federation seemed to be gaining credence. Such a scheme was actively promoted by the British imperialist Joseph Chamberlain during visits to Canada in 1887 and 1888. It called for the binding together of the Empire in one great economic, cultural and military federation. One prominent Canadian imperialist who took up the case for imperial federation was George R. Parkin, a New Brunswick-born teacher and writer. Parkin's views are summarized in this passage from an 1888 article.

Within a short time a remarkable change has come over public opinion in the British Isles themselves. Twenty years ago it almost seemed as if Great Britain was ready voluntarily to throw away her vast colonial empire. A whole school of politicians favored the idea, and seemed to have gained the public ear. 'The Times,' supposed to reflect public opinion, claimed that England was paying too high a price for enjoying the luxury of colonial loyalty, and warned the colonies to prepare for the separation that was inevitable....

All this has now been changed. John Bright in England and Goldwin Smith in Canada still harp on the old string, but get no response from the popular heart, nor even from political parties. Great Britain has found that she still has to fight for her own hand, commercially and politically, and cannot afford to despise her natural allies. The vigor of colonial life, the expansion of colonial trade and power, the greatness of the part which the colonies are manifestly destined to take in affairs, have impressed even the slow British imagination. The integrity of the empire is fast becoming an essential article in the creed of all political parties....

* * * * *

... Mr. Goldwin Smith still argues that trade interests will ultimately draw Canada into political connection with the United States, and apparently does not understand why his opinion is rejected with indignation by the vast majority of Canadians. Yet it seems impossible to conceive how, without a debasement of public sentiment quite unparalleled in history, a people whose history began in loyalty to British institutions, who through a hundred years have been sheltered by British power, who under that rule have attained and enjoyed the most complete political and religious liberty, who have constantly professed the most devoted regard for a mother land with which they are connected by a thousand ties of affectionate sympathy, should deliberately, in cold blood, and for commercial reasons only, break that connection and join themselves to a state in whose history and traditions they have no part. They would incur, and unquestionably would deserve, alike the contempt of the people they abandon and of the people they join. In a Great Britain reorganized as a federation, or union, or alliance, Canada would hold an honorable place, gained on lines of true national development; in annexation to the United States she could have nothing but a bastard nationality, the offspring of either meanness, selfishness, or fear.

George R. Parkin, "The Reorganization of the British Empire", *The Century*, Vol. XXXVII (December, 1888), pp. 188 and 190–91.

Imperial Federation and "Canadian Nationality"—George M. Grant's View, 1889

Most Canadian imperialists believed that imperial federation represented an opportunity for Canadians to secure a full recognition of their political freedom. Canada, according to imperialists like George M. Grant and J. Castell Hopkins, remained a dependency of Britain with little influence in foreign affairs and no real voice in decisions of trade or war and peace. In his speeches, Grant, principal of Queen's University and a leader of the Imperial Federation League, linked imperial federation with the extension of Canadian self-government and the acquisition of full political rights.

Imperial Federation, from a Canadian point of view, means simply the next act in a process of political and historical development that began in 1763, when Canada—with the consent of all parties concerned—was declared to be British. From that day, the development of Canada from the position of a British colony into that of a British nationality has gone on steadily. The colonial condition is one of incomplete political development, and Canada has passed through various stages, each of which marks a greater measure of self-government than the previous stage.... The making of Canada into a nation has been a long process, and the process is not yet ended....

This brief sketch prepares us for a definition. Imperial Federation, then, may be defined as a union between the Mother Country and Canada that would give to Canada not only the present full management of its own affairs, but a fair share in the management and responsibilities of common affairs. As British citizens, ought we to ask for more? As Canadians and full-grown men, ought we to be satisfied with less?

In the meanwhile the object of the Imperial Federation League is to form branches all over Canada to discuss the question from every point of view, with the confident expectation that in due time our Parliament will feel itself warranted by public opinion to instruct the Government of the day to enter into negotiations with the British Government on the subject. Then will be the time to draw up a scheme.

Before forming a branch of the league, all that is necessary is that a number of people in the locality should have two principles rooted and grounded in them: 1. that Britain and Canada must continue to have one flag, in other words that the present union must be maintained; 2. that Canadians are prepared for full citizenship, in other words that they are determined to be the peers and not the dependents of their fellow-citizens in the British Islands....

George M. Grant, *"Imperial Federation": A Lecture Delivered in Victoria Hall, Winnipeg, on September 13th, 1889* (Winnipeg: Manitoba Free Press, 1890), pp. 1–8.

NATIONALISM, CONTINENTALISM OR IMPERIALISM—MAKING THE CHOICE

For most Canadians in the late nineteenth century, the possibilities of nationalism, continentalism and imperialism presented some difficult choices. Underlying each proposition and specific policy were differing ideas and often widely divergent conceptions of Canada's destiny. Often the political solutions lay in finding ways of accommodating extreme positions in the conflict of opinion; and in forging policies of compromise on these fundamental questions.

"She's Outgrown Her Dress"—A *Grip* Cartoon and Commentary, 1889

The dilemma facing Canada in the late 1880s was well illustrated in one of J.W. Bengough's *Grip* cartoons. If "Miss Canada" had outgrown her dress, what choices were open to her? And which choice did John A. Macdonald (shown in the background) prefer?

MISS CANADA—I wouldn't have that Stars and Stripes dress on any account; that Federation affair wouldn't fit me, and besides, I don't like the cut of it; but I just dote on that Independence outfit! One thing is certain, I'm getting too big a girl to continue wearing THIS dress!

SHE'S OUTGROWN HER DRESS

Sir John A. Macdonald's Final Defence of the National Policy, 1891

In his last election campaign John A. Macdonald addressed himself to the Canadian question. The ailing Prime Minister expressed his firm opposition to any proposals for unrestricted reciprocity and commercial union. His 1891 campaign presented a strong defence of the old "National Policy" and rallied Canadians with a stirring appeal to British loyalty. Was Macdonald's famous address an expression of British imperial sentiment, of Canadian nationalism, or of some combination of both?

...As in 1878, in 1882, and again in 1887, so in 1891, do questions relating to the trade and commerce of the country occupy a foremost place in the public mind. Our policy in respect thereto is to-day what it has been for the past thirteen years, and is directed by a firm determination to foster and develop the varied resources of the Dominion, by every means in our power, consistent with Canada's position as an integral portion of the British Empire. To that end we have laboured in the past, and we propose to continue in the work to which we have applied ourselves, of building up on this continent, under the flag of England, a great and powerful nation. . . .

During all this time what has been the attitude of the Reform [Liberal] Party? Vacillating in their policy and inconstancy itself as regards their leaders, they have, at least, been consistent in this particular, that they have uniformly opposed every measure which had for its object the development of our common country. . . . The Reform Party has taken a new departure, and has announced its policy to be Unrestricted Reciprocity—free-trade with the United States, and a common tariff with the United States against the rest of the world. The adoption of this policy would involve, among other grave evils, discrimination against the mother country. . . .

It would, in my opinion, inevitably result in the annexation of this Dominion to the United States. . . .

As for myself, my course is clear. A British subject I was born—a British subject I will die. With my utmost effort, with my latest breath, will I oppose the 'veiled treason' which attempts by sordid means and mercenary proffers to lure our people from their allegiance. During my long public service of nearly half a century, I have been true to my country and its best interests, and I appeal with equal confidence to the men who have trusted me in the past, and to the young hope of the country, with whom rests its destinies for the future, to give me their united and strenuous aid in this, my last effort, for the unity of the Empire and the preservation of our commercial and political freedom.

Joseph Pope, ed., *Memoirs of the Right Honourable Sir John A. Macdonald* (Toronto: Oxford University Press, 1930), pp. 772–777.

Gazing into Canada's Future—Edward Blake's Comments, 1892

The 1891 political controversy over Edward Blake's West Durham letter seemed to raise most of the problems in the whole anguished debate over Canada's proper destiny. The letter not only sparked public discussion; it compelled Blake to speak out again, clarifying his position. In a private letter to a fellow Liberal in 1892, he offered his personal observations on the "Canadian question" of the time. Where did Blake believe Canada's "higher though more arduous destiny" lay?

It is some years since I was constrained to announce the opinion that the scheme of Imperial Federation, which once, notwithstanding its difficulties, I hoped might be accomplished, must be abandoned, as no longer, if indeed it ever had been practicable.

It has seemed to me that, by the courses which of late years Canadian politics have taken, we have been drifting ever nearer to political union with the States.

Notwithstanding some matters of which we have reason to complain I avow feelings of friendship, sympathy, and admiration towards the Union, with whose progress and prosperity the fortunes not only of the new world but of the new era are so closely interwoven. I hope and believe that it will correct what seem its serious errors, overcome its grave difficulties, and achieve a future as glorious as its most patriotic citizen can wish. The Great Republic stands today in the front rank among the nations; its citizens are the political peers of those of any other country; its sovereign states occupy in its system honorable places; and to join them on fair and equal terms would be for any Province of this Dependency no ignoble lot.

Nevertheless this is not the goal at which I aim. I cling to the hope of a higher though more arduous destiny for the great Dominion. I look for the regeneration of my own country. I cling to the hope that—sooner or later, and rather soon than late—there may be born into the world an independent Canadian Commonwealth; nerving itself to solve, after its own fashion, the many racial and religious, moral and political, economic and material problems which confront us; united by enduring links of kinship and sympathy, hope and admiration, with three of the leading nations of the world; advancing, more effectively than now, our own varied interests as well as the true welfare of the old land, the proud mother of free nations as well as free Parliaments; and enjoying under arrangements which a wise and liberal statesmanship on both sides of the Line and of the Atlantic may mature, bright prospects of unbroken peace and absolute security, together with the fullest freedom of trade and the widest measure of intercourse compatible with the provision of our revenue and the preservation of our autonomy.

May these things be!

Ontario Archives, Edward Blake Papers. Blake to David Mills, M.P., April 12, 1892.

CONFLICTING INTERPRETATIONS

Studying the conflict in political, economic and social ideas in late-nineteenth-century Canada is, as historian Carl Berger once remarked, "like trying to nail jelly to the wall". Nationalism, continentalism and imperialism are vague words which must be defined in terms of their historical context. No exact way of measuring the force and impact of these sets of ideas has yet been devised, and major questions still exist about the connections between these ideas, and motivations of the people of power and influence who figured in the critical decisions of the period. A complete and comprehensive picture of the major political and economic choices made in years 1878–1896 requires an understanding of the climate in which the public debates over nationalism, continentalism and imperialism took place. And to this end, many Canadian historians in recent years have applied themselves to the central ideas of the period, offering a variety of interpretations, and drawing often conflicting conclusions.

THE NATIONALISM OF THE NATIONAL PARTY—REAL OR ILLUSORY?

John A. Macdonald and the National Policy—The Creighton Thesis

In the popular version of Canadian development, John A. Macdonald's national policies have often been equated with the very existence and expansion of the Canadian nation itself. Macdonald's brand of nationalism, in this view, is what gave to the Dominion its sense of purpose and confidence in the three decades after Confederation. Problems presented by issues such as Liberal trade policies, provincial rights agitation, the CPR contract and Louis

Riel, are seen as either obstacles to Macdonald's idea of national unity, or threats to the unity of purpose from which Confederation had sprung. The popular interpretation of Macdonald and his nation-building policies owes much to the work of Donald G. Creighton. This passage, taken from Creighton's history, *Dominion of the North* (1944), captures the essence of his view of Macdonald's nationalism and its components and purposes.

In September, 1878... Macdonald returned to power; and from that moment the uncertainty, the hesitation, and the failure which had marked the ten years from Confederation seemed miraculously to end. Macdonald had his mandate; he had settled upon his policies; and he was favoured, far more than perhaps even he was aware, by a brief return of good times. The Conservatives had found their answers to the riddle of national unity; and for the next half-dozen years they plunged into a wild career of economic and political nationalism.

Of the three interrelated national policies of western settlement, transcontinental railways, and protective tariffs, it was the third upon which the Conservatives began. Though this precedence was largely accidental, there was a certain definite appropriateness about it. The tariff was an instrument of vast emotional significance as well as of great practical value; and of the three methods adopted for the attainment of national expansion and unity, the tariff significantly was the only one which ever came to be dignified by the title of the 'National Policy' in capitals. In international affairs, the tariff asserted the principle of independence as against Great Britain and the United States. In domestic matters, it expressed the hope for a more varied and self-sufficient national life. It was intimately and vitally related to the other national policies. By means of the tariff, the settlement of the west would provide a national market; and this national market would supply east-west traffic for Canadian transcontinental railways and areas of exploitation for eastern Canadian industry.

... In place of the uncomplicated revenue tariff the Conservatives proposed and carried an elaborate schedule, with substantially increased rates which included a number of specific duties designed to stiffen the resistance of the tariff in times of depression.... For the whole of Canada, and particularly for the Maritime Provinces, this was the greatest fiscal revolution which had yet occurred in their history....

The Canadian Pacific Railway was a commercial organization which won its astounding success partly through brilliant individual enterprise and partly through heavy government support. The group which George Stephen headed did not look upon itself as an association of financiers engaged in a giant and highly lucrative job of company flotation. They were practical railwaymen who wanted to build, and run, and hold on to a railway.

With the completion of the Canadian Pacific Railway, the Conservative programme of economic unity and expansion had been fully rounded out. Emboldened by the success of its own mission, strengthened by the tide of national feeling which it had itself evoked, the Macdonald government continued to assert its supervisory control over the provinces and began to insist upon a new and more dignified national status in the world at large. For reasons of concrete national interest, as well as on grounds of loyalty and emotional attachment, Macdonald believed in the British connection; but he believed also that, under the new colonial system, the connection between Great Britain and Canada must more and more approximate the relationship of friendly equals....

In the early 1880's the drive and purpose of Macdonald's nationalism were clearly apparent. With a new government, a new series of national enterprises, and a new wave of prosperity, the Dominion stood at the zenith. It was superb with promise and with achievement. It looked confidently into the future. But it could not foresee the long train of disappointments, divisions, and frustrations which in the end were to ruin the Conservative party and very nearly to break the Dominion of Canada itself.

Donald Creighton, *Dominion of the North: A History of Canada* (Toronto: Macmillan, 1957), pp. 345–348, 352 and 353. Selected excerpts.

National Dream or Grand Delusion?—A Critique of CPR Mythology

No aspect of Macdonald's nation-building program has been more closely identified with nationalist mythology than the building of the Canadian Pacific Railway. Much of the epic CPR story derives from the early history of the railway written by Harold A. Innis, and from Donald Creighton's biography of Macdonald. Yet the best known and most widely read version of the building of the CPR is undoubtedly *The Great Railway* by popular historian Pierre Berton. To Berton, the CPR project was nothing less than the realization of Macdonald's "national dream" to bind the British North American colonies together, to forestall American expansion, and to open the way for the settlement of the Canadian West. It was, in his words, "a rare example of a nation created through the construction of a railway."

Berton's CPR history did much to popularize the story of the Pacific railway, but was greeted by predictable scepticism from professional historians. In a review of the first volume in *Canadian Forum*, H.V. Nelles of Toronto's York University raised many questions about Berton's account of the whole enterprise.

It is almost an axiom of Canadian historiography that every generation must write its history of the C.P.R. . . . .

Berton stands four square in what might be called the 'Railroad Now' school of historians which accepts without serious question Macdonald's argument that a transcontinental railroad had to be built immediately, at any cost and by an all-Canadian company over an all-Canadian route, if the west was to be protected against imminent annexation. It follows from this line of reasoning that all other railroad policies become by definition continentalist. Significantly, Berton uses the definite article in his title; there can be only one National Dream. But for some inexplicable reason many Canadians lacked Macdonald's sense of urgency. . . .

Briefly the 'Railroad Now' case rests upon the following assumptions: that the American threat was real rather than apparent or manufactured; that the feared eventuality (i.e. an international railway linking the Canadian and American west) did not in fact come to pass; that the C.P.R. was an all-Canadian national enterprise; and that the country required a transcontinental road immediately (1871 or 1880; take your pick) in order to fill the west with Canadians. Underlying the whole argument is the unstated proposition that a railway connecting a primary producing area with a manufacturing region would also lay the foundation of a harmonious political union. Each of these propositions could be questioned and should be subject to criticism if we are to advance beyond the stage of merely expanding upon Tory election literature.

Did the American railroads seriously threaten Canadian territorial ambitions in the west? Did Macdonald, calling the defensive signals, read the American offense correctly or did he fall for a fake? On this point the 'Railroad Now' case draws heavily upon a rich store of Jay Cooke[2] quotations. Berton, following Macdonald, takes Cooke's promotional literature at face value. Yes, we are reminded by Mr. Berton himself that Cooke was after all a bond salesman who would say anything for a buck; still we are expected to accept his pre-game boasting as assertions of fact. It is this menace, after all, that sanctions the urgency and liberality of terms of the Canadian response. If the threat can be shown to be insubstantial, then the 'Railroad Now' position can only be seen as an over-reaction. Berton uses L.B. Irwin's evidence of Cooke's intentions without accepting his conclusion that the 'imposing financial facade' of the Northern Pacific was in reality a 'false front.' After its collapse the Northern Pacific was in no financial position—nor was any other American transcontinental—to invade the Canadian west in a big way. Nevertheless, all George Stephen had to do was mention the Northern Pacific and Macdonald was good for whatever was needed. There can be no doubting Macdonald's sincerity in this matter; he genuinely believed the wolf was at the door. But, as we have learned from following the current president of the United States, sincerity can only excuse so much. A closer look at the American situation could conceivably remove the force of the immediacy argument. Furthermore, no American railroad could endanger the Canadian purchase on the northwest without the expressed support of the American government. Despite the abundant quotations of known annexationists after the Treaty of Washington that was a remote possibility. Thus, the exact nature of the frightening American design requires a thorough examination before it is accepted as being of whole cloth.

It is assumed though never explicitly stated, that the new C.P.R. syndicate differed substantially in the nationality of its ownership from Hugh Allan's company. In fact, Harold Innis showed long ago that in 1883 almost 53% of the company's shares were held by residents of the United States. Between then and the time Innis wrote (1921) the Canadian share of ownership of C.P.R. stock actually fell slightly from 18% to 17.1%, during that time of course majority ownership shifted from American to British hands. (H.A. Innis, *History of the Canadian Pacific Railway* London, 1923, pp. 276-7)....

The only transcontinental capable of joining the Canadian and American west with rails succeeded; namely, the C.P.R. In fact, as Mr. Berton points out, the Syndicate made its money establishing a rail link between Winnipeg and Minneapolis-St. Paul. So important was this route in the plans of the C.P.R. promoters that they insisted that it remain the sole such connection and in the end Macdonald caved in with the notorious Monopoly Clause....

There seems no good reason for denying that construction of a Canadian transcontinental could have waited for another ten years without seriously impairing national economic development. British Columbia, as everyone soon learned, could be pacified with the expenditure of a million or so annually. That was enough to quiet the handful of railroad promoters and real estate speculators who controlled the government of the province. The mere construction of the railroad worked no wonders in the west. This is not mere hindsight; many critics at the time said as much. Indeed the second most recent company historian, J.L. McDougall, entitled his chapter dealing with the 1886-1896 decade, 'The Dismal Years.' Settlers would not arrive in any great numbers for another ten years after the pounding of the last spike, and then many of them came up from the south. Nor is there any a priori basis for concluding that more north-south railroads would have precluded the eventual construction of a Canadian transcontinental. From this vantage a staged construction programme—in the 'Railroad Now'

2. A wealthy American railway promoter associated with the Northern Pacific Railway.

rhetoric read 'piecemeal'—did possess some merit. Nor should the notion of using the available water routes be dismissed so disdainfully. The C.P.R.'s eventual main contribution to national development consisted of moving western wheat (at uncompetitive prices) to the nearest navigable water. In short it would appear that one could still be a Canadian nationalist and object to Macdonald's railroad policy on rational grounds. There just might be other, equally legitimate National Dreams....

H.V. Nelles, "Ties That Bind: Berton's C.P.R.", *Canadian Forum*, Vol. 50 (November-December, 1970), pp. 271–2. Excerpted.

Macdonald's Nationalism as "Laurentian Imperialism"—A Western Perspective

Westerners have long seen Canada's "national" policies as instruments of central Canadian domination. As early as 1946, Manitoba-born historian W.L. Morton argued that Confederation and Macdonald's National Policy were expressions of "Laurentian imperialism", or, simply put, part of a central Canadian development strategy which cast the West in the role of staple-producing hinterland for industrial eastern Canada. His essay, "Clio in Canada", set out a sweeping critique of the Macdonald scheme of nation-building.

...the West was annexed to Confederation as a subordinate region and so remained for sixty years. Such was the historical schooling of the West. It had, therefore, to fight its way up to self-government and equality in Confederation, nor is the process ended. No more than French Canada can the West accept a common interpretation of Canadian history of a cultural metropolitanism. The West must first work out its own historical experience... and free itself, and find itself. Until it ceases to be either an exploited or a subsidized region it cannot do so. In an imperfect world an unequal incidence of national policies is no doubt inevitable, but even in an imperfect world people may be allowed to shape an interpretation of history and a way of life in accord with their own experience.

If this view appears extreme, it is partly because Westerners seldom enjoy that blessed moderation which descends on those who have dwelt long among the flesh-pots, and partly because metropolitan Canada has seldom appreciated the impact of Laurentian imperialism on the West. One's appreciation of a club depends entirely upon the end from which one contemplates it. It was the fate of the West to become the colony of a colony which brought to its new imperial role neither imagination, liberality, nor magnanimity. To ensure returns from the £300,000 spent in 'buying' the West, the natural resources were retained, contrary to British precedent, the protective tariff, that chief of Canadian extractive industries, was established, and the monopoly clause of the Canadian Pacific Railway charter was imposed. In the events which preceded the rebellion of 1885, Ottawa added neglect to subordination, and after the rebellion was suppressed, neglect from time to time was not unknown.

And Eastern aggression has continued in other and sometimes subtler ways. For two generations the West has been led by the Ontario-born. What this has meant it would be idle to attempt to estimate, but it may be that native Westerners will not be so susceptible to the blandishments of metropolitan 'nationalism.' On the other hand, the Westerner, like the medieval Scot, is poor. Similar in effect is the fact that the West, like a colony, is used as a proving ground in which bright young men in business and the professions prepare themselves for higher positions in the head offices of the East....

> W.L. Morton, "Clio in Canada: The Interpretation of Canadian History", *University of Toronto Quarterly*, Vol. XV (April, 1946), reprinted in Carl Berger, ed., *Approaches to Canadian History* (Toronto: University of Toronto Press, 1967), pp. 43–44, and 47–48.

An Alternative to Macdonald's Nationalism—A Defence of Oliver Mowat's Vision

The popular view that the provincial rights movement of the 1880s constituted a dire threat to the Canadian nation itself has also undergone some re-examination. Recent studies of Oliver Mowat's Ontario (1872–1896), for example, have sought to explain the Ontario movement for provincial autonomy rather than merely condemning it as an obstacle to Macdonald's grand design for Canada. In this revisionist piece, Christopher Armstrong, a historian at York University, sees Mowat's vision as an equally legitimate prescription for Canada's development.

Sir Oliver Mowat deserves the title, 'father of the provincial rights movement in Canada.' It was he who challenged Sir John Macdonald upon the use of the power of disallowance over the granting of 'better terms' to some provinces without the others being consulted, and over the functions of the lieutenant-governor. He took a hand in the calling of the first Interprovincial Conference, which dutifully passed a number of resolutions he had drafted demanding for the provinces sovereign control of their affairs within their sphere of jurisdiction. He appeared personally before the Judicial Committee of the Privy Council with conspicuous success and persuaded them to accept his contentions in a number of important constitutional cases. All in all, he made it certain that the provinces would be far more than the glorified municipalities which some Fathers of Confederation, not least himself, had envisaged....

Mowat's first objective then was to secure the fullest control over the province's economic development. Federal policies which threatened to restrict this must be strenuously resisted. Indeed, there developed a sort of dialectic in federal-provincial relations: any 'interference' by Ottawa was opposed by provincial politicians, almost as a conditioned reflex. Whenever federal policies failed to meet Ontario's needs, or threatened to work against her best interests, the province tried to substitute its authority for that of the federal government....

Because of its vast domain, Ontario was rich enough to resist the efforts of the federal government to bully it or bribe it into line. While the other provinces clamoured for 'better terms,' Ontario held aloof.... Occasionally, however, Ontario might wish the support of the other provinces for some demand it was making upon the federal authorities. Then the premier could unbend a little and ensure the necessary backing by approving the demands of the poor relations for increased subsidies.

Sir Oliver was quick to realize that both of these objectives could better be attained if Ontario were to secure a veto over constitutional change. He could not only torpedo those amendments of which he disapproved but demand favours in return for his assent. Since the British North America Act contained no formula for its own amendment, there was no statutory basis for such a demand, but the 'Compact theory' of Confederation, which explained the constitution as a treaty between the provinces, offered a historical and conventional justification for this claim. Mowat early became an ardent exponent of the theory....

Where Mowat led his successors have followed. He taught them all the moves: how to rally the other provinces against Ottawa; when to form accords and when to go it alone; above all, he revealed the value of persistence and tenacity. He was not an enemy of the national spirit, but one who understood how it would develop in a new country, by grafting itself onto older, deeper, loyalties. His vision of Canada's development was different from Macdonald's, but time has proved him more far-sighted....

Christopher Armstrong, "The Mowat Heritage in Federal-Provincial Relations", in Donald Swainson, ed., *Oliver Mowat's Ontario* (Toronto: Macmillan, 1972), pp. 92–96, and 118. Footnotes deleted.

VIEWS OF CANADA'S DESTINY

R.C. Brown on the Nationalism of Canada's National Policy

Canadian politicians of the late nineteenth century rarely acted like political theorists or philosophers. For the most part men like John A. Macdonald and Edward Blake remained preoccupied with the everyday problems of government. Yet, according to R.C. Brown of the University of Toronto, a look at Macdonald's National Policy illustrates that (even within the framework of practical politics) their thoughts and acts were decidedly nationalist in character:

...the idea of protection embodied in the tariff became equated with the Canadian nation itself. The National Policy, by stressing that Canadians should no longer be 'hewers of wood and drawers of water' for the United States, as Tilley[3] put it, recalled and reinforced that basic impulse of survival as a separate entity on this continent that had been born of the American Revolution, made explicit in Confederation, and remained the primary objective of Canadian nationalists. Protection and the National Policy, then, took on a much larger meaning than mere tinkering with customs schedules.

The same idea was evident in the building of the Canadian Pacific Railway and the opening of the Northwest. The Northwest was the key to the future of both the National Policy and the nation, and an expensive and partially unproductive railway through Canadian territory was the price Canada had to pay to 'protect' it from American penetration and absorption. It was to be the great market for Canadian industry and the foundation of a 'Canadian economy'. Emphasizing that building the railway was 'a great national question', Sir Charles Tupper remarked that 'under the National Policy that Canada has adopted we must look forward not only to building up thriving centres of industry and enterprises all over this portion of the country, but to obtaining a market for these industries after they have been established; and I say where is there a greater market than that magnificent granary of the North-west?' He added that upon the success of the venture 'the rapid progress and prosperity of our common country depends'.

The United States played an interesting role in the National Policy that emphasized

---

3. Leonard Tilley, Macdonald's Minister of Finance, introducing the protective tariff of 1879.

its nationalistic assumptions. Fundamental to the thinking of the framers of the policy was the idea that the United States was much less a friendly neighbour than an aggressive competitor power waiting for a suitable opportunity to fulfill its destiny of the complete conquest of North America. The National Policy was intended to be the first line of defence against American ambitions. And this, I think, is the reason any Canadian alternative to it was unsuccessful. It was the 'national' implications of the National Policy that hindered the Liberals in their attempt to formulate an opposition policy before 1896. They could not accept Commercial Union because it meant the total surrender of tariff autonomy. Unrestricted Reciprocity was adopted as a compromise that retained autonomy. But its distinction from Commercial Union was too subtle for much of the electorate to grasp and left the party open to skillful exploitation by Macdonald's 'loyalty' cry. . . . Rather. . . most Liberals simply wanted a more extensive reciprocity agreement with the United States than the Conservatives. Or, to put it another way, the Liberals were only interested in somewhat less protection from American competition than their opponents . . . .

I have tried to suggest that the National Policy was a manifestation of Canadian national sentiment. Its basic assumptions, protection against the United States, the need for a 'Canadian economy' with a strong industrial base and secure markets, and the implicit assumption of achieving greater autonomy within the Empire all crystallized that ill-defined, but deeply felt, sense of difference that set Canadians apart from both their neighbours to the south and the mother country. . . .

Craig Brown, "The Nationalism of the National Policy", in Peter Russell, ed., *Nationalism in Canada* (Toronto: McGraw Hill Ryerson, 1966), pp. 157–158.

Frank Underhill on the Canadian Dilemma of the 1880s

Frank H. Underhill, professor of history at the University of Toronto from 1927 to 1955, identified the major questions of the decade in one of a series of lectures on the CBC in 1963, in which he analyzed the controversy over imperialism, nationalism and continentalism in the late nineteenth century. He sympathized with Liberal nationalists who favoured Dominion autonomy and accepted the basic tenets of Canadian isolationism.

. . .The late eighties and early nineties mark the point when our national self-confidence reached its lowest level. 'We have come to a period in the history of this young country' wrote Wilfrid Laurier to Edward Blake, 'when premature dissolution seems to be at hand. What will be the outcome? How long can the present fabric last? Can it last at all? All these are questions which surge in my mind and to which dismal answers suggest themselves.' There must have been a good many conversations along these lines in those days.

Out of this situation emerged a movement in 1887 for Commercial Union with the United States. The controversy that went on for the next five or six years raised deeper questions about the nature of the Canadian identify than Canadians had yet faced . . . .

Let me go back to Goldwin Smith. His book on *Canada and the Canadian Question* of 1891 is the most pessimistic book that has ever been written about Canada, and he advanced the most radical solution for the frustrations of the day—union with the United States . . . .

To Smith. . . the United States represented the quintessence of everything he admired in English society and civilization, purified of all the elements he detested. The hope of democracy in the English-speaking world rested upon the United States. This was why he dreamed of a reunion of the two separated branches of the race, and why he saw the union of Canada and the States as a possible first step towards... 'moral federation of the English-speaking peoples', as he called it....

Smith had the early nineteenth-century, romantic, mystic faith in the miracle-working powers of nationhood. When, after experience in Canada, he decided that we had not the capacity for nationhood on our own, there was no other destiny for us than absorption into the great American nation that was the hope of democracy....

The best answers to the Goldwin Smith thesis about the destiny of Canada came from two Maritimers: George M. Grant, Nova Scotian by birth, then Principal of Queen's University; and George R. Parkin, a New Brunswicker, and a missionary for the cause of imperial federation, for which Grant was also an enthusiastic preacher....

Grant was an enthusiastic Canadian as well as an imperialist. He had accompanied his friend, the engineer Sandford Fleming, across Canada on the expedition that explored the Yellowhead route through the sea of mountains to the Pacific, and he was thrilled by the potentialities of his country. The challenge of difficulties only roused him to greater energy; these difficulties were only the growing pains in our history. His objections to Smith's ideas were temperamental almost as much as intellectual. His real objection was that Smith in his cold rational analysis paid no attention to all the traditions and sentiments that had grown up in our Canadian past....

The best answer of all to Smith came from Parkin. Before he made his name as a propagandist for imperial federation, Parkin had been headmaster of the collegiate school in Fredericton, which he had vainly tried to persuade his community to turn into a residential school modelled on the English public schools. His object had been to train the minds and characters of young men, some of whom would in due course show themselves capable of a higher form of politics than was current in New Brunswick. Parkin and Grant and all our later imperialists have been moved by one great vision, that of raising the standards, moral and intellectual, of Canadian public life. One of the great attractions of imperial federation to them was that Canadian statesmen, by becoming partners in a wider enterprise, would acquire wider viewpoints and a more mature sense of responsibility.

Parkin's reply came in a book that he published in 1892: *Imperial Federation, the Problem of National Unity*. One word in that title reveals more than Parkin quite realized, the word 'national'. The nation of which he was thinking was the British Empire as a whole. Canadian nationality seemed to him relatively insignificant. He continuously uses the words 'nation' and 'national' to apply to the wider entity. This was implicitly a denial of the thesis on which Canadian Liberals by the 1890s were beginning to unite, that the relations between Canada and Great Britain must be diplomatic relations between two national states and not constitutional relations within one federal state. And the Liberals, of course, had the future with them....

Frank H. Underhill, *The Image of Confederation: The Massey Lectures, Third Series* (Toronto: Canadian Broadcasting Corporation, 1964), pp. 27–33.

A Liberal Nationalist View of Imperialism

The conflict between imperialism and nationalism which marked the late 1880s and early 1890s in Canada has also served as a focus for debate among historians. Exponents of the Liberal nationalist view of Canadian development, like O.D. Skelton and John W. Dafoe, saw in British Canadian imperialism an attachment to colonial ties which posed a threat to Canada's slowly emerging sense of nationalism. In a 1955 article on Wilfrid Laurier's concept of imperialism, H. Blair Neatby of Carleton University set out the essential premises of the Liberal nationalist analysis.

> ...there was yet another form of Canadian imperialism; another way in which Canadians were conscious of belonging to the Empire and of being indebted to England. And this form is especially relevant because Sir Wilfrid Laurier was such an imperialist. This was the imperialism based on a respect for the principles, and especially the political principles, which Great Britain seemed to represent. To such imperialists, pride in the Empire was based on the belief that the British Empire was the bulwark of liberty and justice in the world. This might be described as intellectual imperialism rather than racial or emotional imperialism. Being a reasoned rather than an emotional attachment to England, it was the most moderate form of imperialism, but it was nonetheless significant.
>
> In French-Canadians, Canadian imperialism evoked much different responses. Appeals to the unity of the Anglo-Saxon race could arouse nothing but repulsion. Indeed, the counterpart of the racial imperialists among French-Canadians was that group of extreme *nationalistes* who looked forward to the creation of a French-Canadian nation in North America. Similarly, the sentimental attachment felt by English-Canadians for the Mother Country was duplicated among French-Canadians by a love for the land of their birth. And the political attitude of French-Canadians was to a large extent determined by their desire for survival as a racial, linguistic and cultural group. Any form of political unity for the Empire would so reduce their influence as to endanger this survival. Many French-Canadians respected and appreciated an Empire in which Canada had been granted self-government, and in which the minority in Canada were given certain guarantees of language, religion and law. Yet even here, their concern was with the preservation of what they considered to be their rights. In view of the Riel episode and the Manitoba Schools Question, it seemed unlikely that their rights would be extended. Thus French-Canadians in general were suspicious of any form of imperialism....
>
> ...Imperial federation—or any other scheme of imperial centralization—was out of the question for a French-Canadian or for any politician interested in racial harmony in Canada. But also, the principle of individual liberty in imperial relations meant local autonomy. Laurier believed that it was the recognition of the political rights of the separate colonies which made the survival of the Empire possible. Thus he regarded imperial federation as the negation of the principles upon which the Empire rested. To him it was such a visionary scheme that it bore no relation to practical politics....
>
> H. Blair Neatby, "Laurier and Imperialism", in Carl Berger, ed., *Imperial Relations in the Age of Laurier*, Canadian Historical Readings Series (Toronto: University of Toronto Press, 1969), pp. 1–2 and 5. Originally published in the Canadian Historical Association *Report*, 1955.

Imperialism as Nationalism—The Berger Thesis

Recent studies view Canada's nineteenth-century imperialism differently. Carl Berger, a University of Toronto scholar specializing in Canadian intellectual history, was one of the first to identify "imperialism" with Canada's struggle for survival against continentalist pressures. In *The Sense of Power* (1970), Berger offered a challenge to the prevailing liberal nationalist interpretation of imperialism, arguing that the movement for "imperial unity" which surfaced in the late 1880s espoused a unique variety of Canadian nationalism.

Twenty years after Confederation, there was a good deal of concrete evidence in support of those who predicted Canada's collapse; there was only faith on the side of those who defended it. The cultural conflict triggered by the execution of Louis Riel and the long depression which had lasted intermittently since 1873, underlay the general mood of despondency. The depression also proved that the national policy had not worked and this led the Liberal party to commit itself to a policy of freer trade with the United States. Unrestricted reciprocity, or the elimination of tariff barriers between the two countries, imparted by way of reaction the initial impulse to the campaign for imperial unity. Those who repudiated reciprocity did not treat it as an innocuous commercial proposition, nor did they rest their case against it upon the grounds of economic profitability alone. They equated it with continentalism, the gradual assimilation of Canada to the United States, and ultimate political absorption. This spectre of annexation forced them into a defence of Canada, forced them, that is, to say exactly why it was worth preserving Canada at all. That is why the three major spokesmen of imperial unity in Canada— Colonel George Taylor Denison of Toronto, Principal George Monro Grant of Queen's University, and Sir George Robert Parkin, teacher and writer—dealt not only with the relative economic merits of alternate commercial policies, but with history, tradition, power, and religion. In retrospect, it is clear that this debate was inflated, that the threat of continental union was exaggerated, and that Macdonald's narrow victory in the election of 1891 was affected by many other factors. But the net effect of this challenge was to galvanize the defenders of Canada and the British connection into action, and bring out into the open the ideas and sentiments, tradition and hopes, that constituted their sense of nationality. . . .

These developments whetted the appetites of those who hankered for a more influential and less subordinate place within the Empire and grew ever more determined to remove the last vestiges, psychological as well as legal, of colonialism and dependence. Where Canadians were once asked to preserve and defend the connection, they were now summoned to take up the imperial mission and behave like the citizens of the major power their country had already become. The campaign for imperial unity attained a few of its objectives, but . . . [these] were only devices intended to secure a meaningful and co-operative alliance between Canada and Britain, and, in this, its central ambition, imperialism failed. It was a victim of its own zeal; in another sense, it was a casualty of the First World War.

This fact of failure has been the main influence in shaping the interpretations and characterizations of Canadian imperialism in historical literature. Had the movement for the union of the British North American colonies miscarried in the 1860s, its history would read somewhat like the story of the struggle for imperial unity. . . .

Canadian imperialism was one variety of Canadian nationalism— a type of awareness of nationality which rested upon a certain understanding of history, the national character, and the national mission. When critics belaboured imperialism because of its hostility to 'Canadian nationalism' what they really meant was that they believed in incompatible with that kind of nationalism which they endorsed. There have been many varieties of Canadian nationalism, and, while they have all been inspired by the same nation, the manner in which the character and interests of Canada have been interpreted vary enormously.

> Carl Berger, *The Sense of Power: Studies in the Ideas of Canadian Imperialism, 1867-1914* (Toronto: University of Toronto Press, 1970), pp. 4-6, and 9-10. Selected excerpts.

Canada's "Arduous Destiny"—P.B. Waite's Interpretation

Professor P.B. Waite's *Arduous Destiny* (1971), a survey of Canada in the 1874-1896 period, did much to tie the divergent strands of interpretation together. In his concluding section, entitled "Fin de siècle", the Dalhousie University historian offered this assessment of Canada's progress—and its probable destiny.

> In the twenty-three years since 1873, despite great inherent difficulties, much had been done; the physical strength, the muscular development of the fledgling of 1873 had been prodigious; the thin gangling frame had been filled out, strengthened with factories, western farms, Nova Scotian and British Columbian orchards; and with the arterial power of railways, there came an energizing circulation of trade between the Maritime provinces, central Canada, and the West; Canada was ready to sustain the massive weight thrown upon it by the great immigration of the Laurier years. It had not been easy; one is tempted again to say that nothing in Canada is easy. Canada's destiny was an arduous one achieved at tremendous cost; the immense capital and energy that went into transportation was a material symbol of a great political and perhaps moral practice to Canada's people. It was easy to despair, easy to be faint-hearted; many did and many were; but even Sir Richard Cartwright, for all his blue ruin speeches of years past, made his amends to the House of Commons and Canada, in March, 1896; and John Willison, writing from Calgary on his first trip west, in September, 1895 was even better:
>
> > If we compare what has been accomplished with the predictions of the boom traders and political prophets we shall be disappointed. If we are content with reasonable expectations and take account of mistakes of policy and acquired knowledge of the characteristics and capabilities of the country we shall be encouraged and hopeful in the future. . . .
>
> Canadians have sometimes forgotten, said Willison in that sensible way of his, 'that this Confederation is not much more than a quarter of a century old . . . you cannot build a nation in a day.'

> P.B. Waite, *Canada 1874-1896: Arduous Destiny*, The Canadian Centenary Series (Toronto: McClelland and Stewart, 1971), pp. 280-281. Footnotes deleted.

A Guide to Further Reading

1. *Overviews*

Creighton, Donald, *Canada's First Century 1867-1967*. Toronto: Macmillan, 1970, esp. chapter 3, "Time of Troubles".

_____, *John A. Macdonald, Vol. II—The Old Chieftain*. Toronto: Macmillan, 1955.

Levitt, Joseph, *A Vision Beyond Reach: A Century of Images of Canadian Destiny*. Ottawa: Deneau, 1982.

MacNutt, W.S., "The 1880s" in J.M.S. Careless and R. Craig Brown, eds., *The Canadians, Part One, 1867-1967.* Toronto: Macmillan, 1968.

Robeson, Virginia R., ed., *Debates About Canada's Future, 1868-1896.* Toronto: OISE Press, 1977.

Russell, Peter, ed., *Nationalism in Canada.* Toronto: McGraw-Hill Ryerson, 1966.

Waite, P.B., *Canada 1874-1896: Arduous Destiny.* Toronto: McClelland and Stewart, 1971.

_____, *Macdonald: His Life and His World.* Toronto: McGraw-Hill Ryerson, 1975.

2. Specialized Studies

The National Policy Tariff

Acheson, T.W. "The National Policy and the Industrialization of the Maritimes, 1880–1914", *Acadiensis*, Vol. 1 (Spring, 1972), pp. 3–28.

Bennett, Paul W., "Frederic Nicholls, the Old National Policy and Canadian Manufacturers, 1879-1911", *Quarterly of Canadian Studies.* Vol. 5, No. 1 (1981), pp. 84–95.

Bliss, Michael, *A Living Profit: Studies in the Social History of Canadian Business, 1883-1911.* Toronto: McClelland and Stewart, 1974.

Brown, R.C., *Canada's National Policy 1883-1900: A Study in Canadian-American Relations.* Princeton: Princeton University Press, 1964.

Dales, John H., "Canada's National Policies" in *The Protective Tariff in Canada's Development.* Toronto: University of Toronto Press, 1966, Chapter 7.

McDiarmid, O.J., *Commercial Policy in the Canadian Economy.* Cambridge: Harvard University Press, 1946, Chapters 7 and 8.

Phillips, Paul, "The National Policy Revisited", *Journal of Canadian Studies*, Vol. 14 (Fall, 1979), pp. 3–13.

The CPR

Berton, Pierre, *The Great Railway, Vol. 1: 1871-1881—The National Dream; and Vol. II: 1881-1885—The Last Spike.* Toronto: McClelland and Stewart, 1970 and 1971.

Glazebrook, G.P. de T., *A History of Transportation in Canada.* Volume II. Toronto: McClelland and Stewart, 1964.

Innis, Harold A., *A History of the Canadian Pacific Railway.* Toronto: University of Toronto Press, 1971. Originally published 1923.

Keefer, T.C., *Philosophy of Railroads and Other Essays.* Edited with an introduction by H.V. Nelles. Toronto: University of Toronto Press, 1972.

Dominion-Provincial Relations/The JCPC Decisions

Browne, G.P., *The Judicial Committee and the British North America Act.* Toronto: University of Toronto Press, 1967.

Russell, Peter H., *Leading Constitutional Decisions.* Toronto: McClelland and Stewart, 1965.

The Provincial Rights Movement

Armstrong, Christopher, "The Mowat Heritage in Federal-Provincial Relations", in Donald Swainson, ed., *Oliver Mowat's Ontario.* Toronto: Macmillan, 1972.

Biggar, C.R.W., *Sir Oliver Mowat: A Biographical Sketch*, Two Volumes. Toronto: Warwick Bros. & Rutter, 1905.

Cook, Ramsay, *Provincial Autonomy: Minority Rights and the Compact Theory, 1867-1921.* Ottawa: Queen's Printer, 1969.

Evans, A. Margaret, "The Mowat Era, 1872-1896: Stability and Progress", in *Profiles of*

A Province: Studies in the History of Ontario. Toronto: Ontario Historical Society, 1967.

Howell, Colin D., "W.S. Fielding and the Repeal Elections of 1886 and 1887 in Nova Scotia", *Acadiensis*, Vol. VIII (Spring, 1979), pp. 28–46.

Miller, J.R., *Equal Rights: The Jesuits' Estates Act Controversy*. Montreal: McGill-Queen's University Press, 1979.

Morrison, J.C., "Oliver Mowat and the Development of Provincial Rights in Ontario: A Study in Dominion-Provincial Relations, 1867–1896", in *Three History Theses*. Toronto: The Ontario Department of Public Records and Archives, 1961.

Rawlyk, George, "Nova Scotia Regional Protest, 1867–1967", *Queen's Quarterly*, Vol. LXXXV (Spring, 1968).

The National Question: Imperialism, Nationalism and Continentalism

Berger, Carl, *The Sense of Power: Studies in the Ideas of Canadian Imperialism 1867–1914*. Toronto: University of Toronto Press, 1970.

_____, ed., *Imperialism and Nationalism, 1884–1914: A Conflict in Canadian Thought*. Toronto: Copp Clark, 1969.

Denison, George T., *The Struggle for Imperial Unity*. Toronto: Macmillan, 1909.

Gagan, David P., "The Relevance of 'Canada First'", *Journal of Canadian Studies*, Vol. V (1970).

Schull, Joseph, *Edward Blake: Leader and Exile, 1881–1912*. Toronto: Macmillan, 1976.

Smith, Goldwin, *Canada and the Canadian Question*. Toronto: University of Toronto Press, 1971. Originally published 1891.

Underhill, Frank, *The Image of Confederation*. Toronto: CBC, 1964, Chapter 3 in particular.

Warner, Donald F., *The Idea of Continental Union: Agitation for the Annexation of Canada to the United States, 1849–93*. Lexington: University of Kentucky Press, 1960.

13

THE WORKING
CLASS RESPONSE TO
INDUSTRIALISM, 1860–1896

A 'Living Wage' or
Workers' Control?

Much of the traditional history of late-nineteenth-century Canada has focused on John A. Macdonald's national policies, the building of the Canadian Pacific Railway, Louis Riel's rebellions and execution, and the outcome of national elections. Political leaders and rival élite groups have usually dominated the historical stage, engaged in a continual epic struggle to shape the Canadian nation. Ordinary working people rarely appear in this version of Canada's past. Yet the real makers of Canada in the late nineteenth century were the ordinary men and women who shared the hardships and benefits of daily life and work. This problem study will deal with late-nineteenth-century Canada, the experience of the "workingman"[1] and woman, and their responses to the forces of industrialization.

Working people in the late nineteenth century expressed two different reactions to the onset of industrialism. Many Canadian workers, particularly orthodox trade unionists, fought for a share of the material benefits of increased industrial production, or a bigger slice of the growing capitalist "pie". Their goals were apparent in traditional union demands for a "living wage", shorter hours and improved working conditions. In the words of American Federation of Labor president Samuel Gompers, they simply wanted "More!" But some workingmen and women went beyond the traditional demands of labour. Confronted with the hardships of economic depression and the advance of mechanized production, these workers began to

---

1. The terms "workingman" and "working girl" were widely used to describe male and female labour in Victorian Canada. Earlier in the century employers and those of the upper classes often referred to working people as "the lower orders". The phrase "the working class", popular among Canadian historians, did not enjoy wide currency in this period.

question the industrial capitalist system itself. To the labour radicals, who often were skilled artisans and craftsmen, industrialism had increased the employer's control over the workplace by imposing factory discipline and displacing many pre-industrial craft skills. They responded by organizing new forms of labour associations and seeking a radical restructuring of industrial capitalist society in which workers would be given a voice in the management of the workplace.

Canada experienced an industrial revolution during the period from 1850 to the mid-1890s. Industrialization came to Victorian Canada as part of the transformation of the pre-industrial economy, characterized by small, independent commodity producers and handicraft production, to a new form of so-called industrial capitalism, marked by the rise of mechanized factory production. Older forms of handicraft production were slowly consolidated into manufactories in the 1850s, either through uniting different craftsmen, as in carriage-making, or through increasing the division of labour, as in shoemaking. Although certainly larger than the artisan's small workshop and displaying more specialized operations, the first manufactories were still based on hand production. Only later, between the 1860s and early 1890s, did the introduction of steam power and large machinery begin to show its effects in Canada's factories, mills, and mines.

Increasing industrialization in the latter half of the nineteenth century helped revive Canada's scattered and relatively weak trade unions. The first labour unions had emerged in the early 1800s among craftsmen attempting to improve their working conditions and wages. These local work societies or craft unions had sprung up in spite of the British law (extending also to the colonies), which prohibited unions. Between the 1820s and 1860, however, many British immigrants had come to the British North American colonies, often bringing with them strong trade union traditions. In these times numerous isolated local unions had been formed, mainly to fight against wage cuts or employers' attempts to hire apprentices rather than skilled workers, at lower rates.

The Canadian industrial experience after 1860 was greatly influenced by world and North American business conditions and shaped, to some extent, by Canada's own national polices. A disastrous world-wide depression which hit Canada in 1873 (and lasted into the 1890s) produced hard times for working Canadians—a period of unemployment, wage cuts, demoralization and trade union disintegration. The slow return of prosperity in the 1880s may have helped in reviving trade unionism, particularly among traditional crafts and trades. Macdonald's national policies also played a part. Under these policies in the 1880s and early 1890s, factories and mills sprang up in central Canada and elsewhere. On the other hand, the protective tariff of 1879 acted to raise the prices of goods for workers and immigration caused intense competition for "living wages" and scarce jobs between Canadian and immigrant labour. Faced with these national policies, thousands of workers chose to emigrate to the United States between 1871 and 1901; Canada's net population loss during those thirty years numbered around 800 000 people.

Industrialism produced a variety of responses from labour. The growth of factory production after 1860, rising demands for a shorter (nine-hour) working day, and a bitter, highly publicized Toronto printers' strike in 1872 all generated a spurt of union activity. Although the vast majority of the labour force consisted of unorganized workers suffering from harsh conditions, by strenuous efforts unions achieved some gains for their members. Higher wages, laws regulating the hours of work, and measures preventing the exploitation of female and child labour were gradually granted by Canadian employers and men of capital. In spite of periodic setbacks, the union movement survived. One reason was the extension of the franchise (through lowering property qualifications for voting), which compelled successive Dominion governments to heed the reform demands of unionists. Another factor was the expansion into Canada of American unions, notably the Holy and Noble Order of the Knights of Labor in the 1880s and, later, the American Federation of Labor. The Knights spearheaded the struggle for "workers' control", appealing to working people with ideas of commonweal and social justice, while the AFL added its financial strength to support Canadian workers in their union demands for "more" of the fruits of their labours.

Much of this problem study focuses on industrialism in central Canadian cities like Toronto, Montreal and Hamilton, reflecting the present limitations of historical study in the field. Comparatively little is known about working-class experiences in New Brunswick mill towns, Cape Breton coal towns, Western bunkhouse camps, or the Quebec City dockyards. Questions are now being raised about whether industrialization evolved in similar ways in various regions, among various Canadian cultural, religious and ethnic groups.

In this historical problem, workers are examined not as isolated figures, engaged only in trade unions, strikes and radical politics, but as an integral part of a society undergoing industrialization. What role was the working class to play in the emerging industrial society? How were workers affected by changes in the forms of production and in working conditions? Did workers in this period of transition to large-scale industrial production develop a sense of common class identity or "working-class consciousness"? What did most working people want—a "living wage" or a greater measure of control over the workplace and over their own lives?

SELECTED CONTEMPORARY SOURCES

ORIGINS OF THE CANADIAN WORKING CLASS

The onset of industrialism in Canada in the years 1860 to 1896 had widespread effects on working people. Industrial growth held out the promise of a "living wage" and more plentiful jobs. The introduction of machinery dramatically increased the rapidity and scale of production. But factory labour conditions grew more inhumane as workers became more and more merely "handmaidens" to machines. Trade unions, which had existed since the early 1800s, showed a major resurgence. Whether these changes produced a definable "working-class consciousness", however, remains a matter of debate.

The Nine-Hour Movement—A Statement of Purpose, 1872

A key development in the rise of Canadian labour was the advent of the Nine-Hour Movement in the early 1870s. The issue which galvanized Canada's trade unionists into action was one with British and American roots—the demand for a shorter working day. Indeed the bitter struggle of British workers for a nine-hour day and American labour agitation for an eight-hour day not only stirred Canadian workers, but also served as a model for collective action.

In a major address to the founding meeting of the Canadian Nine Hour movement in Hamilton in January 1872, James Ryan, a machinist with the Great Western Railway, explained the purposes of the campaign, linking it with an emerging class consciousness.

Fellow workmen, I am proud this evening to see you so unanimous in your support of the cause we are here to advocate.... Our country, though young, is destined to be great and glorious. Working men want their share in this glory and seek it in reduction of labor, not in increase of pay. We want to better our physical constitutions, and to increase our mental power, so that if we cannot equal our Yankee neighbors in the variety of our undertaking, we can at least compete with them in the artistic finish of our productions. Under the pressure of continuous toil for the bare subsistence we can neither do justice to ourselves nor our masters. In the past capital has had inordinate power. Half a century ago a man retiring with £50,000 was thought to have done well; lately some have realized as high as £7,000,000 by twenty-five years devoted by business. This has been partly at the expense of the workingman, and partly owing to the introduction of improved machinery. We must become more skillful to use this machinery. We want time to study and learn. We wish also time to cultivate social and domestic virtues. With this accomplished, saloons will be less frequented. Merchants need the new system, if possible, more than we, as they are more closely confined. We must institute this reform and *both* shall reap its benefits. We want not more *money*, but more *brains*: not to be richer *serfs*, but better *men*. This system once established cannot retrograde. The hours of labor may become less, but never again *more*. England has conceded the principle of our claim. What is right there, cannot be wrong *here*. Working men are not alone in this movement. Several of our largest manufacturers favor it, and are only waiting that it be unanimously adopted. We want fair dealing, not strikes, no lock-outs. There is no real antagonism between capital [and] labor, but mutual dependence. We have not only justice on our side but men of intellect—those whose enterprise has made Hamilton what it is—are with us.... All depends upon our behavior and good spirit in agitating our cause. Let mutual esteem and respect between employers and employed continue.

'Thrice is he armed who knows his cause is just'.

Hamilton *Spectator*, January 29, 1872.

Benefits of Industrialism—Modernization in a Montreal Boot and Shoe Manufactory, 1885

The rise of industrialism brought benefits to workers in certain manufacturing trades. For some classes of workers large-scale production in government-inspected factories was an improvement over employment in the often dank, dingy and cramped workshops. Techniques of "scientific management" may have increased the control of employers over the work process, but in some cases they also made for a cleaner, more salubrious workplace. A report in The Toronto *Globe* in November, 1885 painted a glowing picture of one Montreal boot and shoe factory.

> Your correspondent in making enquiries on the firm of J. & T. Bell, Notre Dame-street, finds that this firm is engaged in the finer class of boots and shoes, and is by the way the oldest manufacturing firm in Canada.... They were just now preparing samples for the coming season, and would start their travellers out with a wider range of goods than usual, having taken up men's boots in addition to ladies' boots, which had been their specialty, and that the prospects of a good trip were very bright. They had, of course, taken special precautions regarding the smallpox, such, for instance, as withdrawing all work previously given to outsiders and having it done in their own premises, having special visits of inspection from independent physicians, and having regular weekly visits from a medical man among their employees at the factory and at their homes, and these precautions, of which they had given proof to their customers, may have saved them from the results of panic among their own section of the trade. A visit through the factory seemed to justify all that was claimed by the firm for their establishment. The factory is remarkably well equipped, and the light and sanitary advantages excellent.... As an instance of the progress made in boots and shoes manufacturing, it may be mentioned that the first introduction of machinery in the business in Canada was about 1845, when this firm imported from New York a Ginger machine for sewing the uppers: to-day they have machines capable of doing almost every branch of the work, from skiving and trimming to sole sewing and heeling—a revolution which has been wrought almost entirely within the last 30 years. Indeed, there were several employees of both sexes, some of whom came to the firm as children, whose experience compasses nearly all the improvements in boot and shoe machinery.... The operation of lasting is the only one which at present cannot be done to satisfaction on machines, but in most of the other processes it is said that the machines do the work not only more regularly and quicker, but with the result of a better finish than by hand.
>
> The Toronto *Globe*, November 18, 1885.

RESPONSES TO INDUSTRIALISM—MATERIAL WELFARE OR WORKERS' CONTROL?

Canadian working people reacted in different ways to the advance of industrialism in factories, mines and mills. Many ordinary workers, like the unskilled street cleaners, dock hands or brewery workers, always fearful of being consigned to the ever-present ranks of the unemployed, sought higher wages and secure jobs. Skilled workers such as the printers, shoemakers and carpenters responded differently. Once proud craftsmen practicing their traditional skills in artisanal workshops, they now found themselves labouring in large factories, surrounded by scores of workers, where their craft skills had been slowly displaced and rendered irrelevant by the process of mass production. To many of these workers, at least, regaining some control over the workplace was a matter of concern.

An Appeal for "A Living Wage", 1889

Wages and the cost of living were among the main worries of workers in the late nineteenth century. Common labourers, engaged in a daily struggle to earn a "living wage", left few records. A rare exception is this testimony by an Ontario machinist before the 1889 Royal Commission on the Relations of Labor and Capital.

> By Mr. WALSH: Q.—Are the wages in your trade higher in Toronto than in the old country? A.—When I lived there we worked nine hours a day or fifty-four hours per week at the place I left; fifty-one hours per week constitutes a week's work. Taking it by the hour I was as well off at home as here. We had as much per hour as here.
>
> By Mr. HEAKES: Q.—Would the purchasing power of money in England be greater than in Canada? A.—We could live cheaper at home than here.
> Q.—Money goes further there than here? A.—Yes, a great deal further. House rents are nothing there as compared with here, and coal was very cheap there.
>
> By Mr. GIBSON—   Q.—Did you have a good house for less money than you can get one here? A.—At home there are more tenements; you are not isolated as you are here. The working classes, especially in Toronto, like to live more on the cottage system, while at home there will be perhaps ten or twenty tenants in one building in flats.
> Q.—Do you get more accommodation for less money? A.—A workingman at home has generally a kitchen and two rooms. I would sooner live the way we do here than the way they do there; at the same time houses give more comfort there.
> Q.—Take the house in which you live now: would you obtain the same accommodation and the same number of rooms in the old country for the same money? A.—You would get a better house for the same money.
> Q.—Then it is better in the Old Country than here? A.—Yes so far as rent is concerned....
>
> Canada, Royal Commission on the Relations of Labor and Capital in Canada, 1889, *Evidence*—Ontario, pp. 62–63.

The Outcry of A Craftsman—A Montreal Shoemaker, 1889

Boot- and shoemakers were a prominent labour group in Victorian Canada with a strong sense of loyalty to their craft traditions. In testimony before the 1889 Labor Commission, a Montreal boot- and shoemaker voiced concerns common to many in his craft about the effects of industrialism on managerial or employer control of the workplace.

By Mr. HELBRONNER: Q.—There are very few boot and shoemakers to-day, who are able to make a pair of boots or shoes? A.—There are in the factories very few boot and shoe men who can make a boot or shoe; they are so few, indeed, that they can hardly be found at present. . . .

Q.—Has the introduction of machinery in the boot and shoe trade, resulted in a lowering of wages? A.—Yes; and that is the reason that I came here, before this Commission to say that our wages have been lowered, and not only the wages but the work has decreased, inasmuch as to-day one machine most certainly takes the place, on the average, of five or six men.

Q.—Does machinery have, as a result, the lowering of prices in boots and shoes? A.— Well, machinery brought on competition, and competition has been spread and been distributed over hand work, I think, and I am certain that, so far as the goods themselves go, if they have been lowered in price, it is the workmanship that has suffered.

By the CHAIRMAN: Q.—What you are asked is this—whether the prices that rule to-day are the same as the prices of other days, that is, a boot or shoe of the same quality is cheaper to-day than it was before the introduction of machinery into the boot and shoe trade. Is that so? A.—It is precisely the same thing with the exception of the few cents more or less one way or the other.

By the CHAIRMAN: Q.—It follows hence that it is possible to make a boot or shoe as cheaply by hand as by machinery, and machinery has been of no injury to you at all, if you can make shoes as cheaply by hand? A.—I do not see how you can say that machinery has not injured us.

Q.—But if you can make a shoe as cheaply by hand as by machinery how can you make out that machinery is harmful to you? A.—Yes; but you must consider that one machine can be put down as equivalent to twenty men, and that I, for instance, may be thrown upon the street. In that case who enjoys the benefit? It is the man who manufactures.

Canada, Royal Commission on the Relations of Labor and Capital in Canada, 1889, *Evidence—Quebec*, pp. 364–5.

ORGANIZING THE WORKINGMAN—THE CASE OF THE KNIGHTS OF LABOR

In the 1880s the most common organizational response to the problems of industrialism was the formation of labour unions. The first great labour organizations, the Knights of Labor, the AFL and Canada's Trades and Labor Congress, were all growing in strength and influence among the working classes. Unemployment, worker dislocation, and social unrest, stemming from the business depression that lasted from 1873 to the mid-1890s, were focusing public attention on the abuses of the emerging industrial system. Workers seemed to be slowly awakening to the impact of industrialism, and to evidence of a growing inequality in wealth and income between the new capitalists and the mass of wage-earners. Of all labour unions, the Knights of Labor was the organization most closely associated with the ideas of radical labour reform.

"Dreaming of What Might Be"—The Knights of Labor Vision, 1885

As a feature writer for the Knights of Labor's chief Canadian organ, *The Palladium of Labor*, T. Phillips Thompson gave strong expression in the mid-1880s to the ideals and goals of the Order. Writing under the *nom de plume* "Enjolras", he set out the Knights' critique of "industrial capitalism" and their vision of an ideal egalitarian society.

WHAT MIGHT BE

If the World's Workers were Only
Educated and Organized

SOCIAL REORGANIZATION

Universal Democracy and Co-operation
—No Wars or Monopolies

A BEAUTIFUL IDEAL

Which Can Never be Realized While
Labor is uneducated, Apathetic
and Divided

AN AIM TO WORK FOR

By Doing Our Part in Spreading the
Light

IT IS PRETTY GENERALLY UNDERSTOOD by this time among those who are interested in Labor Reform that it is a much wider and more comprehensive question than the mere matter of wages or hours— that it includes everything relating to the mental, moral and physical advancement of the worker, and implies a war to the death against every influence which tends to depress the condition of Labor. Yet there are still many whose sympathies are with us to a certain extent who do not realize to the full the ideal which ought steadily to be kept in view. . . . Let us picture to ourselves

THE SOCIAL CONDITION

that would result were our ideals realized by the resolute determination of the masses in all civilized lands to use their power for the good of the whole people, instead of letting the selfish few play upon their prejudices and passions, and rule them for the benefit of the upper class. . . .

PAUPERISM WOULD BE UNKNOWN.

Those who were by disease, accident or old age unable to work would be pensioned not as a charity, but as a right—as their share of the returns from the common inheritance— the earth. All industry would be co-operative. The interest of the workingmen and women in the great enterprises of industry and commerce would be recognized by law—and while organizing capacity, and brain work received its just return, it would not be permitted as now, to treat Labor as a mere commodity. And Labor would get the benefit of all the wonderful discoveries and inventions, such as steam, electricity and Labor saving machinery in a shortening of the hours of toil by abolishing much of the useless work caused by the competition and the waste of war. The really necessary Labor of the world, all men being workers, could probably be done in three or four hours a day.

By this time, no doubt, the readers who have followed me so far are ready to exclaim 'utopian!' 'visionary!' 'Altogether wild and impracticable!' I know it. Look back a little and you will see that I based the whole picture on the supposition that the great majority of

THE WORLD'S WORKERS

were educated as to their true interests and resolute in carrying out their purposes. Nobody can say that that state of things I have endeavoured to outline would not be to the best advantage of Labor—that we should not gladly welcome such a condition of society were it possible. Why then is it 'utopian?'—why is it the dream of a visionary? If it would be for the benefit of the immense majority of mankind, why cannot it be realized? Why? Simply because the people who do the world's work, and physically at least have the immense advantage over all opposing forces

ARE NOT EDUCATED,

—are not self-reliant—are not ready to make sacrifices. There you have the whole thing in a nutshell. The picture is merely a faint presentation of what might be—what cannot be at present solely because of the blindness, ignorance and want of union among workingmen—but what I trust yet will be when the scales of error, of misleading education and of temporary self-interest have fallen from their eyes—so they can see the light.

ENJOLRAS

The Palladium of Labor, December 26, 1885.

The Knights of Labor—A Critical View, 1886

The meteoric rise of the Knights of Labor in the mid-1880s aroused many fears in the upper reaches of the Toronto establishment. One of Canada's leading journals of literary opinion, *The Week*, published by Goldwin Smith, denounced the Knights and their alleged role in fomenting the Toronto street railway strike of 1886.

The organization of Knights of Labour is ... far more formidable than a Trade Union. It is secret, and sure in the end to fall into the same sort of hands into which other secret societies have fallen; it extends over the whole continent, having its centre in New York; it avows itself political, and has already appeared in that character; by laying a trifling tax on its innumerable members it can command almost any sum of money for its operations; it is aggressive in the highest degree, and as every column of commercial intelligence shows, has already kindled war at many points of the industrial world....

It is almost heartbreaking to consider the gross and palpable character of the fallacy by which the bulk of artisans who take part in these labour insurrections are misled, and under the influence of which they may in the end lay destructive hands on the trades by which they live. The enemy against which they are waging war is Capital, which they are taught by their chosen guides to regard as a tyrant robbing them of their bread. Suppose they are completely victorious in the war, as, after a struggle more or less protracted, they are pretty sure to be—suppose the capitalist, finding that all his profits are gone, that nothing but the risk of loss and vexation is left, retires discomfited from the field, realizes whatever remnant of property may remain to him, transfers it to some community where commercial liberty still exists, and shuts up his works or mill, what will follow? Will the artisans without capital, with nothing but their bare sinews, and, perhaps, without the means of subsistence for a week, be able to set up works, or a mill of their own? If not, what can they do but remain unemployed and starve? The expulsion of all capital from the country is the goal towards which these agitations ultimately lead. Does any sane artisan believe that his condition would be really improved by that result?

The Week, March 18, 1886, p. 248.

WORKING-CLASS LIFE AND CULTURE—A SOURCE OF CLASS SOLIDARITY?

If working people did develop a distinct sense of class consciousness in Victorian Canada, it would be reflected in their culture.[2] Faced with the advance of industrialization, they would seek solace in familiar social practices and rituals and look for ways to resist the growing control of employers over modes of production. Thus, workers' lives in the street, tavern and friendly societies may provide clues to the ways in which they sought to preserve a measure of stability and some control over their own experiences. But questions arise. Did a unique working-class culture exist which transcended divisions of religion, ethnicity and skill among workers? And if such a culture existed, was it potent enough to create a sense of common interest and to guide workers in collective action?

A Glimpse of Working-Class Montreal in the 1870s—Joe Beef's Canteen

JOE BEEF, OF MONTREAL.

Who will feed a Poorman, if is hungry,
Cure him if he is sick ...
He never let a poorman die on
The floor and never went back on the Poor !

---

2. Culture may be defined in this sense as "a style of social and artistic expression peculiar to a society or class". (*The American Heritage Dictionary of the English Language*. New York: Dell, 1973.)

Joe Beef's Canteen, a notorious part of the Victorian underworld of old Montreal, provided one remarkable example of late-nineteenth-century working-class life and culture. Located in the waterfront district, it was the haunt of sailors and longshoremen, the unemployed and petty thieves. Middle-class Montreal saw this tavern, with its performing bears, rowdy patrons and sawdust-covered floors as a "den of iniquity" and a threat to the social order of industrial society. The working-class residents along the waterfront claimed the Canteen's owner, Charles McKiernan as their spokesperson, and his tavern as a source of aid and comfort in times of unemployment, sickness or hunger.

Joe Beef's Lecture on the "Almighty Dollar", Chaboillez Square, Montreal, 1877

My friends, I have come here tonight to address you on 'the Almighty Dollar.' The very door bells of Montreal ring with the 'Almighty Dollar.' The wooden-headed bobbies nail you, and you have to sleep on the hard floor provided by the City Fathers, and the next morning the fat Recorder tells you: 'Give me the "Almighty Dollar," or down you go for eight days.' The big-bugs all have their eyes on the 'Almighty Dollar,' from the Bishop down, and if you die in the hospital, they want the almighty dollar to shave you and keep you from the students. No one can blame you for demanding the 'Almighty Dollar' a day. The man who promises 90¢ a day and pays only 80¢ is no man at all. The labourer has his rights.

Montreal *Witness*, December 21, 1877.

The Ordeal of Mrs. Tope—A Hamilton Charivari, 1890

Charivaris[3], a traditional method of community control, were a surprisingly common occurrence in scattered towns and cities of late-nineteenth-century Canada. In the city of Hamilton, for example, the charivari survived as a common cultural practice until the turn of the century, often functioning in its traditional manner, but also was adapted to new purposes. Between 1865 and 1895 there were at least sixteen reported instances of charivari parties, complete with evening marches, rough music and the proverbial sound of the fish-horn.

The Hamilton Cotton Mill strike of 1890 touched off a rash of incidents which may be described as charivari parties. In one such highly publicized instance, Mrs. Tope, a woman who quit the strike to return to the mills, was singled out for intimidation by a band of charivaring weavers. A Hamilton *Spectator* news report on the subsequent trial of the ringleaders described the entire episode.

Great interest was taken in the trial of the weavers who charivaried Mrs. Tope because

---

3. The charivari ritual originated as a kind of mob action used to expose sexual offenders, cuckholded husbands, wife beaters and social deviates to the collective wrath of the community.

she returned to work, at the police court yesterday. [sic]. Many of the strikers were in court. The defendants—William Carlisle, George Maxwell, Robert Irwin, Mary A. Kinsley and Elizabeth Wright—were charged with following the complainant and acting in a disorderly manner, with a view to compel her to abstain from working for the Ontario Cotton Mills Company. . . .

Mrs. Tope testified that she had worked at the mill for eight years. The mill had been shut down for five weeks because of the weavers' strike. She did not attend any meetings of the strikers and at the request of Manager Snow she went to work last Monday. When she was on her way home that evening she went along Ferrie Street. At the corner of John and Ferrie streets she was followed by a crowd of men and women. The defendants Maxwell and Irwin had fish-horns and were blowing them. She estimated the crowd at a couple of hundred, many of them being weavers. Mrs. Tope turned down Catharine Street and was followed by the crowd. She stopped to the let the crowd pass, and Mrs. Wright struck her. She tried to strike back and Carlisle pushed her into the road, and she fell down, injuring her hip. Tope found his wife surrounded by the crowd, and took her home.

Hamilton *Spectator*, June 10, 1890.

CONFLICTING INTERPRETATIONS

The "labour question" in nineteenth-century Canada has emerged in recent years as one of the most lively and fertile areas of Canadian historical discussion. A new generation of labour historians, mostly the product of Canadian universities in the late 1960s and early 1970s has turned its attention to the nineteenth-century working-class experience and directly challenged many of the traditional assumptions and interpretations in Canadian labour history. The work of the "working-class historians", has injected radical perspectives into nineteenth-century labour history and all but revolutionized long-standing views of the relationships between labour and capital in Canada's period of industrialization.

The nature of the working-class response to nineteenth-century industrialism has been at the heart of this historical debate. Traditional labour historians—following the work of Harold Logan in the late forties and early fifties—have interpreted working-class attitudes and actions almost entirely from the perspective of trade unions, and emphasized union efforts to organize labour for material gains. Historians of the new "working-class school", notably Gregory S. Kealey and Bryan D. Palmer, have focused on the relationship between the onset of industrialism and the making of a Canadian working class committed to a struggle for control over the workplace and its own communities. Many of their interpretations, however, have recently been called into question by a number of labour historians, including David J. Bercuson and Irving Abella, whose work centres on the history of twentieth- century Canadian labour. Some of the contentious points are raised in the following reading selections.

THE EMERGENCE OF A WORKING-CLASS MOVEMENT—TWO PERSPECTIVES

The Making of a Canadian Working Class—A Preliminary Analysis

If Canadian workers did indeed pursue a nineteenth-century class struggle for workers' control, a working-class consciousness would have been of critical importance. One of the first labour historians to seek out the origins of a Canadian working-class consciousness was Steven Langdon, a labour historian heavily influenced by the work of British Marxist scholar E.P. Thompson and the English "working-class school". In this passage from a 1973 essay, Langdon examines the Nine-Hour Movement of the early 1870s as part of a slowly emerging sense of working-class solidarity in central Canada.

Out of the TTA (Toronto Trades Assembly) and other similar coordinating efforts, the Nine-Hours Movement grew. It . . . should be seen in the context of capitalist industrialization; having gained some cohesion, workers tried to advance against the impersonal labor market and the ongoing mechanization of the new system.

This can be seen in the arguments workers used. Some emphasized that it was 'necessary to have the hours of labour shortened, in order that the workingmen might have an opportunity to improve themselves intellectually and physically.' And other arguments tied the case for shorter hours even more firmly to the social dislocations of industrial capitalism. 'They wanted to bring the unemployed workingmen of the country into work,' [John] Hewitt explained in Toronto in 1872. 'It was better to have the whole community working four hours a day than to have a portion working for twelve hours.' The Nine-Hours Movement, he stressed later in Hamilton, was 'a demand for a more equal distribution of labour among the human family, which had become a crying want.' . . . .

Such a co-ordinated initiative to reshape industrial growth had to involve many workers if it were to succeed. So the Nine-Hours Leagues acted as forerunners of CIO-style industrial unionism, pulling in everybody, unionized and non-unionized, skilled and unskilled. And in that context, the consciousness of collective workers' interests—working-class consciousness—was inevitable. . . .

The collective reaction of capitalists to the expanding labour movement was critical in this process of class definition. Spurred by union strength, Toronto employers had formed their association 'to resist any attempt on the part of our employees to dictate to us by what rules we shall govern our business or how many hours shall constitute a day's work.' And that reaction, supported by so many powerful industrial capitalists, clearly made the nine-hours struggle the start of a fight for power in the whole political economy, not just a simple trade dispute. So the TTA had to look for support well beyond its own city, wherever its working-class interest in reshaping industrial capitalist society was shared . . . .

* * * * *

This study has shown that a conscious working-class movement emerged in central Canada over 1845–75, and that this emergence was directly related to the rise of industrial capitalism. The evidence is clear that this social process took place. However, the evidence *doesn't* show how widespread and deeply-held the class attitudes and radical perspectives of this process actually were. *Some* leaders of *some* workingmen clearly shared this class feeling; *some* of *them* took steps toward political action. But what were the dimensions of the movement as a whole? Some answer to that is a necessary prelude to gauging the significance of the process I have been tracing, either for understanding events at the time, for analysing roots of the present democratic socialist movement in Canada, or for questioning the classlessness of conventional interpretations of Canadian history....

... the working-class movement I have described was not a mature, confident force capable of transforming Canadian society in the collective egalitarian image it sometimes expressed. It was not even close to that sort of strength. But, nevertheless, the consciousness which the movement expressed *was* widely shared by central Canadian workers. This view is justified by the numerical support the movement seemed to draw by 1872, and by the course of political events of the period.

Steven Langdon, *The Emergence of the Canadian Working Class Movement 1845–1875* (Toronto: New Hogtown Press, 1975), pp. 18–20 and 23. Footnotes omitted.

The Nine-Hour Pioneers—A Different View of the Movement at its Origins

Steven Langdon's central argument that an emergent working-class consciousness can be discerned in the 1845 to 1875 period has met with skepticism in some quarters. Professor John Battye of St. Mary's University raised some questions about the Langdon thesis in a 1979 *Labour/Le Travailleur* article focusing on the Nine-Hour Movement and its failure in the early 1870s.

The nine-hour movement failed primarily because of the primitive condition of the organization of labour in Canada, a condition the movement itself did much to remedy. Despite the intense efforts of men such as James Ryan in Hamilton, John Hewitt in Toronto, and James Black in Montreal, labour organization was far from complete, largely untested in conflict on any scale, inexperienced in the art of negotiation, and financially incapable of supporting sustained strike action....

Perhaps the best assessment of the movement at the time was that made by John Carter of the Painters Union. In a letter written to the *Leader* in July [1872], Carter acknowledged 'it is true that we have not many signal victories to record,' but, continued Carter, the main result of the movement was 'not so much in the direct success that has attended our efforts as from the steady and lasting impressions that have been made upon the minds of the classes.' Specifically, Carter was pointing to the fact that, 'The working class all through the struggle, have gained for themselves, through their leaders, a systematic, yet pure and simple education into the principles of unionism.' Carter, who would be the first president of the Canadian Labor Union formed in the following year, was pointing to the development, not of a class consciousness, but to a growth among the working class of a trade union consciousness. To some extent this was manifested in the organizational activity apparent during the nine-hour struggle; carpenters in Belleville, mechanics in Kingston, machinists in Oshawa, carpenters and printers in Ottawa, bricklayers, masons, tinsmiths, lathers, harness makers, and painters in Toronto, and tinsmiths, boiler makers and harness makers in Hamilton all organized, or sometimes reorganized, themselves into trade unions....

* * * * *

...Trade unions were seen primarily as vehicles through which members might improve their material condition, and perhaps incidentally their social class position, but were not seen as agents for changing the social basis of North American society. Trade unionism was based on the concept of class-for-itself unionism rather than class-in-itself unionism.

The failure to confirm its own independent political structure; the ease with which fledgling working-class leaders were induced into a collaborative alignment with middle-class leadership and into the realm of established bourgeois politics; the careless indulgence with which political and pecuniary palliatives were accepted during the nine-hour agitation, argues against anything but an inchoate sense of class consciousness among Canadian workers during the early 1870s. There certainly was developing a class identity; while working-class spokesmen, such as Hewitt, displayed an obvious sense of awareness in regards to the conflicting interests of capital and labour, but we cannot impute consciousness to Canadian workers as a class based on the apparent consciousness of some few of its leaders. Yet to talk of the making of the working class is not to imply that it is ever finally made. It is continually changing its occupational composition, its internal and external relations, and with these its conception of itself; its present and its future; and its class consciousness. Nor is class consciousness necessarily ever complete....

John Battye, "The Nine Hour Pioneers: The Genesis of the Canadian Labour Movement", *Labour/Le Travailleur*, Vol. 4 (1979), pp. 51–56. Footnotes omitted.

THE KNIGHTS OF LABOR: AN EPHEMERAL TRADE UNION OR A MODEL OF WORKER'S UNITY?

The KOL and American "Labour Imperialism"—A Standard Account of the Order

Traditional histories of the Canadian trade union movement have tended to interpret the Holy and Noble Order of the Knights of Labor as a tame offshoot of American trade unionism which did little to improve the material welfare of working people. In his labour history, *Trade Unions in Canada* (1948), Harold Logan treated the KOL as a relatively minor phenomenon, significant mainly as an example of American "labour imperialism" in Canada.

The Canadian labour movement took its lead from its American membership for the first time in the eighties. Although American organizations were in the majority earlier, it was to British ideas and precedents, as we have seen, that the Canadian unions looked for leadership. But with the great incursion of the Knights of Labour about 1885, with their missionaries and their ideals, the mind of the movement, as well as its organization seems to have been captured by the Americans. It was not until a decade later that a reaction came, bringing with it a critical attitude toward the close American connection and an attempt by a large element to extricate the Canadian membership and operate a more independent national movement.

Although the period of the later eighties was one of very rapid expansion of both Knights and unionist organizations, the methods of labour were not aggressive in any offensive sense. The former was not primarily a striking organization. As expressed by D.J. O'Donoghue in 1887, the tendency of its principles and methods was 'in direction of intellectual development, peaceful and lawful agitation, and an intelligent and united use of the ballot as a remedy' for grievances. It looked for arbitration ultimately 'to remedy the necessity for strikes', and was depending on co-operation—productive and distributive—eventually to take the place of the wage system. Nevertheless, the phenomenal rush of the hitherto unorganized unskilled workers into great assemblies with their pretentious inclusiveness was soon challenged by certain employers in Ontario, and strikes against the employer's closed shop became a necessity....

During the decade or less when the Knights of Labour were showing their strength, the labour movement was characterized by a great deal of idealism and by expectations of rapid improvement to be brought about by different types of reform. Later the idealism waned, but with the general stagnation in industry and consequent hopelessness of industrial action, considerable attention, as we have seen, was turned toward political action, taxation reform, monetary reform, arbitration, and other methods and palliatives. Socialism made a bid for favour, but with the exception of British Columbia the Canadian worker appears to have been suspicious of it.

H.A. Logan, *Trade Unions in Canada* (Toronto: Macmillan, 1948), pp. 73–75. Footnotes deleted.

The Noble Order—A Bond of Workers' Unity

Gregory S. Kealey and Bryan D. Palmer, two "working-class school" historians, have argued that the KOL in Ontario, far from being a weak, conservative Order, was really the leading edge of an emergent "movement culture", an organization committed to a unified working-class action and the radical transformation of industrial society.

...the Noble and Holy Order of the Knights of Labor represented a dramatic shift away from past practices within the history of Ontario workers. Although the Knights built very much on the accumulated experience of the working class, they channelled that experience in new directions. In the words of Raymond Williams[4] they took a whole series of residual aspects of the class experience, built upon them, and erected a structural and intellectual apparatus that was the beginning of emergent purpose. In short, the Knights of Labor in Ontario created, for the first time, what Lawrence Goodwyn[5] has called a movement culture of alternative, opposition, and potential. In the breadth of their vision, the scope of their organization, and the unique refusal to collapse the cause of workers into this reform or that amelioration or restrict entry to the movement to this stratum or that group, the Knights of Labor hinted at the potential and possibility that are at the foundation of the making of a class.... But as the first expression of the social, cultural and political emergence of a class, the Knights of Labor understandably groped for answers more than they marched forcefully towards solutions. The Order was itself inhibited by the context of late nineteenth-century Ontario which, aside from its own peculiar 'regional' divisions, stood poised between an economy of competitive capitalism, but recently arrived, and the monopoly capitalism which stood literally around the corner with the Laurier boom years of the twentieth century. The Knights, in many ways, straddled each epoch, looking simultaneously forward and backward, longing for the rights they knew to be justly theirs,

4. See Raymond Williams, "Base and Superstructure in Marxist Cultural Theory", *New Left Review*, Vol. 82 (November-December, 1973), pp. 1–16.
5. The concept is drawn from Lawrence Goodwyn, *Democratic Promise: The Populist Movement in America*, (New York: Oxford University Press, 1976).

attacking the monopolists they saw controlling the business, politics and culture of their society. . . .

* * * * *

The 1880s were a critical decade in Canadian history—a decade which witnessed the fulfillment of the National Policy industrial strategy with a rapid expansion in Canadian manufacturing, especially in textiles. Yet these years also saw the breakdown of the previous consensus on industrial development, as Canadian workers, especially in the country's industrial heartland, began to raise their voices in an unfamiliar, concerted fashion to join the growing debate about the nation's future. Ontario's mainly British and Canadian workers, many with previous trade-union and industrial experience, provided leadership to the emerging working-class movement which found its most articulate expression in the Knights of Labor. The challenge which this movement mounted in all realms of Ontario society—the cultural, intellectual and political as well as the economic—engendered in turn a class response from employers and from the state. The employers engaged in a virulent, open warfare with their worker-Knights, especially in the period of economic decline after 1886. In the 1890s they began as well to turn to the ever-increasing concentration and centralization of capital and later to the modern management devices of a rampant Taylorism in their battle with labour. Meanwhile the state and the political parties responded in a more conciliatory fashion. Mowat and, to a lesser degree, Macdonald interceded to provide workers with many of the protections they demanded—factory acts, bureaux of labour statistics, arbitration measures, suffrage extension, employers' liability acts and improved mechanics' lien acts. The political parties proved even more flexible and managed through patronage and promises to contain much of the oppositional sentiment which flared in the 1880s. Thus the Canadian political system functioned effectively to mediate the fiery class conflict of the 1880s.

In the following decade, with the exception of eastern Ontario, the Knights were moribund. Their precipitous decline was halted by a slight resurgence in the late 1890s, but the 1902 Berlin decision delivered the final *coup de grâce*. Yet as we suggested earlier, the heritage of the Order lived on. Its major contributions to working-class memory centred on its oppositional success as a movement which for the first time provided *all* workers with an organizational vehicle and, further, which, for a moment at least, overcame the splintering forces which so often divided the working class.

Gregory S. Kealey and Bryan D. Palmer, "The Bonds of Unity: The Knights of Labor in Ontario, 1880-1900", *Histoire sociale/Social History*, Vol. XIV (November, 1981), pp. 372-3 and 410-11. Footnotes edited.

THE WORKING-CLASS RESPONSE TO INDUSTRIALISM—A VARIETY OF VIEWPOINTS

The Right to A "Living Wage"—A Business Historian's View of the Workingman's Welfare

Canadian businessmen and workers in the late nineteenth century shared a common desire for their rightful share of the production wrought by Canada's industrial revolution. Just as businessmen sought a "living profit", so workers demanded a "living wage". Business historian Michael Bliss of the University of Toronto, gave this account of the working man's lot in Canada's age of enterprise:

By the 1880s Canadians had begun to discover the social problems and conflicts that seemed everywhere a consequence of the Industrial Revolution. They were already aware of the British experience half a century earlier; it apparently demonstrated that subsistence wages, harsh discipline, and the exploitation of women and children were the dark underside of the coming of the age of factories. Now that the rapid development of Canadian manufacturing through a protective tariff was officially the country's National Policy, governments and middle-class reformers were concerned to minimize the incidence of these abuses in Canada. So, too, were the leaders of the highly vocal Canadian labour movement, spokesmen for both the skilled artisans whose craft unions were now reviving from the debacle of the depression of the 1870s, and for thousands of unskilled workers who, in the middle of the decade, were organized for the first time when the American-born Knights of Labor sowed hundreds of assemblies across Ontario and Quebec....

Particularly when petitions were backed with the threat of political action by organized labour, governments responded to these concerns with investigations and legislation. The Royal Commission on the Relations of Labor and Capital, formally established in 1886 and popularly known as the Royal Labor Commission, was a major inquiry into working conditions and wages, taking evidence from some 1800 witnesses in every industrial and commercial centre in central and eastern Canada. Already by the time of its report in 1889 Ontario and Quebec had passed their first Factory Acts to regulate safety conditions, child labour, and hours of work. Although these actions had little significant immediate effect on the welfare of workers, they did mean that employers now had to explain and justify the physical conditions of work in their establishments, the wages they offered to various classes of help, and the hours they expected workers to toil. Employers were being called upon to accept responsibility for their workers' welfare....

In this individualistic system, the employer had done his part in contributing to the worker's welfare when he offered a man a job, and had done a little bit more when he provided work for the man's wife and children. The employer provided men with wages...and with an opportunity to put their skill and ambition to work and make something of themselves. It was always assumed that employers would reward good and faithful service....

Most Canadian businessmen thought the workers' material welfare was being adequately served without the presence of unions. Nothing had worsened since the coming of the National Policy factories. Things were as good as or better than they had ever been. Businessmen were impressed by the evidence of New World affluence in Canada. They thought that by virtue of the employment they offered and the attitudes they were instilling in their workers—industry, integrity, thrift—they were already in the vanguard of progress. Surely the opportunities for thrifty and industrious workers to prosper were greater than ever before. True, some tinkering and adjustments in the system were necessary from time to time, a factory act here, divided watercloses and a fire-escape there; businessmen too had been horrified by the pictures of the Lancashire miners in the Sunday-school books. On the whole, though, the system was working well. Therefore it is not surprising that the intrusion of trade unions with their demands for drastic change, their rhetoric of conflict and distrust, and their destructive insistence on having their own way, was met with shock, alarm, and hostility.

Michael Bliss, *A Living Profit: Studies in the Social History of Canadian Business, 1883-1911* (Toronto: McClelland and Stewart, 1974), pp. 55-56; 63-66; 69 and 73. Footnotes omitted.

Labour's Demand for a Slice of the Capitalist Pie—A Labour Historian's Interpretation

Traditional labour historians offer a completely different view of the state of working people and the goals of labour in the period of Canadian industrialization. In the following passage from Eugene Forsey's *The Canadian Labour Movement, 1812–1902* (1974), he argued that labour primarily sought "more!" of the fruits of production.

> So much for the history of the Canadian Labour Movement during its first ninety years. What were its aims, and what methods did it use to attain them?
>
> The aims, then as now, may be summed up in Gompers' famous phrase, 'more, more, more.'
>
> More of what?
>
> First, more money: higher wages (or salaries), and the demands were not always modest. The Charlottetown Shoemakers, in 1874, threatened to strike for 'a nearly 40 per cent increase.' The Telegraphers, in 1883, wanted a minimum of 27 per cent.
>
> Second, more leisure. Here, also, the demands were not always modest. The Saint John Caulkers seem actually to have won an eight-hour day in 1866, and the Telegraphers, in 1883, tried to get an eight-hour day and a seven-hour night. The Congress repeatedly voted for the eight-hour day. But most of the unions, at the end of the century, were still doing well if they got nine hours. From 1890 on, also, the TLC was vigorously demanding 'protection of the Lord's Day.' But no one seems to have dreamt of paid statutory holidays or vacations.
>
> Third, extra pay, higher rates, overtime, for work beyond normal hours.
>
> Fourth, recognition of unions by employers as what we now call 'collective bargaining agents,' and protection against defaulting union officials (a very common species in the nineteenth century). In the struggle for union recognition, the unions had no help from the law. Where they were strong, they got recognition, and they kept it as long as they were strong. Where they were weak, they did not get it.
>
> The skilled crafts tried for, and often got, a *de facto* closed shop. Other forms of union security seem to have been almost unheard of, though the PWA,[6] by 1894, had got the check-off for most of its locals....
>
> Eugene Forsey, *The Canadian Labour Movement, 1812–1902* (Ottawa: Canadian Historical Association, 1974), Historical Booklet No. 27, pp. 13–14.

The Struggle for Workers' Control—A Revisionist Interpretation

Practitioners of the new labour history argue that workers, particularly those in the skilled trades, wanted far more than simply higher wages and satisfaction of a set of union demands. Skilled workers in cities like Toronto, Hamilton and Montreal, under attack by mechanization, were engaged in a larger struggle for control over their working lives. Much of the experience of Quebec's working class has been documented by Fernand Harvey in *Revolution industrielle et travailleurs* (1978).

---

6. The Provincial Workmen's Association, a Nova Scotia union founded in 1879.

But Gregory S. Kealey, of the English-Canadian "working class school", has carried the revisionist argument even further in his study, *Toronto Workers Respond to Industrial Capitalism, 1867–1892* (1980).

Industrial capitalism, born in the 1850s and 1860s in Toronto, grew to maturity in the 1870s and 1880s. The working class emerged in these decades and struggled to keep pace with the vast changes wrought by the new economic system. In its attempt to comprehend and to cope with the wrenching transformation of capitalist industrialization, the working class tenaciously maintained the political and cultural traditions of its ancestors. These traditions ranged from the peculiar Orange trinity of crown, prince, and Protestantism (reminiscent of eighteenth-century 'church-and-king' crowds in England) to the customary methods of work associated with pre-industrial craft production. But Toronto workers adapted these traditions to the new context of industrial capitalist society. Those that failed to be adapted, such as the Orange ritual riot, slowly disappeared in these transitional decades. The Orange Order itself, however, continued to play an important institutional role in the world of Toronto workers. . . .

The artisan traditions deeply entrenched in the pre-industrial world provided Toronto workers with innovative strategies to combat their employers who tried to enforce industrial capitalism's new work styles. From medieval craft lore, the shoemakers brought forth St. Crispin as a symbol of their historic roots and of their importance to the community. Building on traditions of craft pride and solidarity, Toronto shoemakers even resorted to breaking machines in their desperate attempt to maintain decent wages and conditions in the shoe industry. Most striking was their ability to adapt the older means of artisan resistance to their new situation. Thus they extended craft traditions to encompass all workers in the industry, including women, quickly realizing that a narrow view of production was destined to fail. . . .

The experiences of the 1870s made a deep impact on many workers whose skills were increasingly undermined by the development of industrial capitalism. They began to recognize that their strength no longer lay in their skill but rather in their ability to organize all workers. This strategy became the keynote of the Knights of Labor, who preferred arbitration to strike action as a way of resolving industrial conflict. The Knights arrived in Toronto in the early 1800s and proceeded to organize large segments of the Toronto work force previously untouched by craft unionism. As had been true in 1872, when labour united in the nine-hours movement, however, capital responded vigorously to this new challenge and defeated the Knights dramatically in the second street-railway strike in 1886 and in a series of lesser struggles in 1887. These defeats, together with an economic downturn, decreased the Knights' influence. . . .

The transitional nature of the 1870s and 1880s bred a labour reform ideology and a labour movement which simultaneously looked backward and forward. Much of the movement's strength lay in the workers' knowledge of a past that was totally different from their present. They knew that industrial capitalism was a social system with a history: it was neither natural nor pre-ordained. This realization injected their struggles with a precocious vigour, based on their comprehension that the economy had been, and thus could be, organized in radically different ways. This commonly shared understanding disappeared in the twentieth century, and only socialist workers maintained an alternative social vision. The precision of the socialist critique was a major gain for the Toronto working class, but the declining numbers of those whose vision transcended the established system was a major loss. Class conflict, of course, continued.

Gregory S. Kealey, *Toronto Workers Respond to Industrial Capitalism, 1867–1891* (Toronto: University of Toronto Press, 1980), pp. 291–5. Footnotes omitted.

THE WORKING-CLASS CULTURE—AUTONOMOUS OR INDISTINGUISHABLE FROM LARGER SOCIETY?

Much of the new labour history in Canada is explicitly Marxist and primarily concerned with exploring the "culture" of the working class. Following the lead of E.P. Thompson in Britain and Herbert Gutman in the United States, the new labour historians apply a culturalist approach to the Canadian experience by studying workers to discover the patterns of their culture. To those historians who see the Canadian labour experience as a story of class conflict and an ongoing struggle for workers' control, a concern with culture is basic. If workers in the late nineteenth century had developed a working-class consciousness, the unifying force must be found in their cultural experience.

A "Culture in Conflict"—The Case of Hamilton's Skilled Workers

One scholar who has attempted to identify a late nineteenth-century working-class culture is Canadian Marxist historian Bryan D. Palmer. Starting with E.P. Thompson's theory that culture and conflict were interrelated processes, Palmer set out to describe the working-class experience of Hamilton's skilled workers and to explore the intricacies of their culture and community life.

... The culture of the nineteenth-century skilled workingman embraced a rich associational life, institutionalized in the friendly society, the mechanics' institute, sporting fraternities, fire companies, and workingmen's clubs. Complementing these formal relationships were the less structured but equally tangible ties of neighbourhood, workplace, or kin, manifesting themselves in the intimacy of the shared pail of beer, or the belligerence of the charivari party. Lingering at the edge of this culture, and illuminating its contours, stood events of importance to the community of the skilled: Confederation, marked by celebration and trade procession; self-proclaimed working-men's holidays, later legitimized by government proclamation and declared Labour Day; or less momentous happenings, such as the coming of a circus, or the visit of a minstrel troupe. By the early twentieth century, it is true, realms of this culture would be emasculated, if not destroyed. The mechanics' institute, poisoned by the condescension and contemptuous patronage of the city's elite, had withered and died, while professionalization siphoned off much of the cultural essence of the baseball teams and fire companies. Yet the passing of institutions or the sublimation of once specifically working-class activities hardly signified the obliteration of a culture. Much lived on, transplanted to other formal settings, craft unions being particularly fertile ground; other cultural forms and traditions continued to thrive in their own right.

Cultural continuities, then, testify to the basic resiliency of working people in the face of the industrial-capitalist transformation of the nineteenth-century. It was perhaps this fundamental continuity which lent coherence and stability to the working-class community, mediating the disruptive impact of massive population turnover, pervasive upward and downward social mobility, and the chaotic upheavals associated with the transition from handicraft production to modern industry—all prominent in the years 1860–1914. And, finally, this essential cultural continuity may be seen as the background of coherence against which new forms of working-class protest evolved, forms that in Hamilton assumed importance in the struggle for the nine-hour day, the rise of the Knights of Labor, and the emergence of an aggressive craft unionism in the pre-World War I years. For culture is nothing if not *used*: a process that constantly brings into relief the specific social relationships of a given society, relationships that often reflect basic antagonisms under industrial capitalism. . . .

It was, perhaps, in just this kind of way that culture operated in past times in Hamilton's community of skilled workers. Despite the irksome fact that working-class involvement in friendly society and fire-engine hall, mechanics' institute and baseball team, is shrouded in obscurity, a ubiquitous anonymity being imposed on historical knowledge by the lack of surviving sources, it is possible, and even probable, that the associational life of skilled workers cultivated a sense of solidarity that strengthened the ability of the skilled to resist the encroachments of industrial-capitalist disciplines and development. And it is undeniable that within a shared cultural context there were age-old customs and traditions—the charivari, to name but one— that could be turned to the purposes of protest. . . .

* * * * *

Both the charivari and whitecapping[7] . . . illustrate a process of cultural continuity and adaptation. Traditional mechanisms of community control had become converted into tools of working-class protest. Other realms of working-class culture also highlight this process of continuity and adaptation. The workingmen's clubs, for instance, in their evolution from the jocular associations of the 1860s and 1870s to the organized forums of radicalism in the 1898–1914 years, exemplify an important trend. Even such superficially mundane activities as baseball games, picnics, and suppers could bring into relief the class interests of Hamilton workingmen. Finally, the institutional sphere of associational life, centred in the friendly society, mechanics' institute, fire company, and craft union, provided a stability and coherence to working-class life that, over time, fostered an important solidarity. It was in this context that events like the nine-hour movement of 1872, the Knights of Labor parades of the 1880s, or the Hamilton street railway strike of 1906 would draw universal support.

This, then, was a rich and vibrant culture; its subtle interconnections speak of an important continuity. Conscious of the transformation of economic life over the course of the nineteenth century, historians have perhaps emphasized change too much, ignoring the cultural continuities in working-class life. And these continuities were not without meaning, for they could soften the blows of industrial-capitalist development, ease the strain of the many disciplines seemingly engulfing the Victorian mechanic. In certain circumstances, too, cultural continuities could be adapted to new purposes, confronting directly the harsh realities of the new order. But even this was not enough. The impingements of capitalist society were often too oppressive, the strains of everyday life too exhausting, the toll, in human terms, too great.

Bryan D. Palmer, *A Culture in Conflict: Skilled Workers and Industrial Capitalism*

---

7. Whitecapping, a traditional form of community control, involved vigilante groups patterned after secret societies in the American South. The "White Caps" operated in many U.S. and Canadian communities in the years 1890 to 1905, upholding community standards and morality.

in Hamilton, Ontario 1860–1914 (Montreal: McGill-Queen's University Press, 1979), pp. 38–39, 66 and 69. Footnotes edited.

The New "Working-Class History" and the Question of Culture—A Critique of the Culturalist Approach

Many historians question the theoretical assumptions and almost doctrinaire approach to the study of working-class culture taken by such scholars as Kealey and Palmer. In a historiographical essay, University of Calgary historian and former *Canadian Historical Review* editor David Jay Bercuson offered this assessment of the new labour historians' approach to the working-class experience.

The first major treatment of working-class culture to appear in Canada was Bryan Palmer's *A Culture in Conflict.* Part 2, 'Culture' contains chapters touching on workers' lives in street, sports field, and friendly society, as well as a discussion of struggles for workers' control and the development of what Palmer says is reform thought.

Using Palmer's criteria and evidence, what do we see when we look at Hamilton's working-class culture? Was it unique to the working class?

First, we see that workers, merchants, clerks, professionals, and propertied men all belonged to friendly societies such as the Orange Lodge, the Masons, the Foresters, and so on. Although Palmer says that the non-worker members exerted 'disproportionate amounts of influence in many friendly society circles...' he also says that the workers were 'certainly...common' and that 'their role was far from subservient.' Palmer would like to be precise about worker participation but he admits that the 'data are extremely rare.' The only membership lists he has show that the Masons and the St. George's and St. Andrew's societies contained 'a particularly weak working-class constituency....' His evidence clearly shows that some skilled workers belonged to some friendly societies; it does not show that those societies were exclusively composed of workers or even, in some cases, dominated by them. The picture is one of workers, clerks, merchants, and others rubbing shoulders in these clubs. So too with the volunteer fire companies. Palmer presents convincing evidence to show that a large percentage of the members of such companies were skilled workers, but from 20 to 33 per cent were not. We are not told why workers joined.

Similarly with the Mechanics' Institute. It was, according to Palmer, 'directed by men far removed from working-class life;' there was 'little...working-class leadership.' In 1861 two officials of the Institute pointed out that 'classes of the community other than operatives constitute not infrequently the majority of subscribers and attendants.' Palmer presents evidence that some workers were not happy with the way the Institute was being run, but this evidence is not extensive enough to support the claim that 'working-class opposition...seethed below the surface.' Even if it did, it is clear that the Institute was run by non-workers and had worker and non-worker members.

These institutions, as well as sporting events, labour day parades, union dances, suppers, and festivals, and other gatherings constitute what Palmer calls the 'collectivist culture.' Added to it were associational institutions such as the charivari and whitecapping. Here too the evidence hardly supports the contention that charivaris and whitecapping were in any way an exclusive, or even a worker dominated, activity. On the charivari, Palmer states that identification of the participants is not easy. He says, in fact, that we 'would be hard pressed to place Hamilton workers at the scene of any of these boisterous gatherings.' Of the 16 incidents he discovered in a 30 year period, only one can be definitely said to have been used by working men and women to achieve a specific working-class purpose. . . .

Both Kealey and Palmer stress workers' shared experiences in shop, union hall, and street. Both are forced to deal with ethnic and religious division among workers. This is only realistic in face of the considerable body of evidence which shows that ethnic and religious division has rent the Canadian working class from its very beginnings. As far back as the 1830s Ottawa Valley Irish Catholic lumber workers clashed violently with French-Canadian workers. Catholic Irish and Protestant Irish battled each other along Canada's canals in the 1840s. Through much of the nineteenth century the Orange Lodges, that Kealey and Palmer point to as representative of working-class culture, fought with Irish Catholic workers in the streets of Hamilton and Toronto. If skilled workers formed part of a common working-class culture in Canada in the 1870s, how do we account for the continued existence of deep religious divisions within that culture and periodic violence directed against other workers of a different religious persuasion? . . . .

That there was ethnic division among Toronto skilled workers is abundantly clear from Kealey's book. They were deeply divided. Kealey's history of the Orange Lodge in Toronto, and his detailed analysis of working-class politics, speak for themselves. Yet, in at least one instance, his analysis may hide more than it reveals. Kealey is aware of the presence of religious division, even strife, but asserts that 'no examples of ethnic or religious riot at the workplace have been found.' This is not surprising if workplaces were predominantly of one religious and ethnic grouping or another. Kealey does not say. But it seems highly unlikely, for example, that many Irish Catholics could be found in Toronto printshops or were initiated into the Knights of St. Crispin. Kealey is eager, perhaps too eager, to relegate Orange-Catholic violence to the realm of the 'ritualistic' and he may be equally too willing to celebrate the lack of such violence at the workplace. In fact, sectarian division among Toronto workers was great. Politically, and to some degree organizationally, Toronto workers were divided into lines that strongly resembled the battle lines of the Orange-Catholic riots with Liberals, Catholics, Irish, and the Knights of Labor on one side and Tories, Protestants, Ulstermen, Englishmen, and craft unionists on the other. There was little class unity based on culture there. Class unity cannot be built on the rioting crowd that supported the striking street car workers in 1886, as Kealey seems to do, without prompting the conclusion that such unity was fleeting indeed.

David Jay Bercuson, "Through the Looking Glass of Culture: An Essay on the New Labour History and Working-Class Culture in Recent Historical Writing", *Labour/Le Travailleur*, Vol. 7 (Spring, 1981), pp. 99–101 and 102–103. Footnotes omitted.

A Guide to Further Reading

1. *Overviews*

Belanger, Noel et al., *Les Travailleurs Québécois, 1851–1896*. Montreal: Les Presses de l'Université du Québec, 1975.

Bercuson, David J., "Through the Looking Glass of Culture: An Essay on the New Labour History and Working Class Culture in Recent Canadian Historical Writing", *Labour/Le Travailleur*, Vol. 7 (Spring, 1981), pp. 95–112.

Bliss, Michael, *A Living Profit: Studies in the Social History of Canadian Business, 1883–1911*. Toronto: McClelland and Stewart, 1974.

Cross, Michael S., ed., *The Workingman in the Nineteenth Century*. Toronto: Oxford University Press, 1974.

———, and Gregory S. Kealey, eds., *Readings in Canadian Social History, Vol. 3: Canada's Age of Industry, 1849–1896*. Toronto: McClelland and Stewart, 1982.

Harvey, Fernand, *Révolution industrielle et travailleurs*. Montreal: Boréal Express, 1978.

Kealey, Gregory S., "Labour and Working-Class History in Canada: Prospects in the 1980s", *Labour/Le Travailleur*, Vol. 7 (Spring, 1981), pp. 67–94.

Linteau, Paul-André, René Durocher, and Jean-Claude Robert, *Quebec: A History, 1867–1929*. Trans. Robert Chodos. Toronto: James Lorimer & Company, 1983.

McNaught, Kenneth, "E.P. Thompson vs. Harold Logan: Writing About Labour and the Left in the 1970s", *Canadian Historical Review*, Vol. LXII (June, 1981), pp. 141–168.

Morton, Desmond, *Working People: An Illustrated History of Canadian Labour*. Ottawa: Deneau & Greenberg, 1980, especially Chapters 5, 6 and 7.

Palmer, Bryan D., *Working-Class Experience: The Rise and Reconstitution of Canadian Labour 1800–1980*. Toronto: Butterworths, 1983.

2. Specialized Studies

Origins of the Working-Class Movement

Babcock, Robert, "A Note on the Toronto Printers' Strike, 1872", *Labour/Le Travailleur*, Vol. 7 (Spring, 1981), pp. 127–129.

Battye, John, "The Nine-Hour Pioneers: The Genesis of the Canadian Labour Movement", *Labour/Le Travailleur*, Vol. 4 (1979), pp. 25–56.

Creighton, Donald G., "George Brown, Sir John Macdonald and the 'Workingman'", *Canadian Historical Review*, Vol. XXIV (December, 1943), pp. 362–76.

Langdon, Steven, *The Emergence of the Canadian Working Class Movement, 1845–1875*. Toronto: New Hogtown Press, 1975.

Ostry, Bernard, "Conservatives, Liberals and Labour in the 1870's", *Canadian Historical Review*, Vol. XLI (June, 1960), pp. 93–127.

Zerker, Sally, "George Brown and the Printers' Union", *Journal of Canadian Studies*, Vol. X (February, 1975), pp. 42–48.

Working-Class Response to Industrialism

Hann, Russell, "Brainworkers and the Knights of Labor: E.E. Sheppard, Phillips Thompson, and the Toronto News, 1883–1887", in Gregory S. Kealey and Peter Warrian, eds., *Essays in Canadian Working Class History*. Toronto: McClelland and Stewart, 1976, pp. 35–57.

Kealey, Gregory S., *Toronto Workers Respond to Industrial Capitalism, 1867–1892*. Toronto: University of Toronto Press, 1980.

———, ed., *Canada Investigates Industrialism*. Toronto: University of Toronto Press, 1973.

MacLeod, Donald, "Colliers, Colliery Safety and Workplace Control: The Nova Scotian Experience", *C.H.A. Historical Papers 1983*, pp. 227–253.

McKay, Ian, "Capital and Labour in the Halifax Baking and Confectionery Industry During the Last Half of the Nineteenth Century", *Labour/Le Travailleur*, Vol. 3 (1978), pp. 63–108.

Ostry, Bernard, "Conservatives, Liberals and Labour in the 1880's", *Canadian Journal of Economics and Political Science*, Vol. XXVII (May, 1961), pp. 141–161.

Thompson, T. Phillips, *The Politics of Labor*. Edited with an Introduction by Jay Atherton. Toronto: University of Toronto Press, 1975.

Trofimenkoff, Susan Mann, "One Hundred and Two Muffled Voices: Canada's Industrial Women in the 1880s", *Atlantis*, Vol. 3 (1977), pp. 67–82.

Working-Class Culture

DeLottinville, Peter, "Joe Beef of Montreal: Working Class Culture and the Tavern, 1869–1889", *Labour/Le Travailleur*, Vols. 8 and 9 (Autumn/Spring, 1981–82), pp. 9–40.

Kealey, Gregory S., *Hogtown: Working Class Toronto at the Turn of the Century*. Toronto: New Hogtown Press, 1974.

_____, "The Orange Order in Toronto: Religious Riot and the Working Class", in Kealey and Warrian, eds., *Essays in Canadian Working Class History*, pp. 13–34.

Palmer, Bryan D., *A Culture in Conflict: Skilled Workers and Industrial Capitalism in Hamilton, Ontario, 1860–1914*. Montreal: McGill-Queen's University Press, 1979.

_____, "Discordant Music: Charivaris and Whitecapping in Nineteenth-Century North America", *Labour/Le Travailleur*, Vol. 3 (1978), pp. 5–62.

_____, "'Give Us the Road and We Will Run It': The Social and Cultural Matrix of An Emerging Labour Movement", in Kealey and Warrian, eds., *Essays in Canadian Working Class History*, pp. 106–124.

Roberts, Wayne, *Honest Womanhood: Feminism, Femininity and Class Consciousness Among Toronto Working Women, 1893–1914*. Toronto: New Hogtown Press, 1976.

Watt, F.W., "The National Policy, the Workingman and Proletarian Ideas in Victorian Canada", *Canadian Historical Review*, Vol. XL (1959), pp. 1–26.

Trade Unions and Strikes

Babcock, Robert, *Gompers in Canada: A Study of American Continentalism Before the First World War*. Toronto: University of Toronto Press, 1975.

Forsey, Eugene, *Trade Unions in Canada, 1812–1902*. Toronto: University of Toronto Press, 1982.

Kealey, Gregory S. and Bryan D. Palmer, *Dreaming of What Might Be: The Knights of Labor in Ontario, 1880–1900*. Boston: Cambridge University Press, 1982.

Kennedy, Douglas R., *The Knights of Labor in Canada*. London: The University of Western Ontario, 1956.

Lipton, Charles, *The Trade Union Movement of Canada, 1827–1959*. Montreal: Canadian Social Publications, 1968.

Logan, Harold A., *Trade Unions in Canada*. Toronto: Macmillan, 1948.

MacEwan, Paul, *Miners and Steelworkers: Labour in Cape Breton*. Toronto: Hakkert, 1976, esp. Chapter 2.

Phillips, Paul, *No Power Greater: A Century of Labour in British Columbia*. Vancouver: B.C. Federation of Labour and Boag Foundation, 1967, esp. Chapter 2.

Robin, Martin, *Radical Politics and Canadian Labour, 1880–1930*. Kingston: Industrial Relations Centre, Queen's University, 1968, esp. Chapter 2.

14

THE ECONOMIC BOOM
IN THE LAURIER ERA, 1896–1911

Prosperity for Whom?

The years 1896 to 1911 are commonly regarded as a golden age of economic growth in Canada. Wilfrid Laurier's rise to power in 1896 coincided with a revival in world trade and marked the return of prosperous times. It was the greatest boom Canada had yet known. A new wave of immigration commenced, the "Last Best West" was settled, two transcontinental railways were built, and all parts of the country appeared to share in the unprecedented economic activity. The chief political beneficiaries of this boom, Laurier and the Liberals, fell from power in 1911, yet good times continued almost up to the outbreak of the Great War in 1914. By that time, modern Canada was taking shape, and the prosperous nation was developing a new and confident spirit.

The surge of economic growth after 1896 is usually attributed to Laurier's Liberal government and to the beneficial, if somewhat delayed, effects of Canada's National Policy. During its fifteen-year term the Laurier government adopted and sustained the basic strategy of John A. Macdonald's national policies. The Liberal tariff, presented by Finance Minister W.S. Fielding in April 1897, retained a system of protection for Canadian manufacturers with the exception of an imperial preference and minor concessions to freer trade. Between 1896 and 1905, Clifford Sifton, Laurier's Minister of the Interior, promoted an aggressive immigration drive which brought thousands of agricultural settlers into the Canadian West. In the midst of the boom times, two new transcontinental rail lines, the Canadian Northern and the Grand Trunk-Transcontinental were built, linking all regions together much more than before in a strong web of steel. Construction of the new trunk lines across the Shield to the Pacific seemed to act as a stimulus to frontier resource development, opening the door to mining and lumbering booms in northern

Ontario and the British Columbia hinterland. Yet the most significant feature of the new age of prosperity was the creation of a more viable east-west economy. For as the Prairie West was settled and wheat production mounted, Canada's east-west trading system seemed to flourish as never before. It appeared, in the words of historian J.M.S. Careless, that the prosperity and economic growth of the Laurier era had "spelt success at long last for the National Policy".

While most analysts agree that the Laurier years were times of remarkable growth and economic expansion, the extent to which all regions—and all groups in society—shared in the prosperity has emerged as the focus for a lively historical debate. Many historians, following the interpretation set out by O.D. Skelton and the Rowell-Sirois Report, have presented the Laurier era as a classic period of "economic boom" when most social groups and parts of Canada benefited from domestic prosperity and new national economic unity. More recently, however, historians studying the social experience of various regions, social groups and classes have begun to suggest otherwise.

Out of the recent writings of Canada's social historians, a new set of interpretations has started to emerge. Laurier's national policies, like those of Macdonald, have been credited with spurring the establishment of factories and mills in central Canada, but blamed for casting the Maritimes and the West in the role of staple-producing hinterlands. While immigration policy might have racked up impressive figures in bringing over two million prospective settlers to Canada between 1896 and 1911, historians have pointed out that over one million people emigrated, mainly to the United States, and that thousands more collected in cities like Winnipeg, Toronto, and Montreal, depending on charity and menial jobs for their subsistence. Studies of organized labour and industrial relations have suggested that the period from 1896 to 1911 was a time of intense industrial conflict, due mainly to large-scale immigration and the consequent rapid increase in the labour supply which caused a continuing lag of wages behind prices. Investigations of Canadian society have also drawn sharp contrasts between the grand and opulent style of living among Canada's wealthy entrepreneurs, merchants and industrialists, and the abject poverty of life in Toronto's "Ward" district, Winnipeg's "North End" and Montreal's "City Below the Hill". Other analysts of Laurier's Canada have seriously questioned whether the country was indeed a "land of opportunity" for poor European immigrants without capital or agricultural skills, for the "navvies" and "bunkhouse men" working on the transcontinental railway lines, and for "working girls" who entered the workforce in Canada's expanding industrial cities.

In this problem study we will examine the popular conception of the "economic boom" in the Laurier era. Why is this 1896-to-1911 period usually viewed as a great age of economic growth and prosperity in Canada's development? Did all parts of Canada, all social groups, and all classes share equally in the fruits of prosperity? Did the pattern of development favour some regions at the expense of others? Did people's living standards—their real wages, their housing and their working conditions—really improve during this "golden age" of prosperity? Or was the Laurier era in fact a period of social neglect as much as one of unparalleled economic prosperity?

SELECTED CONTEMPORARY SOURCES

THE EXTENT OF PROSPERITY—DIMENSIONS OF GROWTH AND EXPANSION

An Account of the Coming of Prosperity

One of the earliest descriptions of the Laurier era as an age of prosperity is found in O.D. Skelton's 1913 account of Canada's economic history, written for the multi-volume study known as *Canada and Its Provinces*. Skelton, a professor at Queen's University at the time, was a close and partisan observer of the boom years 1896–1914. In this passage he heralds the arrival of prosperity with the opening of the West:

At last Canada's hour had struck. The settlement of the western plains had long dragged on with disheartening slowness, and eastern development, except in the two or three largest cities, had kept the same pace. Then after 1896 a fortunate conjuncture brought a sudden and remarkable change. World-wide factors played a part; population and consumption were again overtaking production, and increasing gold supplies and other forces were raising prices; wheat and cattle rose once more to profitable levels. The United States situation was of determining importance; the rapid growth of its urban population, simultaneously with the ending of fertile homestead areas and the substitution of corn and coarse grains on much of the old land, exhausted by reckless wheat-mining, made it eminently necessary to seek new sources of wheat supply. Western Canada offered limitless land, cultivated by the methods familiar in the western states, and available at a fraction of the price for which the emigrant's Iowa or Minnesota farm would sell. Individual farmers and land companies saw the harvest to be reaped in the inevitable rise of land values, and the northward trek began. In Canada itself, experience was enabling the western farmer to cope more effectively with frost and drought, and bountiful harvests in areas once stamped barren lured the home-seeker.

The treasures below the soil were discovered and developed in the same period as the treasures in the soil. The gold and silver and lead and copper of Southern British Columbia, the bonanza creeks of Klondike, the rich ores of Cobalt, proved lodestones of population. Here as elsewhere it is questionable whether the wealth taken out equalled the wealth put into prospecting and development, much less the money paid for stock; but the discoveries served a purpose by giving a spectacular advertisement of the country, and leading to consideration of its permanent sources of wealth. The more prosaic but more paying riches of the coal-mines of British Columbia and Alberta, of the iron ores of Newfoundland's Wabana, or of Michipicoten, were now exploited. The approaching exhaustion of the timber and especially the pulpwood resources of other countries gave new value to Canada's forests....

O.D. Skelton, "General Economic History, 1867–1912", in Adam Shortt and Arthur G. Doughty, eds., *Canada and Its Provinces* Vol. IX (Toronto: Glasgow, Brook & Company, 1913), pp. 191–192.

The Economy in Expansion—What Were the Signs of Prosperity?

Table 14–1   Production of Wheat in the Prairie Provinces and Canada, 1871–1921.

	PRAIRIE PROVINCES			CANADA
	Wheat acreage (millions)	Yield Per Acre (bushels)	Output (millions of bushels)	Output (millions of bushels)
1871	—	—	—	16.7
1881	—	—	—	32.4
1891	—	—	—	42.2
1901	—	—	—	55.6
1911	10.0	20.8	208.4	230.1
1921	22.2	12.6	280.1	300.9

Adapted from Vernon C. Fowke, *The National Policy and the Wheat Economy* (Toronto: University of Toronto Press, 1957), p. 75.

Table 14–2   Immigrant Arrivals in Canada, 1891–1920.

1891 — 82 165	1901 — 55 747	1911 — 331 288
1892 — 30 996	1902 — 89 102	1912 — 375 756
1893 — 29 633	1903 — 138 660	1913 — 400 870
1894 — 20 829	1904 — 131 252	1914 — 150 484
1895 — 18 790	1905 — 141 465	1915 — 36 665
1896 — 16 835	1906 — 211 653	1916 — 55 914
1897 — 21 716	1907 — 272 409	1917 — 72 910
1898 — 31 900	1908 — 143 326	1918 — 41 875
1899 — 44 543	1909 — 173 694	1919 — 107 698
1900 — 41 681	1910 — 286 839	1920 — 138 824

Extract from *Historical Statistics of Canada*, M.C. Urquhart and K.A.H. Buckley, eds. (Toronto: Macmillan, 1965), Series A254, p.23.

Table 14–3   Estimated Changes in Population Ten Years and Over, by Decades, 1881 to 1921 (in Thousands)

Decade	Natural Increase	Net Migration	Population at End of Decade	Immigration	Emigration
1881–1891	669	−205	3 628	903	1 108
1891–1901	654	−181	4 101	326	507
1901–1911	711	+715	5 528	1 782	1 066
1911–1921	916	+233	6 677	1 592	1 360

Extract from *Historical Statistics of Canada* (1965). The figures are based on Nathan Keyfitz's estimates derived from *Census of Canada*, 1931, Vol. 1, Table 8, p. 387.

The extent of economic growth in the years 1896 to 1914 can be seen in the official production, immigration and population figures for the period. Which sectors of the economy seemed to provide the impetus and set the pace for economic growth—the staple product exports or secondary industry? And to what extent were the boom years a "take-off" stage in Canada's economic growth?

Table 14-4   Net Value of Production

	1900 ($000)	1910 ($000)	1923 ($000)
Rubber Products	606	3 438	30 178
Tobacco	8 078	13 199	41 889
Boots and Shoes	7 623	16 000	22 958
Textile & Textile Products	32 874	67 282	157 995
including Clothing	19 960	43 657	79 470
Cotton Textiles	6 537	13 032	39 342
Furniture	4 280	8 018	16 582
Iron and its Produce	34 967	106 313	208 821
including: Agricultural Implements	5 469	10 667	14 434
Boilers, Tanks & Engines	2 842	7 585	2 786
Machinery	831	2 332	19 857
Primary Iron & Steel*	3 111	14 919	17 500
Railway Rolling Stock	5 178	25 221	28 008
Wire & Wire Goods	769	2 239	11 500
Automobiles	—	2 444	33 462
Chemicals and Chemical Products	3 910	12 167	56 800
Electric Light and Power	1 960	12 892	67 500
Total of Above**	94 298	239 309	602 723
Other Manufactures	120 228	325 158	701 834
Grand Total, All Manufactures	214 526	564 467	1 304 557

* Excludes Iron-smelting in 1900 and 1910
** Includes Total of textiles and textile products and of iron and its products.
   W.A. Mackintosh, *The Economic Background of Dominion-Provincial Relations* (Toronto: McClelland and Stewart, 1964), p. 51.

PROSPERITY FOR WHICH REGIONS?

The Promise of "Prosperity for All"—A Testimonial of Optimism, 1905

As Canada entered the new century the return of prosperity seemed to produce a wave of optimism in Canadian life. The gloom of much of the late nineteenth century seemed to almost vanish as train-loads of settlers rushed into the prairie West. Where once the regions outside central Canada had seemed barren and inhospitable, the vast resources of timber, pulp, minerals and waterpower in the hinterlands now held the promise of prosperity for all.

Henry Morgan and Lawrence Burpee, two Canadians speaking before a British audience, seemed to capture the spirit of optimism in Laurier's Canada:

Fate holds in store for this Dominion a golden future. From whatever point of view we regard it, the Canadian prospect is full of promise. It is safe to say that the natural resources of the country, viewed as a whole, are absolutely unequalled. Even the United States does not possess either the extent or the variety of resources found in Canada. In her vast forests, her coast and inland fisheries, her exhaustless coal deposits, her gold and silver mines, iron, copper, nickel, and nearly every other known variety of mineral, and, above all, in the tremendous possibilities of her grain fields, Canada holds the promise of such commercial prosperity as the world has seldom seen....

...Canada will always be primarily an agricultural nation.... [But it is also] destined to take no mean place among the manufacturing nations of the world.... Even now she produces all the staple articles of modern industry, and as her population increases, and home and foreign capital becomes available for the development of Canadian industries, she will not only supply most of her wants, but will be in a position to compete, and compete successfully, with her foreign rivals in the markets of the world.

Henry J. Morgan and Lawrence J. Burpee, *Canadian Life in Town and Country* (London: George Newness Ltd., 1905), pp. 238 and 241.

The Prairie West as a Land of Opportunity—The Interior Department's Appeal, 1903

For most immigrants the Canadian West held out the attractive prospect of one hundred and sixty acres of free land and the economic opportunities of a "land of the open doors". The Interior Department, headed by Sir Clifford Sifton, did much to create these expectations with a massive advertising campaign between 1897 and 1905. While the promotional literature conjured up glowing and alluring images of a "prosperous West", the Deputy Minister of the Interior made it clear that settlers would fare better on the prairies with "a little capital".

The man we have in mind is, simply the able-bodied man who is willing to work. As soon as he arrives in Winnipeg, he can put in a claim, and have allocated to him 160 acres of fertile land, free of timber and stones. The only conditions are that a fee of $10 be paid for recording the entry, and that the party receiving the homestead reside thereon six months out of the year for the first three years and cultivate at least five acres a year.

If he has a little capital, the newcomer may buy a wagon and horses and start farming right away. If not, he may enter under another man, at $10 per month, with board and lodging, guaranteed by the Immigration Commissioner. A knowledge of farming, acquired beforehand, will secure him double this wage; thrift is easy in a land with a splendid climate; and he can put his spare time into improvements on his grant.

James A. Smart, Deputy Minister of the Interior, 1903, as cited in Jean Bruce, *The Last Best West* (Toronto: Fitzhenry & Whiteside, 1976), p. 72.

Patterns of Immigration and Settlement—The Official Records, 1901–1911

Immigration and settlement patterns provide one indicator of the rate and extent of development in Canada's various regions. Out of the more than two million immigrants who arrived between 1896 and 1914, most told immigration officials that they were agriculturalists bound for the West. Yet many newcomers ended up working in mines, laying railway track, or drifting into the urban working class. Furthermore, immigration from abroad was also accompanied by a massive internal migration in Canada. Patterns of internal migration varied from one region to another.

Table 14–5 Population of Canada and the Provinces, 1901–1911

	1901	1911	% change
Nova Scotia	459 574	492 338	7.1
New Brunswick	331 120	351 889	6.3
Prince Edward Island	103 259	93 728	−9.2
Quebec	1 648 898	2 003 232	21.5
Ontario	2 182 947	2 523 274	15.6
Manitoba	255 211	455 614	78.5
Saskatchewan	91 279	492 432	439.5
Alberta	73 022	374 663	413.1
British Columbia	178 657	392 480	119.7
CANADA	5 371 315	7 206 643	34.2

Canada Year Book, 1913, p. 51

Table 14–6   Birthplaces of Population by Province in 1911 (Percentages)

	Canadian-Born		Immigrants	
	Born in Province	Born in another Province	British-Born	Foreign-Born
Nova Scotia	90.2	2.5	5.1	2.2
New Brunswick	90.7	4.1	2.9	2.3
Prince Edward Island	95.4	1.8	1.8	1.0
Quebec	91.1	1.6	3.6	3.7
Ontario	76.6	3.3	14.2	5.9
Manitoba	37.5	20.6	20.9	21.0
Saskatchewan	20.7	29.8	16.5	33.0
Alberta	19.7	23.6	18.6	38.1
British Columbia	21.5	21.6	30.1	26.8
CANADA	70.2	7.8	11.6	10.4

Canada Year Book, 1913, p. 51

A "Bonanza" in the Resource Hinterland—Reports on the Cobalt Mining Boom

A prime example of the impact of resource development in the Laurier years was the Cobalt mining boom of 1904–1906 in northern Ontario. Within two years of the discovery of silver, the area around Cobalt and Kerr Lakes had been staked out in thousands of small overlapping forty-acre claims, some 580 mining companies had been formed and $450 million worth of stocks sold to an eager and grasping public. Cobalt had grown from the barren marshes to a frontier town of 7 000, bursting at the seams and plagued by myriad problems. Two Ontario government reports provided an inkling of the less glamorous aspects of "instant prosperity".

The Boom in Mining Stocks, 1906

... the signs are too evident that the Cobalt mining district is to be the scene of another joint stock company 'boom.' The undoubted richness of the district is attracting to it not only those who wish to engage in legitimate mining, but also that class of speculators which descends upon every rich mining camp in order to turn to personal advantage the hopes of gain aroused in the public breast by the sight of the suddenly revealed mineral wealth. Their *modus operandi* is, of course, to form so-called 'mining' companies and float their stock while the public's expectations are yet big and their hopes high. Too often these stocks are greedily bought by those quite unable to discriminate between good and bad, only with the object of selling them at an advance. The whole process is a species of gambling and has no more relation to real mining than betting on a race track has to the raising of thoroughbred horses. The result is invariably disastrous. It might have been thought that the exploded booms of the past would have warned the Canadian public against the folly and danger of gambling in mining stocks; but evidently no one learns wisdom from the experience of others, and each few years sees another generation succeeding its predecessor quite as anxious to acquire wealth without working for it, and, therefore, quite as ready to fall into the snares spread by the unscrupulous promoters of bogus mining companies.

Ontario Department of Lands and Forests, *Annual Report of the Bureau of Mines*, 1906, p. 10.

A Breeding Ground for Disease—Cobalt, 1906

The water is got from a couple of very questionable springs amongst the houses and through holes in the ice from Cobalt Lake. Previous analyses of these waters have shown all of them to be infected with intestinal bacteria.... There have been five cases of typhoid in the district since Christmas, three of which have probably been infected elsewhere, but the other two seem to have got their infection in the town.

The settlement is scattered over three more or less parallel ridges radiating somewhat to the north. Nearly one quarter of the houses at the present time drain towards Cobalt Lake, which has an area of about 50 acres. Its infection is thus accounted for. The other three-quarters drain into the valleys between the ridges. The ridges are covered with houses and the valleys are filled with them. There is one water closet about to five houses. Some of them seem filled to above the seats, and otherwise in a most filthy condition. Those houses having none have discharged on the ground. Garbage, wash water, urine and faeces all mixed together in frozen heaps out in the open, on top of rock, practically bare in its greater area. The cold has been steady so far and all is frozen, but when the thaws come the accumulations will all be washed into the valleys and the lake, polluting all the water sources.

Ontario Board of Health, *Annual Report*, 1906, p. 98.

Life in the Cities—A View from the North End of Winnipeg, 1909

Not every Canadian city was a bustling, prosperous, and harmonious community. From most reports Winnipeg at the turn of the century was a city divided. The city's foreign quarter, the "North End", was figuratively as well as literally the other side of the CPR tracks. To respectable WASP Winnipeg, it was a "howling chaos, a slum full of foreigners" and overcrowded rooming houses. The Reverend James Shaver Woodsworth, then a young Methodist clergyman and Superintendent of the All People's Mission, commented on the racial and class divisions the city.

> In country districts people are to a large extent on a level but in the cities we have the rich and the poor, the classes and the masses, with all that these distinctions involve. The tendency is that the well-to-do gather together in more or less exclusive suburbs, while the poor are segregated in slum districts, and between these there is comparatively little direct intercourse. The employer may meet his employee at business, but there is little bond of connection beside what Carlyle called the 'cash nexus'. A woman may superintend laundry operations in her own house, but she knows little or nothing of the home life of her washerwoman who has come several miles to give her days [sic] service. They live in two worlds. ... This condition is intensified and more complicated when large numbers of foreigners are brought into our civic life. Differences of language, of race and of religion, often running parallel, deepen and broaden the chasm. The people who most need help are separated from those who best could help them.

J.S. Woodsworth, Superintendent of All People's Mission in Winnipeg. Woodsworth Papers, Vol. 28, "Some Aspects of the Immigration Problem", in *The Young Women of Canada* (December, 1909).

PROSPERITY FOR WHICH SOCIAL CLASSES AND GROUPS?

The Rise of Big Business—Comments on the "Age of Enterprise"

The Boom Years 1896–1911 were popularly regarded as the high point of the "golden age" of Canadian business enterprise. Close associations between businessmen and politicians, the small size of the Canadian labour movement, the support for "entrepreneurship" provided by tariff, transportation and tax policies, and the readiness with which Canadian resources were dealt out to capitalists, all suggested that Laurier's Canada was a paradise for business opportunity and unfettered "profit-making". Some comments from the popular and business press even claimed that Canada's "captains of industry" had come to epitomize the prosperous, nation-building spirit of the time.

> The development of the last few years has been magnificent; the development of the next few years depends on our having confidence. The country is rich, immigration is proceeding apace, the Government is doing its duty, and the rest lies with the people—the capitalists, the bankers, the businessmen, and the other classes.
>
> *Canadian Magazine* (March, 1905), p. 487.

> ...at the base of the financial structure in Canada is to be found a triangular formation consisting of twenty-three capitalist financiers upon whom depend, in a very large measure, the type and direction of material prosperity.
>
> Nathaniel S. Fineberg, "The Canadian Financial Triangle", *Moody's Magazine*, Vol. VIII (November, 1909), p. 381.

Combinations and Mergers—An Indicator of Business Prosperity

The rise of big corporations and monopolies, which was a dominant feature of American business enterprise in the late nineteenth century, was duplicated after 1900 on a smaller scale in Canada. A spate of mergers and consolidations—reaching its peak in 1909 and 1910—suggested that Canadian business was prospering and expanding.

Table 14-7 Growth in Capitalization of Canadian Industry, 1900-1912

Year	Companies formed with Dominion Charter	Total Capitalization. New Companies.	Increased Capitalization. Existing Companies. ($000)	Grand Total ($000)
1900	53	9 558	3 351	12 909
1901	55	7 662	3 420	11 082
1902	126	51 182	5 055	56 237
1903	187	53 405	5 584	58 989
1904	206	80 597	5 366	85 963
1905	293	99 910	9 685	109 595
1906	374	180 173	32 403	212 576
1907	378	132 686	19 091	151 777
1908*	64	13 299	865	14 164
1908-09	366	121 624	72 293	193 917
1909-10	493	301 788	46 589	348 377
1910-11	544	458 415	24 715	483 130
1911-12	658	447 626	42 939	490 565

* First three months of 1908.

H.G. Stapells, *The Recent Consolidation Movement in Canadian Industry*, unpublished M.A. thesis, University of Toronto, 1922, p. 11.

Table 14–8   Industrial Mergers, 1900–1914

Year	Number	Firms Merged	Capital Authorized ($ million)	Capital Issued ($ million)
1900–08	8	57	$ 43	$ 33
1909	11	160	139	84
1910	22	112	157	113
1911	14	44	96	65
1912	13	37	97	75
1913	5	16	n.a.	n.a.
1914	2	4	n.a.	n.a.

Adapted from Stapells, "The Recent Consolidation Movement...", p. 12; *Monetary Times*, September 24, 1910, pp. 1328–30; and Royal Commission on Price Spreads and Mass Buying, *Report*, 1932, p. 28.

"The Masseys and the Masses"—A Worker's View of Big Business, 1904

The rise of large corporations and great concentrations of wealth did not go unnoticed in Canadian cities like Toronto and Montreal. In Toronto the inequalities of wealth and economic power were glaring— as is evidenced by the popular refrain, "Toronto has two classes: the Masseys and the masses". A poem published in 1904 in the *Toiler*, a working-class paper, expressed more elaborately the undercurrent of indignation.

I came to a works at a railway side,
A half a mile long and nearly as wide,
With millions of lumber and an army of men,
Toiling at furnace, hammer and pen.
'What a most magnificent plant,' I cried;
And a man with a hump on his back replied,
'It's Massey's'

I entered a hall so grand and gay,
To witness a concert, the best of the day
Presented to people, the rich of the land
In a palace supposed for the laboring hands
'A monstrous edifice this,' I sighed:
And a man with a diamond ring replied,
It's Massey's'

I stopped at the door of the city church
Where sinner and saint the truth go to search,
And wisdom from above is imparted
To the meek and humble hearted;
I asked for a seat unoccupied
And a man with a plug in his hand replied,
'It's Massey's'

I went to the only place left, I'll take
A chance in the boat on the brimestone lake;
Or perhaps I may be allowed to sit
On the gridless floor of the fathomless pit.
But a leering lout with horns on his face
Cried out as he forked me off the place,
'It's Massey's'

    Toiler, January 29, 1904.

The Condition of the Urban Working Class—Living Standards in Toronto, 1890–1914

Toronto's working class, which made up the majority of the city's population, was highly differentiated and employed in a wide variety of industries, from printing to building to the needle trade. Even though Toronto was transformed by the economic boom, poverty seemed to persist as an integral part of working-class life. The two graphs which follow, compiled from federal Department of Labour statistics, can be used to compare average daily wages with the relative prices of commodities in the period.

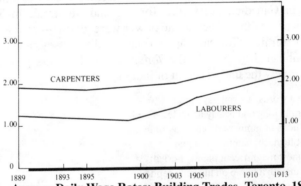

Figure 14–1   Average Daily Wage Rates: Building Trades, Toronto 1889–1913

Figure 14–2   Wholesale Price Chart: Canada, 1890–1909

Source: *Poverty and the Working Class in Toronto, 1880–1914*, Canada's Visual History Series, Vol. 33.

The Homesteading Experience—"Shifting for Yourself", 1904

Once immigrants from eastern Canada, the United States, Britain and contintental Europe had been settled on their homesteads they were expected, in the words of Interior Minister Clifford Sifton, to "shift for themselves" on the Western prairie. While Sifton's Department sought primarily farmers and farm labourers to settle the West, thousands of American and European urban workers also emigrated to the prairies. The British gentlewoman Lucie Johnson, who arrived in Manitoba in the summer of 1903, described the struggle of the city-born and -bred to succeed in the West.

> In this our. . . first year naturally we had not been able to get a crop in, coming too late, but we. . . had been busy all summer preparing for the spring of 1904; breaking and cultivating this virgin land. The task was not an easy one for city born people but we loved this country, the freedom of it all—the wide open spaces, and the love of adventure was in our blood. This, with a determination to make good whatever the hardships, was all the incentive we required to make a success of farming. . . .
>
> When I think of the silly pink teas in the cities, how small a way it does seem to spend one's time, after working in the great open air in the large wide spaces, tilling the sod under wonderful blue skies and making a home out of barren virgin land.
>
> Manitoba Archives, Lucie Johnson, "Against the Wind", MS. reprinted in Linda Rasmussen et al., *A Harvest Yet to Reap: A History of Prairie Women* (Toronto: The Women's Press, 1976), p. 32.

The Plight of "Unfit" Immigrants—The Miseries of Michael Prazilowski's Family, 1906

Not all immigrants met with success in the West. Yet Sifton and his Department refused to assist impoverished newcomers in any material way—insisting that those "unfit for settlement" should "drift somewhere else". Many, in fact, drifted into Canadian cities and were forced to endure wretched conditions. One such case was that of Michael Prazilowski and his family, East Europeans left destitute in Winnipeg in the spring of 1906.

> On the 26th of April, 1906, Mr. Prazilowski and his family reached Winnipeg in a penniless, absolutely destitute and starving condition, and at the time the eldest girl, Maria, was sick and had been sick on the train, so the father stated. Seeing their condition, they were placed in the Immigration Hall, and provided with provisions at the expense of the Department from that time on until they left the building.
>
> On the 3rd or 4th of May, 1906, Dr. Corbett, our Medical Officer, became suspicious of certain symptoms which were present in the child, Rosalie, ten years old, and the family were placed by themselves in the upper flat of the Immigration Building. At this time the eldest girl, Maria, was suffering from bronchitis and quinsy, [tonsillitis] and was being treated therefore by Dr. Corbett.

[On the 6th of May 1906 Maria died in the Immigration Hall, followed on the 10th of May by Rosalie. For Maria the immediate cause of death was quinsy, for Rosalie it was Scarlet Fever. An eight year old son, Vladaslof, also became ill and died of Scarlet Fever on May 12th 1906. All three children were buried "at the expense of the Department."]

... The family left the Immigration Hall and joined other families living at 184 McFarlane Street [in which there were several other families] the father intending to wait there until he heard from his brother with the money. On the 16th of May the baby in this family died at 184 McFarlane St. aforesaid from mal-nutrition and was buried by Undertaker Gardner at the expense of the Department.

All this time the father of the family kept writing to his brother to send the money, but none came and on the 16th of May Officer Genik went with him to the General Post Office and instituted a thorough search in the hope that some letter might be there for Prazilowski. Their efforts were rewarded, and a registered letter just about to be sent to the Dead Letter Office was discovered addressed to Michael Prazilowski at the General Delivery, Winnipeg. This letter contained money from his brother, payable to himself and was thereupon cashed upon his being identified by Officer Genik.

J. Obed Smith, Commissioner of Immigration, Winnipeg, October 13, 1906, reprinted in Jean Bruce, *The Last Best West*, pp. 56–7.

Conditions Among Rural/Frontier Workers—The Lot of the "Bunkhouse Men" and "Blanketstiffs" in British Columbia

Since at least the 1880s, gangs of itinerant workers known as "bunkhouse men", "blanketstiffs" or "navvies" had been imported to the frontier to build Canadian railways. In the railway-building boom of Laurier's time, these workers were paid better wages than in the 1880s, but were usually put up in makeshift bunkhouse camps and often mercilessly exploited by the "company store". A report on bunkhouse camp conditions provides an insight into the lot of itinerant railway construction workers.

The camp at No. 52 was the headquarters of a contractor with one hundred miles of the National Transcontinental. The buildings were closely grouped on the bank of a deep

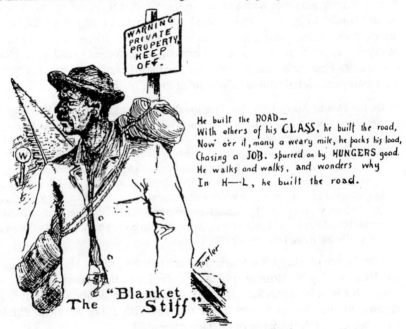

He built the ROAD—
With others of his CLASS, he built the road,
Now o'er it, many a weary mile, he packs his load,
Chasing a JOB, spurred on by HUNGERS good.
He walks and walks, and wonders why
In H—L, he built the road.

The "Blanket Stiff"

clay cut, the bunkhouse was not oblong (as is usually the case), but square. Two small windows lighted the building.

The bunks were built to accommodate forty-eight men, but, on train nights when a fresh lot arrived, it would often have a hundred men. This, with the men coming down the grade or waiting for a settlement at the office, caused the building to be always crowded, the overflow being forced to find the softest spot on the floor for a bed. Hardly could one sleep a night in those bunks and be clean in the morning. A man who used them admitted, 'I'm lousy; I'm good and lousy; but what's a fellow to do? Got to sleep! And I don't think they will let a "wiper" have a bed in the office during the day!' The whole surroundings were fitter far for the stabling of cattle than the abode of men; at a whiff therefrom a well-reared pig would grunt disapproval.

Edmund Bradwin, *The Bunkhouse Man: A Study of Work and Pay in the Camps of Canada* (New York: Columbia University Press, 1928), pp. 85–86.

The Experience of Ethnic Minorities—Asian Immigrants in British Columbia, c. 1908

Asian immigrants, imported as contract labour by the fish, coal, rail and lumber barons of British Columbia, suffered from more than economic deprivation. During the recession of September 1907, anti-Oriental riots broke out in Vancouver. When the Canadian government responded with a "gentleman's agreement" to cut Asian immigration, the Chinese Board of Trade reacted with this dire warning (to prospective immigrants), thirty thousand copies of which were sent from Port of Vancouver on June 3d, 1908, by the S.S. Empress of Japan to Tung Wah Hospital, Hong Kong, for distribution at all Treaty Ports of China.

At present business of all kinds is dull all over Canada, and employment in any kind of labor is hard to obtain. Only about one-third of the Canneries are in operation. The Shingle Mills, Factories of every industry, and Working Mines industry have shut down to more than one-half of their usual activity. Besides, Japanese and Hindu laborers have come in large numbers, hence wages have been reduced. White laborers look upon these with ill feeling, and are organizing to force out our people from all kinds of works.

On September last White laborers gathered in large numbers, marched through the streets, and smashed the doors and windows of our people. We were forced to stop business for several days. Besides all this, owing to the stringency of the money market in the States, business in Canada is greatly affected. At present many of our people are out of employment. . . .

As all immigrants have to pay a head tax of $500 gold, which is more than a $1000 in our money, and that money, many of them, may have to borrow or sell their property to obtain the same, thinking that they can easily earn it back and many times over on their arrival here, will be sorely disappointed. They will find that the conditions here are very hard, without work, and perhaps much harder than in China. It is doubly so, because the cost of living, here is about 5 times more than in our own country. If he should be without work for a single month he will find his savings will soon be gone. . . .

Public Archives of Canada. W.L.M. King Papers, Vol.13, MG26, J4. Translation of Circular Letter issued by Chinese Board of Trade.

CONFLICTING INTERPRETATIONS

THE NATURE AND EXTENT OF PROSPERITY—A CLASH OF VIEWS

The "Wheat Boom"—A Phase of National Economic Expansion and Integration

The popular view of the Boom Years 1896–1914 was expressed in the first volume of the 1940 Royal Commission Report on Dominion-Provincial Relations, better known as the Rowell-Sirois Report, Book I. According to the Report, an economic boom generated by prairie wheat production had transformed the disparate regions of the Dominion into a fully integrated transcontinental economy. In this passage, the authors of the Report explain the economic underpinnings of the "Wheat Boom" and the effects of prosperity on regional and provincial attitudes toward Confederation.

> ...For twenty-five years the new nation had languished and even the most sanguine were troubled by forebodings about the success of Confederation. Then a fortuitous conjuncture of world circumstances brought with a rush the fulfilment of hopes long deferred. Life began to stir in the frame erected years earlier for a transcontinental economy. Directed by the national policies of all-Canadian railways, western settlement and protective tariffs, it grew with a rapidity surpassing all expectations. A vast and sudden transformation was wrought by the magic of wheat. The wheat boom brought a flood of settlers into the West and created two new and flourishing provinces. It precipitated a new era of railway development and spurred on the industrialization of Central Canada. Immense capital expenditures were necessary to equip the West and the growing urban and metropolitan areas of the East. Wheat worked a new integration of economic life and linked together the fortunes of the different regions.
>
> In the optimism and prosperity of the day, the Federal Government recovered the initiative it had lost in the stagnation of preceding years and plunged again into the work of national development which the Fathers had assigned to it. The boldness and success of its new enterprises stimulated national pride. The development of the West was a national achievement and the participation of all areas in a common effort fostered a new sense of nationhood. Sons and daughters of the Maritimes and Central Canada migrated to the plains and built up the West, thus forging innumerable links between the older Canada and the new. Expansion on the distant frontier either solved or postponed the problems of provincial adjustments and regional interests. ...
>
> The wheat boom had finally brought the realization of the economic objectives of the Confederation scheme. The Northwest was settled and the Federal Government was able, through its policies and projects, to ensure expansion in the older communities of Canada on the basis of that settlement. These communities, restricted by the exhaustion of their own frontiers and confined to a precarious dependence on their own foreign outlets, received a new stimulus from the highly specialized exporting industry on the Prairies which had become the country's principal economic contact with the external world. Wheat transformed the static and isolated regions into an integrated and expanding national economy. The rising prosperity which accompanied this growth in interdependence fortified the political structure of Confederation with a common material interest and a national spirit such as had never existed before. ...

Donald Smiley, ed., *The Rowell-Sirois Report, Book I*. Abridged from Book I of the Royal Commission Report on Dominion-Provincial Relations, 1940 (Toronto: McClelland and Stewart, 1963), pp. 91–3.

The Lessons of Development—A Radical Critique of the "Laurier Boom"

The nature and impact of economic growth in the Laurier era has become in recent years a major point of controversy among Canada's economic historians. Scholars such as Tom Naylor and Gary Teeple see the period not as a formative phase in the development of a national economy, but as a period of regression into colonial economic dependence. In this section from his two-volume history of Canadian business, Naylor sets out the thesis that national economic prosperity was achieved at the cost of making Canada an "economic colony" of American and British capitalism.

[In the "golden age" of Canadian economic expansion, inflows and outflows of capital reflected] something more basic, namely the pattern of dependent development of Canada within the broad confines of the British empire. It was its hinterland status that led to unbalanced development, to a staple orientation of the economy, and therefore to the flow of funds that occurred. Huge imports of capital were required to finance the construction of trunk railway lines and other works. Enormous sums were diverted into land speculations. At the same time, funds moved abroad into railway extensions or financing commodity flows. . . .

. . . 'Lack of entrepreneurship' as a cause of industrial underdevelopment and reliance on American patterns and capital is either true but trite, or patently false, depending upon how it is interpreted. It is false in the sense that entrepreneurship can be either industrial or commercial, and Canadian business history shows no lack of commercial capitalists of undisputed ability. In railways, utilities, commercial banking, and finance, 'Canadian' entrepreneurs (often domiciled British ones) were strong, and their hold on those sectors of the economy increased over time. The vigour of Canadian finance, utility, and railroad promotions at home was matched by those abroad. British support in the form of portfolio loans was available to these sectors, and with this assistance Canadian entrepreneurs clung to, and replicated, the familiar patterns of development.

This strength was not matched by industrial efforts. Rather, the strength of the commercial sector went hand-in-hand with industrial weakness, by virtue of the absence of funds due to the twisting of the capital market so that funds flowed freely into commerce and staple movements, and away from industry, and because of the absence of independent innovative capacity. . . .

The strength of commercial capitalism in Canada was the result of the British colonial connection, and together they served to lock the Canadian economy into the staple trap. The domination of the Montreal commercial community in the colonial economic and political structure was the outgrowth of the pattern of dependence, and the stultification of industrial entrepreneurship followed from their control of the state and state policy, most notably with regard to the structure of the federally controlled banking system. The resulting vacuum led directly to the reliance on American industrialism, the form of entrepreneurs, patents, or direct investment.

... Dependence, like protection, was addictive. The very ease of access to British portfolio investment and markets and to American direct investment and technology ensured a particular pattern of development culminating in the reinforcement of the principal structural weaknesses of the Canadian economy during the 'wheat boom'. This 'golden age' of Canadian growth was in some respects an economic catastrophe. British funds were readily available to be misallocated into overextensions to commercial infrastructure or for floating huge mergers, both of which projects led to drastic liquidation after the war and bequeathed to the Canadian economy a huge burden of fixed interest debt owing to British investors. The capital market was shifted increasingly to servicing the production and movement of staples. And American direct investment in manufacturing and resource industries accelerated. As a result, the Canadian economy never fully made the vital transition from commercialism to industrialism....

Tom Naylor, *The History of Canadian Business, 1867–1914*, Volume Two (Toronto: James Lorimer & Company 1975), pp. 280–4. Footnotes omitted.

The Myth of "Commerce Against Industry"—An Indictment of Naylor's Thesis

Tom Naylor's reinterpretation of the "economic boom" has drawn criticism from business historians, including Michael Bliss of the University of Toronto and Douglas McCalla of Trent University. Bliss, author of *A Living Profit* (1974) has attacked Naylor's hypotheses and research methodology. In a review of Naylor's book in *Histoire sociale/Social History*, he offered this commentary:

The central argument of these remarkable volumes is that Canada remained an economic colony from 1867 to 1914 because concentration on the production and movement of staple products diverted capital away from industrial development. Such manufacturing as developed was largely foreign-owned. The country's financial institutions and commercially-oriented businessmen were primarily responsible for this state of affairs.

Assume for a moment that Naylor makes his case. He does not explain why it happened. There are only two possible explanations: businessmen were investing capital 'rationally' (i.e. to maximize their return) or they were not....

... Naylor seems to want us to believe that patterns of Canadian investment were irrational, that there was a 'twisting of the capital market' (II, 282) caused by a colonial situation which created a social and economic structure biased towards commercial and staple enterprises. Canadian businessmen did not perceive their own best interests, and did not maximize their real opportunities.

No explanation is offered about why this should have taken place. By definition the explanation would have to involve a failure of entrepreneurship (i.e. a failure to perceive the best money-making opportunities). Naylor is not sure whether or not he wants to maintain this, perhaps in part because another major thesis of his study is that Canadian businessmen were constantly being driven by their lust for profits into bursting all sorts of institutional and legal barriers. Perhaps they were greedy in breaking the law so often, but stupid in not realizing that honest manufacturing offered a better living.

This discussion is academic, however, because Naylor does not prove his case. Although it is asserted often enough, no evidence is presented to establish that the main problem with Canadian manufacturing was a shortage of capital. The one table on business failures due to 'Lack of Capital' (I, 85) is meaningless for several reasons, the most obvious being that it includes mercantile failures. The apparent fact that banks and other financial intermediaries did not put their capital into indigenous manufacturing cannot in logic lead to the conclusion that manufacturing would have been profitable if they had. There might simply have been more bank failures. As well, Naylor's discussion of municipal bonusing as a means of creating industrial capital seems to contradict the shortage hypothesis, especially when he repeatedly states that there was more bonusing than necessary....

> Michael Bliss, A Review of Tom Naylor, *The History of Canadian Business*, 2 vols. (1975) in *Histoire sociale/Social History*, Vol. IX (November, 1976), pp. 446–447.

PROSPERITY IN THE REGIONS—DID ALL REGIONS BENEFIT EQUALLY?

The Opening of the Prairie West—A "Land of Opportunity"

The widely accepted view of the prairie West as a "Land of Opportunity" was expressed in Robert Craig Brown and Ramsay Cook's synthesis of the period, *Canada 1896–1921: A Nation Transformed* (1974). The remarkable success of western settlement, according to Brown and Cook, sparked economic growth and prosperity which spread all through the national economy.

> The successful settlement of the prairies had long been seen as fundamental to the fulfilment of the grand plan of a viable east-west economy. Its agricultural products would provide the freight needed to ensure the profits of the C.P.R., and its demand for manufactured goods would give eastern industry a long-awaited prosperity. W.S. Fielding, in his budget speech in 1903, explained the Laurier government's developmental policy in terms that Sir John A. Macdonald would have heartily applauded. 'The best way you can help the manufacturers of Canada,' he maintained, 'is to fill up the prairie regions of Manitoba and the Northwest with a prosperous and contented people, who will be consumers of the manufactured goods of the east.' In the years between 1896 and 1921, the prairies became the most dynamic element in the country's economic growth. The potential of the plains attracted capital and labour in amounts never before experienced by Canada, and the results filtered through the entire economy.
>
> The west benefited enormously from changed world economic circumstances, as did the whole country. Of particular importance were declining interest rates, which indicated an increasing availability of investment capital, and lowered freight rates, which greatly assisted in keeping the price of Canadian wheat competitive. Farmers constantly complained about the Canadian Pacific Railway, but it was nevertheless a fact that the railway was absolutely indispensable to their well-being: it brought in new settlers and their effects and hauled out their produce. Moreover, settlement growth was determined by the increasing price of wheat and other foodstuffs on the overseas markets. A bushel of wheat that brought eighty-four cents in Liverpool in 1896 was worth one dollar and thirteen cents by 1913. And, of course, there was much more grain for sale as more land was broken and better grains and improved farming techniques were developed....

> Robert Craig Brown and Ramsay Cook, *Canada 1896–1921: A Nation Transformed* (Toronto: McClelland and Stewart, 1974), pp. 50–51. Footnotes omitted.

Economic Growth in Quebec—A Revisionist View of Quebec's "Economic Lag"

The "industrial takeoff" period in Ontario and other regions has traditionally been viewed as a time of "economic lag" in Quebec. This interpretation, first proposed by Albert Faucher and Maurice Lamontagne of Laval University in 1952, rests on the premise that Quebec's pattern of economic growth has been largely determined by her state of technology and natural resources in various time periods. According to the Faucher-Lamontagne thesis, the period 1866 to 1911 was one in which Quebec's growth slowed down. Because this was a period of expansion in iron and steam production, Quebec, a region poor in iron and coal, was left behind. Only with the advent of hydroelectricity after 1911, they contended, did Quebec begin its delayed industrial takeoff.

Faucher and Lamontagne's position, however, has now been seriously challenged. A recent synthesis of Quebec history, written by Paul-André Linteau, René Durocher and Jean-Claude Robert, argued that Quebec's traditional manufacturing industries did produce a measure of sustained industrial growth throughout the Laurier years.

> The new and sometimes spectacular installations of the resource-oriented industries and their entry into new regions made them an object of interest, even fascination, in their early days. Historians have also been affected by this infatuation, and some of them have tended to identify the industrialization of Quebec with these sectors and to have seen their establishment as the sign of Quebec's industrial takeoff. This is, at the very least, a truncated vision of Quebec's economic history.
>
> ... during the second half of the nineteenth century Quebec became endowed with a manufacturing structure based primarily on light industry (shoes, textiles, clothing) and secondarily on heavy industry (iron and steel, transportation equipment). This existing structure did not disappear in the twentieth century. Rather, it was extensively reorganized, and it continued to dominate manufacturing production even if its proportion of the total decreased....
>
> * * * * *
>
> ... more recent research has made it possible to demonstrate the importance of Quebec's initial, late-nineteenth-century industrial base, and the significance within that base of the iron and steel sector. On the basis of this research, the new resource-oriented sectors can also be seen in a more accurate perspective, as a powerful stimulus to—but still only a partial dimension of—the industrialization of Quebec.
>
> To be sure, levels of production in Quebec and Ontario showed a gap in Ontario's favour, but this should not lead to the conclusion that Quebec's development was slow or lagged behind. André Raynauld [a Quebec economist] has shown that over the long term the rates of growth of Quebec and Ontario industries were entirely comparable. He concludes that between 1870 and 1957, 'manufacturing production grew at an annual rate of 5.48 per cent in Ontario and 5.53 per cent in Quebec.' While the gap might have widened during a short period—as in the decade 1910–20—it narrowed again in later years. According to Raynauld, 'the problem in Quebec is not one of lagging growth but rather of growth with structural and demographic characteristics different from those of some of the other provinces of the country.' Specifically, Quebec's industrial structure included a higher ratio of light industry to heavy industry than Ontario's. In addition, Quebec's high birth rate meant that it had a younger

population and thus a lower rate of participation in the labour force. The income obtained by people with jobs was therefore distributed among a larger number of people outside the labour market, so that per capita income was lower in Quebec than in Ontario....

By whatever measure and whatever point of comparison, there is no doubt that in the first decades of the twentieth century Quebec had attained the status of an industrial society, in which the production of manufactured goods was the driving force of the economy.

Paul-André Linteau, René Durocher, and Jean-Claude Robert, *Quebec: A History 1867–1929*, trans. Robert Chodos (Toronto: James Lorimer & Company, 1983), pp. 322 and 330–331.

The Maritimes in Economic Transition—A Period of Mixed Prosperity

Scholars specializing in Maritime history, such as T.W. Acheson and George A. Rawlyk, have contended that the Boom Years were a period of economic transition and somewhat mixed prosperity for the Maritime provinces. Unable to compete with expanding central Canadian enterprise, Maritime entrepreneurs turned increasingly to resource-based industries like iron and coal. While the Maritimes experienced a new spurt of industrial expansion, they also suffered a transfer of financial control and a flight of capital to central Canada and the West.

...during the decades spanning the turn of the century the thrust of Maritime business initiative shifted from a locally-owned, diverse manufacturing sector back into a resource-based industry, centred on the iron and coal potential of north-eastern Nova Scotia. By 1900 the Nova Scotia Steel and Coal Company had emerged as 'the most fully integrated industrial complex in the country.' Using the coal resources of Cape Breton, Pictou and Cumberland Counties in Nova Scotia, and the iron ore deposits of Belle Isle, off Newfoundland, the company was able to provide primary, secondary and tertiary steel and iron manufacturers for the Canadian market.... While this second wave of industrial expansion was not as diverse or widespread as the earlier one in the 1880s, it had spectacular results in the communities affected. It has been contended that 'between 1900 and 1920, Nova Scotia's capital investment in manufacturing increased over 400 percent to $149.3 million while New Brunswick's multiplied five times to $109.5 million. The population in most of the leading towns along the (Intercolonial) road, including Moncton, Amherst, New Glasgow and Sydney, virtually doubled within the same period'.... The consolidation movement, begun in the 1890s, was completed towards the end of the first decade of the twentieth century. Typical of the more serious casualties was the 1909 merger of the locally-owned Rhodes, Curry Co. of Amherst, manufacturing railway cars, into the Canada Car and Foundry Company of Montreal. While the largest merger of all, the take-over of the Nova Scotia Steel and Coal company by outside interests, did not take place until 1920, the pressure on this regional firm began to be exerted from outside before 1914.

Concomitant to the absorption of what remained of the Maritime manufacturing industries by largely Montreal interests was the consolidation of the region's financial institutions. During what has been described as a 'two-fold process of centralization,' the Halifax-based financial structure and the Central Canadian banks competed for the spoils, as the several smaller private and public banks throughout the three Maritime Provinces were swept into the larger firms....

...The effective headquarters of both [Halifax] banks (the latter re-named The Royal Bank of Canada) were, by 1914, moved to Montreal, and for all intents and purposes, the banks became integrated into the Central Canadian banking structure.

The loss of financial control by the Maritimes meant, as well, that there was a flight of capital from the region. In Nova Scotia, before World War I, capital investment in manufacturing had remained relatively steady, at about 7% of the national total, reaching peaks in 1870 and 1900. But in New Brunswick, during the forty years between 1870 and 1910, investment declined from 7.5% in 1870 to a dismal 2.9% of the national total; in P.E.I. it declined from 1.3% to 0.2%. During the wheat boom period of the two decades before World War I, capital moved steadily out of the Maritimes to the West; such a move was facilitated by the centralized financial institutions which eagerly sucked the substantial bank savings of Maritimers outside of the region to be used elsewhere to build the new Canada in what Laurier called 'Canada's Century'.

G.A. Rawlyk and Doug Brown, "The Historical Framework of the Maritimes and Confederation", in Rawlyk, ed., *The Atlantic Provinces and the Problems of Confederation* (Halifax: Breakwater Publishers, 1979), pp. 22–24. Footnotes omitted.

Development in the Northern Ontario Mining Frontier—A New Hinterland for "Empire Toronto"

The "mining boom" in northern Ontario has held much fascination for popular historians with its tales of instant riches and shattered dreams. Only recently, however, have serious studies been undertaken of the impact of "boom and bust" cycles on the people and communities of northern Ontario. In this summary of recent research, Gilbert A. Stelter points out that while the boom had a lasting significance for the region, the chief beneficiary of the mineral wealth was the financial metropolis of Toronto.

The lure of gold, silver, and other metals has led to dramatic movements of people to new frontiers in North America.... In much the same way, the discovery of precious metals stimulated the development of 'New' Ontario in the late nineteenth and early twentieth centuries. This mining boom witnessed the discovery of nickel and copper at Sudbury in 1883, silver at Cobalt in 1903, and gold in the Porcupine district in 1909. These mining camps may have lacked some of the colour and excitement of the Cariboo and the Klondike, but each was of greater long-term significance than these spectacular but short-lived rushes. The production of Northern Ontario mines provided Canada with a major portion of its staple export of minerals.

The opening of this new territory is largely the story of thousands of bold individuals, most of whom discovered the hardships of a pioneer existence instead of quick fortunes. Both the Sudbury and Cobalt camps were accidental by-products of railway construction, but the individual prospector, nevertheless, played an important part in finding the ore bodies. In Cobalt, the Cariboo, and the Klondike, it was possible for a prospector to both discover and mine a property. Prospectors in Sudbury and the Porcupine, on the other hand, staked claims with the intention of selling them to a company with the necessary capital and technical knowledge to develop the complex ores. Buying these mining properties was a gamble with the odds heavily against success. Canadian and British financiers were reluctant to invest in such questionable schemes and, as a result, much of the original capital came from the United States....

One of the major consequences of any mining boom is the sudden appearance of a number of frontier urban communities....

All of these mining towns had one economic factor in common— they were all single enterprise communities whose destinies were determined by the success or failure of the local mining operations. Diversification was difficult for a number of reasons: mining regions are usually unsuitable for the support of agriculture, the camps were isolated from the major markets, and the relatively high wages in the mining industry discouraged the introduction of secondary industry. These communities have remained colonial towns, part of the economic, cultural, and political empire of Toronto. As on other mining frontiers, the major beneficiary of the mining booms in Northern Ontario has been the metropolitan centre. The mining camps have served merely as agents for the extraction of an exportable staple.

Gilbert A. Stelter, *The Northern Ontario Mining Frontier, 1880-1920*, Vol. 10, Canada's Visual History Series (Ottawa: National Museum of Canada and National Film Board, 1974), pp. 1 and 2.

PROSPERITY AMONG SOCIAL CLASSES AND GROUPS—DID ALL SHARE EQUALLY?

The "Golden Age" of Canadian Businessmen—Captains of Industry or Plutocrats?

Almost every historian, economist and popular analyst of the Laurier years has agreed that no social group benefited more than Canadian businessmen from the wave of prosperity. Yet a bitter debate has emerged over whether men of capital reaped enormous profits in excess of their real contributions to production and, in some cases, at the expense of other social groups and classes. In his study of Canadian businessmen and their attitudes, *A Living Profit* (1974), Michael Bliss set out the main claims made by each side— claims which still animate debates among historians.

... To many, probably most, Canadians before the social disruption of 1914-1918, the country's business leaders were captains of industry; they were the men who were building a nation by driving steel through the wilderness, raising the tall chimneys of thriving manufactories, blasting metals out of the Canadian Shield, unlocking the power of Niagara. A popular poll in 1909 named four railway presidents among 'Canada's Ten Biggest Men,' and a journalist noted enthusiastically, 'in the knapsack of every Canadian schoolboy there is—not a marshall's baton—but a millionaire's bank book.' Another writer could not believe that Donald Mann and William Mackenzie were motivated by self-interest in the creation of their personal transcontinental railway, the Canadian Northern; their actions could only be explained as an act of patriotism.

Others, though, were less enthusiastic about the achievements and values of men of wealth. Throughout the pre-1914 decades spokesmen for labour and agrarian movements attacked the Canadian plutocrats as oppressors of the industrial worker and the homesteader. Clergy of both Protestant and Catholic denominations stopped automatically identifying wealth with virtue and began to question the assumptions of what seemed to be an age of unrestrained acquisitiveness. Intellectuals ranging from Goldwin Smith through Principal Grant, Henri Bourassa, Andrew Macphail, and Stephen Leacock condemned the way in which 'business values' turned everything human into cold yellow metal. In 1914 the American muckraker, Gustavus Myers, published *A History of Canadian Wealth*, arguing that most of the great Canadian fortunes were based on special privilege, subsidies, and corruption. In the same year, in *Arcadian Adventures with the Idle Rich*, Stephen Leacock sketched the new Plutoria (Montreal) peopled by ruthless amoralists and feather-brained pseudo-aristocrats whose lives corroded religion, education, politics, and common morality. Already in 1900, a poet had summarized the intellectuals' response to the advent of that new Canadian phenomenon, the millionaire: he was, wrote Archibald Lampman, 'A creature of that old distorted dream/That makes the sound of life an evil cry.'

Michael Bliss, *A Living Profit: Studies in the Social History of Canadian Business, 1883-1911* (Toronto: McClelland and Stewart, 1974), pp. 12-13. Footnotes omitted.

The Condition of the Urban Working Class—Terry Copp's Thesis

Recent studies of the boom years have begun to explore the distribution of wealth in the midst of this apparent "age of prosperity". Among the first to question whether the economic benefits of increasing production and rapid industrialization were shared by all classes in society was Terry Copp, a social historian trained at McGill University in Montreal. His studies focused on Montreal and examined the economic and social conditions among the city's working class population. Michael J. Piva has taken the same approach in studying the conditions of Toronto's working class, and reached similar conclusions. In this excerpt Copp contends that during the period of economic expansion the real income of Montreal's average wage earner was actually in decline.

The most important single measure of the consequences of a period of sustained growth is the effect of 'national prosperity' on real income. The Department of Labour's index of wage rates in 13 Canadian cities, 1901-1920, indicates that wages moved steadily upwards for the 21 classes of labour examined. Average weekly wages increased by almost 33% from 1901 to 1911, a further 33% increase was obtained between 1911 and 1913 and in the following two years wage rates jumped by an unprecedented 38% . . . .

Even if the Department of Labour's figures are used, a comparison of wage increases with the changes in the cost of living suggests that there was a slight decline in real income 1901-1920. If figures on actual income rather than wage rates were generally available it would be possible to show that there was a significant decline in real income for most wage earners in Canada over the entire twenty year period. Certainly this was the case in Montreal.

The weekly income required by a family of five to reach the 'typical expenditure' level in 1901 was $9.37 for the basic items of expenditure or $11.23 if these basic items are calculated at eighty per cent of total family needs. How close to this figure could the average working man come in 1901? . . . .

The average income for 6543 workers in those categories of 'manufacturing' which did not have significant numbers of women and children workers was calculated. This list excluded almost all of the classically low wage industries, yet the average income was only $405.00 per year or $7.78 per week. Average income for this group fell $3.45 below the sum required to meet the expenses of an ordinary family of five.

For 1911 the same method was used and the income of 9043 adult male workers averaged $549.00 a year or $10.55 a week. The typical expenditure level in 1911 had risen to $15.68 a week....

Average income for the five categories of building trades craftsmen who were heads of families came to $711.00 per year or $13.70 a week. Labourers averaged $531.68 or slightly over $10.00 per week. Trainmen, traditionally among the highest paid wage earners averaged $971.07 or $18.67 a week. They were the only category of wage earner in the Department of Labour sample to receive an income high enough to place a family above the poverty line without the assistance of a second wage earner....

There is a good deal of contemporary descriptive evidence of the plight of the working poor in Montreal during these years. The Committee which organized the Montreal Child Welfare Exhibit of 1912 tried to draw up a family budget on the basis of earnings of $10.50 a week (which it suggested an unskilled labourer could hope to earn if continuously employed). The Committee noted that the budget made no provision for 'sickness, recreation, church, house furnishing, lectures and savings.' A family of five would with careful planning to able to allot 75 cents a day to food, but the Committee quoted its domestic science experts who suggested that a minimum of 25 cents a day was required for food for a growing child. The rent allowance in this budget came to $9.00 a month which the Committee noted could only pay for 'unsanitary quarters, sometimes below street level.'

It seems necessary to conclude that as far as real income is concerned the average wage earner in Montreal was less well off during the period of economic expansion than during the 'depression' of the late nineteenth century. There has been a general awareness that increases in the cost of living outstripped wage gains during the war and immediate post-war years but the overall trend of the first two decades has not been widely recognized. Given the small percentage of the labour force that was organized and the weakness of most components of organized labour the decline in real income should occasion no surprise.

It should be noted that the situation in Montreal was not unique, but part of a national pattern....

Terry Copp, "The Condition of the Working Class in Montreal, 1897–1920", Canadian Historical Association, *Historical Papers* 1972. Footnotes omitted.

The Economic Opportunities of "Foreign" Immigrants—One Ethnic Historian's View

Many Anglo-Canadians in the Laurier years saw "foreign" immigrants as not only a serious threat to the dominant culture, but also as a source of competition in the market for employment. One ethnic historian who has explored the dominant attitudes of English-speaking Canadians toward the new immigrants and the impact of those views on job opportunities is Howard Palmer of the University of Calgary. According to Palmer, strong attitudes of "anglo-conformity" in the West and elsewhere contributed to a vicious circle of discrimination which extended into the job market.

What developed throughout English-speaking Canada during this period was a vicious circle of discrimination. Non-Anglo-Saxons were discriminated against because they were not assimilated, either culturally or socially, but one of the reasons they were not assimilated was because of discrimination against them. As one researcher noted in a 1917 report on 'Social Conditions in Rural Communities in the Prairie Provinces,' the group 'clannishness' of immigrants which was so widely deplored by the public was caused as much by the prejudice of the 'English' as it was by the groups' desire to remain different.

There is no need to catalogue here the extensive patterns of social, economic and political discrimination which developed against non-Anglo-Saxons. Patterns of discrimination paralelled preferences of immigrant sources with northern and western Europeans encountering relatively little discrimination, central and southern Europeans and Jews encountering more discrimination and non-whites encountering an all pervasive pattern of discrimination which extended to almost all aspects of their lives. Discrimination was one of the main factors which led to the transference (with only a few exceptions) of the same ethnic 'pecking order' which existed in immigration policy to the place each group occupied on the 'vertical mosaic,' with the British (especially the Scots) on top, and so on down to the Chinese and blacks who occupied the most menial jobs. Non-British and non-French groups not only had very little economic power; they also would not even significantly occupy the middle echelons of politics, education or the civil service until after World War II.

The ethnic stereotypes which developed for eastern European and Oriental groups emphasized their peasant origins. These stereotypes played a role in determining the job opportunities for new immigrants and functioned to disparage those who would climb out of their place. Opprobrious names such as 'Wops,' 'Bohunks' and especially 'foreigner' indicated class as well as ethnic origin and these terms were used as weapons in the struggle for status. The very word 'ethnic' carried, for many people, such an aura of opprobrium that even recently there have been attempts to expurgate the use of the word. Ethnic food and folklore were regarded by most Anglo-Canadians as not only 'foreign,' but 'backward' and lower class....

Howard Palmer, "Reluctant Hosts: Anglo-Canadian Views of Multiculturalism in the Twentieth Century", in *Multiculturalism as State Policy*. Report of the Second Canadian Conference on Multiculturalism (Ottawa: Canadian Consultative Council on Multiculturalism and Supply and Services Canada, 1976), pp. 95–96. Footnotes omitted.

The Plight of Frontier Labour—The "Forgotten Men" Bypassed by Prosperity

Recent historical research also suggests that in Canada's frontier regions low-status unskilled workers such as the railway "navvies" and the "blanket-stiffs", did not share in many of the benefits of a rapidly expanding economy. In this passage A. Ross McCormack, a labour historian, describes the problems of the "forgotten men" in Canada's second phase of transcontinental railway construction from 1905 to 1914.

... Because the Laurier government, like the rest of Canadian society, was committed to the rapid expansion of the economy, it developed a new immigration policy to supply the railways with unskilled, inexpensive, and potentially exploitable labour. Central Europe became the one most important source of construction hands. Peasants from the provinces of the Austro-Hungarian Empire were attractive to the companies because experience with these workers since the turn of the century had convinced railway executives and contractors that the Slavs were 'obedient and industrious' and therefore excellent for the difficult work on the grade. After 1905, as construction began on the National Transcontinental (NTC) in northern Ontario and Quebec and on the Canadian Northern (CN) and the Grand Trunk Pacific (GTP) in the West, thousands of unskilled central and southern Europeans entered the country. The work on these national projects was to be done mainly by unassimilated immigrants.

In addition to being 'foreign', the other important characteristic of the railway construction labour force was its mobility. Indeed, the term 'blanketstiff' was derived from their mobility; itinerant workers 'jumped' from job to job packing their blanket-beds. To maintain a work force of 2,800 on a section of the NTC, the company had to engage as many as 5,100 men in the period of one month. In part, this mobility was a function of the fact that many jobs were available in the unskilled labour market. Itinerants also sawed trees in British Columbia and harvested wheat in the prairies. Farmers, anxious to harvest their crops in early autumn, bid up the price of unskilled labour, and many stiffs left the grade to secure higher wages in the fields. At the end of the harvest season the itinerants could work in the woods for the winter and return to the construction camps when operations resumed in the spring. Cultural and economic factors also contributed to this mobility. Slavic workers would leave jobs to rest among their families and countrymen in immigrant quarters like Winnipeg's north end thereby retaining something of the seasonality of an agricultural economy. Italians who were often supporting families in their homeland periodically returned to their villages, some making the Atlantic crossing a number of times. English-speaking hoboes, after having made a stake, drifted south to find winter work in California or Louisiana. In their travels from job to job, itinerants tramped along the tracks they had laid or rode in 'side-door Pullmans'.... Clearly a distinct rhythm developed in the life of the blanketstiffs: a job, a spree, another job, another spree.

A. Ross McCormack, *The Blanketstiffs: Itinerant Railway Construction Workers, 1896-1914*, Vol. 13, Canada's Visual History Series (Ottawa: National Museum of Man and National Film Board, 1975), pp. 1-2.

A Guide to Further Reading

1. *Overviews*

Brown, R.C. and Ramsay Cook, *Canada 1896-1921: A Nation Transformed*. Toronto: McClelland and Stewart, 1974.

Clippingdale, Richard, *Laurier: His Life and His World*. Toronto: McGraw-Hill Ryerson, 1979.

Dafoe, John W., *Laurier: A Study in Canadian Politics*. Toronto: McClelland and Stewart, 1963.

Skelton, O.D., *Life and Letters of Sir Wilfrid Laurier*. 2 vols. Toronto: Oxford University Press, 1921.

2. *Specialized Studies*

The Economic Boom

Alexander, David, "Economic Growth in the Atlantic Region, 1880-1914", *Acadiensis*, Vol. VIII, (Autumn, 1978), pp. 47-76.

Ankli, Robert E., "A Note on Canadian GNP Estimates, 1900-25", *Canadian Historical Review*. Vol. LXII (March, 1981), pp. 59-64.

Fowke, V.C., *The National Policy and the Wheat Economy*. Toronto: University of Toronto Press, 1957.

Linteau, Paul-André, René Durocher, and Jean-Claude Robert, *Quebec: A History 1867–1929*. trans. Robert Chodos. Toronto: James Lorimer, 1983.

Mackintosh, W.A., *The Economic Background of Dominion-Provincial Relations*. Toronto: McClelland and Stewart, 1964, esp. Chapter 4.

Skelton, O.D., "General Economic History, 1867–1912", in Adam Shortt and Arthur G. Doughty, eds., *Canada and Its Provinces*. Vol. IX. Toronto: Glasgow, Brook & Company, 1913.

Smiley, Donald V., ed., *The Rowell-Sirois Report/Book I*. Toronto: McClelland and Stewart, 1963, esp. Chapter 3, "The Wheat Boom".

The Protective Tariff, Business and Labour

Bennett, Paul W., "The National Policy and the Rise of American Business Enterprise in the Laurier Era, 1896–1911", *Quarterly of Canadian Studies*. Vol. 4, Nos. 3 & 4 (1977).

Bliss, Michael, *A Living Profit: Studies in the Social History of Canadian Business, 1883–1911*. Toronto: McClelland and Stewart, 1974.

_____, "Canadianizing American Business: The Roots of the Branch Plant", in Ian Lumsden, ed., *Close the 49th Parallel*. Toronto: University of Toronto Press, 1970.

Ellis, L. Ethan, *Reciprocity 1911: A Study in Canadian American Relations*. New Haven: Yale University Press, 1939.

Heron, Craig, "The Crisis of the Craftsman. Hamilton's Metal Workers in the Early Twentieth Century", *Labour/Le Travailleur*. Vol. 6 (Autumn, 1980), pp. 7–48.

_____, and Bryan D. Palmer, "Through the Prism of the Strike: Industrial Conflict in Southern Ontario 1901–14", *Canadian Historical Review*. Vol. LVIII (December, 1977).

Jamieson, Stuart, *Times of Trouble: Labour Unrest and Industrial Conflict in Canada, 1900–1966*. Ottawa: Task Force on Labour Relations Study, 1971.

Naylor, R.T., *The History of Canadian Business, 1867–1914*. Vol. 2. Toronto: James Lorimer and Company, 1975.

Porter, Glenn, and Robert D. Cuff, eds., *Enterprise and National Development: Essays in Canadian Business History*. Toronto: Hakkert, 1972.

Roberts, Wayne, "Toronto Metal Workers and the Second Industrial Revolution, 1889–1914", *Labour/Le Travailleur*. Vol. 6 (Autumn, 1980), pp. 49–72.

Immigration and the West

Avery, Donald, *"Dangerous Foreigners": European Immigrant Workers and Labour Radicalism in Canada, 1896–1932*. Toronto: McClelland and Stewart, 1979.

_____, *Immigration to Western Canada, 1896–1914*. Vol. 2, Canada's Visual History Series. Ottawa: National Museum of Man and National Film Board, 1974.

Berton, Pierre, *The Promised Land: Settling the West, 1896–1914*. Toronto: McClelland and Stewart, 1984.

Bruce, Jean, *The Last Best West*. Toronto: Fitzhenry and Whiteside, 1976.

Dafoe, John W., *Clifford Sifton in Relation to His Times*. Toronto: Macmillan, 1931.

Gray, James, H., *Boomtime: Peopling the Canadian Prairies*. Saskatoon: Western Producer Prairie Books, 1979.

Hall, D.J., *Clifford Sifton, Vol. I: The Young Napoleon*. Vancouver: UBC Press, 1982.

Jackel, Susan, ed., *A Flannel Shirt and Liberty: British Emigrant Gentlewomen in the Canadian West, 1880–1914*. Vancouver: UBC Press, 1982.

McCormack, A. Ross, *Reformers, Rebels and Revolutionaries: The Western Canadian Radical Movement, 1899–1919*. Toronto: University of Toronto Press, 1977.

Troper, Harold, *Only Farmers Need Apply*. Toronto: Griffin House, 1972.

Railway Building

Regehr, T.D., *The Canadian Northern Railway*. Toronto: Macmillan, 1976.

Skelton, O.D., *The Railway Builders*. Vol. 32. Toronto: Brook and Co., 1916.

Stevens, G.R., *The Canadian National Railways, Vol. II: Towards the Inevitable*. Toronto: Clarke Irwin, 1962.

Frontier and Hinterland Development

Acheson, T.W., "The National Policy and the Industrialization of the Maritimes, 1880–1910", *Acadiensis*. Vol. I (Spring, 1972).

Phillips, Paul, *The British Columbia Mining Frontier, 1880–1920*. Vol. 21, Canada's Visual History Series. Ottawa: National Museum of Man and National Film Board, 1975.

Ryan, William F., *The Clergy and Economic Growth in Quebec, 1896–1914*. Quebec: Les Presses de l'Université Laval, 1966.

Stelter, Gilbert A., *The Northern Ontario Mining Frontier, 1880–1920*. Vol. 10, Canada's Visual History Series. Ottawa: National Museum of Man and National Film Board, 1974.

Social Conditions

Allen, Richard, "The Social Gospel and the Reform Tradition in Canada, 1890–1928", *Canadian Historical Review*, Vol XLIX (December, 1968).

Barber, Marilyn, "Nationalism, Nativism and the Social Gospel: The Protestant Church Response to Foreign Immigrants in Western Canada, 1897–1914", in Richard Allen, ed., *The Social Gospel in Canada*. Ottawa: National Museums of Canada, 1975.

Copp, Terry, *The Anatomy of Poverty: The Condition of the Working Class in Montreal 1897–1929*. Toronto: McClelland and Stewart, 1974.

Levitt, Joseph, *Henri Bourassa and the Golden Calf*. Ottawa: Les Editions de l'Université d'Ottawa, 1969.

Piva, Michael J., *The Condition of the Working Class in Toronto, 1900–1921*. Ottawa: University of Ottawa Press, 1979.

Roberts, Wayne, *Honest Womanhood*. Toronto: New Hogtown Press, 1976.

Roy, Patricia, "Vancouver: 'The Mecca of the Unemployed', 1907–1929", in A.F.J. Artibise, ed., *Town and City: Aspects of Western Canadian Urban Development*. Regina: Canadian Plains Research Centre, 1981.

15

THE CANADIAN WOMEN'S MOVEMENT, 1880–1920s

A Struggle for Political Rights or Social Reform?

A women's movement emerged in late Victorian Canada just as public attention was being drawn to a host of pressing political and social issues. As in Britain and the United States, the movement seemed to spring from a variety of different sources. More women in late Victorian Canada were remaining single, the size of families was declining, and many Canadian women were no longer willing to accept domestic life as their only legitimate concern. A new generation of women, symbolized by the "new woman" in Canadian novels of the 1890's, began to question whether a woman's "proper sphere" was indeed only in the home as wife, mother and homemaker. For some of these women, broadening the franchise to allow full female suffrage was of paramount importance. Other women activists joined in the demand for a wide range of social reforms in response to the problems of Canada's emerging industrial society. Scattered across the country in cities and towns where economic advances had brought more leisure time, these "new women" entered in far greater numbers into public life, ready to join together, to assert their rights, and to apply their talents for the betterment of society.

Historical studies of the Canadian women's movement from 1880 to the 1920s are still in a stage of infancy. Yet a historical debate already has emerged over what constituted the primary motivation for the women's movement. Traditionally, historians have focused on the campaign for female suffrage and often implied that the main purpose behind the movement was political equality and the right to vote. Recent studies in Canadian social history, on the other hand, have suggested that the women's movement may have been driven by a strong desire for "progressive reform" common to many other groups in the period. The central question turns on whether woman's suffrage was seen as the means to achieve more societal changes, or as an end in itself.

Whatever the main motivations, the women's movement sprang from modest origins and endured many setbacks. Signs of the emerging movement could first be seen in suffrage societies of the late 1870s and 1880s. Ontario suffragists[1] pioneered the movement with the discreetly named Toronto Women's Literary Club, formed in 1876. The club's members "went public" in 1883 when, at a meeting in Toronto's City Hall, they became the Toronto Women's Suffrage Association. From the mid-1880s onward, suffragists were active in Ontario, Manitoba, British Columbia, Quebec, and to a lesser extent, in the Maritime provinces. Though the degree of activity varied from province to province, the patterns of events and results were similar. A handful of women led small activist groups in Canada's cities. National women's organizations like the National Council of Women and the Dominion Women's Enfranchisement Association sprouted up in the period 1880 to 1920 to facilitate co-ordinated political efforts. Small gains were made when unmarried women who met property qualifications were given the right to vote in municipal and school board elections. Yet a host of petitions and women's delegations to legislatures asking for suffrage met with little success until the war years 1914 to 1918.

The Canadian women's movement can also be seen as part of the broader-based and rising demand for progressive reform at the turn of the century. Many women, like many men, were disturbed by the industrial transformation of Canadian society between the early 1880's and the end of the Great War. The abuses of the factory system, the overcrowding and disorder of the cities, the influx of new immigrant groups and the changing ethnic composition of the population worried many Anglo-Canadian social reformers who feared "social degeneration". Some social reform groups also viewed with alarm the rise of strong farm and labour organizations, the growth of Western protest and French-Canadian nationalism.

For many women activists, the suffrage campaign was closely connected with the reform cause. Actively campaigning for investigations, laws and petitions concerning a wide variety of social maladies may have made them acutely aware of their own lack of political power. Certainly many members of women's groups who began by championing more "genteel" causes like access to higher education, female dress reform and bicycle-riding for women eventually branched out into public activities which included campaigns for female suffrage, temperance, child welfare, public health and stricter factory regulations.

Whether the cause was political rights or progressive reform, the main impetus for change among women came from those in the middle class and professional ranks. Many of these women had joined voluntary clubs and

---

1. Women—and men—who worked to get the vote for women in Canada were called "suffragists". The term "suffragette" was a label used by the British press to refer to England's militant suffrage campaigners. When Canadian women were called "suffragettes" it was usually by opponents seeking to discredit their cause by associating them with the militant tactics of their British counterparts.

friendship societies or had entered the labour force in the newly expanded fields of social service and those professions to which women had access (i.e. nursing, teaching and social welfare). In taking on new roles or entering public life, middle-class women became more conscious of such political and legal disabilities as the absence of female voting rights, the inequities of provincial divorce laws, and property laws which denied married women the right to control their own earnings. Similarly, many of these women developed a kind of "maternal feminism". For those who advocated female suffrage, took up careers or joined in social reform causes did so often in the name of children and family—and saw their mission as one of applying their unique nurturing and "mothering" capacities to the righting of society's wrongs.

In sharp contrast with the militancy displayed by suffragettes in Britain and the United States, female suffrage in Canada was achieved through a peaceful—and piecemeal—process. By 1872 women property owners in British Columbia, single or married, were permitted to vote in city elections. The municipal franchise was won in Ontario in 1883, but only for spinsters and widows who met the prescribed property qualifications. Manitoba granted single and married women the municipal vote in 1887. The provincial franchise, however, came much later. The first province to grant female suffrage was Manitoba in 1916. All other provinces extended the franchise in the next few years except Quebec, which did not do so until 1940. Spurred by the suffragist agitation and the war, the Dominion government finally granted women the right to vote in the federal enfranchisement acts of 1917 and 1918.

This problem study explores the motivations behind the Canadian women's movement between the 1880s and the end of the First World War. Were the early women activists primarily struggling to break out of the "woman's sphere" and to win political equality for its own sake? Were they largely motivated by either "maternal feminism" or a desire to maintain and improve a Christian social order? In short, were early feminists mainly seeking political equality or pursuing the vote as a means to furthering goals of social reform?

SELECTED CONTEMPORARY SOURCES

VIEWS OF THE WOMAN'S "PROPER SPHERE"

In the late nineteenth and early twentieth centuries, most Canadian women were expected to assume a traditional role in the home as wife, mother and homemaker. The contention that "woman's place was in the home" was deeply rooted in Victorian society. The family was considered the fundamental social unit; men were to be the providers and women were responsible for holding the family together and instilling moral values in children. The spheres of male and female were so well defined that mothering was regarded as the only natural role for women. The Victorian family was considered the bulwark of social stability and any deviation from woman's proper sphere was considered an attack on an essential institution.

By the late 1880s and 1890s groups of educated, middle-class women emerged to challenge the traditional role. They asserted that "true womanhood" required them to assume new roles outside the home, or to apply their nurturing and mothering abilities to society's problems at large. Some sought to reform an often selfish and materialistic world for the sake of their children while others aimed to break down political and legal barriers to the full participation of women in Canadian life, asserting that women should enjoy the same rights as men.

The Woman's Sphere—A Common Nineteenth-Century View, 1856

A lecture delivered by Reverend Robert Sedgewick, a Nova Scotian minister, to the local Young Men's Christian Association in 1856 expressed a prevailing attitude toward the role of women in Victorian Canada.

... One would have thought that this at least was a settled question—that it had been decided by universal consent, and that the unanimous voice of civilized and Christian man had definitely and permanently fixed the sphere and influence of woman in Christian society; but it is not so, and at this present time, and especially on this continent, this very question is agitated with a freedom and a fierceness too which augur badly for its settlement on reasonable and scriptual grounds, by those who view it in its moral aspects.

The errors and blunders which are interwoven with the subject of woman's rights and woman's place in modern society are, as these points now engage public attention, to be traced either to the ignoring of the fact or the omission of the fact that in the economy of nature or rather in the design of God, *woman is the complement of man.* In defining her sphere and describing her influence, this fact is fundamental. Unless this fact be admitted as an axiom in every way self-evident, no reasoning on this subject is sound....

In many respects woman is the equal of man. Save in the matter of sex, she has similar form and features. In the higher departments of human nature, she is man's fellow. Her mind comprehends similar powers—her heart similar passions and affections....

... [W]oman is the equal of man, alike in the matter of intellect, emotion, and activity, and ... she has shewn her capabilities in these respects.... It would never do, however, from these premises, to draw the conclusion that woman behoves and is bound to exert her powers in the same direction and for the same ends as man. This were to usurp the place of man—this were to forget her position as the complement of man, and assume a place she is incompetent to fill, or rather was not designed to fill. This were to leap out of her sphere and attempt to move in another, in which, to move rightly, the whole moral relations of society would behove to be changed, and suited anew to each other, but which, because they are unchangeable, every attempt is fraught with damage, it may be with ruin, and woman becomes a wandering star, which, having left its due place, and violated its prescribed relations, dashes itself into shivers against some other planet, whose path it crossed in the eccentricity of its movements, and goes out in the blackness of darkness for ever.

> Reverend Robert Sedgewick, *The Proper Sphere and Influence of Women in Christian Society*, a lecture to the YMCA, Halifax, Nova Scotia, November 1856, reprinted in Ramsay Cook and Wendy Mitchinson, eds., *The Proper Sphere* (Toronto: Oxford University Press, 1976), pp. 8–9.

Trained for Dependence—"A Girl of the Period" Questions Her Role, 1880

Many women in late Victorian Canada grew dissatisfied with their seemingly pre-ordained roles. The sentiments of an anonymous "Girl of the Period" echo an often-voiced complaint about the limitations of the woman's sphere:

> I want to know why it is that I, a well-brought-up lady-like (excuse my self-conceit— but this is the remark people make of me) girl, am so utterly helpless and dependent. I have not been taught anything that is of the slightest earthly use to anybody in the whole world. Of course I can sing correctly; but have no special power or compass of voice. It is only soft and low—a peculiarity of voice which Milton (?), or some of these old poets, says is nice in a woman, because it keeps her from scolding, I suppose. As a pianist I am a *brilliant success*, and yet a humbug as regards the science of music. That goes without saying. I can waltz— well! 'divinely'—but no thanks to anybody for that; it comes *con amore*; I can sew—fancy work; but I could not cut out and 'build' a dress, even if I was never to have another. I can't make up a bonnet, nor even a hat; but I do know when the milliner has made a mess of either. I am self-conceited enough to think I have extremely good taste in such matters as a critic, yet I don't see how I could turn my good taste into a single solitary dollar if I had to. I just love parties, balls, concerts and—shall I confess it?—theatres, and yet, if I had to earn the money with which to gratify myself in these indulgences, I fancy I must perforce go amusementless for many a year. My dear old 'Pater' and my good kind mamma are fairly well-off, I believe (but I really don't know), and are very willing to give me a good share of all these enjoyments; but it does make me often 'feel mean' to know that I am utterly dependent on them for everything, and can't do anything to lighten their load. Why mamma won't even let me into the kitchen to learn how to do things. She says it is not lady-like.

> "Confidences" by 'A Girl of the Period', Rose-Belford's *Canadian Monthly*, Vol. IV (1880), p. 624.

The Woman's Mission—Lady Aberdeen's Address to the National Council of Women, 1894

A nation-wide federation, known as the National Council of Women of Canada (NCWC), was formed in 1894 to provide a measure of coordination and a common meeting ground for various women's groups. In this passage from Lady Ishbel Aberdeen's presidential address to the NCWC's first annual meeting, the Countess sets out her conception of the woman's mission:

> . . . how can we best describe this woman's mission in a word? Can we not best describe

it as 'mothering' in one sense or another? We are not all called upon to be mothers of little children, but every woman is called upon to 'mother' in some way or another; and it is impossible to be in this country, even for a little while, and not be impressed with a sense of what a great work of 'mothering' is in a special sense committed to the women of Canada.

It is one of the great glories of this country that almost all its people are workers, and that there are very few drones. Its sons are all engrossed in the battle of life, striving for a sufficiency for themselves and their dear ones; and therefore on the women, hard-worked though they often are with domestic duties, must devolve the duty of building up the homes of the nation in the truest sense. And what sort of homes? Homes where the love of all that is beautiful and artistic and cultured is natural; where the true dignity of labour of every kind is recognized and acted upon; where a spirit of patriotism inspires young men and maidens to count it a high privilege to serve their country with single-minded disinterestedness, in however humble a way; where mutual love, consideration, forbearance, are the common rule, and the spirit of self-sacrifice is accounted the first necessity in the glorious work of helping others....

...The woman who aspires to make home a place for rest after work and for strengthening before labor, a centre of holy associations and inspiring memories, has need herself to be in touch with every side of our manifold life. She must realize that no walls can shelter her dear ones from the temptations, the sorrows, the discouragements of life. She must [be armed then] with armour suited for the fray. She must learn that if the poor around her doors are not cared for, the orphans not housed, the erring not reclaimed, because she was too much engrossed in her own house to lend a helping hand, the results of her self-absorption may be in the future to provide pitfalls for her own children, whom she so desires to cherish. If she is to be truly her husband's companion, her children's friend and guide, the maker of a home that will shed light and blessing, not only on its own inmates, but on the strangers who pass from time to time within her gates, she must needs understand the changes that are taking place in social conditions, the progress of thought in all directions.

Women Workers of Canada (Ottawa: National Council of Women of Canada, 1898), pp. 10–11.

Joining the Labour Force—A Woman's Experience in A Wartime Munitions Plant, 1916–18

Women's attitudes about their own proper role, and in turn prevailing attitudes about women, were changed dramatically by the Great War. Some women's groups opposed the savagery and wanton destruction of the war. Yet most women joined in the war effort in various ways. One of some 35 000 women who worked in war production was Elaine Nelson, a Toronto woman in her early twenties. Nelson worked first as a "knitting girl" for the Red Cross, then joined the 1916–17 rush of women into the munitions industry. In an interview conducted years later, she gave this answer when asked why she chose munitions work over "pretty jobs" with the Red Cross:

Because anybody can do those other things—the older people could do that. It took young vigorous people of a good will to do that kind of work, you know. Things were bad for the war, for us, and we just felt we had to get our shoulder to the wheel and get down to business. When you're young, you do what everybody's doing. . . . There was a kind of *esprit de corps*. Everybody wanted to be there; you were in the swim of things; everything was war, war, war. I think a lot of the girls—there's always some that are miserable and stupid and badly behaved—but on the whole they were a wonderful bunch, and I see so many of them to this day. It enriched my life really.

There was everybody, every single class, from the squire's lady to Judy O'Grady and some a few shades lower than Judy. I thought it was fascinating. You get in the canteen or up in that big restroom there and hear them talking. It was very, very interesting. And there's every kind: wonderful, brave women who were saving every nickel they could so they'd have enough money to buy a home when their husband came back; and some flighty, silly little fools that were running around with other men. You'd just see every kind. . . .

In meeting these people that we had never had any opportunity to meet before, and finding they were just the same as we were, but they just hadn't had the chances that we'd had for education and that kind of thing, we began to realize that we were all sisters under the skins. Wars do bring every class together and I think we need to do a little bit more of that without war if we can.

Another thing too: there's nothing that draws people together more than mutual trouble. When you read the newspapers and you see columns of deaths, of boys being killed, you read those names and you say, 'Oh, So-and-So's gone,' and then somebody's husband's gone, and somebody's fiancé's gone. And things went so much against us so often, so long that we just felt we *had* to. The boys are doing that for us, what are we doing for them? You just rolled up your sleeves and you didn't care how tired you were or anything else. It's a terrible thing that it takes a war and a national tragedy to pull things together. . . .

Interview with Mrs. Elaine Nelson, transcribed in Daphne Read, ed., *The Great War and Canadian Society: An Oral History* (Toronto: New Hogtown Press, 1978), pp. 156–157.

THE CAMPAIGN FOR WOMEN'S RIGHTS

The Canadian movement for women's rights may have begun in the late 1870s but it was not until the early years of the new century that the cause attracted a popular following. Although Canadian women never resorted to acts of civil disobedience or hunger strikes like their counterparts in England and the United States, they displayed much determination in their struggle. Suffrage bills, introduced repeatedly from the 1880s onward in Parliament and the provincial legislatures, were either rejected, often with jeers and derision, or quietly dropped from the order paper. It would take some thirty-five years before repeated petitions, delegations and bills finally earned the right to vote for women. The writings of women themselves provided an insight into their motivations.

A Cautious First Step—The Views of An Early Feminist, 1879

In late-nineteenth-century Canada women who challenged the image of woman in the home risked becoming social outcasts. From the Victorian middle-class perspective, the ideal of woman in the home, caring for her children and husband, not only was an accepted social maxim, but also a measure of respectability. Unmarried women or "working girls" were often looked upon with pity or outright disapproval. Few women entered into public activities without being accused of being a proponent of "women's rights" whose ultimate goal was the destruction of the family. Such prevailing attitudes undoubtedly influenced early feminists like "Fidelis" (an anonymous female writer) who addressed the so-called "woman question" in the late 1870s and 1880s.

> ... in the long run, women will find themselves permitted to do whatever they shall prove themselves able to do well—all *a priori* prejudices to the contrary notwithstanding. The world wants good work so much more than it wants old prejudices—that these must eventually yield to common sense, and the inevitable law of demand and supply. Even the much vexed question of the suffrage, so obstinate before mere agitation, will ultimately, doubtless, be settled by the women who quietly demonstrate their capability of discharging all other duties of life, and of organising and conducting even great undertakings with the calm and judicious judgment, the perseverance and the thorough conscientiousness of highly cultivated women, which, we believe, will not be found inferior to the same qualities in highly cultivated men. If the new ideal of womanhood shall advance as much during the next quarter of a century as it has done in the past, the principle of excluding the holder of otherwise unrepresented property from the franchise on the ground of sex will, we venture to believe, be regarded as an antiquated survival of a semi-cultivation. But this result will never come by empty agitation....
> Charles Kingsley's counsel deserves to be ever borne in mind by all promoters of this movement. 'By quiet, modest, silent, private influence, we shall win....'
>
> Fidelis, "The New Ideal of Womanhood", *The Canadian Monthly and National Review*, Vol. 3 (November, 1879), p. 674.

The British and American Example—A Canadian Suffragist's View

Canadian suffragists certainly drew some of their inspiration from the example set by the highly publicized struggle for women's rights in England and the United States. The British movement spearheaded by Emmeline Pankhurst's Women's Social and Political Union (WSPU) did not get fully underway until 1903. These English "suffragettes" favoured militant actions to achieve their ends. In addition to organizing petitions and sending delegations to Parliament, they interrupted cabinet meetings, hurled stones through windows, chained themselves to the fence around the Prime Minister's residence, and defied authorities by refusing to eat while imprisoned for their offences.

Flora MacDonald Denison, a Toronto writer, dressmaker and suffragist leader, was one who drew strength and a sense of purpose from the bold actions of Pankhurst and the suffrage campaigners in other countries. While Denison was considered more radical than most of her crusading contemporaries, her views were likely shared by many others.

> Possibly the most remarkable character in all history is the frail little leader of the Militant Suffragettes of England.

She is the most talked of person in the world today.

No queen every made such a triumphal march thru [sic] any country as she is making thru the land of Lincoln and Walt Whitman. . . .

I can see that the great Susan B. Anthony,[2] with clear vision and prophetic insight toil for sixty long years, often single handed and alone, sewing [sic] seeds here and there—organizing, working, educating—till in every civilized nation women were feeling the stress, and strain, of their false position. She did a colossal work and left the world ready for a great burst of light— for a great leap forward.

The fetters and bars of prejudice and custom had been slowly filed thru and broken, but authority and power remained obdurate.

American women had gained so much, they seemed satisfied to rest on their oars and drift, quietly and respectably, to full freedom. . . .

But that is not the way freedom is won.

A vigilance committee needs ever to be on guard.

A torch bearer needs ever to blaze the way.

So, while funeral services were still being held for Susan B. Anthony, Mrs. Pankhurst became the torch bearer for the advance guard. . . .

The originality of Mrs. Pankhurst's campaign methods, the masterly alertness, the rare judgment displayed, the willingness always to make herself the supreme sacrifice, has called forth the world's admiration.

The longest and most spectacular procession ever witnessed to uphold the standard of an inspiring cause was organized by this remarkable woman. There is absolutely no examples [sic] among men in their long struggle to secure the suffrage rights, of such devotion, self-denial and compelling earnestness. What a terrible anomaly that the government of England, always first to protect political refugees from whatever nation, and for whatever cause, should obstinately drive her own women to such waste of time, money and energy, and to such terrible sacrifices and horrible suffering.

In seven years Mrs. Pankhurst has written a story with more thrilling climaxes than was ever written before.

In seven years the victories for women have exceeded the victories of all former time.

Flora MacDonald Denison, "Mrs. Pankhurst—An Appreciation", 1909, Thomas Fisher Library Archives, University of Toronto, F.M. Denison Collection, No. 51, Box 8, "Woman's Suffrage" file.

Sweeping Up Society—The Real Purposes of the Suffragists, 1910

The rise of the suffragists in Canada aroused fears in male-dominated society, satirized in this 1910 cartoon from the *Grain Grower's Guide*. Such a view gained some credence from statements by prominent Canadians such as Goldwin Smith, who predicted that the enfranchisement of women would lead to the prohibition of alcohol, an end to tobacco smoking, and domination by a "women's government."

---

2. Susan B. Anthony, a prominent American feminist who helped found the U.S. National Woman Suffrage Association in 1869, visited Toronto to promote the cause in 1889, and worked tirelessly to secure a suffrage amendment to the U.S. Constitution.

"The Door Steadily Opens"

The "Homesteads-for-Women" Movement—A Campaign for the Rights of Prairie Women, 1915

Female suffrage was not the only goal of women's rights movement. Among the many legal issues of concern to the movement was the struggle of prairie women for equality in land rights. The Dominion Lands Act of 1872, known as the homestead law, lay at the root of the problem. The law excluded most women from the right to claim a homestead from the Dominion's public lands. This provision of the act became the target of a spirited "homesteads-for-women" movement waged by western journalists and farmers, without success, from the early 1900s until 1930, when the three prairie provinces inherited control over public lands. The following letter written by a Saskatchewan woman to Premier Walter Scott in May 1915 sets out a strong plea for a dower law:

> I beg of you in the name of justice to women that you give them your most careful consideration and urge upon your Government the necessity of passing a law at this session to give a married woman a legal and equal right to the property they have jointly accumulated.... why should a man have the legal right to will even 1/2 of their joint earnings to his friends, especially where there are no children.... That is what I get in return for my work, money and most of all my entire devotion to a man for 24 1/2 years. And yet the law does not allow me anything better. He is figuring now on selling out in the fall.... He says he has enough to keep him alright and I can rustle for myself.... All I get is the product of the hens and I have to keep the house in groceries first and whatever is left over I can have for myself. Although last year he took $10.00 from me, and the year before he took $3.00 and that means a lot to me when I have so

little to do with. He says the hens are his as he feeds them so I do not own a hen after all these years of toil and sacrifice according to our Western laws. One year ago I was completely done up. I worked on until I could not stand up without fainting... I never got... 1/2 day rest, not even a holiday since 1909.

Now you may ask why did I do all this hard work? My reply is simple. I had no choice in the matter. I was forced to it. I either had to do it or walk out penniless and so I have just held on for the 6 years waiting patiently for the Government of Sask. to wake up and do justice to its women slaves. It may be the Government does not really know the true condition of affairs although I have been told repeatedly that very sad cases have been brought before the Sask. Govt. several times by the L.C. of Regina....

Mrs. Jennie White to the Hon. Walter Scott, Premier of Saskatchewan, May 14, 1915, reprinted in Linda Rasmussen et al., *A Harvest Yet to Reap* (Toronto: Women's Press, 1976), p. 164.

A Classic Statement of the Suffragist Position—Nellie McClung on the Vote, 1915

While the Canadian movement produced its share of leading activists, Nellie Letitia McClung (1874–1951) stood out as one of Canada's most controversial early feminists. As a campaigner for women's rights whose slogan was "Never retract, never explain, never apologize—get the thing done and let them howl", she played an instrumental role in the successful female suffrage drives in Manitoba and Saskatchewan, wrote some 16 books, and eventually served at various times as an Alberta MLA, a Methodist Church leader, and a Canadian diplomatic representative.

In her fourth book, *In Times Like These* (1915), McClung set out a classic formation of the early feminists' position on many different issues. This passage, dealing with "Votes for Women", refuted many of the perennial arguments raised by opponents of female suffrage.

Women have dispensed charity for many, many years, but gradually it has dawned upon them that the most of our charity is very ineffectual and merely smoothes things over, without ever reaching the root....

... If women would only be content to snip away at the symptoms of poverty and distress, feeding the hungry and clothing the naked, all would be well and they would be much commended for their kindness of heart; but when they begin to inquire into causes, they find themselves in the sacred realm of politics where prejudice says no woman must enter....

Now politics simply mean public affairs—yours and mine, everybody's—and to say that politics are too corrupt for women is a weak and foolish statement for any man to make. Any man who is actively engaged in politics, and declares that politics are too corrupt for women, admits one of two things, either that he is a party to this corruption or that he is unable to prevent it—and in either case something should be done.... Women have cleaned up things since time began; and if women ever get in to politics there will be a cleaning-out of pigeon-holes and forgotten corners, on which the dust of years has fallen, and the sound of the political carpet-beater will be heard in the land.

There is another hardy perennial that constantly lifts its head above the earth... and that is that if women were ever given a chance to participate in outside affairs, family quarrels would result.... If a husband and wife are going to quarrel they will find a cause for dispute easily enough, and will not be compelled to wait for election day. . . .

In spite of the testimony of many reputable women that they have been able to vote and get the dinner on one and the same day, there still exists a strong belief that the whole household machinery gets out of order when a woman goes to vote. No person denies a woman the right to go to church, and yet the church service takes a great deal more time than voting. . . .

People are indifferent about many things that they should be interested in. . . . If one woman wants to vote, she should have that opportunity just as if one woman desires a college education, she should not be held back because of the indifferent careless ones who do not desire it. Why should the mentally inert, careless, uninterested woman, who cares nothing for humanity but is contented to patter along her own little narrow way, set the pace for the others of us? Voting will not be compulsory; the shrinking violets will not be torn from their shady fence-corner; the "home bodies" will be able to still sit in rapt contemplation of their own fireside. We will not force the vote upon them, but why should they force their votelessness upon us?

Nellie McClung, *In Times Like These* (Toronto: University of Toronto Press, 1972), pp. 46, 47–48, 48–49 and 56. Originally published by D. Appleton & Company, 1915.

THE STRUGGLE FOR SOCIAL REFORM

The rise of the early Canadian women's movement coincided with a wave of "progressive" reform that swept the country in the late nineteenth and early twentieth centuries. Women's groups, like their male counterparts, arose as a largely urban, middle-class movement in an emerging industrial society beset by problems of poverty, alcoholism, immigration, and the quality of public health.

Many women's organizations, like the Women's Christian Temperance Union (WCTU) and the Young Women's Christian Association (YWCA) were formed for social and cultural reasons as well as strictly political purposes. For some of these groups, the campaign for voting rights was only part of a larger concerted attack on the problems of urban and industrial society. Whether the struggle for social reform loomed larger in importance than the suffrage cause for most women activists remains open to question.

The Crusade for Social Purity—A Call for Christian Womanhood, 1890

The question of "social purity" was a major concern of middle class reformers, male and female alike. Many civic leaders, social gospel preachers and women activists joined in blaming rapid urbanization at the turn of the century for a proliferation of "social vices" in Canadian cities. Of utmost concern to some middle class reformers were bar-rooms and brothels, symbols of social degeneracy and a disregard for domestic Christian values.

A stirring article written in 1890 by Mrs. Dr. Parker,[3] a prominent WCTU

---

3. The use of "Mrs. Dr." as a title of courtesy in itself is a good indication of the way in which many men viewed women in Victorian Canada.

spokesperson, provided some insight into the appeal and motivations of the "social purity" campaigners.

> ... What is to be the physical character of the nation? Shall our sons and daughters be weak and nervous and puny of constitution, or, shall they have strength of bone and muscle and sinew, and vigor of brain? For answer we must look chiefly to the mothers. Whether we shall be a strong, pure, intellectual people depends most of all upon our women, and their just apprehension of all the possibilities attaching to the holy office of motherhood....
>
> Christianity which elevated woman is the force which has given to the world the measure of social organization we now possess, and it is safe to say, when the world reinstates woman, in the place which God originally assigned her as the equal of man, the first step will be taken to introduce the millenium.... A modern writer gives the following pen-picture of society: 'The rich eating up the poor; the poor stabbing at the rich; fashion playing in the halls of gilded sensualism; folly dancing to the tune of ignorant mirth; intemperance gloating over its roast beef, or whiskey-jug, brandy-punch, champagne-bottle, bearing thousands upon thousands down to the grave of ignominy, sensualism and drunkenness.' Does this picture portray a phase of Canadian society? We cannot say nay. Where is the remedy? Not in increasing wealth, for we have all seen wealth prostituted to just such uses. Not in education, for some of the best educated men are victims of drink and licentiousness. Not in culture or refinement, for these have been known to be handmaidens of debauchery. Where then? The remedy is in the hands of Christian womanhood, through the application to society's laws and customs, of that cleansing element, the Gospel of our Lord Jesus Christ, which, as a personal force regenerates the individual. This is the key to the solution of all our social problems. To our bright young Canadian women, just stepping on the sphere of life's possibilities, we appeal. Give your allegiance to reconstructing the social life of the nation, on the line of one standard of virtue for the sexes, that you may command the purity that is exacted of you; the entire abolition of every form of alcoholic beverage, that the fathers of your children may be sober men; the substitution of amusements requiring the exercise of brains instead of heels; the recognition of true worth wherever found, though it walk in fustian; and the knowing of God, His Sabbath, and His teaching. Surely here are aims worthy of your best endeavor....
>
> Mrs. Dr. Parker, "Woman in Nation-Building" in Rev. B.F. Austin, *Woman: Her Character, Culture and Calling* (Brantford: Book and Bible House, 1890), pp. 462–3.

The WCTU and Temperance for Seamen, 1897

For reformers, the abuse of alcohol was one of the most troubling problems in Canadian life. The Woman's Christian Temperance Union (WCTU), formed as a national body in 1883 and boasting 10,000 members by 1900, spearheaded the battle against the bottle. Temperance groups like the WCTU abhorred the suffering which alcohol caused in late Victorian society and feared that the increasing consumption of alcohol among the working class threatened the social order. In Nova Scotia, the WCTU aimed its message specifically at seamen:

> In view of the fact that sailors and fishermen, owing to long absences from land, are specially liable to be the victims of the saloon when on shore, and in view of the

promised plebiscite in the near future, we suggest, that our provincial and local superintendents of this department, pay marked attention to the distribution of suitable prohibition literature as a means of improving the minds, and influencing the votes, of these classes.

We further strongly suggest that when possible, personal canvass be made among these classes, and that the literature distributed be backed up by personal appeal on behalf of prohibition.

BECAUSE

1. It is right;
2. It will reduce criminals;
3. It will exterminate pauperism;
4. It will cut down the cost of penitentiaries, jails, poor houses and asylums;
5. All license systems have proven a failure;
6. The money employed in liquor, if invested in other industries, would employ more men;
7. It would promote thrift, and general business prosperity;
8. It will put more money circulating in legitimate channels;
9. It will provide better homes, better clothes, and better food, for the people;
10. It can be enforced as well as any criminal law;
11. It will make the sailor as happy and as safe on land as he is on sea;
12. It will give the sailor's wife and children continual joy, peace, prosperity and love....

We suggest that in our department we begin work now; that every union be responsible for the work just at hand, at home first, other places next, if possible.

We suggest that in our department we begin work now; that every union be responsible for the work just at hand, at home first, other places next, if possible....

Let our motto for this year in our department be: Our department for Jesus.

Respectfully submitted,

O.C. WHITMAN.

Woman's Christian Temperance Union, Nova Scotia, 1897, reprinted in Cook and Mitchinson, *The Proper Sphere*, pp. 205–6.

Lady Ishbel Aberdeen Lists the NCWC's Achievements, 1898

Lady Ishbel Aberdeen, the wife of Canada's Governor-General, played a major role in the founding of the National Council of Women and served as its president from 1893 to 1898. Looking back over the NCWC's first five years, she ranked many social reform initiatives among the group's main achievements.

1. It obtained the endorsation of the Educational Department to the introduction of Manual Training and the instruction in Domestic Science in the public schools of Ontario, and the training of teachers so that they may be able to give instruction in these arts. It has also given an impetus to the same movement in other Provinces.

2. It has obtained the appointment of Women Factory Inspectors for factories and workshops where women are employed in the Provinces of Quebec and Ontario....

5. It has brought about very desirable changes in the arrangements for women prisoners in various places, notably in the City of Quebec, where matrons are now in charge of the women, and young girls are now sent to a separate institution....

8. It originated the Victorian Order of Nurses and has taken a leading part in its establishment in various centres....

11. It has held an enquiry all over the country into the circulation of Impure Literature, and has been able to do something, as well as to warn parents and teachers as to the very real danger that exists in this direction. It hopes to be able to do more both by legislation and by circulation of healthy and interesting literature. It also inaugurated the Home Reading Union to promote habits of good and systematic reading....

13. It conducted an enquiry into the laws for the Protection of Women and Children, and has laid certain recommendations before the Minister of Justice which it earnestly hopes he will adopt when amending the Criminal Law.

14. It is at the present moment earnestly concerning itself in the Care and Treatment of the Aged Poor, so many of whom now find their only refuge in the jails for want of any other provision for them. On the authority of the Chief Inspector of Prisons for Ontario, some 60 per cent of the jail population of that Province belong to the infirm, aged, destitute, feeble-minded class.

15. It is now calling on all its members to unite in efforts for the Protection of Animal or Bird Life from useless destruction in the interests of fashion.

16. Through one of its affiliated societies it is endeavoring a plan for the Better Care and Wiser Distribution of Women Immigrants than has hitherto been possible.

17. It is pledged to co-operate with Dr. Bryce and other medical authorities, in urging immediate measures to be taken to check the ever-increasing ravages of consumptive diseases in this country, to spread knowledge on the subject, and to press responsibility home on individuals....

Lady Aberdeen, "Address" in *Women Workers of Canada* (Ottawa: National Council of Women of Canada, 1898), pp. 362–4.

The Reform Motivations of Canadian Suffragists—A Cartoonist's View, 1913

"Votes for Women"

In the early twentieth century the demand for a wide range of social reforms was often linked with the suffrage campaign in the popular press. For many women, winning the right to vote was a necessary first step on the path to social reforms in the areas of child welfare, public health, child and female labour and temperance. A cover illustration from *The Montreal Herald* in November 1913 pointed out that one of the major stumbling blocks for the movement was the attitude of certain classes of women themselves.

The Case for "Maternal Feminism"—Francis Marion Beynon's Reply to an Anti-Suffragist, 1913

In the public debate between Canadian suffragists and anti-suffragists after 1910, women's rights leaders frequently campaigned for female suffrage using arguments rooted in "maternal feminism". One leading Canadian suffragist who claimed that society's ills required the unique mothering abilities of women was Francis Marion Beynon, a founder of Manitoba's Political Equality League and women's page editor of the *Grain Grower's Guide*. In reply to one staunch anti-suffragist who contended that men were born to "take the initiative in all things" whereas a woman's main duty was to "preserve her attractions", Beynon left no doubt that she saw the vote as the beginning—rather than the end—of the reform movement's struggles.

... The theory that a woman should appeal to a man through her basest qualities—her vanity, her weakness, for which a more honest word is incompetence; her mental dependence, which is either ignorance or stupidity, revolts me, more especially as these attributes appeal to the basest side of man's nature—his vanity, his sensual passions and his arrogance. I refuse to believe that such a low appeal is necessary to the perpetuation of the human race....

We have too long been contented with the kind of motherhood that can look out of the window and see little children toiling incredible hours in factories or canning sheds over the way, until their small heads grow dizzy and their little fingers are bruised and bleeding, and say calmly, 'Thank God, it isn't my children,' or who can see the poor wayward girl being driven into a life of disgrace and shame by economic conditions and turn coolly away, content that her own daughter is chaste; with the sort of motherhood that can know that in the poor districts of our cities tiny babies are dying like flies and yet feel no responsibility for the conditions that cause their death.

I tell you, sisters, this kind of motherhood isn't good enough for the present day. We want a new spirit of national motherhood— mothers whose love for their own children teaches them love for all children; mothers who will not boast of their weakness but seek for strength to fight the battle for their own and their neighbors' children; mothers who are more concerned with raising the moral and intellectual standards of the community and country in which they live than in applying the latest suggestions of the beauty doctor....

The ballot is one weapon in this fight for the health, chastity and life of these children.... I regard it as an obligation on the part of every woman to arm herself with this weapon....

Grain Grower's Guide, October 1, 1913, Vol. X, p. 1010.

CONFLICTING INTERPRETATIONS

Studies of the struggle for women's rights have long been characterized by a preoccupation with "great women" and "great events". Until the 1970s, writers of women's history seemed to be attempting to reclaim feminine heroes from historical obscurity and to enlarge upon the glories of Canadian womanhood. Biographies of famous women like Nellie McClung, E. Cora Hind and Agnes Macphail tended to portray their subjects as exceptional people capable of outstanding achievements in a man's world yet retaining their essential femininity. Their interpretations of the struggle for women's rights, however, were often coloured by crude sexual stereotypes and sex-based distinctions.

Recent women's history has taken a decidedly different approach to the Canadian women's movement. Interest has shifted from dominant individuals to groups, from the remarkable woman to the ordinary woman. Women's ideology and socio-economic issues are being explored within the broader context of Canada's changing society. Women are seen not as isolated figures, but as persons coming to grips with social changes such as industrialism, urbanization and technological advance. Similarly, women's actions in the suffrage struggle are being viewed less in terms of personal volition than as the human responses to various social, economic and intellectual pressures in late-nineteenth- and early-twentieth-century Canada.

THE CAMPAIGN FOR WOMEN'S RIGHTS—AN END IN ITSELF?

The Struggle for Woman's Suffrage—C.L. Cleverdon's Interpretation

The campaign for voting rights has, quite predictably, received the largest share of attention from popular writers of women's history. Yet Catherine L. Cleverdon's study, *The Woman's Suffrage Movement in Canada* (1950), remains the original, and indeed, the only complete, account of the suffragist struggle in Canada.

> ...Lacking completely the flamboyance, bitterness, and even violence of the English campaign, the Canadian effort to extend democracy to women has been aptly character-ized by one of its own pioneers as 'a struggle, never a fight.' To the women of Quebec, where the struggle came nearest to being a fight and where memories of countless bitter disappointments are still fresh, this general statement may seem unjust; but from the broader viewpoint of the nation as a whole, it appears to be well founded. At no stage of the campaign was there anything remotely resembling militant tactics, even if the patience of women was sometimes severely tested by legislative hostility or indiffer-ence. Persuasion, not force, was the lever which gradually caused the gates of political freedom to swing open for Canadian women....
>
> * * * * *
>
> ... The basic plea of the suffrage forces was for simple justice. Women were forced to pay taxes and obey laws; why not give them a share in making them? The old cry, 'No

taxation without representation,' which had once rung out with such startling consequences in the neighbour country, now re-echoed in Canada in a milder way.

The forces advocating woman suffrage contended that the state, like the home,
needed women's point of view and influence in order to create a more perfectly
balanced way of life. The homemakers of the nation would take a special interest in
laws to protect their homes and families, and find particular scope for their talents in
such matters as health education, and child protection.... It was also argued that
women would influence moral questions, especially prohibition; and certainly there
was a close working alliance between woman suffrage and prohibition forces at all
stages of the campaign. Some optimists even went so far as to claim that if women
voted, war would be abolished; a prediction which unhappily has not been fulfilled.

In the nineteenth and twentieth centuries women have emerged from their homes
into the industrial and commercial worlds, either voluntarily or through pressure of
economic necessity. Flooding the labour market, they forced down not only their own
wages, but also the general wage level. This fact, clearly perceived by labour unions,
was the main reason for their general support of the suffrage cause. Failure of
legislatures to pass protective legislation for women in industry so long as laws were
exclusively man-made became a powerful argument for extending the franchise to
women.

Frankly admitting that many women were not interested in public questions,
suffragists contended that exercising the vote would train them to a higher sense of
social and civic responsibility, broaden their interests, and generally make them better
and more useful citizens.

The last great argument for political equality came with Canada's entrance into the
world war in 1914 and, quite fittingly, was used more by men than by women. This, of
course, was women's magnificent contribution to the war effort, both in war relief and
in filling the places vacated by men on the farm and in the factory. The average
Canadian was unstinting in praise and generous enough to admit that women had
earned their right to help chart the nation's future course....

Throughout the prairie campaign the women received staunch support from their
men. This presents an interesting parallel with the United States where pioneer
communities were invariably the first to enfranchise women. On both sides of the
border the feeling generally prevailed that women as well as men had opened up the
country, had shared the experiences of settling a new land, and were therefore entitled
to a voice in making the laws....

Catherine L. Cleverdon, *The Woman Suffrage Movement in Canada* (Toronto:
University of Toronto Press, 1950), pp. 4–5, 9–11 and 46. Excerpted and footnotes
omitted.

The Role of Prairie Women—A Revisionist View of the Frontier Thesis

C.L. Cleverdon's contention that the frontier experience of the prairie West
was more conducive to feminism than was the more settled society of Ontario
and the eastern provinces has been challenged by Professor Deborah Gorham
of Carleton University.

The undeniable fact that the suffrage was achieved earlier in the West than in the East,
in both Canada and the United States, does seem to support the frontier-as-equalizer

statements of Cleverdon, Cook... and others. Why, then, is the theory not completely satisfactory? Because it implies that in pioneer society, for the first time in human history, women made themselves indispensible, and this is an obvious untruth. The model that Cleverdon, Cook... and others have in mind as a contrast to the pioneer woman is the middle-class Victorian lady who did not perform economically valuable work, but whose function was rather to symbolize by her economic uselessness the economic success of her middle-class husband. The Victorian lady was, however, a new phenomenon, a product of industrialization and the rise of a new middle class, and this fact is generally overlooked by those who advocate the pioneer-as-equalizer explanation. Women had performed indispensible work in European society (as they have in every society that has ever existed) before the nineteenth century, and nineteenth-century working-class women, along with their children, were performing indispensible work at lower rates of pay than working-class men....

Many social historians of the Victorian period have analysed the metamorphosis that the middle-class woman underwent, as the new industrial middle class emerged. It was not the case that the Victorian lady served no function, but rather that her function had changed. From the bustling manager of the dairy, she became 'the angel of the hearth.' Her duty was to make her home a refuge from the world, and to maintain the moral standard....

The effectiveness of the 'separate-spheres' propaganda was manifest in the fact that middle-class Victorian women including most middle-class feminists, generally accepted this new stereotype. But this was true not only of the middle-class Victorian lady who remained at home in Britain. It was also true of those women who came to North America as pioneer wives, and I would suggest that it was this new image of themselves as moral guardians and protectors of the hearth that was decisive in changing their status in the new society. It proved especially effective, because as well as maintaining the role of moral guardian and spiritual centre of the home, those women also had to resume their old roles and become once again economically productive. It seems plausible to suggest that it was a combination of the two roles which altered and improved the status of women....

Deborah Gorham, "Singing Up the Hill", *Canadian Dimension*, Vol. 10 (June, 1975), pp. 35–36.

The Role of the War—Ontario Premier Hearst, the War and the Vote

The woman's suffrage movement may have received its biggest push from the West, but it did not achieve its goal, either in Canada or in Britain, until the final stages of World War I. Some historians of the Canadian suffrage campaign have argued that women's participation in the war effort was the decisive factor in achieving the right to vote. The case of Ontario is particularly notable because William H. Hearst, a Conservative premier and long-standing anti-suffragist, was the one who conceded the vote to women. In analyzing the circumstances surrounding Hearst's eleventh-hour conversion to suffragism in early 1917, Brian D. Tennyson shed some light on both public attitudes and the motivations of politicians in Ontario.

What had changed Hearst's mind on this question? Undoubtedly, he was speaking largely for himself when he referred to the profound impression which the Great War contributions of women had made on the public mind. In addition, he was also just facing the political facts of life to some extent. For Manitoba and Saskatchewan had enfranchised their women in 1916, and Alberta and British Columbia were doing so at this same time. Also, a large number of American states had already given women the vote.

It has been suggested that Sir Robert Borden and the federal Conservatives exerted pressure on Hearst to pass this legislation. For the conscription crisis was already developing and the idea of Union government was in the air. This theory argues that Borden pointed out to Hearst the need for the political support of women in the impending election, and the Wartimes Election Act is cited as evidence of collusion. There is no documentary evidence to sustain this theory, but it cannot be denied merely on that score. One simply cannot determine the effect on Hearst's calculations of the fact that women related to soldiers serving overseas would probably support conscription if it proved necessary.

Another possible factor in his calculations may have been the well-established fact . . . that women were generally strongly behind the temperance movement. This movement was powerful in Ontario by 1917; indeed, in 1916 Hearst had enacted the Ontario Temperance Act, which brought about virtual prohibition in the province. Could he not, therefore, reasonably expect temperance women to stand behind him when the day of reckoning came?

Brian D. Tennyson, "Premier Hearst, the War and Votes For Women", *Ontario History*, Vol. LVII, No. 3 (1965), pp. 119–120. Footnotes omitted.

The Response of Farm and Labour Women—A Critique of the "Common Front" Thesis

The popular perception of the suffrage campaign as a "common front" of organized middle-class women has come in for attack in recent studies. While the campaign seemed to peak in most provinces in the later war years, it was far from unified. Regional differences, traditional rural-urban antagonisms, and even class differences tended to fragment the women's rights movement. By the time of the Great War new divisions surfaced between "militarists" and "pacifists" in the movement. The work of Carol Lee Bacchi has examined the membership of the English-Canadian suffragist movement, the role of rural and working-class women, and the effect of "divided allegiances" on the suffrage cause.

The organized farmers in the Prairie West—the Saskatchewan and Manitoba Grain Growers and the United Farmers of Alberta—and some elements of the Canadian labour movement were among the earliest and staunchest advocates of woman suffrage in Canada. Yet very few farm or labour men or women managed to penetrate the ranks of suffrage societies like the Manitoba Political Equality League and the Montreal Suffrage Association, which remained predominantly urban and middle class. Farm and labour women preferred to work for the ballot through their own associations rather than join the suffragists, who showed little real understanding of the problems of farmers or workers.

The women managed to cooperate in several joint ventures for the specifically female goals of equal homesteading privileges and a dower law guaranteeing a married woman a one-third interest in a deceased husband's estate. But a series of confrontations between the suffragists and the farming and labour women suggest that more divided than united them....

Many women in the suffrage societies endorsed the goals of [a largely Anglo-Saxon Protestant middle class] reform movement. In fact, most were reformers first and suffragists second. A small minority wanted the vote to advance female interests. A few feminists even challenged the middle-class family structure which kept women in subjection. However, these women were going against the tide of middle-class opinion which saw the patriarchal family as the chief bulwark against the forces of social disruption. The majority of female suffragists accepted the traditional allocation of sexual roles and desired the vote simply as the means to an end, to double the representation of both their race and their class. Many farm women and many working-class women found it impossible to work through the 'official' suffrage societies because of their obvious middle-class bias....

* * * * *

Despite many common objectives, women in the turn-of-the-century period were unable to surmount their class divisions. In part, they were caught up in the heightened class consciousness of the era.... Moreover, while the suffragists claimed to speak for all women, they really represented only the urban middle classes. Farm and labour women understood this and refused to join the urban suffrage societies. Although these women managed to cooperate for several female-oriented goals, ultimately they identified with their class rather than their sex.

After enfranchisement, women followed voting patterns which were determined by their political and economic affiliations. The revolution in social values and in woman's social status which the suffragists had anticipated was never realized.

Carol Bacchi, "Divided Allegiances: The Response of Farm and Labour Women to Suffrage", in Linda Kealey, ed., *A Not Unreasonable Claim* (Toronto: Women's Press, 1979), pp. 89–90 and 106–107.

THE STRUGGLE FOR SOCIAL REFORM—THE PRIME OBJECTIVE OF THE MOVEMENT?

The Women's Movement—An Expression of Christian Reformism

Only recently has the women's movement been interpreted as part of the Christian "social gospel" response to the forces of industrialization and urbanization. Ramsay Cook's introduction to the new edition of Catherine Cleverdon's *Woman Suffrage Movement in Canada* (1974) provided a synthesis of this interpretation.

Many of [the professional, middle-class] women turned to social and charitable activities, responding to the urgings of an awakening Christian social conscience. There were church groups and missionary societies for the more orthodox. For those interested in applied Christianity there were the Woman's Christian Temperance Union, founded in the late seventies, and later the University Settlements and City Missions organized to serve, and evangelize, immigrants and underprivileged urban slum families....

...it has been argued that it was the apparent evidence of the disintegration of traditional family life that turned many women toward public affairs and suffragism. Certainly suffragists realized, with much greater perception than opponents like Goldwin Smith, Stephen Leacock, and Henri Bourassa, that in an industrial and urban society there were no longer air-tight compartments; family, home, work, education, politics, and health were increasingly integrated. Consequently the suffragist could turn the old 'woman's place is in the home' argument against an opponent....

Many suffragists could claim a serious interest in the problems of labouring people, even if their own cause found little vocal support in that segment of Canadian society. Indeed, the suffragists were a part of a more general, middle-class reform movement that was concerned to remove a wide range of injustices and evils that afflicted the country. The most obvious features of this broad reform movement were its Protestant ethos (though the Roman Catholic church was certainly not unmoved by social questions), its revulsion at the materialism of 'Canada's Century,' its predominantly Anglo-Saxon nationalism, and its often naive optimism. Combined, these elements made up that amorphous but potent phenomenon, the Social Gospel. It was not a homogeneous ideology; it had left, centre, and right tendencies, as well as Methodist, Presbyterian, Baptist, and Anglican variations....

The spirit of Christian, liberal optimism, the belief that someday, somehow, the Kingdom of God would be established on earth, motivated the reform movement in general and suffragism in particular. As one suffragist put her case in 1896: 'She followed Christ Her Master everywhere else, and she must follow Him too into the legislative halls, for "the government shall be upon his shoulders." And when she went it would be with her hand in His'....

No doubt this conviction of being on the side of righteousness, supported by the inevitable processes of nature, was important to the suffragists. It provided a helpful psychological defence against the repeated rebuffs that the movement met. It was probably also inevitable that the suffrage cause should become part of the wider reform movement and be presented as one of the steps in the establishment of the Kingdom— 'when the world reinstates woman, in the place which God assigned her as the equal of man, the first step will be taken to introduce the millenium.' The result was, however, that many who supported woman suffrage argued for it by claiming that it would result in a far better society....

Ramsay Cook, "Introduction" to C.L. Cleverdon, *The Woman Suffrage Movement in Canada* (Toronto: University of Toronto Press, 1974), pp. xi, xiii, and xvii-xx. Edited and footnotes omitted.

The "Parliament of Women"—A Questionable Experience in Progressive Reform

The National Council of Women in Canada in the years 1893 to 1929 was perhaps the leading organization in the early Canadian feminist movement. It was founded to promote social reforms and laid claim to the title of the "Parliament of Women". In her full-scale study of the NCWC, Veronica Strong-Boag raised questions about the progressive reform motivations of its members.

By the 1890s feminine nationalists everywhere desired some institutional means of expressing their sense of common identity. They wished to take their part in uniting a country split by sectarian and political conflict. Existing [women's] clubs also shared an immediate practical problem. Lack of communication often resulted in duplicated or uninformed efforts. A sentimental patriotism and a hopeful pragmatism made thoughtful observers receptive to plans for a 'Parliament of Women'. Nor should another factor be forgotten. The financial and industrial expansions of the late nineteenth century had produced a masculine elite whose ambitions—whether economic, social or political—encompassed the Dominion as a whole. The female relatives of Canada's powerful men, energized by a changing external environment and by their own recent access to higher education and the professions, had few formal ways of expressing their complementary desires for national leadership and influence. All these public and private forces came together to create a non-partisan and non-sectarian federation, the National Council of Women of Canada. . . .

As western feminists like Nellie McClung and Violet McNaughton angrily appreciated, National Council leaders were not about to advocate major alterations in the authority patterns of the Dominion. Nor for that matter were the majority of the NCWC's critics within the club movement any more ready to propose a revolutionary overhaul of industrial capitalist society. Very few indeed—not even the moderately radical McClung and McNaughton— had either the confidence or the ideological know-how to prepare such a critique. Within and without the federation most Canadian feminists were liberals. Like Lady Aberdeen they accepted the major tenets of the liberal creed—the faith in individual effort, private property, human progress and natural hierarchy. They demanded reforms not revolution. Over time NCWC leaders came to appear especially conservative interpretors of the prevailing ideology. Female activists like the two westerners had more and more difficulty in finding a comfortable home within the bounds of the federation. Radicals, never frequent at any time, became for all practical purposes non-existent by the 1920s.

The middle-class background which undercut the radical potential of most NCW-C'ers helped produce bureaucratically-minded reformers. Along with maternalism, the virtues of efficiency, predictability, centralization and professionalization constituted the National Council's modern pantheon. The creation of the NCWC with its consolidated, large-scale and formal organization was an important step in feminine efforts to rationalize the functioning of society. The Council early dedicated its labours to this end. Whatever the precise nature of reforms, whether in immigration laws, educational programmes, health institutions or prison regulations, changes were legitimized by reference to the intrinsic value of 'good management'. Society would be stabilized and purified by improved organizational structures. . . .

Male progressives were also attempting to create a more orderly community but the feminine contribution was perhaps particularly helpful in lending the transformation some appearance of humanity. The NCWC like many other elements in the woman's movement both legitimized new institutional overseers and contributed to the shaping of the middle-class value system which [social historians] . . . see emerging in the late nineteenth century.

Veronica Strong-Boag, *The Parliament of Women: The National Council of Women of Canada, 1893–1929* (Ottawa: National Museum of Man, 1976), pp. 410 and 420–422.

The Reform Ideology of the Suffragists—A Reflection of Status Anxieties

Canada's English-speaking suffragists, like their British and American counterparts, were members of a movement largely composed of women drawn from similar Anglo-Saxon, Protestant, middle-class backgrounds. While the suffragists were far from being the "batty, prudish old maids" portrayed in crude anti-suffrage propaganda, they did seem to share a strong belief in the prevailing values of late Victorian Canada.

Recent studies by historian Carol Lee Bacchi have examined the attitudes of Canadian suffragists in the context of their predominantly Anglo-Saxon Protestant, middle-class background:

.... Canada's English-speaking suffragists were members of a late nineteenth-century reform coalition drawn from the Anglo-Saxon Protestant middle classes. Such middle-class reformers suggested only minor changes. The family, for instance, remained sacrosanct in their eyes. The suffragists did not want to challenge the accepted female role but only to raise its status.

This paper examines two parts of the reform ideology: the commitment to race regeneration and the crusade for social purity. It shows how both these goals depended on traditional views of women's virtues. The desire to create a strong and healthy race placed an emphasis on woman's role as procreator and nurturer. The crusade for purity, an attempt by the Protestant elite to reimpose its values on a deviant society, made a patriotic virtue of women's asexuality. Given the suffragists' Protestant Anglo-Saxon background it ought not to be surprising that they endorsed this programme. Their allegiance to their sex was not their sole allegiance. In fact, at times, the commitment to race, creed, and class superceded [sic] the commitment to sex....

* * * * *

In order to understand the suffragists' social attitudes we have to understand the values of the group with which they identified....

...the Anglo-Saxon elite in this period were attempting to preserve or regain racial predominance. Two schools advocated different means towards this end. Eugenists concentrated upon applying lessons in animal breeding to humans while a group of environmental reformers argued for the need to improve the living and health standards of the population. Both approaches stressed the importance of woman's role as mother. The suffragists wished to participate in the re-creation of the race and therefore accepted the priority of woman's maternal function....

The same Anglo-Saxon Protestant elite faced another challenge in the growth of large cities, city slums, and resultant intemperance and social vice. The campaign to reinstate Protestant standards of chastity and sobriety naturally attracted the women since it glorified their particular virtues.

With an understanding of the suffragists' background their social attitudes become predictable. It would have been inconceivable to most of these women to suggest serious restructuring of sex roles or to suggest that women imitate male immorality. Rather, they took advantage of the new dignity bestowed on women to achieve certain victories. The vote and the acquisition of higher education facilities, less restricting garments, and a wider range of physical activities ought to be counted among these.

Carol Bacchi, "Race Regeneration and Social Purity: A Study of the Social Attitudes of Canada's English-Speaking Suffragists", *Histoire sociale/Social History*, Vol. II (November, 1978), pp. 460–474. Footnotes deleted.

POLITICAL RIGHTS OR SOCIAL REFORM?—A CLASH OF VIEWS

The Ideals of Maternal Feminism—T.R. Morrison's Interpretation of the "Child Savers"

One of the clearest attempts to define the dominant ideology of Canada's women activists can be found in Terence R. Morrison's studies of child-centred social reform in Ontario. According to Morrison, the emergence of maternal feminist ideas stimulated more than it inhibited a growing interest and involvement in child welfare and other related forms of urban social reform.

Social reform aimed at child welfare in late nineteenth century Ontario was born from deep concern over the possibility of family disruption and sustained by an enduring faith in the ability of the home to shape society. This was notably the case with the early Woman's Rights Movement. A dominant feature of the rhetoric contained in the feminist literature was a belief that society would benefit in moral terms from an extension of woman's maternalism. Women, in this period, fought to enlarge their 'sphere' to include areas beyond the home, not as their critics maintained, to forsake family responsibilities, but to eradicate those forces eroding family stability.

The most visible indication of family instability, to feminists, was the disadvantaged and delinquent child. To women, a male-dominated society had created the disadvantaged child and, thus, only the gentle and affectionate influence of woman could eliminate the causes of this condition. Such an influence would flow through a strengthened family: the only institution over which woman reigned. With this strategy, feminists hoped to guarantee that urban and industrial growth would proceed in accordance with the values underpinning family life. A direct consequence of such a situation would be the removal of those forces impelling children to delinquency, truancy and vagrancy. . . .

A roughly conceived ideal of true womanhood permeated the Woman's Rights Movement. Attempts to fulfill its promise motivated many women in their child welfare activities. This ideal, for men, stood as something noble to which all women should aspire. To the feminist, on the other hand, the ideal was a source of anxiety: for it placed woman high on a pedestal and at the same time prevented her from climbing down to join the rest of society. An ideal woman in the late nineteenth century personified the values of piety in religion, purity in morals, and submissiveness and domesticity in family life. Inconsistency, however, pervaded this ideal. Although her intuitive powers, refined sensibilities, and life giving maternal resources marked her as the moral superior of man, many men argued that woman's physical and intellectual inferiority made her unfit for the harsh realities of life outside the home.

Women in the late nineteenth century reacted to the ideal of womanhood in three ways. The majority of women acquiesced and sought to emulate the ideal in their everyday conduct. A small group of dedicated feminists, cramped by the tight restrictions imposed on them by the ideal, rejected it entirely. Instead, they sought to compete with men on men's terms hoping in the process to etch a new role for woman. Another group of women, the majority of feminists, accepted the values underpinning the ideal, but saw no reason why it should be confined to the domestic circle. These women, convinced of their own moral purity and spiritual genius— and at the same time witnessing what they considered to be serious threats to the institution which nurtured these womanly qualities— launched efforts to secure the vote and specific social reforms which would purge male society of its home-corrupting influences. . . .

As women edged beyond the home in pursuit of the vote or social reform, they rekindled the fires of a long-standing debate on the appropriate sphere of woman. This discussion concerning woman's social role necessarily involved deliberation about the pattern and quality of relationships existing between husband and wife and parent and child. When women explored avenues of emancipation and improvement for themselves, therefore, they did the same for their children. The much praised feminine instincts and maternal responsibilities of womanhood, which only the very radical feminist disavowed, bound the search for woman's rights to efforts directed at improving the welfare of children.

> T.R. Morrison, "'Their Proper Sphere': Feminism, the Family and Child-Centered Social Reform in Ontario, 1875–1900", *Ontario History*, Vol. LXVIII (March, 1976), pp. 45–48. Footnotes omitted.

"Equal Rights" Feminism—An Alternative Interpretation

Professor Deborah Gorham is one who has questioned whether maternal feminism represented the dominant ideology of the late-nineteenth- and early-twentieth-century women's movement. In a series of articles she has argued that the early feminists were also motivated by other concerns:

> The women's suffrage movement, symbol of nineteenth—and early twentieth-century feminism then and now, was the most visible manifestation of women's emancipation, but it was merely the tip of the iceberg. Those who attacked women's suffrage were attacking much more than the idea that women as well as men should enter the polling booth. Unlike the opposition to a wider male suffrage, resistance to women's suffrage was everywhere based not so much on fear of the effects women might have as voters but on the fact that the woman voter challenged the ideal of womanhood which formed an essential part of a social order that many saw slipping away from them....
>
> More often than not, Canadian feminists gave wholehearted support to the idea that women had special duties. However, they insisted that these very duties made it essential that they participate fully in public life. Only then could they carry out their special mission: the protection of the home, the family, and of women and children....
>
> Feminists in the United States and Britain used the same tactics. But this approach may have been a tactic of argument as much as it was a deeply felt belief. One of the most thoughtful commentators on the American movement has suggested that the U.S. suffragists' arguments were shaped not at their own initiative, but more often in response to the arguments of anti-suffragists. Tactically it was wise, at least in the short run, to emphasize the woman's maternal role because this technique turned the arguments of the opposition against itself. But tactics are one thing, inner beliefs are another....
>
> In any case, there were Canadian women who advocated equal rights for its own sake, and who made it their primary reason for insisting that women must have a wider place in society:
>
>> Why should women, who represent half the human family, not have equal rights and privileges... or all the *natural* conditions of their brothers, or civil conditions made by the laws of their country... for the benefit of the human family in general?
>
> asked Flora MacDonald Denison, an activist in the Toronto movement.
>
> Denison and others like her firmly insisted that as human beings they had a *right* to full citizenship. They fought for their rights as individuals and not only because they felt a duty to expand their maternal role into the public sphere. But Denison herself used maternal feminist arguments when it served her purpose. Canadian feminists of the period cannot be categorized as belonging to one or another clearly delineated group; both equal rights feminism and maternal feminism were realities in Canada.
>
> Deborah Gorham, "The Canadian Suffragists", in Gwen Matheson, ed., *Women in the Canadian Mosaic* (Toronto: Peter Martin Associates, 1976), pp. 24–26. Footnotes deleted.

"Rocking the Cradle for the World"—A Revisionist View of Maternal Feminism

Taking issue with Gorham, Wayne Roberts has claimed that Canada's early women's movement may have begun as a late-nineteenth-century struggle for "radical" democratic rights, but it evolved into a conservative brand of maternal feminism. The potential of the "new woman" was never realized, according to Roberts, because women activists gradually became absorbed in efforts to extend their traditional maternal role into society.

The suffrage movement was no mere parlour rebellion, nor was woman suffrage a 'motherhood' issue. On the contrary, suffrage projected a field of possibilities which challenged woman's subordination within the patriarchal family. The fact that the suffrage movement strayed from its early democratic ideals of women's rights cannot be explained mechanically, as a reflection of the intrinsic limitations built into the suffrage question itself.

The prospects of women's enfranchisement undercut many of the restrictive norms embedded in the social and political system of Victorian Canada. On a personal level, the widening of female realms upset traditional sex stereotyping of male-female interaction. The *Globe* despaired on behalf of anxious lovers: how could they wax 'sentimental over a lady whose conversation deals chiefly with the railway subsidies and amendments to the school law'? Politically, coming on the heels of the mass enfranchisement of males, universal female suffrage would dramatically sever the last tie between citizenship rights and property....

.... It is tempting to refer to the upper-class tenor that came to define the movement as the explanation, rather than the problem to be explained, of the eventual course of the movement. However, this view is fundamentally incorrect.

Even the aristocratic pretensions of the National Council of Women, formed in 1893–94, was more a figment of the leaders' imagination than a fragment of Britain's social system. It was really a case of the bland leading the bland. Their conventions bristled with ceremonies lacking only in content....

* * * * *

Far from challenging the terms of [the traditional family relationship with its unpaid housewife], maternal feminism highlighted additional obligations for women in the family. Just as factory production of household goods was diminishing women's productive functions in the home, women's social role in the home was invested with new importance. In the late nineteenth century, as social institutions became less conscientiously moralistic, wives became mothers. A lengthier process of education was increasingly seen as training in morally neutral skills. This kind of development, together with the moral anonymity of an industrial city where work and community were forcefully separated, put a premium on privately-derived restraints and anxieties. Heightened responsibilities for mothers were a prerequisite in this modern, streamlined industrial order. Maternal feelings interpreted their new responsibilities as part of a package deal leading to extended social responsibilities and rights.

Despite the strivings of women in the turn-of-the-century period, they were unable to overcome the occupational and social injunctions of the era. Maternal feminism expressed the adaptation of women's strivings to these overpowering pressures. It is this adaptation which led to the contradictory nature of maternal feminist aspirations and which accounts for the ultimately disappointing and limited ideological and political gains made by the first self-conscious generation of women's activists in Canadian history.

Wayne Roberts, "'Rocking the Cradle for the World': The New Woman and Maternal Feminism, Toronto 1877–1914", in Linda Kealey, ed., *A Not Unreasonable Claim* (Toronto: Women's Press, 1979), pp. 24–5 and 45.

A Guide to Further Reading

1. Overviews

Andersen, Margaret, *Mother Was Not A Person*. Montreal: Black Rose Books, 1972.

Bacchi, Carol Lee, *Liberation Deferred?: The Ideas of the English-Canadian Suffragists, 1877–1918*. Toronto: University of Toronto Press, 1983.

Bassett, Isabel, *The Parlour Rebellion: Profiles in the Struggle for Women's Rights*. Toronto: McClelland and Stewart, 1975.

Cleverdon, Catherine L., *The Woman Suffrage Movement in Canada*. Introduction by Ramsay Cook. Toronto: University of Toronto Press, 1974.

Cook, Ramsay and Wendy Mitchinson, eds., *The Proper Sphere: Woman's Place in Canadian Society*. Toronto: Oxford University Press, 1976.

Kealey, Linda, ed., *A Not Unreasonable Claim: Women and Reform in Canada, 1880s–1920s*. Toronto: Women's Educational Press, 1979.

Labarge, Margaret, Micheline Dumont-Johnson, and Margaret E. MacLellan, *The Cultural Tradition and Political History of Women in Canada*. Ottawa: Information Canada, 1971.

Light, Beth and Joy Parr, eds., *Canadian Women on the Move, 1867–1920*. Toronto: New Hogtown Press, 1984.

Rasmussen, Linda et al., *A Harvest Yet to Reap*. Toronto: Women's Educational Press, 1976.

2. Specialized Studies

Woman's Proper Sphere and Feminism

Bliss, Michael, "'Pure Books on Avoided Subjects': Pre-Freudian Sexual Ideas in Canada" in Michael Horn and Ronald Sabourin, eds., *Studies in Canadian Social History*. Toronto: McClelland and Stewart, 1974, pp. 326–46.

Griffiths, N.E.S., *Penelope's Web: Some Perceptions of Women in European and Canadian Society*. Toronto: Oxford University Press, 1976.

Morrison, T.R., "'Their Proper Sphere': Feminism, the Family and Child-Centered Social Reform in Ontario, 1875–1900", *Ontario History*, Vol. LXVIII (March and June, 1976), in two parts.

Philip, Catherine, "The Fair Frail Flower of Western Womanhood", in A.W. Rasporich and Henry Klassen, eds., *Frontier Calgary*. Calgary: University of Calgary, 1975.

Roberts, Wayne, *Honest Womanhood: Feminism, Femininity and Class Consciousness among Toronto Working Women, 1896–1914*. Toronto: New Hogtown Press, 1977.

———, "'Rocking the Cradle for the World': The New Woman and Maternal Feminism, Toronto, 1877–1914", in Kealey, ed., *A Not Unreasonable Claim*, pp. 15–45.

Stoddart, Jennifer and Veronica Strong-Boag, "...And Things Were Going Wrong At Home", *Atlantis*, Vol. 1 (Fall, 1975), pp. 38–44.

Women and Progressive Reform

Bacchi, Carol, "Race Regeneration and Social Purity: A Study of the Social Attitudes of Canada's English-Speaking Suffragists", *Histoire sociale/Social History*, Vol. 11, No. 22 (November, 1978), pp. 460–74.

Binnie-Clark, Georgina, *Wheat and Women*. Toronto: Bell and Cockburn, 1914. Reprinted in the University of Toronto Press' Social History Series.

Bliss, Michael, "Neglected Radicals: A Sober Second Look", *Canadian Forum* (April/May, 1970), pp. 16–17.

Cook, Ramsay, "Francis Marion Beynon and the Crisis of Christian Reformism", in Carl Berger and Ramsay Cook, eds., *The West and the Nation*. Toronto: McClelland and Stewart, 1976, pp. 187–208.

Kealey, Linda, "Canadian Socialism and the Woman Question, 1900–1914", *Labour/Le Travail*, Vol. 13 (Spring, 1984), pp. 77–100.

Mitchinson, Wendy, "The WCTU: 'For God, Home and Native Land', A Study in Nineteenth-Century Feminism", in Kealey, ed., *A Not Unreasonable Claim*, pp. 151–168.

Prentice, Alison and Susan Houston, eds., *Family, School and Society in 19th Century Canada*. Toronto: Oxford University Press, 1975, esp. the section, "Places for Girls and Women".

Saywell, John T., ed., *The Canadian Journal of Lady Aberdeen, 1893–1898*. Toronto: Champlain Society, 1960.

Speisman, Stephen A., "Munificent Parsons and Municipal Parsimony: Voluntary vs. Public Poor Relief in 19th Century Toronto", *Ontario History*, Vol. LXV (March, 1973), pp. 32–49.

Strong-Boag, Veronica, *The Parliament of Women: The National Council of Women of Canada, 1893–1929*. Ottawa: National Museums of Canada, 1976.

Trofimenkoff, Susan Mann, "Henri Bourassa and the 'Woman Question'", *Journal of Canadian Studies*, Vol. 10 (November, 1975), pp. 3–11.

Women and the War

Geller, Gloria, "The Maritime Elections Act of 1917 and the Canadian Women's Movement", *Atlantis*, Vol. 2 (Autumn, 1976), pp. 88–106.

Ramkhalawansingh, Ceta, "Women during the Great War", in Janice Acton, Penny Goldsmith and Bonnie Shepard, eds., *Women At Work: Ontario, 1850–1930*. Toronto: Women's Educational Press, 1974, pp. 261–307.

Tennyson, Brian D., "Premier Hearst, the War and Votes for Women", *Ontario History*, Vol. LVII, No. 3 (1965), pp. 115–122.

Wilson, Barbara M., ed., *Ontario and the First World War 1914–18: A Collection of Documents*. Toronto: Champlain Society, University of Toronto Press, 1977, esp. Section D, "Women".

The Woman's Suffrage Movement

Bacchi, Carol, "Divided Allegiances: The Response of Farm and Labour Women to Suffrage", in Kealey, ed., *A Not Unreasonable Claim*, pp. 89–107.

Gorham, Deborah, "English Militancy and the Canadian Suffrage Movement", *Atlantis*, Vol. 1 (Fall, 1975), pp. 83–112.

_____, "The Canadian Suffragists", in Gwen Matheson, ed., *Women in the Canadian Mosaic*. Toronto: Peter Martin Associates, 1976, pp. 23–56.

Matheson, Gwen, and V.E. Lang, "Nellie McClung: 'Not A Nice Woman'", in Matheson, ed., *Women and the Canadian Mosaic*, pp. 1–22.

McClung, Nellie, *In Times Like These*. Introduction by Veronica Strong-Boag. Toronto: University of Toronto Press, 1972.

———, *The Stream Runs Fast*. Toronto: Thomas Allen, 1945.

Menzies, June, "Votes for Saskatchewan Women", in Norman Ward and D. Spafford, eds., *Politics in Saskatchewan*. Don Mills: Longmans, 1968, pp. 78–92.

Savage, Candace, *Our Nell: A Scrapbook Biography of Nellie McClung*. Saskatoon: Western Producer Prairie Books, 1979.

Strong-Boag, Veronica, *The Canadian Campaign for Woman Suffrage*. Canada's Visual History Series, Volume 30. Ottawa: National Museum of Man and National Film Board, 1977.

Thompson, Joan Emily, "The Influence of Dr. Emily Howard Stowe on the Woman Suffrage Movement in Canada", *Ontario History*, Vol. LIV (December, 1962), pp. 253–266.

Voisey, Paul, "The Votes for Women Movement", *Alberta History*, Vol. 23 (Summer, 1975), pp. 10–23.

16

REGIONAL PROTEST IN THE WEST AND THE MARITIMES, 1919–1939

Movements of Reaction or Demands for Structural Change?

The inter-war years (1919–1939) in Canada were times of great upheaval, when a variety of political and economic problems came to the fore. A series of protest movements arose, mostly in the prairie West and the Maritimes, voicing deeply felt regional concerns and challenging the Canadian two-party political system. By the 1920s many Canadians in the West and the Maritimes felt that they were not sharing fully in the nation's growth. Canada's national policies had helped to develop an industrial base and to build a transcontinental nation—but in the process alienated many in the so-called "hinterland" regions. Social discontent born in the twenties was further intensified by the economic crises of the Great Depression. Many Westerners and Maritimers who had complained in the 1920s of being neglected by national governments now saw themselves as victims of their policies. Regional feelings of protest found strong expression in farmers' movements, Maritime rights agitation, and "third parties" in federal and provincial politics.

Historical debates over protests in the West and the Maritimes have raised the fundamental question of what motivated the political movements in each region. Some historians and political scientists have viewed these protests as conservative, reactionary movements based on real, or imagined, political complaints against national policies which seemed to favour and benefit central Canada. Other analysts, often more sympathetic to the West and the Maritimes and more sensitive to their regional characteristics, have seen the movements differently. To them, western and eastern protests—rooted in legitimate, deep-seated grievances—have found expression in a variety of demands for a complete reorganization of Confederation, the existing political party system, or the nation's economy.

Regional discontent stemmed from historic roots. From the time of Confederation conditions in the West and the Maritimes have fostered periodic expressions of popular dissatisfaction, usually during periods of economic dislocation, social unrest or sectional conflict. For Westerners, the prime source of discontent was the National Policy tariff of 1879, which many believed favoured central Canadian manufacturers and businesses at the expense of agricultural producers. For many Maritimers, national governments since Confederation were largely responsible for allowing the Maritime provinces to become depressed areas, consigned to a marginal economic existence.

This period, known popularly as "The Roaring Twenties", produced its share of discontent in Canada's western and maritime regions. Most settlers of the West had gone to the prairies in the Laurier years (1896–1911), filled with high hopes of a prosperous, independent, self-sufficient way of life. But by the end of World War I, there were visible signs that these expectations had not been fulfilled. A brief depression in the early 1920s reduced farmers' incomes by half and agriculture continued its decline throughout the decade. With the peopling of the West and the growing dominance of the central Canadian metropolises over the national economy, Maritimers saw their region declining in relative status and influence within Confederation. The political responses in each region, quite naturally, took different forms. Western farmers formed farm cooperatives, organized provincial agrarian movements, then created the National Progressive party, launching a major assault on Canada's traditional two-party system. This agrarian radicalism took hold everywhere in the West except British Columbia, where the farmers' party lacked effective leadership, espoused a different brand of rural conservatism, and failed to attract a mass following.[1] In the eastern provinces a "Maritime Rights" movement arose and attempted, by exerting political pressure on Ottawa, to restore the position of the Maritimes in the Canadian federal system.

The 1930s brought the Great Depression, an economic catastrophe which touched almost every Canadian. The stock market crash of October 1929 and its aftereffects hit Canada very severely. Canada's economy was highly vulnerable to a decline in world trade and falling prices because of its heavy reliance on exports and its close economic ties to the United States. Hardest hit by the Depression were industries dealing in primary products like wheat, pulp and paper and minerals, whose areas of production were centred in the West and the Maritimes. Wheat prices, for example, fell from $1.60 per bushel in 1929 to 34 cents a bushel in 1932. Governments, both federal and

---

1. The United Farmers of British Columbia, formed in 1917, refrained from independent political action until the provincial election of 1923 when it joined forces with the Provincial Party, a tenuous alliance of dissident Conservatives and dissatisfied businessmen led by a maverick millionaire, Major General A.D. McRae. The B.C. farmers' party expired shortly thereafter.

provincial, seemed powerless to relieve the widespread unemployment, or to arrest the drastic economic downswing and regain control of the national economy.

While the Depression was a national problem, it plunged the regions most dependent on primary production, the West and the Maritimes, into a particularly severe crisis. The two traditional parties, the Conservatives and the Liberals, appeared unable to deal with the unprecedented economic situation and they reacted mostly with stop-gap measures. The loss of markets for fish, timber and coal struck the Maritimes, but seemed to arouse little more than a sense of resignation and indifference.[2] In the prairie West the Depression produced a different response. Two new protest movements emerged with grandiose schemes, often charismatic leaders, and radical solutions. The Co-operative Commonwealth Federation (CCF), officially founded at Regina in August 1933, was an amalgam of progressive farm and labour groups; a third party with a clearly defined socialist philosophy. Social Credit, its Alberta counterpart, was a largely rural movement founded by William ("Bible Bill") Aberhart in the summer of 1932 and based on the controversial monetary theories of Scottish army engineer Major C.H. Douglas; it was a protest movement which wove radical doctrines of monetary reform into the fabric of conservative religious fundamentalism. Such was the state of estrangement from the existing party system that both western parties rose almost like a prairie fire out of the depths of the Depression.

In this problem study, our main focus is on regional protests of the inter-war years in the prairie West and the Maritimes. Because of limitations of length, comparable and equally significant protests like the Winnipeg General Strike of 1919 and similar movements of the 1920s and 1930s in Quebec will not be analyzed. While examining the problem, however, it should be remembered that the immediate postwar period produced an outbreak of Western labour radicalism culminating in the Winnipeg strike of 1919 and the re-emergence of nationalism in Quebec expressed in abbé Lionel Groulx's journal, *L'Action française*. The thirties were also a time of economic crisis and political change in Quebec, producing Maurice Duplessis' *Union Nationale*, a conservative third party which except for a wartime interlude would rule the province from 1936 to 1960.

Regional protests in the 1920s and 1930s raise many important historical questions. Were the organized protest movements of the inter-war years conservative reactions against the pattern of national economic development wrought by Canada's national policies? Did the protests constitute hinterland revolts against national policies and institutions like the protective tariff, the freight rate structure and the two-party political system allegedly designed by

---

2. After the severe economic dislocations and the prolonged industrial conflict in Cape Breton in the 1920s, the response to the Depression in the Atlantic region was relatively mild. Only in Newfoundland, where the economic crisis caused a severe drop in the world price of fish and mounting public debt, was there any popular uprising.

central Canadians for the benefit of industrialized central Canada? Or did movements like the western Progressives, the Maritime Rights campaign, the CCF and the Social Credit represent significant attempts at a radical restructuring of the Canadian political and economic system?

SELECTED CONTEMPORARY SOURCES

REGIONAL PROTEST IN THE WEST—THE WESTERN AGRARIAN MOVEMENT OF THE TWENTIES

The first sign of agrarian discontent in the prairie west was the formation of farmers' associations. These associations, heavily influenced by the activities of the Non-Partisan League[3] in North Dakota, began in the war years to educate western farmers about their legal and political rights, to formulate a critique of the existing system, and to encourage farmers to take collective action. With the producers' associations serving as sources of support and publications like the *Grain Growers' Guide* calling for reform, a national "Farmers' Platform" was formulated in late 1916—a program which included demands for lower tariffs, tax reforms and public ownership of major utilities. The end of the Great War only brought a re-emergence of western grievances, mainly directed against Canadian institutions controlled and dominated by either urban merchant or Eastern business interests. Whether the agrarian protest of the twenties was a reaction against economic changes or a virtual rejection of Canada's established party system remains a contentious issue.

Roots of Western Farmers' Protest—Henry Wise Wood's Ideas of Group Co-operation, 1917 and 1919

Henry Wise Wood, the American-born president of the United Farmers of Alberta (1916-31), saw the farmers' movement as a clear expression of the awakening of an agrarian class identity. Wood argued that farmers were an exploited, poorly rewarded economic and social group in need of organization. His main interest lay in promoting the ideal of class co-operation and unity among farmers, while preventing the movement from being turned into a conventional "third party". Wood's concept of "group government", amounted to a radical departure from the existing party system.

The Theory of "Class Organization", 1917

> We are a class organization, it is true, but we are the basic class and, I am sorry to say, have suffered many wrongs at the hands of other classes. These wrongs must be

---

3. A branch of the American Populist movement composed of mid-western farmers organized for direct political action.

righted, every one of them, but we must remember that two wrongs do not make a right, and we must be ever ready to show to all that we are willing to adjust our relationships with all other legitimate classes on the basis of right and justice. Of course any class that does not give a needed service to society has no rights. The only way to accomplish readjustments of wrong relationships is by conflict or treaty. Conflict is clearly justifiable when treaty fails. But I take it that no clear thinking will justify conflict until treaty has failed....

... Class co-operation means inter-class competition. In this competition of class with class ours is the losing class at every turn, because we are the least organized, the least co-operative, consequently the weakest....

... It is feared by some that when we get this power [which organization bestows] we will use it to wrong other classes.... [But] we cultivate an ambition to re-adjust all class relationships.

H.W. Wood, First Presidential Address to the U.F.A., *Edmonton Daily Bulletin*, January 23, 1917.

The Concept of "Group Government", 1919

We, as a group of farmers, are affected alike by wrong economic conditions. That gives us a common viewpoint. Labour is affected in a different way. That gives them another viewpoint. We can scarcely organize with a common viewpoint. Now, when we get all of our classes properly organized, and we learn and develop leadership amongst our class that is capable of representing us intelligently, and we select the best representatives of each class, and we get Proportional representation, then each class will send representatives commensurate with its strength. These representatives will go down there (to Parliament or Legislature) not as hired lobbyists, but belong as a body to their class, ready to defend the interests of their class with their lives. We go down there as farmers, we ask something we are not entitled to! The other classes are just as thoroughly organized as we, and they will resist any unjust demands, and that resistance of each other will eventually bring them to a common level, on which these great class differences will be settled, and they will never be settled any other way.

H.W. Wood, Crossfield, Alberta, October 21, 1919, excerpted in *The Canadian Annual Review of Public Affairs*, 1919, p. 388.

The Farmers' Entry into Politics—A New National Policy, 1921

As western farmers came to feel that Canada's two parties, the Liberals and the Conservatives, were impervious to their plight, the farmers' organizations were compelled to take the next logical step—direct political action. Under the aegis of the Canadian Council of Agriculture, a new "Farmers' Platform" was ratified by the four main provincial farmers' associations in the prairie West and Ontario. At a convention in Winnipeg in 1920, the United Farmers' groups from the various provinces joined together, under the leadership of Thomas A. Crerar, to form the National Progressive Party. The New National Policy became the basis for the party's platform in the 1921 federal election.

The Tariff

3.   Whereas Canada is now confronted with a huge national war debt and other

greatly increased financial obligations, which can be most readily and effectively reduced by the development of our natural resources, chief of which is agricultural lands; . . . .

And whereas the war has revealed the amazing financial strength of Great Britain, which has enabled her to finance, not only her own part in the struggle, but also to assist in financing her Allies to the extent of hundreds of millions of pounds . . . we believe that the best interests of the Empire and of Canada would be served by reciprocal action on the part of Canada through gradual reductions of the tariff on British imports, having for its objects closer union and a better understanding between Canada and the Motherland and at the same time bring about a great reduction in the cost of living to our Canadian people; . . . .

And whereas the Protective Tariff has fostered combines, trusts and 'gentlemen's agreements' in almost every line of Canadian industrial enterprise, by means of which the people of Canada—both urban and rural—have been shamefully exploited through the elimination of competition, the ruination of many of our smaller industries and the advancement of prices on practially all manufactured goods to the full extent permitted by the tariff;

And whereas agriculture—the basic industry upon which the success of all our other industries primarily depends—is unduly handicapped throughout Canada as shown by the declining rural population in both Eastern and Western Canada, due largely to the greatly increased cost of agricultural implements and machinery, clothing, boots and shoes, building material and practically everything the farmer has to buy, caused by the Protective Tariff . . . .

Therefore be it resolved that the Canadian Council of Agriculture, representing the organized farmers of Canada, urges that, as a means of remedying these evils and bringing about much-needed social and economic reforms, our tariff laws should be amended as follows:

(a) By an immediate and substantial all-round reduction of the customs tariff.
(b) By reducing the customs duty on goods imported from Great Britain to one-half the rates charged under the general tariff, and that further gradual, uniform reductions be made in the remaining tariff on British imports that will ensure complete Free Trade between Great Britain and Canada in five years.
(c) By endeavoring to secure unrestricted reciprocal trade in natural products with the United States along the lines of the Reciprocity Agreement of 1911.
(d) By placing all foodstuffs on the free list.
(e) That agricultural implements, farm and household machinery, vehicles, fertilizers, coal, lumber, cement, gasoline, illuminating, fuel and lubricating oils be placed on the free list, and that all raw materials and machinery used in their manufacture also be placed on the free list.
(f) That all tariff concessions granted to other countries be immediately extended to Great Britain.
(g) That all corporations engaged in the manufacture of products protected by the customs tariff be obliged to publish annually comprehensive and accurate statements of their earnings.
(h) That every claim for tariff protection by any industry should be heard publicly before a special committee of parliament . . . .

The Farmers' Platform, 1921, reprinted in W.L. Morton, *The Progressive Party in Canada* (Toronto: University of Toronto Press, 1950), pp. 302-303.

Division in the Ranks—T.A. Crerar's Letter of Resignation, 1922

The farmers' program gained widespread support, particularly in the prairie West and Ontario. The first political breakthrough came in 1919 when the United Farmers of Ontario (U.F.O.) swept into power in a provincial election. Two years later, the Alberta Farmers' party, later the United Farmers of Alberta (U.F.A.), captured 38 of 59 seats in the Alberta legislature. In the ensuing 1921 federal election, the newly formed National Progressive Party elected 64 members—mainly from the West—and held the balance of power in Ottawa. In 1922, the United Farmers of Manitoba (U.F.M.) also formed a government in their province.

In spite of their electoral success, the National Progressives were racked by internal division over political philosophy and tactics. Since the party's formation fundamental differences had arisen between T.A. Crerar's "Manitoba wing" and H.W. Wood's "Alberta group". As party leader, Crerar advocated forward-looking liberal reform, repudiated Wood's concept of a "class" party, and favoured an appeal to all segments of Canadian society, rural and urban. Crerar's letter of resignation, in November 1922, revealed the extent of the party's factional problems. Such divisions persisted until the Progressives, torn by internal strife and robbed of key party members by Mackenzie King's Liberals, lost most of their public support in the 1925 election.

My retention of the leadership of the Progressive party would depend upon a clear understanding and statement of the Progressives' program, not on questions of policy... but on questions of organization and upon the vital question of whether the Progressive movement in our politics shall descend into a class movement or not.

The greatest obstacle the Progressive movement had to combat in the last federal election was the fear in the hearts of thousands of electors in Canada who were in general sympathy with its policies, that it would become purely a class movement. The attitude of Mr. Wood in Alberta, and of Mr. Morrison in Ontario— and I do not here question the sincerity of either—I am bound to say gave grounds for this fear. Mr. Morrison's attitude is perfectly clear. He says the farmers have never been represented in our legislatures as they should have been, and he says to the farmers of the constituencies where they are strong enough to have a chance of doing it, 'Elect your own man as a farmer, and keep him independent in the House to voice your interests.'

In Alberta Mr. Wood advocates a new theory which, he says, if applied, will revolutionize and correct all the abuses that have hitherto existed in the mechanism of governments. It is that the evils in our political system have grown from the so-called 'party system', and that we shall never be right until we introduce a new order of things. This he proposes to do by having members of parliament or legislatures elected upon the occupational basis. . . .

This view is further amplified in a recently published statement by a U.F.A. constituency executive officer in Alberta, in which it was seriously laid down that their federal member of parliament should be guided and directed in his work by the U.F.A. locals in his constituency. . . . [This] betrays a complete misunderstanding of the duties and responsibilities of a member. . . . [In this argument you] would have 235 members, each guided and directed by his constituents, some of whom were thousands of miles away, attempting to seriously carry on the work of government.

T.A. Crerar's Letter of Resignation as Leader of the Progressive Party, November 10, 1922, *Grain Growers' Guide*, XV, November 15, 1922.

THE MARITIME RIGHTS MOVEMENT OF THE 1920s—POLITICAL OPPORTUNISM OR A GENUINE DRIVE FOR REGIONAL RECOGNITION?

"Maritime Rights" was the slogan of the regional protest movement which erupted in the Maritime provinces in the years after the war. Unlike the West, the vehicle for the strongest expression of eastern grievances was the provincial wing of one of Canada's established political parties. The Conservative Party of Nova Scotia, having been defeated by a Farmer-Labour coalition in the provincial election of 1920, emerged as the foremost defender of Maritime Rights. Discontent was a manifestation of the region's economic decline and loss of political status in the early decades of the twentieth century, rather than the product of agrarian demands for reform.

For the Nova Scotia Conservatives, Maritime Rights were a potent political issue. By reviving the cause, the party rejuvenated itself and returned to power in 1925 with the promise of "better terms" for Nova Scotia and her sister provinces. A federal Royal Commission was appointed in 1926 to investigate Maritime claims, though the outcome did little to solve the region's problems. But looking back, was the Maritime Rights movement the work of opportunistic Nova Scotia politicians or more the expression of genuine regional economic and political frustrations?

The Call to Action—A Halifax Herald Editorial, 1922

The public campaign for Maritime Rights was spearheaded by W.H. Dennis, owner of the Halifax *Herald*, H.S. Congdon, editor of the Dartmouth *Patriot*, and members of the Maritime Board of Trade with connections in the neighbouring Maritime provinces. A stirring editorial in the Halifax *Herald* heaped ridicule on the "solid sixteen" Liberal M.P.s representing Nova Scotia in Ottawa and signalled the official birth of the "Maritime First" movement:

Are we in these Maritime Provinces hopeless and helpless watching Portland while it forges ahead and waxes fat and prosperous on Canadian trade fed to it by Canadian railways—content to let Maritime ports dry up and wither? Or can the 'Solid Sixteen' do anything to save us from such a condition?

Are they without hope or remedy?

Are they able to do anything save murmur that we cannot fight geography?

We want to say that it is time for the people of the Maritime Provinces to put shoulder to shoulder and fight for their rights. And cease not until those right [sic] are acquired. We have the lesson of the Western Members of Parliament who stand like a rock and compelled the Government to DELIVER THE GOODS. Our 'Solid Sixteen' marched up the hill and then marched down again.

What did they bring home to Nova Scotia? Frothy assurances and fulsome promises are the only things they offer the people. We have had enough of these. Now we want action and practical national results; and if the people of this province and the other Maritime provinces desire such results they will have to take a resolute stand for their rights; be no longer humbugged by political claptrap; but insist upon Canadian railways feeding Canadian trade to Canadian ports.

Halifax *Herald*, July 27, 1922.

The Triumph of Maritime Rights, 1925

Regional discontent marshalled under the banner of Maritime Rights carried the Conservatives in October 1925 to the biggest margin of victory they had ever scored in the Maritimes. In Nova Scotia the party won 11 out of 14 seats and a record 56.4 percent of the popular vote. The Conservatives enjoyed similar success in New Brunswick, winning 10 of 11 seats and 59.7 percent of the vote, and split the Prince Edward Island seats evenly with the Liberals. In this cartoon, Cape Breton-born Donald McRitchie conjured up visions of a "Great Delegation" to Parliament Hill:

The Duncan Report—A Royal Commission's Diagnosis and Prescription, 1926

Prime Minister Mackenzie King addressed the problem of Maritime Rights in early 1926 by appointing a Royal Commission on Maritime Claims. The commission, headed by Sir Andrew Rae Duncan, conducted investigations into the problems of the Maritimes and developed a plan for economic rehabilitation. The Government responded in 1927 with political palliatives, increasing financial aid and reducing freight rates.

...The outstanding fact, it seems to us, is that the Maritime Provinces have not prospered and developed, either in population, or in commercial, industrial and rural enterprise, as fully as other portions of Canada. We are unable to take the view that Confederation, is, of itself, responsible for this fact. The trend and nature of economic development generally throughout the last sixty years has made within the Maritimes changes in the structure of business and employment which are unrelated to Confederation, and which would have taken place whether or not the Maritime Provinces had been independent units outside of Confederation. Even within Confederation there has been such a measure of responsibility resting on each province for its own development that much at least of what has happened within the Maritime Provinces must be related to their responsibility and not to the responsibility of the Dominion.

We are far from saying that the Dominion, within its sphere of control, has done all for the Maritime Provinces which it should have done. But it must not be overlooked that the task which has been placed upon the Federal authorities in bringing such a vast territory as Canada to its present point of growth and prospect has been colossal.... It is not possible in such an undertaking as the making of Canada, with its geographical and physical conditions, and its variety of settlement and development, to maintain always an accurate balance, apportioning to every section of this extensive country the exact quality of benefit and quantity of advantage which would be theoretically and justly desired. But reasonable balance is within accomplishment if there be periodic stocktaking. We venture to regard the present occasion as such a period of stocktaking, so that in the future progress of the common great enterprise the prospects of the Maritime Provinces may be brought into line with the prospects of other parts of Canada and the prospects of the Dominion as a whole.

Report of the Royal Commission on Maritime Claims (Ottawa: King's Printer, 1926), pp. 9–11.

THIRD PARTIES IN THE THIRTIES—ATTEMPTS TO REFORM OR TO SCRAP THE SYSTEM?

The Great Depression was an economic disaster for many Canadians in the "Dirty Thirties". The economic downswing, which was both severe and uneven in its regional effects, began in 1929 and bottomed out in 1933. Recovery was slow, interrupted by a serious recession in 1937–38, and far from complete when World War II began. The human costs of the Depression—mass unemployment, despair and a feeling of hopelessness—were such that for many the Second World War actually came as a welcome relief. Under the weight of the economic crisis, many Canadians had begun to question whether the existing system should be reformed or scrapped.

The Rise of the CCF—Prairie Radicalism or Urban Social Gospel?

The Depression, acting as a catalyst, hastened the growth of new forms of regional dissent. Widespread discontent over the inadequacies of the capitalist economy and the insensitive policies of the "old line" parties contributed to the formation of a new socialist alternative, the Cooperative Commonwealth Federation. Like the farmers' organizations and the Progressive party of the twenties, the CCF found great support in the Canadian West. It differed from the earlier movements, however, in two important ways. The initial ideology of the CCF was avowedly socialist and, secondly, the main impetus for its formation was not confined to the rural western provinces. The CCF, from its inception, was also shaped by urban labour and eastern intellectual elements.

From the beginning the CCF set out to build a national coalition of farmers, workers and intellectuals. The party, founded in 1932 under the leadership of J.S. Woodsworth, was a "federation of organizations" committed to achieving "a planned and socialized economy" in which national resources and the principal means of production were "owned, controlled and operated by the people". By emphasizing fundamental social change, the CCF hoped to avoid the fate of the earlier Progressives who never really distinguished themselves from the rhetoric of Liberal reform.

The Co-operative Ideal—A Utopian View, 1931

One of the most important organizational bases for the CCF were the farmers' associations of the prairie West. For amid the economic crisis of the Depression, many people in the region turned to all kinds of agrarian co-operative action. The CCF, organized around co-operative principles, appealed to members of the thriving Prairie co-operative movement. An editorial from *The Scoop Shovel*, the journal of the Manitoba wheat pool, gave expression to the Utopian ideals:

> The co-operative commonwealth, which is the ultimate goal of co-operators, we suggest, is an economic and social system under which all the activities in which the people are engaged will be carried out with the object of the mutual benefit of all the people.
>
> In the co-operative commonwealth every activity connected with the production and distribution of goods—agriculture, mining, manufacturing, transportation, wholesaling and retailing, banking and insurance (if banking and insurance do not become unnecessary)—will be carried on not for the profit of any individual or group, but for the benefit of all.... All the activities in which people engage, economic and social, educational and recreational, literary and artistic, will be organized in such a way that all the people will contribute according to their ability and share according to their needs.
>
> Under these conditions, selfishness, in a sense of a desire to enjoy advantages at the expense of others, will have no place, and the individual will realize that he can promote his own welfare only by promoting that of the community as a whole. Under these conditions there would be no poverty, except as a result of famine; no wars, no crime, but instead a world of peace and good will.
>
> *The Scoop Shovel*, April 1931, p. 12.

J.S. Woodsworth's Founding Address—Regina, 1933

At the first annual convention of the CCF, the Regina Manifesto drafted by Frank Underhill and the League for Social Reconstruction, a small group of Montreal and Toronto intellectuals formed in the hard winter of 1932, was approved with minor revisions. J.S. Woodsworth, the former Superintendent of the All People's Mission and Labour M.P. for Winnipeg, was selected as the party's first president. In his presidential address Woodsworth set out his conception of the CCF and its mission:

> ... The C.C.F. is essentially a drawing together of the common people.... (The Labour movement, Canadian farmers, small businessmen and the clerical and professional groups) have found a place in the C.C.F. There lies ahead of us the great task of overcoming prejudices, of gaining understanding of one another's problems, and of mobilizing our forces for the common good.
>
> The C.C.F. is undoubtedly a movement of protest born of the discontents of our time; a disgust at the inefficiency of the old parties, and the inadequacy of their policies. But it must be recognized that a merely negative position will get us nowhere. We must develop both a philosophy of life and a constructive program. Thanks to the pioneers in the Socialist and Co-operative movements we have at least the fundamental principles on which we may base our teaching with regard to the Co-operative Commonwealth. We do not believe in unchanging social dogma. Society is not static. Knowledge grows, and each age must work out a new and higher synthesis. Such growing knowledge is dependent upon experience and action. Each new development, each new member of our organization should mean a fuller content in our body of Socialist doctrine....
>
> Perhaps it is because I am a Canadian of several generations, and have inherited the individualism common to all born on the American continent; yet with political and social ideals profoundly influenced by British traditions and so-called Christian idealism; further with a rather wide and intimate knowledge of the various sections of the Canadian people—in any case, I am convinced that we may develop in Canada a distinctive type of Socialism. I refuse to follow slavishly the British model or the American model or the Russian model. We in Canada will solve our problems along our own lines. We have a goodly heritage, not only in natural resources but in pioneer traditions and social equipment. If we have the spirit of our fathers we can overcome the difficulties even of our complex modern world.
>
> The C.C.F. advocates peaceful and orderly methods. In this we distinguish ourselves sharply from the Communist party which envisages the new social order as being ushered in by violent upheaval and the establishment of a dictatorship. The decision as to how Capitalism will be overthrown may of course not lie in our hands. Continued bungling and exploitation, callous disregard of the needs and sufferings of the people, and the exercise of repressive measures may bring either a collapse, or riots, or both. But in Canada we believe it possible to avoid chaos and bloodshed which in some countries have characterized economic and social revolutions.
>
> 'Democracy'—the rule of the people—is a much discounted word. Little wonder. The democracy which we have known in this country has been government of the people by party machines for the profiteers. The parliamentary machine is antiquated and its procedure obsolete. Government has functioned largely in the interests of the exploiting classes. The untrained masses are quite unfitted to pass judgment on the complicated problems that face modern executives. But having said this, I must confess that I still believe that the will of the people should prevail. This may appear a hangover from the high-sounding but empty doctrine of Liberalism. But fundamentally it is sound. An intelligent and alert citizenship is the only guarantee of freedom....
>
> ...[O]urs is more than an organization. It is a movement—a movement that is already producing a goodly fellowship of earnest and capable men and women.
>
> J.S. Woodsworth, Presidential Address, Regina, July 19–21, 1933, reprinted in Edith Fowke, ed., *Towards Socialism: Selections from the Writings of J.S. Woodsworth* (Toronto: Ontario Woodsworth Memorial Foundation, 1948), pp. 38–41.

The Social Credit Movement in Alberta—A Radical Departure from the Existing System?

When the Depression struck Alberta in the early thirties, the massive decline in world prices for farm produce and other commodities severely affected the province. All parts of the economy suffered, but in southern Alberta dust bowl conditions made the situation even worse. Alberta's agricultural economy was less dependent on wheat than Saskatchewan's, but, as the last part of the West to be settled, the province had some special problems of its own. The burden of debt—personal, municipal and provincial—was particularly difficult to bear at a time of economic decline and high fixed interest rates. The U.F.A. government which had ruled Alberta since 1921 seemed badly discredited by a scandal involving the Premier, J.E. Brownlee, and incapable of responding to the Depression.

The Social Credit movement may have grown out of a seemingly conservative agricultural society, but it advocate 1 some radical policies of monetary reform.

The Message—A William Aberhart Sermon, 1935

William Aberhart, the teacher-turned-radio evangelist and founder of Calgary's Prophetic Bible Institute, often mixed religion and politics. Converted to the doctrines of Social Credit in the summer of 1932, he wove the Social Credit message into his sermons.

> Never has there been a time for centuries when the Easter message of hope has been more acceptable than today. People are suffering untold misery and intense privation because of their helpless economic condition. If I were to paint the Easter scene I would have the sun rising in the East in all its glory and an open tomb on the hillside, the road winding up through the darkened valley. I think I might label it something like this 'The hope of mankind lies only in the open tomb.' We talk about constitutional impossibilities and physical improbability. We talk about the greed and the selfishness of wicked men and all things that may be imagined which will prevent the emancipation of the human race. But the open tomb is our guarantee, our source of all hope. . . .
>
> * * * * *
>
> I had a splendid letter from Calgary this week. May I read a part of it?
>
> 'The cry of don't mix religion with politics is due to the fact that they have been divorced for so long. We welcome the day when religion will enter into our every effort. The charge that Social Creditors are cheap politicians is because we have all got used to the expensive variety. The same spirit that ascribes ulterior motives to men of Christian principles charged our Blessed Lord with all sorts of crimes. Even going so far as to say he worked his wonders by power of the devil. I am sure the Lord would not be displeased with us, his followers, if we imitate his Divine example, whipping the money changers out of the temple. He at all times had compassion on the multitude, both their spirit and temporal needs. Can we do more?
>
> Why say, my dear sir (I am still reading the letter) this movement may be

the means under Divine guidance of driving all Christians closer together, drawing all Christians closer together, in answer to His prayer that we be one linked with one another. Did He not say "Love one another that the world may know that I sent you?" You are advocating the very same principles as our Holy Father at Rome and his pleas to the world for social justice and our Father Coughlin over the radio and many others including the Anglican Bishops of England. In fact the whole Christian world so lamentably divided.'

I was rather glad to read that. You know I think it's touching on the right chord. The chord that must be struck today. That chord that consists of the many varied notes but harmonizing together in one thing—the love of fellow man. It's helping to blot out that bias and blind prejudice that has separated us for so long. Why cannot we not see that after all we are all sojourners here below. We might as well make it more pleasant for one another. . . .

William Aberhart's Sermon, April 21, 1935. W. Norman Smith Papers, File No. 57, Glenbow-Alberta Institute Archives, Calgary.

The "Ten Plank" Platform, 1935

The Social Credit party of Alberta swept the provincial election of 1935 and elected a majority of the federal Members of Parliament from Alberta later that year. Aberhart and his followers fought and won the 1935 campaign on a platform which combined agricultural reform, Christian moralism and Social Credit monetary theories. The party's "Ten Plank" platform called on Albertans to elect a "good, clean, honest government", to end "poverty in the midst of plenty", and to usher in a "new social order". Even though much of Social Credit policy was later declared unconstitutional, the platform served as a touchstone for a Social Credit régime which governed Alberta for 36 unbroken years.

TEN PLANKS MAKE ONE PLATFORM

1. Finance and the Distribution of Goods

    a) The Cessation of Borrowing from Outside Sources and the creation of our own Credit, thus gradually eliminating heavy interest charges and retaining our own purchasing power.

    b) The Distribution of Purchasing Power to bona fide citizens by means of Basic Dividends sufficient to secure the bare necessities of food, clothing and shelter.

    This distribution is to be based upon active willingness on the part of the individuals to co-operate in the welfare of the people of the Province.

    c) The Establishment of a Just Price on all goods and services, and the regulation of the price spread on all goods sold or transferred within the bounds of the Province.

    This Just Price is to be just and fair:

    i.   To the producers and to the distributors. They should not be required to sell goods for less than the cost of production or of import.

    ii. To the consumers. They should not be exploited or unduly deprived of fair returns for their purchasing power.

    d) The Establishment of an authority to deal with production loans . . . .

* * * * *

5. The Basic Industry—Agriculture
   a) The Just Price for all products will remove the necessity of selling under the cost of production.
   b) The Marketing of Agricultural and Dairy products must be assisted:

   i.   By taking definite steps to find export markets.
   ii. By pressing for lower and more equitable freight rates.
   iii. By seeking a revision of the system of grading farm products.
   iv. By attending regularly to the Market Roads.
   v.   By encouraging the feeding, breeding, and finishing of better livestock in Alberta.

   c) The Development of the Industry should be encouraged in the following ways:

   i.   By a careful investigation of the irrigation projects of the Province.
   ii. By an aggressive policy of Noxious Weeds eradication.
   iii. By a survey and the formation of a definite policy regarding the Drought Area of Alberta.
   iv. By improving the regulations regarding grazing and hay leases.
   v.   By amending the Homestead Laws to make it possible for settlers to establish homes for themselves.
   vi. We are heartily in favor of assisting in the continuance of Rural School Fairs, and Boys' and Girls' Club Work within the Province....

1935 Social Credit Election Platform. Glenbow-Alberta Institute Archives, Calgary.

CONFLICTING INTERPRETATIONS

Much of the historical writing on social protest in the West and the Maritimes during the inter-war years has been influenced by the longstanding views of the regions. To many historians, Western prairie protest has conjured up certain images, evoked by key phrases such as "agrarian revolt", "Western Progressivism", or "third party dissent". Such interpretations have evoked the impression that the West was populated by irascible farmers or religious crusaders complaining about the tariff, the banks, Eastern capitalists, freight rates, or the weather. Regional protest in the Maritimes has often been treated in a similar way. When the Maritime Rights movement of the 1920s has been mentioned at all, it has traditionally been depicted as a manifestation of Maritime conservatism. Some Canadian scholars have drawn sharp contrasts between the Westerner's radicalism and the Maritimer's "settled ways", strong party loyalties and conservative social ideas.

Recent studies of the prairie West and the Maritimes in the inter-war years have challenged traditional images of both regions. Older visions of rural, agrarian-oriented western protest movements seen from the perspective of the British majority group have been called into question as historians begin to grapple with the effects of urban social reform, religion, social class and ethnicity. Regional agitation in the Maritimes, as well, has undergone re-examination. Earlier hypotheses depicting the Maritime Rights movement as a political gambit by opportunistic Maritime politicians have been challenged by historians who see the movement as more the reflection of a "vigorous Maritime progressivism".

WESTERN PROGRESSIVISM IN THE TWENTIES—WHAT KIND OF MOVEMENT?

Western Progressivism and the National Policy—W.L. Morton's Thesis

Much of the popular view of Western progressivism was set out in the works of the late W.L. Morton, a Manitoba-born historian known as an interpreter of events in the prairie West. In *The Progressive Party in Canada* (1950) and a number of related essays, Professor Morton presented the Western Progressive movement as a reaction against what he once termed "the imperialism of the National Policy".

> The Progressive Movement in the West was dual in origin and nature. In one aspect it was an economic protest; in another it was a political revolt. A phase of agrarian resistance to the National Policy of 1878, it was also, and equally, an attempt to destroy the old national parties. The two aspects unite in the belief of all Progressives, both moderate and extreme, that the old parties were equally committed to maintaining the National Policy and indifferent to the ways in which the 'big interests' of protection and monopoly used government for their own ends.
>
> At the root of the sectional conflict, from which the Progressive Movement in part sprang, was the National Policy of 1878. Such conflict is partly the result of the hardships and imperfect adaptations of the frontier, but it also arises from the incidence of national policies. The sectional corn develops where the national shoe pinches. The National Policy, that brilliant improvisation of Sir John A. Macdonald, had grown under the master politician's hand, under the stimulus of depression and under the promptings of political appetite, until it had become a veritable Canadian System Henry Clay might have envied. Explicit in it was the promise that everybody should have something from its operation; implicit in it—its inarticulate major premise indeed— was the promise that when the infant industries it fostered had reached maturity, protection would be needed no more.
>
> This, however, was but a graceful tribute to the laissez-faire doctrine of the day. This same doctrine it was which prevented the western wheat grower from demanding that he, too, should benefit directly from the operation of the National Policy. That he did benefit from the system as a whole, a complex of land settlement, railway construction, and moderate tariff protection, is not to be denied. But the wheat grower, building the wheat economy from homestead to terminal elevator in a few swift years, was caught in a complex of production and marketing costs, land values, railway rates, elevator charges, and interest rates. He fought to lower all these costs by economic organization and by political pressure. He saw them all as parts of a system which exploited him. He was prevented, by his direct experience of it, and by the prevailing doctrine of laissez-faire, from perceiving that the system might confer reciprocal benefits on him. Accordingly, he hated and fought it as a whole. Of the National Policy, however, the tariff was politically the most conspicuous element. Hence the political battle was

fought around the tariff; it became the symbol of the wheat growers' exploitation and frustration, alleged and actual. Like all symbols, it over-simplified the complexities it symbolized.

W.L. Morton, "The Western Progressive Movement, 1919–1921", Canadian Historical Association *Annual Report*, 1946, p.41.

The Progressive Movement—A Co-Operative Impulse in Politics

Professor Ian MacPherson of the University of Victoria has recently studied western Progressivism within the context of the thriving farm co-operative movement in the early decades of this century. MacPherson depicted the Progressive movement as a political expression of the farmers' co-operative experience:

The outburst in co-operative activity by farmers was, of course, intricately associated with the Progressive movement. Progressivism was ultimately a series of political, religious, social, and economic impulses that pulled its supporters in several directions. Its incoherence and inability to find a stable consensus rapidly destroyed its involvement in the politics of the Dominion and of most of the provinces. In contrast, the economic activism of the Progressive movement did not fade: among farmers it stimulated powerful drives for increased government regulation of marketing and, just as importantly, for co-operative action. In fact, in retrospect, the Progressive era, far from being the brief, curious eruption its political history seems to imply it was, was of vital importance in defining the way in which the rural hinterlands would try to relate to their metropolitan centres, especially in economic matters.

The ultimate emphasis upon economics naturally emanated from normal self-interest, but it would be incorrect and unfair to assume that the dominance of economics meant that wider reform interest necessarily declined. The point is that most of the agrarian movement and the related co-operative movement recognized in the failures of Progressive political action that only limited social objectives were immediately attainable. Or, put another way, many co-operators, already exposed to the movements apolitical traditions, had their suspicions reinforced by the Progressive experience. Inevitably, these co-operators became more aloof from political activity, especially at the federal level, during and after the early twenties. Never again would co-operative institutions be as sympathetic to a political movement as they were to the farmer and labour outburst that occurred at the end of the First World War.

Nevertheless, while Progressivism blossomed, it was difficult to know where it started and where the co-operative movement ended. Most of the issues raised by Progressivism—political reform, economic inequality, group action, educational uplifting, attacks on privilege, moral regeneration—had been integral components of co-operative thought for decades. The two movements shared common fears, notably of industrialization and urbanization, corruption and depersonalization, and they postulated the same kinds of solutions, greater democratization and better education. The carryover in leadership figures from one movement to the other was impressive enough: T.A. Crerar, E.C. Drury, J.E. Brownlee, W.C. Good, Agnes Macphail, J.J. Morrison, to mention only a few. But it was even more impressive at the grassroots level....

...at the same time that the older leaders were gaining prominence in federal political life, some found their power bases fast eroding. The problem was that the leaders had created political movements they could not control. Ultimately, the memberships of the farm co-ops had diverse political sympathies and gathering behind the Progressive banner had been a temporary phenomenon. Thus, when federal Progressivism faltered, the unity broke down, especially when so many federal leaders proved to be no more than dissatisfied Liberals. Thus, though co-operatives served as superb stepping stones for many aspirant politicians up to 1923, they were poor political power bases thereafter....

> Ian MacPherson, *Each for All: A History of the Co-operative Movement in English Canada, 1900-1945* (Toronto: Macmillan, 1979), pp. 77-79. Footnotes omitted.

The Social Gospel and the Agrarian Revolt—A Revisionist View

Richard Allen, a leading authority on the Social Gospel movement in Canada, saw the Western agrarian revolt in a different light. Professor Allen contended that, while the agrarian movement did seek a modification of existing institutions, its leadership in the West was rooted in the Christian social gospel.

No man lives by bread—or wheat—alone, and movements with ostensible economic beginnings invariably find themselves clothed with ideas and hopes which provide frameworks for action not reducible to economics or even politics....

The identification of western agrarianism with religious motives was even closer than the foregoing implies, for both the leadership and the membership generally espoused religion with a will. Henry Wise Wood, the great Alberta agrarian leader of the time, though not an active churchman in his Alberta days, was a very religious man who viewed the United Farmers of Alberta as a religious movement. The Regina *Leader* described the Saskatchewan Grain Growers' Association as 'a religious, social, educational, political and commercial organization all in one, and in the truest and deepest meaning of these several terms.' W.R. Wood, Secretary of the Manitoba Grain Growers, wrote that 'we are practically seeking to inaugurate the Kingdom of God and its righteousness....' and Norman Lambert, Secretary of the Canadian Council of Agriculture, suggested that the aim of the Progressive party was 'to give 'politics' a new meaning in Canada,' and 'hand in hand with the organized farmers movement on the prairies has gone religion and social work.'

Such remarks were in the first instance a consequence of the formative influence of the churches in the years of prairie settlement. Even allowing for the ease with which members were lost in those vast expanses of plain and parkland, the church had been a major educative influence. The leaders of the Grain Growers were often (though not always) churchmen of note and even clergy; and most of the participants were church members who could sing 'Onward Christian Soldiers' with great vigour and conviction....

This interpretation of agrarian and church leadership, especially in the period of the agrarian revolt, was not of itself, however, only a consequence of the past services of the church in the settlement process. It was still more a reflection of the impact of the social gospel in prairie Protestantism and the farm movements themselves. As the prairie farmer faced the gargantuan task of marketing his ever-growing grain crop in the complex, impersonal international market, the agrarian myth of the virtuous individual yeoman, wresting his due from the soil by his own skill, broke down. Only in combination and co-operation could he cope with the forces arrayed before him:

elevator companies, railroads, grain exchanges, even political parties and governments. He was in need not only of new organizations and techniques, but also of a new
social faith. The social gospel supplied it....

Richard Allen, "The Social Gospel as the Religion of the Agrarian Revolt", in Carl
Berger and Ramsay Cook, eds., *The West and the Nation: Essays in Honour of W.L.
Morton* (Toronto: McClelland and Stewart, 1976), pp. 174–5. Footnotes omitted.

THE MARITIME RIGHTS MOVEMENT—WHAT LAY BEHIND THE AGITATION?

Maritime Regional Protest—An Expression of the "Paranoid Style" in Nova Scotia Politics

Traditional interpretations of the Maritime Rights movement in the twenties
have focused on the activities of politicians. Queen's University historian
George Rawlyk, a specialist in Maritime history, adopted Richard Hofstadter's term "the paranoid style" to describe the attitude of Nova Scotia
politicans involved in a succession of regional protest movements.

Nova Scotia's distrust of Confederation can be seen in numerous statements made by a
host of provincial patriots. Most of these declarations have two important characteristics in common— First, Confederation is considered to be directly responsible for the
economic decline of Nova Scotia since 1867. Second, it is contended that 'Repeal' or
'Secession' would bring back the never-to-be-forgotten glorious 'Golden Age' of the
Reciprocity period of 1854–1866....

It may be argued that the anti-'Upper Canadian' and anti-Confederation attitudes
have combined to produce what may be called the 'Paranoid Style in Nova Scotia
Regionalism'. Such a 'Paranoid Style', to use Professor Richard Hofstadter's term, is
not unique to the Atlantic province. The 'Paranoid Style' approach could also be used to
examine regionalism in other areas of Canada as well as Canadian attitudes towards the
United States....

In the Nova Scotia context, the spokesman of the regional 'Paranoid Style'.... felt
that the hostile and almost conspiratorial world of 'Upper Canada' was directed
specifically against their beloved Nova Scotia. Their extreme political rhetoric reveals
a great deal about the nature of their regional protest movements.

Confederation was seen by the 'Paranoid Style' spokesman as a blatant example of
the vicious power of a hostile enemy. It was argued that the British North America Act
had brought to a sudden end the material and cultural growth of Nova Scotia. Almost
overnight Nova Scotia was transformed into an economic, political, social and cultural
backwater. The province was carefully bypassed by the flood of immigrants to Canada;
old industries left the province because of the advantages of 'Upper Canada' and new
industries never came. Young Nova Scotians were compelled to emigrate and old Nova
Scotians grew increasingly bitter and disillusioned subjects. They usually remained
sullen and quiet until those periods of extreme, economic crises when the embers of
their discontent and suspicion were fanned into the flames of regional protest by the
propagandists of the 'Paranoid Style'.

G.A. Rawlyk, "Nova Scotia Regional Protest, 1867–1967", *Queen's Quarterly*,
Vol. LXXXV (Spring, 1968), pp. 106–107.

Maritime Rights—A Deep-Seated Regional Movement

In *The Maritime Rights Movement* (1979) and a companion essay, Ernest R. Forbes of the University of New Brunswick presented the regional protest as a genuine expression of Maritime progressivism:

> There was much more to 'Maritime Rights' than the conspicuous wail of the politicians. . . .
>
> The issues involved went much deeper than mere political manoeuvering or even, as professor G.A. Rawlyk has suggested, the attempt by the local 'Establishment' to undercut other forms of social protest. All classes in the region, although often in conflict on other issues, were united in their support of Maritime Rights. Each was aware that its own particular aspirations were incapable of realization until the region's declining influence was checked or reversed. . . .
>
> The development of Maritime regionalism, of which the Maritime Rights movement formed the climax, took place largely in the first two decades of the century. Previously, popular loyalties had been focused upon larger imperial or national entities or upon smaller political, cultural or geographical units. The shift was dictated by a growing realization of the need for co-operation. Co-operation was essential if the three Atlantic Provinces were to counteract the eclipse of their influence which resulted from the rise of the West and the growing metropolitan dominance of Central Canada. Another factor contributing to the growth of regionalism was the progressive ideology of the period, which increased the pressure upon the small governments for expensive reforms while at the same time suggesting the possibility of limitless achievement through a strategy of unity, organization and agitation. Consequently, regional awareness increased sharply in the three provinces. . . .
>
> * * * * *
>
> The Maritime Rights agitation which had emerged by 1919 was a regional protest movement which saw all classes united in their demands upon the rest of the country. This did not mean that different classes did not have distinct aspirations of their own; on the contrary, they were probably more conscious of them in 1919 than in any other period before or since. Each held a dream of progressive development in which its own collective interests were directly involved: for the manufacturers, their growth as the major industrial suppliers of the country; for the urban merchants, the final attainment of their communities' status as the entrepots of Canada's trade; for labour and farmers, the emergence of a new more democratic society in which they would break the economic and political dominance of the business classes; for the fishermen, the chance to rehabilitate their industry through the new fresh fish trade; and for the professionals, the elevation of Maritime society through education. But none of these aspirations was capable of realization with the continued decline of the economic and political status of the Maritimes in the Dominion. Just as electricity might channel the usually conflicting molecular energies of an iron bar to produce a magnetic force, so the federal government's adverse policies served to re-align the various 'classes' in the Maritimes to produce a powerful social force— regionalism. This force, dressed up in a variety of complex rationalizations, became the Maritime Rights movement of the 1920's.
>
> Ernest R. Forbes, "The Origins of the Maritime Rights Movement", *Acadiensis*, Vol. V (Autumn, 1975), pp. 55–57 and 66. Footnotes omitted.

REGIONAL PROTEST IN THE THIRTIES—TWO SEEMINGLY CONTRADICTORY PRAIRIE RESPONSES

The CCF: What Kind of Party—or Movement?

A Movement of Agrarian Socialism—S.M. Lipset's Thesis

The nature of the CCF has always provoked a lively debate among Canadian historians and political scientists. Much of the initial controversy was stirred up by the work of American political sociologist Seymour Martin Lipset. Professor Lipset's study of the CCF in Saskatchewan, *Agrarian Socialism* (1950) set out a thesis in which, focusing almost solely on the party's organizational structure, he contended that the CCF was a class-based movement of "agrarian radicalism" committed to socialism.

> Though it was a new radical party, the C.C.F. did not have to build up an organization from scratch. It was organized from the start by the local 'class' and community leaders of rural Saskatchewan. The fact that the province was so well organized on an occupational basis enabled the new party to obtain the support of the politically conscious community leaders. By the early 1940's, C.C.F. committees, composed in the main of the same people who were the officials of the other rural organizations, were operating in almost every district in the province. It was this 'machine' that brought the C.C.F. to power....
>
> At first glance the relationship between the C.C.F. and other rural community organizations appears similar to the pattern of party-society relations advocated by the Communist Party. Communists want to be the vanguard of the working class, the class leaders. To accomplish this, they attempt to permeate working-class organizations and become their officials. In the Soviet Union, Communists are placed in key positions in trade-unions, cooperatives, and local governments. In democratic countries they use the tactics of 'boring from within' to achieve positions of leadership.
>
> In Saskatchewan, however, the 'vanguard,' the leaders of the farming community, started the C.C.F. As a result, C.C.F. activity and community activity are closely interrelated. This situation is not a result of any planned action, but is, rather, a consequence of the tight organization of the farming community on an occupational basis. The C.C.F. is the class party, the farmers' party, and thus controls the farmers' organizations. Many leaders of the C.C.F. and of rural organizations are not aware of this close interrelationship. The party makes no direct efforts to influence other institutions and has no explicit policy for its members to follow in them. There are no C.C.F. caucuses in the coöperatives or other rural groups. In practice, however, most of the secondary leaders are C.C.F. members and therefore support the policy of the party and the C.C.F. government. The leaders are, in fact, continually engaged in political activity.
>
> S.M. Lipset, *Agrarian Socialism: The Cooperative Commonwealth Federation in Saskatchewan* (Berkeley: University of California Press, 1950), pp. 206 and 207–8. Footnotes omitted.

Socialism Forsaken—A Different View of the Saskatchewan CCF

Lipset's central thesis has been challenged by historians and political scientists on many fronts. Some analysts, like K.W. McNaught and Walter D. Young, have argued that the CCF was more of an amalgam of radical agrarian and urban labour forces than a purely agrarian socialist movement. More recently questions have been raised about the depth of the Saskatchewan CCF's commitment to a radical reform of the economic system.

Peter R. Sinclair is one historian who has argued that the Saskatchewan CCF was transformed from a social movement into a pragmatic party, sacrificing some of its socialist principles *en route* to power in that province.

[The] Saskatchewan CCF responded to electoral results by pragmatically adjusting its policy and attitudes on co-operation with other reform groups, especially Social Credit. In this the CCF clearly demonstrated that its performance was that of a political party, despite frequent claims by CCF members that it was a movement rather than a party.

The radical eclipse of the socialist land policy provides a good example of a familiar dilemma for parties which propose social change but are also committed to gaining power by popular election: should ideology be compromised for immediate reformist gains or should the original goal be explicitly retained and energy diverted into educating the electorate? If such a party fails to provide what the people will accept, it must become reconciled either to taking power by force or remaining a powerless educational organization; to win power quickly by election it must compromise and adopt a reformist rather than a revolutionary programme. This pressure toward revisionism seems to be especially great in rural dominated areas, such as Saskatchewan, where people tend to be strongly committed to existing property institutions. Changes in the CCF's land policy were possible in Saskatchewan because almost nobody in the party adopted a doctrinaire position which would have involved abandoning the ideal of the family farm as the basis of rural life. Therefore, the adjustment of the party to a pragmatic reformist position was relatively painless. Basically, CCF members accepted small-scale capitalist production and only flirted briefly with a socialist solution to the agrarian crisis of the thirties.

Peter R. Sinclair, "The Saskatchewan CCF: Ascent to Power and The Decline of Socialism", *Canadian Historical Review*, Vol. LIV (December, 1973), pp. 419-20 and 432-33. Footnotes omitted.

The Social Credit Movement—Psychological Reaction or Revolt Against the Party System?

The Social Credit Phenomenon—John A. Irving's "Mass Movement" Thesis

The nature and purpose of the Social Credit movement have proven even more baffling to historians and political analysts. Although Social Credit has been studied more thoroughly than any other political movement in Canada— with the possible exception of Confederation—many questions remain. John A. Irving's 1959 study, for example, argued that Social Credit was as much a mass psychological reaction to the Depression as a radical political movement.

The Social Credit upsurge in Alberta was essentially a people's movement which sought to reform, but not to revolutionize, the existing social order by changing the pattern of certain institutions.... During the years it rose to political power, this movement passed through the stages of social unrest, popular excitement, formalization, and institutionalization; and it exhibited, in the course of its evolution, the mechanisms of agitation, *esprit de corps*, morale, ideology, and operating tactics....

As the depression increased in severity, Alberta passed into a phase approaching social disorganization; psychologically considered, conditions could scarcely have been more ideal for the setting up of new social norms. Social Credit thus satisfied the desire for meaning and intelligibility amidst a chaotic social environment. On its positive or constructive side, Social Credit advocated new norms, and the upsurge of the movement represented an active attempt to realize a new social order through a specific programme of monetary and financial reform. It was maintained that if the Social Credit proposals could only secure legislative approval, the horrors of the depression would automatically end and a new world would surely come into being. There are also indications that to many of Aberhart's personal religious following the philosophy took on the character of an eschatology, a prophetic vision of a divinely ordained future for the world....

The social context, the desire for meaning, and the prospect of satisfying their needs combined to produce in Albertans a psychological condition in which they were extremely open to the appeal of Social Credit. At the same time, most of them lacked sufficient knowledge of philosophy and the social sciences to enable them to assess its claim to be *the* authentic interpretation of their world. Unable to deal with Social Credit in any critical way, thousands of people accepted it because it brought order into their confused world. They were at once bewildered and had the will to believe. They were in a condition of readiness to respond, and the philosophy of Social Credit lent itself admirably to shortcut rationalizations in the form of slogans and symbols. For those who could not understand the philosophy as a whole, slogans like 'Control of Credit,' 'Monetization of Natural Resources,' 'Basic Dividend,' 'Just Price,' and 'Cultural Heritage' became crowded with meaning. No small part of the appeal of Social Credit was simply due to the fact that it met so well the conditions of suggestibility which existed in Alberta at the time that Aberhart began his crusade in 1932.

An emphasis on the profound and multivalent appeal of the philosophy of Social Credit to the people of Alberta must not obscure the importance of the leadership of William Aberhart as a major factor in the rise of the Social Credit movement.... Aberhart brought to the movement his great prestige as an educationist and religious leader; it is doubtful if the movement would have won political power in Alberta without his leadership....

John A. Irving, *The Social Credit Movement in Alberta* (Toronto: University of Toronto Press, 1959), pp. 334–339.

William Aberhart's Social Credit—A Pragmatic Reform Administration

Many analysts of William Aberhart's Social Credit, following the interpretation of John Irving and the critics, have characterized the Aberhart version of Social Credit as a populist, right-wing reactionary movement with overtones of fascism.

Lewis H. Thomas was one Western Canadian historian who attempted to evaluate Social Credit in the light of Aberhart's accomplishments in office rather than by the rhetoric of his defenders and critics. In spite of his public reputation as an apostle of Major C.H. Douglas' radical Social Credit theories, Thomas argued that his administration implemented many pragmatic reforms.

It is apparent from the record of legislation and executive action that Aberhart was as much, if not more interested, in the reform and expansion of the provincial government's administrative services as he was in social credit. The former involved both innovations and building on foundations laid during the U.F.A. regime.

The most radical reforms were the creation of the larger units of school administration and of the county system. The larger units, a change long favoured by teachers, were established in the face of opposition of the trustees of the 3,750 small school districts. These were combined into 50 and as a result, the standard of education in rural areas was made more uniform and greatly improved.

A similar principle was involved in the substitution of 60 counties for the many small rural municipalities.

In addition to these reforms there were significant improvements in agricultural services, the encouragement of co-operatives, public health care, and assistance to municipalities. Progressive legislation was adopted with respect to minimum wages, maximum hours of work, guarantee of collective bargaining and methods for settling industrial disputes. A revolutionary new system for guaranteeing protection for the homesteader settling on provincial lands was adopted in 1939.

In brief, under Aberhart a social welfare state was established....

Lewis H. Thomas, "The First Term", in L.H. Thomas, ed., *William Aberhart and Social Credit in Alberta* (Toronto: Copp Clark, 1977), pp. 86 and 90–91.

REGIONAL PROTESTS IN THE WEST AND THE MARITIMES— SOME COMPARATIVE INTERPRETATIONS

Canada's regional protest movements in the 1920s and thirties have generated great interest and prompted a host of studies. The Western Progressives, the Maritime Rights agitation, Social Credit and the CCF have all been subjected to intensive analysis by historians, political scientists and contemporary analysts. Yet with rare exceptions the studies undertaken were of certain movements in particular provinces. Only recently have scholars turned to comparative studies in an effort to assess the similarities and differences in political responses from province to province, region to region. In the process some common stereotypes and long standing images of the West and the Maritimes have been seriously questioned.

Western Radicalism and Maritime Conservatism—A Study in Contrasts

Most studies of regional protest in the inter-war years have drawn a sharp contrast between Western radicalism or Progressivism and the Maritimer's "conservative" responses to regional decline and Depression. The traditional view, drawn largely from W.L. Morton's works on the Western Progressives, lays particular stress on the "steady ways" of the Maritime provinces. One recent study which reaffirmed this traditional dichotomy was Walter D. Young's *Democracy and Discontent* (1978), a comparative look at Progressivism, Socialism and Social Credit in the Canadian West.

The disappearance of a 'pure' two-party system began with the expansion of Canada's population and the development of the western provinces. The people living at extreme distances from Ottawa, Montreal and Toronto—the real centres of power and influence— soon came to appreciate the disadvantages of isolation and political insignificance.

The two old parties were based in the east, financed by the east and controlled by the east. For the people in the west this meant frustration and unrest: they had neither the arm nor the ear of the ruling parties. It was thoroughly consistent with the frontier tradition of self-sufficiency and independence that they should form their own political machines to influence or wrest power from the old and insensitive engines of government in the east. Their economic situation also placed them in the position of vassals to the eastern potentates of the CPR, Massey-Harris; and other large firms that set prices, held mortgages and, to a large extent, influenced governments. This factor gave further impetus to the development of indigenous parties and movements in the west....

If the combination of federalism and the parliamentary system was a major factor in the rise of protest movements, why were such movements largely confined to the western plains? Surely one could have expected similar developments in the perenially depressed areas of Canada—the Maritime provinces. The locale of the protest movements is an indication that there were other factors involved. There was the difference of expectation. The settlers of the prairies had gone to the west filled with high hopes of a prosperous, independent, self-sufficient existence. Like many men before and after, they believed implicitly in the agrarian myth of solid honesty, purity and rewarding nature of the rural life. Life was supposed to be good in the west. To the people of the Maritimes, on the other hand, marginal living was accepted as inevitable. The depression certainly brought additional hardship, but it was relatively less severe than that visited upon the west. The Maritimer's expectations were not those of the new settlers in the west and their political attitudes were based on settled habits and inherited preferences. When one is hip-deep in mud, another inch or so makes little difference; but the man who is dry-shod expresses concern when he steps into a puddle....

Walter D. Young, *Democracy and Discontent: Progressivism, Socialism and Social Credit in the Canadian West*, Second Edition (Toronto: McGraw-Hill Ryerson, 1978), pp. 110–111, 112–113.

Progressivism in the Maritimes—A New View of the Crosscurrents

Traditional assumptions about the differences in regional protests between the West and the Maritimes have been strongly challenged by Ernest R. Forbes in *The Maritime Rights Movement, 1919–1927* (1979). According to Forbes, the Maritime Rights agitation of the 1920s was not a conservative movement of reaction, but a vigorous form of Maritime progressivism that transcended party affiliations.

For a brief period in 1919 and 1920 the spectacular protests of farmer and labouring groups obscured the growth of regional consciousness in the Maritimes. Allied with and sometimes dominated by similar groups from outside the region, the local movements appeared as cross currents in the thrust for regional expression. But a closer view suggests that farmers and labourers in the Maritimes realized that they too had a stake in the achievement of regional goals. Their regionalism, conflicting with that of their external allies, partially accounts for the failure of the farmer-labour political movement in the Maritimes, especially at the federal level. Canadian scholars have tended to ascribe this failure to an innate Maritime conservatism. They have implied a sharp contrast between the Westerner's radicalism or progressivism and the Maritimer's 'steady ways,' strong party allegiance, and presumed rejection of the advanced social thought which underlay the Prairie movement. This interpretation overlooks two important factors: the strength of progressive sentiment in the Maritimes at the beginning of the Twenties and the contrasting role of regional sentiment in the two parts of the country. Progressivism, of course, was not the monopoly of any group or class; each tended to emphasize those aspects of reform ideology which best served their own interests. To professionals, progressivism might be an expression of humanitarian concern and/or an attempt to expand their role in government bureaucracies. To the business-oriented it might mean a search for efficiency, the replacement of old-fashioned party structures, and the development of governments which would more effectively serve the interests of the entrepreneur. To farmers and labour it usually meant an attempt to improve the lot of the weak and exploited, namely themselves. In the Maritimes as in Western Canada their efforts towards this end found expression in cooperative, social gospel, militant trade union, syndicalist, socialist, and independent farmer and labour political movements. In the West, where progressive sentiment was popularly identified with the region and conservative reaction with eastern big business, regionalism and the farmer-labour movements were mutually reinforcing. Dominated by its Western adherents, the Progressive Party provided a vehicle for the expression of regional interests. Its 'real character,' as W.L. Morton pointed out, was that of 'an agrarian and sectional bloc from the continental West, the representation of the monolithic wheat economy.' In the Maritimes the 'national' farmer and labour political movements conflicted with regional sentiment. When Maritimers realized that these movements could not serve their regional aspirations, many withdrew their support in favour of a campaign for Maritime Rights....

Ernest R. Forbes, *The Maritime Rights Movement, 1919–1927: A Study in Canadian Regionalism* (Montreal: McGill-Queen's University Press, 1979), pp. 38–39. Footnotes omitted.

Western Political Protest—A Reflection of the Region's Uniqueness and Diversity

Recent studies of western Canadian history have begun to place prairie radicalism within the context of a more varied, multi-faceted Western society, demonstrating its often unique regional characteristics. Political scientist David E. Smith of the University of Saskatchewan was one scholar who saw Western radicalism springing from diverse sources, assuming different forms and pursuing a variety of objectives.

The dissent found in Western Canada today stems almost as much from grievances that arise out of its political culture as it does from economic unrest. Here, because of a singular combination of events among which must be numbered the influx of an ethnically heterogeneous population settling on homesteads spread over thousands of square miles where services were expensive and attainable only through local initiative, a unique set of attitudes, beliefs, values, and skills developed. Consider the place of cooperatives, which, from the great provincial elevator companies to the village store, were a pillar of the prairie community; or the interrelationship of politics and religion as witnessed in the Social Gospel of T.C. Douglas and J.S. Woodsworth or the Social

Credit of William Aberhart. The prairie experience with both has no Canadian equivalent. Nor is labour's turbulent history in the West duplicated elsewhere in Canada, although of course this is no measure of its respective import for the nation's history. At the same time, although the prairie provinces share a regional political culture, each of them can claim its own distinctive set of characteristics. It is this very pluralism which explains the region's rich heritage of protest....

* * * * *

Social Credit and the C.C.F. represented a new form of dissent. W.L. Morton describes them (particularly Social Credit) as 'Utopian' in the sense that they sought 'to merge the nation in the section.' Unlike the Progressives, who wanted to reform the existing economic and political system, the new parties each sought to replace the old order with one constructed according to new principles. At its English inception, Social Credit was an economic theory that saw politics as a means to attain a goal, but later, in Alberta, because of the Canadian Constitution, this idea was abandoned. Social Credit quickly emerged as a regional protest party whose political ambitions led it to clash most resoundingly with Mackenzie King and his Liberals and with the federal government and its offspring, the Rowell-Sirois Commission.

Because of its socialist doctrine and diverse origins, the C.C.F. was never a regional party like Social Credit. In Saskatchewan, the strong base provided by the United Farmers of Canada (Saskatchewan Section) and the eventual victory of the C.C.F. over the ruling provincial Liberals gave the new party an agrarian aura. Yet its urban-industrial supporters always exerted great influence in the party's organization. The achievement of the C.C.F. and its successor, the New Democratic Party, was the revolution it wrought in political and social thought after the Regina Manifesto— governments and individuals today accept as reasonable many of the movement's principles. But this national success deprived the party of any special claim to representing regional interests, particularly those of the West.

David E. Smith, "Western Politics and National Unity", in David J. Bercuson, ed., *Canada and the Burden of Unity* (Toronto: Macmillan, 1977), pp. 150–156.

A Guide to Further Reading

1. Overviews

Clark, S.D., J.P. Grayson and L.M. Grayson, eds., *Prophecy and Protest: Social Movements in Twentieth Century Canada*. Toronto: Gage, 1975.

Forbes, Ernest R., *The Maritime Rights Movement, 1919–1927: A Study in Canadian Regionalism*. Montreal: McGill-Queen's University Press, 1979.

Graham, Roger, *Arthur Meighen, Vol. II: And Fortune Fled, 1920–1927*. Toronto: Clarke Irwin, 1963.

Horn, Michiel, ed., *The Dirty Thirties: Canadians in the Great Depression*. Toronto: Copp Clark, 1972.

Neatby, H. Blair, *The Politics of Chaos: Canada in the Thirties*. Toronto: Macmillan, 1972.

———, *William Lyon Mackenzie King, Vol. II, 1924–32: The Lonely Heights*. Toronto: University of Toronto Press, 1963.

Safarian, A.E., *The Canadian Economy in the Great Depression*. Toronto: McClelland and Stewart, 1970.

Smith, David E., "A Comparison of Prairie Political Developments in Saskatchewan and Alberta", *Journal of Canadian Studies*. Vol. 4, No. 1 (1969), pp. 17–25.

Smith, Denis, "Prairie Revolt, Federalism and the Party System" in Hugh G. Thorburn, ed., *Party Politics in Canada*. Scarborough: Prentice-Hall, 1967, pp. 189–200.

Trofimenkoff, Susan Mann, ed., *The Twenties in Western Canada*. Ottawa: National Museum of Man, 1972.

Young, Walter D., *Democracy and Discontent: Progressivism, Socialism and Social Credit in the Canadian West*. Toronto: McGraw-Hill Ryerson, 1978.

2. Specialized Studies

The Western Progressive Movement

Allen, Richard, "The Social Gospel as the Religion of the Agrarian Revolt", in Carl Berger and Ramsay Cook, eds., *The West and the Nation*. Toronto: McClelland and Stewart, 1976.

Betke, Carl, "Farm Politics in an Urban Age: The Decline of the United Farmers of Alberta after 1921", in Lewis H. Thomas, ed., *Essays on Western History*. Edmonton: University of Alberta Press, 1976, pp. 175–192.

Griezic, F.J.K., "The Honourable Thomas Alexander Crerar: The Political Career of a Western Liberal Progressive in the 1920s", in Trofimenkoff, ed., *The Twenties in Western Canada*, pp. 107–37.

MacPherson, Ian, *Each for All: A History of the Co-operative Movement in English Canada, 1900–1945*. Toronto: Macmillan, 1979.

Morton, W.L., *The Progressive Party in Canada*. Toronto: University of Toronto Press, 1950.

_____, "The Social Philosophy of Henry Wise Wood, the Canadian Agrarian Leader", *Agricultural History*, Vol. 22 (1948), pp. 114–123.

Ormsby, Margaret A., "The United Farmers of British Columbia: An Abortive Third-Party Movement", *British Columbia Historical Quarterly*, Vol. 17 (1953), pp. 53–73.

Parker, Ian D., "The Provincial Party", *BC Studies*, Vol. 8 (1970–71), pp. 17–28.

Robin, Martin, "British Columbia: The Company Province", in Robin, ed., *Canadian Provincial Politics*. Second Edition. Scarborough: Prentice-Hall, 1978.

Rolph, William K., *Henry Wise Wood of Alberta*. Toronto: University of Toronto Press, 1950.

Sharp, Paul F., *The Agrarian Revolt in Western Canada*. New York: Octagon Books, 1971.

Wood, Louis Aubrey, *A History of Farmers' Movements in Canada*. Introduction by F.J.K. Griezic. Toronto: University of Toronto Press, 1975.

The Maritime Rights Movement

Beck, J.M., *The Government of Nova Scotia*. Toronto: University of Toronto Press, 1957.

Forbes, Ernest R., "The Origins of the Maritime Rights Movement", *Acadiensis*, Vol. V (Autumn, 1975), pp. 55–66.

Lotz, Jim, "The Historical and Social Setting of the Antigonish Movement", *Nova Scotia Historical Quarterly* (1975).

MacPherson, Ian, "Appropriate Forms of Enterprise: The Prairie and Maritime Cooperative Movements, 1900–1955", *Acadiensis*, Vol. VIII (1978).

Rawlyk, G.A., "Nova Scotia Regional Protest, 1867–1967", *Queen's Quarterly*, Vol. LXXX (Spring, 1968), pp. 105–123.

The Co-operative Commonwealth Federation

Cross, Michael S., ed., *The Decline and Fall of a Good Idea: CCF-NDP Manifestoes 1932–1969*. Toronto: New Hogtown Press, 1974.

Horn, Michiel, *The League for Social Reconstruction: Intellectual Origins or the Demo-cratic Left in Canada, 1930-1942.* Toronto: University of Toronto Press, 1980.

Lipset, S.M., *Agrarian Radicalism: The Cooperative Commonwealth Federation in Saskatchewan.* Berkeley: University of California Press, 1950.

Milnor, A.J., "The New Politics and Ethnic Revolt, 1929-1938", in Norman Ward and D.S. Spafford, eds., *Politics in Saskatchewan.* Don Mills: Longmans, 1968, pp. 151-177.

Sinclair, Peter R., "The Saskatchewan CCF: Ascent to Power and the Decline of Socialism", *Canadian Historical Review*, Vol. LIV (December, 1973), pp. 419-433.

Young, Walter D., *The Anatomy of a Party: The National CCF, 1932-61.* Toronto: University of Toronto, 1969.

Zakuta, Leo, *A Protest Movement Becalmed.* Toronto: University of Toronto Press, 1964.

The Social Credit Movement

Barr, John J., *The Dynasty: The Rise and Fall of Social Credit in Alberta.* Toronto: McClelland and Stewart, 1974.

Boudreau, Joseph A., ed., *Alberta, Aberhart and Social Credit.* Toronto: Holt, Rinehart and Winston, 1975.

Elliott, David R., "Antithetical Elements in William Aberhart's Theology and Political Ideology", *Canadian Historical Review*, Vol. LIX (March, 1978), pp. 38-58.

Irving, John A., *The Social Credit Movement in Alberta.* Toronto: University of Toronto Press, 1959.

Johnson, L.P.V. and Ola MacNutt, *Aberhart of Alberta.* Edmonton: Institute of Applied Art, 1970.

Macpherson, C.B., *Democracy in Alberta.* Toronto: University of Toronto Press, 1953.

Mann, W.E., *Sect, Cult and Church in Alberta.* Toronto: University of Toronto Press, 1955.

Shultz, H.J., "Portrait of A Premier: William Aberhart", *Canadian Historical Review*, Vol. XLV (September, 1964), pp. 185-211.

Thomas, Lewis H., ed., *William Aberhart and Social Credit in Alberta.* Toronto: Copp Clark, 1977.

17

CONSCRIPTION IN THE TWO WORLD WARS

A Case of Military Necessities or Broken Promises?

Few political issues have divided Canadians as sharply as conscription for overseas service in time of war. In World War I and again in 1942 and 1944, the question of conscription opened up old wounds, setting English-Canadian patriots and French-Canadian nationalists against each other. Canada's political parties were severely tested as old and partisan loyalties virtually crumbled under the stress of war. In each case the imposition of conscription produced widespread opposition, acts of civil disobedience and rioting in the streets, particularly in French-speaking Canada. Cries of racial hatred swept through the country, almost blurring the question of whether conscription was a military necessity. Compulsory military service proved to be more than a military and diplomatic issue; it became a trial by fire for the national leadership, and a formidable threat to national unity.

Conscription was a bitterly divisive question which forced Canadians to weigh military and domestic political considerations. In both wars, political leaders, conscious of the need to preserve unity between French-and English-speaking Canadians, promised that overseas conscription would not be imposed to raise manpower, except as a last resort. Many patriotic Canadians, on the other hand, argued that the military need to raise troops, provide reinforcements, or help win the war necessitated conscription. Conscription eventually was introduced in each war—and the decisions to do so fueled a raging debate over whether it was a question of "military necessities" or "broken promises", a debate which persists to the present day.

The First World War seemed initially to unite and later to divide Canadians. Canada entered the Great War in August 1914 as a colony of Britain. Robert L. Borden, Canada's Prime Minister, strongly supported the war effort, while maintaining that Canadians would not be conscripted to serve overseas. Few

Canadians questioned the need for Canada's participation to preserve the Empire, aid France, and extinguish German militarism in Europe. As part of the Empire, most Canadians accepted that Canada was at war when Britain was at war. But as the fighting dragged on from months to years, voluntary enlistment declined, and enthusiasm for Canada's involvement waned. Popular support for the war effort dwindled as tensions mounted between French and English-speaking Canadians. Many French-Canadian nationalists, like Henri Bourassa, came to view the European conflict as "Britain's war", an imperialist struggle being waged under the direction of Britain. After living for three centuries in North America, most French Canadians owed their primary allegiance to Canada—and lacked the emotional links with Britain and Europe shared among their English-speaking countrymen. Yet French-speaking Quebeckers were not alone in resisting voluntary enlistment. Farmers in Ontario and the prairie West showed some reluctance to lose their sons and suffer consequent labour shortages on their farms. Some ethnic and religious minorities, notably Ontario Mennonites, German Canadians and recently settled immigrants on the prairie wheatlands, resisted the appeal for troops. Under these conditions, recruitment began to decline.

The introduction of conscription by the Borden government in May 1917 met the high demand for recruits due to the heavy casualties at the front but left Canada rent with divisions between French and English-speaking peoples. The eventual passage of the Military Service Act, the formation of a Unionist coalition, and the divisive "Khaki Election" of 1917 drove a deeper wedge between the Canadian peoples and left a lingering legacy of bitterness and suspicion. To French Canadians the 1917 crisis was a breach of trust and a brutal demonstration of power; the Borden government had violated its earlier promise not to enact conscription and had bowed to the will of ardent English-Canadian conscriptionists.

Political decisions concerning conscription in World War II were conditioned by vivid memories of the great schism of 1917. At the beginning of the war, Prime Minister Mackenzie King and his Quebec lieutenant Ernest Lapointe, mindful of the 1917 crisis, pledged no conscription for overseas service. Underlying King's wartime policy was a firm commitment to avoid conscription and thus preserve Canadian unity. But when the Allies' fortunes in Europe, North Africa, and the Far East reached their lowest point in the summer of 1942, demands for conscription threatened to engulf the King government.

The conscription crises of the Second World War were less damaging than that of 1917. Mackenzie King employed all possible techniques of obfuscation, delay and political manoeuvering to keep the conscriptionists at bay. King promised "conscription if necessary, but not necessarily conscription", conducted a national plebiscite in April 1942 to relieve him of his no-conscription pledge, fired his defence minister in November 1944, and then finally relented, sending 16 000 home service troops overseas. Yet by the time King was forced to abandon his tactical position by the 1944 reinforcements crisis, it was clear to most Quebeckers that he had done all he could. King's policy of compromise and delay, hesitation and caution infuriated a legion of critics, but probably did much to defuse the crisis.

Conscription is a question which has severely tested Canadian unity in wartime. In neither war did a majority of French-Canadians want or accept the need for compulsory military service overseas, yet in both wars previous commitments to voluntary recruitment were set aside and conscription was imposed under pressure from vocal patriotic elements in English-speaking Canada. The two wars were vastly different conflicts, but in both, Canadian territory was rarely, if ever, threatened in a sustained and direct fashion. The relative safety of Canada in North America helped to dampen the potential military ardour of Canadians prepared to fight in defence of their native land, and it led to persistent claims that British imperial ends, not national interests, were being served by Canada's participation in the wars.

Was the imposition of conscription a military necessity in the First World War or the Second World War, or in either? What promises concerning manpower policy were made at the outset of each war—and to what extent were they violated? What critical forces in Europe and in Canada prompted the Canadian governments of Borden and King to introduce conscription in 1917, and later in 1944? In each case, what was achieved and what were the costs to Canada and Canadians? These are some of the questions raised in this problem study.

SELECTED CONTEMPORARY SOURCES

THE CONSCRIPTION CRISIS OF 1917

Prime Minister Robert Borden's Position on Conscription, 1914–1916

Prime Minister Robert L. Borden reacted quickly to the startling events of August 1914. In his view, if Britain was threatened, all members of the Empire were threatened, and if the mother country was at war, Canada was at war. At the outset of the conflict, he assured Canadians that Canada's manpower requirements in the Great War would be met by voluntary recruitment. But as the war worsened, official British pressure mounted, and with the supply of volunteers beginning to dry up, the Prime Minister's attitude changed. By January 1916 Borden announced that the Canadian Expeditionary Force would be raised in strength to 500 000 men to match the commitments of other self-governing Dominions—a commitment which many felt could only be met by conscription.

> ...under the laws of Canada, our citizens may be called out to defend our own territory, but cannot be required to go beyond the seas except for the defence of Canada itself. There has not been, there will not be, compulsion or conscription.
>
> P.A.C., Robert L. Borden Papers, Address, 18 December 1914, Halifax, Nova Scotia, f. 34672.

We have more than two and half million French Canadians in Canada and I realize that the feeling between them and the English-speaking people is intensely bitter at present. The vision of the French Canadian is very limited. He is not well informed and he is in a condition of extreme exasperation by reason of fancied wrongs supposed to be inflicted upon his compatriots in other provinces, especially Ontario. It may be necessary to resort to compulsion. I hope not, but if the necessity arises I shall not hesitate to act accordingly.

Borden Papers, Borden to Sir Charles Hibbert Tupper, 2 January, 1916.

More than a twelvemonth ago our Empire consecrated all its powers and its supreme endeavour in a great purpose which concerns the liberties of the world and the destinies of its nations. . . . The Canadian Forces at the Front have indeed fought a good fight and they have crowned the name of Canada with undying laurels. To them and to all the Overseas Forces now under arms and awaiting the opportunity to do their part we bid God-speed, in the sure faith that they will never fail in their duty. On this the last day of the old year the authorized Forces of Canada number 250,000 and the number enlisted is rapidly approaching that limit. From tomorrow, the first day of the New Year, our authorized force will be 500,000. This announcement is made in token of Canada's unflinchable resolve to crown the justice of our cause with victory and with an abiding peace.

Sir R.L. Borden's New Year's Message, 1916, in Henry Borden, ed., *Robert Laird Borden: His Memoirs* (Toronto: McClelland and Stewart, 1969), Vol. I., pp. 250–251.

The Military Situation—Strength, Enlistments and Casualties, Canadian Expeditionary Force, 1914–1917.

By the end of April 1917, Canada had sent some 312 000 men overseas and was maintaining four infantry divisions in France, a total of 125 000 men. The Borden government planned to send a fifth division to France, but

Table 17–1   Appointments and Enlistments in Canadian Expeditionary Force By Months, 1914–1917

Month	1914			1915			1916			1917		
Month	Off	N/S	ORs	Off	N/S	ORs	Off	N/S	ORs	Off	N/S	ORs
January	—	—	—	324	43	9 363	1 002	108	28 185	238	66	6 690
February	—	—	—	460	43	8 211	1 024	75	26 638	186	19	5 311
March	—	—	—	318	41	9 002	932	21	33 960	143	159	4 886
April	—	—	—	321	225	7 094	681	88	20 200	143	126	4 492
May	—	—	—	310	53	7 539	735	52	14 572	152	166	6 211
June—	—	—		436	49	10 465	502	58	10 059	89	42	5 298
July—	—	—		465	75	14 819	364	64	7 961	93	38	3 515
August	1 117	9	20 838	494	16	17 357	319	73	6 597	94	18	2 902
September	454	95	9 531	464	29	16 229	318	22	5 717	102	11	3 559
October	132	10	5 152	427	40	12 410	255	27	5 262	108	36	4 814
November	449	2	13 015	711	29	17 282	259	49	5 540	84	83	9 284
December	290	2	8 048	1 102	32	22 581	209	61	4 930	90	46	4 317
TOTALS	2 442	118	56 584	5 832	675	152 352	6 600	698	169 621	1 522	810	61 279
		59 144			158 859			176 919			63 611	

Key: Off = Officers; N/S = Nursing Service; ORs = Other Ranks

Table 17–2: Voluntary Enlistments By Provinces and Nationalities, August 1914 to 31 October 1917

Enlistments By Provinces	Population 1916†		Voluntary Enlistments
Ontario	2 713 000	—	191 632
Quebec	2 154 000		48 934
Nova Scotia and Prince Edward Island*	597 000	—	23 436
New Brunswick	368 000	—	18 022
Manitoba	554 000	—	52 784
Saskatchewan	648 000	—	26 111
Alberta	496 000	—	36 279
British Columbia and Yukon*	463 000	—	42 608
			439 806
Enlistments By Nationalities			
Canadian born			197 473
British born			215 769
Other nationalities			26 546
			439 806

† Population figures are estimates derived from Canada Year Book, 1938, p. xxxi.

* The fact that Nova Scotia and Prince Edward Island, and British Columbia and the Yukon are bracketed together suggests that this table was based on statistics compiled by Military Districts, since these areas comprised respectively Military Districts 6 and 11. This being the case, enlistments in four relatively thinly populated western counties of Quebec, which formed part of M.D. 3 (H.Q., Kingston) would be credited to Ontario, and those in a similarly thinly populated area of Ontario forming part of M.D. 10 (H.Q., Winnipeg) would be credited to Manitoba.

Table 17–3: Strength, Enlistment and Casualties, January–December, 1917

Months	Officers	Strength Other Ranks	Strength All Ranks	Enlistments Total	Casualties Total
January	16 790	286 359	303 149	9 194	4 396
February	17 181	286 977	304 158	6 809	1 250
March	17 458	287 127	304 585	6 640	6 161
April	17 802	283 494	301 296	5 530	13 477
May	17 815	285 369	303 184	6 407	13 457
June	17 872	287 160	305 032	6 348	7 931
July	18 231	287 402	305 633	3 882	7 906
August	18 179	285 035	303 214	3 117	13 232
September	18 387	285 220	303 607	3 588	10 990
October	18 273	285 454	303 727	4 884	5 929
November	18 213	288 577	306 790	4 019	30 741
December	18 182	288 947	307 129	3 921	7 474

Tables derived from G.W.L. Nicholson, *Canadian Expeditionary Force 1914–1919*. Ottawa: Queen's Printer, 1962, pp. 546-7 and 548; and C.P. Stacey, ed., *Historical Documents of Canada, Vol. V, 1914–1945*. Toronto: Macmillan, 1972, pp. 568-569.

escalating casualties and slumping enlistment at home prevented such an action. To keep the four divisions up to strength, an estimated 10 000 men were required every month as infantry reinforcements. The official figures from the standard history of the Canadian Expeditionary Force and Defence records provide an inkling of the military situation at the time conscription was introduced.

Borden's Announcement of Conscription, 1917—Promise Violated or Commitment Fulfilled?

During a tour of the European front conducted in the spring of 1917 in between sessions of the Imperial War Cabinet in London, Prime Minister Borden visited the Canadian Corps in France, camps in England and a host of military hospitals. Upon his return to Canada he announced his introduction of the Military Service Act, providing for conscription for overseas service.

> We have four Canadian divisions at the front. For the immediate future there are sufficient reinforcements. But four divisions cannot be maintained without thorough provision for future requirements.... Hitherto we have depended on voluntary enlistment. I myself stated to Parliament that nothing but voluntary enlistment was imposed by the Government. But I return to Canada impressed at once with the extreme gravity of the situation, and with a sense of responsibility for our future effort at the most critical period of the war. It is apparent to me that the voluntary system will not yield further substantial results. I hoped it would....
>
> All citizens are liable to military service for the defence of their country....
>
> I have had to take all these matters into consideration and I have given them my most earnest attention. The responsibility is a serious one, but I do not shrink from it. Therefore, it is my duty to announce to the House that early proposals will be made to provide by compulsory military enlistment on a selective basis, such reinforcements as may be necessary to maintain the Canadian army in the field.
>
> ...The number of men required will not be less than 50,000 and will probably be 100,000...."
>
> Sir R.L. Borden, House of Commons, May 18, 1917, quoted in Henry Borden, ed., *Borden: His Memoirs*, Vol. II., pp. 77–79.

Two Views of Conscription—Images from the Popular Press, 1917

The bitterness and intensity of feeling aroused by the conscription issue were graphically reflected in election posters, campaign slogans and political cartoons. Among pro-conscription English Canadians, Henri Bourassa was regularly denounced as a "Hot Shot for the Empire's Enemies" and Liberal Opposition Leader Wilfrid Laurier pilloried as a "traitor" bent on undermining "the boys at the front". In Quebec anti-conscriptionists dramatized Borden's "broken promises" and depicted the Military Service Act as a measure aimed squarely at French Canadians. Some political cartoons conveyed the impression that English and French Canadians were fighting two different wars.

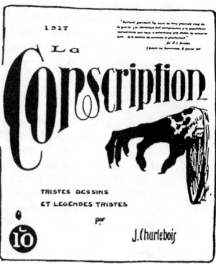

THEY WOULD CUT THE BRIDGE FROM UNDER OUR BOYS

Henri Bourassa's Case Against Conscription, 1917

Henri Bourassa led the fight of the *nationalistes* against conscription in Quebec. Since he viewed the European conflict as "Britain's war" and saw no real Canadian interests at stake, Bourassa claimed that those who opposed conscription were the most patriotic Canadians, and if French Canadians adopted this stand, it was because unlike Anglo-Canadians they owed their allegiance to Canada and Canada alone. In the following article written originally for the New York *Evening Post*, the editor of *Le Devoir* described the great harm being inflicted upon Canada by its war effort:

We are opposed to further enlistments for the war in Europe, whether by conscription or otherwise, for the [following] reasons: (1) Canada has already made a military display, in men and money, proportionately superior to that of any nation engaged in the war; (2) any further weakening of the man-power of the country would seriously handicap agricultural production and other essential industries; (3) an increase in the war budget of Canada spells national bankruptcy; (4) it threatens the economic life of the nation and, eventually, its political independence; (5) conscription means national disunion and strife, and would thereby hurt the cause of the Allies to a much greater extent than the addition of a few thousand soldiers to their fighting forces could bring them help and comfort....

* * * * *

Without any previous declaration of war, Canada has thrown herself into the conflict as a mere satellite of Great Britain. She was not forced to do so, either by constitution or previous understandings. On the contrary, a well defined agreement with Great Britain made it clear that, in case of war, Canada had no other duty to perform than that of defending her own territory, if attacked.

When war broke out, it was specified that military service was and would remain voluntary. Under that pledge, the number of men to be enlisted for overseas' service was gradually raised from 20,000 to 500,000. When, in January 1916, parliament, at the request of the government, decided to allow the latter increase, the prime minister, Sir Robert Borden, made the following declaration:

'In speaking in the first two or three months in the war, I made it clear to the people of Canada that we did not propose any conscription. I repeat that announcement with emphasis to-day.'

The leader of the opposition, Sir Wilfrid Laurier, was no less emphatic:

'Conscription has come in England. . . . but conscription is not to come in Canada.'

A few days later, a newly appointed member of the cabinet, Mr. Sevigny, was re-elected in a Quebec constituency upon the specific and solemn pledge that 'conscription would never be established.' That pledge has been repeatedly given by every represent-ative of Quebec in the government. . . .

So that, in the eyes of all French Canadians, the adoption of conscription would not only result in an economic collapse of the country: it would also shake their faith in the honour and truthfulness of their public men.

Finally, the economic readjustment of the country is sure to bring dispute between the rural provinces of the West and the industrial provinces of the East. . . .

Opposition to conscription and war-madness in Canada is not anti-patriotic: it is essentially patriotic and clear-sighted.

Henri Bourassa, "Win the War and Lose Canada", *Le Devoir*, July 12, 1917, reprinted in Joseph Levitt, ed., *Henri Bourassa on Imperialism and Bi-culturalism 1900–1918*, (Toronto: Copp Clark, 1970) pp. 170 and 174–5.

Conscription and the Wartime Election Acts—A Case of Political Expediency?

The conduct of Borden and his government in the summer and fall of 1917 raised many suspicions about their real purposes in imposing conscription. Between the passage of the Military Service Act and the "Khaki Election" of 1917 held six months later, two important laws were enacted affecting the franchise. The Military Voters' Act gave the vote to all men in Canadian uniform, and disenfranchised conscientious objectors. A second statute, the Wartime Elections Act, enfranchised close women relatives of men serving overseas, but denied the vote to all citizens born in enemy countries and naturalized in Canada after 1902. In the election Borden's Unionist govern-ment was returned with a substantial majority, carrying most of English-speaking Canada and the military service vote. Quebec showed its displeasure by giving Laurier's Liberals 62 of the province's 65 federal seats.

Opposition leader Sir Wilfrid Laurier, faced with the impending desertion of many English-speaking Liberals to the Unionist coalition, offered this interpretation of Borden's decision to enact compulsory military service:

I am just as anxious as you are yourself to win the war. The only question is which is the best policy: is conscription the best means to the end? . . .

What is the reason for the change? The military situation being the same, the reason must be sought elsewhere, and elsewhere there is no other reason than a purely political one, and the object not to win the war but to win the elections. Permit me to look over the situation with you a moment.

Is it not true that the main reason advocated for conscription—not so much publicly as privately, not shouted but whispered—is that Quebec must be made to do her part, and French-Canadians forced to enlist compulsorily since they did not enlist voluntarily? If this is not the main reason advanced in Winnipeg for conscription, I hope you will tell me frankly that I am in error, and then I will know that Winnipeg is an exception to all other centres where conscription is advocated.

It is quite true that Quebec has not enlisted proportionately as the other provinces. No one regrets it more than I do, but could any other result be expected? ...

If you want any further evidence that the conscription act was passed for political purposes alone, you find it in the infamous act just passed for the disfranchisement of men who are by the laws of the land our fellow-citizens. By the conscription act all British subjects resident in Canada between the ages of 20 and 45 are liable to be called, but by the War Times Election Act subsequently passed, all naturalized subjects born in enemy countries, and naturalized after the 31st of March 1902, are disfranchised, unless they enlist. Do you see in these two acts any evidence that the government intend to win the war, or to win the elections?

These are the main reasons which have directed my attitude in the present contest. We have gone voluntarily into this war for a noble object, and I still believe that we can reach the end by adhering to the principle collectively and individually....

> Wilfrid Laurier to a Winnipeg correspondent, September 27, 1917, reprinted in O.D. Skelton, *Life and Letters of Sir Wilfrid Laurier* (Toronto: McClelland and Stewart, 1965), Vol. II, pp. 192–193.

CONSCRIPTION IN THE SECOND WORLD WAR

The Promise of "No Conscription"—Two Official Statements, 1939

Prime Minister Mackenzie King, looking back to the crisis of 1917–18, was quick to promise that his government would never impose conscription. Indeed, King first issued this pledge in March 1939, six months before the war began. King's promise was reiterated by his Quebec cabinet ministers. Engaged in a political campaign to prevent Quebec Premier Maurice Duplessis from gaining re-election in October 1939 on a platform opposing Canada's participation in the war, the Quebec ministers all pledged to stand against the imposition of compulsory overseas service. Here are two official statements made by Prime Minister King and by Ernest Lapointe, the Minister of Justice and King's Quebec lieutenant:

> The present government believes that conscription of men for overseas service will not be a necessary or an effective step. No such measure will be introduced by the present administration. We have full faith in the readiness of Canadian men and women to put forward every effort in their power to defend free institutions, and in particular to resist aggression on the part of a tyrannical regime which aims at the domination of the world by force.

> W.L.M. King, House of Commons *Debates*, September 8, 1939, p. 36.

> ... The whole province of Quebec—and I speak with all the responsibility and all the solemnity I can give to my words—will never agree to accept compulsory service or conscription outside Canada. I will go farther than that: When I say the whole province

of Quebec I mean that I personally agree with them. I am authorized by my colleagues in the cabinet from the province of Quebec... to say that we will never agree to conscription and will never be members or supporters of a government that will try to enforce it. Is that clear enough?...

May I add that if my hon. friends and myself from Quebec were forced to leave the government I question whether anyone would be able to take our place. If my hon. friends in the far corner of the house opposite [the Social Credit group]; if the Ottawa *Citizen*, which just now is waging a campaign for conscription, think they are serving Canada by splitting it at the very outset of the war, then I say they are gravely and seriously wrong.

Ernest Lapointe, House of Commons *Debates*, September 9, 1939, pp. 65–68.

The Plebiscite of 1942—Arguments For—and Against—Conscription

After the Japanese attack on Pearl Harbor and the entry of the United States into the war in December 1941, the King Government came under greater public pressure to approve unlimited conscription for service abroad. The beleaguered Prime Minister decided to ask the Canadian public in a plebiscite to release the government from its pledge against overseas conscription—not with a view to introducing such a measure, but in the hope of diverting the pro-conscription movement. The holding of the plebiscite, however, only inflamed the bitter antagonism between English-and French-speaking Canadians and forced King to seek other methods of avoiding full conscription for overseas service. After the plebiscite, the Prime Minister issued his famous dictum: "not necessarily conscription, but conscription if necessary".

The plebiscite, held in April 1942, provided a graphic demonstration of Canadian public opinion on the conscription question. While 79 per cent of English-speaking Canada voted "Yes" and some 72 per cent of Quebeckers voted "No", many saw the plebiscite as merely a register of patriotism. The following campaign materials illustrate some of the main arguments used by each side in the plebiscite.

The Manifesto of the Ligue pour la défense du Canada, 1942

The reply to the plebiscite must be: *No*. Why? Because nobody asks to be freed of an obligation if he does not already have the temptation to violate it, and because, of all the promises he has made to the people of Canada, there remains only one which King would prefer not to be obliged to keep: the promise not to conscript men for overseas.

Now we do not want conscription for overseas:

—Because, in the opinion of our political and military leaders, Canada is more and more threatened by the enemy, and our chief and supreme duty is to defend our own country first;

—Because, according to the statistics given by the recruiting officials and the government itself, the voluntary system is still supplying, in February 1942, twice as many men as our different services can absorb;

—Because a small country, of eleven million inhabitants, which is claimed to be the granary and arsenal of the democracies and the allies, cannot be simultaneously an inexhaustible reservoir of fighting men;

—Because Canada has already reached and even passed the limit of her military effort, and because, in victory, we do not want to be in a worse situation than those defeated;

—Because, considering her population and financial resources, Canada has already given the allied cause as much, at least, as any of the great nations at war;

—Because none of these great nations has yet—so far as we know—undertaken to destroy its internal structure, and Canada, in no way responsible for the present war, has no right nor even duty to destroy itself.

So it is not as a province nor as an ethnic group that we take our stand. If we refuse to release the government from its pledges of 1939 and 1940, we act as Canadians, placing the interest of Canada above everything else....

L'Action nationale, January 1942, trans. in C.P. Stacey, *Historical Documents of Canada* (Toronto: Macmillan, 1972), Vol. V, pp. 631–633.

A Vote "Yes" Committee Advertisement, 1942

Canada's Wartime Contribution—Materials and Manpower, 1943

From the outset of the Second World War Mackenzie King's government emphasized Canada's contribution of "materials" over that of "manpower". By early 1943 Canada was almost fully mobilized and the war's demands were affecting almost everyone. Statistics concerning Canadian mobilization compared favourably with those in Britain and the United States, two countries with major world responsibilities in time of war. A statistical table in Defence Minister J.L. Ralston's files compared labour force distribution (figures in thousands of persons) in the three countries with interesting results:

Table 17-4   Comparative Labour Force Distribution

	Canada 31 Jan. 1943		USA 1 Jan. 1943		UK Mid–1942	
War Employment Industry	1 036	9.0%	8 700	6.4%	5 110	10.9%
Essential Non-Agricultural Ind.	1 089	9.5	7 700	5.7	4 566	9.7
Less Essential Non-Agricultural Ind.	1 317	11.4	26 600	19.7	7 000	14.9
Agriculture	1 020	8.9	8 900	6.6	1 107	2.4
TOTAL INDUSTRY	4 462	38.8	51 900	38.4	17 783	37.9
Armed Forces	778	6.8	10 800	8.0	4 500	9.6
Total Industry and Forces	5 240	45.6	62 700	46.4	22 283	47.5
Population	11 500		135 000		47 000	

P.A.C., J.L. Ralston Papers, Vol. 144, Table, Comparative Labour Force Distribution.

Responses of the Various Regions to Voluntary Recruitment

The statistics of voluntary enlistments for the various Canadian provinces provided one measure of regional responses to the war effort. While the figures are a crude approximation, and subject to some qualifications, they do offer a general indication of the different regional responses which can be compared to those of 1914–1918. It also should be noted that whereas in the First World War the Canadian Army was only 51.3 per cent Canadian-born, the figure rose in 1939–45 to 84.6 per cent.

Table 17-5   Voluntary Enlistments By Provinces, 1939–45*

Province	Population 1941†	Male Population 18–45 years	Voluntary Enlistments* (Three Services)
Prince Edward Island	95 047	19 000	8 939
Nova Scotia	577 962	123 000	56 797
New Brunswick	457 401	94 000	41 516
Quebec	3 331 882	699 000	131 618
Ontario	3 787 655	830 000	374 486
Manitoba	729 744	159 000	70 529
Saskatchewan	985 992	191 000	72 512
Alberta	796 169	178 000	71 634
British Columbia	817 861	181 000	85 350

* Voluntary enlistment figures calculated by subtracting totals for NRMA (conscripts) from total intake. The women's services (which did not exist in 1914–18) are not

included. Figures for the Territories are included under Saskatchewan and British Columbia.

† Population figures based on *Census*, 1941.

Table adapted from C.P. *Stacey, Canada and The Age of Conflict, Vol. 2: 1921–1948: The Mackenzie King Era.* Toronto: University of Toronto Press, 1981, p. 371; and Stacey, *Arms, Men, and Governments: The War Policies of Canada, 1939–1945.* Ottawa: Queen's Printer, 1970, Appendix R.

Settling the Crisis—Prime Minister King's Explanation of the Conscription Decision, 1944

By the autumn of 1944 a new crisis was looming on Parliament Hill. After surveying the heavy casualties on a visit to the front in North-west Europe, Colonel J.L. Ralston, the Minister of National Defence, had recommended that Canada's home defence troops (raised under the National Resources Mobilization Act of 1940) be sent overseas to meet a serious shortage of reinforcements. To avoid conscription King replaced Ralston with General A.G.L. McNaughton, the former Commander of the Canadian Army, and a firm believer in voluntary enlistment. When McNaughton tried—and failed— to convince NRMA home defence conscripts to volunteer for overseas service and rumors began circulating of a mass Cabinet resignation, the Prime Minister had run out of options.

In the critical days of November 1944, King was fearful of a conspiracy to topple his Liberal government. A memorandum of November 20th from the Army Council to McNaughton, pointing out the futility of the voluntary system and signs of restiveness among the B.C. Pacific Command, convinced the Prime Minister that the generals were in revolt and that the supremacy of civil control was in danger. In his Diary, King gave this account of the motives behind his change in policy issuing an Order-in-Council sending 16 000 NRMA men overseas:

ON THE MORNING of Wednesday, November 22, the Prime Minister was just beginning to prepare for the day's programme when General McNaughton telephoned with 'quite serious news'. 'That the Headquarters Staff here had all advised him that the voluntary system would not get the men. He had emphasized it was the most serious advice that could be tendered and he wished to have it in writing. Said he would come and see me as soon as he had the written statement. He expressed the opinion that it was like a blow in the stomach. He also said that he had the resignation of the Commander in Winnipeg. That if the Commanders, one after the other, began to resign, the whole military machine would run down, begin to disintegrate and there would be no controlling the situation.'

To this news, Mackenzie King reacted quickly. 'Instantly there came to my mind the statement I had made to Parliament in June as to the action the Government would necessarily take if we were agreed that the time had come when conscription was necessary. It is apparent to me that to whatever bad management this may have been due, we are faced with a real situation which has to be met and now there is no longer thought as to the nature of the military advice tendered, particularly by General McNaughton. And if so tendered by General McNaughton who has come into the

Government to try to save the situation, it will be my clear duty to agree to the passing of the order in council and go to Parliament and ask for a vote of confidence, instead of putting before the House the motion that I have drafted and intended to hand the Clerk. This really lifts an enormous burden from my mind as after yesterday's Council it was apparent to me that it was only a matter of days before there would be no Government in Canada and this in the middle of war with our men giving their lives at the front. A situation of civil war in Canada would be more likely to arise than would even be the case were we to attempt to enforce conscription.'

> J.W. Pickersgill and D.F. Forster, eds., *The Mackenzie King Record* (Toronto: University of Toronto Press, 1968), Vol. 2: 1944–1945, p. 229.

Three Viewpoints on the Conscription Policy, 1944 and 1945

King's dramatic about-face on conscription attracted its share of controversy. The Prime Minister was roundly denounced by ardent conscriptionists and harangued in the English-language press of his "half-way" measures. To many French-speaking Canadians, it seemed that King had done everything possible to avoid conscription and only given in as a last resort. Louis St. Laurent, the Minister of Justice and King's leading Quebec minister, "Chubby" Power, the Minister of Defence for Air who resigned on principle, and John Bracken, the Conservative Opposition leader, all voiced different views on King's manpower policy:

> I still felt and I hoped that compulsion might not be necessary to secure in time the required number of fit and trained men.... But no chance could be taken about it, and I decided that I would stand or fall with the Prime Minister. I may add that I have taken and I still take both comfort and pride in that decision....
>
> The all-important fact is that the reinforcements will be neither insufficient nor delayed....
>
> The will of the majority must be respected and it must prevail. But I trust that, here in Canada, the majority will always, as it is doing in this case, assert that will only after giving due consideration to the feelings and views of the minority and to the reasons for such feelings and views, and then only to the extent to which the majority is sincerely convinced that the general interests of the whole body politic require that it be thus asserted....
>
> Louis St. Laurent, House of Commons *Debates*, December 6, 1944, p. 6860.

Conscription as such, though I hate, does not worry me much any more. 'Freedom has shrieked' so many times since this war started, as one after another of our cherished principles, or prejudices, fell, or were cast aside on the plea of war expediency, that even the most Liberal mind has become warped. 'The end justifies the means' is the war credo. But to use a word of which the Prime Minister is so fond, the 'timing' was all wrong. To all intents and purposes as a nation we were out of the conscription morass, and suddenly we plunged right back into it with all its evil consequences to the country, when we might, I think, particularly at the early stages of the Ralston crisis, have avoided it. I don't think we could have held Ralston or Macdonald, but we could have carried on and had an election. Conscription was a long way from being anywhere necessary at this stage. It was certainly convenient to send the zombies,[1] but convenience should give way before future national interest.

Of course, we can argue interminably on the definition of 'necessity' and God knows we did. We will, in all probability, never agree on this, but 'absolute necessity' in the logical sense had disappeared. The war is won and none of the essential conditions which, to the ordinary Liberal mind might justify coercion, any longer exist....

I faced the prospect of a government defeat in the House, and a party minority in the country, and was not discouraged. I envisaged the prospect of one-third of our population uncooperative, with a deep sense of injury, and the prey to the worst elements amongst them, and worst of all, hating all other Canadians.

Don't forget, the chief was right when he hinted in a phrase which he stole from Brooke Claxton: 'Conscription in the mind of the French Canadian, as such, is not so bad. It is because it is considered to be a symbol of British domination that it is anathema. To them it means being forced to fight for the 'maudit Anglais.'

C.G. (Chubby) Power, in Norman Ward, ed., *A Party Politician: The Memoirs of Chubby Power* (Toronto: Macmillan, 1966), pp. 169–170.

Our position is that there is not proof that the reinforcement program was sufficient. Our position is that the Home Defense Army should be sent before they take any more of your boys. Our position is that for 27 years Mr. King has said to one section of Canada that never again will we send your boys in an expeditionary force and that you will not be required to bear your fair share of the load and of the sacrifice.

'Is it any wonder they did not enlist in equal degree?', asked Mr. Bracken. 'Is it any wonder that only 22 per cent of the eligible men of that Province responded while 44 per cent of your boys have gone?'

That is not our policy. Our policy is equal sacrifice in war as in peace....

John Bracken's speech at Clarksburg, Ontario, Feb. 3, 1945, reported in *The Globe and Mail*, February 5, 1945, p. 3.

CONFLICTING INTERPRETATIONS

Conscription emerged as a divisive question in Canada during each of the two World Wars. As a major political issue which aggravated strained relations between French and English Canadians, it has raised difficult questions and attracted its share of attention from Canadian historians. In both 1917 and 1942 to 1944 conscription assumed a character all its own as a political and almost a moral question. Did every citizen, regardless of race and language, owe military service to the state? In each of the wars, was conscription a military necessity? Should a nation conscript men if this action threatened to upset the tranquility, stability and social peace of the home front, something that the troops on the battlefield were ostensibly fighting to preserve? Was "equality of sacrifice", a gruesome phrase favoured by conscriptionists in

---

1. A term of derision applied to Canada's "home service" troops conscripted under the National Resources Mobilization Act of 1940 for the defence of Canada.

both wars, a reasonable conception in a nation so divided by race, religion and ethnicity? And how effectively did Canadian political leaders deal with the thorny questions brought about by wartime crisis?

THE CONSCRIPTION CRISIS OF 1917—A CLASH OF VIEWPOINTS

The Threat to Biracial Unity—The Liberal Interpretation

The great schism of 1917 has been subjected to considerable historical analysis. O.D. Skelton's 1921 biography of Sir Wilfrid Laurier set down a line of interpretation which was closely followed by subsequent "Liberal" historians. Essentially, the Liberal view lays the blame for the 1917–18 crisis on Robert Borden's conscription policy, which, it is argued, unnecessarily split Canada along racial lines and imperiled the national unity achieved in the Laurier era. In the official biography of Laurier, Skelton interpreted the introduction of conscription in 1917 as a direct threat to Canadian biracial unity undertaken by Borden and the Unionists for partisan political purposes.

By the end of 1916, the stock of the Borden government had fallen very low. That did not mean that the Liberal party gained in prestige all that its opponents lost. It did gain in some measure. The charges against the government brought a strong negative reaction in its favour.... Men looked back with regret to the firmness and sureness of administration in Sir Wilfrid's day. Yet against him one strong count lay. He was a French-Canadian, and French-Canadians, it was declared, were not doing their duty in the war. The resentment felt in other provinces, some of it spontaneous, some of it judiciously fostered as a means of diverting attention from the government's failures, was turned against Wilfrid Laurier. With the increasing strain of the war, from this time onward, the racial cleavage grew deeper, and thanks to the ceaseless slandering of opponents and the weak-kneedness of friends, the indiscriminate passion aroused in English-speaking Canada, flamed to the political hurt of the man [Laurier] whose whole life-work it had been to avert the situation that now arose....

* * * * *

Prime Minister Borden's return to Canada in May 1917 led directly into the conscription crisis. The government, influenced by a combination of motives that are still highly controversial, announced its decision to introduce a system of compulsory military service. Laurier immediately declared his intention of opposing conscription, which he did not feel was either necessary or expedient at this time. The decision, he believed, was a gamble; a gamble which you would certainly create havoc in the biracial community of Canada....

The public discussion had made it plain that the compulsory-service proposals would not have plain sailing. On May 29, Sir Robert Borden proposed to Sir Wilfrid the organization of a coalition government, with equal representation for the two parties, aside from his own premiership, with the enforcement of conscription as the basis, and with elections postponed if possible. Later he modified this proposal to provide for the passing of a Military Service Act with a pledge not to enforce it until a general election at which the coalition should seek a mandate from the people. The negotiations continued until June 6. While Sir Wilfrid felt that the offer of coalition after the determination, without a gesture or thought of consultation, of the all-important policy the coalition was to carry out, was insincere, while he felt that a proposal to have him join in carrying out a policy from which the premier would score all the political gain and he incur the political loss and the loss of principle, was preposterous, yet he was anxious to sound out every possibility of co-operation, and to consult his friends. When the prime minister made it clear that he would not agree to a coalition except on the acceptance of compulsory service, Sir Wilfrid definitely declined to take office. He could not take responsibility for a policy which he had no share in making, a policy devised to cover the failures of the government, and a policy for which he would have to bear the chief brunt of the attack. With the adoption of conscription, the chief argument for coalition had vanished; it was obvious to any one who faced realities that an election must be held, and that the country would be bitterly divided.

O.D. Skelton, ed., *Life and Letters of Sir Wilfrid Laurier* (Toronto: McClelland and Stewart, 1965), Vol. II, 1896–1919, pp. 166, 187 and 189. Originally published in 1921 by S.B. Gundy, Oxford University Press, Toronto.

The Necessity of Conscription—A Brief for the Defence

A.M. Willms was one of the first to attack the prevailing Liberal interpretation of the 1917 conscription crisis. In a 1956 essay in the *Canadian Historical Review*, Willms claimed that Borden and his allies underestimated its political appeal and based their position mainly on legitimate military considerations.

... The figures of actual reinforcements available are hard to find and can be deduced only approximately, yet it would seem that at the end of April Canada had reinforcements for approximately six months, under normal circumstances. There were, however, some complications with regard to existing reinforcements. Losses were heaviest in the infantry, but the men available were not all infantrymen. The voluntary enlistment of infantry in the first four months of 1917 was so low that normal wastage in Canada left very few men for overseas. Thus April and May produced a gross total of 3,000 infantry recruits who still had to be trained, with a percentage of wastage resulting. In these same two months Canadian battle casualties in France were 20,045. Approximately 10,000 of these casualties, or about 80 per cent of the wounded, could be expected to return to the trenches eventually, but the loss of men still exceeded the gain by over 7,000. Normal infantry re-inforcement requirements were 7,800 per month. At the rate of the 1917 spring enlistment it would take more than four months' enlistment to make up one normal month's loss—and enlistment had not yet reached its lowest point. These were the figures as they appeared at the time conscription was introduced. In actual fact the existing reinforcements together with the reduced voluntary enlistments were adequate for a year; a year that had, however, much lighter casualties than were expected....

It would appear that by the spring of 1917 the Canadian Government had exhausted the potentialities of voluntary recruiting. In the first three years of war the Government and the Militia Department had made many mistakes, some of them gross errors in tact and common sense. The greatest offender was the Minister of Militia, but the rest of the cabinet and especially the Prime Minister must share the blame. They had antagonized over-sensitive Quebec; they had authorized the recruiting of units and then broken them up; they had commissioned too many officers and lacked the courage to put them to work or discharge them; they had failed to recruit wealth as they recruited manpower and they had not stopped profiteering or patronage. By 1917 many of these mistakes had become obvious even to the Government, but the damage was done. The trend of enlistment showed a fairly steady downward curve from about 30,000 a month in January, 1916, to under 5,000 a month in April 1917....

It would appear, then, that the consequent Military Service Act could have played a dual role in the Government's plans; it did help to win an election and it was also required as a most necessary spur to the war effort. Probably both of these roles were incentives to its adoption, but it is quite evident that the political potential of this move, if it was actually recognized, was vastly underrated. In fact, when the Conservatives introduced the Military Service Bill they were not at all certain that it would get the support of the majority of the country. They were afraid to trust it to a referendum, for they saw what had happened in Australia. The restrictive franchise laws are probably the best indication of the Government's lack of confidence in conscription as a vote-getter....

Conscription was not introduced specifically to win an election; for at the time of its introduction a wartime election was no certainty. Many Conservatives were vigorously urging Borden to have the life of Parliament further extended.... Moreover, Sir Robert certainly did not see compulsory recruitment as a political stepping-stone, for having introduced the measure, he offered to resign in favour of anyone who could form a coalition government. In fact, there were men who apparently sacrificed all their political achievements in backing this measure, men such as Fielding and Graham. On the other hand, it seems no less apparent that the Borden Government did not envisage the long-term effects of conscription on the fortunes of the Conservative party. In any case one might doubt that such a realization would have swayed them from this measure. Assuredly, men on both sides of the question were most sincere.

There seems to be no proof, in short, that the leaders of the Conservative party saw conscription as a political expedient, while there is some evidence to show that the Military Service Act was introduced with fear as to its political effect. It is difficult to believe, however, that the Government was so far out of touch with popular feeling that it introduced the Act without at least a strong hope that the measure would improve the political outlook.

A.M. Willms, "Conscription 1917: A Brief for the Defence", *Canadian Historical Review*, Vol. XXXVII (December, 1956), pp. 343–346. Footnotes omitted.

Conscription in 1917—A Military Success

In the Liberal view of the 1917 crisis, conscription is often judged not only a political blunder but a military failure, since the Military Service Act raised only 83 000 men before the end of the war, and few of these saw active service in France. This interpretation, however, has been strongly challenged by a military historian, G.W.L. Nicholson, in the official history of the C.E.F.

It will be remembered that the objective set the Military Service Act was the raising of a maximum of 100,000 reinforcements. An Order in Council issued on 10 August 1918 took pains to define reinforcements as 'men ultimately selected and actually despatched for Overseas service'. The order specified that the Act should continue to operate until it had produced and *despatched* from Canada 'not less than one hundred thousand efficient soldiers for overseas service'. According to figures of the Department of Militia and Defence the number of draftees that proceeded overseas was 47,509, of whom 24,132 were taken on strength of units serving in France. There seems no doubt whatever that had the demand persisted, the objective of sending 100,000 draftees overseas would have been achieved. But the fighting in 1918 had not produced the heavy Canadian casualties that had been expected. Indeed it had become possible, in August of that year, to instruct registrars in all districts outside the province of Quebec to stop temporarily the call of men in order that Quebec might catch up. Then in October, when full scale call-ups were about to start again, the outbreak of the influenza epidemic halted proceedings in most districts.

It must be concluded that while the administration of the Military Service Act was often inefficient and attended by many gross malpractices, the Act itself was neither a failure nor ineffective. Statistics show that it did produce the military results which it was designed to produce.

G.W.L. Nicholson, *The Canadian Expeditionary Force, 1914-1919* (Ottawa: Queen's Printer, 1962), pp. 219 and 353.

Wartime Recruitment in French Canada—A Cause of the Crisis

Professor Desmond Morton, a military historian at the University of Toronto, has argued that military policy played a significant part in producing the crisis of 1917. If conscription had become necessary, it was, in his view, largely because of the failure of French Canadian recruitment policies since the time of Confederation.

... The voluntary nature of the Canadian war effort until 1917 was inevitable. The kind of foresight that could anticipate the dimensions of the eventual Canadian military commitment would not have been politically influential in 1914. However, the frenzied patriotism, frequently from non-combatants of both sexes, which accompanied voluntary recruiting, the head-counting and the comparisons, the contradictions about whether or not French Canada was playing her part, all tied in with the completely emotional debate about Ontario French-language schools, were what really drove Canada apart in 1915 and 1916. By 1917 conscription could seem to many in English-speaking Canada as a vengeance which, with its carefully adjusted exemptions, would fall exclusively on Quebec.

There was also division within French Canada between those who moved to Bourassa's position of standing apart from the war and those who, like Laurier, the higher clergy and even Talbot [and] Papineau, were terrified of the consequences for Quebec of isolating herself and who therefore struggled, by making speeches, trying to raise troops and, in the case of Papineau, actually fighting and dying, to prove that French Canada was really playing her part.

In all of this, the military institutions of Canada really gave very little help. By 1914 French Canadian representation in the Militia was a mere formality. Thanks to Sam Hughes, even the formality was forgotten when the moment of crisis came. A weak prime minister, a minister of militia who behaved like a stage generalissimo, a recruiting campaign based on confusion and deception, these were no instruments for persuading French Canadians to enlist in a war for which they had little basic inclination.

Desmond Morton, "French Canada and War, 1868–1917: The Military Background to the Conscription Crisis of 1917", in J.L. Granatstein and R.D. Cuff, eds., *War and Society in North America* (Toronto: Thomas Nelson and Sons, 1971), pp. 102–103. Footnotes deleted.

Conscription in the Prairie West—A Response of Race, Region or Class?

The traditional interpretation of the Conscription Crisis as a straight English-French "racial" confrontation has been questioned by historians of farm and labour movements in the West. In studies of organized labour in Western Canada, Martin Robin found "fierce opposition" to conscription from organized labour and parallel studies show evidence that farmer discontent was aggravated by Borden's conscription policy.

John Herd Thompson's recent study of the Prairie West in wartime examined the conscription controversy and pointed out that, although some labour and farm elements actively resisted the manpower policy, most English-speaking Westerners seemed to accept the military need for both conscription and a non-partisan Union government.

Evidence does exist to support the hypothesis that English Canadians in the West and elsewhere were not of uniform mind on the question of conscription, but it is important not to exaggerate the divisions which existed and thus obscure the essential validity of the original interpretation. When faced with the choice at the ballot boxes in the election of December, 1917, English-speaking Westerners chose to vote on the basis of race rather than region or class....

* * * * *

What did the overwhelming support of the West for Union government mean? Undoubtedly, many Westerners were motivated by a desire to enforce conscription when they cast ballots on December 17. To vote for a Laurier Liberal would have meant denying support to the CEF, 'an army which has brought forth praise from military experts of other countries' and was 'deserving of all the support which a grateful and resourceful people can give.' To reject conscription would not only have broken faith with Canada's soldiers, it would have allowed French Canadians to dictate the nation's position on the Great War. To the English-speaking West this was unacceptable and 'The Union Government was the only thing to save Canada...from the plots of the French Jesuit Priests.' By touching this raw racist nerve in the West, the Union government won the support of a substantial part of the West's English Protestant majority.

But there was more substance behind the West's support of Unionism than this determination to make Quebec 'do its duty' with regard to the Great War through the means of the Military Service Act. The idea of a non-partisan national government had strong appeal in Western Canada, both in war and peace, since it seemed to promise an end to a two-party system in which Central Canada was able to dominate both parties. The West had been skeptical that true Union government could come from men so identified with that party system, but the new Union platform and the ostentatious measures to control profits seemed to suggest that Borden and his colleagues sincerely intended to listen to the voice of the West....

John Herd Thompson, *The Harvests of War: The Prairie West, 1914–1918* (Toronto: McClelland and Stewart, 1979), pp. 116 and 144–145. Footnotes omitted.

CONSCRIPTION IN THE SECOND WORLD WAR—THE CRISIS REVISITED?

Mackenzie King and Conscription—R. MacGregor Dawson's Liberal Interpretation

Like the historical debate on the 1917 Conscription Crisis, the dominant interpretations of Mackenzie King's manpower policies were first staked out by contemporary partisans and the biographers of the principal combatants. King's famous Diary provided much of the raw material for the Liberal interpretation of conscription in the Second World War. As an official biographer of King, R. MacGregor Dawson drew heavily on the diary and advanced a defence of King's manpower policy.

> ... For him to be the one to introduce conscription with its coercion of Quebec and its possible destruction of Canadian unity was almost unthinkable; he would thereby be forsaking a fundamental tenet of the Liberal party, violating the great tradition of Laurier, and turning away from a policy which he as leader had faithfully upheld and which had in no small measure been the secret of his political success. So complete a reversal could be satisfactorily explained and extenuated in his own mind only by magnifying the importance and impact of the circumstances which had brought it about. No mere rift in the Cabinet, no simple failure of voluntary enlistment, no trifling military lapses would suffice. The cause must be commensurate with the effect. Having dwelt so often on the emergency which alone would change his policy, it must be an emergency in the real sense of the word. 'The soup he took was Elephant soup, and the fish he took was Whale.' King's mind was instinctively searching for the catastrophic, and it found a satisfactory answer in the threatened army collapse, the possible conflict between the military power and the Government, and the menace of civil war. Any departure, no matter how unprecedented, could find its justification in primary issues such as these, and he was therefore disposed to exaggerate and not minimize them.
>
> King's sudden decision on November 22, however, did not rest alone on real or imaginary difficulties with the army. The situation on the political front had been pushing him reluctantly to the same conclusion. If he continued to support the voluntary system the resignation of the conscriptionist Ministers would be almost inevitable, and the ensuing crisis would probably force him and the residue of the Cabinet out of office. What then would follow might be uncertain in detail, but he was bound to regard its general effect as calamitous. A coalition of Liberal conscriptionists with one or more of the Opposition parties would be formed; Quebec would be isolated, and a national schism on racial lines, already threatening, would be rapidly accelerated. The Liberal party would again be torn apart. The effects of King's unremitting efforts of twenty-five years to rebuild and maintain a united nation and a united party would be completely and perhaps irrevocably destroyed.
>
> R.M. Dawson, *The Conscription Crisis of 1944* (Toronto: University of Toronto Press, 1961), pp. 96–97.

Military Needs and Conscription—A Military Historian's Interpretation

Early studies of the manpower problem in World War II tended to approach conscription as an aspect of military administration. Looking at the 1942–45 period of crisis, General E.L.M. Burns argued that the creation of separate

"general service" and "home defence" armies contributed to the reinforcement problems, and by late 1944 made sending the NRMA men overseas a
virtual military necessity.

In November 1944, there occurred the manpower crisis, after the divisions of the
Canadian Army had been fighting on the average for eight and a half months....

The 16,000 men were required to make up the deficit in the anticipated requirements for infantry reinforcements for early 1945. At the time of the crisis, infantry
battalions were only five per cent under strength. As it turned out, the severity of the
fighting, and consequently the casualties for the remainder of the war against Germany,
had been over-estimated. In fact, only some 2,400 of the NRMA men reached the front
line units before the end of hostilities, or about seventy men per battalion, if they had
been evenly spread among all the thirty-five infantry battalions.

Yet, when the manpower crisis arose, and the responsible officers in the Army
declared that it would be impossible to reinforce the infantry of our five divisions
without using the NRMA men, there were 465,750 men and women in our Army. Of
these, 59,699 were NRMA and 16,178 were nurses of the medical corps or personnel
of Canadian Women's Army Corps, leaving 389,873 soldiers and officers available for
'general services'....

... The establishment strength of the Canadian divisions was about 85,000, and
that of the infantry battalions for which, as it was thought, reinforcements could not be
provided, was about 37,817.

These figures mean that with some 390,000 'general service' (GS) men on its
strength, the Army could not find the bodies to reinforce the 38,000 infantry.

This statement, unqualified, would imply that the Army's organization must have
been inefficient; that there were indeed too many men behind the fighting line and not
enough in it or available to go in it. But simple, unqualified statements regarding
complicated human activities are seldom accurate....

The manpower in the armed forces has to be divided between the fighting corps,
i.e., those whom prime function is to destroy enemy manpower and material, and the
supporting corps, which exist to do work which will enable the fighting corps to carry
out their task. During World War II there was a tendency common to the Canadian,
British and United States Armies for the supporting corps to increase relatively to the
fighting corps. To adapt Churchill's metaphor: the tail kept growing vastly, the teeth
little.

E.L.M. Burns, *Manpower in the Canadian Army* (Toronto: Clarke Irwin, 1956),
pp. 5–6. Footnotes omitted.

The Reinforcements Crisis Reconsidered—C.P. Stacey's Assessment

One of Canada's military historians, Colonel C.P. Stacey, has directly challenged the "Liberal" interpretation of Mackenzie King's response to the
manpower crisis. In his 1970 study, *Arms, Men and Governments*, he offered
a different look at King's approach to crisis management.

It can be and has been suggested that the removal of Ralston and the appointment of
McNaughton played a vital part in convincing the people of Quebec that the government was determined to go to the utmost length to avoid overseas conscription, and that
the final three-week attempt under McNaughton to make the voluntary system work
gave Quebec time to reconcile itself to what was becoming inevitable. But while this

may all be true it must be said that King's diary contains no indication whatever that any such ideas entered into his calculations. On the basis of his written record, it appears that he was moved entirely by a sudden access of fear for his own immediate personal and political position; that, acting purely on an intuition—and an intuition which was in fact baseless—he struck out, blindly but with deadly effect, at the nearest and the most prominent of those he thought his enemies. That the ultimate result in Quebec was probably favourable to him seems to have owed nothing to forethought on his own part. In spite of defective or non-existent strategy, he won a victory, thanks to remarkable good luck, to the ruthless excellence of his tactics—and to the fact that the man he victimized was entirely innocent of the sort of political ambition that was King's whole existence. . . .

* * * * *

The question inevitably arises in retrospect, how genuine was the emergency at this time when the reinforcement crisis arose in the autumn of 1944? Was it really necessary, at that late stage of the war, to resort to overseas conscription with all the domestic difficulties which that action entailed?

The basic facts were summarized in General Sansom's report.[2] It confirmed the statements made earlier by General Stuart that the reinforcement holdings at the outset of the Normandy campaign were adequate in overall numbers to meet the field requirements, 'but that they were not in the proper proportion of the arms in which the casualties occurred'. The report pointed out the fact, already noted, that an actual shortage of infantry reinforcements existed in the Canadian fighting units in North-West Europe 'during the period August to early October, 1944'. In other words the actual shortage *in units* had been overcome before the decision was taken to send N.R.M.A. soldiers overseas . . . .

Since the very worst aspect of the situation had been overcome without drawing upon the conscript soldiers, one is driven to inquire what the situation would have been if the conscripted men who were sent overseas had not been available. It is evident that in the actual circumstances of the first months of 1945 the field units could probably have been kept up to strength without these men, but the reinforcement pool behind them would have been dangerously low . . . .

Another point of importance might easily escape observation. As a result of the decision to send N.R.M.A. men overseas, the Army got far more men than the 16,000 conscripts who were authorized, or the 12,908 who were actually sent. As soon as the decision was announced on 23 November 1944, N.R.M.A. soldiers began to go active in large numbers, knowing that they were likely to be sent overseas anyway and presumably preferring to go as volunteers.

The fact is that the crisis late in 1944 concerned, not so much the actual existing situation, as the situation that would inevitably arise if the war with Germany went on and Canadian troops were involved in continuous heavy fighting. Had this been the case, far more than the 16,000 men authorized for dispatch overseas on 23 November would have been urgently required. It was the business of military planners and of the government to make provision, if not for the worst possible conditions imaginable, at any rate for normal conditions of warfare. As it turned out, the German war came to a

---

2. A comprehensive Department of National Defence report on the reinforcements situation overseas conducted by Lieut.-General E.W. Sansom and released March 29, 1945.

rapid conclusion, and during its final months the conditions, in terms of Canadian casualties, were exceptionally favourable... But in October or November 1944 nobody could possibly have forecast those conditions.

   C.P. Stacey, *Arms, Men and Governments: The War Policies of Canada 1939–1945* (Ottawa: Queen's Printer, 1970), pp. 459–60 and 481–2.

Mackenzie King's Conscription Policy—A Necessary Broken Promise?

York University historian J.L. Granatstein has offered a distinctly different view of King's political manoeuvres during the conscription crisis. In his major works Granatstein has argued that Mackenzie King's political skills and sensitivity to the Quebec problem kept Canada from splitting apart in the critical wartime period:

   ... there can be no doubt that the conscription crises of the Second World War were not as damaging as that of 1917.

   Why? It is too simplistic to say that the difference was Mackenzie King, but there is much truth in this. King was a political animal who lived and breathed politics. He was not above political trickery—as when he sprang a snap election on Manion in January, 1940. He was not above ruthlessness—as when he wielded the axe on Colonel Ralston on November 1, 1944. Clearly, King could be an unpleasant man. But he had a dream. He saw that unity between English and French Canada was essential, and he saw that conscription, involving as it did the deepest emotions of both nations, was one of the few issues that could sever relations between Quebec and the rest of the country.

   This was the greatest motivation for his wartime policy: prevent conscription to preserve unity. As a policy it was dangerous at times for King. If Meighen had been a more skillful politician, he might have been able to create a situation in which King would have had to step down in 1942. If Ralston had cared to campaign against King after the November, 1944 crisis, he probably could have brought down the Prime Minister. But Meighen was incapable of mounting a sustained attack and Ralston would not. King was saved in some respects by his opponents' weaknesses.

   King's policy was by no means a glamorous one. It looked, frankly, silly for a country to have two armies—one for fighting and one for home defence. It was wasteful in terms of equipment, money and training time. It took men out of industry and agriculture where they could be usefully employed and stuck them in NRMA battalions where they did nothing. But it was necessary, necessary for French Canada, necessary for Canada.

   And when King finally was forced out of his carefully constructed position by the 1944 conscription crisis, it was clear to Quebec that he had done all he could. He had done as much as any man could do. That is why the Liberals captured fifty-six of the sixty-five Quebec seats in the 1945 general election. King had remembered 1917 when the country was divided and when Quebec had gone virtually without representation in the cabinet. He had remembered, and even more, he had learned. . . .

   Quebec's attitude was certainly not an idealistic one. It was narrow, selfish, isolationist. But it existed. So long as it was there, all that the government could do was try to 'educate' Quebec—and English Canada. . . .

   In fact, he was strikingly successful. In the Great War, probably no more than 35,000 French Canadians served in the armed forces. Between 1939 and 1945, however, between three and four times that number saw service. French Canadians in large numbers had come to realize that there was no security for Canada unless there was peace in the world. . . .

. . . [S]ometimes compromise and delay, hesitation and caution are better than rigidly held positions. Expediency is a nasty word that is sometimes thrown at politicians when they hedge their bets or try to compromise. But sometimes it is better to practice expediency than to follow the wrong policy.

J.L. Granatstein, *Conscription in the Second World War 1939–1945: A Study in Political Management* (Toronto: Ryerson Press, 1969), pp. 73–76.

The Decision to Impose Overseas Conscription—A Product of Political Expediency and Imagined Conspiracies

The theory of a "generals' revolt" concocted by Mackenzie King and supported by Defence Minister McNaughton has stirred much controversy among historians. It was a story popularized by the late Bruce Hutchison, one of King's early biographers, and repeated in Dawson's short study of the 1944 Conscription crisis. Recently, however, historians of the King period have come to regard the "conspiracy" theory as fanciful. In his biography of General George Pearkes, Reginald H. Roy explained some of the reasons why.

In a sense, Pearkes had the same opinion of the N.R.M.A. soldiers as McNaughton, only at a different time. It was really not until the spring of 1944 that Pearkes began to realize the degree of resistance towards volunteering for overseas service that existed. The summer-long propaganda campaign further convinced him that if reinforcements for overseas were to be maintained at a rate the Chief of the General Staff felt necessary, then the N.R.M.A. men must be conscripted. He had reached that conclusion several weeks before McNaughton became minister, and it would be fair to estimate that almost every other senior officer in Canada felt the same. He did not, as it sometimes intimated, attempt to help sabotage McNaughton's plan by calling together his officers rather late at a moment when time was of the essence. Train schedules, the distances involved, and the unpredictable flying weather in British Columbia in November were such that he could not have collected together 130 senior officers faster than he did. Pearkes and others, at the time and later, were accused of giving the authorities in Ottawa a false impression when they suggested there would be no trouble once conscription was invoked. Officers all across Canada had heard for months if not years the same refrain from the N.R.M.A. soldiers—'if the government really wants us, they must tell us by ordering us overseas.' For many this was merely a convenient shield used as the ultimate argument against serving overseas, but certainly it had been used long enough and widely enough for it to gain credence. At that, such trouble as did arise in British Columbia came in large measure as a result of political decisions in Ottawa. It was McNaughton's decision to investigate the so-called 'press conference' in Vancouver which resulted in senior officers being absent from their units at a critical time. It was Mackenzie King's decision to switch suddenly from a voluntary to a conscription policy, so sudden a decision indeed that in numerous instances the N.R.M.A. soldiers in barracks heard about it over the radio even before their own officers. . . .

Reginald H. Roy, *For Most Conspicuous Bravery: A Biography of Major-General George R. Pearkes, V.C., Through Two World Wars* (Vancouver: UBC Press, 1977, pp. 232–233.

CONSCRIPTION IN THE TWO WORLD WARS—WHAT WERE THE LESSONS?

A Legacy of Broken Promises—J.L. Granatstein's Thesis

Only recently have Canadian military and political historians begun to speculate and comment on the lessons that were learned from Canada's two conscription crises. Much of the "broken promises" thesis has been advanced in a number of studies by J.L. Granatstein. Conscription, according to Granatstein, has been a "cursed" question which colours all memories and interpretations of Canada's role in the two World Wars.

Lamentably, inescapably, one must conclude from Canada's experience with conscription that history repeats itself. Always when conscription has been seriously mooted or implemented, military necessity has been cited as the overriding reason; and yet conscription has never produced any military results of significance. In each case compulsion has been introduced to the accompaniment of broken promises and broken pledges that instantly alienated a large part of the population. In each case, except one, English Canada's pressures for a greater military effort, occasionally carefully thought out but often little more than gut responses to sometimes misperceived needs, ran headlong into the resistance of French Canada, into the refusal of Quebec to be bullied into fighting someone else's war. . . .

The political leaders in both wars . . . had to break promises. Again and again through the first two years of the war, Sir Robert Borden expressed his faith in the voluntary system and his assurances that conscription would not be implemented. Those promises were broken in May 1917. And such was the impact of the Military Service Act on Canadian politics that Mackenzie King made his first promise against conscription five months before war broke out. He and his leading ministers repeated the pledges time and again in the months that followed. When in 1942 King called a plebiscite and then moved to pass Bill 80, Quebec came to the realization that King's promises had little more value than those Borden had made 25 years before. The 1944 crisis merely confirmed the inevitable, simply demonstrating that English Canada, no matter who led it, would insist on its way. . . .

To be fair, by the Second World War many Canadians had learned something from the experience of 1917–18. Men such as Dr. Manion took their political lives in their hands and opposed conscription; some, like Manion, paid a heavy price. Few politicians wanted another race war in Canada, and until the crisis of 1944, except for the brief Meighen interlude, the Conservative Party behaved cautiously. Indeed much of its effort was devoted to manoeuvering so that the Liberals this time would have to assume responsibility for imposing conscription. Mackenzie King's great skill at squaring the circle helped him avoid that burden and its costs until late 1944, and when he was finally forced to assume it in a partial way, it was to the cheers of the Tories and with their cries for more draconian measures loud in the air. King had broken his promises, but he had done so in a fashion that did not completely alienate French Canada. That was the difference between King and Borden, between conscription 1917 and conscription 1944. . . .

Above all, the government of King had learned something from the mistakes of 1917. The propaganda was different in tone, far more nationalist than in 1914–18. The organization of the economy and of the war effort was infinitely better, and even the Army was marginally more sympathetic to French Canada and aware of the problems than had been the case in the Great War. And King himself, fully aware that Canada could founder on the rock of conscription, paid full attention to the situation....

The evidence then seems clear. Conscription may theoretically be the best, the fairest, and the most expeditious way to raise an army; it may equalize the demands and equalize the suffering far better than the hazards of voluntarism. All this may be so, but not in Canada. Here conscription has divided French-speaking Canadians from their compatriots. Here conscription has created chaos, shattering the political system and fostering mistrust and division in the country. And here conscription has had scant military impact, certainly not enough to provide a *post facto* justification for it. Conscription has simply not worked in Canada, and there seems no reason to believe that it ever will.

> J.L. Granatstein and J.M. Hitsman, *Broken Promises: A History of Conscription in Canada* (Toronto: Oxford University Press, 1977), pp. 264, and 276–9.

Conscription in 1917 and 1944—Political Responses to Military Necessities

In a recent synthesis of Canada's war experiences, *Canada and War* (1981), Desmond Morton has countered the Granatstein thesis. As a military historian, he treated the conscription crises as episodes in Canada's evolving military role in war and peace. To Morton, conscription was essentially an "anticlimactic issue".

When the prime minister (Sir Robert Borden) returned to Ottawa (in the spring of 1917) to announce his commitment to conscription, British officials could smugly conclude that their efforts had succeeded. In fact, Borden believed that conscription was now the price Canada must pay for a new and more dignified status in the world. Not only victory but Canadian autonomy were at stake, he told Parliament on May 18....

Like so many of the disputes between French and English in Canada, the conscription debate was a dialogue of the deaf. Borden dismissed Bourassa as a narrow-minded provincialist, fanning grievances which were petty by the scale of the world conflict. To Bourassa, Borden was an imperialist, pouring out Canadian money and lives at England's command. Both, in fact, were nationalists, pursuing utterly divergent versions of Canada's destiny that would, ironically, intersect in the postwar world.... Defying the stereotype of Canadians as a cold and materialistic people, Borden sought a higher national destiny and his reputation would perish in the attempt.

On the means, he was flexible. To the dismay of some Tory colleagues, Borden set out at once to forge a national coalition with Laurier. The Liberal leader refused. Borden offered to delay conscription until a national government had won a general election. Again Laurier refused. The Liberal leader was angry that Borden had announced conscription before opening coalition negotiations. Laurier also believed that his party would stick with him.... Above all, Laurier feared that if he went with Borden he would again be humiliated in his own province by Bourassa....

* * * * *

...[By the late autumn of 1944] the prime minister [Mackenzie King] was almost beside himself. The war was virtually over and won. It seemed incredible to him that an army of half a million men, half of them overseas, could not find 15,000 infantry reinforcements. Why had he been assured repeatedly by Ralston, Stuart, Crerar and other generals that each expansion of the army would not lead to conscription? Surely there must be some way out. . . .

King's response to the crisis was agile and desperate. His sense of outrage was understandable. He had triumphantly kept his Liberal party united to the eve of victory. He had placated pro-conscriptionists and anti-conscriptionists. He had bowed to the right wing in 1943 and to the left in 1944. Now his political resourcefulness faced an ultimate test. . . .

[Defence Minister] McNaughton's message [reporting a breakdown in the military system] was alarmist to the point of being unbalanced. Officers who resigned could be replaced. [Lt. General J.C.] Murchie, a senior officer at Army Headquarters, had given an opinion which, on the evidence available at the time and since, was irrefutable, but it was no act of mutiny for a soldier to give his honest views. Yet the notion of a 'generals' revolt' was a godsend to King. It fitted his well-developed suspicion of soldiers. It would frighten his more timid anti-conscriptionist colleagues and switch their votes. Indeed, he had probably already come to his own conclusion that the NRMA men must go.

On the afternoon of November 22, instead of making a triumphal first appearance in the House of Commons, it was McNaughton's melancholy chore to go to the bar of the House (he was and would remain unelected) to announce that by order-in-council, the government proposed to send 16,000 NRMA men overseas. . . .

In the former war, conscription had been a desperate, divisive and, ultimately, an anticlimactic issue. So it proved again, though in a more muted form. . . .

Desmond Morton, *Canada and War: A Military and Political History* (Toronto: Butterworths, 1981), pp. 71–72 and 144, 145–46 and 147.

A Guide to Further Reading

1. Overviews

Eayrs, James, *In Defence of Canada, Vols. I and II*. Toronto: University of Toronto Press, 1964 and 1965.

Graham, Roger, *Arthur Meighen, Vol. I: The Door of Opportunity and Vol. III: No Surrender*. Toronto: Clarke Irwin, 1960 and 1965.

Granatstein, J.L., "That Cursed Question: Conscription in the Two World Wars", *Quarterly of Canadian Studies*, Vol. 5, No. 1 (1978), pp. 16–22.

_____and R.D. Cuff, eds., *War and Society in North America*. Toronto: Thomas Nelson and Sons, 1971.

_____ and J.M. Hitsman, *Broken Promises: A History of Conscription in Canada*. Toronto: Oxford University Press, 1977.

Morton, Desmond, *Canada and War: A Military and Political History*. Toronto: Butterworths, 1981.

Stacey, C.P., "Nationality: The Experience of Canada", Canadian Historical Association *Annual Report, 1967*. Ottawa: C.H.A., 1967, pp. 10–19.

Wade, Mason, *The French Canadians 1760–1945*. Toronto: Macmillan, 1956.

2. Specialized Studies

The Conscription Crisis of 1917

Armstrong, Elizabeth, *The Crisis of Quebec, 1914–1918*. Toronto: McClelland and Stewart, 1974.

Berger, Carl, *The Sense of Power: Studies in the Ideas of Canadian Imperialism, 1867–1914.* Toronto: University of Toronto Press, 1970.

_____, ed., *Conscription 1917.* Toronto: University of Toronto Press, 1968.

Borden, Henry, ed., *Robert Laird Borden: His Memoirs.* 2 vols. Toronto: McClelland and Stewart, 1969.

Bray, R. Matthew, "'Fighting as an Ally': The English-Canadian Patriotic Response to the Great War", *The Canadian Historical Review*, Vol. LXI, No. 2 (June, 1980), pp. 141–168.

Brown, Robert Craig, *Robert Laird Borden: A Biography, Vol. II: 1914–1937.* Toronto: Macmillan, 1980.

_____ and Ramsay Cook, *Canada, 1896–1921: A Nation Transformed.* Toronto: McClelland and Stewart, 1974.

Durocher, René, "Henri Bourassa, Les Evêques et la guerre de 1914–1918", Canadian Historical Association, *Historical Papers 1971.* Ottawa: C.H.A., 1971.

Frost, Leslie M., *Fighting Men.* Toronto: Clarke Irwin, 1967.

Hyatt, A.M.J., "Sir Arthur Currie and Conscription", *Canadian Historical Review*, Vol. L (September, 1969), pp. 285–296.

Levitt, Joseph, ed., *Henri Bourassa on Imperialism and Bi-culturalism, 1900–1918.* Toronto: Copp Clark, 1970.

Morton, Desmond, "French Canada and War, 1868–1917: The Military Background to the Conscription Crisis of 1917", in Granatstein and Cuff, eds., *War and Society in North America*, pp. 84–103.

Nicholson, G.W.L., *The Canadian Expeditionary Force, 1914–1919.* Ottawa: Queen's Printer, 1962.

Prang, Margaret, *N. W. Rowell: Ontario Nationalist.* Toronto: University of Toronto Press, 1975.

Read, Daphne, ed., *The Great War and Canadian Society: An Oral History.* Toronto: New Hogtown Press, 1975.

Skelton, O.D., ed., *Life and Letters of Sir Wilfrid Laurier, Vol. II: 1896–1919.* Toronto: McClelland and Stewart, 1965.

Stacey, C.P., *Canada and the Age of Conflict, Vol. I: 1867–1921.* Toronto: University of Toronto Press, 1977.

Swettenham, John, *To Seize the Victory.* Toronto: Ryerson Press, 1965.

Thompson, John Herd, *The Harvests of War: The Prairie West, 1914–1918.* Toronto: McClelland and Stewart, 1979.

Willms, A.M., "Conscription 1917: A Brief for the Defence", *Canadian Historical Review*, Vol. XXXVII (December, 1956), pp. 338–351.

Wilson, Barbara, ed., *Ontario and the First World War.* Toronto: University of Toronto Press, 1977.

Young, W.D., "Conscription, Rural Depopulation and the Farmers of Ontario, 1917–1919", *Canadian Historical Review*, Vol. LIII (September, 1972).

Conscription in the Second World War

Burns, E.M.L., *Manpower in the Canadian Army.* Toronto: Clarke Irwin, 1956.

Chisholm, Elspeth, "'Never: Ernest Lapointe and Conscription, 1935–1944", *Canada: An Historical Magazine.* Two Parts. Vol. 3, Nos. 3 and 4 (March and June, 1976).

Dawson, R. MacGregor, *The Conscription Crisis of 1944.* Toronto: University of Toronto Press, 1961.

Douglas W.A.B. and Brereton Greenhous, *Out of the Shadows: Canada in the Second World War.* Toronto: Oxford University Press, 1977.

Eayrs, James, *The Art of the Possible.* Toronto: University of Toronto Press, 1961.

Granatstein, J.L., *Canada's War: The Politics of the Mackenzie King Government, 1939–1945*. Toronto: Oxford University Press, 1975.

———, *Conscription in the Second World War, 1939–1945*. Toronto: Ryerson Press, 1969.

———, *The Politics of Survival: The Conservative Party of Canada, 1939–1945*. Toronto: University of Toronto Press, 1967.

Kendle, John, *John Bracken: A Political Biography*. Toronto: University of Toronto Press, 1979.

Keyserlingk, Robert H., "The Canadian Government's Attitude to Germans and German Canadians in World War Two", *Canadian Ethnic Studies*, Vol. XVI, No. 1 (1984), pp. 16–28.

Pickersgill, J.W., *The Mackenzie King Record, Vol. I: 1939–44; Vol. II: 1944–45*. Toronto: University of Toronto Press, 1960 and 1968.

Pierson, Ruth Roach, "'Jill Canuck': CWAC of All Trades, But No Pistol Packing Momma", Canadian Historical Association *Historical Papers 1978*. Ottawa: C.H.A., 1978, pp. 106–132.

Roy, Reginald H., *For Most Conspicuous Bravery: A Biography of Major-General George R. Pearkes*. Vancouver: UBC Press, 1977.

Stacey, C.P., *Arms, Men and Governments: The War Policies of Canada 1939–1945*. Ottawa: Queen's Printer, 1970.

———, *Six Years of War*. 3 vols. Ottawa: Queen's Printer, 1955.

Stratford, Philip, ed., *Andrew Laurendeau: Witness for Quebec*. Toronto: Macmillan, 1973.

Swettenham, John, *McNaughton, Vol. III: 1944–1966*. Toronto: Ryerson Press, 1969.

Ward, Norman, ed., *A Party Politician: The Memoirs of Chubby Power*. Toronto: Macmillan, 1966.

18

CANADIAN-AMERICAN RELATIONS, 1945–1980s

Harmonious Partnership or Dependent Relationship?

It is impossible to discuss Canada's foreign policy since the Second World War without touching on the question of Canada's relations with the United States. Like Britain, the United States and most of the Western world, Canada faced the test of world conflict from 1939 to 1945, engaged in rearmament to meet apparent Soviet and Chinese threats in the early 1950s, and participated in the continuing post-war struggle to secure a more peaceful and stable world order. This period also saw the transformation of Canada from a self-governing Dominion in the British Commonwealth into more of a North American nation, less closely tied to Britain. The economic power, military might and sizeable population of the United States have weighed heavily in the shaping of Canadian foreign policy. This American presence in North America has afforded Canada military security and considerable domestic prosperity, but, at times, has placed the country in a vulnerable, almost precarious, position. As Prime Minister Pierre Trudeau aptly quipped to Washington's National Press Club in March of 1969: "Living next to you is in some ways like sleeping with an elephant. No matter how friendly and even-tempered is the beast, one is affected by every twitch and grunt."

Like Canadian and American policy makers, interpreters of Canadian-American relations since 1945 have engaged in a continuing debate over the fundamental nature of this relationship. Staunch defenders of the postwar diplomatic, economic and military record have touted Canada's relationship with the United States as a model of "harmonious partnership"—one based, for the most part, on mutual co-operation, and setting high standards of enlightened international relations. Critics of Canadian foreign policy, however, argue that Canada's postwar policies have reduced the nation virtually to the status of a military, economic and political satellite in a dependent relationship with the United States. In exploring the broad issues in this historical debate, we will focus on three areas in Canada-U.S. foreign relations since 1945: perceptions of, and approaches to, the Cold War (1945–53); the defence and diplomatic crises of the Diefenbaker-Pearson years (1957–67); and the changing bilateral relationship in the Trudeau era (1968–84).

Close economic and military association with the United States is largely a legacy of the Second World War. The roots of growing interdependence in North America, however, can be found in the Depression years. The onset of the Great Depression in 1929 found Canada and the U.S., like other countries, unprepared. In an effort to allay the economic disaster, Prime Minister R.B. Bennett initiated trade talks which eventually led to mutual tariff reductions and closer economic cooperation between the two countries. The influence of American cultural phenomena, from popular radio programmes to Hollywood movies to big-league baseball contributed to a growing similarity of cultural tastes on either side of the border. Furthermore, the initial trade dealings of the mid-1930s both foreshadowed and smoothed the way for Mackenzie King's wartime military and economic agreements: the Ogdensburg Agreement (1940) and the Hyde Park Declaration (1941).

As continental neighbours sharing a tradition of friendship, similar political ideologies and comparable economic systems, Canadian and U.S. policymakers since the war have sought to fashion a "special relationship" unique in international affairs. King's wartime agreements, which established a permanent Joint Board on Defence and provided for cooperative defence production, served as precursors of further Canada-U.S. collaboration in the Cold War years. From the late 1940s to the early 1960s, Canada and the United States acted as friendly allies and both sought to establish a Western system of collective security against the threat of Soviet post-war expansionism and the spectre of nuclear war. Fears of Soviet communist aggression in eastern Europe and Asia and a firm belief in America's role as the defender of the Western ("free") world led Canadian policy-makers to assist in the formation of the United Nations system in 1945, play an active part in the founding in 1949 of the North Atlantic Treaty Organization (NATO), and to join in the establishment nine years later of the North American Air Defence (NORAD) Command, a common nuclear defence system for North America. In addition to entering into the Western system of alliances, Canada also undertook military commitments in support of American and Western post-war policies, such as joining the United Nations operation in Korea (1950–53) and finally accepting, in 1963, nuclear warheads for Canadian aircraft and BOMARC missiles.

Canada gained world-wide recognition in the 1950s and early 1960s as a UN peacekeeper in Egypt, Lebanon and other world trouble spots, and its relations with the U.S. seemed to serve as a model of harmonious international cooperation. In the tense atmosphere of the Cold War years, and later during the Vietnam War, Ottawa accepted Washington's pre-eminence in the Western alliance, and most bilateral issues were settled by quiet accommodation. Although Canadian policy-makers often sounded more moralistic than their American counterparts, the "special relationship" followed the principles of "Quiet Diplomacy", a mode of conduct developed by U.S. and Canadian officials and enshrined in the famous Merchant-Heeney Report of 1965. There were periodic disagreements between Ottawa and Washington, but the practice of quiet, conciliatory diplomacy helped to ensure that the two partners publicly supported each other's policies, and assiduously avoided public confrontations, expressing any policy disagreements in private discussion behind the scenes.

Yet the North American relationship was not always a model of harmony. The Canadian government of John G. Diefenbaker (1958–63), for example, repeatedly resisted public inducements from the Kennedy administration to join the Organization of American States (OAS), an alliance of U.S.-aligned states in the Americas. In the Cuban Missile Crisis of October 1962, Diefenbaker refused to endorse President Kennedy's actions and publicly chastised Washington for its unwillingness to consult with Canada, a continental defence partner. America's protracted involvement in Indochina (the Vietnam War) and popular resistance to the growing U.S. economic presence in Canada contributed in the late 1960s to public questioning of Ottawa's ability to pursue a foreign policy independent of Washington. Throughout the 1970s a series of vexing political, economic and environmental issues, such as proposed continental energy deals, the "Nixon Doctrine" of 1971, Canadian foreign investment restrictions, acid rain, and the 1980 National Energy Program emerged as major irritants in bilateral relations. Sharp policy differences such as these produced a variety of responses from the governments of Pierre Trudeau (1968–79 and 1980–84), ranging from "quiet" to "public" diplomacy, but no panacea for reducing Canada's alleged "vulnerability" to the United States.

Events in Canadian-American relations from 1945 to the present day raise a host of critical questions concerning the nature of the continental relationship. In joining the United States in the formation and support of the Western system of alliance since 1945, were Canadian prime ministers like Mackenzie King and Louis St. Laurent pursuing a peaceful, stable global order, toeing the Washington line, or pragmatically looking after Canada's own security and economic needs? During the critical Diefenbaker-Pearson years, was Canada's role that of a "middle power" or a "satellite" of the United States? Was the Canadian-American relationship in the Trudeau era marked by a mutual acceptance of national interests or by severe constraints on Canada's ability to pursue foreign policies independent of the U.S.? Overall, have Canada's relations with the U.S. over the last 40 years produced a dependent relationship or a model of harmonious partnership?

SELECTED CONTEMPORARY SOURCES

PERCEPTIONS OF—AND APPROACHES TO—THE COLD WAR— SEARCHING FOR WORLD ORDER OR FOLLOWING AMERICAN LEADERSHIP?

The "Cold War" which developed after 1945 destroyed the wartime alliance between the Soviet Union and the Western allies. With the defeat of Hitler and Nazism in Europe, there emerged a new state of tension between the East and the West. The Soviet occupation and advances in eastern Europe from 1945 to 1947 raised widespread fears of Soviet expansion in the United States and Canada. The spread of communism was seen in both countries as a dire threat to all "free" political and economic systems in the Western world. Canada and the U.S., with most of the Western powers, sought in the early Cold War years to create collective security in a more stable, peaceful world order to counter the Soviet threat.

The foreign policies pursued by Canada and the U.S. in the early Cold War years were strongly influenced by the images of the Soviet Union held by key policy-makers in Washington and Ottawa. While leading American policy-makers from President Harry Truman to Secretary of State Dean Acheson to senior diplomat George F. Kennan differed in their approaches to the Cold War, most Washington officials saw the Soviet Union as an aggressive, expansionist power driven by its communist ideology. It was assumed that Canada, as a staunch North American ally, shared the prevailing American Cold War view and would support U.S. postwar policies in the interests of Western security.

Louis St. Laurent on the NATO Alliance, 1948—A Reflection of U.S. Cold War Views?

The concept of a North Atlantic defence alliance, first advocated in August 1947 by Escott Reid and Lester B. Pearson in Canada's Department of External Affairs, won strong support in Washington. From the opening of negotiations in March 1948 until the signing of the North Atlantic treaty in April 1949, the United States joined with Britain and the other Western allies in working to create a "collective security" alliance for the common defence of Europe against Soviet expansionism. In making the case for NATO before the House of Commons in April 1948, Canada's Minister of External Affairs, Louis St. Laurent, summed up the official Canadian view.

> One thing we must constantly keep in mind as we approach this fateful decision is that the western European democracies are not beggars asking for our charity. They are allies whose assistance we need in order to be able successfully to defend ourselves and our beliefs. Canada and the United States need the assistance of the western European democracies just as they need ours. The spread of aggressive communist despotism over western Europe would ultimately almost certainly mean for us war, and war on most unfavourable terms. It is in our national interest to see to it that the flood of communist expansion is held back.

Our foreign policy today must, therefore, I suggest, be based on a recognition of the fact that totalitarian communist aggression, endangers the freedom and peace of every democratic country, including Canada. On this basis and pending the strengthening of the United Nations, we should be willing to associate ourselves with other free states in any appropriate collective security arrangements which may be worked out under articles 51 or 52 of the charter.

In the circumstances of the present the organization of collective defence in this way is the most effective guarantee of peace. The pursuit of this course, steadfastly, unprovocatively, and constructively is our best hope for disproving the gloomy predictions of inevitable war.

House of Commons *Debates*, April 29, 1948, pp. 3449–3450.

Canadian Images of Soviet Intentions and Conduct—A Department of External Affairs View, 1947

In the years 1946–47, with the Cold War over Soviet expansion into eastern Europe at its height, Canada's Department of External Affairs gave attention systematically to the question of Soviet intentions and conduct. A top-secret memorandum, prepared by Assistant Under-Secretary of State Escott Reid between February and August of 1947 and based on an earlier draft by senior diplomat Charles Ritchie, set out a cogent analysis of Soviet objectives and revealed some difference of opinion between External Affairs officials in Ottawa and their counterparts in Washington:

[In a section entitled "The Source of Conflict" Escott] Reid said that events over the previous two years revealed that the Soviet strategy was to consolidate already acquired positions, to probe for weak spots and to undermine and divide the Western powers. The 'governing class' of that country was 'anxious to maintain the existing system in the areas now under Soviet political control,' and hence 'to expand the defence area of that system.' . . .

But the Soviet Union alone was not perceived by Reid to be *the* source of conflict.

'It is obvious,' he argued, 'that both the Soviet Union and the United States are expanding powers.' The USSR had annexed a number of areas, including Estonia, Latvia, Lithuania, eastern Poland, and the Kurile Islands, and were attempting to establish sole influence over the Eastern European countries, northern Korea, and other areas. While the United States had not actually annexed territory, 'it occupies Japan, dominates Greece, and it has developed Arctic defences from Alaska to Greenland.' Like the Soviet Union, 'the United States is anxious to maintain the existing system of democratic values and of free enterprise in the areas under United States political control, and this involved a desire to expand the defence area of that system.' These objectives, as with those of the USSR, are based on the American desire to retain its way of life and the belief that the capitalist system is superior. . . . The mutual desire to expand brings the two powers into conflict 'in all the borderlands between their present defence areas from Korea to Finland.' . . .

* * * * *

In the concluding section of his memorandum Reid summarized the overall argument:

. . . the Western powers should be able to prevent war within the next ten years, if, by the pursuit of adequate political, economic and social policies, they remain stronger than the Soviet Union, and if at the same time they pursue a firm, patient and fair-minded policy towards the Soviet Union which would not arouse fear in the Soviet Union of Western aggression and thus goad the Soviet Union into war.

Department of External Affairs Memorandum, File 52-F(S), "The United States and the Soviet Union: A Study of the Possibility of War and Some of the Implications for Canadian Policy", August 20, 1947, as summarized in Don Page and Don Munton, "Canadian Images of the Cold War 1946–7", *International Journal*, Vol. XXXII (Summer, 1977), pp. 585–6, 589–91 and 597.

Canada's Response to the Dollar Crisis of 1947—A Policy of Economic Self-Interest?

Canadian policy-makers in the early Cold War years pursued other postwar aims besides collective security for the Western world. Canada's diplomatic efforts to ease the severe postwar Dollar Crisis and to secure economic benefits from the U.S. Marshall Plan seemed to indicate that economic self-interest prevailed, at least on certain issues.

In the summer of 1947 Canada faced a worsening financial crisis caused by a critical shortage of American dollars. In private meetings with U.S. officials, Canadian policy-makers sought help through a variety of means, including a five-hundred-million-dollar U.S. loan and more stringent import restrictions on American-produced goods. Ottawa officials even sought possible off-shore procurements flowing from the Marshall Plan, a bold and far-reaching U.S. economic aid programme proposed by Secretary of State George C. Marshall in June 1947 and designed principally to provide for the post-war rehabilitation of Britain and Europe. A confidential report composed by Andrew B. Foster of the U.S. State Department in September 1947 described the vigorous efforts of Clifford Clark, the Canadian Deputy Minister of Finance, and Hume Wrong, Canada's Ambassador to Washington, which eventually proved successful in easing the crisis and winning a share of offshore purchases under the Marshall Plan.

... [Mr. Clifford] Clark [who was accompanied by Hume Wrong] emphasized the gravity of the Canadian problem.... He wanted to know whether we could give him any indication whether Canada was being included in our framing of the Marshall plan (not in terms of direct aid but as a partner in the reconstruction of the U.K. and western Europe). If Canada was included in our thinking, and he appreciated that we couldn't say what Congress may do, his Government would apply the least drastic remedies to the present emergency and would declare them to be temporary. But if Canada was not included and if it felt that a 'multilateral' world of comparative free trade and comparatively interchangeable currencies was a thing of the past, Canada would be obliged to apply very drastic and long-term remedies.

Mr. Ty Wood[1] underlined to Mr. Clark and Ambassador Wrong that we were deeply concerned by the Canadian problem and anxious to do what we could to assist;

---

1. C. Tyler Wood, Deputy to the Assistant Secretary of State for Economic Affairs.

he added, however, that there was no magic cure available to us in Washington. He said that ITO[2] and the Marshall plan would simply have to be made to succeed but he said he thought it would be a mistake for Canada to rely on either for any immediate solution of her problem. Even under optimum conditions the effect of the ITO and the Marshall plan might not be felt for a long time, perhaps years.

We feel that the meeting served two useful purposes. It brought us up to date on details concerning the problem and Canadian thinking about its solution. Secondly, it acquainted the Canadians with the fact that there is no easy remedy available at present at this end.... There isn't much sign that Congress will give us in the Marshall plan, even if it is adopted, any great degree of flexibility in placing procurement in Canada or making US dollars available to the U.K. and western Europe for purchases in Canada.

Memorandum, Assistant Chief of the Division of British Commonwealth Affairs (A.B. Foster) to the Director of the Office of European Affairs (J.D. Hickerson), September 27, 1947, in *Foreign Relations of the United States 1947* (Washington: Government Printing Office, 1972), Vol. III, pp. 124–125.

CRISES IN THE DIEFENBAKER-PEARSON YEARS—MIDDLE POWER OR DEPENDENT?

A series of diplomatic and defence crises focused much attention on the nature of the Canadian-American relationship in the critical years 1957–1967. The North American Air Defence (NORAD) Command Agreement, signed by the Diefenbaker Government in 1958 had created an integrated continental air defence system and seemed to assure Canadian security against the threat of a Soviet bomber attack in the northern hemisphere. Yet the NORAD Agreement left defence issues far from settled. Diefenbaker's tiff with U.S. President J.F. Kennedy over the Cuban Missile Crisis of 1962, the nuclear warheads controversy of 1963, and public protests over American involvement in the protracted Vietnam war all produced grave disquiet in the minds of Canadians over the state of Canada-U.S. relations. In each of these situations, had Canada assumed the role of a "middle power", a medium-sized nation recognizing America's global responsibilities and aware of her own limitations? Or was Canada becoming little more than a dependent satellite of the United States?

The Cuban Missile Crisis and Canadian Defence Policy—The Reaction of the Diefenbaker Government, 1962

Like other NATO allies, Canada was caught by surprise when the Cuban Missile Crisis occurred in October 22, 1962. U.S. President John F. Kennedy, already irritated by John Diefenbaker's repeated refusal to carry out his commitment to accept nuclear weapons for Canada, sent a special envoy, Livingston Merchant, to inform the Prime Minister of his plans to place the island of Cuba under naval blockade. Yet, during the five critical days when

---

2. The International Trade Organization, a world body for the promotion of multilateral trade favoured by the U.S. State Department.

the world teetered on the brink of nuclear disaster, Washington made no effort to consult the Canadian government.

Prime Minister Diefenbaker's cool initial response to Kennedy's announcement of the naval quarantine and the internal Cabinet squabble (which led to Defence Minister Douglas Harkness' resignation) were indicative of a breach in the harmonious continental relationship.

Prime Minister Diefenbaker's Statement in the House of Commons, October 22, 1962

This is a time for calmness. It is a time for the banishment of those things that sometimes separate us. Above all, it is a time when each of us must endeavour to do his part to assure the preservation of peace not only in this hemisphere but everywhere in the world. The existence of these bases or launching pads is not defensive but offensive. The determination of Canadians will be that the United Nations should be charged at the earliest possible moment with this serious problem.

The President has stated that the matter will be brought before the security council at once, and whatever the reactions of the U.S.S.R. are to the statements made by President Kennedy, I think what people all over the world want tonight and will want is a full and complete understanding of what is taking place in Cuba. What can be done? Naturally, there has been little time to give consideration to positive action that might be taken. But I suggest that if there is a desire on the part of the U.S.S.R. to have the facts, if a group of nations, perhaps the eight nations comprising the unaligned members of the 18 nation disarmament committee, be given the opportunity of making an on-site inspection in Cuba to ascertain what the facts are, a major step forward would be taken.

This is the only suggestion I have at this moment; but it would provide an objective answer to what is going on in Cuba . . . .

House of Commons *Debates*, October 22, 1962, pp. 805–806.

The Recollections of Two Cabinet Ministers

PIERRE SEVIGNY [Associate Defence Minister]: [Livingston] Merchant [special envoy from the U.S.] met with Diefenbaker and [Howard] Green—Harkness wasn't there— and explained what was happening. A cabinet meeting was immediately convened and the serious situation described.

Then something happened—one of these ridiculous little things which have such an effect. President Kennedy announced on his own that he had the full cooperation of the Canadian government. This was never described before but I am telling you this. Well the only one who had spoken was me, saying that I would relay the information that Merchant was coming and would arrange for the meeting. Kennedy took it upon himself to jump the gun and say this, probably because he believed that he had the full cooperation of Canada.

At any rate, Diefenbaker got mad and said, 'That young man has got to learn that he is not running the Canadian government,' and so on. He said, 'What business has he got? There is no decision which has been made as yet. I am the one who is going to decide and I am the one who has to make the declaration. He is not the one.' . . .

* * * * *

DOUGLAS HARKNESS [Minister of National Defence]. What precipitated the whole nuclear matter was the Cuban crisis. Here we were in Canada with the CF-101 Voodoos and the Bomarcs essentially unarmed. So then I became absolutely insistent that we should immediately conclude the arrangement with the United States and secure the warheads for these systems.

The cabinet, I think, unanimously except for Howard Green, agreed that we should start negotiations with the United States immediately to secure the warheads, and we did start negotiations, but then once more they were stalled—stalled by Howard and the External Affairs people. Eventually it came down to a situation where it was clear that there was perhaps going to be an election fairly shortly, and I was insistent that this question had to be settled, that I couldn't go through an election campaign and attempt to defend defence policy in which we had spent all this money for these weapon systems and then refused to put effective warheads on them. The matter became more and more acrimonious, but for some months beforehand I kept on saying whenever the matter was up for discussion, which was very frequently, that unless we came to a decision on this matter and completed the agreement with the United States and got the warheads, I would have no option except to resign. I couldn't possibly continue.

Oral Interviews in Peter Stursberg, *Diefenbaker: Leadership Lost, 1962–67* (Toronto: University of Toronto Press, 1976), pp. 14–15 and 20.

Canada's Position on the Vietnam War—An External Affairs Minister's View, 1967

American involvement in the Vietnam War, which began in 1956 and escalated sharply under the Lyndon Johnson administration, put Canada's foreign policy to supreme tests of principle. As a member with India and Poland on the International Control Commission (ICC) charged with supervising the observance of the 1954 Geneva Agreement[3], Canada attempted to maintain the position of peaceful mediator. Yet because it was a faithful ally of Washington, Canadian authorities also defended U.S. involvement in Indochina as necessary to prevent international communist aggression and hence to safeguard the security of the Western world. To many, Canada's Vietnam policy by the mid-sixties seemed paradoxical. Some, like political scientists James Eayrs, claimed that the Canadian government of Lester B. Pearson was attempting—for the sake of maintaining friendship with Washington—to perform two incompatible roles.

An official statement delivered by Pearson's External Affairs Minister, Paul Martin, in April 1967 at the height of the conflict offered a clear exposition and defence of the Canadian position.

The *first* point which I think needs to be made is that Canada has no direct national interest to assert or maintain in Southeast Asia. Nor do we have any formal military or other commitments there. If we have been drawn into that part of the world, it has been

---

3. The "Geneva Accords", reached at the Geneva Conference on Indochina in 1954, brought a negotiated end to hostilities in the French Indochinese war. The Accords prescribed a settlement of the conflict, but most importantly, established three international commissions to "supervise and control" the peace in Cambodia, Laos, and Vietnam. Canada, along with India and Poland, was selected for membership on the commissions.

solely as citizens of the wider world community. What we are doing in Southeast Asia in twofold: we are there on a peace-keeping mission on behalf of countries which do have a direct national interest in that area; and we are also there as a contributor to the collective effort to meet the rising expectations of the people in that area for a better life.

Second, there are responsibilities which we have in Vietnam as members of the International Commission. We have endeavoured to carry out these responsibilities with fairness and impartiality and we will continue to do so. I would be the last to deny that the course of events in Vietnam has in some important respects overtaken the mandate of the Commission. But there is agreement among all the parties that, as the representative of the Geneva powers, the Commission cannot simply wish its hands of the situation. . . .

Third, apart from whatever role Canada may be able to play as a member of the International Commission, we have tried to use our national influence in promoting the course of peace in Vietnam. We have done this on the basis of our close relations with the United States and the access we have to the Government of the Democratic Republic of Vietnam in Hanoi, as well, of course, as the Government of the Republic of Vietnam in Saigon. I do not want to exaggerate the influence which a country like Canada can command in a matter of this kind, which has engaged the power and prestige of at least three of the great powers. . . .

Fourth, the Canadian Government has made it clear that it is prepared to make its own contribution to an eventual settlement in Vietnam. Such a settlement is almost certain to involve some form of international presence which will afford to the parties concerned the necessary guarantees that the terms of settlement are being fairly and effectively carried out. If, in the light of our first-hand experience of the Vietnam problem over the past thirteen years, Canada were to be asked to participate in an international peace-keeping effort in Vietnam, whether under the auspices of the Geneva powers or under those of the United Nations, I am sure that we would be prepared to accept such a responsibility within the limits of our capacity. . . .

Hon. Paul Martin, Statement to the House of Commons Standing Committee on External Affairs, April 11, 1967, as reprinted in *Paul Martin Speaks for Canada: A Selection of Speeches on Canadian Foreign Policy 1964–67* (Toronto: McClelland and Stewart, 1967), pp. 113–115.

The Official Enshrinement of "Quiet Diplomacy", 1965

The escalating involvement of the United States in Vietnam in the mid-1960s placed L.B. Pearson's government in a difficult position, publicly supporting the American cause and suppressing any misgivings for the sake of the "special relationship". Finally, in April of 1965, Pearson decided to speak out publicly. In a speech at Temple University in Philadelphia, he accepted a World Peace Award and urged the U.S. to "suspend" its bombing in North Vietnam. The celebrated speech drew the immediate ire of American President Lyndon B. Johnson and made a long-lasting impact on Canadian-American relations. Canada's prime minister was summoned to the presidential retreat at Camp David for, in Pearson's words, "a severe talking to" and the two governments subsequently commissioned a joint report, prepared by Livingston Merchant and Arnold Heeney, which set out some essential "principles" governing the Canada-U.S. partnership.

A Canadian Diplomat's Account of the Camp David Meeting, April 3, 1965

Lunch was over and there had been no mention of the speech. Over coffee the Prime Minister took the leap. 'What,' he enquired, 'did you think of my speech?' The President paused before replying. It was the pause when darkest clouds lower pregnant with the coming storm. 'Awful,' he said and taking Mike [L.B. Pearson] by the arm he led him onto the terrace.

What followed I witnessed mainly in pantomime, although from time to time the President's voice reached us in expletive adjuration. He strode the terrace, he sawed the air with his arms, with upraised fist he drove home the velvet hammer blows. He talked and talked... expostulating, upbraiding, reasoning, persuading. From time to time Mike attempted a sentence—only to have it swept away on the tide. Finally Mac [McGeorge Bundy, Johnson's key White House security advisor] suggested that he and I should take a walk through the wooded hills and leave our two masters together.

Our conversation was a reproduction in minor key of what we had just been witnessing. Mac, with the gentleness of a deft surgeon, went for the crucial spots. Perhaps, he suggested, he had not got his message across to me in our last conversation when he had reminded me of the undesirability of public prodding of the President.... I countered by saying that the substance of the speech was a Canadian policy statement and in our view a wise one. The Prime Minister was speaking as Nobel Prize lecturer at an academic occasion—he must deal with issues affecting the peace of the world. The thought of interfering in United States policy was far from his mind. Finally, losing patience with unanswerable questions about the choice of place and occasion I added that I could assure him that the United States would never have a better or more understanding friend than the present Prime Minister.

By this time we had wound our way back again to the house. In the dining room we found Jack Valenti [an aide]. The three of us looked out again at the terrace—the two figures were still there and the drama seemed to be approaching a climax of physical violence. Mike, only half seated, half leaning on the terrace balustrade, was now completely silent. The President strode up to him and seized him by the lapel of his coat—at the same time raising his other arm to the heavens. I looked at Mac in consternation but he was smiling. 'It will be all right now,' he said, 'once the President has got *it* off his chest.' Shortly thereafter LBJ and the Prime Minister reentered the house and we took our departure. The President this time accompanied the Prime Minister to the airport and parted with him with geniality.

Charles Ritchie, "The Day the President of the United States Struck Fear and Trembling into the Heart of Our PM", *Maclean's*, January, 1974, p. 42.

The Heeney-Merchant Report, June 28, 1965

29. The mutual involvement of the two countries and peoples has also complicated, on both sides, the problems arising from the disparity in power. In most—though not all—of their bilateral affairs the capacity of the United States to benefit or harm Canadian interests is greater than that of Canada to affect the prosperity and security of the United States. Canadians are more conscious than Americans of this element in their dealings with the United States. On the other hand, the United States, pre-occupied with the responsibilities of world power, may sometimes be inhibited in its bilateral dealings by considerations which do not operate directly on Canadian attitudes. Here restraint is required of both sides....

39. We are convinced that the cornerstone of a healthy relationship between our two countries is timely and sufficient consultation in candour and good faith at whatever

level or levels of government is appropriate to the nature and importance of the subject. To consult in this fashion, however, cannot be taken to imply that agreement must always result. The purpose rather is that each be enabled to hear and weigh the other's views. The outcome will depend upon the circumstances of the case and, ultimately, upon the judgment by each of its national interest....

55. We recognize that the kind of consultation which we have described has different implications for our respective governments. These derive primarily from the wide disparity in power and international responsibility which we have already underlined. In consultations with the United States, Canadian authorities must have confidence that the practice of quiet diplomacy is not only neighbourly and convenient to the United States but that it is in fact more effective than the alternative of raising a row and being unpleasant in public. By the same token, the United States authorities must be satisfied that, in such consultations, Canada will have sympathetic regard for the worldwide preoccupations and responsibilities of the United States....

A.D.P. Heeney and Livingston Merchant, *Canada and the United States—Principles for Partnership* (Ottawa: Queen's Printer, 1965), pp. 17, 23 and 33.

THE CANADIAN-AMERICAN RELATIONSHIP IN THE TRUDEAU ERA—NEW ISSUES AND OLD CONSTRAINTS?

A new set of issues arose in the Trudeau years (1968–79 and 1980–84) which seemed to produce a change in the nature and scope of the relationship. Close continental cooperation remained the dominant characteristic of summit diplomacy and collaboration in most economic and military matters. But some issues created disharmony. U.S. policy in the Vietnam War, Canada's diplomatic recognition of the People's Republic of China, the "Nixon Doctrine" of 1971 (placing a 10 per cent surcharge on all dutiable U.S. imports) and the 1974 curtailment of energy exports to the U.S. all produced sharp differences of opinion. Although Prime Minister Trudeau professed his faith in the principles of harmonious partnership, his various governments pursued the so-called "Third Option" of more diversified trade and investment and adopted *ad hoc* policies supported by Canadian "economic nationalists". By the late 1970s and early 1980s, a series of public disputes over vexing issues such as acid rain and Canada's 1980 National Energy Program seemed to signal that the relationship had entered a phase of conflicting national interests.

Pierre Trudeau's Concept of the Canadian-American Relationship—Two Views

On his first official visit to Washington in March 1969, Prime Minister Pierre Trudeau formulated a unique definition of the Canadian-American relationship. Canada, Trudeau told a gathering of the American media at the National Press Club, had launched a systematic review of its foreign policy, and part of the process involved questioning the benefits and the drawbacks of sharing a continent with the United States. Popular Canadian cartoonist Terry Mosher, ("Aislin"), offered a commentary on Trudeau's speech and its real meaning.

"On Sleeping With An Elephant", *Speech to National Press Club, Washington, DC, 1969*

As an example to others we hope that we are able on occasion to serve a beneficial purpose. Our close relationship with the United States is an important illustration of what I mean. The fact that Canada has lived and flourished for more than a century as the closest neighbour to what is now the greatest economic and military power in the history of the world is evidence to all countries of the basic decency of United States foreign policy.

And I add in all seriousness that every occasion on which our policies differ from yours in an important fashion, that difference—if of course it is founded on good faith and sound evidence, as we hope is always the case—contributes to your international reputation as a good citizen as much as it does to ours.

When Canada continues to trade in non-strategic goods with Cuba, or proposes the recognition of the Peoples' Republic of China, or—as sometimes happens—finds itself supporting a point of view different from yours in the United States, the world is given evidence of your basic qualities of understanding and tolerance.

Let me say that it should not be surprising if our policies in many instances either reflect or take into account the proximity of the United States. Living next to you is in some ways like sleeping with an elephant: No matter how friendly and even-tempered is the beast, one is affected by every twitch and grunt....

Pierre E. Trudeau, National Press Club, Washington, D.C., March 25, 1969, in *Conversations with Canadians* (Toronto: University of Toronto Press, 1972), p. 174.

Aislin's Commentary, 1971

AISLIN'S CROSS HATCH

"Living next to you is in some ways like sleeping with an elephant."

A Diplomatic Row—A U.S. Ambassador's "Parting Shots", 1975

Canadian policies of economic nationalism emerged by the mid-1970s as thorns in the American side of the relationship. In December of 1975, departing U.S. Ambassador William Porter astonished a group of journalists he had invited over for cocktails by recounting a list of "unfriendly acts" by Canada toward the U.S.. Topping Porter's list of "irritants" were Canada's decision to phase out oil exports to the U.S., the creation of the Foreign Investment Review Agency (FIRA), Saskatchewan's nationalization of American-owned potash mines, the Canadian Radio and Television Commission's rulings on TV commercial deletions, and the proposed removal of special tax exemptions for *Time* and *Reader's Digest*. A news report three years later seemed to reveal that Ambassador Porter's parting remarks had tested the fabric of the harmonious partnership.

The diplomatic row came about following a private reception for 10 Canadian reporters at which Mr. Porter made some statements about the relationship between the two countries.

Later, he was quoted as saying that nationalistic attitudes in Canada were causing alarm in Congress and in the U.S. news media, adding that Canada-U.S. relations had deteriorated during his term in Ottawa.

Mr. Trudeau, to use Mr. Porter's word, 'erupted'. The Prime Minister accused Mr. Porter of going well beyond the bounds in which an ambassador should stay.

'The comments came as a surprise to me, in substance and form, and do not reflect in any way what I have heard from President [Gerald] Ford, Secretary of State Kissinger or our own ambassador [to Washington].'

Mr. Trudeau also was surprised that 'an experienced diplomat like Mr. Porter would not find other channels for expressing views if he thinks they are right.'

Says Mr. Porter: 'I tried twice to see Mr. Trudeau before leaving Ottawa, once through the regular channels of protocol and once through a member of his staff. Neither worked.

'The reason I was given by the External Affairs Department was that it was a ceremonial thing and that it was not his custom to see departing ambassadors .... I then tried with a member of the Prime Minister's staff and received no reply to that one.'

Did Mr. Kissinger know about the planned approach to the media? 'All I can tell you is that if he didn't, with a matter which bothered a very important Government and country like Canada, if somebody didn't read him the telegram, then he had very bad staff work or was personally remiss....'

By now back in Washington, while the furor raged in Ottawa, Mr. Porter received a call from the Statement Department early in the morning telling him that Mr. Kissinger was planning to disavow the ambassador's action....

'I told [two senior aides] that he [Mr. Kissinger] should keep in mind that if there were any disavowal he would need to find another ambassador to Saudi Arabia.'

Finding a new ambassador 'was too high a price to pay, even for calming down MacEachen and, presumably, Trudeau.'

Subsequently, there was no disavowal. 'After I had telephoned that message, Mr. Kissinger ordered that nobody should say anything more about the matter on the American side, and nobody did.'

Canada's then-External Affairs Minister, Allen MacEachen, and Mr. Kissinger were attending a conference in Paris on international economic cooperation, and Mr. MacEachen was instructed by the Prime Minister to lodge a complaint with Mr. Kissinger about the ambassador's performance.

'Kissinger reacted as he had done before on other occasions—not with the Canadians, necessarily, but other similar occasions—by saying he knew nothing about it (the approach to the news media) and that relations with Canada were great.'

"Kissinger, U.S. Envoy Tangle Over Relations with Canada", *The Globe and Mail*, February 20, 1978.

The Rules of the Game—Ambassador Allan Gotlieb's Case for "Enlightened Self-Interest", 1982

Pierre Trudeau's appointment of Allan Gotlieb as Canadian Ambassador in Washington early in 1982 signalled Ottawa's desire for a more "public" approach in its dealings with Washington. Gotlieb, a bright and highly regarded External Affairs diplomat, was charged with the difficult task of bridging the widening gap between the Trudeau and Ronald Reagan administrations in critical areas of policy and economic philosophy. In an important address at Washington's John Hopkins School of Advanced International Studies in April 1982, Gotlieb laid out the guidelines which served as a framework for bilateral relations in the early 1980s:

I keep getting asked here, 'What's going *on* up there'? And when I'm up there, I'm asked, 'What's *happening* down there'? There have been changes, in each country, and in the relationship. These have added to differences which already existed between the countries. Issues on which we differ may be more numerous now, and some of these may be pretty fundamental in a narrow sort of way, but this is after all more or less par for the course of a relationship which is the most complex and richest of any bilateral relationship in world affairs.

The point is that we shouldn't be embarrassed by this, or anxious, or alarmed. We are, after all, different countries. What we should do is make sure that the rules of the game for managing the relationship have kept up with the changes which have taken place....

Canada, too... is an actor on the world stage, as a function of our national interests.

But our *biggest* foreign policy challenge is our bilateral relationship with the United States. To tell the truth, its implications are pretty awesome for developments in Canada. So much so, that there has been a deliberate effort to reduce the Canadian vulnerability, economically and otherwise, to events and intentions here. Some of the issues where there are short-term differences between the two Governments are related to that effort, even though paradoxically, its overall longer-term intent is to reduce friction by reducing overall dependency....

As a counter-face to its constitutional emphasis, the Canadian government is trying to forge a successful, competitive national economy and society which will enable Canadians to defy some of the harsher facts associated with our rigorous geography and the influences of a gravitational North/South economic pull which has costs as well as benefits....

This requires economic development policies which some have labelled nationalist, but which Canadians consider essential instruments for bringing a minimum amount of national control to economic forces now largely controlled outside the country.... Let me say that we have not been dogmatic about these policies (i.e., NEP and FIRA), not inflexible. We have made important changes which correspond to US interests....

Nor do we have a doctrinaire attitude toward foreign capital *per se*. Many if not most countries do. Canada and Canadians have always welcomed foreign partnership, and foreign investment. We shall continue to do so. We need them both.

I can defend Canadian economic policy with confidence. The obviously important point... is that the willingness of the Canadian Government to pursue these policies has caused a different order of bilateral policy difference with the United States. Along with Acid Rain, and other highly important environmental and boundary-type issues, these investment-related disputes represent a new sort of policy difference between the two countries reflecting in part different economic development priorities or techniques....

My purpose in sketching it all is more than academic—it is to promote an understanding of these national interests. It is to promote above all a sense of the whole relationship, whose tone should be set by a view from both sides which takes account of the really enormous amount each country has at stake in its relationship with the other, and isn't vulnerable to each and every action, reaction and over-reaction. The differences between us, natural as they are, have to be kept in the perspective of what we truly share. The hopes for a continent, for a concept of the New World, and for the enhancement of human values deeply shared by the very closest friends.

Notes for an Address by Ambassador Allan E. Gotlieb, "Canada/U.S. Relations: The Rules of the Game", April 1, 1982. Canadian Embassy, Washington, D.C., pp. 1-2, 6-7, 11, 12-13 and 33-34.

CONFLICTING INTERPRETATIONS

The nature of the Canadian-American relationship since 1945 has attracted a great deal of attention from external affairs experts, historians, economists, and political commentators. While there is a rich motherlode of remarkably diverse (and often strongly opinionated) studies, and identifying definite schools of thought can be a dubious proposition, three main lines of interpretation are discernible. The first and perhaps dominant school of interpreters, whose members might be termed the "liberal realists", takes an optimistic view of Canada's postwar collaboration with America for a peaceful, stable world order, often emphasizing the practical necessities and frequent benefits of the North American partnership. To an older and influential second school of "conservative nationalist" scholars, notably George Grant and the late Donald Creighton, Canada has degenerated since the war—under a succession of "Liberal continentalists"—from the status of a British dominion into a state of economic, cultural and political dependence on the United States. In response to the optimistic liberal realist view, a third more disparate group of interpreters has ventured into "New Left revisionism" and offered radical critiques of Canada's accommodation of what they see as an arising American global empire. Serious analysts as well as popular journalists have almost without exception been influenced to varying degrees by contemporary biases and the immediacy of events.

CANADA, THE UNITED STATES AND THE COLD WAR—A CLASH OF INTERPRETATIONS

The Rise of Canada as a "Middle Power"—A Classic Interpretation of Canadian Postwar Policy

The liberal realist version of Canadian foreign policy during the early Cold War years has always emphasized the rise of Canada to "middle power" status, its casting off the old isolationism of Mackenzie King and its embarcation on a new era of constructive international involvement. Dr. John W. Holmes, a former External Affairs diplomat and longtime director of the Canadian Institute of International Affairs, expressed a pragmatic view of Canadian postwar policy in this excerpt from a 1963 essay in the CIIA's *International Journal*.

> ...Canada went through a remarkably swift transition from the status of a wartime junior partner in 1945 to that of a sure-footed middle power with an acknowledged and applauded role in world affairs ten years later. The change was accentuated by the passing from the political scene of Mr. King in 1948 and his replacement by Mr. Louis St. Laurent, a prime minister less inhibited by the phobias that had prevented both nationalists and imperialists in the past from seeing Canada's place in the world clearly and confidently. Mr. St. Laurent, furthermore, worked in close harmony with his new secretary of state for external affairs, Mr. Pearson, who had been trained as a professional diplomat. Mr. Pearson became a major architect of the United Nations and of N.A.T.O., and the rapid growth of Canada's stature was inextricably associated with his position as one of the most respected foreign ministers of the post-war era. The new approach was encouraged also by the national pride of a country in the course of unparalleled economic expansion, capable even of assisting the ruined great powers of the pre-war world. The rise of the United Nations, which acknowledged the formal equality of states regardless of size, set the stage for accomplishments by lesser powers with will and skill to play the new kind of diplomatic game.
>
> It can be said of Canadians as of Americans, however, that their new international activity was the result more of responding to a need than of thrusting themselves forward as world salvationists in accordance with preconceived notions of national mission. The precarious state of the world after 1945 required the forceful intervention in far corners of a benevolent great power like the United States. It turned out also that the preservation of order often enough required the services of middle powers whose principal value was their very incapacity to threaten or command. Canada was no longer reluctant to be useful. Canadians coveted responsibilities, and Canadian diplomatic missions multiplied from seven in 1939 to sixty-five in 1962....
>
> John W. Holmes, "Canadian External Policies Since 1945", reprinted in *The Better part of Valour: Essays on Canadian Diplomacy* (Toronto: McClelland and Stewart, 1970), pp. 5–6.

Canada's Search for American Dollars—A Foreign Policy of Self-Interest?

Recent studies by Canadian revisionist scholars have called into question the traditional interpretations of Canada's postwar policies in support of collective security and in defence of Western perceptions of the free world. York University historians Robert Cuff and J.L. Granatstein, drawing on insights from American revisionist Gabriel Kolko, have mounted an assault on traditional views. Basing their analysis on a study of Canada's dollar crisis of 1947–48 and official reactions to the U.S. Marshall Plan, Cuff and Granatstein have argued that Canadian postwar policy, like that of the United States, was motivated in large measure by economic interests and a desire to maintain American hegemony in the postwar order.

> Canada...had—and recognized—an enormous stake in maintaining Europe as a free market for its goods. Trade with Eastern Europe was negligible but very extensive with the North Atlantic nations, and self-interest was clear. And if the Americans were prepared to negotiate toughly with their desperate friends, so, too, were we.
>
> Despite [Mackenzie] King's caution about [being accused by the Tory opposition of selling out the British to join the Americans] the government did have to work out a series of economic arrangements with Washington in the immediate postwar years. King baulked at the idea of free trade, but he did accept other arrangements that raised serious questions about the degree of economic independence that remained to the Dominion. At issue in 1947 was a serious dollar exchange crisis. The unexpectedly slow rate of British recovery had forced the United Kingdom to draw on the Canadian loan[4] very quickly, and at the same time the high level of Canadian consumer spending produced an unprecedented flow of American imports into Canada with serious results on Canada's U.S. dollar reserves.... The result was a series of measures to cut imports and to reduce tourist spending abroad in the hope that the drain could be checked. Ironically, on November 17, 1947, the same day that the restrictions were announced, Mackenzie King announced that Canada had signed the General Agreement on Trade and Tariffs. Among other things, GATT reduced tariffs on seventy percent of American imports and similarly lowered U.S. barriers to Canadian products....
>
> In this state of affairs, the Americans could afford to be generous when Canadians tried to win some benefits under the Marshall Plan arrangements. It was not aid they were after, but the right to have Marshall Plan dollars spent by Europeans for Canadian goods. And, of course, any general European recovery would enhance Canadian trading prospects. What this meant, put into cold political terms, was that Canadian leaders became firm advocates of American aid to Europe, and Canadian publicists became just as anxious as the Truman administration to have Congress go along with an aggressive and generous policy....
>
> Although Canadian exports to the United States increased in 1948 to help right the balance, the Marshall Plan played a crucial role, as government officials willingly acknowledged. By April, 1949 fully $706 million had been spent in Canada for the Europeans, and soon the barriers erected in November, 1947 were down, soon

---

4. As part of its policy of extending postwar aid to traditional European customers, Canada had lent Britain $1 billion in 1942. A loan of $1.25 billion followed in 1946, a sum more than double Canada's entire federal budget of 1939.

American capital was flowing north once more, soon the Korean War would spur the rearmament of the West and Canadian prosperity would return. All that must be said on the issue of European aid is that Canadian economic needs contributed substantially to a foreign policy that converged at very much the same point reached by Washington decision-makers. The situation north of the 49th parallel, however, did put Canada into a double dependency, and it also produced the peculiar argument that aid to Europe, whether from Canada or the United States, lessened Canadian dependency on American markets....

> R.D. Cuff and J.L. Granatstein, *Ties That Bind: Canadian-American Relations in Wartime*, 2nd ed. (Toronto: Samuel Stevens Hakkert & Company, 1977), pp. 140–143. Footnotes omitted.

Canada, the United States and the Korean War—A Diplomacy of Constraint

A different view of Canada's response to American postwar policy can be seen in the case of the Korean War (1950–53). Most foreign policy analysts and historians agree that by the outbreak of the Korean conflict in 1950 North American public attitudes toward Soviet communism had hardened, and that policy makers in Washington and Ottawa shared a common commitment to United Nations intervention to resist the spread of "communist aggression" in Asia.

In his 1974 monograph, *The Diplomacy of Constraint*, Denis Stairs of Dalhousie University's Department of Political Science saw Canada's role in Korea as primarily one of moderating and constraining American policy:

> The North Korean attack was... perceived in the west, and especially in the United States, as an aggression authorized, if not actually engineered, by the Soviet Union. In accordance, therefore, with the view that 'communism' had to be firmly opposed wherever and whenever it attempted to expand, the American government unilaterally decided to intervene in the hostilities and counter the North Korean assault. As an important but not crucial adjunct of its policy, it sought to take the United Nations with it, acquiring in the process a substantial measure of international legitimacy for its cause, together with a smaller portion of military support for its forces.
>
> The American recourse to the Security Council in June 1950 nevertheless had profound implications for Canada, for without this formal involvement of the United Nations the government in Ottawa would no more have embroiled itself in the conflict in Korea than it did later in the war in Vietnam. To this extent American policy-makers were very successful in recruiting, through the UN, the active support of a foreign government (Canada's was of course only one among several) that would otherwise have remained aloof. The price the Americans had to pay, and the advantage the Canadians (along with others who were similarly affected) were able to gain, was a measure of participation in the formulation of allied, or 'United Nations' policy. For a variety of reasons—most of them relating in one way or another to the desire to prevent the Americans from becoming bogged down in Asia at a time when there was a more vital theatre to defend across the Atlantic—Canadian officials felt it was essential to moderate and constrain the course of American decisions. In attempting to do so, they acted in concert with other powers of like purpose, and their instrument was the United Nations itself. They met with only marginal success—they would say now that they did

as well as conditions allowed, and that in any case a small advance is better than none at all—but the effort itself was fundamental to their diplomacy throughout the conduct of the hostilities as well as in the political negotiations which preceded them and which later followed in their wake.

> Denis Stairs, *The Diplomacy of Constraint: Canada, the Korean War, and the United States* (Toronto: University of Toronto Press, 1974), pp. ix-xi.

CRISES IN THE DIEFENBAKER-PEARSON YEARS—TENSIONS IN THE RELATIONSHIP

The Defence Policy of the Diefenbaker Government—A Critical View

Popular interpretations of Canada-U.S. defence problems in the early 1960s have tended to place the blame on the doorstep of John Diefenbaker's government. Some of the harshest critics, such as journalists Peter C. Newman and Blair Fraser, have argued that Diefenbaker himself precipitated the problems through his "dithering and indecision" on the nuclear weapons issue. Other analysts, like the American political scientists John McLin, have contended that the Diefenbaker regime caused a rupture in the North American defence partnership by failing to recognize—and adjust to—a shift in alliance politics.

> ... [By the late 1950's] an unhappy conflict [had arisen] between Canada's old aspiration (which for a brief time had been successfully realized) to exercise within the alliance a general influence going beyond specific Canadian interests, and the new reality of the rising cost of such influence. The initial Canadian response, which was far from deliberate, was to pay the increasing cost in order to retain the influential position. This cost was measured not only in financial terms, but in terms of the readiness to perform roles requiring the most advanced weapons. Such a policy could only be successfully pursued as long as its underlying assumption was valid: that the kind of military tasks which it entailed could be performed by Canada at a cost that was both politically and economically acceptable. This assumption ceased to be true after 1957, not only because of Europe's resurgence and the waning importance of Canadian territory, but also because of the increasing sophistication of the advanced weapons which such a role entailed. Their production was rendered uneconomic for any but the largest countries; while to use the weapons and *not* produce them in Canada proved unacceptable for political reasons.
>
> The government of John Diefenbaker entered office in 1957, in the midst of this changing situation. This coincidence may have been fortuitous. Or, the change in political atmosphere that led to the Conservative victory may have been caused at least partly by the same international factors—Canada's diminishing influence and the frustrations associated with that—which produced the dilemma in defense policy. In any case, the presence in office at this time of a government which started as inexperienced and proved to be inept made a situation that was already difficult more painful and prolonged than it need to have been. Ironically, the mishandling of defense issues was permitted by the same factor which helped create the initial problem: it was only because Canada's military forces were so marginal to its security that a Canadian government could permit itself the luxury of emasculating those forces for primarily

political reasons. To be sure, Canadian diplomatic effectiveness suffered more than Canadian security. . . .

Jon B. McLin, *Canada's Changing Defense Policy, 1957–1963* (Baltimore: The Johns Hopkins Press, 1967), pp. 213–215.

In Defence of Diefenbaker Nationalism—George Grant's View

A strong defence of Diefenbaker's defence policies may be found in political philosopher George Grant's work, *Lament for A Nation* (1965). In this conservative nationalist interpretation, Grant claimed that Diefenbaker's defeat in the 1963 election relegated Canada to the status of a mere satellite in an emerging "American Empire".

The gentler regime of Eisenhower was a thing of the past. In 1962, Kennedy had made clear that the United States was no longer going to take any nonsense from its allies. An air of innocence pervades Green's statements about the United States.[5] He spoke as if his comments would be taken in friendship. He seemed unaware that he was an official in a satellite country. Can an ant be an ally with an elephant?

Diefenbaker stood for a much more limited nationalism. He did not criticize American world policy, but insisted that Canadian defence policy should not be determined in Washington. Only at one point did he by implication criticize American world policy. In calling for the UN to investigate Cuba, he implied that he did not automatically accept Kennedy's account of the facts. At no other time did he imply any criticism of America's world role; he simply affirmed his brief in Canadian sovereignty.

Diefenbaker and General Pearkes, the Defence Minister before Harkness, had negotiated the acceptance of the Bomarcs when they scrapped the Arrow program. The Bomarcs were useless without nuclear warheads. It was claimed that in refusing the warheads Diefenbaker was reneging on his own commitment to the United States. It was even claimed that he might not have understood the nature of the original commitment. In refusing to make up his mind about accepting the warheads, he was accused of being 'indecisive.' The 'bad ally' and 'the man of indecision' became Liberal images for the campaign.

Diefenbaker answered these charges in his speech to Parliament on January 25, 1963. He claimed that the acceptance of warheads for the Bomarcs had always been conditional on needing them for the defence of the alliance. Defence technology was in constant flux, and it was no longer clear that warheads were necessary. He maintained that the decision should await the NATO meetings in May of 1963, when there was to be an over-all assessment of the military needs of the alliance. The interests of world peace demanded that warheads should be kept off Canadian soil until it was certain that they were needed. This speech illuminates his assumptions about Canada's place in the world. He was no pacifist, no unilateralist, nor was he sentimental about Communism. If nuclear arms were necessary for North-American defence, Canada would take them. He also assumed that NATO was an alliance and not simply an American instrument. (After all, it was the Russians who had maintained the contrary for many years.)

---

5. In a series of speeches from 1961 to 1963, Howard Green, Diefenbaker's Minister of External Affairs, publicly questioned American actions around the world, and particularly in Vietnam, Cuba and Laos.

Canada's sovereignty entailed that our defence policy be determined in Ottawa. These last two assumptions did not correspond with reality and could not be politically sustained in the climate of Diefenbaker's own country. . . .

George Grant, *Lament for A Nation: The Defeat of Canadian Nationalism* (Toronto: McClelland and Stewart, 1965), pp. 29, 30–31.

Diefenbaker's Response to the Cuban Missile Crisis—A Revisionist View

In the standard accounts of Canada's official response to the Cuban Missile Crisis of 1962, Diefenbaker and his government have been vilified for their indecision, peevishness and stubborn refusal to accede immediately to Washington's wishes in a time of world crisis. Recently, however, Jocelyn Maynard Ghent has attempted to assess the official reaction within the context of Canada's differing perceptions of Fidel Castro and his government.

Underlying Canadian-American interaction during the missile crisis were profoundly different perceptions of Fidel Castro's Cuba. To Canada, Cuba was remote and of negligible economic importance. No less anti-Communist than Americans, Canadians were more flexible and pragmatic in dealing with Communist governments. . . . Many Canadians also felt that they shared with Cuba the status of economic satellite to American industry. Hence they tended to view Castro's expropriations of United States property as the 'legitimate efforts of a small economy to free itself from excessive foreign influence.' Canadians further regarded American involvement in the Bay of Pigs fiasco[6] as deplorable and condemned a presumed American right of forceful intervention as a means of blocking 'communist penetration' of the hemisphere.

Misunderstanding clouded communication between Washington and Ottawa on the Cuban issue. Canadians might attribute it to ignorance and emotion in the United States, a former Canadian diplomat observed, but equally, he added, too many Canadians had given 'the impression that we were differing with the Americans out of prejudice and perversity. . . .' Neither country understood, realistically, the other's imperatives. Canadians thought the Americans had vastly over-estimated and were seriously overreacting to Cuba's potential threat. Americans expected Canadians to cooperate in containing Cuban communism, because Canada was not only part of the Western Hemisphere, but part of an alliance system designed to contain Russian communism. Thus on the Cuba problem there had begun what Richard Neustadt[7] calls the 'spiral' effect of 'muddled perceptions, stifled communications, and disappointed expectations.' These became consequential factors in determining political behaviour patterns during the missile crisis. . . .

* * * * *

The Cuba confrontation was harrowing for everyone, but beneath the veneer of 'playing it cool' the crisis may well have been even more frightening to the Canadian political leadership than it was to the American. Canadian fears intensified because

---

6. An aborted invasion of Cuba at the Bay of Pigs, planned by the U.S. Central Intelligence Agency and carried out by the John F. Kennedy administration in April 1961.

7. An American political scientist and advisor to President J.F. Kennedy.

Canadians found themselves at the brink without consent and because after the proclamation of the alert, they found themselves helpless to influence the course of events in which they were nonetheless inextricably involved.

> Jocelyn Maynard Ghent, "Canada, the United States and the Cuban Missile Crisis", *Pacific Historical Review*, Vol. XLVIII (May, 1979), pp. 160–2 and 184.

Canadian Complicity in Vietnam—An Indictment of "Quiet Diplomacy"

No issue in the late 1960s and early 1970s tested the Canadian-American relationship more severely than U.S. involvement in—and Canadian support of—the Vietnam War. Yet with few exceptions, contemporary analyses and historical treatments of Canada's role in the conflict have generated more heat than light. One of the most damning critiques of Canadian "complicity" was journalist Charles Taylor's *Snow Job* (1974).

> ...for nearly two decades, Canada promoted American interests on successive truce commissions, gave public endorsement to American war aims, provided the Americans with political and military intelligence, became diplomatically entangled in Americans' escalation policies and fed millions of dollars worth of military hardware into the American war machine. Although Canadian leaders sometimes expressed *private* opposition to specific American actions, their efforts to diminish the warfare or hasten negotiations were a total failure.
>
> It should be stressed that Canadian support was given willingly and often voluntarily....
>
> If Ottawa was such a willing accomplice, it was partly because successive Canadian governments—starting with Mackenzie King's—had so thoroughly entwined Canadian economic, military and diplomatic interests with those of Washington that Ottawa had virtually lost the habit—if not the possibility—of independent action. It was also because Pearson, Martin and other Canadian officials of their generation had an outlook that was based upon their experience of the League of Nations, appeasement, World War Two and its immediate aftermath. Strongly committed to the Atlantic Alliance and collective security, they reacted in terms of European history, with too little understanding of Asian nationalism and Communist polarities and too much readiness to accept the domino theory and other phobias of the Acheson-Dulles tradition of militant anti-Communism....
>
> Even when they began to doubt American methods—if not American aims— Pearson and Martin were incurably wedded to the doctrine of Quiet Diplomacy and to Pearson's belief that Canadian-US differences should be played down, and Canadian policies even modified on occasion, because of the effect that open disputes might have on the many problems between the two nations....
>
> Charles Taylor, *Snow Job: Canada, The United States and Vietnam, 1954–1973* (Toronto: House of Anansi Press, 1974) pp. 185–188

A New View of Canada's Diplomacy in Indochina

Opinionated popular indictments of Canada's Vietnam policy like Taylor's *Snow Job* and John W. Warnock's *Partner to Behemoth* (1970) have come in for much criticism in academic and diplomatic circles. One of the most recent studies of Canadian diplomacy in Indochina, written by Douglas A. Ross and based on his 1979 doctoral thesis, repudiated earlier critiques.

The few journalistic and academic appreciations of Canadian policy in Southeast Asia have generally implied or assumed that there was a fundamental attitudinal uniformity in Canadian policy-making during the 1950s. Furthermore it has been assumed that Canadian policy-makers shared United States perceptions of the conflict and supported American foreign policy objectives in the region. Such assumptions are inaccurate and reflect a basic ignorance of the complex policy dynamics which have animated the Department of External Affairs over the past three decades. In fact, there were fundamental differences between Canadian and United States policy towards Indochina, and these differences were frequently quite disturbing to American leaders. Not until after 1960 was there any real meeting of minds in Washington and Ottawa concerning the Indochina issue.[8] . . .

There was no solid and enduring policy consensus on the Indochina problem. The consensus changed and evolved over time. The respective advocates of each policy tendency saw the conflict in very different terms. The conservatives looked at Vietnam and saw communist aggression which was all the more dangerous because it was deviously indirect. The liberal moderates felt that the northern regime was attempting to impose its will on the southern population by force of arms, but they also saw the conflict as in essence a civil war. The left liberals, for their part, perceived not merely a civil war but a conflict which was at root the bitter legacy of French colonial intrusion, a problem that was then compounded by an utterly misguided effort by American 'free world' ideologues to impose their values on a poor Asian nation.

Not surprisingly, the interplay among these policy tendencies generated over time an incrementally complex and not infrequently contradictory line of policy outputs concerning the work of the international supervisory commissions. Only with strong qualifications can one say that any particular approach 'controlled' the internal debate at any given time. From mid-1954 through mid-1956 the liberal-moderate tendency was the primary determinant of Canadian actions. From mid-1956 until 1966 the conservative perspective went into the ascendant. From 1967 until 1973 the liberal-moderate approach once more moved back to a position of relative 'control'. . . .

Douglas A. Ross, "The Dynamics of Indochina Diplomacy: Pearson, Holmes and the Struggle with the Bureaucratic Right 1955", in Kim Richard Nossal, ed., *An Acceptance of Paradox* (Toronto: Canadian Institute of International Affairs, 1982), pp. 58–62.

THE CHANGING RELATIONSHIP IN THE TRUDEAU ERA—THREE PERSPECTIVES

Getting On with the Americans—A Liberal-Realist Interpretation

Political analysts and contemporary observers of Canadian-American relations have characterized the Trudeau years as a time of alternating cooperation and conflict in the "special relationship". Most observers agree that the massive foreign policy review launched by Prime Minister Pierre Trudeau in

---

8. Douglas A. Ross, *In the Interests of Peace: Canada and Vietnam 1954–1973* (Toronto: University of Toronto Press, 1985).

the euphoric atmosphere of the 1968 federal election raised fears and apprehensions in Washington, yet few agree on the effects of the Trudeau government's subsequent reactive and *ad hoc* approach to problems in bilateral relations. Taking up these issues, Robert Bothwell, Ian Drummond and John English offered what might be termed a "liberal-realist" interpretation in their recent history of postwar Canada.

... in August 1971 President Nixon's protectionist economic measures startled Canadians and their government into recognition of the dependence of this country upon the United States. The shock was twofold: Canada was not given special treatment, and the measures themselves revealed for all the end of post-war American economic dominance. Many Canadians felt they had been set adrift. Even those who had called upon the government to cut loose the American anchor worried openly about where we would land. The government's response—one of the most curious foreign policy statements in Canadian history—was External Affairs minister Mitchell Sharp's *Canada-US Relations: Options for the Future*, published during the election campaign in October 1972. This became known as the Third Option paper. Option one was maintaining Canada's present relationship with the United States; option two was closer integration with the Americans; and option three, reduction of 'Canadian vulnerability' to American actions....

Since the 1972 paper, options one or two had become more palatable to Canadians, if only because alternatives were so manifestly lacking. American involvement in Vietnam had ended in 1973, and with it vanished the most useful target opponents of American influence in Canadian life possessed. Moreover, the Nixon-Kissinger policy of détente coincided well with the apparent direction of Canadian policy since 1968. Indeed, since Canada had moved independently to recognize China in October 1970, it now took some credit for the so-called American opening to China. The satisfaction of having acted first was almost all Canada got, however, for with the American initiative most of its hopes for economic advantage from the recognition vanished....

By 1977 the polls were showing that the majority of Canadians had 'very great' or considerable confidence in American foreign policy. They also showed that only in the prairie provinces was there a majority of poll respondents who were willing to make an economic sacrifice to buy back Canada. No longer was there embarrassment in pilgrimages to Washington, and, after the 1976 Parti Québécois victory, both René Lévesque and Pierre Trudeau courted the American capital's favour. The debate about Canada's future was carried on most eloquently in the depths of Wall Street and the halls of Congress. Trudeau, who had been called an 'asshole' on the Nixon tapes, developed a good relationship with Nixon's successor, Gerald Ford, and with Ford's successor, Jimmy Carter. In contrast to the Vietnam years, when close ties with an American president would have given rise to charges of sell-out or 'complicity', Trudeau's warm reception in Washington and his equally warm response garnered press and public approval in Canada.

There was, then, much irony when the Liberal campaign committee decided in 1979 that it must emphasize Trudeau's role on the world stage and the esteem shown him by leaders of other countries, especially the Americans. In 1968 Trudeau probably had won support because of his intention to reduce Canada's international role to a bit part. In the 1979 and 1979–80 campaigns it was clear that a different approach was required. Although Trudeau was less fervent in support of American actions during the Afghanistan crisis than was Joe Clark, he did speak in language that in 1968 would have labelled him a Cold War warrior. Both he and Canadians had become more aware of the dangers of standing aside and more sensitive to the congruity of Canada's interests with those of other states....

> Robert Bothwell, Ian Drummond and John English, *Canada Since 1945: Power, Politics and Provincialism* (Toronto: University of Toronto Press, 1981), pp. 376–78. Selected excerpts.

Canada and the Reagan Challenge—A Conflict of Two Divergent Nationalisms

Canadian-American relations in the early 1980s appeared to enter a phase of contention and, at times, open conflict. The accession to power of Ronald Reagan in the 1980 U.S. presidential election, combined with the restoration of the Trudeau régime in Ottawa, seemed to signal a deterioration in relations and an outpouring of popular analyses in the press. In his study of Canada-U.S. relations in the Trudeau-Reagan era, Professor Stephen Clarkson assessed the effect of the Trudeau government's "economic nationalist" policies from 1968 to the early 1980s on the relationship.

> Two factors account for the startling transformation of the Liberal government's orientation between May 1979, when it lost power, and February 1980, when it returned to office. First was the emergence of a new nationalism in certain sectors of the Canadian business community. In all parts of the economy, nationalist refrains, which a decade previously had only been sounded by dissident academic choruses, were now being heard from some of the most successful and aggressive business leaders in the country....
>
> This new thrust in the business community, which took a positive view towards government intervention, found a response in the second transmogrification—a drastic revision in the thinking of the Liberal party after it went into opposition in 1979....
>
> [In the ensuing 1980 election] the Liberals on the stump promised to launch a broad energy policy aimed at self-sufficiency, higher Canadian ownership levels, more industrial benefits for Canadian industry from mega-projects, and a price of energy maintained below world levels. Trudeau also committed his future government to expand the scope of FIRA's activities and to renegotiate the Auto Pact's disastrous imbalances....
>
> [In the April 1980 throne speech] the Liberal government was declaring a new centralism in its governing objectives, a determination to reaffirm the power of the national government by claiming a greater share of the projected increases in Canada's energy revenues and greater control over the development of those strategic fuels, oil and gas, for Canadian economic development.[9] The new centralism implied that the government was determined to play a larger role in directing the economy. Although greater government intervention in the economy would necessarily have a great impact on an industry overwhelmingly owned and controlled by American companies, there was no thought among the architects of the new Liberal strategy that their plans would lead them to a confrontation with Washington. Such features of the NEP as the target of 50 per cent Canadian ownership, which were later to be denounced by the *Wall Street Journal* and by enraged oil executives as nationalist and anti-American, were seen by

---

9. The National Energy Program, introduced in the October 1980 federal budget and popularly known by the acronym NEP.

their designers as necessary to achieve the centralizing goal of gaining greater revenues for Ottawa. . . .

The American and Canadian governments had been at loggerheads many times before over one issue or another without any crisis arising. The spat over the Cuban missiles in 1961, the arguments over the duty remission policies for the Canadian automotive industry in 1964, the criticism of the guidelines for American multinational corporations proposed in 1968 had, like many another issue, been resolved without the disputed issues escalating into a full crisis between the two governments. Now that a recentralizing, assertive, state-capitalist government on the banks of the Rideau Canal had set its sights on restructuring its energy industry, and that a remilitarizing, straight-capitalist administration had taken power on the banks of the Potomac River, future disputes might be less easy to reconcile. The ideological changes of both governments signalled the end of a long period of national uncertainty and the start of a more self-confident assertion of each country's interests. The two systems had moved into a potentially antagonistic stance that only needed a serious issue to bring their relationship under severe stress. . . .

> Stephen Clarkson, *Canada and the Reagan Challenge: Crisis in the Canadian-American Relationship* (Toronto: James Lorimer & Company, 1982), pp. 17–22. Footnotes omitted.

Looking Back on "Life with Uncle"—A Diplomatic View

John W. Holmes attempted to put the troubles of Trudeau-Reagan diplomacy in historical context. In a recent essay he maintained that tactful Canadian diplomacy, in spite of its frustrations, still remained the most effective approach for dealing with the American colossus in the 1980s.

The United States of America is greater than any administration, and its progress has always been cyclical. Many administrations have scared us, but we have found new terms of agreement. Dr. Jekyll usually triumphs. . . .

The American sin was not selfishness but hubris. I wonder if we might have done more to restrain their excesses, to help them learn how to live with the poor and work with their peers. We have our own sour reputation for nauseous holiness and hypocrisy to cope with, our rhetoric too often outpacing our contribution. Dean Acheson[10], whose parents were part of the Toronto Establishment, resented the homilies Canadian ambassadors were constantly delivering to him, urging him to do things he was trying his damdest [sic] to do. He later wrote an essay about Canada called 'Stern Daughter of the Voice of God.' Could we, nevertheless, as best friends, have prepared them better for the resentments that now overwhelm and discourage them by pointing out how we have resented and respected them for two centuries?

Americans, of course, would furiously resent this kind of condescending talk from a small and backward neighbour, but they talk that way all the time about other mixed-up peoples they sincerely want to help. They need best friends to tell them when their breath is bad. The fanatical anti-Americanism which has become such a destructive force in the world threatens not just the United States but world equilibrium. We remain Number One exhibit to prove that American influence is limited by moral inhibitions.

---

10. Dean G. Acheson, the American architect of NATO and Secretary of State in the Harry Truman administration.

To make that point convincingly, however, we have to continue being not a submissive but a stubborn, opinionated, tiresome, and, of course, always wise friend. We have to protect our heritage to show the world that on the borders of at least one superpower, that can be done. It can't be done, however, unless the Americans climb off their godlike perch to see Canada as it really is and see it steadily and see it whole.

John W. Holmes, *Life with Uncle: The Canadian-American Relationship* (Toronto: University of Toronto Press, 1981), pp. 136–138. Footnotes omitted.

A Guide to Further Reading

1. Overviews

Axline, W. Andrew, James F. Hyndman, Peyton V. Lyon and Maureen A. Molot, eds., *Continental Community?: Independence and Integration in North America*. Toronto: McClelland and Stewart, 1974.

Bothwell, Robert, Ian Drummond, and John English, *Canada Since 1945: Power, Politics, and Provincialism*. Toronto: University of Toronto Press, 1981.

Bowles, R.P. et al., eds., *Canada and the U.S.: Continental Partners or Wary Neighbours?* Scarborough: Prentice-Hall of Canada, 1973.

Clarkson, Stephen, ed., *An Independent Foreign Policy for Canada?* Toronto: McClelland and Stewart, 1968.

Creighton, Donald, *The Forked Road: Canada 1939–57*. Toronto: McClelland and Stewart, 1976.

Granatstein, J.L., ed., *Canadian Foreign Policy Since 1945: Middle Power or Satellite?* Toronto: Copp Clark, 1973.

Grant, George, *Lament for A Nation: The Defeat of Canadian Nationalism*. Toronto: McClelland and Stewart, 1965.

Holmes, John W., *The Better Part of Valour: Essays on Canadian Diplomacy*. Toronto: McClelland and Stewart, 1970.

_____, *Life with Uncle: The Canadian-American Relationship*. Toronto: University of Toronto Press, 1981.

Mahant, Edelgard and Graeme S. Mount, *An Introduction to Canadian-American Relations*. Toronto: Methuen, 1984.

Martin, Lawrence, *The Presidents & the Prime Ministers. Washington and Ottawa Face to Face: The Myth of Bilateral Bliss 1867–1982*. Toronto: Doubleday, 1982.

Swanson, Roger Frank, ed. *Canadian-American Summit Diplomacy, 1923–1973*. Toronto: McClelland and Stewart, 1975.

Warnock, John W., *Partner to Behemoth: The Military Policy of A Satellite Canada*. Toronto: New Press, 1970.

2. Specialized Studies

Canada, the United States, and the Cold War, 1945–57

Creighton, Donald. "Canada and the Cold War" in *Towards the Discovery of Canada: Selected Essays*. Toronto: Macmillan, 1972, pp. 243–255.

Cuff, R.D. and J.L. Granatstein, *American Dollars—Canadian Prosperity: Canadian-American Economic Relations, 1945–1950*. Toronto: Samuel Stevens, 1978.

Eayrs, James, *In Defence of Canada: Growing Up Allied*. Toronto: University of Toronto Press, 1980.

_____, *In Defence of Canada. Indochina: Roots of Complicity*. Toronto: University of Toronto Press, 1983.

Granatstein, J.L. and R.D. Cuff, "Canada and the Marshall Plan, June-December, 1947", Canadian Historical Association *Historical Papers, 1977*, pp. 197–213.

Holmes, John W., *The Shaping of Peace: Canada and the Search for World Order, 1943–1957, Vol. 2*. Toronto: University of Toronto Press, 1982.

Mackay, R.A., ed., *Canadian Foreign Policy 1945–1954*. Toronto: McClelland and Stewart, 1971.

Munro, John A., and Alex I. Inglis, eds., *Mike: The Memoirs of the Rt. Hon. Lester B. Pearson, Vol. 2: 1948–1957*. Toronto: University of Toronto Press, 1973.

Page, Don and Don Munton, "Canadian Images of the Cold War 1946–7", *International Journal*, Vol. XXXII (Summer, 1977), pp. 577–604.

Pickersgill, J.W. and D.F. Forster, *The Mackenzie King Record, Vol. 4: 1947–1948*. Toronto: University of Toronto Press, 1970.

Stairs, Denis, *The Diplomacy of Constraint: Canada, the Korean War and the United States*. Toronto: University of Toronto Press, 1974.

Thomson, Dale C., *Louis St. Laurent: Canadian*. Toronto: Macmillan, 1967.

Defence Problems in the Diefenbaker Years, 1957–63

Blanchette, Arthur E., ed., *Canadian Foreign Policy 1955–1965*. Toronto: McClelland and Stewart, 1977.

Diefenbaker, John G., *One Canada: Memoirs of the Right Honourable John G. Diefenbaker, Vol. II: Years of Achievement, 1957–62; and Vol. III: The Tumultuous Years, 1962–1967*. Toronto: Macmillan, 1976 and 1977.

Ghent, Jocelyn Maynard, "Canada, the United States and the Cuban Missile Crisis", *Pacific Historical Review*, Vol. XLVIII (May, 1979), pp. 159–184.

_____, "Did He Fall or Was He Pushed?: The Kennedy Administration and the Collapse of the Diefenbaker Government", *International History Review*, Vol. 1 (April, 1979), pp. 246–279.

Lyon, Peyton V., *Canada in World Affairs, 1961–1963*. Toronto: Oxford University Press, 1968.

McLin, Jon B., *Canada's Changing Defence Policy, 1957–1963: The Problems of A Middle Power in Alliance*. Baltimore: The Johns Hopkins Press, 1967.

Newman, Peter C., *Renegade in Power: The Diefenbaker Years*. Toronto: McClelland and Stewart, 1973.

Reford, Robert W., *Canada and Three Crises*. Lindsay: John Deyell and the CIIA, 1968.

Stursberg, Peter, *Diefenbaker: Vol. 1, Leadership Gained, 1956–62 and Vol. 2, Leadership Lost, 1962–67*. Toronto: University of Toronto Press, 1975 and 1976.

Canada and the U.S. in the Pearson Years, 1963–67

Girard, Charlotte, *Canada in World Affairs 1963–1965*. Toronto: Canadian Institute of International Affairs, 1980.

Godfrey, Dave and Mel Watkins, eds., *Gordon to Watkins to You, A Documentary: The Battle for Control of Our Economy*. Toronto: New Press, 1970.

Heeney, A.D.P., and Livingston T. Merchant, *Canada and the United States: Principles for Partnership*. Ottawa: Queen's Printer, June 28, 1965.

Holmes, John, "Canada and the Vietnam War" in J.L. Granatstein and R.D. Cuff, eds., *War and Society in North America*. Toronto: Thomas Nelson and Sons, 1971, pp. 184–199.

Levitt, Kari, *Silent Surrender: The Multinational Corporation in Canada*. Toronto: Macmillan, 1970.

Munro, John A., and Alex I. Inglis, eds., *Mike: The Memoirs of the Rt. Honourable Lester B. Pearson, Vol. III: 1957–1968*. Toronto: University of Toronto Press, 1975.

Newman, Peter C., *The Distemper of Our Times: Canadian Politics in Transition, 1963–1968*. Toronto: McClelland and Stewart, 1968.

Ross, Douglas A., *In the Interests of Peace. Canada and Vietnam 1954–73*. Toronto: University of Toronto Press, 1985.

Safarian, A.E., *Foreign Ownership of Canadian Industry*. Toronto: McGraw Hill, 1966.

Smith, Denis, *Gentle Patriot: A Political Biography of Walter Gordon*. Edmonton: Hurtig Publishers, 1973.

Stursberg, Peter, *Lester Pearson and the American Dilemma*. Toronto: Doubleday, 1978.

Taylor, Charles, *Snow Job: Canada, the United States and Vietnam, 1954 to 1973*. House of Anansi Press, 1974

Canadian-American Relations in the Trudeau Era

Beigie, Carl E., and James K. Stewart, "New Pressures, Old Constraints: Canada-United States Relations in the 1980s", *Behind the Headlines*, Vol. XL, No. 6 (1983).

Blanchette, Arthur E., ed., *Canadian Foreign Policy, 1966–1976*. Toronto: Gage Publishers, 1980.

Clarkson, Stephen, *Canada and the Reagan Challenge*. Toronto: James Lorimer and Company, 1982. Revised edition, 1985.

Cuthbertson, Brian, *Canadian Military Independence in the Age of the Superpowers*. Toronto: Fitzhenry & Whiteside, 1977.

Doran, Charles, *Forgotten Partnership: Canada-United States Relations Today*. Baltimore: Johns Hopkins University Press, 1984.

Dobell, Peter C. *Canada's Search for New Roles: Foreign Policy in the Trudeau Era*. London: Oxford University Press, 1972.

Gray, Colin, *Canadian Defence Priorities: A Question of Relevance*. Toronto: Clarke Irwin, 1972.

Hertzman, Lewis, John W. Warnock, and Thomas A. Hockin, *Alliances and Illusions: Canada and the NATO-NORAD Question*. Edmonton: Hurtig Publishers, 1969.

Holmes, John W., "Most Safely in the Middle", *International Journal*, Vol. XXXIX (Spring, 1984), pp. 366–88.

Kirton, John, "Canada and the United States: A More Distant Relationship", *Current History* (November, 1980), pp. 117–149.

Leyton-Brown, David, "The Nation-State and Multinational Enterprise: Erosion or Assertion", *Behind the Headlines*, Vol. XL, No. 1 (1982).

Nelles, Viv, "The Unfriendly Giant", *Saturday Night* (February, 1982), pp. 28–34.

Regehr, Ernie, *Making A Killing: Canada's Arms Industry*. Toronto: McClelland and Stewart, 1975.

_____ and Simon Rosenblum, eds., *Canada and the Nuclear Arms Race*. Toronto: James Lorimer & Company, 1983.

Shaffer, Ed., *Canada's Oil and the American Empire*. Edmonton: Hurtig Publishers, 1983.

Swanson, Roger Frank, "The Ford Interlude and the U.S.-Canadian Relationship," *American Review of Canadian Studies, Vol. VIII* (Spring, 1978), pp. 3–17.

Thordarson, Bruce, *Trudeau and Foreign Policy: A Study in Decision-Making*. Toronto: Oxford University Press, 1972.

19

THE QUIET
REVOLUTION AND BEYOND

Who Speaks for Quebec?

During the quarter-century that has elapsed since the death of the controversial Union Nationale leader and provincial Premier Maurice Duplessis in 1959, Quebec has undergone transformations and attracted attention across Canada and even beyond the country's borders. One major topic of debate—surely the most important one for outsiders—has concerned the province's links with the Canadian Confederation, and on this subject a variety of voices have made themselves heard. Since the advent of this "Quiet Revolution", proponents of provincial autonomy and an expanded Quebec state have claimed to represent the aspirations of Quebeckers for a more progressive, modern and "national" society. Voices of Quebec separatism have argued that Quebeckers would only find fulfilment in an independent, sovereign state. Defenders of federalism and bilingualism have contended that strengthening "French power" in Ottawa would assure that Quebeckers could "feel at home" in all parts of Canada. And advocates of sovereignty-association have countered that the true aspirations of *Québécois* could only be realized through self-government and a new economic association with the rest of Canada. Most leading Quebec voices and political groups, ranging from federalist to decentralist to separatist in orientation, have claimed to speak "on behalf of French Canadians" or "Québécois". And only by exploring the nature and extent of their influence in Quebec's rapidly changing society can we weigh the relative claims of each to be the true voice of Quebec.

The term "Quiet Revolution" is commonly applied to Quebec's movement of reform, technological advance and modernization which found its origins in the later years of the Duplessis régime and burst forth in the sweeping reforms of Jean Lesage's Liberal Government from 1960 to 1966. In many ways Quebec by 1960 had already become an urban industrial society, so much so that the Quebec depicted in *Maria Chapdelaine*[1] was little more than a nostalgic memory. Yet intellectuals and liberal-minded activists saw a clear need for far-ranging reforms. Education, particularly at higher levels, was the privilege of an élite. The Church's temporal role had expanded beyond the capacities of its financial and human resources. American and Anglo-Saxon interests dominated the province's economy, politics were notoriously corrupt, and the rights of labour were trampled underfoot. In addition, the Union Nationale's much-vaunted defence of provincial autonomy had yielded few fruits and the party's small-town conservatism led it to recoil from any notion of broad state intervention in the affairs of society. It was, as the Liberals proclaimed in the 1960 Quebec election, *"temps que ça change"*. And the alterations in Quebec society begun in the early 1960s are, in the minds of many Quebeckers, far from finished today.

Since 1960 most French-speaking Quebeckers seem to have supported constitutional changes that would enhance the power of the Quebec state. However, a minority of francophones, which the polls usually placed at around 15–20% of the population, were favourable to outright independence. In the early 1960s, their voice was heard through a variety of separatist movements, notably the Rassemblement pour l'Indépendance Nationale (RIN). Then, in 1968, the Parti Québécois was established in the hope of bringing together all advocates of independence. The party took power in 1976 but its option was defeated in the Quebec referendum held in May 1980. Amongst those who voted "no" to sovereignty-association, many, like Claude Ryan, favoured constitutional change within Confederation, and felt cheated by the proposals introduced by Pierre E. Trudeau's government in the fall of 1980, and eventually written into the new Canadian Constitution, which the Queen proclaimed in April 1982. Quebec thus remains a "province like the others" with the same legislative powers it had possessed in 1960. Still, it should be noted that, politically, Quebeckers like to hedge their bets—did voters not re-elect the Parti Québécois in 1981 after defeating its option in the referendum a year earlier? Humorist Yvon Deschamps was perhaps not far from the truth when he jested that Quebeckers really favoured "a strong Quebec within a strong Canada"!

Although Quebeckers have devoted a great deal of energy to the issue of Quebec's links with Canada and to related questions like language, they have also spent much time attempting to define, and even create, the type of society in which they wished to live. On such issues, however, the spectrum of opinion has been quite as broad as on the constitutional question. At the risk of oversimplifying, it could be stated that one large group has called for change by the creation of a "modern" and "progressive" Quebec. These people sought to reform educational structures and increase access to the system; they put forth a wide variety of social measures, in areas such as health care

---

1. *Maria Chapdelaine* (1916) by Paul Hémon—a classic novel set in rural Quebec.

and consumer rights, generally aimed at middle and lower-income groups; they came down on the side of unions against business and even against government, in its role as employer, and they were strongly nationalistic. Their instrument for change was a strong Quebec state and they set about creating it.

On the other hand, a substantial body of conservatives was critical of change that often appeared to be disruptive; they were more respectful of traditional values, they distrusted big labour and big government, and they attached priority to economic issues. Fringe groups, too, were active, both on the right, among those who longed for a return to the security of the Union Nationale era, and on the left, where a multitude of socialist and Marxist groups clamoured for the abolition of the capitalist system. Generally speaking, change was the catchword of the early 1960s and late 1970s while conservative voices spoke more loudly in the late 1960s and early 1970s. Since 1980, though, the province's difficult economic situation, the high rate of unemployment, poor labour relations, particularly in the public sector, and a government fiscal crisis have contributed to resuscitating conservative opinion.

Quebec, it is clear, has not been speaking with one voice. But, in spite of the wide diversity of opinion within the province, some public figures and groups have commanded more general support than others. Who, then, has spoken for most Quebeckers since 1960? Was it the advocates of provincial autonomy and an expanded Quebec state, like Jean Lesage or Daniel Johnson, with his call for the recognition of "two nations" within our federal system? Or the radical separatists of the Front de Libération du Québec (FLQ) who planted bombs and conducted political kidnappings in an attempt to "liberate" Quebec from English Canadian domination? Was it Pierre Trudeau and the defenders of bilingualism with their plans of extending and promoting linguistic equality across Canada? Or did René Lévesque and the Parti Québécois government with their prescription for political sovereignty within an economic association with the rest of Canada? The debate continues well into the 1980s.

SELECTED CONTEMPORARY SOURCES

The Quiet Revolution, a movement whose effects are still being felt in Quebec, expressed the new hopes of many French Canadians for the political power to set and achieve their own goals. It also challenged English Canadians to confront the perplexing problem: What does Quebec want? And, conversely, many English Canadians had to decide what they wanted: the status quo, equal partnership with French Canadians or a Canada without Quebec. The main alternatives facing Quebec and Canada—greater provincial autonomy or self-government, complete separation for Quebec, federalism with bilingualism, and sovereignty-association—all have had, and continue to have, their own spokespersons and active supporters. Determining which voice has spoken for most Quebeckers at various times is left in this problem study for the reader to decide.

THE ADVOCATES OF PROVINCIAL AUTONOMY AND AN EXPANDED QUEBEC STATE

Jean Lesage's Liberal Party—The Promise of "Maîtres Chez Nous", 1962

Convinced that Duplessis' conservatism and political nationalism had held back the modernization of Quebec, the Liberal party of Jean Lesage, and particularly its more dynamic members like René Lévesque and Paul Gérin-Lajoie, championed the idea of a much more interventionist role for the state in Quebec society to achieve social and educational reform. The growth of government also held great promise for many nationalists who saw it as the major tool that French Canada could use in promoting its national interests. In the 1962 Quebec election, Lesage's Liberals, using the slogan *"Maîtres Chez Nous"* campaigned for the nationalization of the province's private electrical companies.

On June 22, 1960, the population approved the Quebec Liberal Party's programme and gave it a mandate to organize national and economic life in such a way as to favour the distinctive identity of Quebec's citizens and promote their welfare. . . .

Serious studies have shown that the unification of the electrical power system—the key to the industrialization of all regions of Quebec—is necessary as the primary condition for our economic liberation and for a dynamic policy of full employment. This important step necessitates the nationalization of eleven companies responsible for producing and distributing electricity. . . .

The magnitude and complexity of the task as well as the domination of the Legislative Council by the Union Nationale, a party opposed to the complete nationalization of these eleven companies, have convinced the government that the entire population of Quebec should be associated with this great and profitable enterprise. . . .

. . . Jean Lesage and his team are asking the entire population of Quebec to give them a clear and unequivocal mandate to pursue, with the utmost vigour, the fulfillment of the Quebec Liberal Party's 1960 programme. . . . Now or never 'masters in our own house', that is the objective that the Quebec Liberal Party is proposing . . . .

* * * * *

It should not be necessary to add that the Quebec Liberal party does not intend to promote a general policy of nationalization. Its only interest is to build a broad and secure base for the expansion and decentralization of industry. Its only interest is to give Hydro a dimension equivalent to the needs and hopes of Quebec.

. . . the Liberal Party of Quebec is convinced that the nationalization of electricity is a magnificent and profitable undertaking, not only as regards the material welfare of Quebec but just as much as from the perspective of French Canada's social health and national future.

Manifeste du parti liberal du Québec, 1962, pp. 1, 2, 9. trans. Richard A. Jones.

Daniel Johnson and the Union Nationale—Recognizing "Two Nations" Within A New Constitution, 1965

Daniel Johnson, chosen leader of the Union Nationale opposition party in 1961, carried Quebec nationalism one step further when he began campaigning in favour of a fully revised Canadian constitution; in 1965, he even published a book outlining his proposals. For the future prime minister of the province (from 1966 until his untimely death in 1968), the choice was between equality of the two founding nations, to be ensured by a new constitution, and independence for Quebec, implying the destruction of Canadian confederation.

Our current difficulties are caused mainly by the absence of a constitution adapted to the political and sociological realities of modern Canada. Our country is composed of two cultural communities which, to varying degrees and for different reasons, are hindered in their development by today's [constitutional] structures. Because of these structures, there is a danger that our two nations come to consider each other as natural enemies, whereas they are really natural allies in view of their many common interests. Before positions harden on both sides, it is urgent to put an end to this disastrous misunderstanding.

We often hear it said: let us forget what separates us and increase our awareness of what unites us. In my opinion, that is the wrong way to approach the question. It is the obsession with unity, of which Durham has not been the only victim, that prevents real union. Our first duty is to arrive at a clear understanding of the things that separate us. Then it will become possible to unite what can be united. . . .

* * * * *

. . . History proves that it is impossible to merge our two nations. Such forced unity, which would violate nature, would be a constant source of quarrels and enduring conflict. What is possible and desirable, in a binational country, is not national unity, an expression whose meaning is always ambiguous, but national union, national harmony, founded upon the respect for legitimate identities. . . .

In our opinion, it is time for a new departure. A constitution elaborated a century ago in the context of the realities and needs of that period cannot simply be reworked. It is easier to build a new mechanism than to correct the defects of one which has gone radically awry. . . .

In order to work, the new constitution must resolve the internal contradiction that tends to oppose French Canada and English Canada in a juridical framework unsuited to their respective needs and curtailing their growth. For situations of conflict, it will have to substitute possibilities for cooperation. It will have to enable the two nations to pursue their development freely. . . .

* * * * *

I believe the time is ripe and that it has become not only possible but imperative and urgent to give Canada an entirely new constitution, founded on the alliance of two nations each possessing the sovereignty necessary to fulfil its own destiny, working together, as equal partners, in the administration of their common interests.

Daniel Johnson, *Egalité ou indépendance* (Montreal: Editions Renaissance, 1965), pp. 83–85, 92. trans. R.A.J.

Claude Ryan's "Beige Paper"—Proposals for A Decentralized Federation, 1980

In the midst of the campaign leading up to the Quebec Referendum of May 1980, the Quebec Liberal Party under the leadership of former *Le Devoir* publisher Claude Ryan answered the Lévesque government's scheme of sovereignty-association with its own proposals for a "New Canadian Federation". Claude Ryan's "Beige Paper", like the Parti Québécois White Paper, sought an institutional means of enshrining the equality of the francophone minority with the anglophone majority in Canada. But it advocated a decentralized form of federalism which promised to provide the minority with "equality" in areas affecting its security.

It is certainly necessary to review in depth the constitutional arrangements bequeathed to us in 1867. The venture has become urgent in the light of current tensions which have been generated not only in Quebec but elsewhere, and particularly in western Canada. But a realistic and honest evaluation of the Canadian federation can lead to only one conclusion: The assets far outweigh the liabilities. Starting from this premise, the most useful and promising approach is to work constructively and with confidence to renew and modernize the Canadian federal structure, rather than attempt to destroy it. . . .

We would establish the following as our fundamental goals:

1. We must aim at providing the people of this country with a written constitutional document, modern and Canadian.

2. We must affirm the fundamental equality of the two founding peoples who have given, and still provide, this country its unique place in the family of nations. . . . The objective can be realized:

a. by proclaiming in the constitutional text certain fundamental linguistic rights which will protect francophones and anglophones equally across the country;

b. by the granting to Quebec of guarantees capable of facilitating the protection and the affirmation of its distinct personality.

3. We must ensure the judicial primacy of the rights and fundamental liberties of individual citizens in the Canadian political system.

4. We must affirm and give faithful recognition to the fundamental rights of the first inhabitants in this country.

5. We must acknowledge the richness of the cultural heritages of the different regions, and affirm Canada's interest in their preservation and development. . . .

6. We must aim to provide equal access to economic, social and cultural development for all individuals, regions and provinces.

7. We must maintain in Canada a federal system of government. . . .

8. We must ensure the existence of a central power strong enough to serve the whole country in the face of whatever new challenges the modern world presents, whether internally or externally. This government's major tasks will be to manage the economic union, to ensure the smooth operation of national policies in certain aspects of industry and commerce, to ensure a reasonable redistribution of wealth between the provinces and between individual citizens, and to act in the name of the whole country in the pursuit of peace and national security.

9. We must ensure the existence of provincial powers strong enough to take charge, in their respective territories, of the tasks related to the development of their physical and human resources. This implies, among other things, the management of their natural resources, land use, local and provincial commerce, regional economic devel-

opment, education and culture, social and sanitary services, the administration of justice, and social insurance schemes.

10. We must aim at establishing a clear division of legislative and fiscal responsibilities between the two orders of government....

11. We must aim to ensure that the very great disproportion in size among the member-states of the federation can be corrected by the eventual amalgamation of some services, while still respecting the acquired rights of each province.

12. We must establish a system of arbitration for constitutional disputes which recognizes the fundamental dualism of the population and the judicial institutions of this country, and which is above all suspicion....

13. We must aim to recognize in the text of the constitution the fact that in almost all fields, any governmental action has international repercussions.... We must affirm the need to harmonize provincial initiatives with the broad orientation of federal foreign policy... so that the provinces' role in those international activities relating to its areas of jurisdiction is recognized....

A New Canadian Federation. Report of the Constitutional Committee of the Quebec Liberal Party, 1980, as reprinted in *The Toronto Star*, January 10, 1980.

THE VOICES OF SEPARATISM

Marcel Chaput—"Why I Am A Separatist", 1961

One of the founders of the Quebec separatist party, the *Rassemblement pour L'Indépendance Nationale* (RIN) in the early 1960s, Marcel Chaput, set out the classic arguments for a fully sovereign state of Quebec. Many English Canadians were jolted into recognizing the existence of separatism by the publicity generated by Chaput's 1961 book, *Pourquoi je suis séparatiste*, and by the public rallies of the RIN.

I begin with the postulate that the French Canadians form a nation like any other. And like all other nations, the French-Canadian nation has its good and bad points, a soul capable of love and reaction, aspirations to grandeur, a need for dignity and self-expression, the capacity for joy and tears, a feeling of solidarity. In short, the French Canadian needs a national identity, within the framework of concrete political structures and incarnated in universally accepted symbols....

* * * * *

The hour of decision
French Canada has arrived at its hour of decision. Its real problem is to decide now, once and for all, what it wants to be— an eternal minority, in eternal retreat in an immense country which doesn't belong to it, or a living and progressive majority, in a country which is smaller but all its own.

To those who choose to be a minority
The experience of ninety-four years of Confederation is enough to convince us that minority status in a two-nation country can lead only to mediocrity. To hope that by some sort of miracle the French-Canadian people should suddenly reform, demand with one voice that it be respected, become anxious to speak correctly, desire culture and great works, without the inspiration of an animating ideal—that is a dangerous case of delirium.

Let us suppose that the miracle should happen, and that our people should acquire the desired virtues of resistance—we would still remain a numerical minority, whose democratic responsibility would still and forever be to bow to the wishes, legitimate or not, just or not, generous or not, of a majority which is foreign to us in language and spirit.

The urgent need for orientation

Through the fault of its élite groups, the French Canadians are a people which doesn't know where it is going or what it wants. It is the victim of an immense confusion, torn between proposals that are as fantastic as they are contradictory.

Faced with this tangled mass of choices, it is absolutely necessary to choose one, once and for all; we must answer the one question we are allowed to ask—which of the choices, a bilingual Canada or an independent Quebec, will ensure the French-Canadian nation its greatest development? Personally, I have chosen independence.

Marcel Chaput, *Why I Am A Separatist*, trans. Robert A. Taylor (Toronto: Ryerson Press, 1962), pp. 91–4.

The Front de Libération du Québec—An FLQ Manifesto, October 1970

A few months after the April 1970 Quebec provincial election, in which the *Parti Québécois* won 23 percent of the vote and only 7 of 110 seats in the National Assembly, the FLQ separatist group took matters into its own hands. Two small "cells" of the FLQ abducted James Cross, a British trade commissioner, and a few days later, Pierre Laporte, the Quebec Minister of Labour, thus plunging the entire country into a series of dramatic events known as the "October Crisis" of 1970.

During the few tense weeks of the October Crisis, the FLQ released a series of manifestoes stating their demands and offering a radical critique of the state of Quebec society. Shortly after the Cross kidnapping, the group issued this manifesto which, in response to their demands, was read over French-language television.

The Front de Libération du Québec is not a messiah, nor a modern-day Robin Hood. It is a group of Quebec workers who have decided to use all means to make sure that the people of Quebec take control of their destiny.

The Front de Libération du Québec wants the total independence of Quebecers, united in a free society, purged forever of the clique of voracious sharks, the patronizing 'big bosses' and their henchmen who have made Quebec their hunting preserve for 'cheap labor' and unscrupulous exploitation.

The Front de Libération du Québec is not a movement of aggression, but is a response to the aggression organized by high finance and the puppet governments in Ottawa and Quebec (the Brinks 'show,' Bill 63, the electoral map, the so-called social progress tax, Power Corporation, 'Doctors' insurance,' the Lapalme boys...)....

We once believed that perhaps it would be worth it to channel our energy and our impatience, as René Lévesque said so well, in the Parti Québécois, but the Liberal victory showed us clearly that that which we call democracy in Quebec is nothing but the democracy of the rich. The Liberal party's victory was nothing but the victory of the election riggers, Simard-Cotroni. As a result, the British parliamentary system is finished and the Front de Libération du Québec will never allow itself to be distracted by the pseudo-elections that the Anglo-Saxon capitalists toss to the people of Quebec every four years. . . .

We are the workers of Quebec and we will go to the end. We want to replace the slave society with a free society, functioning by itself and for itself. An open society to the world.

Our struggle can only be victorious. You cannot hold back an awakening people. Long live Free Quebec.

Long live our comrades who are political prisoners.

Long live the Quebec revolution.

Long live the Front de Libération du Québec.

Montreal *Gazette*, October 9, 1970.

The Quebec Left—A Manifesto for a Socialist Quebec, 1981

For a time during the mid-1970s, René Lévesque's Parti Québécois seemed to forge a coalition among the various elements of the Quebec independence movement. Although the PQ government elected in November 1976 did implement some major social reforms during 1977 and 1978, its program of "social democracy" failed to satisfy many socialists in the Quebec left. In addition, the referendum defeat of 1980, the deepening recession, and a serious Quebec budget crisis forced the PQ government into an increasingly conservative stance. Bitterly disappointed though scarcely surprised, representatives of the left decided to form a Socialist Movement that would carry on the struggle.

The Socialist Movement that we today undertake to construct, as well as its strategy of implantation and development, are determined by the political project that we put forth. Our project implies radical transformations in the political, economic, social and cultural organizations of Quebec society. It affirms the necessity for the working and popular classes to conquer not only the State power, but all sites of power, and to appropriate, transform and democratize them in such a way that socialism is one that is lived by the men and women workers in their daily lives, and the sovereignty acquired be that of the collectivities—autonomous and solidary—over their development and their future.

This represents a profound change that cannot be realized by the simple election of deputies. . . . It is not sufficient to simply decree that Quebec is henceforth socialist, independent and democratic, for it to become so!

The changes to which we aspire will not take place overnight. We must first bring together a constellation of political conditions: transcend divisions and realize the political unity of the working and popular classes; deeply implant our project in all the regions and spheres of life and work; arouse and develop a will to struggle and change, construct a relationship of strength, develop international solidarities; in short, put into operation a social dynamic capable of carrying out our political project.

We must bring about a true political and unitary mutation in the midst of the working and popular classes. It is through the construction, as of today, in our working and living environments, of a large movement for socialism, independence, democracy and equality between men and women, that we will get there.

Le Comité des Cent, "Pour un Québec socialiste", *Canadian Journal of Political and Social Theory*, Vol. 6, Nos. 1–2 (Winter-Spring 1982), p. 135.

THE DEFENDERS OF FEDERALISM AND BILINGUALISM

Pierre Trudeau's Federalism—An Explanation of Federal Bilingualism, 1969

Much of the debate over Quebec's place in Confederation since the late 1960s has touched on Pierre Trudeau's conception of Canadian federalism. Though recognized as an outspoken champion of French Canadian rights, Trudeau came to power in Ottawa in 1968 as a Prime Minister who consistently denied the need for special status for Quebec, rejected the idea of a new Canadian constitution, and strongly condemned the notion of an independent Quebec. Trudeau's brand of federalism was, in part, a response to the Report of the Royal Commission on Bilingualism and Biculturalism, released in 1965, which recommended a major extension of bilingualism to help alleviate the disharmony in English-French relations.

From the time he took office in 1968, Trudeau attempted to meet the aspirations of Quebeckers by promoting linguistic equality across Canada. Trudeau believed that if minority language rights were guaranteed in all parts of Canada, Quebeckers would be made to feel "more at home" in the country, and most French Canadian grievances would be satisfied. The Official Languages Act of 1969 was a key part of that strategy.

WHY ARE THEY FORCING FRENCH DOWN OUR THROATS?

That question has been asked by English-speaking Canadians who are concerned about the government's bilingual policy and about the Official Languages Act, which was recently [1969] enacted by Parliament. The question is based on a widely shared misunderstanding of what our policy on bilingualism means.

In fact, everyone in Canada will not be required to speak French, any more than everyone will be required to speak English. You can grow up in parts of Quebec and never use English a day in your life. You can live in many parts of the country and never hear a single word of French. Most of the people who deal with the government of Canada speak only one language. It is because everyone in the country is not expected to speak both languages, and never will be, that the federal government must be able to speak to Canadians in either French or English wherever there are enough French speakers or English speakers to justify it. Nothing is more important to a person than to understand and to be understood. The most common and most effective tool we can use for this purpose is our language. Any policy which affects such an important aspect of our lives is bound to stir up some controversy. . . .

* * * * *

Some people claim that the Official Languages Act will result in discrimination against those whose mother tongue is neither English nor French. This is one of the most widespread and the most unjustified misconceptions. The Act itself states categorically that the rights and privileges of any language other than English or French, whether acquired by law or by custom, will in no way be diminished as a result of the Act. For instance, the right of people who do not understand English or French to be heard in court through an official interpreter will be maintained . . . .

A second misconception is that the Act will prevent Canadians who speak only one language from working for the government, the armed forces or the Crown corporations, or from being promoted to important government jobs. There is no clause in the Act which states this, or which will have this result. The object of the Act is to provide government services in both languages where required by the population.

This does not mean that everyone who works for the government must be bilingual. In many areas of the country, including almost all of Western Canada and much of Quebec, government services will be provided in only one language and people working for the government in those areas will need only that language. . . .

* * * * *

As I travel around the country I find that the advantages of bilingualism are becoming more widely accepted by Canadians, particularly among the young. However urgent it may be to introduce such a policy, and I believe the very survival of our country depends on it, we should not expect to reap its full benefits overnight. That will require fundamental changes in attitudes and institutions which may take years, or even generations. In this historic process the Official Languages Act is an important forward step.

Pierre E. Trudeau, Statement on the Official Languages Act, Canadian Press, July 1969. Courtesy of Press News Limited.

Robert Bourassa's "Fédéralisme Rentable"—The Case for Profitable Federalism, 1973

One Quebec leader who placed heavy emphasis on the economic benefits of federalism for Quebeckers was Robert Bourassa, the Liberal premier of the province from 1970 to 1976. Bourassa's 1970 election campaign was based principally upon economic issues, and his promise to create 100 000 new jobs in 1971 as well as his slogan, "Quebec At Work", attracted much attention in a climate of economic slowdown. Yet, while Bourassa condemned separatism as a risky and potentially costly venture, he appealed to nationalist elements with a call for greater Quebec autonomy in social policy and a promise to make French "the language of the workplace".

Bourassa and his government were committed to *"fédéralisme rentable"*, profitable federalism. In his speeches Premier Bourassa stressed that for Quebec separatism from Canada as proposed by the Parti Québécois would be disastrous, and that federalism offered Quebeckers some tangible economic benefits.

The most striking aspect of recent developments in Canadian federalism is the fact that the provincial governments have been adopting increasingly similar attitudes towards most problems. The provinces have in fact arrived at an identity of views on how to approach and solve most of Canada's economic and social problems. This identity of views finds expression in joint efforts to bring about a greater decentralization of the federal system, particularly in the following areas:

1. Federal finances: it is hoped to obtain a distribution of the resources that is more in keeping with the constitutional responsibilities of the federal government and the provincial governments.
2. Economic development, particularly respecting the problems of regional disparities and unemployment;

3. Social development, with special emphasis on social security programs.
4. Cultural identity. . . .

The Canadian federal system is a powerful instrument for developing national [Quebec] resources, as may be seen from some recent examples:

— Quebec will be receiving an additional $78 million annually following changes in equalization payments announced in Mr. Turner's last budget speech,
— Quebeckers will be getting $315 millions in family allowances following the successful conclusion of negotiations between Mr. [Marc] Lalonde and Mr. [Claude] Castonguay,
— Quebec received over half—$93 million of $167 million—of the federal funds allocated to the bilingualism program between September 1970 and March 1973,
— Over the next three years, Quebec will be getting one billion dollars, payable at the rate of $300 million annually, for housing and waste-water [sic] treatment,
— Quebec takes in over half—$66.5 million out of $128.6 million—of the federal funds distributed by the Department of Regional Economic Expansion in the form of regional expansion grants.

Communiqué of December 22, 1973, Gouvernement du Québec, Conseil Exécutif, Information, mimeo, pp. 10–12.

Pierre Trudeau's Renewed Federalism—Statements on Quebec and the New Constitution, 1980–81

In the aftermath of Quebec's May 1980 Referendum on the Parti Québécois proposals for a "New Deal" between Quebec and Ottawa, Prime Minister Trudeau resumed—and stepped up—his efforts of the 1970s to address the problems of Quebec and other provinces through constitutional reform. While most federalists rejoiced at the resounding victory of the "No" forces in the Referendum (60 percent), many who hoped for constitutional change resisted Trudeau's proposals for a new Canadian constitution. His plan attempted to extend linguistic equality to the provinces, yet seemed designed to reassert federal authority in many areas of jurisdiction. The Prime Minister's determination to patriate the BNA Act from Britain and to create a new Constitution sprang largely from his promise, made at the height of the Quebec Referendum campaign, that a "No" vote would be rewarded with a new made-in-Canada constitution. The struggle for a new Constitution eventually was settled in a November 1981 compromise between Trudeau and all the provincial premiers except René Lévesque. The government of Quebec refused to sign the accord, and thus the province was excluded from the final act of constitutional "rebirth" in April 1982.

The following statements, excerpted from Trudeau's constitutional speeches of 1980 and 1981, illustrate his attempts to meet the aspirations of Quebeckers through a new Constitution.

I know that I can make a most solemn commitment that following a 'No' vote we will immediately take action to renew the constitution and we will not stop until we have done that.

And I make a solemn declaration to all Canadians in the other provinces; we, the Quebec MPs, are laying ourselves on the line, because we are telling Quebeckers to vote 'No' and telling you in the other provinces that we will not agree to your interpreting a 'No' vote as an indication that everything is fine and can remain as it was before.

We want change and we are willing to lay our seats in the House on the line to have change.

Pierre E. Trudeau, Address at Paul Sauvé Arena, May 16, 1980, as reprinted in Robert Sheppard and Michael Valpy, *The National Deal: The Fight for A Canadian Constitution* (Toronto: Fleet Books, 1982), p. 33.

This past spring, when Quebeckers were urged by their provincial Government to separate from Canada, people in all parts of the country confirmed the bargain, the social contract, which made Confederation possible; the promise that all can share fully in Canada's heritage.

The Canadian Government's commitment was clear. So was the commitment of all national party leaders and of each of the premiers. Hundreds of thousands of individual Canadians signed petitions; schools, churches, and city councils declared themselves.

It was more than a commitment to Quebeckers, even though the Quebec referendum was the immediate reason for it. The commitment was from each Canadian to every other Canadian to change our country for the better.

The people, through Parliament, can now redeem that pledge. Freed of the paralysis of the past, with our constitution home, with our full independence beyond question, with our rights and freedoms guaranteed, the process of reform and renewal can truly proceed. Our Government is willing, indeed it is anxious, to resume discussions on the constitution with the provinces, once the way has been provided to make progress.

The Globe and Mail, October 3, 1980.

I realize that this resolution has caused deep division among members of both houses of Parliament, members of all political parties, within the ranks of provincial premiers and indeed among the Canadian population. However, I find some consolation in the fact...that the division seems to arise not so much on the substance of what we are debating as on the process and on the timing....

On the substance, the motion before us poses two things; firstly, that Canada give itself a Canadian constitution with an amending formula which would allow Canadians to amend their constitution themselves in their own country and, secondly, the charter of fundamental rights and freedoms.

As for the first factor, patriation and the amending formula, it is enough to say that since 1927 Canadians have wanted this.

Canadians have sought this systematically. Under six different prime ministers. Under dozens of provincial premiers. At innumerable federal-provincial conferences....

In all cases, whatever part of the country we look to, there is a clear majority in favor of patriation....

It is time to stop turning in circles; it is time to act; it is time to cut the Gordian knot. We have no more time, lest the forces of self-interest pull us apart....

And so to the charter of rights and freedoms, because this is a sensitive question with our opposition, the question was asked (in polls): Should the charter be included before patriation, after patriation or not at all? The answers: In Saskatchewan, before patriation 70 per cent; in Alberta, before patriation 55 per cent; in British Columbia, before patriation 56 per cent.

The Canadian people are not afraid of this tag of colonialism which has been attached to this action of Parliament by the opposition, and they are right. . . .

* * * * *

The next two decades will see the gestation of the 21st century in Canada. I do not know what kind of country our successors in this place will leave behind them. But I do know, and I deeply believe, that it is our duty to leave behind us at least the ability to our successors to choose Canada's destiny.

The Toronto Star, March 24, 1981, p. A14.

THE PROPONENTS OF SOVEREIGNTY-ASSOCIATION

René Lévesque's Option for Quebec—"We Are Québécois", 1968

The idea of sovereignty-association first surfaced as a policy proposal considered by the Quebec Liberal party in the mid-1960s. When the party formally rejected the policy in late 1967, René Lévesque and other advocates of the proposal left the Quebec Liberals and formed the Mouvement Souveraineté-Association (MSA). A year later, in 1968, the Parti Québécois was formed in a merger between the RIN and the MSA. The PQ billed itself as a moderate democratic separatist party, committed to the idea of making Quebec a sovereign state in an economic association with the rest of Canada.

In his book, *Option for Quebec* (1968), Lévesque made the case that French-speaking Quebeckers were Québécois who could only really feel at home in an independent, sovereign Quebec. Sovereignty-association, he argued, was the solution to the problems faced by Québécois in preserving their cultural identity.

We are Québécois.

What that means first and foremost—and if need be, all that it means—is that we are attached to this one corner of the earth where we can be completely ourselves: this Quebec, the only place where we have the unmistakable feeling that 'here we can really be at home.'

Being ourselves is essentially a matter of keeping and developing a personality that has survived for three and a half centuries.

At the core of this personality is the fact that we speak French. Everything else depends on this one essential element and follows from it or leads us infallibly back to it. . . .

The dangers are striking enough.

In a world where, in so many fields, the only stable law seems to have become that of perpetual change, where our old certainties are crumbling one after the other, we find ourselves swept along helplessly by irresistible currents. . . .

* * * * *

The only way to overcome the danger is to face up to this trying and thoughtless age and make it accept us as we are, succeeding somehow in making a proper and appropriate place in it for ourselves, in our own language, so that we can feel we are equals and not inferiors. This means that in our homeland we must be able to earn our living and pursue our careers in French. It also means that we must build a society which, while it preserves an image that is our own, will be as progressive, as efficient, and as 'civilized' as any in the world....

René Lévesque, *An Option for Quebec* (Toronto: McClelland and Stewart, 1968), pp. 14–16 and 21.

The Parti Québécois "New Deal, Between Equals"—The "Yes" Side Referendum Proposal, 1980

During the 1976 election campaign, the Parti Québécois promised, if elected, to hold a referendum on the issue of sovereignty-association. Its victory demonstrated that it had succeeded in distinguishing, in electors' minds, the issue of independence from the question of voting for the party. Finally, after three and a half years of waiting for the referendum, May 20, 1980 was announced as the day of reckoning that would decide Quebec's future. But, in line with the Parti Québécois strategy of *étapisme* (or step-by-step approach), the actual referendum question was worded so as to avoid a definitive judgement and, instead, merely requested from Quebeckers a "mandate to negotiate" and a "new form of association between equals".

Here is a document stating the position of the "Yes" side, which was rejected by nearly 60 per cent of Quebec voters in the referendum.

In the last three decades, an ever-growing number of Quebec[k]ers have expressed a deeply felt desire to reshape this relationship in order to endow the Quebec Government with all the powers it needs to ensure the development of one of those two founding peoples, since nine French-speaking Canadians out of ten live within our Quebec borders. As a result, we have had a plethora of Royal commissions, reports and federal-provincial conferences, aimed at finding a solution. All in vain.

No surprise. For, within a federal system, it is practically impossible to satisfy Quebec's demands without stripping Ottawa of those powers it requires as a 'national government'. And, naturally, no other province is ready to let Quebec have a 'special status' within Confederation. This is why all efforts at 'renewing' federalism from within are doomed to failure from the start. Let those who would still be hopeful consider a series of recipes for a revamped federalism: the Ryan Beige Paper. By all accounts, it is a lame duck: too little for Quebec, and too much for the rest of Canada!

If you want to preserve the Quebec-Canada relationship, you must therefore look in a different direction. And you will find a more promising approach in the new forms of association which have cropped up in Europe and other continents in recent years: the European common Market, the Nordic Council, the Andean Pact, etc.... These are associations of sovereign states that provide for extensive and structured relationships between the partners, notably in economic matters, while allowing each government to remain fully in charge of all its own affairs. There you can find the blueprint of a new and viable deal between Quebec and Canada.

The formula proposed by the Quebec Government and explicitly described in the referendum question, therefore, is not aimed at the separation of Quebec from the rest of Canada but, on the contrary, at a new form of association between equals.... It is no mandate for secession, but a mandate for negotiation. And not a mandate to negotiate the separation of Quebec, but a mandate to negotiate a new association with Canada....

Referendum Oui (Quebec: Directeur général des Elections, 1980), pp. 9–11.

Which Way Ahead? —Aislin's Commentary on the State of Quebec, 1979

The referendum campaign over sovereignty-association revealed that the people of Quebec were deeply torn between contending loyalties. While the "No" side scored a victory, the issue of Quebec's place in Confederation remained far from resolved. The situation was further complicated by the re-election in April 1981, of the Parti Québécois government, which had pledged not to hold another referendum during its second mandate. A political cartoon by Terry Mosher, popularly known as "Aislin", which appeared in 1979, offered a trenchant commentary on the "real" options open to Quebec.

CONFLICTING INTERPRETATIONS

The contemporary history of Quebec since the Quiet Revolution has stirred tremendous scholarly interest and produced its share of lively debate. Quebec historians and social scientists, among others, have written abundantly on the fundamental question of "Who speaks for Quebec?". Moreover, the Quebec constitutional crisis and its implications for Canada's future have prompted many English-Canadian analysts, and a few American scholars, to turn their attention to the nature and complexity of Quebec politics. Like most contemporary history, however, recent studies have often reflected the strong biases generated by the ongoing clash of Quebec ideologies.

Almost every major public leader and group claiming to speak on behalf of Quebeckers has been subject to study and analysis. While all observers agree that the Quiet Revolution was a period of considerable and rapid change, sharp differences of opinion have emerged over who best expressed and represented the aspirations of most French Canadians or Québécois. Many analysts have disagreed over which party or group today can claim to be the rightful heir to the Quiet Revolution. And, since the early 1980s, fundamental questions are being raised about the future of Quebec nationalism and the long-term viability of French Canada as a distinct cultural entity.

THE NATURE OF THE QUIET REVOLUTION—A CLASH OF VIEWS

The New Era of Reform and Modernization—A Liberal Viewpoint

Early interpretations of Jean Lesage's Quiet Revolution were heavily influenced by popular perceptions of Maurice Duplessis' Union Nationale régime as a narrowly nationalist, anti-trade union and blatantly corrupt administration. Indeed, a whole generation of Liberal analysts greeted the beginning of the Lesage era as a needed break from the past. One such interpreter was Herbert F. Quinn, a political scientist known for his study of the Union Nationale party from its origins to its decline in the 1970s.

> Like the Union Nationale in 1936, the Quebec Liberal party came to power in 1960 as a party of reform. Unlike Duplessis' party, however, the Liberals not only carried out their promised reforms but in most respects went far beyond them. During the period between 1960 and 1966 they put through sweeping educational, economic, and administrative reforms which had a profound impact on the modernization and democratization of Quebec society. Although the extensive changes we will be describing must for the most part be credited to the initiative of the Lesage government, at the same time they were also a response to pressures and demands which had been building up for some time from various segments of Quebec society and which had been held in check by the restrictive policies of the Duplessis regime. Like any revolution, the one we are discussing did not start from scratch in 1960; it had been slowly developing since the end of the Second World War. The Lesage regime acted as the catalyst which set it in motion....

* * * * *

> The magnitude of the task facing the Liberal party when it came to power lay in the fact that the Duplessis era had left Quebec in the contradictory position of being an advanced industrial society with institutions, ideologies, and attitudes which were largely pre-industrial. This contradiction was to be found in the educational system, the attitude of the government toward the economy, the administrative and electoral systems, labour legislation, and social welfare services.

> Although some advances had been made in the educational system since the Second World War, when the Liberals came to power it still was deficient both quantitatively and qualitatively, and it was almost entirely under the control of the Church. For financial and other reasons too many young people dropped out of the school system too early and without the adequate intellectual and specialized skills which one Quebec

educationist called, 'la clé de la société moderne.' ... in higher education the system of classical colleges was geared to turning out priests, doctors, and lawyers, rather than the engineers, accountants, and technicians needed in an industrial society; further-more, these colleges were beyond the reach of those who could not afford the fees.

After education, the area in which the policies of governments in the past had been most inadequate was in regard to the economy and the development of natural resources. We have seen that both the Taschereau and Duplessis administrations, with their strong commitment to private enterprise, had a restricted and negative attitude towards the intervention of the state in the economy. This led to the uncontrolled activity of the large multinational corporations and the wasteful exploitation of natural resources, and it did little to increase the participation of the French Quebecer in the English-dominated economy of the province. . . .

* * * * *

Social welfare services were outdated and inferior compared to other provinces, and like education, were almost entirely in the hands of the clergy. The Church's hospitals, orphanages, homes for the aged, and other charitable institutions had performed a useful service in the heavily agrarian society of the past, but its human and financial resources were no longer adequate to meet the needs of an urbanized and industrialized state. Moreover, many of the religious principles underlying the provision of these social services were being increasingly questioned by the growth of secular values.

Herbert F. Quinn, *The Union Nationale: Quebec Nationalism from Duplessis to Lévesque*, 2nd ed. (Toronto: University of Toronto Press, 1979), pp. 187–190. Footnotes deleted.

The "Noisy Evolution"—A Recent Synthesis

Recent histories of modern Quebec, Maurice Duplessis' regime, and the Quiet Revolution have tended to depart from the Liberal view, contending that Quebec under "le chef" was anything but a "backward place". And recent interpreters of Jean Lesage's so-called *révolution tranquille* from 1960 to 1966 have suggested that, although the state's role was significantly expanded over this period, government priorities remained remarkably simi-lar to those of the Duplessis era. Susan Mann Trofimenkoff, a historian at the University of Ottawa, has attempted to tie the recent threads of interpretation together.

The Quiet Revolution fooled a lot of people. For six years the Liberal party of Quebec convinced itself and most onlookers that it had created something new and done so peacefully. By using the provincial government in a daring and innovative way, the Liberals had succeeded in slaying the ghost of Duplessis. Out of the ashes of his *grande noirceur* (great gloom) had arisen a thoroughly modern Quebec, glowing with enthusi-asm and purpose and, except for language, looking and behaving very much like any other political entity in North America. In the hands of bureaucrats in pinstripe suits, planning had succeeded in wiping out the past. For awhile almost everyone applauded. And then they began to wonder. For those within Quebec, the pace of change was either too fast or too slow. To those outside Quebec, the changes at first appeared welcoming but then became menacing. Just as Quebec was becoming so similar, it began reiterating its difference. Given all the modern trappings of that difference, it might well threaten the stability of Canada itself. Quebecois wondered uneasily, what next? And English Canadians demanded fretfully, what does Quebec want?. . .

* * * * *

By 1966 both the noise and the evolution had left a number of people uneasy. Traditionalists distrusted the notion of an *état providence*, a providential state that did everything for everyone. They regretted the state's undermining of previous forces of social cohesion, such as the church. Radicals, on the other hand, suspected that the makers of the Quiet Revolution were too middle class and were fashioning the new Quebec too much in their own image. Rural dwellers eyed the urban pace and direction of change warily. Regional sensibilities chafed under the increasing economic dominance of Montreal and the new bureaucratic dominance of Quebec City. If workers, particularly those in public service employment, saw their wages rise, they also watched taxes increase and inflation eat away their gains. Federalists were surprised by the nationalist cloak that increasingly covered the activities of the provincial government and took their surprise to Ottawa. Nationalists on the other hand thought the cloak should envelop even more, perhaps as much as an independent Quebec. English Canadians both inside and outside Quebec wondered unhappily about the outcome of all this French fervour; for a while it had seemed so familiar, but gradually it became frightening. And in spite of the bomb throwers, women may have tossed the most explosive suggestion into the public forum in that their problems appeared to be related neither to class nor to nation. What that might mean for the future was anyone's guess. In the present, all of the protest combined to carve off ten percent of the Liberals' popular vote, offering two percent to the *Union nationale* and eight to the separatists. It still left the Liberals with the most votes, but fewer seats. The *Union nationale* victory of June 5, 1966, was, the Liberals liked to think, the end of the Quiet Revolution. But many of the groups that that noisy evolution had spawned went on to develop their own dreams of nation.

Susan Mann Trofimenkoff, *The Dream of Nation: A Social and Intellectual History of Quebec* (Toronto: Macmillan of Canada, 1982), pp. 298–299, 313–314.

VIEWS OF SEPARATISM AND SOVEREIGNTY-ASSOCIATION

The Goal of An Independent Quebec—René Lévesque's Case for A Great "Collective Project"

Many social scientists and politicians in Quebec came to view the Quiet Revolution as a period of modernization which, in many ways, threatened French Canada's cultural identity. For, while Quebeckers were "catching up" with the rest of North America in these years, concerns were expressed that they were losing their cultural distinctiveness. Some analysts, such as Laval University sociologist Fernand Dumont, argued that if Quebeckers were to remain "a unique cultural species" in a modern technocratic society, they would have to join together in support of great "collective projects" like national independence or social reconstruction.

For René Lévesque and his Parti Québécois, the great "collective project" has been the pursuit of an independent, sovereign Quebec. Since the formation of the PQ in 1968, Lévesque and the party have followed a strategy of *étapisme*, but the ultimate goal has always been the political independence of Quebec in a loose economic union with the rest of Canada.

What of Quebec's own national future, both internal and international, in this context of sovereignty-cum-interdependence?...

* * * * *

One thing sure, is that Quebec will not end up, either soon or in any foreseeable future, as the anarchic caricature of a revolutionary banana republic which adverse propaganda has been having great sinister fun depicting in advance....

In actual fact, French Quebec, with its normal share of troubles, disquiet and, now, the same kind of social turmoil and search for new values that are rampant all over the Western world, remains at bottom a very solid, well-knit and nonviolent society. Even its new and demanding nationalism has about itself something less strident and essentially more self-confident than its current pan-Canadian counterpart. For Quebec has an assurance of identity, along with a relative lack of aggressiveness, which are the result of that one major factor of national durability lacking in the rest of Canada: a different language and the cultural fabric that goes with it.

Now how does the Parti Québécois see this society begin to find its way as an independent nation?...

The way we have been trying to rough it out democratically through half a dozen national party conventions, ours would call for a presidential regime, as much of an equal-opportunity social system as we could afford, and a decent measure, as quickly as possible but as carefully as indicated, of economic 'repatriation.' This last would begin to happen immediately, and normally without any great perturbation, through the very fact of sovereignty: with the gathering in of all of our public revenues and the full legislative control which any self-respecting national state has to implement over its main financial institutions, banks, insurance companies and the like....

As to non-resident enterprise, apart from the universal minimums concerning incorporations and due respect for Quebec taxes, language and other classic national requirements, what we have been fashioning over the last few years is an outline of a policy which we think is both logical and promising....

In brief, Quebec's most privileged links, aside from its most essential relationship with the Canadian partner, would be first with the United States—where there is no imaginable reason to frown on such a tardy but natural and healthy development (especially during a Bicentennial year). Then Quebec would look to other Francophone or 'Latin' countries as cultural respondents, and to France herself—who would certainly not be indifferent to the fact that this new nation would constitute the second most important French-speaking country in the world. In brief, such is the peaceful and, we confidently hope, fruitfully progressive state which may very well appear on the map of North America before the end of the decade.

René Lévesque, "For an Independent Quebec", *Foreign Affairs*, Vol. 54, No. 4 (July 1976), pp. 742-744.

Separatism—A Critical Point of View

There can be no doubt that, while the dream of an independent Quebec enthused a large minority of French-speaking Quebeckers, virtually all Canadians outside Quebec remained bitterly opposed to separatism. No one argument is common to all foes of separatism, but Douglas Fullerton's perspective, that of a well-known civil servant long involved with Quebec, might be considered representative:

An open letter to Prime Minister Lévesque
Cher René, ...
Do you remember the open letter I wrote you (back in 1967)? . . . .
I urged you to 'draw back from a policy of potential disaster,' and closed with the suggestion if the decision to separate or not is largely an internal one for Quebec, 'the matter of how much it will cost will be determined largely by those outside Quebec.'

Nearly ten years have passed and nothing which has occurred in that decade leads me to change my mind. In fact, Quebec is more dependent than ever on borrowed capital, and on federal transfer payments and equalization grants, to keep its economy alive, if in a sickly state. . . .

By the time your April 1, 1977 language white paper appeared, I had acquired a certain scepticism about any public statements or releases of you or your ministers . . . . The language white paper and Bill One which emerged four weeks later, hit a new low. I had no quarrel with the general objectives of the language legislation, which seeks to establish the primacy of the French language in Quebec . . . . What I personally found most repugnant about the white paper was its Chapter One—'The situation of the French language in Quebec.'

What a monstrous tissue of twisted facts, misleading statements, and biased analysis! Yet it is on this superstructure, René Lévesque, that Bills One and 101 were mounted; it is with such products of devious minds that it has been defended, justified, rationalized. This legislation, which even you yourself admit to finding humiliating, and which could prove to be the most divisive ever produced in this country, polarizing and envenoming opinion, pitting English against French, splitting Quebec families. This legislation, which any objective observer of the Quebec scene knows is unnecessary. . . .

But what of the other side of the coin, your case for association with Canada, after independence? You are already beginning to see some backlash from your activities to date, and the language issue will inevitably worsen French-English relations in this country. Think of the impact of the thousands of anglophone Quebecers, now scattering across this country, made to feel like second class citizens, forced to leave a Quebec homeland . . . . if you honestly believe that association would be possible after the great divide, you had better start reshaping your thinking. Your government's language policies will be the kiss of death for it.

If, however, the purpose of the 'association' argument is simply to quieten the fears of francophone Quebecers that they will lose out economically if Quebec separates, then you should be shining up a new propaganda weapon. Even péquiste supporters in the media will be unable to conceal the truth from the average French-Canadian worker, who is more interested in his daily bread than in being a pawn in a struggle for power and glory by the intellectually élite group which surrounds you . . . .

But no matter what you do now to escape the walls closing in on you, most of the blame for what happens will be yours, in your dual role as Prime Minister and party leader. You are no longer a knight in shining armour to me, of course, and I may have succumbed too readily to your natural persuasiveness. Still, I remember the good years, when the things we did were based on solid economic sense, not on perverted religious doctrine; when the Hon. René Lévesque was more concerned about improving the quality of life in Quebec, and giving good government to the people, than in aspiring to be the George Washington of a new, unilingual, ghetto-like state. Perhaps you yourself are wondering if you made the right choice ten years ago. Could it be that you will look at yourself in the mirror, one of these mornings, and say to yourself, 'My God—what have I done to my beloved Quebec?'

En amitié—

(As ever)

Doug Fullerton

Douglas H. Fullerton, *The Dangerous Delusion: Quebec's Independence Obsession* (Toronto: McClelland and Stewart, 1978), pp. 208–209, 210–211.

VIEWS OF FEDERALISM AND BILINGUALISM

Federalism and the French Canadians—Pierre Trudeau's Analysis

Much of the debate over Quebec's role in Canadian federalism since the early 1960s was dominated by the ideas and initiatives of Pierre E. Trudeau, who gained recognition as one of the country's strongest defenders of federalism and bilingualism. He strenuously opposed all proposals for "particular status" for Quebec, and instead insisted that the economic, social and cultural goals of Quebec would best be achieved by a new brand of federalism based on extended bilingualism and a greater French Canadian presence in Ottawa. In his book of essays entitled *Federalism and the French Canadians* (1968), Trudeau set out his main arguments.

We French Canadians are terribly lacking in tenacity. Rather than devote all our efforts to the real improvement of our intellectual, social, and economic condition, we let ourselves be carried away by legal superstructures without even inquiring whether they will work.

All the various kinds of 'special status' which have been discussed until now, whatever their content, lead to the following logical problem: how can a constitution be devised to give Quebec greater powers than other provinces, without reducing Quebec's power in Ottawa? How can citizens of other provinces be made to accept the fact that they would have less power over Quebec at the federal level than Quebec would have over them? How, for example, can Quebec assume powers in foreign affairs, which other provinces do not have, without accepting a reduction of its influence in the field of foreign affairs through the federal government? How can Quebec be made the national state of French Canadians, with really *special* powers, without abandoning at the same time demands for the parity of French and English in Ottawa and throughout the rest of the country?

These questions remain unanswered, because they are unanswerable. For to think about them is to realize that we must have the courage and lucidity to make a choice.

Either the federal government exercises approximately the same powers over Quebec as it does over other provinces; Quebeckers will then be entitled to be represented in Ottawa in exactly the same way as other Canadians. This option would obviously not prevent Quebeckers from adopting whatever special policies they wished *within their provincial jurisdiction*, for example through the Civil Code, social legislation, development of resources, or a completely revised *provincial* constitution. This option would also allow parity between English and French languages in all federal institutions, and the same parity would eventually be negotiated with other provinces.

Or, the central government's power over Quebec is substantially reduced compared to what it is over other provinces. Quebec's constitutional position having thus become

The Quiet Revolution and Beyond   517

really special, its electorate would not be entitled to demand complete representation at the federal level; and, more specifically, it would have to accept that the French fact be limited, legally and politically, to the province of Quebec.

The second alternative is the 'special status' one. We can adopt it, or not. But those who think that they can have both options are deceiving themselves . . . .

Pierre Elliott Trudeau, *Federalism and the French Canadians* (Toronto: Macmillan, 1968), pp. xxiv-xxvi.

The "Polarization" of Quebec—A Political Scientist's Assessment of Trudeau Federalism

Not every analyst concurred with the Trudeau approach to Quebec and the constitutional problem. Professor Donald V. Smiley, an English-Canadian political scientist, was one of many who suggested that Trudeau's position "polarized politics" within Quebec and heightened the tensions between Quebec and Canadian forms of nationalism.

As a scholar and publicist and later as Minister of Justice and Prime Minister of Canada, Pierre Elliott Trudeau has forcefully supported the bilingual and bicultural alternative as an integral part of his general formulation of Canadian federalism. This formulation can be summarized in five propositions:

(1) *The distribution of legislative powers between Ottawa and the provinces under the British North America Act corresponds to the needs of the French Canadian community in Quebec . . . .*

(2) *The federal authorities must respect provincial jurisdiction . . . .*

(3) *A special status for Quebec is unacceptable . . . .*

(4) *There must be an enhanced recognition of the French fact in Canada as such . . . .*

(5) *Liberal and nationalist values are diametrically opposed and the latter are incompatible with Canadian federalism . . . .*

Pierre Elliott Trudeau has thus formulated a coherent view of Canadian federalism, and as Prime Minister he has lost no opportunity to try to polarize politics within Quebec and throughout Canada on this issue. In pressing this polarization Trudeau has defined as unacceptable the views of some of those whose allegiances are basically federalist. For example, during the 1968 election campaign the Prime Minister attacked the Progressive Conservative party as supporting the 'two nations' solution, because of the views of the Quebec Conservative leader, Marcel Faribault, although Faribault had spoken and written extensively in support of federalism. Within his own party Trudeau had previously taken a very strong position against the very cautious special status position elaborated by Maurice Lamontagne in 1966, although Lamontagne was like Trudeau both a federalist Liberal and a distinguished student of Canadian federalism . . . .

The new linguistic regime in Quebec[2] and the emergent pattern of French-English relations in that province does not in my view challenge the essentials of Confederation. The government of Quebec is the most effective instrument for the survival of the French language and culture in North America and will no doubt by itself find the practical limits to these majoritarian policies. Neither need such changes as those

2. A reference to the Quebec language law (Bill 22) passed by Robert Bourassa's Liberal Government in 1974, which made French the working language and established language tests for admission to English schools in the province.

embodied in Bill 22 cause any retreat from the bilingual and bicultural alternative as this relates to the institutions of the federal government rather than the French Canadian minorities outside Quebec. What is, however, needed is more realism from supporters of this alternative, a realism which dissociates dualism within the shared institutions of the government of Canada from dualism within Quebec or the other provinces and which recognizes that the strength of Quebec nationalism is decisively determined by other factors than the degree of recognition of cultural and linguistic duality outside that province....

The polarization of Quebec society on the national issue— either as this involves the relations between Quebec and the rest of Canada or French-English relations within Quebec itself— constitutes dangers for the Canadian federation. So long as Quebec elections are in effect plebiscites on the continuance of Confederation, there will be incentives for external political actors to involve themselves; these are absent in the case of the other provinces. Even more critically, the rapid changes in Quebec since 1960 appear to have resulted in the weakening of legitimacy in the province's political institutions to the extent that it may be possible to govern it if at all only by the use of measures which are by Canadian standards repressive....

Donald V. Smiley, *Canada in Question: Federalism in the Seventies*, 2nd ed. (Toronto: McGraw-Hill Ryerson, 1975), pp. 174–75, 190–91.

DEBATING THE FUTURE—SPEAKING FOR QUEBEC IN THE EIGHTIES

The Impact of the Referendum Defeat—Some Hypotheses

During the 1970s, it was tempting to conclude that Quebec's movement towards independence, though gradual, was irreversible. The Parti Québécois had dynamic leadership, a fervent membership, a vast social and national project. Youth seemed irrevocably committed to the dream, while federalism's supporters were aging. With each election, the Parti Québécois's vote increased until finally it took power from the Bourassa government in 1976. Yet it lost the referendum vote on sovereignty-association and was compelled to abandon, for the time being, its plans to negotiate a new partnership "between equals" with Ottawa. Two York University political scientists, Kenneth McRoberts and Dale Postgate, were among the first to speculate on the impact of the referendum on the Quebec independence movement.

The referendum defeat has delivered a staggering challenge to the Parti québécois, and to the independence movement in general. It is too early to determine whether the Parti québécois will survive this challenge. But it is clear that the independence movement, per se, will persist. If anything, it may become stronger as the alternatives between federalism and independence narrow. On this basis, the need to find a new accommodation for Quebec within the federal system is more acute than ever before. Yet, given the massive 'no' vote, there is a risk that the challenge will not be fully appreciated in English Canada. Since not even a clear majority of Quebec Francophones were ready to support the referendum proposition, with all its careful hedging, there will be a temptation to presume that most Québécois can now be reconciled to the federal system as it now stands, or that their demands for change are essentially the same as those in other provinces. This would be an error. Surveys show that most Quebec Francophones share three basic assumptions: there must be an expansion of the powers held by the Quebec government; the Quebec state is the government of a distinct 'national' collectivity; and the relationship between Quebec and the rest of Canada should be based on equality. These were, of course, key themes of the 'yes' campaign. But they also became important elements of the 'no' campaign, as federalists sought to mobilize support. They must, in turn, be central elements in any 'renewed federalism.'

Kenneth McRoberts and Dale Postgate, *Quebec: Social Change and Political Crisis* Rev. ed. (Toronto: McClelland and Stewart, 1980), pp. 280-281.

Nationalism in Decline—Dominique Clift's Thesis

With the failure of the referendum vote and the proclamation of a new Canadian constitution, Quebec's movement towards political sovereignty, or even towards greater autonomy within Confederation, reached an impasse. Many Quebec analysts and commentators in the early 1980s began to point to signs that Quebeckers were becoming more conservative in their attitudes and more preoccupied with economic issues. The Parti Québécois government, for its part, seemed to be turning its attention to controlling the costs of adminstration and reducing the size of the Quebec state.

In interpreting these recent changes in Quebec society, journalist Dominique Clift concluded that Quebec nationalism was in a period of decline. The main thrust of his interpretation in *The Decline of Nationalism in Quebec* (1982) was summarized in this article.

There are unmistakable signs that once again Quebec is engaged in one of its periodic mutations that outsiders always find so disconcerting. Political disorientation is now so prevalent that it suggests a kind of ideological collapse usually preceding the appearance of a completely new set of values.

The last time this happened was during the 1950s as the province came to terms with urban life and industrial organizations. It was marked by a dramatic drop in the birth rate and led to the rapid decline of the Catholic Church. This time, the change has to do with the collective self-image and it may completely transform the historical attachment to nationalism, particularly that aspect of it which tends to paint the French as victims of the English, of capitalism and of history itself. . . .

* * * * *

Nationalist ideology sees the state as crucial for its aims. But confidence has been eroded by burdensome taxation and stifling bureaucracy. Public servants are viewed increasingly as parasites. However, the major failure of the state could well be harsh legislation enacted last month to force illegally striking teachers back to work.

Belief in the benevolence of the state was shattered as the law foisted on the strikers a presumption of guilt by suspending the application of certain rights granted by federal and provincial charters. There were strong protests by the Quebec Bar Association and from the provincial Human Rights Commission. Opinion leaders are making the point that excessive force has been used in defence of authority.

The current mood signals the end of that period which has come to be known as the Quiet Revolution and which was launched in 1960 by former premier Jean Lesage. The nationalism it had initially proposed was aimed at achievement and self-assertion. But under the pressure of ultra-nationalists such as René Lévesque, Mr. (Pierre) Bourgault and Mr. (Pierre) Vallières, it became obsessed with liberation politics and victimization....

* * * * *

The victim representation has worked well in Quebec for specific objectives such as the election of the Parti Québécois in 1976 and the referendum on sovereignty-association in 1980. But it has serious drawbacks in an urban, industrial and capitalist society such as Quebec has become. There comes a moment when leaders must focus on pressing requirements of productivity and economic growth, and this is the point where liberation politics will break down. The problem is the existential victims are not achievers and they are not prone to the kind of action required in the prosaic and workaday world....

Even though Quebec is undergoing a rapid ideological transformation, it remains very difficult to shake off the behaviour patterns associated with liberation politics. French society has now become so conflict-oriented that negotiated settlements are sometimes impossible, particularly if provincial authorities are involved.

Confrontation has become a way of governing in spite of the fact that it has produced far more defeats than victories. Indeed, there is an incredible string of failures in a number of areas that would have brought down any other government: in constitutional reform, public-service bargaining, budget policy, relations with business and with minority groups, not to mention diplomatic intrigues with France. Instead of destroying the Parti Québécois, these failures are simply discrediting the idea of the state as the instrument of collective liberation.

This could be the last intellectual construct to fall before the coming onslaught of individualism and pragmatism. Or maybe populism.

Dominique Clift, "Beyond Nationalism in Quebec", *Globe and Mail*, March 22, 1983. p. 7.

The Possibilities for Quebec's Independence—A Quebec Nationalist View

Political forecasts like that of Dominique Clift looked very prophetic indeed by the mid-eighties. Leading authorities on modern Quebec, from Professor Ramsay Cook of York University to editorialists with the French-language press saw in the 1980 PQ Referendum defeat and in the subsequent disintegration of public support for the Parti Québécois signs that the Quiet Revolution was perhaps coming to an end. In addition, news reports in the popular press were suggesting that Quebec's youth no longer rallied to the PQ and its project as they had in the 1970s.

In the face of such adversity, Quebec independentists and their intellectual allies remained hopeful. Even though most conceded that Quebec's separation was not imminent, they continued to insist that predictions of the demise of Quebec nationalism were premature. One Québécois commentator, Pauline Vaillancourt of the Université de Québec in Montreal, argued that, in spite of a series of setbacks in the early 1980s, Quebec's independence remained a real possibility.

The historical forces which first gave rise to Quebec nationalism have not changed. The centuries of second class citizenship, national oppression, English assumed superiority, economic exploitation through English domination of commerce and industry, and discrimination within confederation cannot be erased even were they to completely disappear tomorrow. Quebecois are no more comfortable in English Canada now than they were 100 years ago. Anti-French racism has not disappeared.

The PQ has not been completely without success in the struggle to move Quebec out of Canada, though its limited victories receive little attention in English Canada and are sometimes overlooked within Quebec. The 1980 referendum was defeated. But a precedent was set. By permitting Quebec to hold its referendum and by accepting the results, Ottawa acknowledged that Confederation can be called into question democratically and peacefully in the future. What would happen if in a subsequent referendum a majority supported sovereignty-association? It would be exceedingly difficult for the federal government to reject the legitimacy of this mechanism....

Almost imperceptibly, and certainly unintentionally, *the structures and mechanisms which may one day permit Quebec's peaceful separation from Canada have fallen into place over the last several years.* The stage for Quebec's citizens may once again consider the possibility of opting out of Confederation. What will influence whether or not independence is put back on the agenda?

Whether Quebec stays in Confederation or separates will be influenced not just by events in Quebec but by the federal government and the English Canadian provinces. Decisions made in other provinces and in Ottawa will increase or decrease the Québécois consciousness of the necessity to separate....

Other political events also weigh in the balance. Trudeau's resignation is of substantial importance. In Quebec it is generally interpreted as boosting the possibility of independence. Trudeau's policy of bilingualism from Atlantic to Pacific was deeply resented in English Canada. In Quebec it was received with mixed emotion. Even those who supported it saw it as a very temporary gain....

The large number of francophones in high posts in Ottawa was testimony to Trudeau's promise to make room for Quebec within Confederation. Quebecers were constantly cross-pressured between Quebec City and Ottawa. Trudeau effectively reduced popular support in Quebec for sovereignty-association and nationalist consciousness in general. It is hard to imagine anyone else, Conservative or Liberal, being able to replace him in this respect. Quebec nationalists almost unanimously agree that support for Confederation within Quebec will inevitably wane over the next few years as 'French power' in Ottawa diminishes....

Of course, much depends on the kind of leadership offered from Ottawa and the sort of policies pursued. If Ottawa chooses a decentralized rather than a centralized form of Confederation, Quebec may become comfortable within Confederation. If provincial powers are reduced to mere administrative responsibilities, tension will increase. The judiciary could use its powers in interpreting the new constitution to protect provincial autonomy. But to date Supreme Court decisions, especially the unqualified rejection of Quebec's veto, signal that judicial interpretation will favor Ottawa....

Whether Quebec stays or leaves Confederation is related to the fortunes of the PQ....

...If the PQ makes a mistake it could disappear from the Quebec political map as quickly as it appeared. But if it correctly assesses the political situation it could re-emerge united and stronger than ever before and again mobilize Quebec toward independence. In any case it is far from clear that Quebec's efforts to gain independence are a thing of the past.

Pauline Vaillancourt, "Will Quebec Still Separate?", *Canadian Dimension*, Vol. 18, No. 5 (October/November, 1984), pp. 12–16. Sub-headings omitted.

A Guide to Further Reading

1. Overviews

Bernard, André, *What Does Quebec Want?* Toronto: James Lorimer and Co., 1978.

Coleman, William D., *The Independence Movement in Quebec, 1945–1980.* Toronto: University of Toronto Press, 1984.

Dion, Léon, *Quebec: The Unfinished Revolution.* Translated by Thérèse Romer. Montreal: McGill-Queen's University Press, 1976.

Dumont, Fernand, *The Vigil of Quebec.* Translated by Sheila Fischman and Richard Howard. Toronto: University of Toronto Press, 1974.

Jones, Richard, *Community in Crisis: French-Canadian Nationalism in Perspective.* Toronto: McClelland and Stewart, 1972. Carleton Library no. 59.

Latouche, Daniel, "La vraie nature de . . . la Révolution tranquille". *Canadian Journal of Political Science*, Vol. VII, no. 3 (September 1974), pp. 525–536.

McRoberts, Kenneth and Dale Postgate, *Quebec, Social Change and Political Crisis.* rev. ed. Toronto: McClelland and Stewart, 1980.

Milner, Sheilagh Hodgins and Henry Milner, *The Decolonization of Quebec.* Toronto: McClelland and Stewart, 1973.

Quinn, Herbert F., *The Union Nationale: Quebec Nationalism from Duplessis to Lévesque*, 2nd ed. Toronto: University of Toronto Press, 1979.

Rioux, Marcel, *Quebec in Question.* Translated by James Boake. Toronto: James Lorimer and Co., 1978.

Saywell, John T., *The Rise of the Parti Québécois.* Toronto: University of Toronto Press, 1977.

Thomson, Dale C., ed., *Quebec Society and Politics: Views from the Inside.* Toronto: McClelland and Stewart, 1973.

Trofimenkoff, Susan Mann, *The Dream of Nation: A Social and Intellectual History of Quebec.* Toronto: Macmillan, 1982.

2. Specialized Studies

Arnopoulos, Sheila McLeod and Dominique Clift, *The English Fact in Quebec.* Montreal: McGill-Queen's University Press, 1980.

Black, Conrad, *Duplessis.* Toronto: McClelland and Stewart, 1977.

Bourgault, Pierre, *Ecrits polémiques, 1960–1981. 1. La politique.* Montreal: VLB Editeur, 1982.

_____, *Ecrits polémiques, 1960–1983. 2. La culture.* Montreal: VLB Editeur, 1983.

Clift, Dominique, *The Decline of Nationalism in Quebec.* Montreal: McGill-Queen's University Press, 1982.

Cook, Ramsay, "Has the Quiet Revolution finally ended?" *Queen's Quarterly* Vol. 90 (Summer 1983), pp.330–342.

Desbarats, Peter, *René: A Canadian in Search of a Country.* Toronto: McClelland and Stewart, 1976.

Fraser, Graham, *The PQ: René Lévesque and the Parti Québécois in Power.* Toronto: Macmillan, 1984.

Fullerton, Douglas H., *The Dangerous Delusion: Quebec's Independence Obsession.* Toronto: McClelland and Stewart, 1978.

Jones, Richard, *Duplessis and the Union Nationale Administration.* trans. by author. Ottawa: Canadian Historical Association, 1983. Historical Booklet no 35.

Latouche, Daniel, "It Takes Two to. . . Divorce and Remarry". *Journal of Canadian Studies*, Vol. 12 (July 1977), pp. 24–32.

Lévesque, René, "For an Independent Quebec". *Foreign Affairs*, Vol. 54, no 4 (July 1976), pp. 734–744.

McRoberts, Kenneth, "The Sources of Neo-nationalism in Quebec" *Ethnic and Racial Studies*, Vol. VII (January 1984), pp. 55–85.

Milner, Henry, *Politics in the New Quebec*. Toronto: McClelland and Stewart, 1978.

Murray, Vera, *Le parti québécois: de la fondation à la prise du pouvoir*. Montreal: Hurtubise-HMH, 1976. Collection Science politique.

Pelletier, Gérard, *Years of Impatience 1950–1960*. Toronto: Methuen, 1984.

Pelletier, Réjean, ed., *Partis politiques au Québec*. Montreal: Hurtubise-HMH, 1976. Collection Science politique.

Pinard, Maurice and Richard Hamilton, "The Parti Québécois Comes to Power: An Analysis of the 1976 Quebec Election", *Canadian Journal of Political Science*, Vol. XI, no. 4 (December 1978), pp. 739–775.

Robert, Jean-Claude, *Du Canada français au Québec libre: Histoire d'un mouvement indépendantiste*. Paris: Flammarion, 1975.

Thomson, Dale C.,*Jean Lesage & The Quiet Revolution*. Toronto: Macmillan, 1984.

Vallières, Pierre, *White Niggers of America*. Translated by Joan Pinkham. Toronto: McClelland and Stewart, 1972.

Vaillancourt, Pauline, "Will Quebec Still Separate?" *Canadian Dimension*, Vol. 18, no. 5 (Oct/Nov 1984), pp. 11–16.

Wilson-Smith, Anthony, "Changing Course in Quebec" *Maclean's*, Jan. 21, 1985, pp. 14–18.

20

THE CHALLENGE OF
CANADIAN DIVERSITY, 1960–1980s

Emerging Identities or Portent of Deconfederation?

"Unity in Diversity" is a hopeful phrase which has been widely applied to Canada since the heady days of Expo '67 and the centennial celebrations. Yet Canada in the mid-1980s seems to be experiencing as much division as unity. The Canadian community has been beset with a seemingly infinite variety of tensions involving conflicting regional, cultural and territorial interests. This contemporary diversity of regions and cultures has roots which grow deep in our history. Indeed much of what is distinctive about the Canadian experience in the latter half of the century can be found in what historians Ramsay Cook and J.M.S. Careless have termed our "limited identities" of region, culture, class and territory. In today's Canada, these identities—whether in the form of the Quebecker's assertion of nationalism, the Westerner's sense of alienation, the Maritimer's feeling of economic deprivation, or the recent immigrant's pride in his ethnicity—continue to animate much public discussion concerning the present state and future shape of Canadian Confederation.

Over the past two decades the challenges of Canadian diversity have come to assume a central place in debates among historians, political scientists and popular commentators. The growing interest in Canada's diverse regions and cultures has to a large extent mirrored the evolution of Canada itself into a community of divided loyalties, English-French cleavages and remarkable ethnic diversity. Like our contemporary political leaders, interpreters of Canada's recent history have harboured differing notions of the nature of Canadian Confederation and have offered a variety of prognoses for Canada's future. Out of this ongoing debate, however, two fundamentally different positions have emerged. Many contemporary analysts, mostly strong upholders of "national unity" and centralized federalism, have argued that recent trends toward rampant provincialism, ethnic diversity and regional alienation threaten to fragment Canada and to bring about "Deconfederation", or the political breakup of the Canadian community. On the other side, a second school of interpretation—often more sympathetic to regional, ethnic and cultural interests—has contended that Canada's growing diversity of regions, cultures, and ethnic communities is a healthy development and a source of strength for Canadian federalism. While both views recognize the recent emergence of Canada's regional, ethnic and cultural diversity, they differ greatly on whether or not such a trend bodes well for Canada's future.

In exploring the problems of Canadian diversity from 1960 to the early '80s, we will examine three major challenges within our national community—the emergence of provincialism in federal-provincial relations, immigration and the development of multiculturalism, and the recent assertion of regionalism. All three of these will be considered, with the purpose of determining whether they constitute healthy expressions of Canada's "emerging identities" or ominous signs of impending national disintegration.

Each of these challenges of Canadian diversity has sprung from different sources and assumed different forms in the years since 1960. Resurgent provincialism can be traced back to the public demand for social welfare programs after 1945, and the consequent increase in the scale of expenditures under provincial areas of jurisdiction. Such changes precipitated a shift in power that set the stage for a "tug-of-war" between Ottawa and the provinces, beginning at the time of Quebec's Quiet Revolution. Later, in the 1970s, Quebec, Alberta, Newfoundland and the other provinces fought for greater provincial autonomy in the Canadian federal system: in the case of Quebec, for the right to negotiate sovereignty-association and in the case of Alberta and Newfoundland, for the right to full control over resources. The challenge of ethnic diversity is a legacy of Canada's postwar wave of immigration, which brought to Canada a succession of ethnic groups ranging from the Italians, Germans and Hungarians to more recent Third-World immigrants. Much of the dramatic change in Canada's ethnic composition since 1960 can be attributed to alterations in immigration regulations and the official adoption in 1971 of multiculturalism as Canadian state policy. Canada's recent regionalism, on the other hand, is more a response to the uneven character of Canadian development. For parts of Canada like the West and the Maritimes, regionalism, while originating in historic grievances such as the tariff, freight rates and central Canadian financial control, came to a head in the 1960s and 1970s over new issues like official bilingualism, oil supply and pricing and federal regional economic policies.

Many of the hopes and prospects for meeting Canada's challenges of diversity were conjoined in the Herculean struggle for a new Canadian constitution. Prime Minister Pierre Trudeau had set out a far-reaching plan in 1978 for constitutional reform. Trudeau and most provincial premiers had joined in the successful Quebec Referendum campaign of May 1980 promising to reward a "*Non*" vote on sovereignty-association with a new "made-in-Canada" constitution. But any consensus on reform dissolved in the temporary euphoria surrounding the federalist triumph. Canada's provincial leaders assumed the role of regional and cultural champions—and attempted to articulate the concerns of groups as diverse as nationalist Quebeckers, disaffected Westerners and neglected Newfoundlanders. Eventually, after months of negotiations and federal-provincial conflict, a constitutional deal was struck between Ottawa and all provinces except Quebec. The new Constitution, patriated from Britain in April 1982, settled some of the constitutional issues, yet did little to alleviate the immediate problems associated with Quebec's secession movement, a resurgence of Western alienation, or the economic development concerns of Atlantic Canada.

To delve into the multiple challenges of Canadian diversity from 1960 into the 1980s requires a closer analysis of the social and economic underpinnings of popular thought, political rhetoric and public policies in recent years. How have recent trends like the rise of provincialism, the emergence of ethnic pluralism, and the assertion of regionalism affected the viability of the Canadian community? Can the aspirations and demands of the provinces for Quebec sovereignty-association or full control over resources continue to be accommodated within a restructured federal system? Does the encouragement of Canada's multicultural diversity serve to perpetuate ethnic isolation and possibly accentuate Old-World prejudices? Or will recognizing the contributions of newer ethnic groups heighten the feelings of belonging to Canada and thus strengthen Canadian unity? Can the often competing interests of regions like the West and the Maritimes be harmonized within our Confederation? And most importantly, are these challenges of Canadian diversity a positive reflection of Canada's emerging regional, cultural and ethnic identities—or a portent of eventual Deconfederation?

SELECTED CONTEMPORARY SOURCES

THE CHALLENGE OF PROVINCIALISM—THE PROVINCES VS. OTTAWA

Every Canadian government since 1960 has had its problems with the provinces. While federal administrations after 1945 had expanded the government's role in the Canadian economy, the services provided—such as health care, roads, education and social assistance—were constitutionally a provincial responsibility. The accession to power of Jean Lesage's Liberals in the 1960 Quebec election seemed to signal the start of a new period of increasing provincialism. By the early sixties, Quebec was demanding an expanded role in the management of its own affairs—and all the provinces required more money to finance their programs. Finally, after a series of federal-provincial conferences, the federal government of Lester B. Pearson (1963–68)— adopting a form of "cooperative federalism"—allowed the provinces to opt out of federal shared-cost programs in return for a larger share of federal tax revenues. Political battles between the provinces and Ottawa continued, however, in the 1970s and into the early 1980s. Deep-seated economic, social and political grievances came to the surface. Attempts by Pierre Trudeau's governments (1968–79 and 1980–84) to reassert federal authority in areas like official bilingualism, oil pricing and constitutional reform were all resisted as examples of centralization aimed at perpetuating federal, and/or central Canadian, domination over the country.

Premier Jean Lesage's Appeal for "Special Status", 1965

The Quebec government of Jean Lesage, which ushered in the massive reforms of the Quiet Revolution in the early 1960s, often grappled with the problem of defining its prescription for a reformed federal system. The Premier and his colleagues called for a recognition of Quebec's "particular status" within Confederation—but seldom elaborated on the concept. In a landmark speech during a trip through western Canada in the fall of 1965, Lesage issued an appeal which spelled out clearly his view of Canada's cultural duality and Quebec's claim for "particular status".

> We are sometimes told, or given to understand, that Quebec is only one of Canada's ten provinces and that it need not concern itself with what happens in the other nine. This is tantamount to a denial that Quebec is the mainstay on which all French Canada relies....
>
> Our problem is to determine which factor is more characteristic of our country: Is it the political division of Canada into ten provinces, or is it the presence across the same vast territory of the two peoples who founded that country?
>
> Quebec feels that the second factor is the one which really counts. Those who stick to the first one... make the mistake of overlooking the historic role of the French-speaking element in Canada.
>
> What is more, their decision is based on a political situation which has nothing permanent about it: the present division of Canada into ten provinces, one predominantly French and the other nine predominantly English. That situation could have been and still could be quite different. This view of Canada as a series of water-tight provinces makes it difficult for us to find solutions to our current problems. It shuts us into a framework which may make us lose sight of the fundamental question: How can we guarantee the dynamic coexistence in Canada of both French and English societies?
>
> Jean Lesage, Address to the Saskatchewan Franco-Canadian Cultural Association, Saskatoon, September 19, 1965, reprinted in John Saywell, ed., *The Canadian Annual Review for 1965* (Toronto: University of Toronto Press, 1966), p. 38.

The Assertion of Provincial Identity—A British Columbian's Perspective, 1964

Quebec was not the only province to assert its claim of uniqueness in the early 1960s. Because of its geographic position, separated from the rest of Canada by the Rocky Mountains, and its relative wealth of resources, British Columbia exhibited a different regional response. Many British Columbians, conscious of Quebec's emerging separatist movement, sought to assert their province's distinct identity and to consider ways of preserving "the B.C. way of life". Responding to the "Quebec Question" in April 1964, one British Columbian commentator asserted that the two provinces were "different in the same way".

While Canada as a whole stands mesmerized by the upsurge of separatism in the province of Quebec, what is in many ways the most separatist unit of all, the province of British Columbia, continues to be ignored.

British Columbia has never really been a part of Canada at all, in the sense of belonging. It has stood outside the Canadian story from the beginning, and its attempts to join the Canadian mainstream such as it is have been steadfastly rebuffed, perhaps unconsciously.

...while these two parts are very different from the rest of Canada, *they are different in the same way*. Quebec and British Columbia could, as a matter of fact, understand one another very well if they ever set about doing it....

British Columbia is a motherland. The reason is simple. It got its own start, had its own history, and developed its own way of life before it somewhat reluctantly joined Confederation....

The differences between B.C. and Canada will remain so vast that I sometimes doubt whether they will ever be bridged. They result partly from B.C.'s youth. This province in many ways is still frontier country. The differences are also partly a result of geography. The Rocky Mountains remain at least a psychological barrier between B.C. and Canada, while, at the same time B.C.'s pride in empire has restricted its intercourse with the neighbouring American states of Oregon and Washington.

But overriding the geographical causes is the fact of history.... To Canada, B.C. is just something tacked on to the end of the country. But B.C. was created in a different era under different conditions, and in a different way by different men. These differences still have their effect. They are, to a large extent, what makes a British Columbian....

...[British Columbians] find themselves cut off by their Canadian homeland. This has always been so and it is demonstrably true. The most immediately evident symptom of it is the appalling lack of B.C. news in eastern papers....

So we sit smugly upon our beauty spots, express our confidence that this is the best of all possible lands and that in it we live the best of all possible ways of life, not awfully caring whether Quebec secedes or not, but understanding their feelings and being quietly interested in its mechanics. We can't help thinking that geography would make a parallel operation at the western end of Canada a very logical, neat and tidy affair.

Donald Stainsby, "Separatism is Old Stuff in B.C.", *Saturday Night*, April, 1964.

The Practice of Opting Out—An Assessment of Its Dangers, 1966

The Pearson government's decision to permit provinces to opt out of federal conditional grant (shared-cost) programs provoked a storm of controversy in federal-provincial relations. Critics of Pearson's brand of flexible, "cooperative federalism" contended that opting out would lead to excessive decentralization and a one-way flow of power from Ottawa to Quebec and the other provinces. One recognized authority on federal-provincial relations, J. Stefan

Dupré, offered this assessment of the Pearson government's 1964 proposals for "contracting out" and their possible long-term implications:

> Quebec lost no time in announcing its wholesale acceptance of the Pearson proposals. Other provinces appear content to await the outcome of the deliberations of the important Federal-Provincial Tax Structure Committee, whose terms of reference include the future of conditional grant and shared-cost programs. For the interim, the contracting out arrangements amount to little more than a symbolic rerouting of conditional grants to Quebec through tax abatements and lump sum compensation. The substantive programs in all instances are unaffected. It is the longer run that is the object of open speculation. . . .
>
> As to the long run implications of contracting out for Canadian federalism, there are doubtless prophets of doom who would see it as sounding the death knell of Canadian Confederation. Present contracting out arrangements, whether in the domain of wholly federal programs, in that of contributory schemes, or in that of conditional grants, are but the prelude to a great *Gotterdamerung* whereby Quebec will contract its way out of Confederation altogether. Let me say that I personally find this view untenable. I believe that contracting out is an important step in the direction of maintaining the integrity of Canadian federalism. Confederation is far more likely to contain the province of Quebec through the use of contracting out provisions than it is to lose Quebec as a result of such provisions. . . .
>
> J. Stefan Dupré, "'Contracting Out' A Funny Thing Happened on the Way to the Centennial", in *Report of the Proceedings of the Eighteenth Annual Tax Conference Nov. 23–25, 1964* (Toronto: Canadian Tax Foundation, 1965), pp. 217–18.

Justice Minister Pierre Trudeau's Views on the "Quebec Problem", 1968

A new federal policy on the "Quebec problem", which had been slowly taking shape since 1965, was unveiled at a major Constitutional Conference in February of 1968. The chief architect of the new approach was Pierre Elliott Trudeau, long recognized as a champion of French Canadian linguistic rights and fierce opponent of Quebec nationalism. In an interview with Ottawa journalist Peter C. Newman, Trudeau outlined his federalist position that Quebec could be treated as a province *comme les autres* in constitutional matters if Ottawa guaranteed linguistic and cultural equality for French Canadians.

> *Newman:* Is the Liberal approach to the constitutional negotiations a status quo position?
>
> *Trudeau:* It is not; it's fighting on principle and it's not giving in on the basic principles of federalism and therefore it looks as though we're holding to the status quo. It amounts to fighting for the only thing that can make Canada united—to take the fuse out of explosive Quebec nationalism—by making sure that Quebec is not a ghetto for French Canadians, that all of Canada is theirs.
>
> I'm kind of happy with developments, because we've reached the point where the struggle between Quebec and Ottawa is beginning to appear more and more as a power struggle. Until now it was made to look like a struggle of principle: only Quebec could speak for the French Canadians and only Quebec could give the French Canadians their

language rights and correspond to their full philosophy. But now with the B & B Commission and our reforms in the civil service and especially with our bill of rights project which guarantees a system of language rights across the country, with all these modifications, it's obvious that we are saying to French Canadians: No, not only the Quebec government can speak for you, on the contrary, only the Ottawa government can give the French Canadians their due across the country.

So if we can get this across, then the rest is a normal power struggle between Quebec and Ottawa, or between Halifax and Ottawa, or between Victoria and Ottawa.... The fight would no longer be between 'French-Quebec' and 'English-Ottawa'.

Interview with P.E. Trudeau, Minister of Justice, *The Montreal Star*, February 2, 1968.

Provincial Control of Resources—Alberta's Position on Energy Supply and Pricing, 1974

Much of the impetus behind a resurgence of provincialism in the 1970s stemmed from a strong resistance to federal energy policies, which were seen as a threat to provincial control over resources. In response to the 1973–74 OPEC oil crisis and the subsequent quadrupling of world oil prices, the Trudeau government had adopted new energy policies which maintained domestic oil prices below world levels and imposed a tax on energy exports to the United States. Federal policies, however, seemed to favour the oil-consuming provinces of central Canada and adversely affect the oil-producing economies of Alberta and its neighbouring western provinces. In the following excerpt, Alberta premier Peter Lougheed, speaking before a 1974 federal-provincial conference, states his province's case for provincial control over resources.

Alberta welcomes the opportunity to participate in this Federal-Provincial Conference on Energy. As the major supplier of energy for Canada, we obviously have a substantial stake in the development of sound and fair national energy policies. They must be national policies though—national in the sense they are developed by agreement between the Federal Government and the Provinces and with full recognition that natural resources located within the provinces, under our Constitution, are owned by the provinces....

It is clear and unequivocal that the Fathers of Confederation decided that the natural resources within provincial boundaries would be owned by the citizens through their provincial governments, rather than through the Federal Government. Implicit in such ownership is the right of the provinces to manage the resources in terms of conserving or selling them....

We view the federal export tax on Alberta oil as contrary to both the spirit and the intent of Confederation. We object to it in principle because it is discriminatory. It is not just an export tax—it is also a price freeze on all of Alberta's oil production at immense cost to Albertans. If the export tax had been part of a total Canadian price freeze on all exported products, including manufactured products, as an anti-inflationary measure to protect Canadian consumers—then it would not have been discriminatory and we in Alberta would have found it less objectionable....

Finally, with regard to the export tax—for the Federal Government to have taken such a major step unilaterally without first even consulting with the producing provinces, is unfortunately firmly implanted in the minds of Albertans in terms of Ottawa's attitude towards the West.

Opening Statement by Premier Lougheed of Alberta, Federal-Provincial Conference on Energy, Ottawa, January 22, 1974.

THE CHALLENGE OF ETHNIC DIVERSITY—IMMIGRATION AND THE RISE OF MULTICULTURALISM

The five million immigrants who have come to Canada since 1945 have dramatically changed the country's ethnic composition. Whereas Canada was once basically a bicultural society, British and French, it is now a fully multicultural society. This great post-war migration has brought a wider diversity of peoples to Canada. Although the majority of immigrants in the immediate post-war years were British or Western Europeans, recent immigration has for the first time introduced large numbers of people from Asia, the West Indies, South America and Africa into Canadian society. The federal government of Pierre Trudeau responded to the changing ethnic character of Canada in 1971 by adopting an official policy of multiculturalism, recognizing the right of all Canadians to retain their ethnic heritage. While government policy is limited to voluntary application, most Canadians have greeted the newcomers with an open attitude, and tolerance has generally prevailed. Yet building a society based on respect for ethnic diversity has presented its problems. Prejudice, fears of prejudice and isolated cases of open discrimination have often made it difficult for recent immigrants to adjust happily to a new life in Canada.

Canada's Policy of Multiculturalism—Prime Minister P.E. Trudeau's Statement, 1971

Canada's official policy of federal multiculturalism, based on the findings and recommendations of Book IV of the Royal Commission Report on Bilingualism and Biculturalism (1970), was introduced in October 1971 by Prime Minister Trudeau in an address to the House of Commons.

It was the view of the Royal Commission, shared by the Government and, I am sure, by all Canadians, that there cannot be one cultural policy for Canadians of British and French origin, another for the original peoples and yet another for all others. For although there are two official languages, there is no official culture, nor does any ethnic group take precedence over any other. No citizen or group of citizens is other than Canadian, and all should be treated fairly.

The Royal Commission was guided by the belief that adherence to one's ethnic group is influenced not so much by one's origin or mother tongue as by one's sense of belonging to the group and by what the Commission calls the group's 'collective will to exist.' The Government shares this belief.

The individual's freedom would be hampered if he were locked for life within a particular cultural compartment by the accident of birth or language. It is vital, therefore, that every Canadian, whatever his ethnic origin, be given a chance to learn at least one of the two official languages in which his country conducts its official business and its politics.

A policy of multiculturalism within a bilingual framework commends itself to the Government as the most suitable means of assuring the cultural freedom of Canadians. Such a policy should help to break down discriminatory attitudes and cultural jealousies. National unity, if it is to mean anything in the deeply personal sense, must be founded on confidence in one's own individual identity; out of this can grow respect for that of others and a willingness to share ideas, attitudes and assumptions. A vigorous policy of multiculturalism will help create this initial confidence. It can form the base of a society which is based on fair play for all. . . .

In conclusion, I wish to emphasize the view of the Government that a policy of multiculturalism within a bilingual framework is basically the conscious support of individual freedom of choice. We are free to be ourselves. But this cannot be left to chance. It must be fostered and pursued actively. If freedom of choice is in danger for some ethnic group, it is in danger for us all. It is the policy of this Government to eliminate any such danger and to 'safeguard' this freedom.

Pierre Elliott Trudeau, House of Commons *Debates*, October 8, 1971, pp. 8545-6.

The Pattern of Ethnic Diversity—Immigration and Population Data, 1946-81

Canada's growing ethnic diversity is strongly reflected in the official immigration and population data for the period 1946 to 1981. The following tables for immigration and population illustrate the effects of economic conditions, the 1967 Canadian immigration regulations, and the government's policy of official multiculturalism.

Table 20-1   Immigration to Canada by Region of Origin

	1946-1957	1958-1967	1968-1977	TOTAL
Europe	1 467 212	944 080	614 536	3 025 828
United States	111 694	132 585	187 910	432 190
Asia	33 771	74 643	271 598	380 012
Central America & Caribbean	11 356	29 753	115 721	156 830
South America	11 829	20 346	62 860	95 035
Australia & Pacific	25 238	26 832	36 205	88 275
Africa	8 240	24 060	53 485	85 785
TOTAL	1 669 340	1 252 299	1 342 315	4 263 954

Statistics Canada, 1977, as reprinted in Iain R. Munro, *Immigration*. Toronto: Wiley Publishers, 1978, p. 62. Figures as of September 30, 1977.

Table 20-2 Canadian Population by First Language, 1971 and 1981

	1971		1981	
	Number of People	Percentage of Population	Number of People	Percentage of Population
English	12 973 810	60.2	14 918 460	61.3
French	5 793 650	26.9	6 249 095	25.7
Baltic	43 385	0.2	38 610	0.1
Celtic	24 630	0.1	12 135	0.1
Chinese	94 855	0.4	224 030	0.9
Croatian/Serbian	74 190	0.3	87 870	0.4
Czech/Slovak	45 145	0.2	42 825	0.2
Finnish	36 725	0.2	33 385	0.1
German	561 085	2.6	522 850	2.1
Greek	104 455	0.5	122 955	0.5
Indo-Pakistani languages	32 555	0.2	116 990	0.5
Inuit	15 295	0.1	18 840	0.1
Italian	538 360	2.5	528 780	2.2
Japanese	16 890	0.1	20 135	0.1
Hungarian	86 835	0.4	83 725	0.3
Native Indian	164 525	0.8	147 730	0.6
Netherlandic languages	159 165	0.7	156 645	0.6
Polish	134 780	0.6	127 960	0.5
Portuguese	86 925	0.4	165 510	0.7
Romanian	11 300	0.1	12 945	0.1
Russian	31 745	0.1	31 485	0.1
Scandinavian languages	84 335	0.4	67 720	0.3
Semitic languages	28 550	0.1	58 900	0.2
Spanish	23 815	0.1	70 160	0.3
Ukrainian	309 855	1.4	292 265	1.2
Yiddish	49 890	0.2	32 760	0.1
Other/Unknown	41 830	0.2	158 415	0.7
TOTAL	21 568 310	100.0	24 343 180	100.0

Census of Canada, 1971 and 1981. Minister of Supply and Services Canada.

Respecting Diversity—A Report on Progress, 1979

The profound effect of recent immigration on Canadian society was one of many critical issues examined by the 1979 Report of the Task Force on Canadian Unity, headed by Jean-Luc Pépin and John P. Robarts. The final report, *A Future Together*, saw the encouragement and appreciation of cultural and ethnic diversity as an important way of strengthening the bonds of Canadian identity.

The degree to which Canada's growing diversity has enriched and enlivened its cultural life has gained widening recognition, but discussion of Canadian pluralism has also suffered at times from a failure to relate it with sufficient care to other features of Canadian life....

The impact of immigration has...been uneven in geographic terms. Some regions, cities and towns have felt the influence of immigration much more than others. The western provinces, for example, exhibit much greater ethnic diversity than Quebec or the Atlantic region, and Ontario is closer in this respect to the west than to the east. In fact, the original ethnic duality of the Atlantic provinces and Quebec still accounts for about 90 per cent of their populations. The major exception to this pattern east of the Ottawa River is the greater Montreal region, where Canadians of non-British and non-French origin now form about 20 per cent of the community.

Unfortunately the uneven distribution of diversity is frequently neglected in discussion of the cultural character of Canada as a whole. Cultural policy is often conceived as if Canada displayed a pattern and tradition of diversity which is common to the whole country. Yet the fact is that the members of the various ethnic groups have played a much more prominent role in the development of certain provinces and communities than of others, and in some their contribution has been a fundamental one....

...it would be wrong to think that consideration of Canadian pluralism can or should be limited to its cultural dimension. There are many other important social issues which deserve attention from Canadians at large, public authorities, and all those responsible for the welfare of the ethnic communities. Fundamental issues such as equality of opportunity, the sharing of Canada's material benefits, access to public services, and the degree of racial and ethnic discrimination to be found in our country are of at least equal importance to the cultural issues so often discussed. If we are to maintain or strengthen the unity of a country like ours, whose people are drawn from so many backgrounds, we must not allow preoccupation with the cultural side of diversity to distract our attention from these basic social issues. In line with our objective of treating diversity as a source of strength, and responding to the concerns proposed by many ethno-cultural groups we met, we have proposed that both the public and private sectors make efforts to reflect in their institutions more adequately the cultural diversity of Canada. The future we hope to share together must include all Canadians, and provide equality of opportunity for all.

A Future Together: Observations and Recommendations, Report of the Task Force on Canadian Unity (Ottawa: Minister of Supply and Services Canada, January 1979), pp. 55–6.

THE CHALLENGE OF REGIONALISM—THE WEST AND THE EAST VS. CENTRAL CANADA

Regionalism has emerged in recent years as one of the most predominant features of Canadian life. While strong regional attitudes and loyalties are hardly new, only recently has regionalism come to be perceived as a fundamental cleavage within the Canadian community. The phenomenon itself, while deeply rooted in history, has been reflected since 1960 in differing views of bilingualism, Quebec nationalism, energy policies, and constitutional reform. Its influence can be seen in the persistent popular belief that the West and the Atlantic region are either regularly ignored or victimized by federal policies—policies designed by and for central Canadians. Many contemporary analysts even suggest that regional forces, such as the threat of Quebec's independence, have the potential—if ignored or not effectively dealt with—to break up the country.

The Provincial Premiers' Analysis of Biculturalism—A Cartoonist's View of Regional Identities, 1963

The response of Canada's provincial premiers to proposals for Canadian bilingualism and biculturalism in the early 1960s provided a prime example of regional perspectives and "limited identities". A *Toronto Telegram* cartoon, which appeared shortly after the L.B. Pearson government's establishment of a Royal Commission on Bilingualism and Biculturalism in July of 1963, offered a perceptive commentary on the various provincial conceptions of a bicultural Canada. The cartoonist, Allan Beaton, drew his inspiration from a Hindu fable about the attempts of seven blind men to describe an elephant which none of them had seen or felt in its entirety.

Beyond Bitterness—The Views of A Western Separatist, 1971

Historically, western regional protest had always been aimed at gaining a larger share of political power within the Canadian system. By the late 1960s, however, the demands of Westerners began to take a different form. The idea of Western independence was taken up by small groups of conservative-minded college students, journalists and artists based in Alberta. Some early

Western separatists believed that a policy of independence might revive the sagging fortunes of Alberta's Social Credit party; others argued that only through secession could Alberta achieve full control over the benefits of its new-found oil wealth. One of the first Albertans to consider Western separatism, John Barr, saw independence as an opportunity for the political revitalization of the West.

> I can't really claim to come from a long line of Western separatists nor does my hostility to the present role of the West in Confederation date back to when my family first lost their farm to an Eastern mortgage company during the Depression—we were city people....
>
> * * * * *
>
> Consider, just for a moment, the paradoxes posed for a Westerner by the existence of a corporation like Canadian Pacific. Here is a company, one of the largest in the world, which is both Canadian-owned and very much in the forefront of technological change.... Canadian Pacific ought to make every Westerner who believes in competition, technology, and Canadian control of our economy, feel warm inside. Instead, it breeds Western socialists and separatists. Why?
>
> It does this because, as anyone who has read Canadian history knows, Canadian Pacific is an Eastern-controlled institution that regularly rides roughshod over Western interests and Western sensibilities.
>
> It is a growing consciousness that we are powerless that lies at the heart of Western unrest today....
>
> And one of the surest tests of the development of an *anti*-colonial movement is when people discover, as they are discovering today in the West, that their own problems *are* interesting, are certainly important to their exploiters, and are capable of being tackled.
>
> ... For more than two generations it has not been possible to get a fair hearing in this country for the Western case; the general reaction of the national media has been the kind of sneering viciousness displayed by Douglas Fisher and Harry Crowe in their column in the Toronto *Telegram* during the last Tory leadership convention, when they characterized Westerners as the most depraved and mean-spirited reactionaries in the nation. In a nation, as in a marriage, there are some things said which can never be forgotten or forgiven....
>
> But the time for bitterness is past. Canada is in deep trouble today and may well founder from the consequences of past acts. This is not something I celebrate: Canada has not been a bad country for me and I would not greet her death with celebration. It is, alas, a country torn by strong regional loyalties—so torn by them, in fact, that those in each region are forced by the rules of the national power-game to fight as hard as they can for the interests of their own area. Those who do not fight go to the wall.
>
> John J. Barr, "Beyond Bitterness: The New Western Radicalism", in John Barr and Owen Anderson, eds., *The Unfinished Revolt* (Toronto: McClelland and Stewart, 1971), pp. 11–13, and 32.

The Failure of Federal Policies in the West—A Western Premier's View, 1973

The depth of Western discontent with federal Liberal policies in the early 1970s was dramatically revealed by the results of the 1972 federal election. Pierre Trudeau's government was reduced to precarious minority status and the Liberals' federal representation in provinces west of the Great Lakes was decimated. In direct response to this evidence of widespread disaffection, Trudeau convened a Western Economic Opportunities Conference in Calgary in July of 1973 and made an unsuccessful attempt to redress Western grievances. Saskatchewan premier Allan Blakeney reacted to Trudeau's Western initiative with a trenchant criticism of Liberal policies in the West.

We agreed with Mr. Trudeau when he stated that the old national policy of John A. Macdonald, based on a Central Canadian 'metropole' with an agricultural and resource 'hinterland' in the West, could not have foreseen the 'fully developed Western society of today.' But after stating that it was the Government of Canada's belief that the time had finally come to shape a new national policy, we were presented with ad hoc programme alterations, rather than new policy directions....

Perhaps the time had come to ask whether we are not putting the cart before the horse. Should we not emphasize regional economic development objectives as the bases around which to build 'national policies?' I fully recognize the difficulties in this process. Much accommodation would have to occur to ensure that the national interest is fully served. It may well be, however, that this shift in emphasis will offer the only effective way to come to grips with the forces of economic and human concentration now at work in Canada. These centralizing forces divide rather than unify; they exact high costs both in the cities and the countryside.

In this policy vacuum, an all-embracing commitment to a national settlement pattern may well provide the focus for a new national policy. The operative guidelines of this new emphasis might well be:

1) that each region should be free to develop fully those opportunities which naturally occur there. Where a region possesses a natural advantage, therefore, no disadvantage should be created by discriminatory or inadequate national policies; and

2) that the federal and provincial governments, working together, should set a course that will promote the distribution of development and population across Canada in a more uniform, equitable, and humane manner....

I do not share the dissatisfaction reflected in the Prime Minister's closing statement when he said (quote) 'the one and only Western Economic Opportunities Conferences has ended.' I think that we, in the West, will pursue this issue until we are satisfied that we have obtained meaningful results.... It is only through a heightened sensitivity to the full gravity of regional problems that Ottawa will see fit to act in a fundamental way. In the end, surely, Canada will be a better country when we succeed in forging a new national policy which embraces every region of Canada.

Allan Blakeney, Address to the Interprovincial Conference, Charlottetown, August 9–10, 1973, reprinted in John T. Saywell, ed., *The Canadian Annual Review 1973* (Toronto: University of Toronto Press, 1974), pp. 48–49.

The Problem of Economic Dependence—A Newfoundlander's Perspective, 1977

The disaffection of the Atlantic provinces was often rooted in concerns over regional economic disparities. For, in spite of massive intervention by governments in the late 1960s and early 1970s, the Maritimes and Newfoundland continued to lag behind the other parts of the country in levels of economic growth, employment and per capita income. The problem was so acute in Canada's easternmost province that prominent Newfoundlanders—instead of expressing shock or alarm at the prospect of Quebec independence—began to make it clear that they shared Quebec's growing disenchantment with Canadian Confederation.

A news report on Newfoundland presentations before the 1977 Task Force on Canadian Unity provided some insight into the concerns of Newfoundlanders.

Quebec is less threatening to national unity than regional disparity and the lack of economic opportunity in places like Newfoundland, ran the common theme throughout the hearings. Newfoundland was painted as the colony 'of the empire of the St. Lawrence' composed of the Quebec City-to-Windsor corridor by David Alexander, professor of history at Memorial University.

Like colonized people everywhere the natives have become restless and angry. They are frustrated by their lack of power over their own affairs and moreover they are humiliated by their lack of dignity and self-respect as they, in the words of another brief to the task force, 'revel in the sweet death of welfare, unemployment insurance and mothers' allowance.'

Much of the blame for Newfoundland's unhappiness was placed at the feet of the central Government and the concentration of power and influence in the 'empire of the St. Lawrence.' Professor Alexander compared Newfoundlanders to 'Maritimers in the 1920s who saw their industrial revolution dismantled by the transfer to Montreal of regional control over the Intercolonial Railway, and Westerners who still find it impossible to mill grain, dress beef and manufacture petrochemicals for national markets.

'So Newfoundlanders were to see their ocean resources frittered away to national indifference, and the economic benefits of the disputed Labrador frontier safely ensconced in the empire of the St. Lawrence.

'In times past, injustices like this were defended in the name of unity of the British Empire; today it is offered to us as a necessity of national unity. It is imperialism, plain and simple. In its Canadian transmogrification, fiscal transfers have replaced the imperial garrison at least in Newfoundland, where presumably we are too beaten to require guarding.'

Hugh Winsor, "Quebec and Newfoundland in Same Boat, Inquiry Told", *The Globe and Mail*, October 31, 1977.

The "Atlantic Vision"—An APEC Diagnosis and Prescription for Economic Development, 1979

The atmosphere of national crisis hanging over the Canadian state in the 1970s and early 1980s produced a constructive response in the Atlantic region. Threats to Canada's survival, posed by Quebec separatism, and visible signs of Western alienation awakened many Maritimers to the economic vulnerability of a "dependent" region like the Atlantic provinces. In its 1979 report entitled *The Atlantic Vision—1990*, the Atlantic Provinces Economic Council (an independent research group) identified the region's economic problems and proposed a new development strategy.

...the range of instruments employed over the past two decades to promote economic catch-up by the region has not been outstandingly successful. These instruments may have provided some catch-up, but not much. More ominously, they may have been critical in simply keeping the region in the race. If so, then one is forced to conclude that the normal workings of the Canadian economy are such as to encourage an increasing concentration of wealth and opportunity in fewer areas of the country. This in turn raises the question of the value of the whole arrangement.

The prognosis for the instruments in place today, including the policies of DREE, transfer payments, provincial development policies and others, is for more of the same. There will be little growth of these to encourage higher levels of new investment, development and new opportunities. However, they will not be adequate to meet the challenges of the 1980's. New directions are needed. Something extra must be done to 'kick the process into high gear'. APEC, for instance, estimates roughly that if only existing policies are followed, earned income per person in the region will take a century to reach national averages. That is not good enough....

A new set of developmental techniques and technologies is needed. The region is faced now, not with a large list of physical needs, but with a bottleneck of institutional and social problems that slow down development. The most critical areas are the development of a more self-reliant, integrated regional economy and an expansion of regional capabilities in such activities best described as 'developmental software'....

* * * * *

Not only is the Atlantic region faced with the inability of existing federal and provincial policy measures to quickly close the income gap, but today it is faced with the changing nature of both the economic and monetary union of Canada and the rules under which development is stimulated. New measures must be devised and recognition must be made that some of the fundamental assumptions about economic growth and its consequences must be changed....

...Atlantic Canada has moved from poverty to dependency. The region is no longer poor, even if it is not rich.... While dependency obviates serious poverty, it does not provide an opportunity for full employment and pride inherent in being fully employed. The new requirement must therefore be to maintain this new-found non-poverty position while becoming increasingly a more self-reliant economy....

Atlantic Provinces Economic Council, *The Atlantic Vision—1990: A Development Strategy for the 1980's* (Halifax: APEC, 1979), pp. 11–12 and 79.

THE CHALLENGE OF CANADA'S FUTURE—WHICH WAY AHEAD?

Entering the 1980s, Canada seemed to reach a mid-life crisis. The sense of national crisis stirred up by Quebec's demands for secession was compounded by a rising feeling of estrangement from Ottawa, by the Western and the Atlantic provinces. After living together for over 200 years Canadians and *Canadiens* confronted some fundamental questions: Who are we? What are we doing together? And where do we go from here? Such matters as the identity, functioning and purpose of the Canadian community came together in the public debate over a new Canadian constitution. While few political leaders, commentators or thinkers presumed to give definitive answers to these perennial Canadian questions, the critical problems of "community" were brought into sharper focus and the Canadian experiment endured.

Prospects for "A Future Together"—A Commentary on the Canadian Unity Task Force, 1978

The Trudeau government responded to the election of René Lévesque's Parti Québécois government by appointing a Task Force on Canadian Unity in July 1977 and then, a year later, by proposing a new and far-reaching set of constitutional proposals for a renewed Canadian federalism. The Canadian Unity task force chaired by Jean-Luc Pépin and John P. Robarts set out to investigate the "national crisis" and to offer its prescription for "a future together". Controversy dogged the task force on its seven-month trek across the country, holding noisy and often acrimonious public hearings in some 13 different Canadian centres. *The Toronto Star*'s cartoonist, Duncan Macpherson, expressed a view of the Task Force shared by many close observers of the enterprise.

The Unity Task Force

French-speakers hooted at English in Montreal; English-speakers booed French in Winnipeg. Separatists argued their case in Quebec; Leonard Jones, the independent MP for Moncton, berated the Official Languages Act in New Brunswick. Acadians waved flags. Politicians ground axes. Academics floated theories. Labour decried unemployment. Maritimers bemoaned disparities; westerners complained of alienation.

Jeffrey Simpson, *The Globe and Mail*, January 25, 1979.

"Two Concepts of Canada"—Prime Minister Trudeau vs. the Premiers, 1980

A First Ministers Conference held in Ottawa in September 1980 was the scene for a remarkable clash of views over the form and future shape of Canadian federalism. Pierre Trudeau's Liberal government had returned to power in early 1980, the "*Non*" side had triumphed in the May 1980 Quebec Referendum, and the stage seemed set for a resolution of the debate over constitutional reform. But a leaked memorandum prepared by Trudeau aide Michael Kirby was unveiled on the eve of the Conference, confirming the suspicions of several premiers that Ottawa planned to use the failure of the summit as a pretext for unilateral action on the new Constitution. The following heated exchange, which occurred during Trudeau's televised closing remarks to the Conference, revealed the fundamental nature of the disagreement over the future direction of Confederation.

> *The Chairman* [P.E. Trudeau]
> ... there are... two conceptions of Canada and that is why we have failed and that I think it was dishonest on the part of the Premiers who preceded me this morning not to say so.
> ... There is one view which holds that national Canadian policies are contradictory to the national Canadian common good, the common wheal [sic] ought to be what results from each province acting independently to maximize its own self-interest and this is why Premiers, naturally, if they hold that view, demand more and more powers from Ottawa and reject any strengthening of the powers of the national government so that they can pursue vigorously the maximization of the provincial self-interest.
> The other view is that there is a national interest which transcends regional interests and as I said last night in our private meetings that view also goes so far as to say that when there is a conflict between the national interest and the provincial interest the national interest must prevail because Canada is more than just the sum of its parts, more than the sum of 10 provinces, more than the sum of 10 regional economies and that is my view....
> ... but I denied to Premier Lyon and to Premier Peckford and to Premier Bennett the right to hold that we should accept a theory that when the provinces are unanimous on something, we must say 'Aye, aye, sir.' That is not my view of Canada....
> ... we hear from Premier after Premier that they agree with the concept of Canada put forward by Mr. Levesque. I don't even know if that makes me sad. I think it just—I hear Premier Lyon saying it is true, but all I can say—
> *Hon. Sterling Lyon*: He doesn't know that it is true.
> The Chairman: He doesn't know that it is true; well we heard the words this morning from Premier Peckford. Certainly, all I can say is that the people of Quebec showed me last May that they did not agree with the view of Canada held by Mr. Levesque.
> *Hon. Brian Peckford*: Mr. Prime Minister, I must interject because I never advocated a concept of Canada that the Prime Minister of Quebec advocated in the referendum. I was advocating the concept of Canada we all talked about last night, which was a federal state which had a strong federal government and strong provinces.
> The Chairman: A free association of provinces, that is what Newfoundland has been defining Canada as. You have a right to do that, sir, you have said that here, you said it

in private; that is your view of Canada and it is not mine. Canada is more than a free association of provinces....

> Closing remarks at the First Ministers Conference on the Constitution, Ottawa, September 13, 1980, in *Constitutional Reform 1980* (Ottawa: Canadian Unity Information Office, 1980), pp. 52, 55–6, 57–58 and 59–61.

The New Constitution and a Divided Quebec—A Journalist's Prognosis, 1982

Following the collapse of negotiations at the 1980 First Ministers Conference, Prime Minister Trudeau took the offensive, setting in motion a fractious and protracted struggle which ended in a compromise agreement on constitutional reform. The constitutional accord, reached in November 1981 between the Trudeau government and all provinces except Quebec, settled the main issues of patriation, fundamental rights and amendment, but left Quebec deeply divided and seemingly excluded from the symbolic process of constitutional rebirth. In this excerpt from the Toronto *Globe and Mail*, journalist William Johnson offered an analysis of Quebec's response and its possible implications.

Quebec rejoices and Quebec rages and Quebec yawns. Quebec greets the patriated Constitution just as it submitted to the 1867 British North America Act—divided. But perhaps more divided now than ever before.

A son of Quebec, Pierre Trudeau, succeeded where all other prime ministers of Canada failed for more than 50 years: he cut the constitutional colonial bond with the United Kingdom. Only in Quebec was the link with the imperial mother country an issue; the rest of Canada, down almost to the present, took it for granted....

But now that Canada becomes officially the one country of all Canadians, only Quebec—its Government and a substantial part of its people—remains outside the celebrations. Perhaps patriation comes too late for Quebec....

Now the new Constitution will protect French and English school rights throughout the expanse of Confederation, but does not make French an official language in most provinces. And even the protection of school rights, long sought by Quebec, now leaves it divided; many see it as a threat to French predominance in Quebec. Perhaps it also comes too late....

* * * * *

Perhaps as significant as what [Parti Québécois premier René Lévesque] said was what he did not do. He did not call a referendum on the issue, or go to the people in an election; he backed away from a proposed monster rally against patriation at Montreal's Olympic Stadium, opting instead for a 'street march' which, in Montreal on a Saturday, should have no trouble attracting the 25,000 the PQ predicted. Polls clearly showed he could not marshal all-out support for his position; they showed the Constitution was a non-issue in Quebec, and those who did care about it were equally critical of both the provincial and federal governments.

At present, divided Quebec seems to be in a state of equilibrium, with the supporters of Mr. Trudeau and Mr. Lévesque about equal in influence with the public. But the process of constitutional revision has only begun, and by the time the next stage of bargaining reopens the issue of provincial powers, many of the players will be different. Both Mr. Trudeau and Mr. Lévesque are likely to be gone from the scene before serious negotiations can be undertaken.

What will Quebec's mood be in the next round? It will depend on the leaders who emerge to defend the powers of each level of government. It is they who will determine whether the patriation taking place this week is the end of the beginning, as Mr. Trudeau says, or instead is the beginning of the end.

William Johnson, "Conflict Deepens Quebec Divisions", *The Globe and Mail*, April 15, 1982, p. P2.

CONFLICTING INTERPRETATIONS

Studies of contemporary Canadian diversity, like those of most other themes in Canada's recent history, often mirror the biases and prevailing attitudes of the age. Standard surveys of Canadian history, following the "national" school of interpretation, have tended to treat the rise of provincialism, regionalism and even ethnic diversity as flaws in the fabric of Confederation. Some of these challenges of diversity have been admitted but underplayed by nationalist writers more interested in the greater symphony of "national unity". Perhaps it is the preoccupation of English-Canadian historians with the problems and prospects of Canada's survival that has led many of them to expound upon the "virtue" of national unity and to make present biases the standards by which they judge past actions.

Recent historical studies of Canada's regional, cultural and ethnic diversity, however, are beginning to raise fundamental issues. Much of the best recent work, following the directions charted by historians Ramsay Cook and J.M.S. Careless in the late 1960s, has already unearthed a great deal about the "limited identities" of region, culture, class and territory readily discernible in contemporary Canada. Whether the trend toward greater Canadian diversity will make for a more interesting, rich and confident nation or for a divisive, inherently weak one has become the central point at issue.

THE CHALLENGE OF PROVINCIALISM

Federal-Provincial Conflict—A Threat to Viable Federalism

The popular perception of strengthening provincialism as a dire threat to the viability of the Canadian federal state gained powerful support in the studies of some of the country's leading English-Canadian political scientists. Donald V. Smiley and Garth Stevenson, for instance, argued that shifts in economic and political power have transformed Canada into one of the world's most decentralized federal states. In the following selection, Professor Smiley describes the progressive dismantling of centralized Canadian federalism from the late 1950s to the mid-seventies:

The current circumstances of federal-provincial conflict in Canada can be understood only against the background of the piecemeal though rapid disintegration of the

relatively centralized régime which was established during and just at the end of the
Second World War and was perpetuated through the late 1950s....

The story of Canadian federalism from the late 1950s onward is that of the relative
weakening of the power of the national government and the strengthening of that of the
provinces. The redefinition of Quebec from the election of the Lesage government in
1960 was crucial in this process. However, several other factors worked in the same
direction—the failure of national economic policies from the late 1950s onward to
ensure adequate conditions of employment and growth; the shift in the balance of
bureaucratic competence to the provinces; the defeat of the Liberal party in the general
election of 1957 and the minority governments resulting from that election and those of
1962, 1963, 1965 and 1972; the changing balance of public expenditures toward
functions mainly or exclusively within the constitutional jurisdiction of the provinces.
These influences, taken together, have led to a situation in which the most crucial
aspects of Canadian public policy are within the context of federal-provincial negotiation....

Significantly, the early 1970s appear for the time being at least to put aside what
seemed to be one of the most intractable issues of Canadian federalism. This was
whether or not Quebec because of its cultural and linguistic particularity should have a
broader range of autonomy than that wanted or needed by the other provinces. In broad
terms, what has recently happened is that the larger, more prosperous and more
influential of the provinces with English-speaking majorities have come to demand for
themselves the same range of independent discretion that has been defined by Quebec
as its own requirement for cultural survival.

Donald V. Smiley, "Federal-Provincial Conflict in Canada", *PUBLIUS, The
Journal of Federalism* (Summer, 1974), pp. 7–9. Footnotes omitted.

Quebec and the Struggle for Self-Government—A Defence of Provincialism

One of the strongest defences of provincialism is found in Claude Morin's
1976 study of Quebec-Canada relations in the 1960s and early seventies. As
Quebec's Deputy Minister of Intergovernmental Affairs from 1961 to 1971,
Morin played a leading role in shaping his government's position on many
issues from pensions to medical care to constitutional reform.

... Federal pressure on Quebec and the other provinces is a perennial phenomenon of
Canadian life. The fact that it may have seemed more hesitant at certain periods,
especially during the Quiet Revolution, does not mean it has gone. It is resumed with
new vigour, we now realize, as soon as circumstances allow. This pattern will persist
unless our system undergoes basic change....

* * * * *

... The federal authorities have endeavoured to avoid doing anything that might
draw the Quebec public's attention to its control impulses. It has trodden very softly for
fear of arousing some visceral defensive reaction, or fuelling a latent nationalism that
would have made political capital for Quebec City....

The imbalance of power between Ottawa and Quebec is such that all competition
eventually bears witness, barring accident, to the federal government's greater
strength. Ottawa desires this imbalance not through wickedness or political pettifog-

gery, but simply because in its view the 'national' government must naturally be much stronger from all points of view than the provinces. It will then be in a position to secure such 'national' objectives as it decides may flow from its prerogative. Largely for this reason, Ottawa has been refusing any substantial transfer of resources to the provinces since 1966....

...Never before had Quebec's political power been so systematically savaged [as during the first Trudeau government (1968–72)]. On the Ottawa side, as circumstances allowed, there was the intention of taking the full responsibility of a 'national' government. Free rein was given to all the naturally centralizing tendencies of a federal administration. On the Quebec side, we witnessed the arrival in office of a party which either did not know how to face up to this centripetal force or else did not want to. Instead, they had worked out the philosophy of 'paying' federalism, which struck many as a rationalization in political terms of a mere lack of vision and firmness, but did offer Ottawa the advantage of a free hand. Together these two governments, the one in Ottawa and the newly provincial administration in Quebec City, undertook to convince Quebeckers of two new 'truths.' First, federalism as Ottawa conceived it could mean numerous material benefits.... According to the second 'truth,' though it meant almost certain erosion for the Quebec government as a collective instrument, it was possible for Quebeckers to take up the reins of power in Ottawa and wield a decisive influence on the development of the entire country. In short, there was to be established in Ottawa a 'Quebec power' that could normally sit only in Quebec City....

...from the federal viewpoint there were other reasons for greater centralization and a more conspicuous role for the federal administration throughout Canada. After the minority governments of the past decade and Quebec's aggressiveness of the Quiet Revolution years, it was important for Ottawa to reaffirm its authority and confirm its predominance in the country's business. All these factors produced the intensive movement of federal penetration whose characteristics I have been examining. There is certainly nothing fortuitous about the events of 1968–72. They suit the logic of the present system.

Claude Morin, *Quebec versus Ottawa: The Struggle for Self-Government, 1960–72,* trans. Richard Howard (Toronto: University of Toronto Press, 1976), pp. 75, 76, 81 and 84–86.

Federal Power and the Rise of Provincialism—An Alternative View

A completely different view of the trend to provincialism in Canada's postwar years was offered in a study by Robert Bothwell, Ian Drummond and John English, *Canada Since 1945: Power, Politics and Provincialism* (1981). The rise of provincialism, according to these three analysts, was the natural outgrowth of a postwar increase in those governmental responsibilities and expenditures which belonged constitutionally to the provinces. They argue, however, that the growing power of the provinces since 1960 required the reassertion of a "strong national government" to "arbitrate" conflicting provincial claims.

...in the heady prosperity of the sixties, it seemed possible to use the federal spending power to resolve constitutional difficulties by throwing money at the provinces in order to produce a welfare state.

Federal incursions into the sphere of social welfare were encouraged by reductions in spending in areas that were unquestionably national in scope, such as defence. If it had been necessary throughout this period to maintain a defence effort comparable to that of the early 1950s, there would have been less room for much of this. The unexpected and unsought result of social welfare planning and accomplishment was that the national government was weaker in terms of its undoubted responsibilities at the end of the period than at the beginning.

In the case of one provincial government, that of Quebec, an activist outlook exacerbated the tensions that would in any event have been present. The federal government feared, with much justification, that it might soon have little or no direct contact with Canadians in Quebec. Moreover, the Quebec government moved into areas of shared jurisdiction with its own deposit insurance, pension plan, and cultural policy. Other provinces were less adventurous and their motivations less ideological, but their actions contributed to the conflict in the same fashion.

One sees this in the field of natural resources where the interest of the national government in the 1940s and 1950s was directed to the solution of national problems such as unemployment, growth, and imbalances of payment. As constitutional conflict intensified, debate over the exploitation of natural resources which had previously been considered to require co-operation became more bitter. Because provincial governments own these resources, they were naturally interested in using them and especially their revenue for provincial ends. But the national government remained interested in resources, and its underlying reasons for such an interest have not changed, although new concerns have emerged in Ottawa also. Of course all conflict is not federal-provincial; provinces differ among themselves with respect to resource exploitation. Ontario and Alberta would have feuded over oil prices if Ottawa had not existed. Indeed, without a strong national government, a rational arbitration of their differences would likely have proven impossible. Similarly, Ontario, Manitoba, and Quebec would have warred over egg marketing and chicken sales.

Robert Bothwell, Ian Drummond and John English, *Canada Since 1945: Power, Politics and Provincialism* (Toronto: University of Toronto Press, 1981), pp. 458–59.

THE CHALLENGE OF ETHNIC DIVERSITY

Balancing Cultural Diversity and National Unity—A Defence of Multiculturalism

Much controversy has arisen in recent years over the impact of new immigration and the official multiculturalism policy on unity and cohesion within the Canadian community. Some confusion still exists concerning the purposes of multiculturalism as a policy, and wide gaps remain in our understanding of the importance of ethnicity in contemporary Canadian life. In addition, critics of multiculturalism policy contend that the celebration of ethnic diversity may promote forms of ethnic isolation or "ghettoization" and serve to accentuate ethnic, racial or class cleavages within Canadian society.

Two defenders of multiculturalism, Rudolf Kalin and J.W. Berry, attempted to answer this criticism in a 1982 article based on a national survey of public attitudes.

In view of the great ethnic, cultural and geographic diversity of Canada, ethnic relations in this country are remarkably healthy and there is much good will and respect for ethnic diversity. Ethnic attitudes and relations have not always been this good. Bigotry and discrimination against French and other ethnic Canadians are well documented in Canada's history. The relatively healthy state of ethnic relations, as we perceive it, is not generally recognized. Conflict between English and French and between the majority groups and various other ethnic groups frequently receives wide attention in public discussion. In saying that ethnic attitudes are generally positive, we are not saying that ethnic conflict and injustices do not exist, nor that there are no instances of outright bigotry. What we are saying is that the vast majority of Canadians are quite tolerant and accepting of ethnic diversity.

At the same time it must be recognized that tolerance and good will are not uniformly high in the Canadian population. Some intolerance and negative attitudes were uncovered. In the original report on the national survey of ethnic attitudes (Berry et al., 1977) we suggested that this intolerance appears to be occasioned primarily by cultural and economic threat and insecurity. On the basis of secondary analyses described in this paper another possible source of intolerance was uncovered, namely cultural isolation and encapsulation. An improvement of ethnic relations can be accomplished by focusing on these two sources of intolerance. Threat and insecurity can be lessened by new economic arrangements and cultural guarantees. The Task Force on National Unity has in fact suggested some possibilities. For example, it has recommended that 'the principle of the equality of status, rights and privileges of the English and French languages for all purposes declared by the Parliament of Canada... should be entrenched in the constitution' (p. 121). Among a number of other recommendations were minority official language rights in education, health, and social services, and criminal courts. The second source of intolerance, cultural isolation, can be reduced by the sharing of cultures and by promoting the experience of diversity. We have tried to suggest here how to accomplish this goal. The Task Force has also made a number of recommendations designed to increase contact among Canadians of various origins and to promote therefore the experience of cultural diversity. Among these recommendations are youth exchange programmes, low cost travel to enable Canadians to become better acquainted with their country, and the diffusion and distribution of cultural activities throughout Canada. New arrangements for increasing tolerance may not be easy to accomplish, but given the existing good will they will not be impossible.

Rudolf Kalin and J.W. Berry, "Canadian Ethnic Attitudes and Identity in the Context of National Unity", *Journal of Canadian Studies*, Vol. 17, No. 1 (Spring, 1982), pp. 103 and 109–110.

Myths and Realities in the Canadian Mosaic—A Different View

Some critics of Canadian multiculturalism have argued that the "mosaic" ideology, which recognizes the right of ethnic groups to retain their cultural/ linguistic distinctiveness, is not without its deficiencies. Professor Evelyn Kallen, a social scientist at York University, is one who has contended that the "celebration" of ethnic diversity is open to question as a societal ideal, an official government policy, and as an ethno-political social movement.

...the concept of multiculturalism is problematic at all levels of analysis, i.e., as a set of universal social values (ideology), as federal policy, and as an ethno-political movement (social reality)....

...the long-accumulated evidence from the study of ethnic relations clearly demonstrates that maintenance of ethnic distinctiveness requires geo-ethnic segregation and restriction on participation in public life, while the development of national consciousness and commitment requires extensive ethnic interaction through full and equal participation in public life....

...the multicultural policy says nothing and does nothing... about existing racial/ethnic inequality in Canada. Thus the long-term effects of structural racism, such as the 'welfare colonialism' of Canada's indigenous peoples, and the virtual absence of representation among Canadian elites of visible minorities is nowhere addressed in the multicultural policy statement.

The inherent problems and contradictions of the mosaic ideology as societal ideal and as government policy are clearly expressed at the level of societal reality. Here, the built-in problem of reconciling the principles of equality of societal opportunity and freedom of (distinctive) ethnocultural expression is variously articulated in the ofttimes conflicting demands of different ethnic collectivities. Spokespersons for long-oppressed and racially discriminated against minorities such as Canada's indigenous peoples and visible immigrants point out that the unduly expressive (roots and belongingness) emphasis of the present multicultural policy fails to take account of their more immediate, instrumental needs. In the case of Canada's indigenous peoples (initially excluded, under the policy rubric), spokespersons argue that their special status as Canada's original peoples is negated by the policy. Thus they have rejected multiculturalism out of hand and have chosen instead to lobby for constitutional recognition of their treaty and aboriginal rights....

[Entering the 1980s] the prospects for true multiculturalism... are a long way from realization. Indeed, in the thralls of the present constitutional debate, we are witnessing just the opposite, i.e., a disturbing trend towards ethnic and regional fragmentation. Demands for national self-determination put forward by organizations and coalitions representing the interests of Canada's indigenous peoples; the unflagging efforts of the supporters of Québécois sovereignty-association to increase public support for their cause; and the threats of cessation by the Western provinces are in the forefront of an already inflamed public consciousness, stirred out of complacency by the snowballing effects of separatist claims and demands. At present, however, the likelihood that Canada's fragile mosaic will be multiply fractured seems no closer to reality than the likelihood that a true (egalitarian) Canadian mosaic will be realized in the foreseeable future.

Evelyn Kallen, "Multiculturalism: Ideology, Policy and Reality", *Journal of Canadian Studies*, Vol. 17, No. 1 (Spring, 1982), pp. 60, 61 and 62.

THE CHALLENGE OF REGIONALISM

Canada's Burden of of Unity—A Western Canadian Perspective

The resurgence of regionalism in the 1970s and early 1980s caused many historians, political scientists and popular commentators to re-examine the relationship between central Canada and the so-called "hinterland" regions of the West and the Maritimes. Canada's preoccupation with maintaining national unity, according to some analysts, had obscured the nature of regional interests and particularly the impact of federal policies on the western and

Atlantic regions. A collection of essays, edited by University of Calgary historian David Jay Bercuson and entitled *Canada and the Burden of Unity* (1977), set out to right the balance.

Canada is a country of regions. There is nothing new or extraordinary about this observation, and the fact is recognized, sometimes grudgingly, by academics, journalists, and politicians. Our trouble is that, having paid lip-service to the concept, too many Canadians who should know better wish regionalism would go away. If the stubborn regional identification of British Columbians, prairie Westerners, and Maritimers could only be melded with the all too powerful and sometimes parochial 'Canadian' awareness of Ontarians, the land could be neatly split between the French and 'English' of the bicultural illusion. That is the wish of some, but the ever-present reality is quite different. Regions exist, distinguished by geographical setting, economic role, history, culture, and even different ambitions for the same Canada to which they all belong....

...federal policies, far from breaking down the barriers of regionalism, imposed differences of role on the Maritimes and the West, and forced their economies into rigid patterns subservient and contributing to the power of Central Canada. The tariff, the railway, and the political muscle of Ottawa assured the continued existence of regionalism and the certainty of regional discontent. The Maritimes and the West could do little about this 'no win' sitation at the federal level. They could not defend or assert themselves within the cabinet and party structure at Ottawa because a vicious circle of circumstance assured them of continuing weakness of representation in the halls of the federal government.

Industrialization and population growth are necessarily connected, Canada was destined by geography and federal policy to have an industrialized centre and an agricultural and resource-extraction periphery. Population growth in the outlying regions has never kept pace with that of Central Canada because the Maritimes and the West are not industrialized. The Maritimes and the West are not strongly represented at Ottawa because of the relatively low population. National growth might have been more even, if federal policies had been designed to help hinterlands overcome geographic handicaps, but the federal government has always been more representative of the desires and ambitions of Central Canada than the Maritimes and the West together.... The payoff, the bribe, is our institutionalized government-to-government welfare policy of equalization payments; a Band-Aid program used to substitute for radical surgery. Since the hinterland regions are at a permanent disadvantage in federal politics they turn to their provincial governments for protection. The identification of some Canadians with their own regions, as much as or perhaps more than their identification with the whole nation, is a fact of Canadian life that will not easily be made to go away....

David Jay Bercuson, "Canada's Burden of Unity", in *Canada and the Burden of Unity* (Toronto: Gage, 1980), pp. 1–3. Footnotes deleted.

The Myth of the Downtrodden West—a Rejoinder

The popular view that the "hinterland" regions have long been victimized by central Canada has come under fire in historical circles. Approaching contemporary Western regionalism from an historical perspective, J.M.S. Careless of the University of Toronto has claimed that the notion of the "downtrodden West" is more of a popular myth than an accurate reflection of the Western tradition:

Since the nineteenth century, the West has felt exposed to powerful forces beyond its control—not just huge distances, the vagaries of climate and harvests, and the problem of distant market prices, but the power of outside human interests over the West's promised destiny. Nature and the 'natural' laws of the market could be lived with, perhaps to some extent offset. But dependence on eastern-controlled transport and business, and on federal government policies, grew much harder to accept....

Recently this buoyant, increasingly diversifying West was confronted by a fresh outside intervention. Federal power (central Canadian power, in western eyes) sought, it seemed, to seize control of the new western wealth in energy; to draw it off in support of a faltering East and centre. No wonder the West sharply reacted. No wonder western provincial politicians began to raise defensive barriers. No wonder many aroused westerners could ardently agree that the whole history of their region added up to a century of victimization by central Canada.

The reaction is understandable, but not fair. It is grounded in experience, but it sees just one side of history. Western problems have to be judged in the light of the fuller Canadian record: regions are not closed entities, embattled armies of us against them, but interlinked communities in broad national and international frames. At the very least, the historic treatment of the West must be assessed within the wider realm of the Canadian nation....

Westerners have continually protested that the federal protective tariff, originally created by John A. Macdonald's government, compelled them to buy higher-priced, protected central Canadian goods instead of cheaper alternatives from outside the country, where their own primary products went. Thus they were held subservient.... They have argued that this diversion and imbalance retarded the growth of manufacturing within the West itself, keeping it industrially dependent on the centre....

Yet if the would-be nation-builders of the time mainly considered the West a great new property to be developed under central direction—and they did—it's also true that there was virtually no western regional community *until* that progress got under way.... The imposition of the tariff was not just centralist greed and self-interest, but part of a genuine nation-making effort. The achievement of this design, in fact, was the rapid settling of the West, which then increasingly protested central domination—and the policy which had helped make the modern West possible....

It is short-sighted... to view the industrial rise of central Canada from a western perspective alone. The wider record indicates that central economic ascendancy was based on far more than any tariff grip on the West. And later years confirmed as much when the centre continued to expand despite western slowdowns—though in some degree, admittedly, because of north-south trade in the primary products of its resource-rich northern hinterlands.

Whatever the history behind the West's current alienation, history itself is at work to settle the matter. The West that has grown so far has not escaped geography; but the impact of geography is changing over time, as the whole demographic and economic orientation of North American moves westward. This shift may not make grass grow on Yonge Street—a cheerful western fantasy—but it will change the whole Canadian balance. The centre's dominance, not a sinister plot but a joint product of history and geography, will be modified and offset....

What we need, really, is more time to defuse angry issues. We could also use a shrewdly adaptable John A. Macdonald to wangle new political combinations, even a skillfully delaying Mackenzie King, rather than urgent confrontationists in power. If the Canadian genius (of seeming anything but genius) does come through, western alienation could subside without explosions. And history may then confirm that western discontents, while deep in memory, should be seen as no true basis for a belief in steady victimization.

J.M.S. Careless, "The Myth of the Downtrodden West", *Saturday Night*, May, 1981, pp. 31–36 Excerpted.

The Maritimes and the Problems of Confederation—An Analysis of the Region's "Identity Paradox"

While the regions of the West and the Atlantic provinces may share a common antipathy toward federal policies, recent studies tend to confirm that their problems and demands are quite different. Western discontents seem to arise from the region's growing economic strength rather than its economic deprivation—and find expression in demands for a larger share of political power. Yet the contemporary problems of Atlantic Canada seem to stem from different causes and generate conflicting demands. In a study undertaken for the Task Force on Canadian Unity in 1978–79, George A. Rawlyk and Doug Brown offered this analysis of Maritime perspectives on the "unity crisis":

In stressing their 'Maritime-ness'—and in re-articulating the shibboleths of regional protest, Maritimers in the 1960s and 1970s are, it may be argued, not only trying to define their regional identity, but also attempting to come to grips with their status as Canadians. Such a development may, taking into account the historical context, appear to be both a paradox and an ironic mystery. But there is more and more evidence to suggest that at both the mass and elite levels, a growing number of residents of Prince Edward Island, New Brunswick and Nova Scotia have succeeded in blending their local patriotism and a larger Canadianism....

It may seem ironic, that, at the present time, so many Maritimers consider themselves to be such ardent Canadians. Economic dependence and a hardening colonial mentality may help to account for this. But there is more to this 'identity paradox'. It may be argued that during the past few decades a new mature identity has been clicking into place in the Maritime Provinces. Many Maritimers evidently have been able to move beyond the point of merely highlighting their regional distinctiveness to a position where they can freely discuss and contemplate their sense of belonging to Canada. When a person is able to declare that there is compatibility in being an 'Islander' and 'a Canadian', it reveals that the person is able to integrate two quite different, but not incompatible, levels of identity and to move easily back and forth between these two positions. Such a development reveals something about the complex relationship of Maritime regionalism and an English-Canadian sense of identity.

Thus it is not surprising that the region of Canada which feels it has the most to lose should Quebec leave Confederation is the Maritimes. As the twentieth century unfolds, and as economic, cultural, and political ties draw the Maritime Provinces into an ever-closer relationship with Central Canada, the often virulent anti-Confederation and anti-'Upper Canadian' rhetoric of the nineteenth century has been greatly neutralized by a growing dependence on the federal government and a cultural bombardment from Central Canada and the United States... if any Canadian region feels, with considerable justification, that it will be adversely affected by the undermining of the federal government's power to redistribute financial resources and equalize social services, it is the Maritime region.

Furthermore, if any group of Canadians today is firmly and emotionally attached to Canada, and feels especially threatened by the spectre of Quebec's separation, it is the Maritimers. Although often unwilling or unable to articulate their sense of concern about the future, as well as their pride and faith in Canada, these people have blended their 'dollars and cents' pragmatism into their local patriotism, and welded these ingredients into a larger Canadianism. In a fascinating twist of a complex relationship, the region of Canada which was once most vociferously opposed to Confederation has become one of its most ardent and committed supporters.

George Rawlyk and Doug Brown, "The Historical Framework of the Maritimes and Confederation", in G.A. Rawlyk, ed., *The Atlantic Provinces and the Problems of Confederation* (Halifax: Breakwater Publishers, 1979), pp. 41-2. Footnotes omitted.

THE CHALLENGE OF CANADA'S FUTURE

"Dominion Day, 2084"—A Fantasy of Deconfederation

By the late 1970s and early 1980s the multiple problems of Canadian diversity did not seem to bode well for the future. Speculating about the prospects of national survival had become a favourite pastime of not only popular Canadian humorists like Eric Nicol and Peter Whalley, but even normally dour historians. Predictions of "Deconfederation" were satirized and lampooned in speeches, magazines and the electronic media. One humorous scenario was spun by J.M.S. Careless in a 1979 convocation address at Laurentian University in Sudbury, Ontario.

More than a century ago, in 1967, Canadians celebrated the hundredth anniversary of Confederation. Little did they think that 117 years later, here in 2084, we would be celebrating an even greater historic event, the Centenary of the Deconfederation of Canada, which occurred, as any school child with a computer information terminal is well aware, back in the magic year of 1984. In our current centennial year, then, we are properly remembering those great Fathers of Deconfederation—famous names like Levesque, Lougheed, and others who launched our country on its present glorious path, so that we may truly say—the Twenty-Second Century will belong to Canada! ....

It was in 1980 that the first of 72 referenda—known as the Quebec Referendums—was held. There had to be that many, partly to make the question clear, and partly because they were held from coast to coast, as everybody got into the game, and bets were laid on the outcome, so that Lottario was replaced by Referendario as the biggest public revenue raiser and the main diversion on the primitive television system of the day. Voters were progressively asked: Are you in favour of Sovereignty with Association, Sovereignty without Association, Association without Sovereignty, mushrooms or pepperoni, and do you truly mean it? Public pollsters proved conclusively that Yukon preferred sovereignty with pipelines and pepperoni, that Northern Ontario wanted to secede from Southern Ontario, Northwestern Ontario from Northeastern Ontario, Reed from Dryden, and Timmins from everybody. The dominant issues, however, were at length condensed and accurately simplified to these: What does Quebec really want? What does the West actually expect? What will the Atlantic

Provinces have to put up with? And what does Ontario think that it can keep?

Everyone indeed agreed that things could not remain as they were. That was the great outcome of the referenda process, clearly expressing (if at some expense) the ultimate resolution of the national will....

* * * * *

...Quebec declared irrevocably for a free and independent French state joined with an economically strong Canada. Not to be outdone—never to be outdone—the West voiced its unalterable stand for a free and independent Canada joined with an economically strong British Colberta-Saskatchitoba. Ontario expressed its undying readiness to sacrifice for Canadian unity, as long as no one laid a cotton-pickin' finger on its god-given industries; and the Atlantic provinces said, don't call us, we'll call you; except Newfoundland, which had gone fishing—for oil.

The sense that the crucial moment was at hand flashed upon the acutely perceptive mind of the prime minister. Immediately, he went on national television to announce that something would be done—and left for a world pilgrimage to study related global problems in Tokyo, Moscow, Madagascar and at the Vatican. At last, from Jerusalem early in 1983, he announced the vital decision. There would be a conference—to be known forever as the Last, Best Conference on the Deconfederation of Canada....

We cannot go in detail through the weeks of earnest deliberation in which the final scheme was gradually hammered out. It must suffice simply to record the main results. First, Canada was solemnly resolved to have deconfederated and everything was to be totally new. Second, all the province-nations were to be separately equal to the others, though some might be more equal. Third, instead of the old Confederation, there was now to be a Condominium of the Northern Living Space, without a federal system, but with 'some joint authority' to deal with things the tenants had in common, while the things they did not would be known as Apartment Rights—inalienable—unless the Condominium Joint Authority acted otherwise. For convenience, two lists were drawn up: not of powers (heaven forbid) but of housekeeping shares, 'joint' and 'apartmentized'. This eventually became Sections 91 and 92 of the Better North American Action of Agreement, our present constitutional structure, which is now generally referred to as the B.N.A. Action—to distinguish it from the outmoded, superseded B.N.A. Act....

The new scheme was conceivably a bit foggy, but in fact was based upon another deep-rooted Canadian principle—constructive confusion. And so finally, in the spring of 1984, the plan was effectively adopted, by popular ballots cut from the backs of bilingual cereal boxes—one reason why the Deconfederation scheme of 1984 has also been widely termed the Kellogg Pact.

Thus, in consequence of the devoted labours of our forepersons, we now have the transformed system we enjoy today. It went into effect on July 1 a hundred years ago, and was promulgated in our 16 official languages, including that of the Anglo-Saxon Reserve here on Vancouver Island. Granted, there is now a movement for re-de-Confederation, swelling powerfully in the revived strength of Prince Edward Island nationalism. But we have been through a lot and any problems ahead will not lessen the massive jubilations of the eagerly awaited INCOPO festival this summer. The Condominium of Canada-Quebec-Et Al. (now shortened in popular parlance to the Dominium of Canada) still stands. The Dominium of Canada is one and divided—outdoing the mystery of the Trinity by several paces. And as it stands, it remains ever-faithful to its enduring historic motto—plus ça change....

J.M.S. Careless, "Dominion Day, 2084", *The Graduate* (University of Toronto Alumni Magazine), March-April, 1980, pp. 16–18 Excerpted.

Canada's Emerging Identities—A Literary Critic's Perspective

Not every Canadian commentator predicted that Canada's emerging regional identities would lead to national deconfederation. The literary critic Professor Northrop Frye of the University of Toronto, was one of many who read the trends differently. In the introduction to *The Bush Garden* (1971), Frye has drawn an important distinction between "unity" and "identity" in Canada: the former was national in scope and based on a sense of political allegiance, the latter was regional and rooted in works of the imagination. By the beginning of the 1980s, he came to see Canada as a community balanced on a tension between a political feeling of unity and a host of emerging regional identities.

> Every part of Canada is shut off by its geography, British Columbia from the Prairies by the Rockies, the Prairies from the Canadas by the immense hinterland of northern Ontario, Quebec from the Maritimes by the upthrust of Maine, the Maritimes from Newfoundland by the sea.
>
> A generation ago, Hugh MacLennan took a phrase from Rilke, 'two solitudes,' as the title for a novel about the mutual isolation of English and French in Montreal. But everywhere in Canada we find solitudes touching other solitudes: every part of Canada has strong separatist feelings, because every part of it is in fact a separation.
>
> And behind all these separations lies the silent north, full of vast rivers, lakes and islands that, even yet, very few Canadians have ever seen. The Mississippi, running north to south through the middle of the country, is a symbol of the American frontier and its steady advance into the sunset. The largest river in Canada, the Mackenzie, is a symbol of the *terra incognita* in Canadian consciousness. It is what Rupert Brooke called the 'unseizable virginity' of the Canadian landscape. Or, as another British Visitor, Wyndham Lewis, remarked: 'This monstrous, empty habitat must continue to dominate this nation psychologically, and so culturally.' . . .
>
> Soon after World War II, French Canada entered what has been called the quiet revolution, an awareness of belonging both to itself and to the modern world, which shook off most of the isolating features that had been previously restricting its cultural life. I think it was partly a response to the French act of self-definition that made for a sudden and dramatic emergence of English Canadian culture after about 1960. Since then there has been a tremendous cultural explosion, in literature and painting particularly, which as produced a mood that is often called cultural nationalism.
>
> This is a most misleading phrase, and for two reasons. First, nationalism suggests something aggressive, like a 19th-century jingoist waiting for the next war to start, or a 20th-century Third World revolutionary. But culture in itself seeks only its own identity, not an enemy: hostility only confuses it.
>
> Second, contemporary Canadian culture, being a culture, is not a national development but a series of regional ones. What is happening in British Columbia is very different from what is happening in New Brunswick or Ontario . . . .
>
> During the centenary of Confederation, a sour little joke was circulating in Canada to the effect that what had been aimed at in Canada was a combination of British political institutions, American economic buoyancy and French culture, and that what we had, after a century, was French politics, British economic buoyancy, and American culture. However, the growth of an anonymous, mass-produced, mindless sub-culture is American only to the extent that the United States is the world's most highly

industrialized society. Its effect on genuine American culture is quite as lethal as its effect everywhere else. . . .

* * * * *

When I first came to Toronto, in 1929, it was a homogeneous Scottish-Irish town, dominated by the Orange Order, and greatly derided by the rest of Canada for its smugness, its snobbery, and its sterility. The public food in restaurants and hotels was of indifferent quality, as it is in all right-thinking Anglo-Saxon communities. After the war, Toronto took in immigrants to the extent of nearly a quarter of its population, and large Greek, Italian, Portuguese, Central European, West Indian communities grew up within it. The public food improved dramatically. More important, these communities all seemed to find their own place in the larger community with a minimum of violence and tension, preserving much of their own cultures and yet taking part in the total one.

It has always seemed to me that this very relaxed absorption of minorities, where there is no concerted effort at a 'melting pot', has something to do with what the Queen symbolizes, the separation of the head of state from the head of government. Because Canada was founded by two peoples, nobody could ever know what a 100 per cent Canadian was, and hence the decentralizing rhythm that is so essential to culture had room to expand.

Still more important is the Canadian sense of the close relation of the people to the land. Everywhere we turn in Canadian literature and painting, we are haunted by the natural world, and even the most sophisticated Canadian artists can hardly keep something very primitive and archaic out of their imaginations. This sense is not that of the possession of the land, but precisely the absence of possession, a feeling that here is a nature that man has polluted and imprisoned and violated but has never really lived with. . . .

It seems clear that for Canadian culture the old imperialist phrase 'going native' has come home to roost. We are no longer an army of occupation, and the natives are ourselves.

Canada is still a place of considerable natural resources, but it is no longer simply a place to be looted, either by Canadians or by non-Canadians.

It is of immense importance to the United States itself that there should be other views of the human occupation of this continent, rooted in different ideologies and different historical traditions.

And it is of immense importance to the world that a country which used to be at the edge of the earth and is now a kind of global Switzerland, surrounded by all the world's great powers, should have achieved the repatriating of its culture.

For this is essentially what has happened in the past 20 years, in all parts of Canada; and what was an inarticulate space on a map is now responding to the world with the tongues and eyes of a mature and disciplined imagination.

Northrop Frye, "Canada's Emerging Identity", *The Toronto Star*, June 28, 1980, p. B1 and B4.

A Guide to Further Reading

1. Overviews

Bell, David and Lorne Tepperman, *The Roots of Disunity: A Look at Canadian Political Culture*. Toronto: McClelland and Stewart, 1979.

Bercuson, David Jay, ed., *Canada and the Burden of Unity*. Toronto: Macmillan, 1977.

Bothwell, Robert, Ian Drummond and John English, *Canada Since 1945: Power, Politics and Provincialism*. Toronto: University of Toronto Press, 1981.

Byers, R.B. and Robert W. Reford, eds., *Canada Challenged: The Viability of Confederation*. Toronto: Canadian Institute of International Affairs, 1979.

Careless, J.M.S., "Limited Identities in Canada", *Canadian Historical Review*, Vol. L (March, 1969), pp. 1–10.

Carty, R. Kenneth and Peter W. Ward, eds., *Entering the Eighties: Canada in Crisis*. Toronto: Oxford University Press, 1980.

Cook, Ramsay, "The Burden of Regionalism", *Acadiensis*, Vol. VII (Autumn, 1977), pp. 110–115.

Elkins, David J. and Richard Simeon, *Small Worlds: Provinces and Parties in Canadian Political Life*. Toronto: Methuen, 1980.

Geddes, Gary, ed., *Divided We Stand*. Toronto: Peter Martin Associates, 1977.

Meekison, J. Peter, ed., *Canadian Federalism: Myth or Reality*. Third Edition. Toronto: Methuen, 1977.

Rawlyk, G.A., R.P. Bowles and B.W. Hodgins, *Regionalism in Canada: Flexible Federalism or Fractured Nation?* Scarborough: Prentice-Hall, 1979.

Simeon, Richard, ed., *Must Canada Fail?* Montreal: McGill-Queen's University Press, 1977.

Stevenson, Garth, *Unfulfilled Union: Canadian Federalism and National Unity*. Toronto: Gage Publishing, 1979.

Wade, Mason, ed., *Regionalism in the Canadian Community, 1867–1967*. Toronto: University of Toronto Press, 1969.

Walker, Michael, ed., *Canadian Confederation at the Crossroads*. Vancouver: The Fraser Institute, 1978.

Westfall, William, "On the Concept of Region in Canadian History and Literature", *Journal of Canadian Studies*, Vol. 15 (Summer, 1980), pp. 3–15.

2. Specialized Studies

Federal-Provincial Relations in the Sixties

Beck, J.M. ed., *The Shaping of Canadian Federalism: Central Authority or Provincial Right?* Toronto: Copp Clark, 1971.

Black, Edwin R., *Divided Loyalties: Canadian Concepts of Federalism*. Montreal: McGill—Queen's University Press, 1975.

Fox, Paul W., *Politics: Canada*. Second Edition. Toronto: McGraw-Hill, 1966.

Meekison, J. Peter, ed., *Canadian Federalism: Myth or Reality*. First Edition. Toronto: Methuen, 1968.

Newman, Peter C., *The Distemper of Our Times: Canadian Politics in Transition, 1963–1968*. Toronto: McClelland and Stewart, 1968.

Simeon, Richard, *Federal-Provincial Diplomacy: The Making of Recent Policy in Canada*. Toronto: University of Toronto Press, 1972.

Smiley, Donald V., *The Canadian Political Nationality*. Toronto: Methuen, 1967.

Alberta and the Energy Resources Controversy

Laxer, James, *Canada's Energy Crisis*. Toronto: James Lewis & Samuel, 1974.

Nelles, H.V., "Canadian Energy Policy, 1945–1980: A Federalist Perspective" in Carty and Ward, eds., *Entering the Eighties: Canada in Crisis*, pp. 91–117.

Report of the Western Premiers' Task Force on Constitutional Trends. Victoria: Queen's Printer, May, 1977.

Richards, John and Larry Pratt, *Prairie Capitalism: Power and Influence in the New West.* Toronto: McClelland and Stewart, 1979.

Shaffer, Ed, *Canada's Oil and the American Empire.* Edmonton: Hurtig, 1983.

Simpson, Jeffrey, *Discipline of Power: The Conservative Interlude and the Liberal Restoration.* Toronto: Personal Library, 1980.

Toner, Glen and Francois Bregha, "The Political Economy of Energy" in Michael S. Whittington and Glen Williams, eds., *Canadian Politics in the 1980's.* Toronto: Methuen, 1981, pp. 1-26.

Quebec and the Constitutional Debate

Banting, Keith and Richard Simeon, *Redesigning the State: The Politics of Constitutional Change.* Toronto: University of Toronto Press, 1984.

Behiels, Michael D., "Forging Canada's Destiny", *Canadian Ethnic Studies*, Vol. XI, No. 2 (1979), pp. 110-117.

Cook, Ramsay, *The Maple Leaf Forever: Essays on Nationalism and Politics in Canada.* Toronto: Macmillan, 1977.

Latouche, Daniel, "It Takes Two to... Divorce and Remarry", *Journal of Canadian Studies*, Vol. 12 no. 3 (1977).

Lévesque, René, "For An Independent Quebec", *Foreign* Affairs (July, 1976).

_____, *My Quebec.* Toronto: Totem Books, 1979.

McWhinney, Edward, *Canada and the Constitution, 1979-82.* Toronto: University of Toronto Press, 1982.

Morin, Claude, *Quebec versus Ottawa: The Struggle for Self-Government, 1960-72.* trans. Richard Howard. Toronto: University of Toronto Press, 1976.

Olling, R.D. and M.W. Westmacott, eds., *The Confederation Debate: The Constitution in Crisis.* Toronto: Kendall/Hunt Publishing, 1980.

Options. Proceedings of the Conference on the Future of the Canadian Federation, University of Toronto, October, 1977. Toronto: University of Toronto Media Centre, 1977.

Radwanski, George, *Trudeau.* Scarborough: Signet Books, 1978.

Sheppard, Robert and Michael Valpy, *The National Deal: The Fight for A Canadian Constitution.* Toronto: Fleet Books, 1982.

Romanow, Roy, John Whyte, and Howard Leeson, *Canada... Not Withstanding.* Toronto: Methuen, 1984.

Simeon, Richard and Keith Banting, eds. *And No One Cheered.* Toronto: Methuen, 1983.

Smiley, Donald V., *Canada in Question: Federalism in the Eighties.* Third Edition. Toronto: McGraw-Hill Ryerson, 1980.

Task Force on Canadian Unity, *A Future Together: Observations and Recommendations.* Ottawa: Minister of Supply and Services, Canada, 1979.

Trudeau, Pierre E., *Federalism and the French Canadians.* Toronto: Macmillan, 1968.

Immigration and Ethnic Diversity

Berry, J.W., R. Kalin and D.M. Taylor, *Multiculturalism and Ethnic Attitudes in Canada.* Ottawa: Minister of Supply and Services, 1977.

Dahlie, Jorgen and Tissa Fernando, eds., *Ethnicity, Power and Politics in Canada.* Toronto: Methuen, 1981.

Isajiw, W.W., ed., *Identities: The Impact of Ethnicity on Canadian Society.* Toronto: Peter Martin Associates, 1977.

_____, "Olga in Wonderland: Ethnicity in Technological Society", *Canadian Ethnic Studies*, Vol. IX, No. 1 (1977), pp. 77–83.

"Multiculturalism: The First Decade", Special Theme Issue, *Journal of Canadian Studies*, Vol. 17, No. 1 (Spring, 1982).

Palmer, Howard, ed., *Immigration and the Rise of Multiculturalism*. Toronto: Copp Clark, 1975.

Perin, Roberto, "Clio as an Ethnic: The Third Force in Canadian Historiography", *Canadian Historical Review*, Vol. LXIV, No. 4 (December, 1983), pp. 441–467.

Regionalism in Atlantic Canada

Alexander, David, "New Notions of Happiness: Nationalism, Regionalism and Atlantic Canada," *Journal of Canadian Studies*, Vol. 15 (Summer, 1980), pp. 29–42.

Atlantic Provinces Economic Council, *The Atlantic Vision—1990: A Development Strategy for the 1980's*. Halifax: APEC, 1979.

Economic Council of Canada, *Living Together: A Study of Regional Disparities*. Ottawa: Minister of Supply and Services, 1977.

Harris, Michael, "The Promised Land Fights for Its Life", *Atlantic Insight* (March, 1981), pp. 46–49.

Rawlyk, G.A., ed., *The Atlantic Provinces and the Problems of Confederation*. Halifax: Breakwater Publishers, 1979.

Weale, David and Harry Baglole, *The Island and Confederation: The End of an Era*. Summerside: Williams & Crue, 1973.

Regionalism in the West

Barr, John J. and Owen Anderson, eds., *The Unfinished Revolt: Some Views of Western Independence*. Toronto: McClelland and Stewart, 1971.

Bercuson, David Jay, "Regionalism and 'Unlimited Identity' in Western Canada", *Journal of Canadian Studies*, Vol. 15 (Summer, 1980), pp. 121–126.

Careless, J.M.S., "The Myth of the Downtrodden West", *Saturday Night* (May, 1981), pp. 30–36.

Gibbins, Roger, *Prairie Politics and Society: Regionalism in Decline*. Toronto: Butterworths, 1980.

_____, *Regionalism: Territorial Politics in Canada and the United States*. Toronto: Butterworths, 1982.

Morton, W.L., "Clio in Canada: The Interpretation of Canadian History", *University of Toronto Quarterly*, Vol. XV (April, 1946).

Palmer, Howard and Tamara, "The Alberta Experience", *Journal of Canadian Studies*, Vol. 17 (Fall, 1982), pp. 20–34.

Pratt, Larry and Grant Stevenson, eds., *Western Separatism: The Myths, Realities & Dangers*. Edmonton: Hurtig, 1981.

Skene, Wayne, "Will the Prairies Go West?", *Quest* (March, 1981), pp. 11–17.

Thomas, Lewis G., "Alberta 1905–1980: The Uneasy Society" in Howard Palmer and Donald Smith, eds., *The New Provinces: Alberta and Saskatchewan 1905–1980*. Vancouver: Tantalus Research, 1980, pp. 23–41.

Index to Subjects

Historiographic Index

Visual Sources

p. 5 Anonymous French woodcut. Bibliothèque Nationale, Paris. P.A.C. 52.

p. 27 *left* Engraving by I.B. Scotin in C. Bacqueville, *Histoire de l'Amérique septentrionale*, 1722, Vol. I plate p. 51. Metropolitan Toronto Library
right Engraving by Thomas Mower Martin (1838–1934). 58.44.18. Glenbow-Alberta Institute

p. 39 C-102, P.A.C.

p. 56 Engraving in C. Bacqueville, *Histoire de l'Amérique septentrionale*, 1722, C-4696, P.A.C.

p. 80 Engraving, 1759. 63 AA 26. Royal Ontario Museum, Toronto.

p. 122 "This S^R. is the meaning of the Quebec Act" Mezzotint publ. by Frans Adams, 1774. C-25990, P.A.C.

p. 135 Nova Scotia and the American Revolutionary War, 1775–76

p. 171 Lithograph N. Hartnell from sketch by Lord Charles Beauclerk. C-396, P.A.C.

p. 188 C-41067, P.A.C.

p. 225 *left:* *Punch in Canada*, May 19, 1849, reprinted in J.W. Bengough, *A Caricature History of Canadian Politics*. Toronto, 1886, Vol. 1, p. 33 C 78534-P.A.C.
right: sketch by E. Hides. T 15591—Metropolitan Toronto Library

p. 250 C-733, P.A.C.

p. 299 J.W. Bengough, *Grip*, September 19, 1885. Rapid Grip & Batten Ltd.

p. 305 J.W. Bengough, *Grip*, February 2, 1889. Rapid Grip & Batten Ltd.

p. 330 *Le Canard*, Dec. 28, 1878. L8602 National Library

p. 358 *The Industrial Worker*, April 23, 1919. Reprinted in J.L. Kornbluh, ed. *Rebel Voices*: an IWW Anthology (Ann Arbor: University of Michigan Press, 1968)

p. 385 *Grain Growers' Guide*, September 21, 1910

p. 390 *The Montreal Herald*, November 26, 1913. (Bibliothèque de la Ville de Montréal).

p. 414 *left* *The Toronto World*, November 27, 1917 *right* Donald McRitchie, *The Halifax Herald*, Oct. 3, 1925

p. 441 "La Conscription" by J. Charlebois. *Editions du Devoir* (Montreal: Le Devoir, 1917)

p. 445 *The Toronto Globe and Mail*, April 24, 1942

p. 477 Terry Mosher, *Aislin's 100 Caricatures*. (Montreal: Montreal Reporter Publications, 1971)

p. 510 Terry Mosher, *Aislin: Another 180 Caricatures (Did the Earth Move?)* Toronto: McClelland and Stewart, 1980.

p. 524 Alan Beaton, *Toronto Telegram*, July 15, 1963

p. 540 Duncan Macpherson, *The Toronto Star*, January 16, 1978. Reprinted in Macpherson Editorial Cartoons 1978 (Toronto: Toronto Star Limited, 1978).

Reprint Acknowledgements (Listed by Publisher)

American Historical Association: p. 487—J.M. Ghent. ©1979 A.H.A., Pacific Coast Branch. Reprinted with permission.

Butterworth: p. 462—D. Morton. ©1981 Butterworth & Co. (Canada) Ltd. Reprinted with permission.

Canadian Broadcasting Corporation: p. 231—F. Underhill. ©1964 by the C.B.C. Used with permission.

Clarke Irwin: p. 456—E.L.M. Burns. ©1956 by Clarke Irwin Inc. Used with permission.

Council on Foreign Relations, Inc.: p. 514—R. Levesque. Excerpted by permission of Foreign Affairs.

Doubleday: p. 92—G. Donaldson. ©1973 by Gordon Donaldson. Reprinted by permission of Doubleday & Company, Inc.

Labour/Le Travailleur: pp. 334-5—J. Battye and pp. 343-4—D.J. Bercuson. ©Committee on Canadian Labour History, 1979; 1981. Reprinted by permission of the editor.

Harold A. Logan Estate: pp. 335-6—H.A. Logan. Reprinted with permission.

Macmillan of Canada, (a division of Gage Publishing Ltd.)—the following extracts reprinted with permission: p. 43—M. Wade; pp. 47-8—S. Trofimenkoff; pp. 69, 98—M. Wade; p. 102—R. Cook; p. 108—S. Trofimenkoff; pp. 129-30—F. Ouellet; pp. 153-4—G. Stewart and G. Rawlyk; p. 173-4—W. LeSueur; pp. 174-5—H.T. Manning; pp. 175-6, 308-9—D. Creighton; p. 312-13—C. Armstrong; pp. 335-6—H.A. Logan; pp. 422-3—I. MacPherson; pp. 431-2—D. Smith; pp. 439, 444-5—C.P. Stacey; pp. 448-9—N. Ward; pp. 512-13—S. Trofimenkoff; pp. 516-17—P. Trudeau; p. 549—D.J. Bercuson.

P. Martin: p. 401—G. Matheson. ©Peter Martin Associates Ltd. Used by permission.

McClelland and Stewart—the following extracts used by permission of the Canadian Publishers, McClelland and Stewart Limited, Toronto: p. 24—C. Jaenen; pp. 44—M. Trudel; p. 46—W. Eccles; pp. 92-3—G. Stanley; p. 141—J. Brebner; pp. 172-3—A. Dunham; pp. 209-10—A. Prentice; pp. 211-12—J. Careless; pp. 212-13—M. Cross and G. Kealey; p. 235—J. Careless; p. 236—W. Morton; p. 318—P. Waite; p. 338—M. Bliss; pp. 362-3—D. Smiley; p. 365—R. Brown and R. Cook; pp. 369-70—M. Bliss; pp. 423-4—R. Allen; p. 438, 440—H. Borden; pp. 442-3, 450-1—O. Skelton; p. 454—J. Thomson; p. 455—R.M. Dawson; pp. 473-4—P. Martin; p. 481—J. Holmes; pp. 483-4—D. Stairs; pp. 485-6—G. Grant; pp. 508-9—R. Levesque; pp. 515-16—D. Fullerton; pp. 518-19—K. McRoberts and D. Posgate; p. 536—J. Barr.

William Morrow & Company: p. 284—J.K. Howard. Used by permission.

National Museum of Man: pp. 368-9—G. Stelter, 372-3—A. McCormack, 397-8—V. Strong-Boag. Reprinted by permission of the N.M.M., National Museums of Canada.

New Hogtown Press: pp. 333-4—S. Langdon, pp. 381-2—D. Read. Reprinted with permission.

Supply and Services: p. 534—extract. Reprinted by permission of the Minister of Supply and Services Canada.

University of Georgia Press: p. 21—B. Trigger. ©1981 University of Georgia Press. Reprinted by permission.

University of Toronto Press—the following extracts reprinted by permission: pp. 152-3—S.D. Clark; p. 167—H. Innis and A. Lower; p. 180—C. Read; p. 195, 203—R. Splane; p. 230—C. Martin